COMPARATIVE LEGAL STUDIES: TRADITIONS AND TRANSITIONS

This book features fourteen original essays written by some of the world's most distinguished comparatists who bring sophisticated theoretical and interdisciplinary perspectives to bear on comparative legal studies. Arguably the most ambitious intellectual project to date within the field, this collection brings together representatives of many approaches to the practice of comparison of laws and offers a uniquely comprehensive response to the fundamental challenges raised by comparative interventions. Topics covered include universalism, nationalism, colonialism and functionalism. Disciplines addressed include anthropology, history, sociology, philosophy, politics and literary criticism. Problems discussed include contextualization, differentiation, cognition, translation and transferability. Throughout, the contributors present their respective vision of the nature of comparative legal studies and the assumptions that inform their work. This book will engage all lawyers wishing to operate beyond their national law and will be required for everyone taking a specific interest in the comparison of laws.

PIERRE LEGRAND teaches law at the Sorbonne.

RODERICK MUNDAY teaches law at the University of Cambridge.

COMPARATIVE LEGAL STUDIES: TRADITIONS AND TRANSITIONS

Edited by
PIERRE LEGRAND AND RODERICK MUNDAY

CAMBRIDGE
UNIVERSITY PRESS

CAMBRIDGE UNIVERSITY PRESS
Cambridge, New York, Melbourne, Madrid, Cape Town,
Singapore, São Paulo, Delhi, Tokyo, Mexico City

Cambridge University Press
The Edinburgh Building, Cambridge CB2 8RU, UK

Published in the United States of America by Cambridge University Press, New York

www.cambridge.org
Information on this title: www.cambridge.org/9780521272407

© Cambridge University Press 2003

This publication is in copyright. Subject to statutory exception
and to the provisions of relevant collective licensing agreements,
no reproduction of any part may take place without the written
permission of Cambridge University Press.

First published 2003
First paperback edition 2011

A catalogue record for this publication is available from the British Library

ISBN 978-0-521-81811-7 Hardback
ISBN 978-0-521-27240-7 Paperback

Cambridge University Press has no responsibility for the persistence or
accuracy of URLs for external or third-party internet websites referred to in
this publication, and does not guarantee that any content on such websites is,
or will remain, accurate or appropriate.

CONTENTS

List of contributors   vii

Introduction

1   Accounting for an encounter   3
    Roderick Munday

Comparative legal studies and its legacies

2   The universalist heritage   31
    James Gordley

3   The colonialist heritage   46
    Upendra Baxi

4   The nationalist heritage   76
    H. Patrick Glenn

5   The functionalist heritage   100
    Michele Graziadei

Comparative legal studies and its boundaries

6   Comparatists and sociology   131
    Roger Cotterrell

7   Comparatists and languages   154
    Bernhard Großfeld

Comparative legal studies and its theories

8 The question of understanding   197
   Mitchel de S.-O.-l'E. Lasser

9 The same and the different   240
   Pierre Legrand

10 The neo-Romantic turn   312
    James Q. Whitman

11 The methods and the politics   345
    David Kennedy

Comparative legal studies and its futures

12 Comparatists and transferability   437
    David Nelken

13 Comparatists and extraordinary places   467
    Esin Örücü

Conclusion

14 Beyond compare   493
    Lawrence Rosen

Index   511

CONTRIBUTORS

Upendra Baxi is Professor of Law, University of Warwick, and a former Vice-Chancellor, University of Delhi and South Gujarat.

Roger Cotterrell is Professor of Legal Theory, Queen Mary and Westfield College, University of London.

H. Patrick Glenn is Peter M. Laing Professor of Law, Faculty of Law and Institute of Comparative Law, McGill University.

Michele Graziadei is Professor of Law, Facoltà di Giurisprudenza, Università del Piemonte Orientale 'A. Avogadro'.

James Gordley is Shannon Cecil Turner Professor of Jurisprudence, School of Law, University of California at Berkeley.

Bernhard Großfeld is Professor of Law, Universität Münster.

David Kennedy is Henry Shattuck Professor of Law, Harvard University.

Mitchel de S.-O.-l'E. Lasser is Samuel D. Thurman Professor of Law, University of Utah S. J. Quinney College of Law, and Visiting Professor, Cornell Law School.

Pierre Legrand is Professor of Law, Université Panthéon-Sorbonne.

Roderick Munday is a Fellow of Peterhouse and University Lecturer in Law, University of Cambridge.

David Nelken is Distinguished Professor of Legal Institutions and Social Change, University of Macerata; Distinguished Research Professor of Law, University of Wales, Cardiff; and Honorary Professor of Law, London School of Economics and Political Science.

Esin Örücü is Professor of Comparative Law, University of Glasgow and Erasmus University Rotterdam.

Lawrence Rosen is Professor of Anthropology, Princeton University, and Adjunct Professor of Law, Columbia Law School.

James Q. Whitman is Ford Foundation Professor of Comparative and Foreign Law, Yale University.

Introduction

1

Accounting for an encounter

RODERICK MUNDAY

'[L]'on peut comparer sans craindre d'être injuste.'[1] Safe in that knowledge, the contributors to this book met in a closed seminar in Downing College, Cambridge between 26 and 30 July 2000 to debate comparative legal studies, almost exactly a century to the day after the *Société française de législation comparée* had held its landmark Congress in Paris. The Cambridge Conference was, of course, intended to mark the centenary of the Paris Congress. To this end, fifteen scholars from around the globe, representing widely diverse strands of comparative scholarship, were invited to speak to comparative legal studies at the millennium within their specialist fields and then, drawing freely upon their research, to reflect upon fruitful lines of inquiry for the future. The present volume comprises papers presented and discussed on that occasion in Cambridge. The Cambridge Conference may not have reaped the incidental benefit of a universal exhibition which, in 1900, coincided with the Paris Congress. But like its Paris predecessor, finding itself poised on the threshold of a new century inevitably lent a symbolic edge to the enterprise. In broad imitation of its Parisian forebear, the Cambridge Conference was intended to provide a *tour d'horizon* of the current state of the comparative endeavour in the specific context of legal studies.

The impact exerted by the Paris Congress on the subsequent development of the subject is underscored by Konrad Zweigert and Hein Kötz on the opening page of their well-known textbook:

> Comparative law as we know it started in Paris in 1900 [...]. [...] The science of comparative law, or at any rate its method, was greatly advanced by the

---

[1] Charles Perrault, 'Le siècle de Louis le Grand', in *Parallèle des Anciens et des Modernes*, vol. I (Paris: Coignard, 1688), p. 1. An English version might read: 'One may compare without fear of being unjust.'

occurrence of this Congress, and the views expressed at it have led to a wealth of productive research in this branch of legal study, young though it is.[2]

The proclaimed objectives of the Paris Congress, which took place between 31 July and 4 August 1900, had been 'not only to bring together and to foster contacts between scholars and jurists from all parts of the world, but particularly to seek to provide the science of comparative law with the precise model and the settled direction it requires if it is to develop'.[3] Clearly, a century on, the need to foster contact between scholars within different jurisdictions and even different legally related fields of research remains undiminished. However, the notion of imposing a model on a discipline which is now both fully recognized in its own right and which has already developed a number of disparate but settled directions of its own was not on the Cambridge agenda.

The Parisian organizers' summons issued to all jurisdictions where 'legal science' was well established. Their circular declared that not only would their Congress produce scientific work of the first order, but that it might also indirectly contribute to fostering peace and understanding between nations. It would, of course, be gratifying to imagine that the Cambridge Conference might make some contribution to international peace and understanding, but for obvious reasons this was not a stated objective. Our aim was simply to assemble a dozen or so colleagues, in the context of a challenging round table, to wrangle over the current condition of comparative legal studies within their personal fields of speciality and thereafter to speculate on the future routes the discipline might take.

Depending upon how one chooses to portray the Paris Congress, its programme could variously be described as ambitious, comprehensive or simply diffuse. The proceedings were split into six separate sections, deliberately taking in both theoretical and practical questions. The first, and the most intellectually durable, section was devoted to general comparative theory and method. This was intended by Raymond Saleilles, who designed the programme, to be 'the focal point of the entire

---

[2] Konrad Zweigert and Hein Kötz, *An Introduction to Comparative Law*, 3d ed. transl. by Tony Weir (Oxford: Oxford University Press, 1998), p. 2.
[3] Georges Picot and Fernand Daguin, 'Circulaire', in Congrès international de droit comparé, *Procès-verbaux des séances et documents*, vol. I (Paris: L.G.D.J., 1905), pp. 7–8 [hereinafter *Procès-verbaux et documents*]. Interestingly, it is reported that 127 congresses took place in Paris between 24 May and 13 October 1900. See *Anon.*, 'The Paris Copyright Congress', *The Nation*, 20 September 1900, p. 226.

Congress'.[4] The remaining five sections addressed specific practical themes within the diverse realms of private international law, commercial law, civil law, public law and criminology. The topics prescribed by the organizing committee in the latter five sections reflected preoccupations of the day. Thus, public-law lawyers were to address the theme of 'proportional representation: its progress, its consequences in different countries', private international law specialists were to debate 'means of reaching agreement between states, either by international union or by individual treaties, on jurisdiction and the enforcement of judgements', while the commercial section was to consider 'means of achieving uniformity of law and custom in the context of negotiable instruments'.[5]

Saleilles's report to the organizing committee proclaimed that four aims needed to be kept clearly in mind. First, as art and part of the very notion of a 'science' of comparative law, it was necessary to define the appropriate methods whereby the three activities that together constitute the proper task of comparative law might be carried out, namely, establishing the law, comparing law and then adapting the law. Secondly, from a doctrinal point of view, it was important to clarify comparative law's role as an educational tool. Thirdly, from a practical point of view, the Congress had to consider to what extent legal solutions derived from comparative analysis might be implemented. Finally, means of discovering and exchanging information about foreign law had to be developed.[6] As Saleilles put it, 'being a science whose formulation is far from defined, these matters demand elaboration'.[7] A century later, the objectives of comparative legal studies have become too eclectic to permit of such intellectual dirigism.

Moreover, when one examines more closely what Saleilles designated 'the focal point of the entire Congress', one seems to detect a pronouncedly domestic as well as an international agenda. To be sure, the purposes of the Paris Congress were framed in terms of an objective, international 'legal science' which, if properly applied, was to reveal the deepest secrets of legal existence and ultimately lead to ever-greater uniformity among legal systems. Indeed, Saleilles, in his general report to the Congress, berates would-be comparatists for having hitherto simply juxtaposed institutions

---

[4] Raymond Saleilles, 'Rapport présenté à la commission d'organisation sur l'utilité, le but et le programme du Congrès', in *Procès-verbaux et documents, supra*, note 3, p. 15.
[5] 'Programme et rapporteurs du Congrès international de droit comparé de 1900', in *Procès-verbaux et documents, supra*, note 3, pp. 18–20.
[6] Saleilles, *supra*, note 4, p. 14.   [7] *Id.*, p. 15.

without design and 'without having made the slightest attempt to present any analysis of the scientific laws which must inform comparison'.[8] However, there was a prominently French dimension to the 1900 Congress. Christophe Jamin brought this aspect out to great effect in an elegantly crafted paper presented to the Cambridge Conference one evening under the title 'Lambert and Saleilles's Noble Dream Revisited'.[9] The turn of the century, it was contended, marked an indelible intellectual watershed in French legal thinking. Before 1900, French civil law in particular was dominated by the outlook of an exegetical movement whose faith lay in the ability of the legislative texts, when properly construed, to provide jurists with comprehensive answers to all legal questions. After 1900, however, it is noticeable that another philosophy, another mood took hold. As Jamin shows, the thought of both Saleilles and Edouard Lambert heralds a very different approach that would view legal rules in the context of their historical development rather than in isolation. Hence, Saleilles's famous slogan, 'beyond the Civil Code, but via the Civil Code'.[10] Saleilles's quest for harmony and balance was later to emerge in the form of what he termed 'a national science of comparative law',[11] in which the study of foreign systems was dictated by, and thus subservient to, requirements of national law. If national law was defective, other systems could be ransacked for alternative national models. Comparative law, then, had a practical role to play.

Although Lambert set off from a slightly different point of departure, he too shared this idea that the study of foreign legal systems was meant to serve the interests of national law. Additionally, there was the belief in an international legislative common law – this idea being that universal principles and tendencies could be discerned at work within the various systems and that when these uniformities were absent other disciplines could be prayed in aid to demonstrate statistically, economically or in whichever way the formulation to be preferred. The consequence, as Jamin makes clear, was

---

[8] *Id.*, p. 13. See also *id.*, 'Conception et objet de la science du droit comparé', in *Procès-verbaux et documents*, supra, note 3, p. 167.

[9] This paper, which was delivered after dinner in Christ's College on 27 July, has since been published under the title 'Le vieux rêve de Saleilles et Lambert revisité: à propos du centenaire du Congrès international de droit comparé de Paris', Rev. int. dr. comp., 2000, p. 733. It has been reprinted in Mireille Delmas-Marty (ed.), *Variations autour d'un droit commun* (Paris: Société de législation comparée, 2001), pp. 31–48.

[10] Raymond Saleilles, 'Préface', in François Gény, *Méthode d'interprétation et sources en droit privé positif*, 2d ed., vol. I (Paris: L.G.D.J., 1919), p. xxv ['*Au-delà du Code civil, mais par le Code civil!*'].

[11] *Id.*, 'Droit civil et droit comparé', Rev. int. enseignement, 1911, p. 30.

to accentuate the importance of French doctrinal writing in systematizing the diverse materials and pointing the way to be taken by the courts:

> Saleilles and Lambert essentially employ comparative law as a means of renewing French legal thinking by imposing on French civilian *doctrine* an approach to which it would adhere throughout the following century. Comparative law serves to fill the void left [when French lawyers] abandoned that literal method of reading the texts for which the nineteenth-century writers had been reproached. It provides a broader base for the legal structures founded on the search for the principles that have to replace analytical textual examination, while at the same time conferring on them a much sought-after scientific objectivity. [...] It was inevitable that this very particular role given to comparative law would to a great extent determine the principal directions it would subsequently take.[12]

The search for inspiration from other systems was not necessarily to be unrestricted. For Lambert, it was apparent that certain laws – notably, the English common law – were simply too far removed and lacking in coherent structure to provide the material for valid comparisons.[13] Fruitful comparison might be made only within groups of legal systems with broadly shared attributes.

The scientism of the Paris Congress now looks decidedly antiquated. Similarly, it need scarcely be said that contemporary comparative legal studies no longer particularly seeks after that Grail of universal legal principles which once were assumed to inform the laws of all civilized nations.[14] Nor did participants in 2000 expect to see repeated that renewal within the host country's legal thinking which in 1900 was to coincide with and, to an inevitable degree, become confounded with the birth of modern

---

[12] Jamin, *supra*, note 9, pp. 743–4 and 40–1, respectively.

[13] See Edouard Lambert, 'Une réforme nécessaire des études de droit civil', Rev. int. enseignement, 1900, p. 421. Lack of structure would seem to be an enduring property of the common law. No comparatist will be unaware of Bernard Rudden's penetrating jest in his 'Torticles', (1991–2) 6/7 Tulane Civ. L. Forum 105, p. 110: 'The alphabet is virtually the only instrument of intellectual order of which the common law makes use.'

[14] This sort of view was widely held at that time. Coincidentally, Lord Haldane, speaking extrajudicially in the very year of the Paris Congress, declared that '[t]he jurisprudence of all countries is much the same in its fundamental principles. Strip it of its technical terminology, and the differences in great measure disappear': Richard B. Haldane, 'The Appellate Courts of the Empire', in *Education and Empire: Addresses on Certain Topics of the Day* (London: John Murray, 1902), p. 141. From this, he deduced that '[t]he master of legal principle who has a mind large enough to be free from provincialism is, therefore, in all cases the best kind of judge': *id.*, pp. 141–2.

comparative legal studies. Rather than restrict the territory of comparative law with fancied incompatibilities or predicate any methodological orthodoxy, the Cambridge Conference deliberately sought to be inclusive and consciously all-encompassing. To this end, it attempted to identify and give expression to all leading strands of comparative thinking. This openness is reflected, for instance, in the fact that the fourth and final session of the Cambridge Conference was specifically devoted to 'Comparative Legal Studies and its Futures'.

The two papers in this session set out to explore where the outer bounds of the subject may eventually come to lie. First, against a background of today's tendencies toward the Europeanization and the globalization of law, David Nelken (chapter 12) considers the increasingly prevalent phenomenon of legal transfers. This obviously invokes a series of questions. Can we ever aspire to a full understanding of another system's law and does it greatly matter if we cannot?[15] Are legal transplants largely a product of serendipity and chance, as Alan Watson has argued?[16] Alternatively, are transfers better viewed as deliberate and do we have means at our disposal that enable us to foretell whether particular institutions or rules are likely to prove especially appropriate subjects for transplantation? This, in turn, leads on to the question of how we might measure 'appropriateness' – what counts for success and what counts for failure in this domain? Beyond this, there lies the equally pertinent question, whether law has a social context or, more perplexingly, whether law also simultaneously or independently makes its own context.[17] The harder one looks at all these conceptual puzzles, the more elusive they prove. Then, finally, there is the issue as to what contribution, if any, sociology can make alongside comparative legal studies – two disciplines that are often at odds with one another – in explaining the effects that broader political, economic and social factors can have on the process of legal transfer. Nelken sounds an important word of caution, namely, that the comparatist surveying this phenomenon must not lose from sight

---

[15] The issue of understanding the other recalls a passage in Umberto Eco's introduction to the English translation of his *Diario minimo*, in *Misreadings*, transl. by William Weaver (London: Jonathan Cape, 1993), p. 4, where he recounts the following anecdote: 'Some time ago, a group of anthropologists invited African researchers to France so that they could observe the French way of life. The Africans were amazed to find, for example, that the French were in the habit of walking their dogs.'

[16] For example, see Alan Watson, *Legal Transplants*, 2d ed. (Athens, Georgia: University of Georgia Press, 1993).

[17] For example, see Gunther Teubner, *Autopoietic Law* (Oxford: Blackwell, 1993).

'how different metaphors mobilize and favour different ideas about how law fits society' and, indeed, how the very notion of 'transplant' may be ambiguous and quite inapposite in certain contexts.[18] He also argues that there has been a failure fully to engage in empirical research into these fraught questions. Clearly, in a globalizing world, where there appears to be a strong movement favouring increasing uniformity in many areas of law, these are issues of considerable magnitude and potential import.

This diversity of metaphor to which Nelken alludes – the metaphors are variously musical, culinary, biological, marital, medical – is much in evidence in Esin Örücü's examination of 'Comparatists and Extraordinary Places' (chapter 13). It is the case that places can prove 'extraordinary' in a multitude of different ways. However, Örücü's underpinning argument is that in a world where legal implants, transplants, or whatever one chooses to call them now, frequently take place across jurisdictions that share few legal, social or religious attributes, the focus of the comparatist must shift. Henceforth, comparison between systems which conventional orthodoxy would probably once have dismissed as simply too remote from one another to merit meaningful inquiry are entitled at least to equal attention. Without underestimating the importance of understanding transfers of institutions and rules within, say, the European Union, an activity that currently dominates the comparative agenda, it is argued that 'transpositions from the western legal traditions to the eastern and central European legal systems are of equal, if not greater, importance'. Among the formidable challenges that await tomorrow's comparatist, therefore, are the tasks of tracing the sometimes improbable paths taken by migrating laws, of investigating the ways in which they come to be assimilated, rejected or refashioned within the host system, of analysing the consequences that flow from this process of transplantation and adaptation and, finally, of assessing the inevitable conceptual implications inherent in these phenomena.[19] In the course of time, it may be that globalization will put paid even to the notion of an 'extraordinary place'. The 'extraordinary' may simply wither away as global convergence gathers pace. The comparatist's world in consequence may shrink back to a more familiar size and shape. But for the time being, these fresh vistas offer themselves.

---

[18] For example, see *id.*, 'Legal Irritants: Good Faith in British Law or How Unifying Law Ends Up in New Divergences', (1998) 61 Modern L.R. 1.

[19] See Esin Örücü, 'A Theoretical Framework for Transfrontier Mobility of Law', in R. Jagtenberg, *id.* and A. de Roo (eds.), *Transfrontier Mobility of Law* (The Hague: Kluwer, 1995), pp. 5–18.

To this day, comparative legal studies, as a subject, remains to a surprising degree problematical and is still perhaps regarded by some as the 'Cinderella of the Legal Sciences'.[20] Indeed, the very term 'comparative law' has always invited the *boutade* that it is not really a category of law at all – although, from the time of Harold Gutteridge and beyond, it had been recognized that not all languages by any means encounter this perplexity.[21] Because 'comparative law' is in a sense a subject without a constituency, a clear appreciation of its objectives is especially vital. Indeed, the issue can be stated in a more menacing way, it having even been suggested lately that unless the subject does discover a meaningful sense of purpose, it will find itself altogether without an audience.[22] This reflection, of course, invites the allied question regarding comparative law's proper place within the academic curriculum – a question that sparks into life from time to time.[23] The enduring quality of these foundational doubts is a constant reminder to those engaged in comparative legal studies that, in the eyes of many, its intellectual *raison d'être* may be somewhat precarious. Although these issues inevitably form part of the backdrop to the papers assembled in this book, the editors' and the contributors' posture was anything but one of defensive hand-wringing. Without ignoring the problematic nature of the enterprise, as its title suggests, the purpose behind *Traditions and Transitions* was to demonstrate both continuity and development within the subject, that is, to explore both those habitudes of thinking that have now become established methodologies within comparative legal studies and to tap into the intellectual vigour and generosity of vision with which the comparative approach can now endow the researcher.

It seemed fitting that the proceedings on the first day of the Cambridge Conference should be devoted to consideration of four great intellectual strands that, it appeared to us, have left their enduring mark on comparative scholarship. First, there is what could be broadly termed 'The Universalist

---

[20] H. C. Gutteridge, *Comparative Law*, 2d ed. (Cambridge: Cambridge University Press, 1946), p. 23.

[21] *Id.*, pp. 1–2. The title given to the Cambridge Conference deliberately avoids this academic quagmire.

[22] See Basil Markesinis, 'Comparative Law – A Subject in Search of an Audience', (1990) 53 Modern L.R. 1. Markesinis would further maintain that fresh life can be suffused into comparative legal studies in England only by its judges. For example, see *id.*, *Always on the Same Path: Essays on Foreign Law and Comparative Methodology* (Oxford: Hart, 2001), p. 1.

[23] For example, see Geoffrey Samuel, 'Comparative Law as a Core Subject', (2001) 21 Leg. Stud. 444, who provocatively argues that comparative law ought to be a core subject in each of the years of a law student's university curriculum.

Heritage'. As James Gordley (chapter 2) begins by pointing out, this approach, at least in its classical form as a derivative of natural-law theory in its various guises, lost sway all of two centuries ago. Yet, one can still return with profit to Aristotle, and more particularly to Aquinas, each of whose writings reposed upon an assumption that there existed universal guiding principles and reflect upon questions that continue to perplex the comparatist to this day. The seemingly straightforward problem that Gordley lays before us concerns the relationship between differences in the laws adopted in different jurisdictions and differences of principle. His message is that if we pay proper heed to these lessons from our intellectual history, we may avoid the possible error of jumping too precipitately to the conclusion that a difference between national laws inevitably predicates a difference of principle. Viewed from the natural-law lawyers' perspective, many apparent differences of principle may prove to be merely the different ways in which systems can handle uncertainty which, in turn, owes much to the basic fact that it is just difficult to frame clear rules. Even in the clearest of cases, where conflicting, contradictory principles appear to clash – the example Gordley takes is the tension between freedom of speech and a right to privacy as it has variously been resolved in German and US laws – it may not, in fact, be possible to demonstrate that different principles are at work. If this is correct, of course, this conclusion has a direct impact on the direction in which the comparatist ought to be looking in order to explain difference. The universalist heritage, then, may not have entirely exhausted its utility.

Another vital heritage in comparative legal studies, as it seemed to us, is that of colonialism. Upendra Baxi (chapter 3) shrewdly observes how this historical legacy of imposed legal cultures is a reminder that a notion of 'transaction' lies between the juxtaposed 'traditions' and 'transitions' that appeared on our Conference banner. In an outpouring of *Angst* at the poverty of legal theory, Baxi first traces what is inherent in the process of imposition of alien law by conquest, in terms of both ideology and institutions. He argues that the effects produced include a system whose primary end will often be the economic exploitation of the colony, a law that becomes hybridized, the destruction of local notions of narrative and a perceptibly lower degree of civil freedom. The consequence is a form of 'predatory legality' in which individuals' rights are treated as concessions and are directed to maintaining the *status quo*, in which any broader notion of 'human rights' has no proper place, in which the ethos is inimical to the extension of existing rights or to the creation of new ones and so on. It may be, as Baxi suggests, that legal colonialism, geared as it is to exploitation and domination, nevertheless carries within it the seeds of its own subversion. Perhaps it can be turned upon itself. It may even be possible that we are seeing this reaction taking place around the world today. Like the papers delivered by Nelken and Örücü, Baxi's impassioned examination of the colonialist heritage questions the boundaries of conventional comparative legal thinking. It assaults a conventional wisdom, which instinctively assumes that pre-modern law is antithetical to 'progress'. More importantly, it confronts us directly with the question whether the time is not ripe for comparatists to begin to afford what Baxi terms 'equal discursive dignity' to those legal traditions that emphatically neither share the attributes of, nor identify with, the traditions that animate legal systems falling along the Euro-American axis.

Traditionally, it has been taken as axiomatic that the very act of comparison is contingent upon an ability to define and situate different legal systems. The key has been the nation state. Although the nation state is of comparatively recent invention, nationalist perceptions have wielded enormous influence over the shape and direction of comparative legal studies. As Patrick Glenn (chapter 4) argues, these perceptions presuppose the existence of two primary elements: states and national legal systems. From these two primary elements, by deduction, there must also exist a third element, that is, some conception of the international. The problem today is that both a wide variety of localized and particularist tendencies and a rising tide of globalization are eroding the national legal tradition. Dividing the world's two-hundred-odd nation states into three broad categories – those within Europe, those peopled by Europeans and those largely outside the orbit of European thought – Glenn proceeds to illustrate, in turn, how each of the first two elements, critical to 'The Nationalist Heritage', is threatened in different ways within each of these state groupings. The rise of regionalism, globalism or even universalism then impacts upon the international, a system designed to uphold and legitimate the notion of 'national statehood'. Against this backdrop, it can therefore be claimed with some accuracy that '[r]egions devour the international'. The fundamental question this poses can be stated thus: what is the nationalist heritage's future role, if any, once its ability 'to eliminate both the local and the distant as sources of identity and law' has been sapped?

The fourth unquestionable 'heritage' of comparative legal studies is functionalism. Taking as leading exponents of this approach Konrad Zweigert and Hein Kötz, on the one hand, and Rudolf Schlesinger, on the other, Michele Graziadei (chapter 5) demonstrates just how influential functional method has been and still remains. It serves practical ends and, by placing comparative investigations in a seeming neutral setting congenial to causal explanation, appears to offer satisfying answers that veer toward the universal. The approach, however, carries a price. It tends to assume, for example, that the comparatist's proper role is to establish the basic similarity of legal experience across the world against the background of Zweigert and Kötz's famous '*praesumptio similitudinis*'.[24] It also comports a notion that certain areas of the law may not constitute fit matters for the attention of comparatists simply because they are thought not to lend themselves to this type of explanation. As Graziadei asserts, '[t]he attempt to reduce the legal meaning of any fact to the legal effects of that fact as stated in operative terms is probably flawed'. It is an error to treat functional similarity as synonymous with identity. The interpretation of legal 'facts' is simply incomplete without proper consideration of the culture out of which they grow. Functionalism may, of course, seek to adapt to this insight. This may lead to the kind of 'methodological functionalism', for instance, practised in the European 'common core' project.[25] However, the need to incorporate 'interpretive understanding' alongside causal explanation raises teasing questions concerning what exactly the notion of 'culture' connotes. Besides, there is another meaning of functionalism: the idea of law as a response to a society's needs. This idea, which once found expression, say, in Savigny or in Montesquieu, that law will be, or ought to be, the product of its people,[26] has pretty much had its day. The question today, posed in the context of legal transplantation, rather centres upon whether law is not

---

[24] Zweigert and Kötz, *supra*, note 2, p. 40.
[25] For a presentation, see Ugo Mattei and Mauro Bussani, 'The Common Core Approach to European Private Law', (1997–8) 3 Columbia J. Eur. L. 339.
[26] G. K. Chesterton put the matter well in a newpaper article: 'There are no people so poetical as the English, no people that are so full of a sense of vague distances and perspectives; there are no people so full of a certain fine formless sentiment. They see all things melting into one another like the mists of their Northern sky; the Latin sees everything as clear cut as the crests of the Alps against the hard blue enamel of heaven. The English law, for instance, is uncommonly like an impressionistic picture of a rainy day. The Code Napoleon is like a coloured photograph of Rome. The haphazard, hand-to-mouth quality both in our legislation and our judicature is [...] still more the result of a certain dim kindliness, a sort of desperate kindliness, living in the heart of a confusion and never daring to trust itself to a general rule': 'The English Way', in A. L. Maycock (ed.), *The Man Who Was Orthodox: A Selection from the Uncollected Writings of G. K. Chesterton* (London: Dennis Dobson, 1963), pp. 100–1 [1905].

actually dysfunctional, in the sense that rules and institutions are not peculiarly devised for the specific societies in which they operate and, indeed, that this is not a matter for great concern. Functionalism may not be utterly *passé*, but its limitations as a means of analysing legal phenomena are growing ever clearer. In Graziadei's view, it is preferable, therefore, to see explanation and interpretation as 'alternative, but complementary, ways to the study of legal phenomena'.

Having considered four elements within comparative legal studies that have materially contributed to its development, the second session of the Conference was devoted to 'Comparative Legal Studies and its Boundaries'. The two themes treated on this second day addressed the relationships between comparative legal studies and other areas of scholarly endeavour. What insights, for example, can sociology and languages bring to the comparative enterprise?

The relationship between comparative legal studies and the sociology of law has for long been complex and fraught. While sociologists in the past would have been likely to view certain comparative concepts with suspicion, comparatists may in the past have been drawn to sociology simply because it possessed established responses to those fundamental epistemological and ontological questions that are posed by any species of social inquiry. Roger Cotterrell (chapter 6) perceives the comparatist's attitude to legal sociology today as one of general ambivalence but argues that, in fact, the two disciplines are 'interdependent co-workers in the empirical study of law' sharing, as they do, an identical goal, namely, the desire to understand law as normative regulation in the social setting. Although Jerome Hall may have been the last scholar with pretensions fully to integrate comparative legal studies into the fold of social science,[27] Cotterrell's thesis is that the sociologist of law still has insights that can guide the comparatist, even with such basic issues as what to compare and the validity of those comparisons. Equally, the comparatist's perspective can inform the sociologist's labours. The intellectual traffic is, therefore, two-way. Cotterrell sets out to demonstrate sociology's utility in three contexts where comparatists are seemingly at their most resistant to any form of sociological input. In turn, he suggests how sociology's ability to clarify the nature of the social might be of service as regards the debate concerning legal transplants,[28] how systems theory might be brought

---

[27] See Jerome Hall, *Comparative Law and Social Theory* (Baton Rouge: Louisiana State University Press, 1963).

[28] *Contra*: Watson, *supra*, note 16.

to bear on frameworks that hold up law as autonomous or comprising a functionally distinctive communication system,[29] and how sociological insights and, more specifically, social anthropology's perspective might aid in conceptualizing and elucidating those highly complex notions like 'culture' which increasingly engage the attention of comparatists. The relationship between comparative legal studies and sociology is uneasy, overlapping, awkward to state, but clearly of consuming interest to both callings.

The other theme of the second session was the relationship between comparative legal studies and languages. By virtue of his involvement with the systems of different nations, the comparatist perforce works with foreign materials that require understanding not only of their setting, but also of the language in which they are written. Legal scholars operating in the comparative field are hardly unique in experiencing problems of translation.[30] Translators of literary works, too, persistently encounter similar difficulties. Take the following example. Kathrine Jason published a fine translation of selected short stories by the Italian writer, Tommaso Landolfi (1908–79).[31] The aristocratic and compulsively secretive Landolfi was, in his writing, by turns erudite, archaic, perverse and playful. He has sometimes been described as *lunar*. The following sentence appears in the story, *Parole in agitazione*:

> One thing's for sure, two females and a goose make a market in Naples![32]

What does this mean? What essence is it meant to convey? The original Italian reads: '*è proprio vero che due femmine e una papera misero un mercato a Napoli.*'[33] The principal indicator, I would suggest, lies in Naples. Landolfi, in a story that is nothing short of a verbal *tour de force*, is hearkening back to an original Neapolitan saying, '*Nà femmn e nà papera arrevutarn Nàpule.*' Outside Naples, the meaning of this proverb would not be recognized.[34] In

---

[29] For example, see Teubner, *supra*, note 17; *id.*, *supra*, note 18.
[30] For example, consider Lord Brougham's 'introduction' to his translation of Demosthenes in *The Oration of Demosthenes upon the Crown* (London: Charles Knight, 1840), pp. iii–xxiii, and especially his response to Lord Dudley's misgivings at his having undertaken in the first place to 'attempt to translate the Greatest Oration of the Greatest of Orators into a language so different in its frame and idiom from that noble tongue in which it was pronounced' (p. iii).
[31] Tommaso Landolfi, *Words in Commotion and Other Stories*, transl. and ed. by Kathrine Jason (New York: Viking, 1986).
[32] *Id.*, p. 266. For the original text, see Tommaso Landolfi, *Parole in agitazione*, in *Opere*, ed. by Idolina Landolfi, vol. II: *1960–1971* (Milan: Rizzoli, 1992), pp. 855–8.
[33] Landolfi, *supra*, note 32, p. 857.
[34] In Italian, the proverb can be rendered: '*Una femmina e una papera misero sotto sopra Napoli.*'

the particular context of the saying, the word '*mercato*' does not actually mean 'market' but signifies something akin to the French word '*foire*', when a French person exclaims '*quelle foire!*' ('what confusion!'). Yet, although by a happy coincidence the French word offers us also that comparative rarity, a commercial metaphor, *foire* at the same time fails to convey the full impact of the Italian/Neapolitan *mercato*. *Foire*, meaning both a 'fair' and 'confusion', is simultaneously a thing and an expression universal to France; '*arrevutarn*' or '*mercato*', however, has other levels of meaning. These meanings are intelligible only to those from Naples or to those who share similar cultural values. Thus, in addition to 'making confusion', the expression can mean 'standing out from the crowd', 'deception' and 'conveying the false impression that someone is obtaining a bargain' – all of these being notions intimately connected with the life of a street market. The interest in this example is that Landolfi has successfully conveyed much of the richness of the Neapolitan term in his translation '*mercato*'. What is quite clear is that once one attempts to render any of this intelligible in English, one is doomed to failure. The obstacle is the absence of a common cultural denominator. Confronted with this text, however, other questions also crowd in. How much of this did Landolfi actually *intend* to convey? Was he making deliberate play on these ambiguities? Why did Landolfi alter the conventional '*una femmina*' to '*due femmine*', later even referring to '*tre femmine*'?[35] How does the translator, trying faithfully to render Landolfi's prose, get any of this across to an American or an English readership, each of whom presumably can be taken to interpret meaning through quite distinct cultural frames of reference? How many of these layers of meaning were deliberately omitted by the translator? At what point does one legitimately abandon the struggle to keep faith with the original and to what degree ought one to alert the reader to one's having quit the chase at a certain point?[36] It seems to me that the translator, when wrestling with these perplexities, has strong affinities to the comparatist attempting honestly to convey the

---

[35] His allusions become even more complex. Landolfi may be referring to two women because the passage relates to a squabble between two disputants, shortly to be joined by a third ('*macché due femmine: tre, femmine, dice il proverbio*': Landolfi, *supra*, note 32, p. 857). Alternatively, the intrusion of a third woman is simply a way to emphasize the magnitude of the confusion. The translation of '*femmine*' is further complicated by the fact that in Italian the word '*parola*' is itself feminine and the term '*femmine*' might therefore be taken to refer also to the words themselves that are squabbling with one another in the story.

[36] I am grateful to my friends, Pasquale Cardellicchio and Maria Luisa Pinto, for confirming my suspicions and for inducting me into the Neapolitan language.

very precise shades of meaning and cultural resonances that can reside within what appear to be another system's anodyne legal terminology, rules and institutions. Bernhard Großfeld (chapter 7), who addressed this elusive theme, recalls the difficulty in communicating in accurate, equivalent translation such allied but differing concepts as '*Rechtsstaat*', '*prééminence du droit*' and the 'rule of law'. There is clearly a fundamental problem in any form of cross-cultural communication. The technical setting can only multiply the difficulties. Ought one, therefore, to expect perfect communication in comparative legal studies? In Großfeld's view, such an expectation is plainly unreasonable and the comparatist must settle for imperfect communication. According to him, we should 'avoi[d] perfectionism'. Even if comparatists are condemned forever to miss many of the subtle referents in which foreign legal discourse is inevitably steeped, they cannot just abdicate their responsibilities. It is possible to convey much of the sense by resorting to crafted explanations of the concepts and cultural references that accompany foreign discourse. Imperfect representations seem preferable to none at all. The comparatist's enduring mission, then, is to act as a communicator and as a tireless builder of cross-cultural bridges.[37]

The four papers presented in the third session addressed the general theme of 'Comparative Legal Studies and its Theories'. The evidence is not easily seized and concepts are subtle, but the issues undeniably matter. Like many of the speakers, James Whitman (chapter 10) focuses upon the idea of diversity, repudiating a comparative literature that he finds 'weirdly innocent of the fact that human societies differ'. He seeks to explore via an historical approach the limits of the New Romanticism, which he considers 'difference' methodology has instilled into comparative legal studies. He traces the various intellectual strands that now make up this contemporary Romanticism back to their origins in nineteenth-century German writings – notably, the writings of Herder, Hugo and Savigny – and to the early stirrings of twentieth-century hermeneutics in the work of Hans-Georg Gadamer in particular. This revived Romantic strain in comparative legal thought lays its stress upon the problem of otherness and the question of the ultimate knowability of another law. These developments take a variety of forms – sometimes concerning themselves with the 'inner' perspective of the law, sometimes with the study of those unarticulated premises upon which law

---

[37] The image is borrowed from Basil S. Markesinis, *Foreign Law and Comparative Methodology: A Subject and a Thesis* (Oxford: Hart, 1997), p. 194.

reposes – and different scholars consider the issues intractable to differing degrees. What all these 'exciting and overdue' developments share is that they direct attention to the fact that full understanding in the comparative sphere is not easily acquired. But what exactly is the comparatist required to do? Using the example of what he calls 'dignitary law', Whitman first seeks to show that, unlike cultural anthropology, the comparatist cannot acquire an accurate understanding of other institutions merely by studying the insiders' 'inner' account. Thus, he notes that European laws set out to address a wide range of issues – such as the sale of body parts, protection from sexual harassment and rights of privacy – under the broad banner of 'human dignity'. Curiously, in these selfsame areas, US law is not founded upon such a concept. When he inquired into the reasons why European insiders claim that they have recourse to notions of 'dignity', Whitman found that Europeans appear to have distorted the account of their own law, rewritten their legal history. They actually misunderstand the functioning of their own law and have fallen victims to their own normative reconstruction. Whitman argues that this shows how the comparatist needs more than just that 'inner' perspective for which someone like William Ewald argues,[38] but additionally requires to be alive to those unarticulated assumptions that are simply taken for granted – identified by Gadamer in his studies on juristic hermeneutics under the label 'pre-understanding' or '*Vorverständnis*'.[39] This is not, of course, the sole and exclusive way in which foreign legal systems may be understood. Indeed, the comparatist may produce a kind of Heisenberg effect. Simply by articulating what previously was left unspoken, the comparatist may alter the premise; more likely, by articulating what was previously assumed, he may facilitate its modification. While fully acknowledging the importance of understanding law in its cultural context, Whitman sounds a warning, issuing a reminder that, by its nature, law is a normative endeavour, that it ought to be the subject of vigorous debate and that the valuable commodity that the comparatist can actually bring to bear on this activity is a fully informed awareness of other normative conceptions.

Unlike certain other species of lawyers, comparatists are prone to lay claim to the dry virtue of a scientific neutrality unsullied by political

---

[38] For example, see William Ewald, 'Legal History and Comparative Law', Zeitschrift für Europäisches Privatrecht, 1999, p. 553.
[39] See Hans-Georg Gadamer, *Truth and Method*, 2d ed. transl. by Joel Weinsheimer and Donald G. Marshall (London: Sheed & Ward, 1993), pp. 265–307.

objectives. One notable example of this phenomenon is the European 'common core' project which, in spite of the notoriety of the harmonizing objectives sought by the European Union, claims that dispassionate comparative research can be simply 'devoted to producing reliable information, whatever its policy use might be'.[40] Proceeding from his intuition that comparative legal studies self-evidently is 'political' in the sense of producing political effects, David Kennedy (chapter 11) investigates and begins to map out the, as yet, unwritten story of comparative law's participation in governance. His main hypothesis is that methodology carries political consequences. These may manifest themselves because a comparatist elects to espouse one particular comparative methodology in preference to others on offer, each of these individual methodologies appearing to be possessed of a 'politics'. Alternatively, it may be possible to discern a politics beneath the broad background assumptions that underlie the entire comparative enterprise, regardless of the methodology pursued. Some of the insights this approach can furnish are exemplified in Jorge Esquirol's study of the various effects wrought by comparative scholarship in Latin America.[41] However, the politics of comparative law, as practised today, proves extremely hard to pin down, if only owing to the discipline's contemporary eclecticism. Kennedy sets about drafting in broad brush-stroke a relief map of the politics or 'governance contribution' of contemporary comparative legal studies. The politics is argued to fall under three general headings, these being the political projects actually pursued by the groups and individuals within the field, the comparatists' shared knowledge practices which can, in turn, exert an impact on those who govern and, finally, the enhanced contribution to governance that is a dividend deriving from the comparatists' membership of a recognized discipline in the intellectual class. As Kennedy observes, it is curious that for all the methodological discussion across a century of professionalization, we know so very little concerning the politics of comparative law.

To what extent is meaningful legal comparison possible given the seemingly insuperable problems of understanding that ultimately confront the comparatist? Mitchel Lasser (chapter 8) approaches the difficulty by first testing optimistic assumptions that the comparatist might make as to the

---

[40] Mauro Bussani, 'Current Trends in European Comparative Law: The Common Core Approach', (1998) 21 Hastings Int. & Comp. L.R. 785, p. 796.
[41] Jorge Esquirol, 'The Fictions of Latin American Law: An Analysis of Comparative Law Scholarship', [1997] Utah L.R. 425.

knowability of another law. Using techniques such as immersion in the foreign legal culture, rigorous textual analysis that employs, say, strategies pirated from literary theory, and not confining oneself to consideration of the materials that represent the 'official' version of the law as expressed by the official state agencies, a level of understanding might be reached that permits meaningful dialogue with those within the foreign system. However, objections remain. These revolve around the fact that foreign systems are not truly intelligible as monolithic structures but, on the contrary, are turbulent entities, often in a state of flux. The objections also relate to the fundamental difficulty that the comparatist's choice of methodology serves to construct the very object which he sets out to analyse. Comparison, therefore, is in a real sense an 'intervention'. Like Großfeld, Lasser concludes that for a variety of reasons compromise is not merely unavoidable, but can be justified.[42] The comparatist can, and must, develop a certain familiarity with the foreign 'culture' and its internal view. But complete understanding is not really possible either for those external to, or even to those internal to, the system. The choices of methodology do reflect choices of motivation and policy but these selections may be explicable and capable of justification. In as much as they may relate to what has gone before or set out to cross-reference with other disciplines, these determinations merely show that comparative law is 'a relational practice'. Moreover, rather after the manner of Karl Llewellyn's 'situation-sense',[43] thanks to a kind of trained instinct the comparatist may intuit the methodology best geared to the needs of whatever object he is studying and of the audience he is addressing. The ultimate test, in Lasser's view, is that one's work must 'pass muster' with significant sections of those practising, teaching or otherwise being involved within the foreign system. His solution is not especially crisp, but then the problems it is addressing have thus far proved indomitable.

In different vein, Pierre Legrand (chapter 9) launches an assault on that trend of thinking, prevalent in comparative legal studies at least since the time of Edouard Lambert and the 1900 Paris Congress, which would seek to eliminate or ignore difference. To the extent that representing another's

---

[42] This perhaps recalls Wittgenstein's reflection upon whether a blurred concept is a concept at all. He asked: 'Is an indistinct photograph a picture of a person at all? Is it even always an advantage to replace an indistinct picture by a sharp one? Isn't the indistinct one often exactly what we need?': Ludwig Wittgenstein, *Philosophical Investigations*, 3d ed. by G. E. M. Anscombe and R. Rees and transl. by G. E. M. Anscombe (Oxford: Blackwell, 2001), § 71.
[43] Karl N. Llewellyn, *The Common Law Tradition* (Boston: Little, Brown, 1960), *passim*.

system will inevitably involve an act of prescription, identity is not even something one can necessarily perceive. Indeed, claims to sameness can really hold water only if legal problems can be considered in the abstract, totally dissociated from their cultural environments. Such an approach, however, will tell us little, if anything, about those problems or about the legal systems under examination. Moreover, it may be worth considering that if harmonization is on the political agenda, it may 'secure the allegiance of the various constituencies only by retreating from the imperialist drive to oneness and by doing justice to the profound diversity of legal experience across jurisdictions'. For these and other reasons, Legrand argues that comparatists must 'reverse the intellectual movement which subordinates difference to identity' and that 'comparative legal studies must assume the duty to acknowledge, appreciate and respect alterity'. Like Lasser and indeed several other participants in the Cambridge Conference, Legrand sees difference as the ultimate intractable but self-evident fact confronting comparatists. Several consequences might flow were comparatists to give priority to difference over sameness. They would obviously lose the tunnel vision that otherwise allows them to see only a portion of the range of legal possibilities. No longer would they need to traduce foreign law in order to force it to fit a pre-ordained uniform mould. No more would they be driven to espouse the functionalist viewpoint, with its improbable universalist expectations. Despite a world with globalizing pretensions, they would discover that intensity of contact actually emphasizes a sense of difference, not of sameness. And they could avoid the naive illusion that the object of comparative legal studies is to quest after the best solution to any given legal problem. This is why comparative legal studies ought to 'resist the attempts of conservative academics to reduce alterity to sameness by way of sterile facilitations reminiscent of the *Begriff*-stricken world of nineteenth-century scholarship' and, instead, to appreciate that comparison does 'not have a unifying, but a multiplying effect'.

Lawrence Rosen (chapter 14) offered his general thoughts on comparison in a concluding talk delivered in Peterhouse on the final evening of the conference. In his paper, he takes up themes pursued in earlier contributions, starting with an expression of surprise that comparative legal studies today seems still to be so rooted in the dated scientism associated with the Paris Congress. What he is anxious to emphasize, however, is the positive contribution comparison can make to legal studies. Thus, referring to G. K. Chesterton's dictum that 'the function of imagination is not to make strange things settled, so much as to make settled things strange',[44] he explores the similar dividends a comparative outlook can yield. He draws upon the examples of law and colonialism, where comparative legal studies can claim to have enriched understanding of the colonial experience, of the relationship between culture and legal reasoning in common-law and Islamic systems where, again, comparative analysis reveals some unexpected features, and of universalism and functionalism, with a withering indictment of the influential conceit that functionality ought to be 'the basic methodological principle of all comparative law'.[45] Rosen argues that comparison may assist us in avoiding 'category mistakes' and, more especially, enables us to pick up unforeseen connections. A facet of this positive outlook may entail abandonment of problems that appear insoluble. Thus, if the debate over sameness and difference is incapable of resolution, the answer may be to move on to more productive issues. If, as seems likely, there are no true bases for categorizations, and those with which we operate are in the nature of working hypotheses, the future directions of comparative legal studies are fluid. To be sure, comparative study can enable us to perceive, with fresh eyes, the unfamiliar in what we mistakenly took to be the familiar.[46] It can draw together unexpected combinations of concepts and institutions. Nevertheless, Rosen issues an admonition, pointing out that although comparison can yield a rich harvest of insights, one ought not to assume too much about the subject: 'Comparative law cannot be expected magically to yield answers to every teleological issue or practical effect.'

The papers collected in this book are intended to provide a comprehensive account and critique of ideas that currently dominate comparative legal studies as well as to investigate the traditions on which the subject was founded and the future directions that it might take. Yet, it might be objected, highfalutin theory is all very well. But how does this concern the many comparatists who toil at the coal-face? The answer perhaps is obvious. As contemplation of the issues canvassed in this book reveals, comparison carries with it an intellectual baggage to which one has to

---

[44] G. K. Chesterton, *The Defendant* (London: Dent, 1922), p. 84 [1901]. The passage continues, that the role of imagination is 'not so much to make wonders facts as to make facts wonders'.
[45] Zweigert and Kötz, *supra*, note 2, p. 34.
[46] Perhaps this is not far from what Kipling meant when he penned the line, 'And what should they know of England who only England know?': Rudyard Kipling, 'The English Flag', in *Rudyard Kipling's Verse: Definitive Edition* (London: Hodder & Stoughton, 1940), p. 221 [1891].

be alert. No longer can one simply comply with the curt instruction to the Soviet youth issued by the scientist, Pavlov: 'Learn, compare and collect the facts.'[47] The request is clear enough. Any comparatist, however, will immediately grasp how many questions it begs. What is one to compare? Are the phenomena one seeks to compare truly comparable? What hidden purpose may lie concealed behind the act of comparison? And so on. Furthermore, only if one appreciates the full range of available philosophic stances and of the allied disciplines upon which one may make call does the comparatist also become conscious of the wealth of angles from which to view any given legal object. Rather like a mariner's chart, an understanding of fundamental comparative theory enables us to descry contours in an otherwise submerged intellectual landscape. To deal with the point at a micro- rather than simply at a macro-level, after the manner of Mitchel Lasser, let me try briefly to indicate how these insights might come to inform the activities of one who toils at the coal-face.

Let us consider a feature of legal systems that can probably be treated as fundamental: styles of appellate judicial decision-making in common-law and civil-law jurisdictions. Remarkably, something as seemingly straightforward as establishing the facts can prove highly problematical. This, in turn, may mean that it is problematical to identify with certainty what is actually significant in the topic itself. It has long been assumed that one meaningful point of difference between English law and many Continental systems lies in the decision-making procedures the respective benches adopt. It is assumed that English judges, even when sitting as an appellate bench of three, five or seven, will all hand down individual judgements, even to the extent of merely saying 'I agree'. In this way, English judges can be claimed to be robustly asserting a basic right to have their say. This is an accepted tenet of English judicial procedure. Continental courts, in contrast, behave quite differently when there is a bench of judges, acting collegiately and delivering themselves of composite, collaborative judgements. This is often treated like a self-evident proposition by comparatists. It is also thought to be important. But is it actually self-evident? And is it actually important? When one comes to research the question,

---

[47] The most authoritative source for this well-known quotation is possibly I. P. Pawlow, '[Brief an die Jugend]', in *Sämtliche Werke*, ed. by Lothar Pickenhain and transl. by G. Kirpatsch, vol. I (Berlin: Akademie-Verlag, 1954), p. 14 ['*Studiert, vergleicht und sammelt die Tatsachen*'] (1935).

one discovers that a comparative imagination can 'make settled things strange'.[48]

In 2001, in the Civil Division of the English Court of Appeal, composite judgements were handed down in no less than one in seven cases. Moreover, there are indications that this proportion continues to rise. When one adds to the 14 or so per cent of composite judgements the 40–50 per cent of cases in which, to all intents, only one member of the Court of Appeal delivers a full judgement, the other appellate judges confining themselves to briefly signalling concurrence, one does begin to wonder to what extent that vaunted, robust individualism of the English bench is a central or even significant feature of English judicial method. The fact is that within the space of a decade English judicial method has undergone a possibly radical transformation. The judiciary has effected this change without fanfare, without discussion in the profession, in short as if by stealth – and no one even noticed. In order to understand the possible significance of this change, the temptation is strong to see this as a borrowing or as possibly another step down the road to European harmonization. Is it a vindication of the functionalist claim that, at root, legal systems tend to be similar and to gravitate toward the best method of operation? The comparatist might, therefore, be prompted to look to other systems whose appellate courts manufacture composite judgements. He might be inclined to investigate the hypothesis that the English Court of Appeal has begun to behave like a French, Italian or German court, or more plausibly like the European Court of Justice. But are these courts in fact the same or different?

Were one to begin to look at France, with what is one to compare the English Court of Appeal? It is an intermediate court and, save for one aberrant occasion in recent years,[49] the House of Lords has not become implicated in the particular change of practice I address. Nevertheless, I suggest that it might appear a little odd to French lawyers were one to focus on the operations of their intermediate level of the *cours d'appel*, just as it might look equally odd to focus upon that ever-popular subject of the comparatist, the *Cour de cassation*. Moreover, even if one settled this question, one would still need to consider a host of other variables,

---

[48] The remarks that follow draw on Roderick Munday, ' "All for One and One for All": The Rise to Prominence of the Composite Judgment Within the Civil Division of the Court of Appeal', [2002] Cambridge L.J. 321; *id.*, 'Judicial Configurations: Permutations of the Court and Properties of Judgment', [2002] Cambridge L.J. 612.

[49] *R. v. Forbes*, [2001] 2 W.L.R. 1 (H.L.).

linguistic and institutional. Furthermore, when one takes into account that the English court now occasionally hands down decisions with majority composite judgements together with a dissent,[50] it turns out that the more apposite parallel might be the European Court of Human Rights or that it might not be European at all but could be the courts of the United States or of Australia. One might then struggle to acquire the 'inner' view to explain why judges in these jurisdictions do what they do. Judicial explanations in England oscillate between a quest for efficiency or for authoritative clarity, while practitioners are prone to ascribe the English change to laziness. Hard evidence of the litigants' viewpoint will not easily be come by. How do legal systems that are by tradition proponents of the composite style of judgement assess their own performance and, more beguilingly, how do they compare their composite ways with the individualistic approach taken by judges from common-law systems?[51] History, too, will complicate the picture as French courts, for sure, evolved composite ways for reasons very different to those that induced the various common-law jurisdictions to tread this path. But can one even discover why common-law courts actually developed and retained such a strong tradition of delivering individual judgements in the first place? Interestingly, common-law lawyers have almost never addressed the question. How do we justify the practice of concurring judgements? But this is exactly the kind of awkward question that a comparative perspective is apt to generate. If one does detect differences between the methods followed by courts that deliver composite judgements in a number of jurisdictions, does this illustrate a difference of principle? And what is that principle? And if one can detect similarity of method, if one looks more intently, will one discover that beneath the surface lie deeper convictions – evidence of *mentalités* that are more enduring than would-be grand reforms that barely scratch the legal system's surface? Moreover, just as one may discern a politics, in the sense of an impact on governance, in the judiciary's postures, does one also participate in the politics merely because one's research is an intervention in the field under study? More narrowly, what is the purpose behind pursuing this question at all?

A theme which recurred throughout the Cambridge Conference was that of globalization and convergence. Two further observations might be made in this regard. First, legal change, which is often effected now in the name

---

[50] For example, see *Bellinger* v. *Bellinger*, [2002] 2 W.L.R. 411 (C.A.).
[51] See Jean-Marie Baudouin, 'La collégialité est-elle une garantie de la sûreté des jugements?', Rev. trim dr. civ., 1992, p. 532.

of harmonization, occurs almost everywhere with bewildering speed. The comparatist, therefore, is forever condemned to aim at multiple moving targets. His difficulty is to ensure that knowledge is up to date. But also, in a world where convergence seems to be the watchword, one may just be deceived into believing that the process is linear, that everything is conducing to that one end. To return once more to the subject of judicial decision-making, the tide is not in fact moving entirely in one direction. Once again, unnoticed it would seem,[52] the Judicial Committee of the Privy Council, which in its advice to the sovereign habitually delivers itself of a single composite opinion, has now for the first time acquired a right to deliver individual judgements in appeals in devolution cases from Scotland.[53] And in all the cases that until now have come before it involving devolution issues, every member of that Committee has without fail exercised his power to deliver an individual judgement.[54] The Court of Appeal may have gone half-composite, yet the impulsion to adopt the tried and tested judicial ways seems to have proven equally powerful in another forum. The facts are slippery. What exactly is the significant evidence in this least expected of shifting landscapes?

Comparison complicates. It tests one's suppositions in unexpected ways. If one thing is clear, it is that there is no single key to comparative legal studies. The ideas that there may be universal answers to the comparatist's every question or that there is a single preferred methodology that will fit all cases seem to be an illusion. Illusions, however, can prove tenacious. There is a significant passage in Gabriel García Márquez's long short story, *No One Writes to the Colonel*, when the following exchange takes place between

---

[52] For example, see Lord Hope, '*Edinburgh v. Westminster & Others*: Resolving Constitutional Disputes – Inside the Crystal Ball Again?', (1997) 42 J. L. Soc. of Scotland 140, p. 142; Aidan O'Neill, 'Judicial Politics and the Judicial Committee: The Devolution Jurisprudence of the Privy Council', (2001) 64 Modern L.R. 603.

[53] This is by virtue of the Judicial Committee (Powers in Devolution Cases) Order 1999, art. 4(1)(a). Although not strictly speaking a court, in fact the Judicial Committee has for long been recognized to be just that. For example, see *British Coal Corp. v. R.*, [1935] A.C. 500 (P.C.), pp. 510–11: 'It is clear that the Committee is [...] a judicial body or Court, though all it can do is to report or recommend to His Majesty in Council' (Viscount Sankey L. C.). See also *Ibralebbe v. R.*, [1964] A.C. 900 (P.C.), p. 913 (Viscount Radcliffe).

[54] Ignoring petitions for leave to appeal which are dealt with in the form of composite judgements, the relevant cases are *Montgomery v. H.M. Advocate* (DRA Nos. 1 and 2 of 2000); *Procurator Fiscal, Dunfermline v. Brown* (DRA No. 3 of 2000); *H.M. Advocate v. McIntosh*, [2001] U.K.P.C. D1; *McLean v. Procurator Fiscal, Fort William*, [2001] U.K.P.C. D3; *Millar v. Dickson*, [2002] W.L.R. 1615 (P.C.); *Anderson v. Scottish Ministers* (DRA Nos. 9, 10 and 11 of 2000); *Procurator Fiscal, Linlithgow v. Watson*, [2002] U.K.P.C. D1.

the starving colonel, who persistently clings to an optimism scarcely justified by his predicament, and his starving wife, pointing up their 'two utterly distinct world views':[55]

> 'You can't eat illusions,' said the woman.
> 'You can't eat them, but they feed you', replied the colonel.[56]

It remains to add words of thanks. The editors wish to put on record their gratitude to Professor Kevin Gray for the enthusiastic support he gave this project when the idea was first mooted with him, to the University of Cambridge Faculty of Law for its generous financial assistance which made the event possible, to Downing College, Cambridge for providing the most congenial environment in which to hold an event such as this and to Valentina Steel and her staff at the University of Cambridge Institute of Continuing Education for having organized the practical arrangements so ably. Finally, we express our gratitude to the participants, many of whom journeyed far to attend the Cambridge Conference. Invidious though it will appear, Pierre Legrand and I wish particularly to thank Lawrence Rosen for a contribution which we find it difficult to quantify. Besides offering the summation at the close of proceedings which appears at the end of this book, unbidden, he also commentated on, and initiated discussion of, each of the papers presented. As with a firework, he lit the blue touch-paper enabling conversation to sparkle, occasionally incandesce. Curiously, before the Conference opened, although – reminiscent of Wittgenstein's image of the strands of the rope attaching the ship to the wharf[57] – all participants were personally acquainted with a number of the other contributors, no

---

[55] Stephen Minta, *Gabriel García Márquez: Writer of Colombia* (London: Jonathan Cape, 1987), p. 69.

[56] *Ibid*. For another English rendition of this passage, see Gabriel García Márquez, *No One Writes to the Colonel*, in *Collected Novellas* (New York: HarperCollins, 1990), p. 144 [1961]. This translation is by J. S. Bernstein.

[57] Significantly, what Wittgenstein was discussing on this occasion was the very notion of 'comparing': 'We find that what connects all the cases of comparing is a vast number of overlapping similarities, and as soon as we see this, we feel no longer compelled to say that there must be some one feature common to them all. What ties the ship to the wharf is a rope, and the rope consists of fibres, but it does not get its strength from any fibre which runs through it from one end to the other, but from the fact that there is a vast number of fibres overlapping': *Preliminary Studies for the 'Philosophical Investigations' Generally Known as the Blue and Brown Books*, 2d ed. by R. Rhees (Oxford: Blackwell, 1964), p. 87. See also Wittgenstein, *supra*, note 42, § 67: 'the strength of the thread does not reside in the fact that some one fibre runs through its whole length, but in the overlapping of many fibres.'

single participant appeared ever to have previously met all the others. As Wittgenstein noted, no single fibre runs its entire length, yet the rope is strong. Although unanimity of opinion was absent on many matters, the sense of common enterprise never flagged. Whatever the perceived failings of this undertaking may turn out to be, fifteen academics shared five intense and profitable days in Cambridge in July 2000 meditating and controverting the intellectual foundations of comparative legal studies.

Comparative legal studies and its legacies

2

The universalist heritage

JAMES GORDLEY

Unlike other contributors to this book, I discuss an approach to law which is at least two centuries out of fashion. We associate it with the natural-law schools that flourished before the rise of positivism in the nineteenth century. The jurists of these schools looked for principles which are universal, which underlie all legal systems. Here, I do not consider whether or not there are such principles. I ask what the approach of the natural lawyers can tell us about how laws may differ even when they are based on the same principles. As comparatists, we ought to be interested in how such differences are possible and what they are like. We can see such differences in modern legal systems. If we are sensitive to them, we can avoid the methodological error of assuming that principles must be different whenever we see a difference in laws. First, however, we must distinguish sharply between the approach of some seventeenth- and eighteenth-century natural lawyers who were influenced by philosophical rationalism and that of the earlier natural lawyers whose approach was based on ideas that stemmed ultimately from Aristotle and Thomas Aquinas.

The later rationalist approach was to try to deduce consequences as a mathematician would from supposedly self-evident principles. The difficulties are clear in retrospect. It is far from self-evident what the self-evident principles are. Moreover, many principles do not lead to a single set of consequences. For present purposes, however, it is enough to note that even if this approach did work, and legal rules could be logically deduced from self-evident principles, we could not explain the important differences that we see among legal systems. Either the differences would not matter or they would be the result of some error in logical deduction. Yet, if comparative law has taught us anything, it is that some of these differences do matter and that they are not merely mistakes.

The approach of the earlier natural lawyers differed in two ways. The first difference that I wish to stress concerns the fact that the relationship between principle and rule, and between higher- and lower-level principles and rules, was not only conceptual but teleological. It was based on purpose. As Aquinas said at the beginning of his commentary on Aristotle's *Ethics*, there are two kinds of order to be found in things: the order of part to whole and the order of means to ends, the first being based on the second.[1] The parts of a whole are defined by what they do, and what they do is a means to what the whole does. As Aristotle said, we should explain whatever we study, be it an animal, a man-made object or a political institution, as we would a couch, identifying each element and the contribution it makes to what the thing does.[2]

Viewed in this way, explaining a legal system in terms of its underlying principles would look more like biology or engineering than mathematics. Each rule would be explained in terms of the purpose it achieves in conjunction with other rules, and this purpose in terms of still higher-level purposes, much as a biologist explains the specializations of cells in terms of the functions of organs and these functions in terms of the survival and reproduction of the organism. At the summit of the explanation of a legal system would be the principles that describe what the society and its members ultimately wish it to achieve which, for Aristotle and Aquinas, should not merely be survival and reproduction but a truly human life in which, so far as possible, each person's distinctively human capacities are realized.

The second difference has to do with the way we know which rules or principles are right or appropriate. The later rationalist approach begins with self-evident principles and deduces everything else from them. As we can already see, by the earlier approach, even when one is reasoning systematically, one no more deduces a legal system from a self-evident principle than a biologist would deduce the structure of a sunflower or a starfish from a definition of the creature. He examines its structure and sees what each part contributes to the life of a sunflower or a starfish. Moreover, for Aristotle and Aquinas, systematic reasoning is not the only way that people can tell what rules are appropriate. When people choose the actions that contribute to a distinctively human life, they exercise an ability which

---

[1] Thomas Aquinas, *In decem libros Ethicorum Aristotelis ad Nicomachum expositio*, ed. by Angelo Pirotta (Turin: Marietti, 1934), I, lect. 1, no. 1.
[2] Aristotle, *The Parts of Animals*, I, i, 641a.

Aristotle and Aquinas called 'prudence'.[3] Prudence enables them to see that certain actions are right, even though they cannot explain why. For example, many people can see that murder is not right, even though they could not give a good definition of murder or explain precisely why it is wrong.

While people can and do reason systematically about laws, when they make rules and decide cases, they exercise two aspects of prudence which Aristotle called *synesis* and *gnome*.[4] *Synesis* is good judgement in framing rules. *Gnome* is good judgement in deciding particular cases.[5] People with these abilities can frame a rule well or decide a case well, even though they may not be able to explain systematically why the rule is well framed or the case rightly decided.[6] Aquinas identified these abilities with certain legal roles in society: those of law-maker and of judge.

By the earlier approach, then, systematic reasoning about law is not the same as logical deduction and, moreover, not all our knowledge about the appropriateness of rules and principles comes from systematic reasoning. It can come from *synesis* and *gnome*. Let us now ask how, by this earlier approach, laws might differ even when they are ultimately based on the same principles. Without intending to be exhaustive, I will discuss several reasons why this might be the case.

The first has to do with human fallibility. While, for Aristotle and Aquinas, the abilities just described enable people to know what laws are appropriate, people are not able to know everything they possibly can know all at once. So we must distinguish carefully between how these abilities work and what they could reveal ideally, and how they work under the less-than-ideal circumstances in which we often find ourselves. Ideally, *synesis* would always enable law-makers to see what rule would give the right result in the largest number of cases. At least as Aquinas interpreted Aristotle, *gnome* would complement this ability. It would enable judges to see when the special circumstances of a particular case require a deviation from the rule. According to Aristotle and Aquinas, because rules serve purposes, circumstances can always arise in which following a rule would not serve its

---

[3] Aristotle, *Nicomachean Ethics*, VI, v [hereinafter *Ethics*]; Thomas Aquinas, *Summa theologiae*, II–II, q. 47, a. 2 [hereinafter *Summa*].

[4] In the technical vocabulary of Aquinas, they are quasi-potential parts: *Summa, supra*, note 3, II–II, q. 51, pr.

[5] *Id.*, I–II, q. 95, a. 1; q. 96, a. 6; II–II, q. 51, aa. 3–4; *id., supra*, note 1, VI, lect. ix; *Ethics, supra*, note 3, VI, xi. Throughout, I do not consider to what extent Aquinas's interpretations were faithful to Aristotle.

[6] *Summa, supra*, note 3, I–II, q. 95, a. 2, ad. 3; *Ethics, supra*, note 3, VI, xi.

purpose and consequently a deviation is necessary.[7] Thus, even with the best-framed rules, *gnome* is needed to see when to deviate.[8] Finally, by reasoning systematically, ideally one could explain the appropriateness of each rule and of each deviation in terms of the higher principles which make them appropriate. And while that knowledge is not necessary in order for rules and cases to be well framed and decided, still, it should be of assistance. As Aristotle said, if we know what is good, '[w]ill not the knowledge of it have a great influence on life? Shall we not, like archers who have a mark to aim at, more often hit upon what is right?'[9]

In contrast, in our imperfect world, law-makers may be uncertain what rule to frame, judges may be uncertain how to decide a case and those who reason systematically about law may often find themselves stymied. That is one reason differences may emerge among legal systems even when they rest on the same principles. They may be confronting the same uncertainty and responding to it in different ways, each of which has its own advantages and inconveniences.

Suppose that after giving the matter his best thought, the law-maker has trouble seeing what to do. He finds it hard to frame a law that accurately delimits the class of cases in which a given result is appropriate. One alternative is to frame the best rule he can, even though he knows it fits these cases only roughly. For example, in French law, a person is strictly liable in tort for harm caused by any object in his custody or *garde*.[10] I doubt if the French really think that they have drawn the line just where it should be. But it is not clear just where the line should be drawn. Or, for example, in medieval law, relief was given when the contract price deviated by more than 50 per cent from the fair price.[11] While the rule is clear, one cannot help feeling that more matters than simply the percentage deviation.

That is one option for the law-maker: frame a rule as well as he can and hope for the best. That is all he could do if the only ability that mattered were *synesis*. But an alternative is to dispense with a clear general rule and fall back on the ability to see what result is appropriate in particular cases.

---

[7] *Ethics, supra,* note 3, V, x; *Summa, supra,* note 3, II–II, q. 120, a. 1.
[8] *Summa, supra,* note 3, I–II, q. 96, a. 6.   [9] *Ethics, supra,* note 3, V, i, 1094a.
[10] French *Code civil,* art. 1384, as it is presently interpreted. Here, and in my discussion of §§138(1) and 242 of the German *BGB,* I do not suggest that the drafters of the codes had the current interpretations in mind. I describe the advantages and disadvantages of keeping these provisions as they are now interpreted.
[11] See generally James Gordley, 'Just Price', in *The New Palgrave Dictionary of Economics and the Law,* ed. by Peter Newman, vol. II (London: Macmillan, 1998), p. 410.

Aquinas discussed the possibility of running the entire system of justice that way. Every case would go to the judges with no laws to guide them. He said there were three disadvantages in doing so. First, it is easier to find a small number of able rule-makers than a large number of able judges. Second, rule-makers have more time to think and can consider a larger range of possible cases. Third, the rule-makers are legislating for the future and may be more impartial and dispassionate.[12] Nevertheless, if the law-maker were really unsure what to do, he might find these risks preferable to that of laying down the wrong general rule. Differences between legal systems might then arise, not because of any difference in principle, but because different law-makers deal with uncertainty in different ways.

The law-maker who finds it difficult to frame a general rule and wishes to deal with an area of law case by case has two alternatives. He could make a list of cases himself in which he believes that a given result is proper. Or, he could allow judges to decide what result is proper as cases arise. An example of the first approach is the German law governing strict liability. There is no general rule. There are special statutes imposing liability without fault, for example, for the operation of trains,[13] aircraft,[14] automobiles[15] and electric and gas installations.[16] The judges do not add to the list even when the cases seem analogous.[17] Similarly, in France, there is no general rule against enforcing a hard bargain. The French *Code civil* says that relief will be given only in cases provided for by statute. Special statutes protect, among others, those who sell land at less than five-twelfths of the just price,[18] those who pay an excessive amount for fertilizer, seeds and fodder,[19] those who are rescued at sea[20] or after an aviation accident[21] and those who receive too little for artistic or literary property.[22]

One advantage of making such a list in advance, rather than leaving the matter to judges, is that the law will be more certain. No one has to wonder

---

[12] *Summa, supra*, note 3, I–II, q. 95, a. 1, ad. 2.
[13] *Haftpflichtgesetz* (4 January 1978), § 1, I (BGBl.I.145).
[14] *Luftverkehrsgesetz* (14 January 1981), § 33 (BGBl.I.61).
[15] *Straßenverkehrsgesetz* (19 December 1952), § 7 (BGBl.I.837).
[16] *Haftpflichtgesetz* (4 January 1978), § 2, I (BGBl.I.145).
[17] See Konrad Zweigert and Hein Kötz, *An Introduction to Comparative Law*, 3d ed. transl. by Tony Weir (Oxford: Oxford University Press, 1998), p. 656.
[18] French *Code civil*, art. 1674.   [19] *Loi* of 8–9 July 1907, art. 1, D.P.1907.4.173.
[20] *Loi* of 29 April 1916, art. 7, D.P.1919.4.285. See now *loi* no. 67–545 of 7 July 1967, art. 15, D.1967.L.258.
[21] *Loi* of 31 May 1924, art. 57, D.P.1925.4.41. See now *Code de l'aviation civile*, art. L. 142–1.
[22] *Loi* no. 57–298 of 11 March 1957, art. 37, D.H.1957.L.102.

what the judges will do. A disadvantage is that a law-maker, who must consider these cases abstractly, may be less able to see the proper result than a judge, who considers them in a concrete factual setting. Another disadvantage is that when a law-maker does not think of all the cases that may arise, there will be gaps. As Hein Kötz has said of the German rules on strict liability:

> It is far from obvious why a person should be strictly liable if he decides to move earth by means of a light railway while he is liable only for negligence if he uses heavy bulldozers for the job. And why should an injured person's right to damages depend on whether the accident took place on board a steamer or a train? And if a motorized conveyance causes injury, why should liability turn on whether it is a chairlift, a motor car, a motorboat, a light railway, a hoist, a funicular, or an escalator?[23]

Moreover, whatever the law-maker may say, judges may try to fill these gaps. Then, the advantage of certainty is lost. French courts have given relief for an unfair price outside the statutory list of cases by finding fraud, duress or mistake, even though the victim had neither been told a lie nor threatened and his only mistake concerned the value of what he bought or sold.[24]

Consequently, a law-maker might allow judges to decide particular cases as they arise. Here, again, he has two alternatives. He might list cases, as before, but allow the judges to add to the list. That is the approach, for example, of the German *Allgemeinegeschäftsbedingungengesetz* and of the European Council Directive on Unfair Terms in Consumer Contracts.[25] They list a large number of presumptively unfair terms, but add a muddy general clause which allows a judge to find other terms invalid as well. That approach avoids gaps. It still has the disadvantage that the law-maker, considering some of these cases in the abstract, may find it harder to see the right result than a judge who considers them in the concrete.

Instead, and to avoid that disadvantage, the law-maker might not make a list but simply enact an unclear rule, thereby allowing judges to decide

---

[23] Zweigert and Kötz, *supra*, note 17, p. 658. For a similar criticism, see Karl Larenz and C.-W. Canaris, *Lehrbuch des Schuldrechts*, 13th ed., vol. II, part 2 (Munich: C. H. Beck, 1994), no. 80, I, 2, c.

[24] *Req.*, 27 April 1887, D.P.1888.I.263; *Req.*, 27 January 1919, S.1920.I.198; *Civ.*, 29 November 1968, Gaz.Pal.1969.63; Douai, 2 June 1930, Jurisprudence de la Cour d'appel de Douai, 1930, p. 183; Paris, 22 January 1953, J.C.P.1953.II.7435.

[25] European Community Council Directive 93/13/EEC of 5 April 1993.

cases as they arise. The unclear rule might either be definite enough to give some guidance or it might be completely vague. The US rule on strict liability gives some guidance: the defendant is liable if he conducts an 'abnormally dangerous activity'.[26] The rule is too imprecise to enable a US lawyer to tell what cases it covers. He would never guess from the rule that driving cars is not included while ground damage from aircraft may be, even though aircraft are safer than cars. When he wants to know what activities are included, he turns to a list which is so long that I consign it in a footnote, but which includes blasting, storing explosives or large quantities of water, crop dusting and possible ground damage by aircraft and harm caused by nuclear power.[27] Nevertheless, the rule gives some guidance.

Alternatively, the law-maker could promulgate a vague rule that allows judges to do what seems right in particular cases without much if any guidance. An example is relief from hard bargains under two of the general clauses of the German *BGB*: § 138(1), which says that a contract is void if it violates good morals (*gute Sitten*), and § 242, which says that a contract must be performed in good faith (*Treu und Glauben*). Nobody knows what these rules mean.

Again, there are advantages and disadvantages to each approach. Giving guidance is an advantage but only if the guidance is good. It may not be since, by hypothesis, the law-maker is not sure how to describe the class of cases that call for a particular result. Maybe it is good for judges to consider whether an activity is 'abnormally dangerous'. If George Fletcher is right, however, what should matter is not whether it is dangerous but whether it creates a risk which is non-reciprocal: the defendant endangers others more than they endanger him.[28] Perhaps, then, the US rule points in the wrong direction.

---

[26] *Restatement (Second) of Torts*, s. 519.
[27] '[W]ater collected in quantity in a dangerous place, or allowed to percolate; explosives or inflammable liquids stored in quantity in the midst of a city; blasting; pile driving; crop dusting; the fumigation of part of a building with cyanide gas; drilling oil wells or operating refineries in thickly settled communities; an excavation letting in the sea; factories emitting smoke, dust or noxious gases in the midst of a town; roofs so constructed as to shed snow into a highway; [...] a dangerous party wall' and possibly 'ground damage from aviation' and 'rockets and nuclear energy': W. Page Keeton *et al.*, *Prosser and Keeton on the Law of Torts*, 5th ed. (St Paul: West, 1984), pp. 549–50 and 556.
[28] See George P. Fletcher, 'Fairness and Utility in Tort Theory', (1972) 85 Harvard L. R. 537. For some thoughts about why he may be right, see James Gordley, 'Tort Law in the Aristotelian Tradition', in D. G. Owen (ed.), *Philosophical Foundations of Tort Law* (Oxford: Oxford University Press, 1995), pp. 151–7.

In contrast, one advantage of a vague rule is that it allows us time to gather experience before any guidance is given. The very vagueness of the German rule about good faith has enabled German jurists to see that the term 'good faith' covers different types of cases: for example, the implication of ancillary contractual terms, the abuse of contractual rights and the effect of changed and unforeseen circumstances.[29] That brings jurists a step closer to developing clearer rules for each type of case. Similarly, in the United States, courts initially gave relief for violations of 'privacy' without any clear idea what 'privacy' might mean. Drawing on their experience, William Prosser distinguished four types of cases in which relief was given: commercial appropriation of name or image, intrusion into seclusion, disclosure of embarrassing private facts and putting the plaintiff in a false light.[30] It was then possible to frame more definite rules.

We have seen, then, that when the law-maker is unsure of how to frame a rule, an alternative is to rely on the ability to decide particular cases appropriately even absent a rule. Indeed, some people think that a major difference between civil-law and common-law jurisdictions is that the former rely more on the rules contained in civil codes and the latter on the ability of judges to decide particular cases. I think this contrast can easily be exaggerated. But to the extent it is true, it is a further instance of how the use of these abilities can be alternatives. If they are alternatives, each with its advantages and disadvantages, then, again, laws may differ not because of a difference in principle but because of the way of handling uncertainty.

The other ability described earlier is the capacity to explain rules systematically in terms of principles. Historically, some legal systems have been more interested in finding such explanations than others. Ancient Roman law, as has often been noted, was not very systematic. I have described elsewhere how it was first systematized in the sixteenth century when the late scholastics or Spanish natural-law school tried to explain Roman rules by Aristotelian and Thomistic principles.[31] Similarly, before the nineteenth century, the common law was not organized systematically by doctrines but by writs or forms of action.[32]

---

[29] See Günter Roth, in H. Heinrichs, *Münchener Kommentar zum Bürgerlichen Gesetzbuch*, 3d ed., vol. II (Munich: C. H. Beck, 1994), no. 93 [appended to § 242 *BGB*].

[30] See William Prosser, 'Privacy', (1960) 48 California L.R. 383.

[31] See James Gordley, *The Philosophical Origins of Modern Contract Doctrine* (Oxford: Oxford University Press, 1991), pp. 69–111.

[32] *Id.*, pp. 134–60.

As before, if the law-maker is unsure how to frame a rule, an alternative would be to rely on this ability to explain rules by principles.[33] Even if we cannot frame a rule, it may still be possible to see the principle at stake. Indeed, according to Aquinas, it is often easier for us to see the more general principles than their more specific consequences.[34] Over some domain of cases it must be true that *pacta sunt servanda*, that one who is at fault for injuring another must make compensation, that an owner can do with his property as he wishes and that one who is enriched at another's expense must disgorge the enrichment. Otherwise, there would be no law of contracts, torts, property and unjust enrichment. It is more difficult to get from these principles to clear rules. Thus, in the absence of a clear rule, the law-maker might tell judges to be guided by the principle.

A difficulty, however, is that any single principle is unlikely to be all that matters. General principles of the kind just described nearly always need to be qualified by other principles. Consequently, if the law-maker states only one principle, there is the danger that judges may think they should follow it invariably, as though it is all that matters. One reason that French jurists do not accept relief for *imprévision* or changed circumstances[35] may be that their code does not mention that doctrine but does contain the principle of *pacta sunt servanda*.[36] The reason, I believe, is the historical accident that the drafters worked from the treatises of Jean Domat and Robert-Joseph Pothier who happened not to mention the doctrine of changed circumstances although it was widely accepted at the time. Similarly, the US Supreme

---

[33] The ability to explain rules can also be used to evaluate a rule even when we do not know the principles on which it is ultimately based. We might be able to see that a certain rule is inconsistent with any plausible explanation. For example, there is no generally accepted theory of why the law sometimes gives relief for an unfair bargain. Even without such a theory, however, one could still raise questions about the medieval rule mentioned earlier which gives relief whenever the contract price deviates from a fair price by more than 50 per cent. This rule, unlike § 138(2) of the German *BGB*, ignores the question of whether the advantaged party obtained more favourable terms by exploiting the 'distressed situation, inexperience, lack of judgemental ability or grave weakness of the will' of the disadvantaged party. Without a theory of why relief is given, one cannot tell whether these factors should matter in principle. But one can say that even if they do not – even if all that matters in principle is the extent of the deviation from a fair price – these factors should still be relevant. It is hard to tell what price may have been fair when the contract is concluded. It is more likely to have been unfair when the disadvantaged party is less able to protect himself. His ability to do so should, therefore, matter even if the question in principle should be the extent to which the terms of the contract are unfair.

[34] *Summa, supra*, note 3, I–II, q. 94, a. 4.

[35] See François Terré, Philippe Simler and Yves Lequette, *Droit civil: les obligations*, 7th ed. (Paris: Dalloz, 1999), no. 441, pp. 428–30.

[36] French *Code civil*, art. 1134.

Court protects freedom of expression zealously. Perhaps it would do so less zealously if the US Constitution, as does the German Constitution, also mentioned human dignity,[37] honour[38] and personality.[39]

Nevertheless, there are situations in which a rule-maker may want judges to follow a principle invariably, as though it were all that matters, even if it is not. Where there is no clear rule, deviations from the principle create uncertainty, even though the deviations are necessary to reach the right result in particular cases. Certainty may be worth the price of sometimes reaching the wrong result. In English law, a contract is enforced without regard to whether there has been a violation of good faith.[40] In French law, as just noted, it is enforced without regard to whether circumstances have changed. The reason is probably not that the English and French think *pacta sunt servanda* is all that matters, like the nineteenth-century will theorists. More likely, they fear that people will not be sure when their contracts are enforceable. Similarly, the US Supreme Court has sometimes behaved as though all that matters is freedom of expression. According to the court, the Constitution is violated if *Hustler* magazine is held liable for grossly and obscenely ridiculing the minister Jerry Falwell[41] or if a newspaper is held liable for printing the name of a rape victim while her assailant is still at large.[42] Perhaps the court mistakenly thinks that freedom of expression is all that matters. But it may fear that editors will be unsure of when they will be liable for publishing information or satire.

Legal systems may differ, then, because people are fallible. When they cannot frame clear rules that accurately describe when a certain result is to be reached, they may handle the problem of uncertainty differently. That does not mean that their laws are based on different principles.

Another reason why laws may differ even though the underlying principles are the same is, as Aquinas himself noted, that different laws may be consistent with the same principles.[43] Sometimes, when that is so, which law to enact is a matter of indifference. Theft should be punished but the exact length of the sentence is more or less arbitrary. We all must drive on the right side of the road or on the left so as to avoid head-on collisions, but which side is a matter of indifference. For present purposes, however,

---

[37] German Constitution [*Grundgesetz*], art. 1.   [38] *Id.*, art. 5(2).   [39] *Id.*, art. 2(1).
[40] See G. H. Treitel, *The Law of Contract*, 10th ed. (London: Sweet & Maxwell, 1999), p. 225.
[41] *Hustler Magazine* v. *Falwell*, (1988) 485 US 46.
[42] *Florida Star* v. *B.L.F.*, (1989) 491 US 524.
[43] *Summa, supra*, note 3, I–II, q. 95, a. 2, ad. 3; q. 96, a. 1; q. 97, a. 1.

it is important to see that sometimes the choice of which law to enact is not a matter of indifference even though the underlying principles are the same. Indeed, even when they are, the choice of which law to enact may be one which we rightly regard as shaping our values and culture. There are two reasons this may be so. The first is that circumstances differ and the laws appropriate in one set of circumstances may not be appropriate in the other. The second is that even when the circumstances are the same, laws can differ even when they are based on the same principles.

First, then, different laws may be appropriate because of different circumstances and yet we may rightly perceive the difference as entailing a difference in values or culture. Let me give an example. In pre-commercial societies, when people make gifts, the recipient is often obligated to give back something equivalent but as yet unspecified. When people in these societies exchange, they often form stable trading relationships with particular partners. Each party to the relationship is obligated to exchange when the other asks and to exchange at a price that remains stable despite changes in supply and demand.[44] It is not like our own society where gifts are often made to enrich another party at the donor's expense and where a person can exchange with whomever he wants and charge what the market will bear. But the rules of pre-commercial societies make sense given their circumstances. There are few ways to store wealth. Therefore, it makes sense to give gifts in order to have a claim for help in the future. Markets are thin or non-existent and so supply or demand can swing wildly from day to day. Therefore, it makes sense to trade with a regular partner who will not exploit a temporary advantage and who, in return, is not to be exploited.[45] That is not to imply that people in these societies see their rules as appropriate only under certain circumstances. They might have trouble imagining it could ever be proper for a donee not to give in return or for a person to raise the price he charges a regular customer. They have never had occasion to consider how circumstances might be different and what it would be proper to do then.

People in these societies regard certain conduct as wrongful which we regard as appropriate, and in that sense their values differ from ours.

---

[44] See James Gordley, 'Contract in Pre-Commercial Societies and in Western History', in *Contracts in General*, in *International Encyclopedia of Comparative Law*, vol. VII, ch. 2 (Tübingen: J. C. B. Mohr, 1997), pp. 2–9.

[45] For an attempt to explain the contract law of pre-commercial societies by these considerations, see *ibid*.

Moreover, this difference is likely to be linked to many other differences in attitudes and behaviour. They cannot behave to each other like modern creditors or merchants. Their relationships require trust and for trust to flourish, relationships must be deeper, more personal and not restricted to mere economic need. This difference will, in turn, affect people's character, personalities and their image of themselves and others. In that sense, one can speak of a difference in culture.

My point is a simple one. To speak of a difference in values or culture in this sense is not to speak of a difference in principles. If the principles were different, which set of rules is appropriate would not depend on the circumstances. One could not analyse the rules as a response to the difference in circumstances. And one would fail to see that if one of us were transported to such a society with our values and culture intact, our standard of conduct would then be inappropriate. It would be wrong to accept a gift on the understanding that one would some day give in return and then fail to do so. It would be wrong to trade with someone who demands less than he might because he expects a similar concession in the future and then to fail to make the concession when the time arrives.

Suppose now that the circumstances as well as the principles on which the laws are based are the same. In the Aristotelian tradition, it is still possible that the laws might differ. Moreover, the difference can matter very much. It need not be a matter of indifference like whether we drive on the left or the right side of the street. That sounds odd. As I am using the term, principles are the ultimate standards by which we judge what is better or worse. If two rules are equally consistent with the same principles, neither of them could be better than the other. It would seem that the choice between them must be a matter of indifference. To see why that is not so for Aristotle and Aquinas, we must come back to their idea of how people make choices. As noted earlier, when people choose, they exercise the virtue of 'prudence'. Prudence is an ability to recognize that certain choices contribute to the life that they should live and are, therefore, good choices, whereas others detract from such a life and are bad.[46] When an action contributes in one way and detracts in another way from such a life, prudence enables a person to weigh the good and bad consequences. Of course, he may be mistaken. He may see only the contribution that the action makes to his life and think it is all that matters or he may exaggerate the extent to which it contributes.

---

[46] *Ethics, supra,* note 3, VI, v; *Summa, supra,* note 3, II–II, q. 47, a. 2.

It is also possible, for Aristotle and Aquinas, that after all the good and bad consequences are taken into account, neither choice is superior and yet the choice is important. Suppose, for example, someone is asking himself whom to marry or whether to have a career in law or in medicine. Choices like these are not a matter of indifference. They shape people's lives. Yet there may be no right answer.[47] According to Aquinas, there is no one right way for God to have made the world and that is why He was free to make whatever good world He chose.[48] He did not have to make the 'best of all possible worlds'. The goodness of all possible worlds cannot be rank-ordered. According to Aquinas, that is also why people have free will not simply to choose between good and evil, but to choose which of many possible good lives to live.[49]

Making laws is similar. When the law-maker exercises that aspect of prudence called *synesis*, he weighs the good and bad consequences of a law. Sometimes, a single choice is right. Sometimes, he is left with a range of alternatives. Therefore, it is possible for different law-makers to choose different laws even though they are acting under the same circumstances and even though they are judging what is good and what is bad according to the same principles. An example may be the protection that modern legal systems give to freedom of expression, dignity and privacy. As mentioned earlier, the US Supreme Court has decided that a newspaper is free to ridicule a public figure grossly and obscenely and to release the name of a rape victim while her assailant is still at large. In Continental countries, public figures have recovered for 'insult' much more easily. In France, a radio commentator recovered for being called a 'kosher pork butcher'.[50] In Germany, the German army and its soldiers recovered when the army was called a 'murder machine'.[51] People have also recovered more easily when publicity is given to their private lives. In France, a newspaper was held liable for revealing that a judge had taken a vacation for 'nervous depression'.[52]

---

[47] Some modern philosophers also believe that there may be no right answer when a choice is based on more than one principle and that nevertheless the choice may be important. For example, see Joseph Raz, *The Morality of Freedom* (Oxford: Oxford University Press, 1986), p. 332; Isaiah Berlin, 'Alleged Relativism in Eighteenth-Century Legal Thought', in *The Crooked Timber of Humanity*, ed. by Henry Hardy (Princeton: Princeton University Press, 1991), pp. 70 and 79–80; Christopher L. Kutz, 'Just Disagreement: Indeterminacy and Rationality in the Rule of Law', (1994) 103 Yale L.J. 1023, pp. 1023–9. Here, I cannot describe the ways in which these positions coincide with and diverge from that of Aquinas.

[48] *Summa, supra*, note 3, I, q. 19, aa. 3 and 10.   [49] *Id.*, I–II, q. 10, a. 2; q. 13, a. 6.

[50] Paris, 15 February 1988, J.C.P.1988.II.21115.   [51] *BGH*, 19 January 1989, JZ, 1989, p. 644.

[52] *Civ.2e*, 27 April 1988, *pourvoi* no. 86–13.303 [retrieved from the Lexis data bank].

In Germany, the wife of a *Hohenzollern* recovered for publicity given her divorce.[53]

One might think that the Americans, Germans and French disagree on the importance of freedom of expression as opposed to dignity and privacy. If so, their principles are different. That is certainly possible. My point is that these differences in their laws could exist even if their principles were the same. Americans might resent an insult or unwarranted publicity as much or more than Germans and French. Germans and French might express themselves as forcefully as Americans and with the same or more gusto. Nevertheless, one still has to choose whether to protect privacy and dignity even though people must then be more careful about what they write and say. There may be no right answer. Choices like that shape societies, making one different in character from another. In that sense, one can speak of a difference in values or culture. Yet, there may not be a disagreement about principles. To be a lawyer rather than a physician, I do not have to believe that doing justice is more important than saving lives, even though I will then be more occupied with the former than the latter. I can love my own wife or my own country the best without believing there is something the matter with all the others. The 'freedom of expression' example is one of the clearest instances I know in modern private law in which the principles, or at least the importance accorded these principles, seems to differ. Yet, even here we cannot be sure that it does. The example illustrates how easy it is to make the methodological error of assuming that people must believe in different things because they adopt different rules. If that is our method, we will find ourselves postulating a difference in principles or in the weight accorded them whenever rules differ. In fact, two people whose laws differ, each of whom likes his own laws, might have to talk a long time to discover whether they disagree in principle or not.

Let me make a last point which concerns what comparatists can and cannot hope to know about differences in legal systems. If laws differ because people disagree about principles, comparatists can describe the disagreement. Perhaps they can even help to resolve it. If laws differ because circumstances are different, comparatists can describe how the difference in circumstances makes each law appropriate. Perhaps their explanation can help in redesigning the law to make each even more appropriate to its own circumstances. But if laws differ even though the principles and

---

[53] *OLG* Hamburg, 26 March 1970, NJW, 1970, p. 1325.

circumstances are the same, then comparatists have reached the limit of analysis. The only explanation can be historical: to describe the previous choices which are like this one and which made the societies what they are. The problem is like accounting for what people do. Sometimes, their actions are due to their goals and principles and to the circumstances in which they are acting, including the natural abilities which they possess. But sometimes one can explain what they are doing only by telling the story of how they came to be who they are.

3

The colonialist heritage

UPENDRA BAXI

The 'word' and the 'world'

Notions of 'heritage', no matter howsoever nuanced, privilege certain moments of domination as inaugural. Implied in these notions are constitutive ideas about historic time flattened by certain orders of narrative hegemony. Who fashioned the colonial heritage, with what means of violence and exclusion, what elements were constitutive of 'its' core and who 'received' it, which aspects of 'it' were imposed by force and who resisted 'it' and how, are questions that, once posed, open up vistas of heterogeneity of historic time and space that we symbolize by the words 'colonial'/'post-colonial'. The matter of 'winners' and 'losers' forces our attention to the shifting character of the calculus of interests that animated the imposition and/or the 'reception' of metropolitan legality as well as patterns of resistance. The missing middle term between *traditions* and *transitions* (the thematic of this book) is *transactions*. The addition of this 'dangerous supplement' enables a more differentiated understanding of the sources of violence inherent in patterns of the dominant historiography that silence the voices of the subordinated.

Genres of comparative legal studies determine what may be meaningfully said concerning 'the' colonial inheritance. The positivistic genre of comparative legal studies strictly addresses forms of normative and institutional diffusion of dominant global legality. Instrumentalist approaches, principally the Old and the now 'New' law-and-development genre, remain concerned with issues of efficient management of transition from 'non-' modern to modern law. The sociological genre explores production of difference within, between and across legal cultures, especially through the prisms of legal/juridical pluralisms. The critical comparative genre provides frameworks for understanding the spread of dominant legal-ideological traditions and the transformations within them. Each of these, and related, genres develops its own kinds of (pre-eminently Euro-American) epistemic communities sustaining the practices of inclusion/exclusion that define the distinctive domain of comparative legal studies. My approach in this essay, which is concerned with comparative colonial legality, derives much from these traditions of doing legal comparison but also seeks to go beyond them in mood, method and message. Of necessity, it runs many a narrative risk.

Colonial legal/jural inheritance, at best a bricolage of alien ideologies and institutions, may be viewed at least in three distinct but related modes: as an ethical enterprise, an affair of history and an ensemble of practices of violence.

Kant's 1784 essay 'What is Enlightenment?' (at least in the version offered by Michel Foucault)[1] may be read as constructing an ethical notion of colonial inheritance in terms of a process in which certain 'guardians have so kindly assumed superintendence' over 'so great a portion of mankind'. Kant highlights the tension between *sapere aude* (the courage to use one's own independent reason) and a 'lower degree of civil freedom' (which allows 'the propensity and vocation to free thinking'). This creative tension between autonomy and obedience 'gradually works back upon the character of the people, who thereby gradually become capable of managing freedom', through invention of 'principles of government, which finds it to its own advantage to treat men [...] in accordance with dignity'. Much within the theory and practice of comparative legal studies simply recycles the Enlightenment notions of the moral roots of legal paternalism.

Savigny, in contrast, helps us to think about inheritance in historical rather than ethical terms, as a historical process of social (intergenerational) transmission of law. He suggests that law, like language, is what people inherit as well as invent. Like language, law is necessarily a collective heritage of the people, embodied in *lived* and, therefore, transformative modes of experience (to evoke the Saussurian distinction between *langue* and *parole*) that Savigny, somewhat tragically, identified as *Volksgeist*. In his dispute with Thibaut, Savigny conceptualized this notion as signifying a double split.[2] On the one hand, *Volksgeist* stands for that 'spirit' already

---

[1] Immanuel Kant, 'What is Enlightenment?' ['*Was ist Aufklärung?*'], in Michel Foucault, *The Foucault Reader*, ed. by Paul Rabinow (New York: Pantheon, 1984), pp. 32–50 [1784] (hereinafter *Foucault Reader*). The translation from Foucault's French rendition is by Catherine Porter.
[2] See F. K. von Savigny, *Of the Vocation of Our Age for Legislation and Jurisprudence*, transl. by Abraham Hayward (New York: Arno Press, repr. 1975) [1831].

reconstituted by historic intrusions of the received/imposed law; on the other hand, resistance to further imposition/reception is made legible and legitimate by the invocation of that reconstituted spirit of the people. That 'spirit', in turn, is further split as manifesting a 'popular' dimension and a 'technical' one in ways suggestive of the presence of limits to effective legal change.[3] This notion brings home the insight that the power of epistemic communities to legislate social change must remain bound to the career of popular resistance. The fact that something which constitutes the 'people', in turn, homogenizes/totalizes the law 'givers' and the law 'receivers', not to mention the notion of 'law' itself, is, however, another matter.

Perceived in terms of practices of violence, colonial legality enacts various scripts of the politics of desire for global domination and complicates the notion of 'inheritance'. Too much of the early history of colonial law stands marked by the law and politics of violent exclusion.[4] When all is said and done, the 'character' or the 'spirit' of the 'people' is reshaped by violent imposition of governance practices. The history of the practices of a politics of cruelty seems of very little interest to comparative *jurisprudes* (as Karl Llewellyn was fond of describing 'jurisprudents'). But this history of 'inheritance', when not fully genocidal, disinherits the 'people' at least doubly by divesting them of any epistemic capability to know/create 'law' and by imposing upon them forms of law that, instead of proceeding from domination to liberation, proceed 'from domination to domination' (to quote words from Foucault which he used in another context).[5] The character of modern law's 'infamy'[6] archives for us the violent making of colonial jural and juristic inheritance. At the threshold of the edifice of comparative legal studies, then, lies the Althusserian logic of *indifference*, an order of knowledge/power relation in which all concrete differences are regarded as 'equally indifferent'.[7]

---

[3] On the question of limits to effective legal change, see Julius Stone, *Social Dimensions of Law and Justice* (Sydney: Maitland, 1966), pp. 101–18.
[4] See Upendra Baxi, *The Future of Human Rights* (Delhi: Oxford University Press, 2002).
[5] Michel Foucault, 'Nietzsche, Genealogy, History', in *Foucault Reader, supra*, note 1, p. 85. The translation from the French is by Donald F. Bouchard and Sherry Simon.
[6] Peter Fitzpatrick, *The Mythology of Modern Law* (London: Routledge, 1992), pp. 63–86.
[7] Louis Althusser, *For Marx*, transl. by Ben Brewster (New York: Vintage, 1970), p. 203. In contrast, the pluralization of the notion of 'inheritance' seeks to combat this ' "indifferent" epistemology', assigning a 'primacy of identity' and constructing an 'identitarian logic' which imposes 'ceaseless subordination of the differentiated [...and] of the non-integral'. I borrow this striking phrase regime from another context: Wai Chee Dimock, *Residues of Justice: Literature, Law, Philosophy*

To further complicate the picture, colonial inheritance affects not just those who 'receive' it since those who 'gave'/'bequeathed' it also continue to reproduce themselves. Comparative legal studies, understood as the narratives of the making of 'modern' law, still stands marked by the 'Caliban syndrome', the construction of colonial/post-colonial narrative voices in ways that comfort and confirm the Euro-American images of progress and 'developmentalism'.[8] Caliban is a being, or a history of being, that 'is the excluded, that which is eternally below possibility [...]. He is seen as an occasion, a state of existence which can be appropriated and exploited to the purposes of another's own development.'[9]

This is a complex story. The colonial juristic mind-set survives even as colonies have disappeared. The dominant tradition of doing comparative law still reproduces the binary contrasts between the 'common'- and 'civil'-law cultures or the 'bourgeois' and 'socialist' ideal-types, thus reducing the diversity of the world's legal systems to a common Euro-American measure.[10] In every sphere, the 'modern' law remains the gift of the west to the rest. The large processes of 'westernization', 'modernization', 'development' and now 'globalization' of law present the never-ending story of triumphant legal liberalism despite the recent powerful stirrings of the internal post-socialist, post-modern critiques of the 'modern' law and messages from the worlds of legal pluralism. The only history that can guide the future of law is that of the 'modern' law; our common juristic future resides in a world without alternatives. The 'law' is modern or post-modern; it was not and cannot be anything else.

Thus emerges a history of mentality that maps a unidirectionality of legal 'development' within which pluralism may often construct the logic of difference and expose the late modern law's neo-colonial core. Expressed in the contemporary hi-tech idiom, the image of the modern law as a juridical human genome project, or at least as universal 'cultural software',[11]

(Berkeley: University of California Press, 1996), p. 74. Comparative legal studies practices remain, simply, insensible outside this heterogeneity.

[8] Patrick Chabal, 'The African Crisis: Context and Interpretation', in Richard Werbner and Terence Ranger (eds.), *Post-colonial Identities in Africa* (London: Zed Books, 1996), pp. 45–6.

[9] George Lamming, *The Pleasures of Exile* (London: Alison & Busby, 1984), as cited and further developed in Edward W. Said, *Culture and Imperialism* (London: Vintage, 1994), pp. 256–8.

[10] See Gyula Eörsi, *Comparative Civil (Private) Law: Law Types, Law Groups, The Roads of Legal Development* (Budapest: Akadémiai Kiadó, 1979); Pierre Legrand, *Fragments on Law-as-Culture* (Deventer: W. E. J. Tjeenk Willink, 1999).

[11] J. M. Balkin, *Cultural Software* (New Haven: Yale University Press, 1998).

continues to dominate the performances and uses of comparative legal studies. Unidirectionality leads to perfectibility of global epistemic hegemonic practices which consolidate the view that the masters and makers of the modern law have nothing worthy to learn from the discursive traditions of the Euro-American tradition's Other. For example, strategic comparatists guiding the legal/juridical reconstruction of the so-called 'transitional' post-communist societies resolutely forfeit any possibility of learning from the juristic and juridical traditions of the decolonized worlds (for instance, from India in the middle of the last Christian century and from southern Africa at the end of it).

In this sense at least, comparative legal studies that affords equal discursive dignity to non-Euro-American traditions has yet to emerge. Put another way, comparative legal studies continues to happen, as ever, as decisions centring on the Euro-American world. The importance of these decisions is not in doubt for they determine universes of law: the ways of *seeing* (that constitute the realm of the invisible), of *speaking* (that determine the regimes of silence) and of *feeling* (that devalue the suffering of the colonial Other). Can this book finally enable the inauguration of an *epistemic break*?

Different registers

The making of 'modern law' is almost always presented as a saga of the Idea of Progress. The rule of law, the doctrine of separation of powers, the relative autonomy of the legal profession and the Bill of Rights are usually offered as moral inventions of Euro-American political and legal theory *without* any lineage elsewhere and whose dissemination is then constructed as a Kantian civilizational good. In this first register, the colonial legacy and inheritance mark a decisive discontinuity with the 'pre-colonial' tradition, one that constitutes at once the ways of domination as well as of resistance. Thus, E. P. Thompson was able to write as late as 1975 that even if the 'rules and rhetoric' of modern law were a mask of imperial power, 'it was a mask which Gandhi and Nehru were to borrow, at the head of half a million masked supporters'.[12] In this discourse, the post-colonial mission merely allows the potency of the modern law to unfold, prompting the Eternal Return of the Same as a 'pillar of emancipation' (to borrow a phrase from Santos).[13] As

---

[12] E. P. Thompson, *Whigs and Hunters* (London: Penguin, 1975), p. 266.
[13] Boaventura de Sousa Santos, *Toward a New Legal Common Sense: Law, Globalization, and Emancipation*, 2d ed. (London: Butterworths, 2002), pp. 21–61.

the *spaces* of the post-colony transit to *places* in the emerging global 'order', it becomes the mission of the law's late modernity to arrest deflections from the path of legal liberalism by persuasion when possible and through justified armed intervention when necessary.[14] That mission reworks and harnesses the colonial legacy and the post-colonial experience in the pursuit of visions of the globalizing world's iconic images of 'democracy', 'good governance', 'economic rationalism' – the goal being, in truth, to make the world safe for the foreign investor.

In a second register, these 'irreversible' and 'rational' legacies and inheritances emerge as the mythology of the modern law, as an aspect of the wider phenomenon of White Mythologies.[15] This discourse presents the progress of modern law in terms of the foundational and reiterative violence of 'modern law'.[16] From Walter Rodney to Mahmood Mamdani,[17] we read the modern law's biography as a brutal history of ways of combining the *rule of law* with the *reign of terror*. 'Post-colonial reason' contests in a myriad of modes the notions of 'rationality' that constitute the 'legacy' and the 'inheritance'.[18]

A third register scatters the narrative hegemony of the modern law through devices of legal pluralism. *Activist* legal pluralism contests the 'justice' of meta-narratives of all-pervasive colonial and contemporaneous 'globalizing' modes of domination. *Sedentary* forms of legal pluralism are content to tell us what actually happened, leaving evaluation to the realm of ethical sentiment. For present purposes, both discourses suggest that colonial appropriation of 'customariness' resulting in hybrid legal pluralism,[19] whether of the kind that entailed the creation of bodies of Anglo-Hindu and Anglo-Muslim law in colonial India or the reconstruction of the African chieftaincy, was a function of many, often contradictory, interests of the colonizing and indigenous elites. These distinctive domains of

---

[14] See John Rawls, *The Law of Peoples* (Cambridge, Mass.: Harvard University Press, 1999).

[15] See Robert Young, *White Mythologies: Writing and the History of the West* (London: Routledge, 1990).

[16] See Jacques Derrida, 'Force of Law: The "Mystical Foundation of Authority"', in Drucilla Cornell, Michel Rosenfeld and David Gray Carlson (eds.), *Deconstruction and the Possibility of Justice* (London: Routledge, 1992), pp. 3–67.

[17] See Walter Rodney, *How Europe Underdeveloped Africa* (Dar-es-Salem: Tanzania Publishing House, 1976); Mahmood Mamdani, *Citizen and Subject: Contemporary Africa and the Legacy of Late Colonialism* (Princeton: Princeton University Press, 1995).

[18] See Gayatri Chakravorty Spivak, *A Critique of Post-colonial Reason: Towards a History of a Vanishing Present* (Cambridge, Mass.: Harvard University Press, 1999).

[19] Mamdani, *supra*, note 17, pp. 109–37.

customariness have always troubled the patterns of colonial and post-colonial legality.

In a fourth register, modern law's comprehensive violence stands narrated in very different genres. Feminist narratology constructs the colonial 'legacy'/'inheritance' as so many ways of entrenching the male in the state.[20] This subaltern genre struggles to give a place to the voices of suffering and to the authentic practices of resistance to domination without hegemony. Eco-feminism and eco-history empower us with critiques of the ways of colonial and post-colonial legality that commodified the commons.[21] Psycho-history invites us to consider the ways in which 'modernity' reconstitutes the colonial and post-colonial self.[22]

The constitutive elements of colonial heritages of the modern law thus emerge very differently in these various registers. When we add to this the combined and uneven processes of colonization, the *making* of colonial law presents very different histories, too. In the high-colonial period of the British Empire in India, the presiding deity was Jeremy Bentham, whose utilitarian project finds the highest expression in the 'scientific' reform of law which proves impossible for the metropolitan power at home.[23] The Anglo-French rivalry went so far as to encourage the French dreams of an 'India-in-Africa' form of colonizing,[24] a mimetic desire that would, even

---

[20] For example, see Ann Laura Stoler, *Race and the Education of Desire: Foucault's History of Sexuality and the Colonial Order of Things* (Durham: Duke University Press, 1995); Rajeswari Sunder Rajan, *Real and Imagined Women: Gender, Culture and Post-coloniality* (London: Routledge, 1993).

[21] See Maria Meis and Vandana Shiva, *Ecofeminism* (London: Zed Books, 1993); Ariel Salleh, *Ecofeminism as Politics: Nature, Marx and the Postmodern* (London: Zed Books, 1997); Ranajit Guha, *Savaging the Civilized: Verrier Elwin, His Trials and India* (Delhi: Oxford University Press, 1999).

[22] For example, see Ashis Nandy, *The Savage Freud and Other Essays on Possible and Retrievable Selves* (Princeton: Princeton University Press, 1995); id., *Exiled at Home: Comprising at the Edge of Psychiatry, the Intimate Enemy* (Delhi: Oxford University Press, 1990). Observe that human-rights activism speaks to us not just about the genealogies of governance but also addresses colonial-legality modes of production of the 'absent subject' (see Fitzpatrick, *supra*, note 6) and the contradiction and complexity in the construction of 'subject-citizen' or even the constitutive career of a *citizen-monster*. See Veena Das, 'Language and Body: Transactions in the Construction of Pain', in Arthur Kleinman, *id.* and Margaret Lock (eds.), *Social Suffering* (Berkeley: University of California Press, 1998), pp. 67–91. Colonial law, politics and administration also constitute future histories of post-colonial violence. See E. Valentine Daniel, *Chapters in Anthropology of Violence: Sri Lankans, Sinhalas and Tamils* (Delhi: Oxford University Press, 1997); Donald Horowitz, *Ethnic Groups in Conflict* (Berkeley: University of California Press, 1985).

[23] For references and materials, see Upendra Baxi, *Towards a Sociology of Indian Law* (Delhi: Satvahan and Indian Council of Social Science Research, 1985).

[24] Thomas Pakenham, *The Scramble for Africa: 1876–1912* (London: Abacus, 1992), p. 168.

more outstandingly than the common law, arrange for the reproduction of a civil-law regime in francophone Africa. In contrast, the Portuguese in Mozambique simply exported their laws, decrees and lawyers as they did any other commodity.[25] Despite overarching commonalities in the leitmotiv of domination, colonial legality offers not one but many histories, both on the plane of ideas and institutions. It also offers multitudinous registers of resistance, especially when the life of literature is regarded as mirroring the images of law.[26]

Colonial inheritances make it almost impossible to disengage the 'colonial' from the 'post-' and the 'neo-' colonial. The 'legacies' and 'inheritances' of colonial legality persist in an era of decolonization. Most markedly, they persist in the forms and apparatuses of governance and in the accoutrements which adorn manifestations of the supreme executive power. The neo-colonial consolidates itself in the many phases of the Cold War, a phenomenon that is coeval with the processes of liberation from the colonial yoke. The juridical and legal histories of the Cold War formations of imposed neo-colonial legality await Foucault-like labours in comparative legal studies. It must suffice, for present purposes, to stress that the colonial and neo-colonial legal formations form a seamless web.[27]

Without purporting to be exhaustive, there remains, even for the 'progressive' Eurocentric tradition of doing comparative legal studies, the problem of what can only be referred to as *epistemic racism* – a term less politically correct than Althusser's 'logic of indifference'. This *habitus*, entirely comprehensible in the era of colonial comparative legal studies, has become puzzling since the middle of the twentieth century. A Jürgen Habermas, a John Rawls or a Ronald Dworkin thus remains able to expound theories of justice, public reason or judicial process *as if* the *living law* of the Third World or the south, transcending colonial inheritances, simply does not exist or is supremely irrelevant to theory-construction. The revival of comparative constitutionalism studies almost always ignores the remarkable achievements of decolonized public-law theory, whether as regards the fifty years of Indian judicial and juridical creativity or the extraordinary developments of the South African constitutional court. Outside Laura Nader's pioneering corpus which interrogates the range of hegemonic

---

[25] Albie Sachs and Gita H. Welsh, *Liberating the Law: Creating Popular Justice in Mozambique* (London: Zed Books, 1990), p. 3.
[26] See Said, *supra*, note 9, pp. 320–40.
[27] See Upendra Baxi, 'Postcolonial Legality', in Henry Schwarz and Sangeeta Ray (eds.), *A Companion to Postcolonial Studies* (Oxford: Blackwell, 2000), pp. 540–55.

presuppositions undergirding the practices of comparative jurisprudence, there has been no effort to follow Max Gluckman's studies on Barotse jurisprudence.[28] To the best of my knowledge, even the flowering of legal-pluralism studies remains unmarked by any interest in understanding the ways in which pre-colonial legality may have informed and shaped the legal imagination in the metropolitan cultures.

In the main, when comparative legal studies goes beyond the inner histories of the formation of the western legal tradition, it attends to the pressing and vital needs of doing business abroad as reflected in the so-called new *lex mercatoria* and the corresponding grammars of 'good governance'. Comparative legal 'theory' increasingly assumes an instrumentalist character, forgoing the reflexive richness that informed many of its foundational figures from Max Weber to Max Rheinstein.

The constitution of a *juristische Weltanschauung*

No understanding of the 'colonialist heritage' as a 'progress' narrative seems sensible outside the construction of a 'juridical world outlook'.[29] The juridical world outlook, or JWO, constructs 'modern' law, with all its complexity and contradictions, as a constitutive condition for human emancipation. Marked by a *juridisme* (the notion that, given good laws, all will be well with the world) which replaces 'the rule of the people by the rule of law',[30] the JWO celebrates the maxim that 'all law is bourgeois law'.[31] Indeed, the maxim may well provide a foundation for comparative legal studies in this era of globalization.

The JWO remains hostile to patterns of 'pre-modern' law, thought to be antithetical to 'progress'.[32] The work of 'progress' organizes *double* genesis amnesia. First, the JWO organizes the oblivion of the origins of the making of the western legal tradition from the tenth to the fifteenth century and the multiple histories of class-, race- and gender-based aggression. This effacement/defacement enables an idealistic presentation of the 'modern' law as inherently superior to all pre-colonial legal formations. Second, colonized people have to learn to forget their own genius for law and to forget that

---

[28] See Max Gluckman, *The Ideas in Barotse Jurisprudence* (New Haven: Yale University Press, 1965).
[29] V. A. Tumanov, *Contemporary Bourgeois Thought: Marxist Evaluation of Basic Concepts* (Moscow: Progress Publishers, 1974), p. 30 [referring to Friedrich Engels].
[30] *Id.*, p. 43.   [31] *Id.*, pp. 50–1.
[32] On this count, at least, the socialist reconstruction converged with the bourgeois outlook.

not a shred of evidence exists (if I may be so bold) to suggest that a 'highly developed law' in the lawyerly sense has anything to do with economic and social development.[33]

Of course, neither order of organized amnesia fully achieved what was intended.[34] Many a nationalist critique of colonial legality, notably that of Mohandas Gandhi (in his still inspiring *Hind Swaraj*, written around 1911),[35] in fact invoked its inglorious past, living on in the acts and feats of colonization. In the process, the communitarian virtues and values of the pre-colonial law formations were reconstructed as combating orders of imposed legality.

Even when the 'handiwork of legality' drove the 'panic-stricken bourgeoisie' to 'a general debacle of its principles' (imperialism abroad and fascism at home), the complacencies and complicities of *juridisme* and *Rechtsstaat* reigned triumphant overall.[36] Similarly, in ways unnecessary to archive here, the Marxist–Leninist JWO was also shaped by its own 'debacle of principles'.

The 'debacle of principles' further complicates notions of programmed colonialist inheritance. The imposition of colonial 'law' signified, for the most part, conscious departures from the emergent metropolitan scripts of the rule of law. Colonial governance, in the main, was not (to use Foucault's words in another context) 'a matter of imposing laws on men, but rather of disposing things, that is to say employ tactics, rather than laws, and if need be to use laws themselves as tactics'.[37] Contrary to the progress narrative, the gift of law[38] inscribed as a heritage emerges as a repertoire of 'tactics' of repressive governance.

---

[33] Lawrence Friedman and Stewart Macaulay, *Law and the Behavioural Sciences* (New York: Bobbs-Merrill, 1977), p. 1060.
[34] See Upendra Baxi, 'The Conflicting Conceptions of Legal Cultures and the Conflict of Legal Culture', in Peter Sack, Carl Wellman and Mitsukuni Yasaki (eds.), *Monismus oder Pluralismus der Rechtskulturen?* (Berlin: Duncker & Humblot, 1991), pp. 267–82.
[35] This text may perhaps most conveniently be found in A. J. Parel (ed.), *Gandhi: Hind Swaraj and Other Writings* (Cambridge: Cambridge University Press, 1997).
[36] Tumanov, *supra*, note 29, pp. 63–6 [referring to Lenin].
[37] Michel Foucault, 'Governmentality', in *The Foucault Effect: Studies in Governmentality*, ed. by Graham Burchell, Colin Gordon and Peter Miller (Chicago: University of Chicago Press, 1991), p. 95. The translation from the French is by Rosi Braidotti and Colin Gordon. For a critique, see Alan Hunt and Gary Wickam, *Foucault and Law: Towards Sociology of Law as Governance* (London: Pluto Press, 1994), pp. 39–58.
[38] The proud British boast was that India knew no law and that it was the British Rule which imparted law to India. See Susanne Rudolph and Lloyd Rudolph, *The Modernity of Tradition* (Chicago: University of Chicago Press, 1969), p. 253.

Entailed in all of this is a popular distrust of law in most, if not all, ex-colonial societies. When law itself appears as 'political tactic', it invites Gandhian opprobrium that the law is nothing more than the 'convenience of the powerful'.[39] Moreover, histories of insurgency, the orders of 'popular illegality', present the face of legal nihilism, which leave active residues in the timespace of the post-colony. Statist constructions of these, in turn, become inchoate when national resistance movements variously, and vigorously, contest the colonial right to rule, the natural right to an Empire, the variously embodied ruses and performances of 'legal tactics' of governance.

Comparative legal studies remains unconcerned with the histories of resistance to the formative practices of the JWO which performed a double function: the delegitimation of colonial/imperial legality and its ongoing profound reconstruction. Histories of power and order analytically disengaging 'law' from 'politics' can present narratives of resistance in the lexicon of 'order' and 'security' only as acts and events of 'insurgency', 'treason' and 'political criminality'.[40] The practice of comparative legal studies (at any rate as demonstrated by the taught tradition) thus de-symbolizes peoples' struggles for an alternative legality. Indeed, any acknowledgement of these would necessarily disorient the master-narrative of the progressive Eurocentric legality.[41]

The results are astounding in their ways of reinforcing progress narratives of the colonial inheritance. We are, incredibly, asked to believe that orders of resistance to colonial/imperial legality *owe* their moral/ethical origins, from a Mahatma to a Mandela, to the orders of imposed colonial *juridisme*. The non-Euro-American Other thus stands narrated in a *mimetic* relation to constitutive traditions of the JWO forbidding *in limine*, as it were, 'its' potential to renovate histories of comparative legal studies.[42]

---

[39] See Upendra Baxi, *The Crisis of the Indian Legal System* (Delhi: Vikas, 1982).

[40] See Ranajit Guha, *The Elementary Aspects of Peasant Insurgency* (Delhi: Oxford University Press, 1973).

[41] Thus, fifty years after Indian independence, the dominant juridical historiography still tends to describe the transition as a mere *transfer of power*. Struggles for self-determination are scarcely read as germinal texts providing critiques of colonial/imperial notions of legality and of the felicitous ways of domination these notions sheltered.

[42] For an examination of how the juristic genius of anti-colonial struggles shaped the histories of contemporary human-rights movements, see Baxi, *supra*, note 4. Even Gramsci (by no means the staple cognitive diet of most practitioners of comparative legal studies) was moved to describe the anti-imperial/colonial legality resistance of Gandhi in the image of 'passive revolution' or 'revolution without revolution': Antonio Gramsci, *Selections from the Prison Notebooks*, ed. and transl. by Quintin Hoare and Geoffrey Nowell Smith (New York: International Publishers, 1971),

The JWO, whether bourgeois or socialist, with all its internal variations, combines a profound rejection of the juristic creativity and energies of 'peripheral' peoples, the 'core' being constituted by Euro-American (now including transient socialist) traditions. What it denies *wholesale* stands often conceded in *retail*. Colonial/imperial legal pluralism accepts 'precolonial' legal traditions, which either conform to its ideological configuration (such as patriarchy mirrored in systems of family or 'personal' law or in the practices of agrestic serfdom) or tolerates these when they do not threaten patterns of domination (such as an indigenous law-merchant). What its formations *deny* is the notion that subordinated peoples possessed any potential for conceptions of legality, the rule of law, equality and human rights. The 'civilizing gift' of law was uniquely theirs to bestow. But the gift thus bestowed, as has already been glimpsed, is also a curse.

The first 'legacy': mercantilist governmentality

What has been 'inherited', through the ways of colonial legality, is then both the corpus of practices of freedom and the practices of management of freedom and, simultaneously, the repertoire of the *means* and the *ends* of the law's violence. I have noted elsewhere, in some detail, this history of 'continuities' and 'discontinuities' between the 'colonial' and the 'postcolonial' legality formations.[43] What I require to do here is to expand upon the notions of governmentality inherent in the colonial inheritance.

Of the many 'moments' of colonial imposition (the word 'rule' would legitimate the formation through its excess of meaning), the most intense and enduring is the one which fashions governmentality in sheer mercantilist terms. In the main, the colonized peoples and territories emerge as *commercial* possessions of joint-stock private companies. In so far as any idea of 'public' authority is discernible, it is overlaid with the privileges associated with profit and plunder which are considered as 'moral' ends in themselves. This archetypical moment is the marker of notions of governmentality in which politics becomes commerce and commerce politics. Its institutional form is the multinational corporation, the British East India Company providing a paradigm case. And the 'law' marks its birth as the command of an Austinian sovereign, as a code (to adopt Niklas Luhmann's

p. 100. The same imagery animates E. P. Thompson whom I quoted earlier (*supra*, note 12). Even the modes of empathetic understanding thus stand inescapably located within the JWO.
[43] See Baxi, *supra*, note 27, p. 540.

terminology) of 'positivization of arbitrariness'.[44] Men of commerce (there were, of course, no women) who became law-makers as well as judges and enforcers had little or no knowledge of the profound normative and institutional changes shaping metropolitan legality.

Force and fraud provided the techniques of governance for mercantile state power. The values and virtues of dominance *without* hegemony codifying both the violence of law and the law of violence are institutionalized in the incipient notions of 'state' and 'law'.[45] This phenomenon marks the colonial constitution of the *absent* subject. The 'strength' of early colonial governance also (as is true of all schizoid/paranoid formations of power) lay in its vulnerability, which arose in many contingent combinations. If the rivalry among European powers (truly illustrative of the Hobbesian state of nature) shaped the nature and future of this form of governmentality, so did the emerging conflicts of interest within the factions of merchant capital. And that combination was further riven by a conflict between those (to use Foucault's distinction) who sought governance over bodies and those who struggled for the governance of souls[46] – the emerging conflict between missionaries and merchants was not inconsequential in the period of mercantilist governance. Finally, and without claiming to be exhaustive, the ways of resistance offered by the subordinated peoples fomented political practices of fierce, and catastrophic, cruelty.[47] Governmentality thus *constitutes* the colonial heritage in a myriad of ways, some of which persist in the space and time of the post-colony.

The second legacy: 'high'-colonial legality

The second moment of 'high'-colonial law, very uneven in its historic spread across the colonial possessions, occurs when colonial sovereignty migrates to the 'duly' constituted metropolitan sovereign.[48] Inevitably, some ideas and ideals constitutive of the orders of metropolitan legality then also

---

[44] Niklas Luhmann, *A Sociological Theory of Law*, transl. by Elizabeth King and Martin Albrow (London: Routledge & Kegan Paul, 1985), pp. 147–58.
[45] See Baxi, *supra*, note 23.
[46] See Foucault, *supra*, note 37, pp. 87–104.
[47] For examples of archiving, see Guha, *supra*, note 40; Mamdani, *supra*, note 17; Oliver Mendelssohn and Upendra Baxi, *The Rights of Subordinated Peoples* (Delhi: Oxford University Press, 1994); Pakenham, *supra*, note 24; Rodney, *supra*, note 17.
[48] See David Washbrook, 'Law, State and Agrarian Society in India', (1981–2) 15 Modern Asian Stud. 157.

migrate, though with profound ambivalence, to the orders of colonially constituted space and time. This conjuncture marks many historic beginnings that shape also the beginning of the ends of the Empire.

But the practitioners of comparative law rarely recall the fact that the formative contexts of colonial legality follow the lines of imperial conquest, even when they narrate the resultant juridical spheres such as the 'anglophone' and 'francophone', or more generally the 'common-law' and 'civil-law' legal territories. From the subjectivities of the colonized, however, high-colonial state 'diffusion' of the western legal tradition emerges as a process of continual conquest. Law itself is seen as conquest by other means. It reinvents communitarian legal traditions and puts them to work toward the ends of colonial administration and adjudication. This 'expropriation of law' (to use a Weberian phrase-regime) results in a hybrid legality which, in turn, reconstitutes public memory as well as colonizing the normative means of the production of law and, crucially, the very structures of time and space. *No error in the doing of comparative legal studies is more egregious than that which remains complicit with the politics of organized amnesia of law as a form of conquest.*

In this way, various orders of construction of the colonial legal pluralism arise. If high-colonial law emerges early in some possessions (for example, in British India or in Pondichéry in French India), it does so rather late in others (as in east Africa and south-east Asia) and almost never at all in yet others (I have in mind mostly colonies under Portuguese domination, whether Goa or Mozambique). Almost half a century after decolonization, we still lack a map of the combined and uneven spread of high-colonial law. And an undifferentiating 'cartography' of law, in turn, reproduces the potential for *geographies of injustice* in the constitutive modes of doing comparative law and jurisprudence.

High-colonial law also presents us with a complex of inter-legality (as illustrated, for instance, by Sri Lanka, the former Indochina or Indonesia). This inter-legality becomes a veritable labyrinth when colonially manufactured laws are exported from one jural territory to others (as happened, for example, with the imposition of Indian codes to colonial possessions in anglophone Africa). Control over the interpretation of colonial law by the appellate courts in the metropolis adds further levels of intricacy to the scenario of high-colonial law. Colonial legal pluralism, a salient feature of high-colonial law, appears as a necessity whose mother was imperialism, even if its multitudinous midwives were located in the grid of colonial administration, whether managed through the natives or from Europe.

Hybridity is thus a constitutive feature of high-colonial law and of the colonial legal inheritance in the post-colony. The contradictions between liberalism and the Empire shape conflicted practices of governmentality and influence the career of 'modern' law.[49] The mercantilist practices of governmentality are no longer permissible wholesale; their production and deployment in retail, however, needs to be re-constituted by metropolitan legal theory and practice. Control over land and agrarian relations of production is now to be articulated not by 'force without phrases' but by the 'force of phrases' (to evoke Marx's distinction).[50] Planned de-industrialization of the colonies and the enforced dispersion of its labouring population are to be achieved through languages of rights to property and equitable governance within the Empire. Maintenance of the colonial 'law-and-order', vital to rule by property, stands presented as an aspect of good, even benign, governance. Thus, high-colonial law archives the foundations of legal paternalism in an almost Kantian mode and projects the image of a *caring* colonizing self.

Yet, high-colonial law may never presume the fidelity of colonial subjects. All subjects, by definition, threaten imperial sovereignty. And many, even by the mere fact of their *birth* in legally proscribed social communities (as with British India's Criminal Tribes Act) constituted threats to colonial sovereignty. High-colonial law is a paradigm case of the schizoid/paranoid state seized by its periodic crises of nervous legal rationality. Never unwilling to strike, and not wholly afraid to wound, high-colonial law develops along the grids of obedience and sedition. The construction of a 'loyal' subject of colonial law thus always remained an excessively hazardous enterprise. There were real limits to what 'legal' sanctions and 'co-legal' terror could achieve under conditions of high-colonial legality.

Thus, the colonial legal subject was summoned not only to duties of *obedience* but also to duties of *affection*. The British Indian Penal Code, in a provision that travelled well to other imperial possessions and whose repressive potential has outlasted even the Golden Jubilee of Indian constitutionalism, defines the crime of sedition (a cousin of treason) as inciting *disaffection* toward the lawfully constituted government. All colonial subjects also stand conceived as potential spies. The widely-exported colonial Indian Official

---

[49] See Uday Mehta, *Liberalism and Empire* (Chicago: University of Chicago Press, 1998).
[50] See Karl Marx, *Capital*, vol. I (Moscow: Progress Publishers, 1976), pp. 671–93 [1867]. See also Upendra Baxi, *Marx, Law and Justice* (Bombay: N. M. Tripathi, 1993), pp. 85–94.

Secrets Act renders criminal any spatial movement by the subject within an ascribed 'place' as notified, say, by the executive. Once an area has thus been delineated, the subjects are liable to being treated as 'spies' and exposed to summary military trial. Colonial penal legality is rife with such notions of crimes against the state. It abounds in models of legislation that constitute the political *geographies of injustice*.

Formations of colonial legality, with all the 'normative' weight of their institutional apparatuses, also structure notions of *time*. Colonial legality triumphs by control over rhythms of time. Its law of evidence and procedure sets boundaries as regards what stories may be told concerning human violation and suffering, thus fragmenting and disorganizing narrative voice – a facet of 'modern' law which Ranajit Guha has poignantly archived.[51] In thus (dis-)organizing the time of the subjugated peoples, high-colonial law eliminates all formative contexts of insurrection against public authority.

Colonial law as adjudication confines and often makes impossible the telling of genealogical stories concerning human violation and violence by forces in civil society acting at the behest of state power. In the mightily uncommon 'common-law' jurisdictions, a number of varied devices (in particular, the so-called hearsay-evidence rule) typically structure notions of relevancy and admissibility in ways that strike at the very roots of lived social memory. Meanwhile, contract law provides mechanisms that legalize forced labour and debt bondage. The vaunted distinction between 'public' and 'private' makes familial violence and abuse invisible and inaudible in ways that comfort patriarchy. Revenue law, while promoting large land-holdings, encourages the loyalty of the propertied classes (I am thinking of Nietzsche's slave morality) and legitimates the worst excesses of agrestic serfdom. Forest laws degrade, desexualize and dehumanize indigenous peoples. Laws of limitation render ineligible any 'belated' movement for the redress of wrongs. (Even an English judge, writing on the subject, wondered why it required the Indian Limitation Act to prescribe 163 ways in which a human being can be said to be 'sleeping' on her actionable claims.[52]) Also, the administration of criminal justice structures, in complex ways, the fading of testimonial memories through proverbial adjudicatory process delays while the patterns of penality visit crimes against property and the state with

---

[51] Ranajit Guha, 'Chandra's Death', in *id*. (ed.), *Subaltern Studies V: Writings on South Asian History and Society* (Delhi: Oxford University Press, 1989), pp. 135–65.

[52] See Upendra Baxi, 'Conflict of Laws', in (1967–8) Annual Survey of Indian Law 227, p. 284, n. 305.

savage repression. The colonial subject, constituted by a marked incapacity for truth-telling, is to be socialized, whether by persuasion or coercion, in the ways of production of colonial legal truths. Perjurer by 'nature,' as it were, the colonial legal subject is now destined to another incarnation of life in perjury.

The high-colonial law-and-governance project of construction of a loyal subject has proved, unsurprisingly, of little interest to comparatists concerned as they are, for the most part, with the 'introduction', 'diffusion' and 'reception' in colonial possessions of western laws' norms and institutions. The notion of colonial 'inheritance' as a series of violent and catastrophic practices that constitute the colonial state and the colonial law, however, remains the foundational premise for any meaningful tradition of *subaltern* studies in comparative jurisprudence.

The third legacy: the 'lower degree of civil freedom'

The violence of law and governance stands celebrated, whether overtly or covertly, in the dominant narratives of comparative jurisprudence. This violent penetration, this forced entry, this 'prizing open', is often represented, *pace* Foucault, not as movement from domination to domination but from domination to progress. Progress stands defined in relation to the development of capitalism. Modern law is progressive because it has enabled movement from status to contract (I have in mind Maine's idea), that is, from the 'charismatic'/'traditional'/'patrimonial' forms of domination to a legal-rational domination in the Weberian sense and from the repressive sanctions of 'mechanical' solidarity to regimes of restitutive sanctions of 'organic' (Durkheimian) solidarity.

Despite the foundational colonial politics of social Darwinism, this progress narrative has its roots in Marx's dialectical notion of human emancipation where forces and relations of production generate, simultaneously, the immiseration of the working classes as well as their 'once-upon-a-time' privilege as bearers of the future history of human emancipation through an inversion of the means of 'progressive' bourgeois legality. And, although Marx's own project was confined to the future history of capitalism in the regions of its birth, it furnished several new twists and turns in the life of colonial and post-colonial legality through different modes of nationalist self-assertion in colonized regions. This is too large a theme to be addressed here. But it remains worthy of mention that the spectres of Marx (to invoke

Jacques Derrida) haunted high-colonial law formations. Incipient notions of socialist legality, and their underlying critiques of bourgeois legality, contributed in some measure to the renovation of colonial legal practices, albeit in a way consistent with the overarching patterns of legal imperialism. Comparative histories of high-colonial law, informed by competing and contradictory notions of progressive Eurocentric legality, are as yet unwritten.

The high-colonial/imperial-law formation reflects this movement of law through the installation in the colonies of at least a 'lower degree of civil freedom'. Whereas pre-colonial formations had only notions of authority, high-colonial law brought along the idea of *legality*.[53] Whereas the pre-colonial formations lacked the rudiments of differentiation in the spheres of power, high-colonial law carried with it the notions of separation of powers and of a relatively autonomous judiciary. Whereas 'priestly' knowledge/power combinations sustained the 'legitimacy' of pre-colonial law, the high-colonial state remained increasingly secular, allowing for religious pluralism. The interpretive monopolies established to sustain revealed law gave way to an idea of law as being made contingently by some human beings to govern others. If law still constituted 'fate', it was a provisional destiny rather than an unalterable cosmic force. Networks of professional knowledges validated by state law – known as 'certificatory' knowledges within Foucault's discursive framework[54] – steadily crafted new power/knowledge combinations and new conceptions of the 'common good' which, for one thing, marginalized orders of organic knowledges. The epistemic communities constituted by professional lawyers and adjudicators, the civil service, police and security forces, the public-health professions, revenue and forest officials, practitioners of colonial forensic medicine and census officials, for example, formed power/knowledge grids that combined disciplinarity with sovereign forms of power, imparting the project of construction of the loyal subject with increasing orders of cogency and efficacy.[55]

These stark and generally well-known contrasts should suffice to foreground at least partially the evangelical fervour that animated the discourse

---

[53] See Robert Lingat, *The Classical Law of India*, ed. and transl. by J. Duncan M. Derrett (Delhi: Oxford University Press, 1972).

[54] See generally Michel Foucault, *Power/Knowledge: Selected Interviews and Other Writings 1972–1977*, ed. by Colin Gordon (New York: Pantheon, 1981), pp. 77–108.

[55] The growing contemporary literature concerning the intensification and diversification of bureaucratic development in the high-colonial era is too rich to warrant even summary citation. However, the next two sections of this essay contain various illustrative references.

of high-colonial law-makers and reformers[56] – which, interestingly, is of the same order as that which now characterizes the discourse purporting to bring 'law' to the post-Soviet-Union federations and republics. The law-makers and reformers' original intent was benign and paternal, not amorally sinister. From the explorer-missionary David Livingstone onwards, the original intent was to bring the three Cs: Commerce, Christianity and Civilization (in *that* order, of course) – or, to use Bronislaw Malinowski's three Cs: Codes, Courts and Constabulary.[57] Conquest and belligerent occupation offered, in the high-colonial era, only a vague context of memory within which the original intent had now to be performed (not unlike the Cold War for the 'transitional societies' of eastern and central Europe today). Implicit to their labours, however, was an unproblematized social Darwinism, the imperialism of the Same and the 'ceaseless subordination of the differentiated, [...] of the nonintegral'.[58]

We are all too familiar (thanks to the endless debate among US constitutionalists) with the 'impossibility', as it were, of 'originalism'. But the originalism of high-colonial law (far from representing the hermeneutic hobby of citizen–scholars from a society dedicated, after all, to the 'pursuit of happiness') acted as a *material* force shaping many practices of power over the colonized peoples. Detraditionalization of the communitarian traditions of peoples' law was the first step toward the development of colonial legal authority. The creation of an adjudicative monopoly and a colonial penality constituted further processes aiding the construction of the loyal colonial subject. The colonial prison not only created conditions for the production of 'controlled delinquency' and the management of 'popular illegalities', but it also provided the context in which 'docile bodies' constructed many a truth for high-colonial legality.[59] The colonial police and assorted security forces implemented regimes of surveillance, and at times of terror, which served to contain the emergence of an insurrectionary 'self'. The grid of power/knowledge that gave rise to the modern legal professions, including the adjudicatory vocations, not to mention the 'overdeveloped'

---

[56] For example, see Eric Stokes, *The English Utilitarians and India* (Oxford: Oxford University Press, 1959).

[57] For the reference to Livingstone, see Pakenham, *supra*, note 24, p. xxv. For a general reference to Malinowski, see Bronislaw Malinowski, *Crime and Custom in Savage Society* (London: Kegan Paul, Trench, Trubner, 1926).

[58] Dimock, *supra*, note 7, p. 74.

[59] See generally Michel Foucault, *Discipline and Punish*, transl. by Alan Sheridan (New York: Pantheon, 1977).

civil service, served the material interests of an upwardly mobile indigenous elite providing generational loyalties for the Empire.[60]

This being said, we need to attend to the 'objective' legacy constituted by the 'lower degree of civil freedom'. I describe the legacy as 'objective,' *only* in the sense of the *material effects* that overrun many high-minded colonial-authorial intentions.

Predatory legality and the 'lower degree of civil freedom'

In contrast to the mercantilist colonial formation, high-colonial law seeks to construct, or at any rate to present, the law as a public good. But the notion of 'law' is severely qualified. Designed to structure colonial violence and to promote the prosperity of the Empire, high-colonial law emerges above all as a form of *predatory legality*.[61]

Predatory legality confronted the law with various contradictory tasks. The law was assigned the simultaneous tasks of legitimating the fact and force of colonization and of performing a whole variety of tasks that facilitated massive metropolitan gains from domination. A certain order of legitimation was required if only to produce a class of loyal subjects who not only benefited from the system of domination, but also became convinced missionaries extolling the progressive nature of high-colonial law. The law (whether as norm, policy or administration) had to apportion rewards and sanctions, distribute social opportunities and enhance life choices and

---

[60] One must not ignore the formation of the armed forces that fought many imperial wars on behalf, and at the behest of, colonizing elites. The Sandhurst- and, later in the Cold War era, the West-Point-trained armed forces, provided, at least for the British Empire, the warp and the woof for post-colonial military coups, regimes and dictatorships. These now generate a myriad of forms of western public lamentation at the demise of democratic forms of governance. This complaint masks the bases of 'western' affluence based partly, but substantially, on the arms industry and informal arms trafficking. The complex transactions of material interests thus constituted under the auspices of high-colonial law also sustain, unsurprisingly, the *re-colonization* of the very legal imagination.

[61] In conversations on the role of law in the development of middle- and low-income countries at a conference organized by the Institute of Development Studies on 1–3 June 2000, where I addressed the theme of 'Rights amidst risk and regression' – a notion that has had no takers since I first enunciated it (Baxi, *supra*, note 39, pp. 348–58) – Professor Laura Nader suggested that 'predation' might prove a more acceptable notion. The swift currency the term began to enjoy reminded me of the lamented Julius Stone's constant advice which, alas, I have never been able to internalize, that one ought to learn to respect what he inimitably termed the ways of the 'diplomacy of scholarly communication'.

material gains. High-colonial law also distributed symbolic capital in terms of recognition (without redistribution).[62]

At the same time, predatory legality constructed the logic of colonial *thrift*. Resources, natural and human, had to be harvested for optimal metropolitan gain. Thus emerges high-colonial law's chief concern: to design legal policy and administration in ways that command and control natural resources. General categories of contract and property law were, while important, simply not enough. Specific regimes of natural-resource law were needed, and developed,[63] in which the role of law in the rule of law was not designed to meet the basic needs of the colonial impoverished, except, and circumstantially, as a series of accumulated unintended side-effects. These legal regimes were robust enough to survive decolonization.

The colony furnished a storehouse of raw materials, a surplus industrial reserve army and a conscriptible mass of natives that sustained the consolidation of colonial frontiers and imperial wars. Predatory legality had also to pursue the rather difficult aims of organizing exactions of land revenue and the 'extractive' management of natural and human resources. It had to facilitate the constant supply of 'unfree labour' (both within and across the colony) and create structures allowing for the de-industrialization of the colonial economy. Moreover, colonial law, policy and administration had to achieve somehow the balance of payments within a rather complex pattern of inter-colonial extraction of surplus value.

These were tasks not wholly unfamiliar to the development of capitalist law within the metropolitan tradition. But the means to achieve these goals in metropolitan spaces had to address the formation of progressive legality, which had elaborated, over long stretches of historical time, the notions of the rule of law, human rights and democratic governance. The mission of high-colonial law was, however, to legitimize whenever possible the denial of these ideas to the 'native' subjects or to make them available in severely attenuated forms when necessary – a process which has rightly prompted

---

[62] I refer in particular to Nancy Fraser's rich work, most recently summarized in her 'Rethinking Recognition', (2000) 3 New Left R. (2d) 107.

[63] I have in mind relations of property in agricultural land, the appropriation of the public commons, uses of eminent-domain power for 'public works' serving the pressing needs of colonial capital movement such as irrigation, railways, ports and coastal shipping, mining, power generation and road transport, the productive management of forests and export-driven commodity production (notably, the plantation economy).

Guha to refer to 'mediocre liberalism'.[64] Predatory legal regimes thus invented different forms of *quarantine legality* which empowered local administrators to contain the spread of these novel ideas at the frontiers of the colony.[65] I cannot develop the history of these processes except to say, speaking of predatory legality from the standpoint of British high-colonial law in south Asia, that they varied enormously depending on the law-regions and on the circumstances of colonization.[66]

How, then, was this high-colonial legality constructed? Such question leads us to vastly different response trajectories, each privileging a particular perspective on governance, rights, development and justice.

The subaltern perspectives

On one deeply subaltern view, high-colonial law constructs, yet again, the law as a kind of *fate*. For the colonized masses, long accustomed to law as the desire of the sovereign backed with potentially limitless coercion, high-colonial legality is more of the same experience. John Austin, a name unbeknownst to them, paradigmatically confirms their own lived experience of the *ultimate* social meaning of the law. The law is an order of experience in the shaping of which they have no say or voice; it just *happens* to them as do floods, droughts, famines and being born to a cradle-to-grave struggle for subsistence. High-colonial law, through its invention of new forms of suzerainty, languages, institutions and professional forms of expropriation of just grievances, claims and disputes, added to the repertoire of their immiseration. Even when considered as a 'weapon of the weak' (to evoke Scott James), the experience of law as fate did not undergo any profound shift: it

---

[64] See Ranajit Guha, *Dominance Without Hegemony: History and Power in Colonial India* (Cambridge: Cambridge University Press, 1997), p. 5.
[65] In a sense, the maintenance of colonial legality echoes tasks which the north now faces in genetic policing as it seeks to discipline and punish horizontal gene transfers from genetically modified seeds, plants and foods. Ideas, much like genetic mutations, cross-fertilize in unanticipated and ungovernable ways. When they do, they expose the inherent vulnerability of law.
[66] Notions of European progressive legality varied in their internal evolution among European powers (as any reader of A. V. Dicey's 'rule of law' corpus well knows). There was considerable differentiation in notions concerning separation of powers, judicial autonomy, legislative primacy or supremacy, definitions of criminality and the theory and practice of punishment. Likewise, there were marked differences in the ways of negotiating the circumstance of colonization: the French differed from the British, and these both stood in contrast to the Dutch, Belgian, Portuguese, Italian and Spanish. Not merely is this comparative history of colonial inheritance yet to be fully written but also the ways of constructing different narrative voices in the writing of these colonial histories have yet to be fully addressed.

amounted, at the end of the day, to no more than one more distinct mode of experience for cheating one's ways into rudimentary human survival.

Yet, with some persuasion, and in some colonial contexts, a few subaltern voices have endowed high-colonial law with a liberative potential. This is particularly true as regards India's perennially deprived 'outcasts'.[67] The Dalit leader, a founding figure of the Indian Constitution, Dr B. R. Ambedkar, was a powerful voice applauding colonial legal liberalism as a harbinger of social equality, even emancipation, for millions of *'atisudras'*, as he named the social and economic proletariat whom various practices of Hinduisms relegated to a permanent order of disadvantage and dispossession.[68] According to this conception, high-colonial law emerged as the very antithesis of fate, which pre-colonial legality represented for the *atisudras*.

The colonial mode of production

High-colonial law constituted people under its sway as *subjects*, not as slaves. In political-theory terms, this marks a normative shift away from the 'slave' mode of production and even from the somewhat nebulous 'Asiatic' mode. Legal modernization was not, however, a means of instituting industrial capitalism and its superstructures of legality. Rather, it occurred under the auspices of the colonial mode of production. A highly complex and contradictory affair of history, this mode introduced changes in property relations and forms of dependent industrialization in ways that facilitated the ends of colonial predation. All this now stands amply documented.[69] High-colonial law was the principal instrument in the installation of these processes which 'hindered the development of capitalistic production in agriculture' in ways that promoted systematic de-industrialization and economic growth favourable to the metropolitan economy.[70]

---

[67] See Oliver Mendelssohn and Marika Vicziany, *The Untouchables: Subordination, Poverty and the State in India* (Cambridge: Cambridge University Press, 1998).

[68] See Upendra Baxi, 'Justice as Emancipation: Babasaheb Ambedkar's Legacy and Vision', in *id*. and Bhikhu Parekh (eds.), *Crisis and Change in Contemporary India* (Delhi: Sage, 1995), pp. 122–49.

[69] For example, see Elizabeth Whitcombe, *Agrarian Conditions in Northern India in Late Nineteenth Century* (Berkeley: University of California Press, 1972); Kumar Ravinder, *Western India in the Nineteenth Century* (London: Routledge, 1968); Washbrook, *supra*, note 48. For further references, see Baxi, *supra*, note 23.

[70] Utsa Patnaik, 'Capitalist Development in Agriculture', (1971) 6 Economic & Political Weekly A-123, p. A-146. See also Paresh Chattopadhyaya, 'On the Question of the Mode of Production in Indian Agriculture', (1972) 7 Economic & Political Weekly A-39; Baxi, *supra*, note 23,

State differentiation

High-colonial law introduces significant levels of differentiation in the state apparatuses and modes of governance. The notion of separation of powers emerges as a whole series of ways of constructions of 'decentralized despotism';[71] the apparent *dispersal* of power, the shifting range of distribution of opportunities to coerce and command, the ever-growing diffuse location of powers of *enumeration* (through district gazetteers, census and land records),[72] all these, as well as related devices of separation of powers, merge into the centralized unity of the colonial state.

State differentiation also entails the growth of what Foucault names as the 'certificatory' sovereignty of the state.[73] All professions (whether in the public service, medical and legal practice, town planning, architecture and public works, journalism and education, policing and prisons) now require the imprimatur of the state, negotiated in fine detail through legal norms and processes. It also signifies, to evoke Gramsci, the subjugation of the organic by means of erudite knowledges. High-colonial law shapes, and is in turn shaped by, the bureaucracies it necessarily creates. In this way, it further concretizes the project of construction of the loyal subject, progressively empowered to curb, crib and confine the disloyal.

The ceaseless drive of the Will to Adjudication, a necessary entailment of expanding sovereignties everywhere, assumes in high-colonial law at least two historic forms: the destruction of remnants of pre-colonial adjudicatory forms where necessary and their cooptation where expedient. By dint of the orders of administrative exigency, a relatively autonomous adjudicature becomes a necessary adjunct of the project of high-colonial law. It creates a sorting-out state apparatus for specific disputes among fractions of indigenous and metropolitan capital; enables the rise of the learned legal professions with the attendant creation of whole frameworks supportive of the overall ends of the colonial regimes; provides an arena for the enactment of interest formations congealed in the constructions of crime and punishment (I have in mind Althusser's repressive state apparatuses); and,

---

pp. 29–40. For Africa, see also Rodney, *supra*, note 17; Mamdani, *supra*, note 17; Issa G. Shivji, *The Concept of Human Rights in Africa* (Harare: Africa World Press, 1989).

[71] Mamdani, *supra*, note 17, pp. 37–61.

[72] See Arjun Appadurai, *Modernity at Large: Cultural Dimensions of Globalization* (Minneapolis: University of Minnesota Press, 1996), pp. 114–38.

[73] *Supra*, note 54.

above all, sustains the 'production of belief' (to quote Pierre Bourdieu)[74] in the production of *legitimate* colonial law.

This comes to pass, in turn, in a whole variety of ways: the introduction of the indeterminate 'certainty' of law through legislation and codification; the insertion of minimalist notions of fairness in the administration of criminal justice and of differential standards of 'proof' in civil and criminal justice; the erection of hierarchies of courts and judges. All these, in other words, provide various modes for the production of colonial 'truths' of law. This realm of contestation, in the main, passes by (to evoke John Austin) the 'bulk and generality' of the duly constituted obedient colonial subjects. In its construction of a hierarchy of jurisdictions governing the adjudicatory process and the regimes of *legal* rights, high-colonial law's limits of fairness and of rights stand necessarily determined by the need to sustain the *Grundnorm* of imperial rule. When we bear in mind these features of colonial 'rights', we are better able to discern the nature of 'freedoms' available in a high-colonial era.

Languages of rights

In so far as a reflexion on rights enables a glimpse into the history of imperial colonial formation, it remains useful to undertake a few risky journeys across this enchanting realm. The languages of rights served several measurable functions. They helped to mediate and protect the interests of the competing factions of capital. Necessary as a means of redressing the foundational legitimation deficit, the languages of rights also provided grammars of governance.[75]

The sheer administrative compulsions to raise revenue from agriculture, establish a hegemonic judicature, protect and promote regimes of unfree labour (to different degrees) and foster free markets across colonial boundaries required recourse to languages of rights as aspects of high-colonial governance. So did, in diverse ways, the needs of the construction of a loyal colonial subject. The legal professions, as well as hegemonic judicatures, afforded the subjects some sort of stake in the imperial legal orderings. These projects beset many an authorial intention. Rights, however, served well the functions of *signposts*, even when their logics and paralogics constructed

---

[74] Pierre Bourdieu, *The Field of Cultural Production: Essays on Art and Literature*, transl. by Randal Johnson (Cambridge: Polity, 1993), pp. 40–61.
[75] See Baxi, *supra*, note 4.

wholly ambivalent directions. As signposts, somewhat summarily configured, the congeries of high-colonial rights had the following manifest attributes.

First, rights emerge as *favours* or *concessions* provided, for a whole variety of reasons, by the colonial sovereign to the subject. The bases of colonial rights lie in the will of the colonizer, not in the affirmation of the equal worth of all human beings. *Imperial legality abhors the notion of human rights* – that is, the right of human beings everywhere to share in the order of universal human rights – as any recognition of this entitlement will stultify imperialism. The favours or concessions may be represented as being progressive, in contrast with the mercantilist governance traditions. *Mon Dieu*, this marks *some* progress indeed!

Second, differential rights, being concessions or favours, become legitimate. The state does not have to justify unequal distribution of rights among the various social strata as between owners of land and landless labour, moneylenders and the indebted, industrialists and the working classes. Indeed, some people may not be invested with any rights at all (as with so many varieties of unfree labour). Rights, thus, do not set real boundaries to supreme executive power; rather, they serve as markers of the executive largess.

Third, the grant of rights is all too often a grant of *powers* directed to sustain certain patterns of governance. The rights of *zamindars* over tenants, in late nineteenth-century India, were in effect powers to raise revenue for the state. The power to rule (that is, the performance of sovereign functions) often went hand in hand with the grant of such rights.

Fourth, all rights, of whatever nature, must derive from the established 'sources' of law. In one foul swift stroke, this demand disinherited masses of First Nation peoples. At a technical comparative jurisprudence level, the issue of what aspects and which corpus of imperial law was transferred to the colony has always been a contested site in the history of high-colonial law. Certain rights available in the metropolis have often been transported to the colony through judicial interpretation (I am thinking, for instance, of equitable rights and of their transfer to the British colonies). But, on the whole, it was axiomatic in high-colonial law that the function of judicial processes was to enforce rights where they could be said to exist (albeit with a wide margin of appreciation) and not to enunciate new rights under the guise of interpretation.

Fifth, claims that cannot be legally protected are then not 'rights' and what ought to be legally protected as 'rights' must vary with every order of contingent as well as foundational exigency of colonial administration.

Sixth, no natural rights may be said to exist in a colony. Outside the foundational natural right inherent in colonialism (the *natural right to an Empire for European nations*), colonial legal tradition repudiates firmly any *jusnaturalist* construction of rights.

Seventh, rights stand conceived in the image of a universalistic imperial order of *patriarchy*. High-colonial law enforces this order in somewhat uncomprehending but still comprehensible ways. It finds a grand ally in the pre-colonial patterns of legality that sanctify the myriad of practices purporting to subjugate women. At the same time, it responds to the urge for progressive reform through the formation of lineages of colonial legal paternalism. The latter stands achieved, for example, by suppressing the outrageous practices of female infanticide[76] or by regulating the practice of *sati*. Legal paternalism serves the function of legitimating a 'progressive' high-colonial state formation as well as promoting the reach and sway of colonial administration. The former is achieved through the performative acts of colonial legal pluralism. Among these, the preservation of *personal-law* systems ranks high (for instance, the perpetuation of oppressive systems from the pre-colonial era discriminating on the basis of gender). The colonial inheritance is, in many ways, a narrative of the combinatory ways of production of *legal bodies in pain* which survive in the spaces of the decolonization struggle and beyond, in the timeplace of post-colonial law.[77]

The unintended heritage

Life, even that of high-colonial law, does not quite move according to the original intention of hegemonic projects. In any event, there is simply no *single* trajectory of colonial intention. The historic unfolding of European hegemony was deeply fractured by a mix of 'noble' and savage intentionalities. Radical critiques of colonization from the standpoint of the oppressed address the former as the fables and parables of the Enlightenment project. Meanwhile, the latter live on in the killing fields of many a post-colony. But the mixture of 'noble' and savage intentionalities makes recounting large stories about unintended consequences particularly difficult.

---

[76] See Lalita Panigrahi, *British Social Policy and Female Infanticide in India* (Delhi: Munshiram Manoharlal, 1972).

[77] See Bina Agarwal, *A Field of Their Own: Gender and Land Rights in South Asia* (Cambridge: Cambridge University Press, 1994); Urvashi Butalia, *The Other Side of Silence: Voices from the Partition of India* (Delhi: Viking, 1998); Das, *supra*, note 22.

A first way of telling the story is to opt for a Kantian mode in which 'the character of the people' is shaped by colonial governance in such a way that native subjects collectively seek a higher form of freedom. High-colonial law educates subject peoples in the vocabulary of self-determination and decolonization, in a sense marking the very triumph of the Enlightenment project. On this view, the Other of Europe can learn languages of freedom and rights only through the necessitous visitation upon 'it' of various orders of brutalizing violence and deprivation. In this sense (if the proposition is sensible at all), the latent function of colonial legality as conquest was *jurisgenerative*.[78] This logically fallacious, historically inaccurate and ethically problematic mode of narrating unintended consequences is, however, still in vogue, even as regards human rights. Phoenix-like, it continually reproduces itself.[79]

A second mode of narrating histories of unintended impacts eschews large polemical motifs, concentrating instead on the institutional materiality of the 'modern'/late-modern law. By this, I mean the proliferation of institutions possessed of the power to enunciate norms and standards of law (including models of law reform), administer and implement (or ignore and subvert) these, and enforce (or ignore) dominant legality through the means of state coercion. The development of a sociological structure of coercion (to invoke the distinction that enables Weber to differentiate 'modern' from 'pre-modern' law)[80] entails considerable mobilization of state resources so as to maintain specialized bureaucracies. The construction

---

[78] See Robert M. Cover, '*Nomos* and Narrative', (1983–4) 97 Harvard L.R. 4, pp. 11–23 and 40–5.
[79] This is demonstrated by the current talk about 'good governance' and economic rationalism linking foreign aid to conditions of democratic governance as well as by the related discovery of the late-modern law's global mission to empower the world's impoverished in a world simultaneously, and vigorously, declared safe for direct foreign investment. The failure of decolonization, as it were, put at the doorstep of the political elites and regimes of the developing countries (not wholly unfairly), is now an urgent 'global' concern, so pressing that even the World Bank is moved to define conceptions of good governance and an agenda for institutional legal reforms. The exogenous causes of this failure (for example, the many phases of the Cold War, 'structural' adjustment programmes, the organized effort to replace the paradigmatic Universal Declaration of Human Rights by a Trade-Related, Market-Friendly Human Rights paradigm and arms traffic) are rarely matters that invite attention or cause anxiety. I am aware that a compact footnote is scarcely a vehicle for sustained analytical communication. But it remains possible to observe that the global movement of power and law is still from domination to domination, with the difference that predation now invents the processes of a colonized without a colonizer through the globally sustained structures of 'lower degrees of civil freedom'.
[80] See generally Max Weber, *Economy and Society*, ed. by Guenther Roth and Claus Wittich, t. II (Berkeley: University of California Press, 1978), pp. 880–900 [1922].

of the materiality of the law thus implies a whole range of recursive concrete labours of governance. And the spread of social costs remains uneven among the beneficiaries and victims of legal order. The languages of imposed legality are also a material force, if only because these determine the orders of speech and silence of the colonized subject in ways perhaps more determinative than what gets said by way of literature.

The materiality of the law also introduces the relative autonomy of institutions that seek to carry out high-colonial law's project of domination.[81] The forms of relative autonomy vary with each domain of high-colonial law depending on the intention of the hierarchies of power thus constructed by the labours of governance. Typically, the level of autonomy is relatively highly socially visible in interpretive monopolies gradually established through adjudication and lawyering. It also exists, in less visible forms, in the administration of law and policy through a specialized civil service (such as revenue and forest services) which introduces spaces for indigenous doings within a colonial hierarchy. Even prisons and other fora of detention under vicious security laws develop their own distinctive orders of immunity and impunity.

And the story is not merely one that involves state differentiation for it also explores the autonomy that the people's legal formations develop *inter se* as well as in a counter-hegemonic relation to high-colonial law. The colonial subject emerges in these stories not just as a passive recipient of the truths of high-colonial law but also as its strategic critic and subverter, as an active agent resisting, ambushing, waylaying, dis-orientating the megastructures of high-colonial law. The inaugural figure of a Mohandas Gandhi or a Nelson Mandela leaps to mind as embodiment of the most powerful deconstruction of the claims of colonial law. But there were also (to borrow a phrase from V. S. Naipaul) the 'million mutinies' of everyday life that jeopardized the law's basic structure or essential features through subaltern struggles deploying the imposed norms as social opportunities of resistance to their inner logic.[82]

---

[81] Here, domination assumes at least five forms, highlighted by Roy Bhaskar, *Plato Etc.* (London: Verso, 1994), pp. 212–13: suppression, exclusion, marginalization, idealization and 'tacit complicity'.

[82] V. S. Naipaul, *A Million Mutinies Now* (New York: Viking, 1981). Legal anthropologists have archived memorable examples. My own favourite is the narrative of how the British complained about the *cannibalization of the high-colonial rule of law*. The North Bengal Tenancy Act 1889 sought to order relations of property in the agrarian realm. The petty landholders deployed the new legality to clog the courts through means of what is now termed 'docket' or 'litigation'

A third way of narrating colonial inheritance is to trace the continuities and discontinuities between the colonial and post-colonial legality (a task I have recently attempted).[83] What constitutes these often remains elusive and problematic, mapping the levels of juristic inertia and political intent. To the extent that the normative and institutional continuities persist in ways that perpetuate habits and styles of governance which appropriate the resources to the ruling clique (or even to a single tyrant), one may speak of the failure of decolonization even though it is the more diffuse and generalized exclusion of the impoverished masses from the benefits of decolonization that names it in a far-reaching way. However, the discontinuities, disruptions and departures mark the emergences of wholly new (almost self-originating) forms and functions of legality.

In lieu of conclusion

At the end of the narrative enterprise of colonial inheritance, we begin and end in the middle. In other words, the 'beginnings' of colonial legal experience have no discernible endings. The inheritance/disinheritance processes possess a power of origin without a *terminus*, marking the very successes of decolonization simultaneously as a source of its failure.

All the same, narrative power is not bereft of future emancipatory potential. Just as there exist narrative modes empowering various colonial legacies, the subaltern genre is always at hand to fragment their hegemonic domain. Comparative legal studies needs to resort to a historiography that does not simply thrive on the sound of the trumpet. It needs also, and more than ever before, to listen to the power of lamentation of the millennial losers.

---

explosion. On one single day, they filed 60,000 civil suits asserting competing, often mythical, claims over ownership of land. The so-called Indian 'litigiousness' provides, in another idiom, an archive of collective ways of rendering inoperative the paradigm of 'legal-rational' authority. See generally Bernard S. Cohn, *An Anthropologist Among the Historians and Other Essays* (Delhi: Oxford University Press, 1987), pp. 608–23.

[83] See Baxi, *supra*, note 27.

4

The nationalist heritage

H. PATRICK GLENN

The Chief Justice of the Wisconsin Supreme Court, in the United States, recounts how counsel for the plaintiff cited case-law from Florida and Canada in a case before the court. Counsel for the defendant sought to distinguish the Florida authority but the Canadian case, in the language of the Chief Justice, 'was an entirely different matter altogether'.[1] The defence brief 'noted archly' that '[p]etitioner is not aware if Canadian case law has precedential value in the United States'.[2] In the result, the Canadian case was not relied upon by the court, and this example of judicial reticence before extra-national law was repeated in a case of the United States Supreme Court, in which a justice of the court declared that 'comparative analysis is inappropriate to the task of interpreting a constitution'.[3]

Comparative legal studies, at least in the contemporary judicial world, would therefore be incompatible with the nationalist legal heritage, and the autonomous legal systems of the world would be engaged in autonomous, though surely evolutionary, legal development. Yet, this synchronic and particularist view of the relations between national and extra-national law may not capture past or future relations between local and distant law, nor for that matter the experience of other jurisdictions in the world. There would, therefore, be need for both retrospective and prospective consideration of the subject. Expansion of the national experiences may also be instructive. To what extent, given the relatively recent origin of nation states, is it

---

I am grateful for the research assistance of Marianne Tara and for the financial aid of the Wainwright Trust, Faculty of Law, McGill University.

[1] Shirley S. Abrahamson and Michael J. Fischer, 'All the World's a Courtroom: Judging in the New Millennium', (1997) 26 Hofstra L.R. 273, p. 275. I am grateful to Professor Sarah Harding of the Chicago-Kent Law School for bringing these judicial observations to my attention.

[2] Ibid.

[3] Printz v. United States, (1997) 521 US 898, p. 935 (Scalia J.). For different views in the US Supreme Court, cf. infra, note 64.

thus appropriate to speak of comparative legal studies in the origination of national legal tradition? To what extent, given a contemporary phenomenon of 'globalization', must one speak of present and future erosion of national tradition? To what extent, moreover, must different responses be given to these questions given different national experiences?

Comparison and the origination of national legal tradition

The US example is instructive as to how exclusivist national tradition has covered its tracks, or is at least the result of discontinuity in the comparative use of legal authority. Historical research in the United States has now established that US law-makers, both judges and legislators, made extensive and wide-ranging use of European civil law (English law being regarded in a more ambivalent manner) in the process of establishing a national corpus of US law. Judges and doctrinal writers were the most frequent practitioners of this process of constructive comparison,[4] but the process of legislative borrowing extended well into the twentieth century, notably in the formulation of the Uniform Commercial Code.[5] It has been written that an 'Americanization' of the common (and civil) law was the overall result of this process, an instrumental capturing of European sources for local, national purposes, uninhibited (or largely so) by prior, indigenous forms of North American normativity.[6]

The US experience can be seen as a largely derivative one, since the European experience from the sixteenth century had been one of constructive

[4] For example, see Peter Stein, 'The Attraction of the Civil Law in Post-revolutionary America', (1966) 52 Virginia L.R. 403; W. Hamilton Brison, 'The Use of Roman Law in Virginia Courts', (1984) 28 Am. J. Comp. L. 135; Michael Hoeflich, *Roman and Civil Law and the Development of Anglo-American Jurisprudence in the Nineteenth Century* (Athens, Georgia: University of Georgia Press, 1997); Richard Helmholz, 'Use of the Civil Law in Post-revolutionary American Jurisprudence', (1992) 66 Tulane L.R. 1649; John Langbein, 'Chancellor Kent and the History of Legal Literature', (1993) 93 Columbia L.R. 547; Mathias Reimann (ed.), *The Reception of Continental Ideas in the Common Law World* (Berlin: Duncker & Humblot, 1993).
[5] See Stefan Riesenfeld, 'The Influence of German Legal Theory on American Law: The Heritage of Savigny and His Disciples', (1989) 37 Am. J. Comp. L. 37, addressing the German influence on Karl Llewellyn and giving 'secured transactions' as an example of the borrowing of an abstract concept of civilian origin.
[6] See, notably, William E. Nelson, *Americanization of the Common Law: The Impact of Change on Massachusetts Society, 1760–1830* (Cambridge, Mass.: Harvard University Press, 1975); Morton Horwitz, *The Transformation of American Law 1780–1860* (New York: Oxford University Press, 1992). For a conceptualization of the place of indigenous law, see Robert A. Williams, *The American Indian in Western Legal Thought: The Discourses of Conquest* (New York: Oxford University Press, 1990).

reception of distant law (in the form of Roman law) which was 'decanted' into national receptacles and thus lost its identity as Roman law.[7] The process arguably began with Cujas, who accomplished the major intellectual task of converting (Roman) law into fact, that which had been law for the Roman people but which was not necessarily of 'precedential value' elsewhere in the world, even in Europe. This neutralization of normativity entailed a separation, since French people, with their law, became necessarily distinct from Roman people, with their law. Roman law, as fact, could become law for French people only if it was reconverted ('decanted') into normative form. This was what occurred later in the United States, as the law of the European people now seen as distinct was made into law, in the United States, for the European people who had come to the United States. Revolutions may, therefore, be essentially superficial phenomena, involving no change in underlying ideas, though some change in the actors involved in the unfolding of events.

The tradition of national law which has been passed down to us from this process thus contains two basic elements and implies a third. The two basic elements are the state, that which became separated out in the conversion of norm to fact, and the idea of a (national) legal system – the forward-looking, instrumental consequence of law being localized and factualized. The third element is the idea of the inter-national, which emerged in recognizable form at essentially the same time as the ideas of the state and the national legal system. So, we have a coherent package of ideas which have controlled European and US legal thought for roughly the last three or four centuries and which constitutes the essence of the national heritage. What more can be said of each of them, in the European context, before turning to the possibility of their erosion in contemporary circumstances?

The state

The state has been defined both as an 'imagined community'[8] and as a '*plébiscite de tous les jours*'.[9] The state is thus ephemeral in character, driven

---

[7] See Jean Carbonnier, '*Usus hodiernus pandectarum*', in R. Graveson *et al.* (eds.), *Festschrift für Imre Zajtay* (Tübingen: J. C. B. Mohr, 1982), p. 110, observing that Roman laws were '*transvasées dans des articles de la codification*'. But *cf. id.*, p. 107, noting the current need for a more direct form of reception, of limited nature: '*des gorgées de droit prises de temps en temps, selon la soif, à l'antique fontaine.*'

[8] Benedict Anderson, *Imagined Communities* (London: Verso, 1991).

[9] Ernest Renan, *Qu'est-ce qu'une nation?*, in *Oeuvres complètes*, ed. by Henriette Psichari, vol. I (Paris: Calmann-Lévy, 1948), p. 904.

by the constant menaces of internal entropy and external challenge. This means, as we will see, that states are very diverse, but it also means that it is extremely important for states to anchor themselves, immovably, to territory. Land is essential. So, the foundation of the contemporary state is in territorial control, which is even explicitly recognized in law described as 'international'. It is thus a condition of the existence of a state that it has a 'defined territory'[10] and enormous efforts have been made in recent centuries to define the territory of particular states.

Why is it important that the territory of a state be 'defined'? Why can it not rest undefined in some areas, or be more generally imprecise in diminishing as effective state control might diminish, over distance away from a capital for example? Two reasons exist, both of which involve comparative thought, so we see once again, on the ground, the importance of comparison in the origination of national tradition.

To the extent that a state's territory is not defined it becomes susceptible to occupation by another state (we will have to return to this theme in the discussion of the inter-national) such that delimitation of territory becomes essential given the existence of multiple states. What is not clearly mine may be yours. I only know what is mine by comparing it, delimiting it, in relation to what is yours. If Kashmir does not belong to India it belongs to Pakistan or China, or both. So, given the existence of states, comparative delimitation becomes necessary as a means of identification of the states themselves, rooted as they are in the land.

The second, larger, reason for the need to define the territory of a state is found in the relation between states, their territory and law. The concept of the state developed, in Europe, from the thirteenth century, with acceleration in the process from the seventeenth century.[11] It was not a Greek invention, nor a Roman invention. It did not burst forth as a result of enlightened thought, in different places in the world. It emerged as a phenomenon specific to Europe, developed over a considerable period of

---

[10] J. L. Brierly, *The Law of Nations*, 6th ed. by Humphrey Waldock (Oxford: Oxford University Press, 1963), p. 137; Pierre-Marie Dupuy, *Droit international public*, 3d ed. (Paris: Dalloz, 1995), pp. 30–1, referring to the '*détermination exacte*' of a spatial field of sovereignty and to a delimitation of territory which is '*complète et définitive*'. Cf. Malcolm N. Shaw, *International Law*, 4th ed. (Cambridge: Cambridge University Press, 1997), pp. 140–1, who mentions the 'need for a defined territory' but observes that there is 'no necessity in international law for defined and settled boundaries' so long as a 'consistent band of territory [is] undeniably controlled'.

[11] See generally Martin van Creveld, *The Rise and Decline of the State* (Cambridge: Cambridge University Press, 1999). The designation 'state', applied to abstract political units, came into use in the first half of the seventeenth century.

time, as a result of particularly European circumstances. There were major obstacles to the existence of states in Europe, notably the commonalities of Christianity, the *jus commune* (both very much related to one another),[12] and what is known in Europe as 'custom'.[13] Local monarchs were not enamoured of these commonalities, and neither were those opposed to feudal privilege and serfdom (slavery). So, the state emerged as something relatively, comparatively, better than existing (often corrupted) forms of social organization. Since existing forms of social organization were very entrenched, and very recalcitrant, they had to be positively displaced, in a *binding* manner. State law had to bind because otherwise there would be no state law, and no state. '*L'autorité de l'Etat ne souffre point le vide*',[14] and so state authority had to extend geographically, as far as it could, in a rigorously uniform manner. It had to erase ('*gommer*') all other ensembles or distinctions.[15] Local (state) authority thus extended its normativity as a means of affirming its policy and its identity, in the face of other policies and other identities. This happened, it bears repeating, nowhere else in the world, so contextual, comparative explanation is the best explanation for it.

Once the state became recognizable as a concept it had to be implemented, on the ground. This meant that boundaries which were both political and legal on the one hand, and geo-physical on the other, had to be drawn on both maps and territory. The national boundary is an interesting concept, and it, too, is best understood in relation to other, pre-existing

[12] On the relations between Christianity and the development of the *jus commune*, see Manlio Bellomo, *The Common Legal Past of Europe 1000–1800*, transl. by Lydia G. Cochrane (Washington, DC: Catholic University of America Press, 1995), p. 101 ['The ideology of a unified and Christian empire (the ideology of Dante Alighieri) underlay and governed the legal and cultural potential of a complex of norms that were thought of and experienced as "common law" for all the faithful in Christ within the confines of the empire'].

[13] On the indigenous resistance in Germany to modernizing, romanizing and centralizing lawyers, see Gerald Strauss, *Law, Resistance and the State: The Opposition to Roman Law in Reformation Germany* (Princeton: Princeton University Press, 1986). For the transformation of European chthonic law into 'custom' or habit through the process of redaction, see H. Patrick Glenn, 'The Capture, Reconstruction and Marginalization of "Custom" ', (1997) 45 Am. J. Comp. L. 613.

[14] Daniel Nordman, 'Problématique historique: des frontières de l'Europe aux frontières du Maghreb (19e siècle)', in *Frontières: problèmes de frontières dans le Tiers-Monde* (Paris: L'Harmattan, 1982), p. 19 [hereinafter *Frontières*].

[15] Monique Chemillier-Gendreau, 'Synthèse juridico-politique', in *Frontières, supra*, note 14, p. 30. For the combined process of the growth in ambit of state law, its declining association with morality and its increasing politicization (with the philosophical attention turning away from concepts of justice toward abstract definitions of law), see Uwe Wesel, *Geschichte des Rechts: Von den Frühformen bis zum Vertrag von Maastricht* (Munich: C. H. Beck, 1997), pp. 47–9.

concepts. Prior to the state, there was no idea of a fixed, geo-political demarcation of competing sovereignties.[16] There was a Roman god, Terminus, of the boundaries of fields – himself, necessarily immovable. There was also an idea of the limits of empire, or *civis*, though what lay beyond was 'barbarism', not competing sovereignty. Where neighbouring co-equals did exist, in the form of kings or princes, the space between them was not precisely divided, but rather was the object of reciprocal, diminishing control, with a meeting-point found in zones or border marches in which, at some imprecise location, control of A began to yield to control of B.[17] So, a vocabulary of boundaries had to develop, which occurred from the thirteenth century, first with the word 'frontier' (from the French *front* and *frontie*), then also the German *Grenz*, then very late, approaching the Treaty of Westphalia in the seventeenth century, 'boundary' in English.[18] In France, the tracing of a national boundary began in the sixteenth century and became more systematic in the eighteenth.[19] The process often appeared highly arbitrary, given existing human relations and dependencies. If this village went one way, what about a neighbouring, dependent, hamlet? What about this isolated house? What about this wood, long used by this village?[20] We are told that personal loyalties often controlled the delimitation of space, and not the reverse.[21] The process was facilitated by two parallel, intellectual developments: the map and natural law. The map, in bird's-eye view form, allowed visualization of the 'vertical interface' of a national boundary; it became a model *for* and not a model *of*.[22] Space, for Renaissance cartographers,

---

[16] See Paul Guichonnet and Claude Raffestin, *Géographie des frontières* (Paris: Presses Universitaires de France, 1974), pp. 83–4; van Creveld, *supra*, note 11, pp. 143–4 [writing on the problems of territorial demarcation in Europe and referring to Napoleon's retreat from Moscow, the author notes that 'in *terra* that was largely *incognita* (...) blank patches were still large and numerous'].

[17] See Samuel W. Boggs, *International Boundaries* (New York: Columbia University Press, 1940), p. 7.

[18] See Guichonnet and Raffestin, *supra*, note 16, pp. 11–12. The earliest example of 'boundary' in the *Oxford English Dictionary* is dated 1626 and it is said to originate from the ancient French *bodne, bone, bune, bonne, bunne* and the Anglo-French *bounde*, hence the 'metes and bounds' description of land.

[19] See Nordman, *supra*, note 14, p. 18.   [20] *Id.*, p. 19.

[21] See Michael Biggs, 'Putting the State on the Map: Cartography, Territory and European State Formation', (1999) 41 Comp. Stud. Soc. & Hist. 374, p. 386 ['rule was exercised over subjects rather than land'].

[22] See Anderson, *supra*, note 8, p. 173. For the map as an instrument of political power, see Jeremy Black, *Maps and Politics* (London: Reaktion Books, 1997), pp. 9, 11, 18–21, 123–5 and 136, describing the unsuitability of mapping for mixed jurisdictions and observing that the 49th

became 'pure quantity, abstracted from the qualities of meaning and experience' while the world appeared as 'mundane surface, no longer the hub of a sacred cosmos'.[23] The notion of *carte blanche* was born. Natural law provided the idea of the 'natural boundary'. While nature itself never separates, natural features could be taken as of political and legal significance – the Rhine as 'natural boundary' of both France and Germany. This idea, too, is local and European; it originated in the Renaissance. Nature had to be compliant with the frontier as '*couloir*'.[24]

The national legal system

The states of Europe thus all adhered to the tradition of the state, that is, that mass of non-state information which, in Europe, said that social organization should abandon feudal or religious form and take on some form of governmental organization with a defined boundary. A state is a first and essential element of national legal tradition, but must be complemented by further information which tells us how the particular state is to be justified and how it is to function. The normativity of the state has to be assured. The means of doing this was found in the notion, now itself a widely accepted tradition, at least in the west, of a national legal system.

Systems-thought appears to have its origins in the natural sciences[25] and was developed at approximately the same time that the notion of the 'state' was developed, so we see here Renaissance thought having effect both in science and in law. There was thus interplay, or comparison, in developing the concept of 'system' as an operative element in both scientific and legal thinking. Moreover, in both science and law, the concept of

---

parallel as North American boundary shows the use of European science to subject territory to the European notion of spatiality.

[23] Biggs, *supra*, note 21, p. 377.

[24] Nordman, *supra*, note 14, p. 19. On the Renaissance origins of the 'natural boundary', see Guichonnet and Raffestin, *supra*, note 16, p. 19; Catherine Coquery-Vidrovitch, 'Présentation', in *Frontières*, *supra*, note 14, p. 4; Stephen Jones, 'Boundary Concepts in the Setting of Place and Time', in Harm J. de Blij (ed.), *Systematic Political Geography*, 2d ed. (New York: Wiley, 1973), p. 167.

[25] See Carl von Linne [Linnaeus], *Systema naturae* (London: British Museum, 1956) [1735], founding taxonomic thought. On systems-thought generally, in both science and law, see Thomas D. Barton, 'The Structure of Legal Systems', (1992) 37 Am. J. Jurisp. 291, referring notably to the history of the concept of 'system'; Christophe Grzegorczyk, 'Evaluation critique du paradigme systémique dans la science du droit', Arch. phil. droit, 1986, p. 301, observing that the idea of 'system' is finally not very rich or productive – not '*féconde*' – but necessary if law is to be positive and rational.

'system' was developed in contrast to that which had preceded it. Much of what is known in the west as 'philosophy of law' has been directed toward reinforcement and refinement of this transnational tradition of a legal system.[26] Its foundational element has been variously described as command,[27] a presumed Basic Norm[28] or the fact of obedience.[29] The efforts of justification continue, though perhaps with declining intensity. All of the efforts combine in pointing to the exclusivity of state sources of law, so they are all instrumentally directed toward the process of creating *binding* law, which can be uniformly enforced within the defined territory of the state.

Well-known concepts of western law are found as elements within this tradition of the national legal system. The civil-law jurisdictions codified their national law through the nineteenth and twentieth centuries; in the common law, the concept of national '*stare decisis*' was developed, also in the nineteenth century, as a functional equivalent to codification. In the United States, there was both (local) state codification and (local) state *stare decisis*. Rights became widely used on the Continent and in the United States as a means of articulating national law, though England remained in large measure recalcitrant.[30] Belief in the adequacy of national law, in both civil- and common-law jurisdictions, largely precluded resort to extra-national law, and the examples discussed at the beginning of this chapter find their justification in this process. In some cases, resort to extra-national law was the object of formal prohibition; elsewhere, it flowed from the simple belief

---

[26] For the origins and development of legal-system building, see Werner Krawietz, *Recht als Regelsystem* (Wiesbaden: Franz Steiner, 1984).

[27] See John Austin, *The Province of Jurisprudence Determined*, ed. by Wilfrid E. Rumble (Cambridge: Cambridge University Press, 1995) [1832].

[28] See Hans Kelsen, *Pure Theory of Law*, transl. by Max Knight (Gloucester, Mass.: Peter Smith, 1989), ch. 5 ['The Dynamic Aspect of Law'], ss. 34 ['The Reason for the Validity of a Normative Order: The Basic Norm'] and 35 ['The Hierarchical Structure of the Legal Order'], constituting the pyramid of norms.

[29] See H. L. A. Hart, *The Concept of Law*, 2d ed. (Oxford: Oxford University Press, 1994), p. 116 ['There are therefore two minimum conditions necessary and sufficient for the existence of a legal system. On the one hand, those rules of behaviour which are valid according to the system's ultimate criteria of validity must be generally obeyed, and, on the other hand, its rules of recognition specifying the criteria of legal validity and its rules of change and adjudication must be effectively accepted as common public standards of official behaviour by its officials']. For a legal system understood as a series of successive, momentary systems in time allowing for change and evolution, see Joseph Raz, *The Concept of a Legal System*, 2d ed. (Oxford: Oxford University Press, 1980), pp. 34–5.

[30] See H. Patrick Glenn, 'Law, Revolution and Rights', Arch. Leg. & Soc. Phil., 1990, No. 41, p. 13.

that the richness of local sources obviated any need for foreign assistance.[31] Some jurisdictions did approach legal self-sufficiency, though the process generated major forms of local resistance and deconstruction of national law.[32] National law was identified by the nationality of its sources; its *content*, however, was of diverse origin. The formal discipline of comparative law had its origins in the mining of customary, Roman and canonical sources, from the sixteenth century, in the process of articulating national law. By the beginning of the twentieth century, the nation-building process largely completed, it could be relegated to a more scientific, complementary role.[33] Comparison had been essential, however, in deciding what national law should be.

The international

As they developed, the traditions of the state and the national legal system exercised great, even irresistible, persuasive authority in Europe. The codifications of the nineteenth and twentieth centuries thus settled a process of dividing all of the territory of Europe into state territory. Even before this process was completed, however, it was evident that it had itself generated a second-order problem in terms of the relations between these states, seen now as co-equal institutions. So, the concept of the inter-national was originated, soon becoming distinct and autonomous in its own right as a new field of institutional, formal, state-like law.

The first and primary function of international law, in its public dimension, was to legitimate the 'defined territory' of each state. In the process of formation, each state had 'compressed' as much as possible the potential territory of neighbouring states,[34] and, once a stage of mutual exhaustion

---

[31] For examples of prohibition in Europe (such as in the Swiss cantons or in the French *Cour de cassation*), see H. Patrick Glenn, 'Persuasive Authority', (1987) 32 McGill L. J. 261, pp. 280–1 [hereinafter 'Persuasive Authority']. For the prohibition of resort to foreign law, even in the case of private international law, in Latin America and China, see *id.*, 'Comparative Law and the Judicial Function', in John E. C. Brierley *et al.* (eds.), *Mélanges Paul-André Crépeau* (Montreal: Blais, 1997), p. 317. For the argument from local completeness, citing different national views, see Ulrich Drobnig, 'General Report', in *id.* and Sjef van Erp (eds.), *The Use of Comparative Law by Courts* (The Hague: Kluwer, 1999), p. 21. For a contrary judicial view from the United States, see Abrahamson and Fischer, *infra*, at text accompanying note 65.

[32] See Glenn, 'Persuasive Authority', *supra*, note 31, pp. 262–3.

[33] See *id.*, 'Vers un droit comparé intégré?', Rev. int. dr. comp., 1999, p. 842 and the references cited.

[34] See Chemillier-Gendreau, *supra*, note 15, p. 31. See also Eric J. Hobsbawm, *Nations and Nationalism Since 1780* (Cambridge: Cambridge University Press, 1990), p. 32 ['building of nations was seen inevitably as a process of expansion'].

had been reached, formalization of the result was necessary to create a 'fixed' ('intangible') national boundary. Treaties, as instruments of the new public international law, could declare the results of this process of mutual exhaustion. Thereafter, public international law could undertake the 'impossible search' for a rational principle of allocation of territory,[35] as well as other principles capable of regulating entities perceived as 'sovereign'. Public international law was conceived at the same time as, and on the model of, formal state law. It is profoundly western in character, yet must be constructed in the absence of the foundational element of western law, sovereign authority. 'Dualist' theories of public international law have largely prevailed, according to which public international law is not law, in the western sense, unless it has been converted into normativity by state institutions.[36]

The notion of law as state law prevailed still more clearly, however, in regard to private, international, legal relations. Private international law, it is now widely agreed, is not international law but national law applicable to private international relations or conflict of laws. The division of European law into sets of notionally complete and mutually exclusive private-law rules meant that all private, international, legal relations had to be allocated to one or another of these sets of mutually exclusive rules. Whatever legal unity had existed in Europe had been replaced by a principle of legal disunity as a result of the process of national legal unification. Differences in national laws are seen as conflicts of laws, and in many European jurisdictions the process of allocation to a national law must be undertaken even in the absence of established conflict.[37] There is widespread dissatisfaction with this conflictual, abstract, expensive and time-consuming process.

International law, like state law, was not constructed from scratch. It drew on Roman law (the *jus gentium*) and state law (contract, custom – which had to be resuscitated – and decisional law), so we see, once again, the continuities and comparisons inherent in legal development in the

---

[35] See Chemillier-Gendreau, *supra*, note 15, p. 36.

[36] This is so even in the case of jurisdictions said to accept a 'monist' principle of international law being the law of the land, the principle being qualified in various ways to acknowledge the supremacy of local law-making authority. For example, see Brierly, *supra*, note 10, pp. 86–93; Dupuy, *supra*, note 10, pp. 323–42. For the influence of Vattel in creating 'classical' public international law, founded on the existence of sovereign entities, the application of which '*relevait de l'interprétation subjective de chaque Etat*', see Emmanuelle Jouannet, *Emer de Vattel et l'émergence doctrinale du droit international classique* (Paris: Pedone, 1998), p. 421.

[37] For the application of private international law rules '*d'office*' or '*von Amts wegen*' on the part of the judge, eliminating party agreement as a means of conciliation of legal differences, see H. Patrick Glenn, 'Harmonization of Law, Foreign Law and Private International Law', (1993) 1 Eur. R. Priv. L. 47.

growth of international law. International law, however, had a future beyond Europe, since the concept of the 'state' was soon to spread beyond the area of its origin. It did so in the process of colonialism or imperialism, which is also a major part of the nationalist heritage. This subject is dealt with in this book in the contribution of Upendra Baxi, but it is important to note the inseparability of European nationalism and colonialism. European state-building was a process of expansion of state control, a process of 'compressing' the territory of neighbouring states.[38] Given the Lockean natural-law concept that God had commanded humanity 'to subdue the earth',[39] European states simply had to continue their expansion, beyond metropolitan territory, until effective resistance was met. They all did it. It was first done 'internally', in Europe, as regions were incorporated into the new state structures. It was then done abroad, as overseas territories became responsible to metropolitan territory. It was then reiterated abroad, as 'frontiers' were pushed back in the ongoing expansion process. Again, comparison was important, and the Roman notion of 'empire' played a significant, guiding role in the thinking through of the expansion process.[40]

One of the main legacies of nationalism and colonialism has been the division of the territory of the world into states, as *carte blanche* disappeared from the *mappemonde*. There are now just short of 200 of them. The process is arguably not yet complete, as we will see, but the exportation of European law led inevitably to territorial definition and the emergence of new states.[41] As the concept of the 'state' was imposed or continued abroad, so international law had to expand beyond Europe, continuing the same function of formalization of mutual exhaustion in the search for territory as it had fulfilled in Europe. The 'Scramble for Africa' thus (arguably) ended with the Congress of Berlin in 1884–5.[42] International law is here clearly

[38] See *supra*, note 34.
[39] John Locke, *Two Treatises of Government*, ed. by Mark Goldie (London: Dent, 1993), p. 130 [1690].
[40] On the influence of Roman notions of 'empire', see Anthony Pagden, *Lords of All the World: Ideologies of Empire in Spain, Britain and France c. 1500–1800* (New Haven: Yale University Press, 1995), ch. 1 ['The Legacy of Rome'].
[41] For example, see John C. Wilkinson, *Arabia's Frontiers: The Story of Britain's Boundary Drawing in the Desert* (London: I. B. Tauris, 1991), p. xiii ['It was only when the authority of the East India Company was replaced by the institutions of empire that Britain started to elevate its role as a "civilizing" nation to justify imposing that system of rule which eventually found expression in territorial definition']. More generally, see John R. Schmidhauser, 'Legal Imperialism: Its Enduring Impact on Colonial and Post-colonial Judicial Systems', (1992) 13 Int. Pol. Sc. R. 321.
[42] Wilkinson, *supra*, note 41, p. xxxi. More generally, see Lauren Benton, 'Colonial Law and Cultural Difference: Jurisdictional Politics and the Formation of the Colonial State', (1999) 41 Comp. Stud. Soc. & Hist. 563, p. 588 ['the replication of these patterns of (colonial) conflict (...) helped

hegemonic, a European instrument for the validation of European ideas (notably that of the 'state') and European law. Other ensembles or distinctions or legal traditions had to be erased, or '*gommées*', a process which, if successful, would replicate again the European process. At this point, however, we reach the limits of the expansion of national tradition. Attention has now shifted to its erosion; some even speak of survival.

Comparison and the erosion of national legal tradition

The growth of national legal tradition within Europe met with resistance, but it was a limited form of resistance. States resisted one another, but did so in the name of the same underlying ideas. Some people resisted in the name of religion, 'customary' law or local identity, but the national traditions incorporated some of their ideas or beliefs; they were not alien, or entirely alien, to the peoples eventually bound by them. Outside of Europe, the tradition of national law necessarily encountered greater resistance. It ran up against other legal traditions, the adherents to which did not, at least immediately, see themselves reflected in European law. It also distanced itself from its own, indigenous, intellectual sources. The lifelines had to be extended, often with difficulty. Law books are expensive to ship. Even at home, it became more and more difficult to maintain the exclusivity of national sources. Information is, in any event, impossible to control entirely; the success of European states and the prosperity of European peoples made control still more difficult. To the extent that national legal tradition is today eroding, the process is thus taking place in three areas of the world: within Europe itself; within states peopled and controlled by those of European origin; and within states which, following the decline of empires, remain in large measure outside the orbit of European thought. In all of these places, there are signs of erosion of the constituent elements of the national heritage.

The state

Resistance to defined state boundaries is growing in the world. In Europe, the resistance is not so much directed toward the concept as toward its implementation. People want different boundaries and are prepared to kill

give rise to a global legal order – the interstate system – in which expectations about the location of legal authority became uniform across otherwise quite diverse polities'].

to bring them about. Here, the old social ensembles and distinctions are re-asserting themselves, since an exclusivist state structure is seen as incompatible with many of the social identities it seeks to integrate. The state is not neutral before other 'private' forms of belief, organization or language.[43] It necessarily represents a choice among many; the comparisons inherent in its origination re-assert themselves in its continuation. In Europe, as elsewhere, the number of states increases as new 'fixed' boundaries are painfully drawn.

Outside Europe, in states settled and controlled by people of European origin, there is resistance of the European variety to the actual boundaries of states. Different people, of different European origins, want their own boundaries, as in Europe. In these states, however, there is resistance of a different kind, in the shape of resistance even to the concept of fixed, territorial boundaries. This is the resistance of non-European peoples to the European idea of a national boundary. In North America, the two large states of the United States and Canada are unable to control movement of Mohawk people across their joint boundary in the St Lawrence valley. People move at night, on the water, with what states designate as 'contraband'. The border exists, but not for some people; erosion of the concept of the 'state' is demonstrable. You have only to wait for nightfall and keep your head down.

In other lands, where European, colonial settlement was not permanent, the idea of the 'state' with fixed, territorial boundaries is most fragile. There are problems both with the concept and with its implementation. Conceptually, people do not agree with the idea of 'fixed boundaries of territory'. There are profound reasons for this, which put into question much European thought. In Arabia, where fixed boundaries are a very recent concept, many people do not accept them because they are an impediment to centuries of freedom of movement in the use of natural resources. The word 'arab' means 'nomad' and Arabia is the land of nomads, those who have a millennia-old tradition of the *hijra*, that of 'upping stakes and forming a new community'.[44] When Muhammad left Mecca for Medina, he was affecting a *hijra*, and the Islamic calendar counts (AH) from the year of the

---

[43] See Will Kymlicka, *Multicultural Citizenship: A Liberal Theory of Minority Rights* (Oxford: Oxford University Press, 1995), pp. 53–4 and the references cited ['English liberal institutions were as much English as liberal'; colonizers 'thought it sufficient to transplant, where the need was to translate'].

[44] Wilkinson, *supra*, note 41, p. xi.

hijra. This is not a tradition easy to dislodge. It is also rooted in profound beliefs about the relation of people to land. These beliefs look more to a concept of 'usufruct' than to one of *dominium*. *Abusus* is not a legal right. Scarce resources are thus to be both shared and preserved and the interests of groups can 'overlap and indeed complement each other'.[45] There is also an inherent notion of inter-generational equity. This was the case in pre-state Europe and in much, if not most, of the rest of the world. Such ideas are now increasingly urged in European and US states.

Sedentary, non-state peoples also are sceptical about fixed, national boundaries. Here, the opposition is not so much to boundaries as to fixed boundaries. Authority or control over land would be not 'linear' but 'zonal' or 'polar', extending out from established centres but diminishing to non-existence in what were known in Europe as 'marches'. Border zones or marches would have sharply reduced political connotation;[46] they would represent spaces of transition of *influence*. This thinking has been predominant in Asia and Africa. The Great Wall of China would be an exception to this, but it was above all a defensive measure, marking also a limit of expansion.[47] Space is here measured not in metres but in terms of richness, of human culture and development. In their absence, there is no space for appropriation and eventual control, only nothingness, of no interest.[48] In south-east Asia, the western, bird's-eye-view map replaced two other types, one vertical – showing the relations of heavens and earth – the other horizontal, that of the traveller's eye, showing the path to follow among natural surroundings.[49] There was no encompassing, super-elevation. Mercator's mind had to be imposed on this thinking, and was, in some measure.

Resistance to the concept of 'boundaries' has been accompanied by difficulty in its implementation. In much of the world, it is more appropriate to speak of non-implementation, since in the discipline of geography it is accepted that many boundary-lines drawn on maps have no equivalent on

---

[45] *Id.*, p. xvi.
[46] See Guichonnet and Rafestin, *supra*, note 16, pp. 15–16; Coquery-Vidrovitch, *supra*, note 24, p. 5, referring to centres with 'concentric aureoles'; Jones, *supra*, note 24, p. 162. For the recent emergence of the idea of 'frontier' zones for purposes of regional maritime cooperation ['the zone in the area of the boundary (and on both sides of it)'], see, however, Ian Townsend-Gault, 'Regional Maritime Cooperation Post-UNCLOS/UNCED: Do Boundaries Matter Anymore?', in Gerald Blake *et al.* (eds.), *International Boundaries and Environmental Security* (The Hague: Kluwer, 1997), p. 3.
[47] See Jones, *supra*, note 24, p. 164.
[48] See Oskar Weggel, *Die Asiaten* (Munich: C. H. Beck, 1989), p. 206.
[49] See Anderson, *supra*, note 8, p. 173.

the ground.[50] They, like the states they would represent, are 'imaginary', driven by state theory in both law and geography in spite of impossibility of physical execution. These imaginary boundaries may be the object of theoretical agreement between the states concerned. The situation is more complex in the case of boundary disputes, which have been multiplying as the number of states in the world increases.[51] Here, the state must exist in the absence of a 'defined territory' and many, apparently, do. Many boundary disputes are famous and of long duration. Others are less famous but no less intractable. Between Belize and Guatemala, a boundary would go through the soccer field of the village of Arenal; they have been fighting over it for 150 years.[52] In some cases, as in Africa, colonial boundaries have been preserved *faute de mieux* or, as it is said in international law, in virtue of the principle '*uti possidetis juris*'.[53] Only this 'voluntary rigidity' would compensate for the absence of 'historical evolution' of boundaries.[54] As the number of states continued to increase, so would the number of boundary disputes. States would become undefinable.

The national legal system

The definition of a state suggests uniformity, since all states are composed of uniform elements – a government and a defined territory. International law supports this impression of uniformity, since all states are treated as equal, at least in principle. Yet, national legal traditions crystallize in many different forms, some close to the original European model, or models, others far removed from them. Diversity emerges in the choice which the members of each state make as to its constituent elements. The tradition of a national legal system creates no obstacle to this, since systems are

---

[50] See Yves Lacoste, 'Typologie géopolitique', in *Frontières, supra*, note 14, p. 11; Boggs, *supra*, note 17, pp. 7–8; Husain M. Albaharna, *The Arabian Gulf States: Their Legal and Political Status and the International Problems*, 2d ed. (Beirut: Librairie du Liban, 1975), p. 261.

[51] In the 1950s, the number of states numbered in the fifties. There are now 188 member states of the United Nations. On the relation between boundary disputes and the multiplication of states, see Lacoste, *supra*, note 50, p. 9; Coquery-Vidrovitch, *supra*, note 24, p. 5; Wilkinson, *supra*, note 41, p. ix. For current boundary tensions, see Martin Pratt and Janet A. Brown, *Borderlands Under Stress* (The Hague: Kluwer, 2000), p. 4, observing that 17 per cent of world land borders are now disputed.

[52] See *The Globe and Mail*, 29 April 2000, p. A-17. For the extent of ongoing boundary disputes in Latin America, see *The Economist*, 19 August 2000, p. 32.

[53] Literally, 'since you possess'. This is Latin for the European phenomenon of mutual exhaustion.

[54] Coquery-Vidrovitch, *supra*, note 24, p. 6.

defined only in terms of ensembles with interacting elements. This is why the notion of a system is not '*féconde*'; it is a formal descriptor and almost anything can be conceived of in terms of system.[55] Hence the ubiquity of the expression 'legal system' in describing widely disparate legal phenomena in the world. Since so-called 'legal systems' differ so widely, however, the state is 'polymorphe' and there is no single national heritage.[56] States may be unitary, federal, confederal or consociational; they may be dictatorial or democratic, monarchical or republican, parliamentary or congressional; they may define their citizens through the *jus solis* or the *jus sanguinis*, or complex combinations of them. They may change from one type to another, as the information of one type of national tradition becomes preferred to that of another. Legal systems do not themselves bind; they are traditions like other traditions and bind to the extent that people choose to adhere to them (the 'fact' of obedience).

Is there erosion of the concept of the 'national legal system' in all its diverse forms? Again, the question must be asked within Europe; within states peopled and controlled by those of European origin; and within states which remain in large measure outside the orbit of European thought.

Within Europe, Europeans report that the concept of the 'national legal system' is declining in importance. It is said that '*[l]e droit national n'est plus souverain*'[57] and this striking conclusion would flow from two distinct phenomena: the growth in importance of the law of the European Union and the increasing use of extra-national law. European law is both public and private and has affected national legal systems in both their public and private dimensions. The result is most striking in the area of public law, which Otto Kahn-Freund identified as being the most resistant to foreign influence.[58] Now, it is said, reflecting the growth of European law, that

---

[55] See *supra*, note 25. For concepts of 'systems' which would accommodate even catastrophe, see Ivar Ekeland, *Mathematics and the Unexpected* (Chicago: University of Chicago Press, 1988), pp. 88–90 and 106. For systems in the social sciences which would tolerate even the most 'strategic, innovative or rebellious choice-making', see Sally F. Moore, 'History and the Redefinition of Custom on Kilimanjaro', in June Starr and Jane F. Collier (eds.), *History and Power in the Study of Law: New Directions in Legal Anthropology* (Ithaca: Cornell University Press, 1989), pp. 287–8 and the references cited.
[56] See Norbert Rouland, *Introduction historique au droit* (Paris: Presses Universitaires de France, 1998), p. 107.
[57] *Id.*, p. 386.
[58] See Otto Kahn-Freund, 'On Uses and Misuses of Comparative Law', (1974) 37 Modern L.R. 1, pp. 12–13.

'*[l]e droit public n'est pas un droit uniquement national*'.[59] Use of extra-national law also occurs, however, outside the ambit of European law. In England, this conforms to the floating character of common-law authority in the Commonwealth, but it is now also the law of civil-law jurisdictions which may be invoked by English judges. Between 1994 and 1995, there was a three-fold increase in the number of foreign decisions cited in England and English judges now explicitly call for comparative material.[60] In the Netherlands, Dutch judges are regularly informed of foreign experience by the conclusion and pleadings of private parties and by representatives of the government.[61] In France, use of comparative materials is 'slowly entering into the methods of work';[62] it is regularly practised within the *Cour de cassation*.[63] The exclusivity of state law is here being abandoned, in the home lands of the state.

Outside of Europe, the jurisdictions of the United States have been most faithful to the European idea of an exclusivist legal system in the name of local, popular sovereignty. The unanimity of the US Supreme Court on this question, however, has now been broken, and debate within the court is taking place as to the use of 'comparative experience'.[64] Both in the federal judiciary and in state judiciaries, voices have been raised in favour of greater receptiveness to foreign law, in order to appreciate more fully 'the

---

[59] John Bell, 'La comparaison en droit public', in *Mélanges en l'honneur de Denis Tallon* (Paris: Société de législation comparée, 1999), p. 32.

[60] See Esin Örücü, 'Comparative Law in British Courts', in Drobnig and van Erp, *supra*, note 31, pp. 264–5 and 294. For judicial declarations, see Lord Goff in *Kleinwort Benson Ltd* v. *Lincoln City Council*, [1998] 4 All E.R. 513 (H.L.), p. 534 ['Nowadays (the judge) (...) has regard, where appropriate, to decisions of judges in other jurisdictions'] and Lord Woolf in his preface to Basil S. Markesinis, *Foreign Law and Comparative Methodology: A Subject and a Thesis* (Oxford: Hart, 1997), p. viii ['The Appellate Committee of the Lords are already increasingly demanding comparative materials from practitioners in cases where an appeal before them could involve the development of the law. While in the past the assistance would be expected to be limited to that available from other common law jurisdictions, this is no longer the situation. (...) (J)udicial isolationism is now a thing of the past']. The use of Continental authority renews with nineteenth-century English practice, in which the authority of Pothier was 'as high as can be had, next to the decision of a Court of Justice in this country': *Cox* v. *Troy*, (1822) 5 B. & Ald. 474, p. 480; 106 E.R. 1264, p. 1266 (K.B.; Best J.).

[61] See Sjef van Erp, 'The Use of the Comparative Law Method by the Judiciary – Dutch National Report', in Drobnig and *id.*, *supra*, note 31, p. 243.

[62] Raymond Legeais, 'L'utilisation du droit comparé par les tribunaux: rapport français', in Drobnig and van Erp, *supra*, note 31, p. 121.

[63] See Mitchel Lasser, 'Judicial (Self-)Portraits: Judicial Discourse in the French Legal System', (1995) 104 Yale L.J. 1325, p. 1370.

[64] Compare the remarks of Breyer J. in *Printz* v. *United States*, *supra*, note 3, pp. 970–1, with those of Scalia J. in the same case, *supra*, note 3.

policy issues driving the debate'.⁶⁵ The historical exclusivist position, even emanating from the Supreme Court, has been characterized by US academic writing as 'the kind of self-satisfied strutting that gives chauvinism a bad name'.⁶⁶ The opening of this debate within leading US institutions and in mainstream academic debate itself represents an erosion of national legal tradition; unanimity no longer prevails.

In other jurisdictions outside of Europe which have been settled and controlled by people of European origin, there has never been acceptance of a rigorously European, exclusivist model of a legal system. European law was received, for European people, but the European tradition of an exclusively national legal system was rejected, out of loyalty to Europe. European law could thus be received, where appropriate – the process of comparison is explicit – and the process of reception could be ongoing. Dialogue thus ensues between local circumstance, local authority and distant authority, in much the same way that local custom and the *jus commune* were both invoked, in particular places, in European legal history. No source is hegemonic, or exclusive; illumination is sought where it may be found. This attitude toward law is widespread in the Commonwealth; the declaratory theory of law has been widely used in the process and continues to exercise great influence.⁶⁷ Judges thus do not make law; they declare their present perception of what the law might be. They proceed analogically, not deductively, as in the common-law tradition. *Stare decisis* is now in decline in the common-law world; in most jurisdictions it never achieved a truly

---

⁶⁵ Abrahamson and Fischer, *supra*, note 1, p. 284. See also *id.*, p. 286 [observing that foreign decisions 'frequently see such problems in a light which (...) is fresh and provocative. Those courts inform and illuminate'] and 290 ['the provincial attitudes of American courts are becoming less excusable']. For the federal judiciary, see Roger Miner, 'The Reception of Foreign Law in US Federal Courts', (1985) 43 Am. J. Comp. L. 581.

⁶⁶ J. M. Balkin and Sanford Levinson, 'The Canons of Constitutional Law', (1998) 111 Harvard L.R. 963, p. 1005. For further academic pursuit of the theme, see Mark Tushnet, 'The Possibilities of Comparative Constitutional Law', (1999) 108 Yale L.J. 1225; Annelise Riles, 'Wigmore's Treasure Box: Comparative Law in the Era of Information', (1999) 40 Harvard Int. L.J. 221 and the references cited at n. 2; Kathryn A. Perales, 'It Works Fine in Europe, so Why Not Here? Comparative Law and Constitutional Federalism', (1999) 23 Vermont L.R. 885.

⁶⁷ See Glenn, 'Persuasive Authority', *supra*, note 31; *id.*, 'The Common Law in Canada', (1995) 74 Can. Bar R. 261, pp. 265–6, 271 and 285, n. 96, observing that Canadian trial and appeal courts follow Commonwealth authority rather than the Supreme Court of Canada. For Australia, see H. K. Lücke, 'The Common Law: Judicial Impartiality and Judge-Made Law', (1982) 98 L.Q.R. 29, p. 45; Peter Wesley-Smith, 'Theories of Adjudication and the Status of *Stare Decisis*', in Laurence Goldstein (ed.), *Precedent in Law* (Oxford: Oxford University Press, 1987), p. 75. For references to other jurisdictions, see H. Patrick Glenn, 'Reception and Reconciliation of Laws', Rechtstheorie, 1991, No. 12, pp. 209–14.

dominant position. The model is as much one of 'coordinate persuasion' as one of vertical command or hierarchy.[68] Since the law of the state is not exclusive, this allows recognition of the law of indigenous peoples or other minorities, either through (unacknowledged) recognition of a '*statut personnel*'[69] or through operation of a more incremental notion of 'reasonable accommodation'.[70] The 'erosion' of national legal tradition is here of long standing; it is just as much a case of the inapplicability of European tradition, in its full dimensions, outside of Europe. States do exist outside of Europe; they are not, however, the same types of state. European legal theory has been decidedly unhelpful in dealing with these circumstances, though changes within Europe now suggest a larger field of shared experience.

This rejection of European legal theory for the purposes of maintaining contact with European law is not limited to the common-law jurisdictions of the world. Latin America follows Spanish, French, German and Italian law (in addition to US law) in an ongoing manner, though usually in doctrinal or legislative form. This occurs in spite of these jurisdictions having adopted 'import substitution' economies and theories of radical territoriality of application of local law. Exchange of legal information will accelerate now that these walls are collapsing, under the influence of regional and international trade arrangements.[71] Quebec has long maintained French doctrinal authority high among its leading sources of law.[72] This may have slowed recently under the effect of nationalist theory; it is unlikely ever to disappear and in the future may yield to an even greater range of

---

[68] On 'coordinate persuasion', see Peter McCormick, 'The Evolution of Coordinate Precedential Authority in Canada: Interprovincial Citations of Judicial Authority, 1992–93', (1994) 32 Osgoode Hall L.J. 271, p. 275 ['Coordinate persuasion is clearly as much a part of the modern practice of judicial decision making as is hierarchical authority'].

[69] For the recognition and application of the aboriginal law of adoption in common-law Canada, prevailing even over provincial legislation, see *Casimel* v. *Insurance Corporation of British Columbia*, (1993) 106 D.L.R. (4th) 720 [also citing prior authority]. For the same result in Quebec, see *Deer* v. *Okpik*, (1980) 4 C.N.L.R. 93.

[70] See José Woehrling, 'L'obligation d'accommodement raisonnable et l'adaptation de la société à la diversité religieuse', (1998) 43 McGill L.J. 325.

[71] See Hector Fix-Fierro and Sergio López Ayllón, 'The Impact of Globalization on the Reform of the State and the Law in Latin America', (1997) 19 Houston J. Int. L. 785.

[72] See Pierre-Gabriel Jobin, 'Les réactions de la doctrine à la création du droit civil québécois par les juges: les débuts d'une affaire de famille', (1980) 21 C. de D. 257; *id.*, 'Le droit comparé dans la réforme du Code civil du Québec et sa première interprétation', (1997) 38 C. de D. 477. See generally H. Patrick Glenn (ed.), *Droit québécois et droit français: communauté, autonomie, concordance* (Montreal: Blais, 1993).

extra-national, non-binding authority.[73] Of course, looking at extra-national law does not mean following it; both civil-law and common-law traditions become multivalent in their cross-border relations.

About 60 per cent of the world's population lives in Asia, and European settlement, through colonialism, was there a temporary phenomenon. The same can be said, in large measure, of Africa and the Middle East. Most of the population of the world, therefore, lives outside of the immediate ambit of European thought and in close relation to non-European legal traditions. If the state fits within European legal theory, the fit is less clear in relation to these other legal traditions. They do recognize political authority; it is the primacy of their law-making which is problematical. The primary sources of Islamic, Hindu, Confucian and *adat* normativity are not state sources; it follows that the national heritage is weakest where the population of the world is greatest. This could change if the tradition of a national legal system displaces these other forms of law. It has not yet happened and may never happen. It is true that Hindu law has been either formally repealed or codified in India; it is also true that the majority of the Indian population remains unmoved by state law (there is no 'fact' of obedience) and continues to live much as it has always lived.[74] Castes are evidence of this. In China, Confucianism is undergoing a revival and is seen as a major form of support of state law which cannot bind the way it might in Europe.[75] The French–Dutch civil code is largely in ruins in Indonesia.[76]

---

[73] See Pierre-Gabriel Jobin, 'La modernité du droit commun des contrats dans le Code civil du Québec: quelle modernité?', Rev. int. dr. comp., 2000, p. 72, discussing the need to consider the law of other civilian jurisdictions and US law.

[74] See Upendra Baxi, 'People's Law in India: The Hindu Society', in Masaji Chiba (ed.), *Asian Indigenous Law in Interaction with Received Law* (London: KPI, 1986), p. 216; Marc Galanter, *Law and Society in Modern India* (Delhi: Oxford University Press, 1989), p. 15, observing that the received English law is 'palpably foreign' for the Indian population; Bernard S. Cohn, *An Anthropologist Among the Historians and Other Essays* (Delhi: Oxford University Press, 1987), pp. 568–71, discussing the effect of caste differences on litigation in which the parties are presumed equal.

[75] For the renewed role of Confucianism in China, see Hano von Senger, *Einführung in das chinesische Recht* (Munich: C. H. Beck, 1994), p. 25; Albert H. Y. Chen, *An Introduction to the Legal System of the People's Republic of China* (Singapore: Butterworths, 1992), p. 38, noting that Marxism and Confucianism are converging in their distrust of the rule of law of western origin; Benjamin Gregg, 'Law in China: The Tug of Tradition, the Push of Capitalism', (1995) 21 R. Central & East Eur. L. 65, p. 76 ['Communist China inherited and never rejected this Confucian-based anti-legalism'].

[76] It is, however, difficult to document a lack of documentation. But see Sudargo Gautama and Robert N. Hornick, *An Introduction to Indonesian Law* (Bandung: Alumni Press, 1974), p. 7, observing that the Dutch civil code was amended by legislation since Indonesian independence

African 'customary' law is resurgent; there is a process known as 'Islamicization'. There may still be great loyalty to European tradition in some of these jurisdictions, as in the legal professions of India[77] or Singapore.[78] The lawyers in these places must deal, however, with more than state law. They may also look to European law rather than the law of their own state, in accordance with local tradition and as facilitated by modern technology. In Samoa, the common law has been received as it exists 'from time to time'.[79]

In much of the world, there is also the major problem of corruption of state institutions, officials and judges. State law is thin law and, with its large institutions, provides endless occasions for 'grease'. *Transparency International* is now doing very valuable work in illuminating this problem throughout the world.[80] Vigilance or anti-corruption agencies are essential; they may, or may not, be eventually successful. The forces of corruption are omnipresent; it has been said to the author of these lines, in an Asian country, '[i]f you are innocent, they will get you'. In de-stabilizing other traditions, without adequately replacing them itself, western legal tradition creates much room for manoeuvre. The state here, in many instances, is an 'empty title'.[81] International law has already recognized the phenomenon of 'collapsed, dysfunctional and disoriented States'.[82] *Carte blanche* is re-appearing on the maps of the world, or should be.

in 1945, but that it is no longer clear which provisions are in force since the new legislation does not explicitly repeal the affected texts and there is no 'authoritative edition' of the code.

[77] For the Indian legal profession as effecting an 'inner colonialization' of Indian law, see Weggel, *supra*, note 48, p. 123.

[78] See Andrew J. Harding, *The Common Law in Singapore and Malaysia* (Singapore: Butterworths, 1989); Kevin Tan (ed.), *The Singapore Legal System*, 2d ed. (Singapore: Singapore University Press, 1999). *Cf*. Walter Woon, 'Singapore', in Poh-Ling Tan (ed.), *Asian Legal Systems* (Sydney: Butterworths, 1997), p. 352 ['Chinese-educated Chinese (in Singapore) have a deeply-rooted distrust of courts and the law' while 'English-educated Singaporeans (Chinese, Malay, Indian and others) are more inclined to push for strengthening of institutions. (...) The tension between these two tendencies will characterize the Singapore legal system for some time to come'].

[79] Jennifer C. Care, Tess Newton and Don Paterson, *Introduction to South Pacific Law* (London: Cavendish, 1999), p. 72 ['without a cut-off date'].

[80] See www.transparency.org.

[81] Van Creveld, *supra*, note 11, p. 331. See also *The Economist*, 13 May 2000, p. 17, referring to Sierra Leone as 'an extreme, but not untypical, example of a state with all the epiphenomena and none of the institutions of government'.

[82] Nii L. Wallace-Bruce, 'Of Collapsed, Dysfunctional and Disoriented States: Challenges to International Law', (2000) 47 Neth. Int. L.R. 3, p. 54 ['the phenomenon of a state in which the basic institutions have completely ceased to function is of recent origin. International law does not appear to have foreshadowed this and so it has no defined principles to apply to such situations']. For further references, see Ruth Gordon, 'Saving Failed States: Sometimes a Neo-colonialist Notion', (1997) 12 Am. U. J. Int. L. & Policy 903, p. 904. For the majority of states in

The international

International law has been hegemonic in character, in assuming the universality of states and the primacy of inter-state relations, though these circumstances, to the extent they exist, are the product largely of colonialism. Today, the international faces a future as clouded as that of the national, for some of the same reasons, and for some different ones.

To the extent that the national is challenged by other legal traditions, within states and at their borders, the international is also challenged. The Islamic community, the *umma*, does not define itself in national terms and its law runs through national boundaries. The same can be said for Talmudic law, now resurgent as a means of 'alternative' dispute resolution in many western jurisdictions. The law of aboriginal peoples (as they are known in the west) is also unmindful of state structures and boundaries. Can states successfully and universally relegate these other forms of law to a so-called 'private' sphere? The evidence is increasing that they cannot. Many states already explicitly admit the existence of personal laws (India, Morocco, Israel); others admit the practice or use other language (the Americas and Australasia). The idea of a '*statut personnel*' for minority populations is now being seriously discussed within Europe itself.[83] The Ottoman 'millet' system is seen by political theorists in western writing as worthy of serious investigation.[84] Recognition of such non-state laws implies erosion of the exclusivity of state law, but also of the international, whether public or private. The expression 'inter-personal' already exists as a means of indicating the choice to be made between different non-state laws. The diversity of state structures (from the most exclusivist to the most open and accommodating of non-state laws) means that the international also exists, already, as a matter of degree.

The international is being eroded, however, not only from without the west, but from within. Western law is becoming impatient with itself, with the eighteenth- and nineteenth-century structures it developed at a time

---

Africa south of the Sahara now being in initial, advanced or complete collapse, see *Die Zeit*, 18 May 2000, p. 3. The process is accompanied by new forms of warfare dominated by small arms, machine guns and mortars supplied by western powers and in which increasing numbers of civilians are victims, as to which see George Musser and Sasha Nemecek, 'Waging a New Kind of War', *Scientific American*, June 2000, p. 47. Thirty-four such wars were being fought in 1999, according to the *Frankfurter Allgemeine Zeitung*, 7 June 2000, pp. 4 and 7.

[83] See Yves Plasseraud, 'L'histoire oubliée de l'autonomie culturelle', *Le Monde diplomatique*, May 2000, pp. 16–17.

[84] See Kymlicka, *supra*, note 43, pp. 56–8 and 183–4.

of limited means of communication and, from today's perspective, limited ambition. Today, western law is becoming, in its own perception of itself, regional, global or universal. All are incompatible in some measure with the international, with its *'notion périmée'* of boundaries.[85] Europe represents the regional. The European Coal and Steel Community was probably seen as an international development. The law of the European Union is, however, European law and not international law.[86] Regions devour the international. The world of trade represents the global, facilitated by structures and technology which have grown out of state structures. Globalization would represent the end not of history, but of geography, in terms of the importance of geo-physical and political boundaries.[87] Public international law has been partly revitalized by this process, in the measure that it regulates international trade; it has also been by-passed in significant measure, as the actors of world trade regulate themselves. This has also had serious repercussions on private international law, which is now systematically avoided by nearly all of those with the knowledge and means of doing so, in favour of international arbitration.[88] Human rights would represent the universal, and western international law here remains faithful to its proselytizing and

---

[85] Coquery-Vidrovitch, *supra*, note 24, p. 6.

[86] See C. N. Kakouris, 'L'utilisation de la méthode comparative par la Cour de justice des Communautés Européennes', in Drobnig and van Erp, *supra*, note 31, p. 101 [*'la Cour considère le droit communautaire comme droit interne de la Communauté, et non comme droit international'*].

[87] See Zygmunt Bauman, *Globalization: The Human Consequences* (New York: Columbia University Press, 1998), p. 12 and the references cited. *Cf*., however, for a critical assessment of the 'globalization' phenomenon, Paul Q. Hirst and Grahame Thompson, *Globalization in Question: The International Economy and the Possibilities of Governance* (Cambridge: Polity, 1996), noting that the present level of internationalization is not unprecedented, that there are few genuine transnational companies and that most investment and trade is concentrated in Europe, Japan and North America; Dani Rodrik, *Has Globalization Gone Too Far?* (Washington, DC: Institute for International Economics, 1997), discussing the tension between global market and social stability; The World Bank, *World Development Report 1997: The State in a Changing World* (Oxford: Oxford University Press, 1997), p. 12, observing that half of the people in the developing world are unaffected by the rise in world trade.

[88] See Marielle Koppenol-Laforce *et al*. (eds.), *International Contracts: Aspects of Jurisdiction, Arbitration and Private International Law* (London: Sweet & Maxwell, 1996), p. 86, noting that it is estimated that 90 per cent of international contracts have arbitration clauses. For the growth in arbitration, which would now be 'the accepted method for resolving international business disputes', see Yves Dezalay and Bryant G. Garth, *Dealing in Virtue: International Commercial Arbitration and the Construction of a Transnational Legal Order* (Chicago: University of Chicago Press, 1996), p. 6; H. Patrick Glenn, 'Globalization and Dispute Resolution', (2000) 19 Civil Just. Q. 136, pp. 140–1 and the references cited.

hegemonic character.[89] It now, however, must leap over its own shadow, the state long its exclusive subject, and confer substantive, universal rights directly on human beings. This might, eventually, be universal, common law; it is not international in the way it has traditionally been conceived.

Conclusion

States and national legal systems have been formidable intellectual constructions, which have both generated national identities and produced (relatively) coherent models of national law, in some parts of the world.[90] In their origins, they represented remarkable syntheses of information of variable provenance, and in their ongoing existence they have shown great capacity for self-renewal. They will probably be with us for a long time. There are signs, however, of fatigue, even exhaustion, in the effort to control legal information totally and exclusively, to eliminate both the local and the distant as sources of identity and law. States and national legal systems may thus be demonstrating, once again, the Maimonides phenomenon – that all efforts to reduce, refine, clarify, codify, will eventually yield, in some measure, to the natural flow of information in the world.[91] They will be reeled back in, interrogated and challenged by both the local and the distant. Reductionist and constructed identities are thus not stable, and reductionist and constructed law is not stable. State law may, however, be a useful intermediary between the local and the distant. Conceived as an intermediary, a place of meeting and ongoing dialogue of different sources of information, the state may become no longer a source of conflict but a means of reconciliation of conflict.

---

[89] For the argument that the existence of state structures necessarily implies recognition of the concept of 'rights' as a means of protection against state structures, see Ann E. Mayer, *Islam and Human Rights: Tradition and Politics* (Boulder: Westview, 1991), p. 12

[90] For a recent exploration of national models of company law, see Véronique Magnier, *Rapprochement des droits dans l'Union européenne et viabilité d'un droit commun des sociétés* (Paris: L.G.D.J., 1999), p. 318 ['*Modèle européen et modèles nationaux sont en définitive intrinsèquement liés*'].

[91] On the consequences of Maimonides' twelfth-century codification of Talmudic law, see Elliot Dorff and Arthur Rosett, *A Living Tree: The Roots and Growth of Jewish Law* (Albany: State University of New York Press, 1988), pp. 368, 369 and 372; Robert Goldenberg, 'Talmud', in Barry W. Holz (ed.), *Back to the Sources: Reading the Classic Jewish Texts* (New York: Summit Books, 1984), p. 162 ['no code has brought that history (of Talmudic law) to an end']; Charles Leben, 'Maïmonide et la codification du droit hébraïque', Droits, 1998, No. 27, pp. 122–7.

5

The functionalist heritage

MICHELE GRAZIADEI

Varieties of functionalism

'Functionalism' is a broad term. In the field of comparative law, it denotes at least two distinct, yet related, currents of thought. The first is linked to methodological concerns. In this context, an analysis of the functionalist heritage involves an assessment of the strengths and weaknesses of the 'functionalist method', which is one of the best-known working tools in comparative legal studies. The second understanding of 'functionalism' evokes the idea that law responds to society's needs – a view which some comparatists find more attractive than others in order to explain differences and similarities between the world's legal systems. Today, both varieties of functionalism are being challenged from different angles.

The functional method in comparative law: a standard account

Before considering the basic tenets of the functional method in comparative law, it is worth recalling that it never represented the sole or even the dominant approach to comparative legal studies during the twentieth century. Nor is it the prevailing method today despite the fact that some initiatives, such as the research being conducted by a large number of scholars under the flag of the 'Common Core of European Private Law', have breathed new life into it. There have always been other routes to comparison. Among the best-known ones, especially in Europe and in the United States, there is the tradition which analyses existing institutions and rules in their historical context. Books like John Dawson's *Oracles of the Law*,[1] John Merryman's

---

[1] John P. Dawson, *The Oracles of the Law* (Ann Arbor: University of Michigan Law School, 1968).

The Civil Law Tradition,[2] René David's *Les grands systèmes de droit contemporains*,[3] Gino Gorla's essays on courts and legal doctrine,[4] James Gordley's *The Philosophical Origins of Modern Contract Doctrine*,[5] just to name a few twentieth-century classics, leave no doubt about the fact that the functional method has been just one of the tools employed by comparatists. Indeed, even leading supporters of the functional method do not practise functionalism as if it were the sole approach to comparison. I need only mention Hein Kötz's essay on judicial practices of doctrinal citation by way of illustration.[6] It would be misleading, therefore, to proclaim that there is one method for comparative law and that that method is functionalism. Nowadays, comparative law is practised by individuals professing very different methodological faiths and concentrating on issues having little in common except that they are addressed in a comparative way. In fact, no one could have foreseen the plurality of methods which are currently being practised when comparative law was thought to be a method in itself.[7]

Within the framework of comparative legal studies, the basic features of what is often introduced as the functionalist method have been described on several occasions by different authors.[8] Arguably, Konrad Zweigert and

---

[2] John H. Merryman, *The Civil Law Tradition*, 2d ed. (Stanford: Stanford University Press, 1985). Dawson and Merryman's contributions are discussed by Mitchel Lasser, 'Comparative Law and Comparative Literature: A Project in Progress', [1997] Utah L.R. 471.
[3] René David, *Les grands systèmes de droit contemporains*, 11th ed. by Camille Jauffret-Spinosi (Paris: Dalloz, 2002). For the current English translation, see René David and John E. C. Brierley, *Major Legal Systems in the World Today*, 3d ed. (London: Stevens, 1985).
[4] For a collection of several of these papers, see Gino Gorla, *Diritto comparato e diritto comune europeo* (Milan: Giuffrè, 1981).
[5] James R. Gordley, *The Philosophical Origins of Modern Contract Doctrine* (Oxford: Oxford University Press, 1991).
[6] Hein Kötz, 'Die Zitierpraxis der Gerichte: Eine Vergleichende Skizze', RabelsZ, 1988, p. 644.
[7] The roots of the approach which consists in apprehending comparative law as a method in and of itself have been traced to the writings of Lambert, Pollock, David and others by Léontin-Jean Constantinesco, *Traité de droit comparé*, vol. I (Paris: L.G.D.J., 1972), pp. 176–205. It has been suggested that the notion of comparative law as method became more prominent after the confident view of comparative law as science declined in the aftermath of the Second World War. See Rodolfo Sacco, *Introduzione al diritto comparato*, 5th ed. (Turin: UTET, 1992), pp. 9–10. This author observes, however, that it is reductive to consider comparative law as a method given the variety of methodological options open to comparatists and the range of phenomena traditionally investigated by comparatists. Still, 'the comparative method' is the title of the first chapter in Rudolf B. Schlesinger, *Comparative Law: Cases-Text-Materials*, 6th ed. by Hans W. Baade, Peter E. Herzog and Edward M. Wise (New York: Foundation Press, 1998).
[8] For example, see Mary Ann Glendon, Michael W. Gordon and Christopher Osakwe, *Comparative Legal Traditions*, 2d ed. (St Paul: West, 1994), pp. 11–12; Arthur T. von Mehren, 'An Academic Tradition for Comparative Law?', (1971) 19 Am. J. Comp. L. 624. For a critical perspective, see Günter Frankenberg, 'Critical Comparisons: Re-thinking Comparative Law', (1985) 26 Harvard

Hein Kötz's classic *An Introduction to Comparative Law* contains the best current account of the essential features of the functional approach.[9] These authors remark that the only things which are comparable are those fulfilling the same function. Because '[i]ncomparables cannot be usefully compared', they maintain that the question to which any comparative study is devoted 'must be posed in purely functional terms' and that 'the problem must be stated without any reference to the concepts of one's legal system'. In brief, comparative law must address 'the concrete problem'. Starting from this premise, the comparative exercise focuses on an elementary truth: 'the legal system of every society faces essentially the same problems, and solves these problems by quite different means though very often with similar results.' Hence, the novice and the experienced comparatist are both warned. Successful comparison depends on the comparatist's ability to 'eradicate the preconceptions of his native legal system' while framing comparative research.[10]

The discussion of the examples illustrating these points insists on the similarity of solutions across legal systems 'despite the great differences in their historical development, conceptual structure, and style of operation'.[11] To be sure, there are exceptions to the rule. The notion of *ordre public*, prominent in the field of conflict of laws, hints at these. Nevertheless, investigations within legal subjects that, according to Zweigert and Kötz, are relatively 'unpolitical' would confirm their basic line. Topics in the field of family law and succession, however, appear to them to be 'heavily impressed by moral views or values'.[12] Leaving these areas aside, and assuming that the object of comparison is not impressed by 'strong moral and ethical feelings, rooted in the particularities of the prevailing religion, in historical tradition, in cultural development, or in the character of the people',[13] comparatists could usefully start from a '*praesumptio similitudinis*', a presumption that the practical results are similar because 'developed nations answer the needs

---

Int. L.J. 411, pp. 434–40; David Kennedy, 'New Approaches to Comparative Law: Comparativism and International Governance', [1997] Utah L.R. 545, pp. 588–92 [I regard this paper as being particularly helpful]; Mark Tushnet, 'The Possibilities of Comparative Constitutional Law', (1999) 108 Yale L.J. 1225, pp. 1265–9 and 1281–5.

[9] Konrad Zweigert and Hein Kötz, *An Introduction to Comparative Law*, 3d ed. transl. by Tony Weir (Oxford: Oxford University Press, 1998). For a critical review of the previous edition, see Jonathan Hill, 'Comparative Law, Law Reform and Legal Theory', (1989) 9 Oxford J. Leg. Stud. 101.

[10] For these quotations, see Zweigert and Kötz, *supra*, note 9, pp. 34–5.

[11] *Id.*, p. 39.   [12] *Id.*, p. 40.   [13] *Ibid.*

of legal business in the same or in a very similar way'.[14] By adopting this presumption, comparatists should be able to discover similarities and substitutes in the world's legal systems and, at the same time, check the results of their research.[15]

The functional method: what for?

Zweigert and Kötz's introduction to the functional method is remarkable for what it says and for what it does not say. What does that old saw, 'incomparables cannot be usefully compared', mean after all? What are the preconceptions that comparatists must eradicate? Is *'Rechtsgeschäft'* or 'trespass' a preconception? Do comparatists really learn that legal systems across the world face essentially the same problems and very often solve these problems by reaching similar results, though with the help of different means? And, if so, how and when is the result 'similar'? Is it true that the areas of law where comparatists find the greatest differences are those most closely connected with strong moral and ethical feelings? Or is it possible that very different (and strong) moral and ethical feelings coexist with the application of the same rules?

To understand the functional approach, it is necessary to discuss the theoretical problems that functional comparisons should solve. Arguably, the appeal to the functional method in comparative law is a response to a specific set of rather narrow and difficult theoretical questions. Until we know what the critical questions are, we can hardly hope to be making sense of functionalism.

The methodological assumptions that Zweigert and Kötz summarize in their *Introduction* have been on the market for a long time. Thus, Zweigert published articles illustrating the functional method over forty years ago.[16] But the roots of the functional method reach further back in time. Indeed, I argue that this particular approach originated with the need to solve theoretical problems that became acute in the field of conflict of laws. Specifically, the functional method first emerged as a response to characterization problems which surfaced in late nineteenth-century conflict-of-laws doctrines

---

[14] *Ibid.*   [15] *Ibid.*

[16] For example, see Konrad Zweigert, 'Méthodologie du droit comparé', in *Mélanges offerts à Jacques Maury*, vol. I (Paris: Dalloz, 1960), pp. 579–96; *id.*, 'Des solutions identiques par des voies différentes (quelques observations en matière de droit comparé)', Rev. int. dr. comp., 1966, p. 5.

and which became of great scholarly concern during the first decades of the twentieth century.

The functional method and the clash of legal categories in the field of conflict of laws

Conflict-of-laws scholars point to the fact that there was a fortunate age when the problem of characterization had not yet been discovered.[17] Issues of characterization originate from the structure of a conflict-of-laws system based on categories and connecting factors. The typical example would be any conflicts law which enacts rules like 'succession to immovables is governed by the law of the *situs*'. Conflict-of-laws rules framed in such terms do not provide a description of the facts triggering their application. If these rules are interpreted in accordance with the domestic law of the forum, there is little chance of achieving uniform application of the conflicts rules, even though the same conflicts texts are in force in different countries. Characterization of the same facts will shift from one legal system to another, because the notions employed to frame the conflicts rule are interpreted differently across legal borders. Hence, what is a tort here can be a contract elsewhere, or what is succession here can be marital property in another jurisdiction. While it would be out of place to delve deeper into the debate over characterization, what is interesting for present purposes is how the awareness of the problems raised by questions of characterization has affected comparative legal studies. The clash of legal categories, which becomes apparent when a characterization issue is involved in the decision of a case, stimulated a rich theoretical debate. From a comparative perspective, the most important contribution to that debate originated from the question raised by Ernst Rabel. What is characterized, after all, by conflict-of-laws rules?

Rabel thought that conflicts rules must operate 'directly on the facts of life, not on a legally predicated, abstract subject matter'.[18] He took the view

---

[17] On the 'discovery' of the problem and its relevance today, see Kurt Lipstein, 'Characterization', in *Private International Law*, in *International Encyclopedia of Comparative Law*, vol. III, ch. 5 (Tübingen: J. C. B. Mohr, 1999), pp. 5–8.
[18] Ernst Rabel, *The Conflict of Laws: A Comparative Study*, 2d ed., vol. I (Ann Arbor: University of Michigan Press, 1945), p. 46. For an excellent study of Rabel's intellectual profile and of his contribution to comparative law, see David J. Gerber, 'Sculpting the Agenda of Comparative Law: Ernst Rabel and the Façade of Language', in Annelise Riles (ed.), *Rethinking the Masters of Comparative Law* (Oxford: Hart, 2001), pp. 190–208. On Rabel's legacy in Germany, see

that problems of characterization could be solved by looking through the phraseology of conflicts rules in order to identify the facts of life from which legal consequences flow. Though conflicts rules are apparently framed in the language of legal relationship, Rabel argued that they denote social relationships. The lack of a universal language adopted across jurisdictions forces legislators or judges to frame conflicts rules by using the legal categories coined to express strictly domestic law. However, sophisticated conflicts lawyers should not ascribe to juridical concepts an absolute character, irrespective of their purposes. For Rabel, there is no 'heaven of concepts' in conflict of laws,[19] no more than in other areas of the law, and the way forward is shown by comparative research:

> the factual situation, which is the true premise of any conflicts rule, must be referable indifferently to foreign as well as to domestic substantive law: hence, if legal terms are used to describe this factual situation, they must be susceptible of interpretation with reference to foreign institutions, even those unknown to the *lex fori*. This operation includes comparative research.[20]

The most instructive comparative research would, therefore, be based on the following technique:

> to gather the foreign case-law over a certain matter, to examine carefully the facts and the decisions, to study in which way the same cases would be solved in one's own country and then to try to solve the practical cases which arise in one's own country in accordance with foreign norms. From this, a variety of new points of view on both laws will arise.[21]

This recipe now sounds incredibly naive, and yet Rabel entrusted to it the essential message of functionalism: it is possible to compare the incomparable provided that the focus is on the same facts. Across the world, lawyers use widely different legal categories to denote facts and to indicate their legal consequences: these categories are contingent and instrumental. They cannot provide guidance for comparative legal research. Comparative law must concentrate on isolating the facts from which legal consequences

---

Michael Martinek, 'Wissenschaftsgeschichte der Rechtsvergleichung und des Internationalen Privatsrecht in der Bundesrepublik Deutschland', in Dieter Simon (ed.), *Rechtswissenschaft in der Bonner Republik* (Frankfurt: Suhrkamp, 1994), pp. 539–41. On Rabel and the hermeneutical approach of Joseph Esser, see *id.*, p. 529.

[19] Rabel, *supra*, note 18, pp. 55.   [20] *Id.*, pp. 49–50.
[21] *Id.*, 'El fomento international del derecho privado' (1931), now in *id.*, *Gesammelte Aufsätze*, vol. III (Tübingen: J. C. B. Mohr, 1967), p. 51 [my translation].

follow, quite irrespective of the way they are looked at, or categorized, in any legal system. Rabel's approach laid the foundation for the research that a later generation of comparatists would conduct in different areas of private law.[22] True to this heritage, Zweigert and Kötz now declare that 'the method taught and practised today comes from the research that Rabel evolved and perfected'.[23]

The mistrust of municipal legal categories is a central feature of this method. National legal concepts are the screen behind which comparatists locate what is relevant for their research. Indeed, in accordance with the principle of functionality, when the comparative work based on surveys of national laws begins, each national solution 'must be freed from the context of its own system', so that these solutions may be seen 'purely in the light of their function, as an attempt to satisfy a particular legal need'.[24]

The growth of a methodological tradition

Rabel's insights into comparative-law methodology may have been influenced by his personal experience with the 'Mixed Arbitral Tribunal Panels' established to decide disputes under the provisions of the Versailles Peace Treaty. In the late 1920s, he also served as an *ad hoc* judge on the Permanent Court for International Justice. These appointments, like his education in end-of-the-century Vienna, must have sharpened his thinking on the relationship between facts, language and the law. But, during the second and the third decades of the twentieth century, the same questions also attracted attention in different circles.

In Germany, Philipp Heck's *Interessenjurisprudenz* and its faith in the notion of 'interest' as an *Arbeitsbegriff* stood in opposition to the conceptualistic approach of large sectors of nineteenth-century legal scholarship.[25]

---

[22] However, most conflicts scholars have turned their backs on Rabel's universalist approach, arguing that private international law is, essentially, national law. Conflicts doctrines based on interest analysis, instead of categories, also undermined Rabel's proposals. *Cf*. Rodolfo de Nova, 'The Comparative Method and Private International Law', in *Italian National Reports to the Xth International Congress of Comparative Law, Budapest, 1978* (Milan: Giuffrè, 1978), p. 119.

[23] Zweigert and Kötz, *supra*, note 9, p. 61. This statement is contained in the chapter devoted to the history of comparative law. See now Hein Kötz, 'Comparative Law in Germany Today', Rev. int. dr. comp., 1999, p. 755.

[24] Zweigert and Kötz, *supra*, note 9, p. 44. See also *id*., p. 45.

[25] See now Manfred Wolf, *Philipp Heck als Zivilrechtsdogmatiker: Studien zur dogmatischen Umsetzung seiner Methodenlehre* (Ebelsbach: Aktiv, 1996).

On the other side of the Atlantic, the rejection of conceptualism by legal realism and the ascent of philosophical pragmatism was celebrated by a host of scholars. Felix Cohen's essays on the functional approach represent the tip of this anti-formalist iceberg.[26] To turn again to comparative law after the Second World War and to the use of the functional method outside Germany, in the late 1950s Rudolf Schlesinger launched the project that eventually produced two monumental volumes on formation of contracts published under his general editorship.[27]

In order to conduct multilateral comparative research on formation of contracts, Schlesinger had to ensure that all participants in the project answered the same questions and that no one was unsure or in disagreement about the issues to be addressed. Therefore, the project proposed to take fact situations as its starting-point for discussion:

> It was clear from the outset that these questions [that is, the questions national reporters were required to answer] had to be formulated in such a way that our colleague from India would understand them in the same way as our colleague from Italy. If the questions had been asked in abstract legal terms, each participant might have read particular notions of his own legal system into such terms, and the result would have been the complete lack of a common focus. It was decided, therefore, to ask the questions in factual terms.[28]

The factual approach tested at Cornell was designed to overcome the radical differences concerning the way legal systems considered in Schlesinger's study organize the field of contract law. Working with the factual approach, participants in the project discovered that the method 'cut right through the conceptual cubicles in which each legal system stores its law of contract, and made it possible to proceed immediately to the matching of results reached by the various legal systems'.[29] Once more, this operation purported to free comparative-law research from the 'shackles of existing classificatory systems'.[30]

---

[26] See Felix Cohen, 'Transcendental Nonsense and the Functional Approach' (1935); *id.*, 'The Problems of Functional Jurisprudence' (1937); *id.*, 'The Relativity of Philosophical Systems and the Method of Systematic Relativism' (1939), all repr. in Lucy Kramer Cohen (ed.), *The Legal Conscience: Selected Papers of Felix S. Cohen* (New Haven: Yale University Press, 1960), pp. 33–76, 77–94 and 95–110, respectively.

[27] See Rudolf B. Schlesinger (ed.), *Formation of Contracts: A Study of the Common Core of Legal Systems* (Dobbs Ferry: Oceana, 1968), 2 vols.

[28] *Id.*, 'Introduction', in *id.*, *supra*, note 27, vol. I, p. 31 [hereinafter 'Introduction'].

[29] *Id.*, p. 57.   [30] *Id.*, p. 58.

Schlesinger, however, could not fail to observe some limitations and traps within the factual approach. Not all the 'facts' investigated by comparative research have the same quality. Thus, some facts consist wholly or in part of institutional elements, that is, 'of elements differently formed by the history, the mores, the ethos and – indeed – by the laws of different communities'.[31] Schlesinger thought that such 'facts' were hardly suitable for comparative research based on the factual approach, which would then risk 'the danger of self-deception and circular reasoning'.[32] Furthermore, even when working in an area of the law free from institutional facts such as those just mentioned, differences in procedural and evidentiary law might render uncertain the question of whether the 'same' facts reported in different jurisdictions are really the same. Though taking the view that truly similar fact-situations may occur across legal systems, Schlesinger advised healthy scepticism on this issue.[33] Last, but not least, Schlesinger averted the danger of falling prey to the temptation to conclude that, because two courts of different countries have reached the same result on the same facts, the same rule is applicable to the facts in the two countries. This conclusion may simply be wrong as happens when the New York Court of Appeals lays down a rule of law, while the French *Cour de cassation* merely refuses to disturb a factual finding by the lower court.[34]

Functionalism and beyond: a critical assessment

The methodological breakthroughs I have summarized changed the intellectual landscape of comparative law during the twentieth century. Nevertheless, progress was made at a considerable price.

The intellectual posture sustaining the approach discussed in the previous paragraphs had a component of make-believe, of circularity, that is striking in retrospect. Similarity among legal experiences across the world

---

[31] *Ibid.* On the philosophical arguments raised by the investigation of these social facts, see John R. Searle, *The Social Construction of Reality* (New York: Free Press, 1995). For a perceptive discussion of the same point in the context of a wider assessment of functionalism in comparative law, see Geoffrey Samuel, 'Epistemology and Comparative Law: Contributions from the Sciences and Social Sciences' (2002), on file with the author.

[32] Schlesinger, 'Introduction', *supra*, note 28, p. 32; *id.*, 'The Common Core of Legal Systems: An Emerging Subject of Comparative Study', in Kurt Nadelmann, Arthur T. von Mehren and John Hazard (eds.), *XXth Century Comparative and Conflicts Law* (Leiden: Sijthoff, 1961), pp. 65–79.

[33] See Schlesinger, 'Introduction', *supra*, note 28, pp. 32–3. *Cf.* Pierre Legrand, *Fragments on Law-as-Culture* (Deventer: W. E. J. Tjeenk Willink, 1999), pp. 87–9.

[34] See Schlesinger, 'Introduction', *supra*, note 28, p. 56.

was presented as a fact which – exceptions apart – comparative legal research could take for granted. The image was that of a universal law, which the functional approach to comparative law was going to bring to light.[35] Such an attitude meant the elaboration of an inclusive approach to comparative law which, as it expanded its territorial reach beyond the geographical area marked by the diffusion of Roman law in the era of the *jus commune*, assumed, in advance of empirical investigation, a fundamental consensus among different legal experiences across the world.

On a different level, the sheer quantity of 'facts' that the functional method left out of the picture is impressive. One has only to read the list of factors regarded as impeding or disturbing the application of the functional method to realize how its domain could be circumscribed. Thus, Schlesinger mentions history, the mores, ethics and even the laws of various countries.[36] Zweigert and Kötz consider an even broader list of limiting factors.[37] It is proper to ask whether these limitations are really built into the functional method or whether they do not rather reflect the training and ideology of particular researchers resorting to the functional approach. In the social sciences, for example, functionalism has been used to investigate a vast number of subjects, including those that Schlesinger or Zweigert and Kötz consider as rather unsuitable for functional research. Even within law, an adept of functionalism like Mauro Cappelletti engaged in the study of comparative civil procedure in its social and political context.[38] Likewise, more recent research has explored concepts such as 'good faith', which are traditionally thought to be impressed with moral or ethical values.[39] In this sense, some of the limitations ascribed to the functional method probably reflect a desire to test it on topics traditionally considered to be the

---

[35] See Vivian G. Curran, 'Cultural Immersion, Difference and Categories in US Comparative Law', (1998) 46 Am. J. Comp. L. 43, pp. 66–78, discussing the reasons which inspired some comparatists in particular to favour this understanding in the aftermath of the Second World War.

[36] See Schlesinger, 'Introduction', *supra*, note 28, p. 32.

[37] See Zweigert and Kötz, *supra*, note 9, pp. 39–40.

[38] For example, see Mauro Cappelletti (ed.), *Access to Justice* (Milan: Giuffrè, 1978); *id.*, James Gordley and Earl Johnson, *Toward Equal Justice: A Comparative Study of Legal Aid in Modern Societies* (Milan: Giuffrè, 1975).

[39] For example, see Reinhard Zimmermann and Simon Whittaker (eds.), *Good Faith in European Contract Law* (Cambridge: Cambridge University Press, 2000); François van der Mensbrugghe, 'Migrations juridiques de la bonne foi', Rev. dr. int. dr. comp., 1999, p. 246; Hein Kötz, 'Towards a European Civil Code: The Duty of Good Faith', in Peter Cane and Jane Stapleton (eds.), *The Law of Obligations: Essays in Celebration of John Fleming* (Oxford: Oxford University Press, 1998), pp. 243–59.

preserve of an inner logic of the law more than they do its inherent limitations beyond these topics. Today, it should be openly recognized that even such large subjects as 'law' or 'religion' can be investigated in functional terms.[40] However, if the range of applications of the functional method is abundantly worth re-appraising, there are also good reasons to ponder whether the major limitation of the functional method does not lie in its governing principle.

Criticism focused on this aspect implies an assessment of the reductionist approach that is the birth-mark of functionalism. The functional method brackets whatever is found in between the 'facts' and their 'legal consequences' as reconstructed in operative terms. This is often noticed by scholars who object that functional comparisons are too rule-based or too rule-centred.[41] The same concern suggests that such bias in favour of a rule-centred treatment of the law obscures the larger picture, which the notion of 'legal culture' evokes.[42] It is the whole legal culture that should matter for comparative purposes, because legal rules are embedded in the local dimensions of the law and their meaning depends largely on that context, that is, on the cultural patterns to which they belong.

These critical remarks focus on an essential aspect of the functional method. The method is built to do away with the local dimensions of operative rules. First and foremost, the goal is to do away with their (local) linguistic husk. If the application of the method is radical enough, any local element will be deconstructed and reduced to an operative description of

---

[40] Durkheim's path-breaking sociological work was based on this insight. For example, see Roger Cotterrell, *Emile Durkheim: Law in a Moral Domain* (Edinburgh: Edinburgh University Press, 1999), pp. 50–5. On the definition of 'religion' in a functional perspective, see Jan G. Platvoet and Arie L. Molendijk (eds.), *The Pragmatics of Defining Religion: Contexts, Concepts and Contests* (Leiden: E. J. Brill, 1999).

[41] For example, see John Merryman's views as stated in Pierre Legrand, 'John Henry Merryman and Comparative Legal Studies: A Dialogue', (1999) 47 Am. J. Comp. L. 3, pp. 48–9. A large number of contemporary comparatists express a similar concern including, of course, Merryman's interviewer himself. For some of the problems that a rule-centred approach raises in the context of macro-comparisons, see René David, 'Introduction', in *The Different Conceptions of the Law*, in *International Encyclopedia of Comparative Law*, vol. II, ch. 1 (Tübingen: J. C. B. Mohr, 1975), pp. 3–13.

[42] In this paper, I discuss how 'legal culture' features in some recent methodological discussions about comparative law rather than the relevance of the notion itself. For their part, Roger Cotterrell and David Nelken's contributions to this book address the meaning of 'legal culture' for current research within sociology of law. See also David Nelken (ed.), *Comparing Legal Cultures* (Aldershot: Dartmouth, 1997).

the rule. The proponents of the functional method are, of course, aware of the larger picture. Specifically, they know about the socio-economic implications of legal rules.[43] Yet, the functional approach discounts the broader framework. It assumes that the structure of any law can be reconstructed and described in operative terms. Not surprisingly, these assumptions are unpalatable to scholars who have been exposed to the lessons of legal realism, though Arthur Corbin or Karl Llewellyn would probably have found little to criticize. Indeed, all opponents of positivism would react negatively to the positivistic ring of an analysis of law as a set of rules. Supporters of the functional method, however, would rightly deny any relationship between functionalism and positivism. They would hasten to reply that the history of comparative law speaks against an association between comparative analysis and legal positivism.

Contorted exchanges like these happen because functionalism often runs into problems which, at first sight, would seem common to all cross-cultural comparisons. And it must be said that critics of functional comparisons have made little progress in discussing these, despite the energy put in challenging the functionalist canon through the appeal to the cultural dimension of legal phenomena. The nature of such problems is probably best explored by thinking of those exercise books for the use of foreign-language students showing frozen views of everyday life in an artificial setting. The pictures depict a room packed with objects. The table stands in front of the reader with chairs around it. A boy (nowadays, a girl) is doing his (her) homework, while Mom (nowadays, anybody) is preparing a (generic) cake (nowadays, putting something to defrost in the microwave oven). The window is in the rear of the room, the door on the right. Each person and each object is graphically labelled with a name. What are these pictures asking us to believe? They are an open invitation to assume that a table is a table everywhere and that a cake is a cake everywhere. Their lesson does not stop there, however. They teach us to appreciate that language in the foreign-languages department may look very different from our experience of it in daily life. Stretching this observation a little further, one may note that an identical sensation of estrangement is often provoked by the first reading of a grammar book dedicated to the reader's maternal language. Once more, the

---

[43] For example, see Ulrich Drobnig, 'Methods of Sociological Research in Comparative Law', RabelsZ, 1971, p. 496; *id.* and Manfred Rehbinder (eds.), *Rechtssoziologie und Rechtsvergleichung* (Berlin: Duncker & Humblot, 1977).

handbook speaks of items that do not have a familiar appearance, though, in this case, the 'foreign' element is not a foreign language but rather the distance that exists between the learned professional's view of the subject and the lay person's knowledge of it.

With these remarks in mind, it would appear that functionalism, as it is practised within comparative-law circles, raises problems which are not, in fact, peculiar to cross-cultural comparisons. Functionalism works with models and hypotheses, draws bold inferences and requires wide generalizations. Its practitioners are lawyers fully trained in the intricacies of their laws who choose to speak to colleagues similarly trained. No doubt their work conveys a picture of the law that is remote from life more than the script of a good movie on a civil action or some exciting legal thriller. But, to make a long story short, the problem raised by the above example is not whether we as comparatists are subject to cognitive limitations that prevent us from understanding any culture in the world. Rather, the question is whether it makes sense to seek from functional comparisons an account of acts of comparison as we experience them while venturing to study an unknown legal system. To be sure, it is one thing to listen to old Grandma's tales and quite another to read them in Propp's *Morphology of the Folktale*. Both experiences reveal something about tales, both inform us about the world we live in, both are in some sense enjoyable, and yet they are not really interchangeable.

It is, therefore, accurate that functionalism teaches us an instructive lesson in trying to separate the universal from the local and that that lesson is rather unilateral. The attempt to reduce the legal meaning of any fact to the legal effects of that fact as stated in operative terms is probably flawed inasmuch as it pretends to capture some ultimate truth. A semantic theory based on such a premise would maintain that the meaning of an expression corresponds to its operational content, but operational theories of meaning are far from satisfactory.[44] Thus, despite the many functional equivalents of 'trusts' existing in Continental Europe, it would be foolish to maintain that today French law, Italian law or German law mirrors the English law of trusts, its language, its taxonomy (if any!) and its imagery of trust relationships, quite apart from its working rules.

---

[44] On their difficulties, see Israel Scheffler, *Four Pragmatists: A Critical Introduction to Peirce, James, Mead and Dewey* (London: Routledge & Kegan Paul, 1974), p. 81.

Does this criticism of functionalism lead us to conclude that nothing valuable can be learned by developing functional comparisons? Quite to the contrary, it would seem to me. We constantly resort to functional comparisons in daily life, to play, to work, to teach and learn, and, yes, to communicate with people who share beliefs about the world very different from our own.[45] To play football in the backyard, a ball is anything that rolls and can be kicked. Children understand this meaning, though they may not know all the cultural implications of playing football in a certain country. Lawyers who choose to govern a given transaction by adopting legal techniques developed in a different cultural milieu act in the same way. They do so at their own risk, of course. Legislators communicate across borders by drafting instruments conceived in functional terms; today, these instruments are the backbone of European Community legislation.[46] Furthermore, a negative answer to the question would not do justice to the corrosive impact of functionalism on formalism or conceptualism, that is, on the foundational philosophy of law which governed in Europe and America up until the end of the nineteenth century.

In the course of the twentieth century, functionalism has been deployed more and more frequently in reconstructive efforts, at both the national and the international level.[47] This use of functionalism should not prevent more critical applications casting new light on the interrelationship between legal concepts and legal rules. Thinking of this corrosive effect of functionalism, the claim that functionalism, inside and outside of comparative law, has shaped the modern mind, is not unduly far-fetched. When all is said about the merits of functional comparisons, however, it is still the case that comparative law meets challenges that cannot be addressed by confining comparative-law scholarship within the four corners of the functional method.

---

[45] For example, see Jean-Claude Gémar, 'Seven Pillars for the Legal Translator: Knowledge, Know-How and Art', in Susan Šarčević (ed.), *Legal Translation: Preparation for Accession to the European Union* (Rijeka: Faculty of Law, University of Rijeka, 2001), pp. 111 and 121–5. See also A. L. Becker, *Beyond Translation* (Ann Arbor: University of Michigan Press, 1995).

[46] To return to the example of 'trusts', there is no doubt that in his 'Things as Thing and Things as Wealth', (1994) 14 Oxford J. Leg. Stud. 81, Bernard Rudden introduces a functional analysis of trust law providing unique insights for any comparative study of this institution.

[47] These efforts motivated Rabel's work in the field of private international law and find a clear echo in Zweigert and Kötz, *supra*, note 9, pp. 44–6, introducing comparative law as the source of a universal legal science.

Unpacking law and unpacking legal culture: a dynamic approach to comparative law

Contemporary criticisms of the functional method insist on the complexity of the 'law' as a phenomenon while, at the same time, stressing the importance of doing justice to such complexity when comparing laws. The starting-point of this criticism is the very idea of a *'praesumptio similitudinis'* between the various laws of the world, at least those of the industrialized nations. Comparative law should not be seduced by the idea of uniformity; it should rather support the opposite stance. Comparative law as an academic subject should be strongly attuned to diversity.[48] In this perspective, the notion of 'culture' appears as the best opportunity for comparative legal studies to 'modernize itself, to come of age, by moving away from its oft-repeated commitment to positivism'.[49] 'Culture', of course, includes much more than rule-following. The notion of law as cultural artefact shows also why comparative law should not aim at fostering uniformity. A planet with one culture would be an impoverished habitat (and it would also be a world in which comparatists have very little to do). To be sure, neither the assumption that law consists of rule-following, nor the invitation to look for a common core of solutions widely accepted across the globe, are indispensable tenets of a comparative-law methodology.

Comparatists may choose other epistemologies for their subject. In the pursuit of such alternatives, however, the appeal to the polyvalent notion of 'culture' raises many difficulties. For comparative theory and practice, one crucial problem is the recurrent temptation to consider 'culture' as a homogeneous whole.[50] Far from being an exotic idea, the notion of 'culture'

---

[48] See Pierre Legrand, *Le droit comparé* (Paris: Presses Universitaires de France, 1999), pp. 32–49. In fact, Kötz himself now recommends caution in resorting to the *'praesumptio similitudinis'*. See Hein Kötz, 'The Trento Project and Its Contribution to the Europeanization of Private Law', in Mauro Bussani and Ugo Mattei (eds.), *Making European Law: Essays on the 'Common Core' Project* (Trento: Università degli Studi di Trento, 2000), p. 121.

[49] Legrand, *supra*, note 41, p. 65. Merryman, however, refuses to confine comparative law to the realm of investigations on 'legal culture', because comparisons should pursue scientific explanations as well as the more familiar non-scientific modes of scholarship. See Legrand, *supra*, note 41, p. 65.

[50] Quite obviously, conceptions of 'culture' based on homogeneity are strongly related to strategies of empowerment and disempowerment. The analytical failure of the notion of 'culture' in this respect is well exposed by A. R. Radcliffe-Brown, *Structure and Function in Primitive Society* (London: Cohen & West, 1952), p. 202, a response to Malinowski's suggestion that African societies should be studied like societies in which two or more 'cultures' interact: 'what is happening in South Africa, for example, is not the interaction of British culture, and Afrikander

based on homogeneity is probably the most popular legacy of Romanticism, which aligned factors like language, religion and law in order to build ethnic and national identities. If comparative legal studies accepts this idea of 'culture', it is bound to ignore the very complexity for which the notion of 'culture' should stand. From an anthropological perspective, however, the holistic notion of 'culture' inherited from Romanticism is a hypothesis contradicted by the dynamics of cultural processes around the world.[51] Thus, anthropological studies on the construction of social boundaries make it clear that members of ethnic groups alter their behaviour through contacts with other groups. These changes take place without necessarily destroying previous allegiances to the group. Such observations show the situational and instrumental features of cultural traits. Anthropologists have also noticed that cultural traits often change precisely where the social boundary is drawn on certain issues. These changes depend on the context and on the situation in which the particular issues arise.[52]

How are these observations taken into account by comparative legal studies? Comparatists know that law, just like culture, is not monolithic. To be sure, municipal lawyers are mostly trained to think that any given case is governed ultimately by a rule and that the legal system has a unitary structure, free from inconsistencies. Deviations from this ideal must be momentary, if a legal system is to exist. Functionalism hardly contradicts this opinion, because it sets out to understand what makes law work. On closer scrutiny, however, the municipal lawyer's training turns out to be based on yet another untutored assumption. One of the great merits of twentieth-century comparative legal studies is, indeed, the assault upon the conventional wisdom which extols the unity of the law and ignores the

(or Boer) culture, Hottentot culture, various Bantu cultures and Indian culture, but the interaction of individuals and groups within an established social structure which is itself in a process of change.'

[51] For example, see Rodolfo Sacco, 'Langue et droit', in *Italian National Reports to the XVth International Congress of Comparative Law, Bristol 1998* (Milan: Giuffrè, 1998), p. 20: '*L'homme ne parle pas* une *langue, sa* langue, la *langue de son ethnie. Il utilise un système linguistique, où peuvent figurer une langue (non nécessairement parlée) pour la lecture des textes sacrés et pour le culte, une langue pour la science, une langue pour la poésie, une langue pour l'administration, une langue pour le commerce (y compris le contact avec le touriste), une langue pour l rapport avec les autres ethnies, une langue vernaculaire (non nécessairement écrite) appelée "dialecte" ou "patois"*' [emphasis original] (hereinafter *Italian Reports – Bristol 1998*). Self-styled post-modern approaches to legal culture and to comparative law all too often ignore this reality or fail to work out its implications.

[52] For these observations, see Sebastian Poulter, *Ethnicity, Law and Human Rights: The English Experience* (Oxford: Oxford University Press, 1998), pp. 4–9.

multiplicity of the components making up the world's legal systems. This is the leitmotiv of Rodolfo Sacco's contribution to comparative jurisprudence.

According to Sacco, there exist different 'formants' of the law which must never be collapsed into an undifferentiated discourse on 'the law' of a given jurisdiction. One of the principal aims of the comparative effort, therefore, is to cast light on all the formants at work within a legal system, including those that are implicit, such as practices that shape the law but are not expressly acknowledged – what Sacco refers to as 'cryptotypes' – be they situated at the level of operative rules or at other levels, such as the ideology permeating a given legal system.[53] While his approach welcomes comparative research on operative rules, Sacco nonetheless insists that the law does not consist exclusively of operative rules and emphasizes that operative rules are not in any sense more 'real' than any other component of the law. Specifically, Sacco notes that law is not necessarily dependent upon language and that legal rules that are not expressed in words play a large role in any legal system.[54] Although every student of customary legal systems knows this, the same truth is seldom proclaimed in legal systems that appear to be governed by legislation, case-law or scholarly writings and awareness of the large role that tacit assumptions play in the interpretation of the law remains a rarity among legal scholars who continue to practice their skills under the umbrella of enacted law and judicial precedents. In proceeding to the comparison, Sacco argues that the contribution of the various formants to the making of the law should be separately tracked.

---

[53] See Rodolfo Sacco, 'Legal Formants: A Dynamic Approach to Comparative Law', (1991) 39 Am. J. Comp. L. 1 & 343. These publications consolidate previous research published either in Italian or in French, which is discussed in Pierre Legrand, 'Questions à Rodolfo Sacco', Rev. int. dr. comp., 1995, p. 943 and Rodolfo Sacco, *Che cos'è il diritto comparato*, ed. by Paolo Cendon (Milan: Giuffrè, 1992). Sacco's theory of comparative law as critical knowledge is discussed in P. G. Monateri and Rodolfo Sacco, 'Legal Formants', in *The New Palgrave Dictionary of Economics and the Law*, ed. by Peter Newman, vol. II (London: Macmillan, 1998), p. 531; P. G. Monateri, 'Critique et différence: le droit comparé en Italie', Rev. int. dr. comp., 1999, p. 989; Horatia Muir Watt, 'La fonction subversive du droit comparé', Rev. int. dr. comp., 2000, p. 503. For an instructive discussion of Sacco's and Schlesinger's contributions to comparative jurisprudence, see Ugo Mattei, 'The Comparative Jurisprudence of Schlesinger and Sacco: A Study in Legal Influence', in Riles, *supra*, note 18, pp. 238–56.

[54] See Rodolfo Sacco, 'Mute Law', (1995) 43 Am. J. Comp. L. 455. In a similar vein, see Daniel Jutras, 'Enoncer l'indicible: le droit entre langue et traditions', Rev. int. dr. comp., 2001, p. 781; Nicholas Kasirer, '*Lex*-icographie *mercatoria*', (1999) 47 Am. J. Comp. L. 653; *id.*, 'Dire ou définir le droit', (1994) Rev. jur. Thémis 141; Roderick A. Macdonald, 'Legal Bilingualism', (1997) McGill L. J. 119.

The recognition of pluralism within any given legal system has important consequences in terms of the accuracy of comparisons. It may well turn out, for example, that the rule enacted in jurisdiction A is different from that in jurisdiction B, though the outcome of a certain case in both countries is the same. Should we, therefore, say that 'the law' is the same in the two jurisdictions? What if the operative rules followed in one country do not match the definitions of the law prevailing in that jurisdiction, but fit instead those of a different legal system? Is it not proper to recognize in such cases that similarities and differences are distributed across legal formants and that they are all relevant for comparative purposes? There is no reason why comparatists should iron out these mismatches in order to state 'the' solution received in a certain legal system. Undoubtedly, this approach makes the most of the fact that several of the world's legal systems have been exposed to the circulation of legal models. These dynamics may well explain why the civil code of a given country adopts a given model (or pays lip-service to it), while judges and scholars prefer other models (steadfastly proclaiming all along that they are doing nothing but interpreting the code).

Drawing on these insights, one can renew the methodology used by Schlesinger and expand the programme of multilateral comparisons. This possibility is currently being explored by scholars involved in the 'Common Core of European Private Law' project launched in the mid-1990s by Ugo Mattei and Mauro Bussani.[55] This endeavour is largely based on Schlesinger's method, which Mattei and Bussani have enriched by casting it within the theoretical framework developed by Sacco. Hence, the basic thrust of common-core research is functionalism in a revamped version that brings in a sharper awareness of the multiplicity of factors which must be taken into account so as to provide a reliable analysis of any given law. In my experience, this means that a familiar stick may still be used to chastise some old vices, like the idea that different legal categories are always the signpost for different rules. The proponents of the project insist that the purpose of the exercise is neither to pave the way for law reform, nor to suppress difference, but rather to provide a map of European private law that would

---

[55] See Ugo Mattei and Mauro Bussani, 'The Common Core Approach to European Private Law', (1997–8) 3 Columbia J. Eur. L. 339; Bussani and Mattei, *supra*, note 48. See also Xavier Blanc-Jouvan, 'Reflections on the "Common Core of European Private Law Project"', Global Jurist, Vol. I, No. 2 [www.bepress.com/gj/frontiers/voll1/iss1/art2]. At the time of writing, two volumes in the 'common–core' series have been published: Zimmermann and Whittaker, *supra*, note 39; James R. Gordley (ed.), *The Enforceability of Promises* (Cambridge: Cambridge University Press, 2001).

help private-law lawyers know where they stand.[56] The 'map' metaphor is misleading insofar as it suggests that it is possible to draw a picture unrelated to any point of view.[57] This academic enterprise purports to offer an opportunity for European private-law lawyers to study the limitations of national legal traditions across Europe as they are increasingly exposed by the dynamics of European private-law integration through the action of European Community institutions, such that their task is not reduced to that of codifying the law or commenting upon national and Community legislative initiatives. Beyond this, one of the editors of the project considers the possibility of using the materials collected in the course of the study to press arguments regarding the comparative economic efficiency of legal norms in circumstances where no common features across European laws emerge from the research.[58]

Against this background, one must now explore the other side of functionalism, that is, the relationship between law and society's needs. In this respect, I argue that it is impossible to maintain the thesis that law is the reflection of the spirit of the people or, in contemporary terms, that all law is invariably connected to the constitution of a society and to a society's needs.

Legal transplants, law and society

The idea that law is a product of the living conditions of a people is very old. Bernhard Großfeld finds that Plato hints at it, but there are even more ancient traces of this theme.[59] Considering the intellectual history of modern Europe, it is tempting to list Montesquieu's *De l'esprit des lois* among

[56] See Mattei and Bussani, *supra*, note 55, pp. 340–2. The reproach that common-core research is 'designed to suppress difference' is expressed by George P. Fletcher, 'Comparative Law as a Subversive Subject', (1998) 46 Am. J. Comp. L. 683, p. 694.

[57] Indeed, the very title of the collection of essays edited by Bussani and Mattei, *Making European Law* (*supra*, note 48), implies that the project goes beyond a purely descriptive approach. *Cf.* Ugo Mattei, 'The Issue of European Civil Codification and Legal Scholarship: Biases, Strategies and Perspectives', (1998) 21 Hastings Int. & Comp. L.R. 883, which conveys the impression that common-core research involves policy decisions made only once the researchers' task is over, but where the author also remarks that the question one asks determines the answer one gets.

[58] See *id.*, *supra*, note 57, pp. 898–902. See also *id.*, *Comparative Law and Economics* (Ann Arbor: University of Michigan Press, 1997).

[59] See Bernhard Großfeld, *The Strength and Weakness of Comparative Law*, transl. by Tony Weir (Oxford: Oxford University Press, 1990), p. 75. See also the Greek treatise known under the Latin title *De aeribus aquis locis*, published in the fifth century BC and included as part of the *Corpus Hippocraticum*.

the texts that propagated the same idea on a larger scale, but Montesquieu actually made a rather different point. He argued that the laws *should* be adapted to the people for whom they are made. Thus, Montesquieu claimed that the laws of different countries 'should be adapted in such a manner to the people for whom they are framed, that it is a great chance if those of one nation suit another'.[60] In other words, he intended to build a normative argument, rather than simply to describe what he saw. Sixteenth-century French humanist jurisprudence had already developed a similar view of the relationship between law and society in order to undermine the universal authority of Roman law.[61] Later scholars took for granted what Montesquieu and his French predecessors had intended to demonstrate, that is, the existence of a link between a given people and its laws. The best and most influential nineteenth-century example of this intellectual posture is Savigny's theory of the *Volksgeist*, which enhanced his reputation because it showed how to reconcile the authority of Roman law in Germany with the idea that the law is the expression of national forces and inclinations.[62]

Much twentieth-century comparative scholarship shares in the tradition that considers law to be the product of local conditions and that resists the contrary idea which explains legal change mainly through imitation and borrowing. The categorization of legal systems into legal families probably contributed to the development of this view. Nevertheless, even this classificatory effort could not ignore the diffusion of Roman law across Europe during the Middle Ages. Nor could it ignore that colonization meant the implementation of colonial laws everywhere. As a consequence of this inevitable awareness, twentieth-century comparative law was not entirely blind to the migration of legal systems, though it did not investigate similar topics on a large scale until a few decades ago. Generally speaking, subjects like the circulation of legal models were neglected because the idea that law is the product of local conditions was predominant across the whole

[60] My reference is to Montesquieu, *The Spirit of Laws*, 4th ed. transl. by Thomas Nugent (London: J. Nourse & P. Vaillant, 1766), bk I, ch. 3, p. 7 [1748]. For an unveiling of the complex philosophical background to Montesquieu's work, see Patrick Riley, *The General Will Before Rousseau: The Transformation of the Divine into the Civic* (Princeton: Princeton University Press, 1986), pp. 138–80. I am indebted to Professor Silvia Ferreri for the reading of Montesquieu offered in the text.
[61] See Julian H. Franklin, *Jean Bodin and the Sixteenth Century Revolution in the Methodology of Law and History* (New York: Columbia University Press, 1962), pp. 46–7 [discussing François Hotman].
[62] For example, see James Q. Whitman, *The Legacy of Roman Law in the German Romantic Era* (Princeton: Princeton University Press, 1990), pp. 109–10.

spectrum of social sciences. In legal circles, furthermore, legal positivism and the ongoing nationalization of sources of law seemed to confirm by way of legislative commands the territorial nature of legal orders.[63]

The reversal of fortune for the prevailing approach began when it was noticed that legal systems inspired by opposite political goals shared a good deal of law. In this vein, Schlesinger, for instance, observed that the law of contracts in socialist countries showed several features common to legal systems of the western block.[64] His conclusions undermined the idea that 'what is comparable in this area is relatively unimportant, and what is important is not comparable'.[65] At the same time, Sacco showed the extent to which socialist legal systems were indebted to civilian categories and rules of Romanist origins.[66] He also began working on the general features of the circulation of legal models, which soon became a central theme of his approach to comparative law.[67] He played down the importance of imposition as a motor of diffusion of legal models. Thus, he observed that the generalized application of European models took place in the former colonies only after independence. During the colonial era, European private-law models were applied to European residents only, or governed those legal matters that autochthonous laws did not regulate (such as company law).[68]

In a wider perspective, Sacco argued that one of history's lessons is that prestige is the principal cause of legal change. By 'prestige' is meant that factor – which seems to defy definition – inspiring the desire to acquire tangible or intangible assets deemed to possess superior qualities.[69] Linguistic change by way of imitation and the diffusion of cultural models (such as fashions) are usually explained in terms of prestige. Arguably, legal change on account of imitation is largely dependent on the same factor, at least whenever the variation is not backed by political or economic causes.[70]

---

[63] Of course, the lawyers who cultivated the noble dream of natural law in the era of the *jus commune* would object to these nineteenth- and twentieth-century aberrations.

[64] See Schlesinger, 'Introduction', *supra*, note 28, p. 25.   [65] *Ibid*.

[66] See Rodolfo Sacco, 'The Romanist Substratum in the Civil Law of Socialist Countries', [1988] R. Socialist L., p. 56. The paper had appeared in Italian in 1971.

[67] See *id*., 'La circulation des modèles juridiques: rapport général', in Académie internationale de droit comparé, *Rapports généraux au XIIIe congrès international, Montréal 1990* (Montreal: Blais, 1992), pp. 1–20.

[68] See *id*., *supra*, note 7, p. 148.   [69] *Id*., pp. 148–9.

[70] See Ugo Mattei, 'Efficiency in Legal Transplants: An Essay in Comparative Law and Economics', (1994) 14 Int. R. Law & Econ. 3, who suggests taking into account economic efficiency to explain the diffusion of legal institutions. Of course, it would be simplistic to deny that there is a link between, say, company law and the industrialized economies. The difficult task for

These basic questions, which previous studies on the reception of legal systems had seemingly ignored, moved to the forefront with the publication of Alan Watson's *Legal Transplants* and his subsequent work on the subject.[71] Watson's writings on legal transplants and legal change challenge precisely the view that law is a local phenomenon functionally linked to the living conditions of a given society. Though much law is functional and practical, and facilitates social and economic life, the relationship between law and society cannot always be understood in functional terms.[72] Watson notes that legal borrowings, whether of rules, institutions or doctrines, are extremely common. In fact, such borrowings would account for most legal change in most systems. If borrowings occur, however, it is because the law is not necessarily rooted in local conditions and because it is not always in touch with current needs. The logical consequence is that 'legal rules are not peculiarly devised for the particular society in which they now operate and also that this is not a matter for great concern'.[73] This statement is descriptive rather than normative. The adoption of foreign rules, institutions and doctrines often happens without the benefit of full familiarity with whatever is imported in the receiving country. And, even when the transplanted rule remains unchanged, its impact in the new social setting may be altogether different.[74]

Watson acknowledges that the source which generated the original rule, institution or doctrine does not control the outcome of the process of transplantation or diffusion. The donee, not the donor, has the last word

---

comparatists – and for law-and-economics scholars – is, however, to explain legal change serving no apparent economic need.

[71] See Alan Watson, *Legal Transplants*, 2d ed. (Athens, Georgia: University of Georgia Press, 1993) [hereinafter *Legal Transplants*]. The first edition appeared in 1974. Among Watson's many titles bearing on the topic discussed in the text, see *id.*, *Society and Legal Change* (Edinburgh: Scottish Academic Press, 1977); *id.*, 'Comparative Law and Legal Change', [1978] Cambridge L.J. 313. For an analytical survey of Watson's work, see William Ewald, 'Comparative Jurisprudence (II): The Logic of Legal Transplants', (1995) 43 Am. J. Comp. L. 498. Beyond Watson, the secondary literature is too voluminous to allow for citation since the study of 'legal transplants' has become a central 'paradigm' within contemporary comparative law – the word is used by Ugo Mattei, 'Why the Wind Changed: Intellectual Leadership in Western Law', (1994) 42 Am. J. Comp. L. 195, p. 197. Recent contributions to the debate include David Nelken and Johannes Feest (eds.), *Adapting Legal Cultures* (Oxford: Hart, 2001); Elisabetta Grande, *Imitazione e diritto: ipotesi sulla circolazione dei modelli* (Turin: Giappichelli, 2001); Gianmaria Ajani, 'By Chance and Prestige: Legal Transplants in Russia and Eastern Europe', (1995) 43 Am. J. Comp. L. 93.

[72] See Alan Watson, 'Legal Change: Sources of Law and Legal Culture', (1983) 131 U. Pennsylvania L.R. 1121.

[73] Watson, *Legal Transplants*, *supra*, note 71, p. 96.   [74] *Id.*, p. 116.

on the uses of the imported law. This remark clearly involves a paradox, duly noted first by Pierre Legrand.[75] If the donee controls the outcome of the process triggered by the transplant, how can one claim that foreign models are actually at work in the local ambience? This paradox highlights, once more, the central problem that any theory of legal interpretation must face. The interesting side of Watson's contribution, however, lies precisely in the deconstruction of the very concept of 'legal source' which results from his historical and comparative investigation. The outcome of the process is conveniently summarized by Watson himself:

> Law is power. Law is politics. Law is politics in the sense that persons who have the political power determine which persons or bodies create the law, how the validity of the law is assessed, and how the legal order is to operate. But one cannot simply deduce from that, as is frequently assumed, that it is the holders of political power who determine what the rules are and what the sources of law are to be.[76]

In most fields of law, therefore, and especially within private law, political rulers need not express an interest in determining what some rules are or should be. If the government is silent on a certain point, some other group will speak. The activity of jurists in ancient Rome, of law professors in Continental Europe or of English judges points to the role of legal elites in shaping the law. In Watson's account, the discourses of legal elites are largely self-referential. Members of a professional group, such as lawyers, treat the law as belonging to their professional culture. Through it, they distance themselves from other groups. Among lawyers, reputation establishes authority. Reputation, in turn, depends on argument and invention according to the rules of legal debates, although those rules are implicitly established by participants in the game themselves. This is why lawyers claim to be solving problems by using a legal logic peculiar to their profession. Of course, lawyers are involved in political decisions. Nevertheless, their intellectual outlook does not necessarily depend on their political orientation.

---

[75] See Pierre Legrand, 'The Impossibility of "Legal Transplants"', (1997) 4 Maastricht J. Eur. & Comp. L. 111, pp. 116–20. I agree with Legrand that each culture is the product of a unique historical experience and imagination. Nevertheless, collective identities are established through interaction with others and no culture can claim to be wholly original. See generally Claude Lévi-Strauss, *Race et histoire* (Paris: Albin Michel, 2001), pp. 103–12 [1952]. For a contemporary exploration of this theme, see Ulf Hannerz, *Cultural Complexity: Studies in the Sociological Organization of Meaning* (New York: Columbia University Press, 1993).

[76] Alan Watson, *Roman Law and Comparative Law* (Athens, Georgia: University of Georgia Press, 1991), p. 97.

Needless to say, Watson's arguments have provoked strong reactions from scholars who insist on functional explanations of the law, like Richard Abel and Lawrence Friedman.[77] What is striking about this criticism, however, is how it fails to identify the intellectual roots of Watson's thesis and misses the opportunity to assess it in the light of its proper background.

The first underpinning of Watson's argument that law may be dysfunctional in relation to society lies in the notion of 'survivals'. This idea was a key concept of nineteenth-century and early twentieth-century evolutionary anthropology. It emerges from the work of E. B. Tylor, the Oxford father of anthropology, who, in 1871, published his two-volume study on *Primitive Culture*. It is interesting to note that Radcliffe-Brown, the towering figure of twentieth-century British social anthropology, broke with the previous evolutionary tradition represented by his mentor Rivers precisely over the latter's understanding of the concept of 'survivals'.[78] Rivers had said of a survival like 'custom' that its nature could not be explained 'by its present utility but only [...] through its past history'. His pupil replied that calling a custom 'useless' depended on a prior conception of the 'fundamental purpose or end of society' and that any hypothesis concerning survivals 'must depend on some hypothesis as to the function that such a custom fulfils (or on the nature of the necessary connections between such customs and the other institutions of the society)'.[79] Tylor's influential treatment of survivals inspired Oliver Wendell Holmes's analysis of the permanence of legal rules and institutions after the sunset of beliefs, necessities or customs having generated them – a leitmotiv of Holmes's masterpiece, *The Common Law*.[80] From a functional point of view, however, it was not enough to refer to that mental disposition called 'conservatism' in order to understand survivals. Conservatism itself needed explaining and that explanation, so as to be objective, had to be functional.[81]

---

[77] For example, see Richard Abel, 'Law as Lag: Inertia as a Social Theory of Law', (1982) 80 Michigan L.R. 785; Lawrence Friedman, 'Book Review', (1979) 6 Brit. J. L. & Society 127.

[78] See George W. Stocking, 'Radcliffe-Brown and British Social Anthropology', in *id.* (ed.), *Functionalism Historicized* (Madison: University of Wisconsin Press, 1984), pp. 131–91.

[79] The quotations come from *id.*, pp. 151–2.

[80] See Oliver Wendell Holmes, *The Common Law*, ed. by Sheldon M. Novick (New York: Dover, 1991), pp. 5 and 35 [1881]. See generally John W. Burrow, 'Holmes in His Intellectual Milieu', in Robert W. Gordon (ed.), *The Legacy of Oliver Wendell Holmes, Jr.* (Stanford: Stanford University Press, 1992), pp. 17–26.

[81] The subsequent history of anthropological thought is very instructive in this regard. For example, see Alan Barnard, *History and Theory in Anthropology* (Cambridge: Cambridge University Press, 2000), pp. 158–77; Adam Kuper, *Culture: The Anthropologists' Account* (Cambridge, Mass.: Harvard University Press, 1999).

This remark leads us to consider the second aspect of Watson's thesis, that is, the attempt to explain why the law is quite often borrowed rather than produced by (or within) a given society. If we leave aside outright imposition, Watson's answer is, basically, that much in the law depends on its 'internal logic' and that this 'logic' is very much that of an elite distancing itself from the rest of society and asserting its role as law-maker. In the creation of their product, lawyers enjoy great freedom and legal transplants occur thanks to that freedom.

Once more, it is surprising that the critics engaged in the refutation of Watson's argument have failed to grasp the functional character of his explanation as to why lawyers spend so much of their energies playing self-referential games. Watson's point is that lawyers' activities that apparently do not satisfy *any practical need* establish their identity as an elite. The result of lawyers' discussions may be arbitrary or may respond to specific power pressures, demands or desires. But even when the outcome of the process is arbitrary, it can still be explained functionally.

Thus far, I have discussed criticism levelled at Watson's argument mainly on the basis of different methodological perspectives. It is fair to acknowledge, however, that the criticism Watson has encountered has come mainly from scholars on the left. They have objected that the thesis that law may be dysfunctional in relation to current social needs 'trivializes the political' and intends to 'confute radicals, notably Marx and later Marxists, who maintain that historical trends do exist and should be used to further progressive causes'.[82] Though functionalism in the United States and elsewhere has often played a progressive role, it is far from clear whether that role is necessarily linked to the variety of functionalism defended by Watson's critics. Watson's analysis of legal transplants and of the function of legal elites in the law-making process could well justify a democratic revolt against lawyers.[83] Indeed, other scholars who have explored the relationship between law and society have not been as critical of Watson's work. For example, Gunther

---

[82] Abel, *supra*, note 77, p. 803.
[83] Conventional criticisms of law's autonomy (as analysed by Watson) are 'misconceived and politically naive' according to P. G. Monateri, ' "Everybody's Talking": The Future of Comparative Law', (1998) 21 Hastings Int. & Comp. L.R. 825, p. 840. See also Tushnet, *supra*, note 8, pp. 1285–1301. But Watson's approach could be considered biased inasmuch as he does not explore the dynamics of legal systems where the role of jurists is not as prominent as it is in the west. For a comparison of western and non-western experiences (and on the law-and-development movement in general), see Masaji Chiba, *Legal Pluralism: Toward a General Theory Through Japanese Legal Culture* (Tokyo: Tokai University Press, 1989).

Teubner shows appreciation for many of Watson's arguments, though he also insists on the differentiation and the fragmentation of the national legal system produced by globalizing processes and the decline of the nation state.[84]

Conclusion

Today, both familiar versions of functionalism are coming under attack. This is happening not because they have failed, but because they have both been very successful. Functionalism promised to cut across municipal legal categories, to separate rules from their linguistic husk or their contextual justifications. That promise has largely been fulfilled. Functionalism also promised to cast light on the relationship between law and society. Several topics have, in fact, been investigated from this perspective. The results of sophisticated functional investigations have widened our comparative knowledge and have become part of mainstream legal thinking.

It fits our age, of course, to blame functionalism for its success, just as the nineteenth century blamed interest-based theories of political action, because they had successfully replaced political discourse founded on concepts like 'glory' or 'honour'.[85] The functional method has been charged with stripping the law of all that is interesting. This criticism opposes functionalism, because it favours causal explanation over interpretive understanding. Causal explanations of the effects of other people's actions need not cast light on their thoughts. It is possible to explain why a car being driven at high speed in the rain skidded off the road without knowing what reasons (if any!) the driver had to go too fast. Yet, by investigating in meaningful ways the thoughts and motivations of human agents, we surely get a fuller picture of the world. After all, to ask whether a road accident was caused by reckless passion for racing or by the driver's desire to get back home yields meaningful answers for some purposes.

The theory of legal formants and cryptotypes developed by Rodolfo Sacco is both an alternative and a supplement to the functional approach adopted nowadays by a number of comparatists. This theoretical framework helps us

---

[84] See Gunther Teubner, 'Legal Irritants: Good Faith in British Law or How Unifying Law Ends Up in New Divergences', (1998) 61 Modern L.R. 11. Teubner objects to the flat alternative between rejection or integration of foreign elements.

[85] *Cf.* Albert O. Hirschman, *The Passion and the Interests: Political Arguments for Capitalism Before Its Triumph* (Princeton: Princeton University Press, 1997).

to formulate a realistic account of what we compare. It casts light on the role of definitions, taxonomies and the operative rules of law. It further shows how all these elements are approached through implicit assumptions and illustrates the pervasive influence of this implicit dimension of the law on the way in which the legal system's explicit commitments are implemented, modified or stultified by lay persons and lawyers alike.

The catchword 'culture' has been recently used to express dissatisfaction with functional comparisons. Both Sacco's and Alan Watson's contributions show why we should resist the temptation to consider 'culture' as a monolith rather than as an adaptive and porous multilayered compound, where actors having different stakes in the game are at work.[86] From a functional perspective, however, it still makes sense to ask how much law can go into brackets without losing too much 'culture'. The question is obviously relevant for law-reform purposes, whether legal change is being promoted by comparatists or being advanced by other actors, as happens more and more frequently in today's Europe. Consider, for example, the borderland between 'contract' and 'tort' as defined by national litigation concerning limitation periods. This litigation enjoys a venerable record in each European country; it is certainly part of our cultural heritage. Nevertheless, it is worth asking whether European litigants would not be better off if a common European stance on the issue could emerge, based on intelligible policy considerations.[87] English, French and German lawyers, be they comparatists or not, will remain prisoners of their past (that is, of their culture!), ugly as it is, until they discuss similar issues in the broader perspective provided by functional comparative studies. Of course, as similar questions are raised, the road to legal change is open. If change takes place, there will be winners and losers. The promise of functionalism, however, is not to suppress conflict over change, but to make the process of change more transparent. Possibly, this would also render arguments for and against change more accessible.

---

[86] Sacco's and Watson's treatment of legal change have much in common in that they both reject a positivistic analysis of what counts as a 'legal source'. Nevertheless, the former is more indebted to the theoretical insights of linguistics and anthropology, while the latter draws on legal history and Roman law.

[87] The case-law of the European Court of Justice in areas close to the heart of private law, like judicial jurisdiction, shows the contemporary importance of this approach in Europe. For some of the challenges that the development of European private law poses today, see Antonio Gambaro, '*Iura et leges* nel processo di edificazione di un diritto privato europeo', Europa e diritto privato, 1998, p. 993.

In any case, law-reform projects and their redistributive effects are not the end of the story. In the course of the twentieth century, functionalism emerged as a mode of inquiry and that approach has represented a powerful intellectual challenge to other perspectives. To what extent is functionalism now being challenged or replaced by other methodological insights? Explanation and interpretation are alternative, but complementary, ways to the study of legal phenomena. Though interpretation takes into consideration phenomena that are unique, inasmuch as they are experienced by those who live them, the functionalist's insistence on selecting 'facts' to develop comparisons highlights the theoretical problems involved in interpretive comparative analysis. The bargaining process taking place among participants in multilateral comparative projects to establish what constitutes a 'fact' for comparative purposes is an instructive example of the many ways there are to understand what we share and what is unique to each of us. Such bargaining happens because cultural expressions are largely undetermined by the external world, hence the limits of functionalism. This experience, however, also shows that comparative research is one of the best cures for the analytical poverty of naive functionalism.

Comparative legal studies and its boundaries

6

Comparatists and sociology

ROGER COTTERRELL

I

The relationship between comparative law and sociology has been paradoxical for at least a century. Since the inauguration of modern comparative law as a distinctive field of scholarly practice, conventionally traced to the 1900 Paris Congress, the closeness and necessity of this relationship has been frequently asserted by comparatists. Comparative law and sociology of law have often been said by comparatists to be inseparable. Sometimes, as regards an important part of its activity or aspirations, comparative law has been claimed to be a type of sociology of law or even identical with sociology of law. Yet, the nature of this relationship has rarely been examined in detail. In general, the need to explore it rigorously has been avoided by both comparatists and legal sociologists.

In some ways, this avoidance is understandable. Few scholars claim detailed knowledge of the whole range of the literature of both comparative law and sociology. Few are likely to have sufficient interest in both fields to motivate such an inquiry. And the orientations of comparatists and legal sociologists are often significantly different. The theoretical and empirical concerns of legal sociology go beyond those that interest most comparatists. Comparatists do not necessarily share sociology's ambitions to explain theoretically social change or social stability or to characterize the nature of social life using abstract concepts such as 'structure' or 'system'. They often prefer specific, seemingly far more practical, inquiries closely related to the detail of legal practice and legal doctrine in particular systems. Whereas legal sociology ultimately must put no limits on the range and diversity of legal experience from which it tries to gather empirical material to support its efforts at generalization and theoretical analysis, comparatists tend to distrust broad social or legal theory that might purport to offer matrices for the widest legal and social comparisons. Even comparatists strongly sympathetic to sociology and who see comparative law as itself a social science tend to urge caution, stressing the limits of objectivity in social research and the danger of mistaking ideology for theory.[1]

For the legal sociologist, comparative law should provide an indispensable resource of detail about doctrinal and institutional characteristics of legal systems. But the categories of comparison that comparatists have typically used — for example, those of legal styles or 'families' of law — may seem unhelpful to legal sociologists. Some even dismiss these categories as reflecting 'mandarin' preoccupations with lawyers' professional traditions or outlook and having no clear relation to law as experienced in its effects in social life beyond the courtroom or lawyer's office.[2] Legal sociologists question what and why comparatists compare and how far comparisons of legal doctrine or institutions in isolation from *systematic* study of their social contexts can yield useful knowledge.[3]

If these differences of outlook are easy to identify, why has the link between comparative law and sociology, especially legal sociology, been so strongly affirmed by many comparatists, at the same time as they have usually avoided exploring it in depth? The main reason, I think, lies in enduring uncertainties about the nature of comparative law as a research enterprise. An attraction for some comparatists has been to claim for comparative law a special status as social science, distancing it from other legal studies seen as having less fundamental 'scientific' concerns. More crucial, however, is the attraction of assuming that comparative law can presuppose or ally itself with certain sociological understandings about the nature of social inquiry (including inquiry about law as a social phenomenon) and so avoid being enmeshed in broad epistemological and ontological questions.

Epistemological questions here relate to the *purposes* of comparing social phenomena. What kind of knowledge does comparison give? What makes this knowledge valid? Ontological questions relate to what is to be compared, what can be treated as comparable *entities* or appropriate empirical foci of research. In comparative law, foci of comparison might be, for

---

[1] For example, see Konrad Zweigert, 'Quelques réflexions sur les relations entre la sociologie juridique et le droit comparé', in *Aspects nouveaux de la pensée juridique: recueil d'études en hommage à Marc Ancel* (Paris: Pedone, 1975), pp. 83–4.

[2] See Lawrence M. Friedman, 'The Concept of Legal Culture: A Reply', in David Nelken (ed.), *Comparing Legal Cultures* (Aldershot: Dartmouth, 1997), pp. 33–9.

[3] For example, see Jean Carbonnier, 'L'apport du droit comparé à la sociologie juridique', in *Livre du centenaire de la Société de législation comparée* (Paris: L.G.D.J., 1969), pp. 75–87; Richard L. Abel, 'Comparative Law and Social Theory', (1978) 26 Am. J. Comp. L. 219.

example, legal rules or institutions; or legal styles, traditions or cultures; or social problems (such as 'crime' or 'industrial conflict') addressed by law; or social institutions (for example, 'the family', 'inheritance' or 'the business enterprise') regulated legally.

Sociology has developed concepts that have been useful to comparatists at various times in dealing with these epistemological and ontological problems of comparative law. They have been useful because their provenance from, or association with, social science has meant that comparatists have not themselves felt the need to engage in social theoretical inquiries to validate these concepts. Probably, the concept most widely appealed to in this way has been that of 'function'. It has often been argued that rules or institutions should be compared in terms of their objectively identifiable functions – the contribution they make to wider social processes or the specific, differentiated 'task' that they can be seen to be fulfilling in society – for example, regulating specific aspects of domestic relations, commerce or property regimes. Max Rheinstein, writing in 1938, saw comparative law as focused on functional comparison of legal rules and the 'social function of law in general'. 'In this sense', he suggested, 'comparative law is synonymous with sociology of law'.[4] Legal sociology hardly existed as a distinct field of sociological inquiry at the time Rheinstein wrote (though the idea of functional analysis of law was well established in sociology, mainly through the influence of Emile Durkheim's work).[5] So, it was easy to claim, as many earlier writers had done, that comparative law encompassed sociology of law in some sense. Part of comparative law's legitimacy was thus as a division of social science, its distinctiveness given by its specifically legal focus.

Comparative law has appealed, at various times over the past century, to ideas of 'function',[6] legal and social 'evolution'[7] and 'social

---

[4] Max Rheinstein, 'Teaching Comparative Law', (1938) 5 U. Chicago L.R. 617, pp. 619 and 622. Rheinstein actively promoted early legal sociology. He directed the English translation of Max Weber's writings on law and wrote extensively about the work of Weber, Eugen Ehrlich, Nicholas Timasheff, Georges Gurvitch and other legal sociologists. See generally *id.*, *Collected Works*, vol. I (Tübingen: J. C. B. Mohr, 1979), pp. 151–70; *id.* (ed.), *Max Weber on Law in Economy and Society* (Cambridge, Mass.: Harvard University Press, 1954).
[5] See Emile Durkheim, *The Division of Labour in Society*, transl. by W. D. Halls (London: Macmillan, 1984)[1893]; *id.*, *The Rules of Sociological Method and Selected Texts on Sociology and its Method*, transl. by W. D. Halls (London: Macmillan, 1982)[1895] (hereinafter *Rules*).
[6] For example, see Konrad Zweigert and Hein Kötz, *An Introduction to Comparative Law*, 3d ed. transl. by Tony Weir (Oxford: Oxford University Press, 1998), pp. 34–6 and 62; Vivian G. Curran, 'Cultural Immersion, Difference and Categories in US Comparative Law', (1998) 46 Am. J. Comp. L. 43, pp. 67–8.
[7] See Jerome Hall, *Comparative Law and Social Theory* (Baton Rouge: Louisiana State University Press, 1963), pp. 16–17. See also H. C. Gutteridge, *Comparative Law*, 2d ed. (Cambridge:

facts'.[8] It has referred to social institutions, interests, needs or problems as ideas borrowed from social science or assumed to be validated by sociological discourse. It has done this often to identify what could legitimately be compared and to specify scientific purposes of comparison.[9] However, this strategy always had an unsatisfactory aspect. To make part of the foundations of comparative law dependent on reference (even if only implicitly or in the most general terms) to a different discipline offers many hostages to fortune. Perhaps partly for this reason, many comparatists have strongly stressed purposes of comparison having no particular link to sociological inquiries. Often, they have defined the projects of comparative law in ways that require no reference to social science. Sometimes, they have declared sociological perspectives (as contrasted with historical or philosophical ones) largely unnecessary to comparative law's main concerns.[10]

These considerations, I think, map the ambivalence of comparatists' views of sociology and, specifically, of sociology of law. In the following sections of this paper, I shall try to explore this ambivalence in more detail, suggesting that, in some measure, difficulties in the relations of legal sociology and comparative law arise from difficulties in conceptualizing the scope of each of these enterprises and from changes over time in the way each of them has been understood. My argument, ultimately, is that comparative law and legal sociology are interdependent and, while each of these research enterprises has a wide variety of appropriate aims, their central, most general and most ambitious scientific projects – to understand law in its development and its variety as an aspect of social life – are identical.

II

The literature of comparative law suggests an immense range of possible justifications for the enterprise. Comparison of law might be pursued: (i) to find ideas useful in improving or clarifying one's own legal system;[11] (ii) to

---

Cambridge University Press, 1949), p. 73, stressing the importance of the 'stage of development' (not mere chronology) as a basis for comparison.

[8] See Pierre Lepaulle, 'The Function of Comparative Law', (1921–2) 35 Harvard L.R. 838. Lepaulle's paper, partly a critique of Pound's sociological jurisprudence, shows the strong influence of Durkheimian sociology.

[9] Cf. Zweigert and Kötz, supra, note 6, pp. 10–11.

[10] See Alan Watson, Legal Transplants, 2d ed. (Athens, Georgia: University of Georgia Press, 1993); William Ewald, 'Comparative Jurisprudence (II): The Logic of Legal Transplants', (1995) 43 Am. J. Comp. L. 489.

[11] See Watson, supra, note 10, p. 17; René David and John E. C. Brierley, Major Legal Systems in the World Today, 3d ed. (London: Stevens, 1985), pp. 6–7; Zweigert and Kötz, supra, note 6,

aid detailed communication between lawyers of different systems,[12] for example, in interpreting a uniquely common-law institution such as the trust in civil-law contexts; (iii) to explain legal development in particular systems by tracing lines of legal borrowing and influence;[13] (iv) to harmonize or unify areas of law on a transnational basis to promote trade or economic activity across borders or for other reasons;[14] (v) to provide legal solutions to causes of international conflicts and so promote international understanding;[15] (vi) to give law students and legal scholars a more distanced view of their own system,[16] challenging the sense of naturalness and inevitability of its particular legal arrangements[17] and promoting appreciation of 'difference';[18] (vii) to understand the power of legal cultures,[19] for example, as barriers to harmonization of law; (viii) to find a 'common trunk' of legal ideas to express 'the awakening of an international legal consciousness';[20] or (ix) to contribute toward knowledge of the social world through study of its legal aspects.[21]

Other professed aims of comparative law are found in the literature but their diversity is sufficiently illustrated above. They might be arranged on a scale extending from intensely practical concerns with solving specific and immediate legal problems, for example, in current case-law,[22] to the most abstract ideal of contributing to broad theoretical knowledge of the social world. It is important to note that sociology has also exhibited a somewhat similar range. It has included, at least in the British context, what Philip Abrams terms a 'policy-science conception', which sees sociology as concerned to provide practical knowledge for rational social planning, and a 'socio-technics conception', treating sociologists as technical assistants to policy-makers or negotiators with them, providing 'basic information, analytic data, advice on data-gathering, technical problem-solving,

pp. 18–19; Basil Markesinis, 'Comparative Law – A Subject in Search of an Audience', (1990) 53 Modern L.R. 1.
[12] See Abel, *supra*, note 3, p. 220.   [13] See Watson, *supra*, note 10.
[14] For example, see M. J. Bonell, 'The UNIDROIT Principles of International Commercial Contracts', in Roger Cotterrell (ed.), *Process and Substance: Butterworth Lectures on Comparative Law 1994* (London: Butterworths, 1995), p. 46.
[15] See Lepaulle, *supra*, note 8, p. 855; David and Brierley, *supra*, note 11, p. 8.
[16] See Zweigert and Kötz, *supra*, note 6, p. 21.
[17] See Lepaulle, *supra*, note 8, p. 858; Gutteridge, *supra*, note 7, pp. 19–20.
[18] See Pierre Legrand, *Fragments on Law-as-Culture* (Deventer: W. E. J. Tjeenk Willink, 1999), pp. 10–11 and 134; Curran, *supra*, note 6, p. 44.
[19] See Legrand, *supra*, note 18, pp. 73–4, 134 and *passim*.
[20] See Edouard Lambert, 'Comparative Law', in *Encyclopedia of the Social Sciences*, ed. by Edwin R. A. Seligman, vol. IV (New York: Macmillan, 1931), p. 127.
[21] See Hall, *supra*, note 7, *passim*.   [22] For example, see Markesinis, *supra*, note 11.

identification of technically best courses of action or evaluation of the effectiveness of policy after the event'. But sociology, according to Abrams, has also been understood in terms of three other conceptions: 'clarification' (reformulating problems by elucidating assumptions, dispelling illusions or unmasking myths), 'advocacy' (linking good evidence to good causes as a matter of political persuasion) and 'education' (providing gradual enlightenment about the nature of the social world unconnected directly to immediate policy, advocacy or short-term problem-solving).[23]

It is not difficult to link each of these conceptions to corresponding conceptions of the aims of comparative law. The parallels reinforce the point that, from a certain perspective, comparative legal scholarship and sociology can be seen as engaged in very similar multifaceted enterprises of ordering and making sense of the social world, understanding its normative regulation, and evaluating and comparing the different ways in which different societies have organized that regulation.

Probably, this closeness was never more apparent than at the time of the 1900 Paris Congress. It has been said that 'the principal emphasis in the meeting was on comparative law viewed as a social science, even then called the sociology of law' and 'what bulks large [...] is the enormous influence of nineteenth-century sociology on the Continental scholars'.[24] In the turn-of-the-century mood of optimism and belief in scientific progress, comparative law, like sociology, presented itself in its most ambitious forms. Both fields, in their furthest extension, appeared to embrace the same overarching intellectual project, differences of emphasis being given only by a degree of specialization.

The great comparatist Edouard Lambert, writing in an intellectual climate in France strongly shaped by Durkheim's sociological ideas, recognized comparative legal history as one of three divisions of the broad enterprise of comparative legal studies.[25] He described it in a way entirely consistent with Durkheim's understanding of it as a major branch of sociology.[26] Comparative legal history, according to Lambert, aims to

---

[23] Philip Abrams, 'The Uses of British Sociology 1831–1981', in Martin Bulmer (ed.), *Essays on the History of British Sociological Research* (Cambridge: Cambridge University Press, 1985), pp. 183–5.

[24] Hall, *supra*, note 7, pp. 17–18.

[25] Edouard Lambert, *La fonction du droit civil comparé* (Paris: Giard & Brière, 1903), pp. 913–16; id., *supra*, note 20.

[26] See Roger Cotterrell, *Emile Durkheim: Law in a Moral Domain* (Edinburgh: Edinburgh University Press, 1999), pp. 7–8. Durkheim, in a review of Lambert's *La fonction du droit civil comparé*,

create 'a universal history of law' so as to reveal 'the rhythms or natural laws of the succession of social phenomena, which direct the evolution of legal institutions'. Its practitioners had been 'up to the present principally interested in the reconstitution of the most obscure phases of the legal history of human societies'[27] and Lambert criticized the speculative nature of their work,[28] often compromised by naive assumptions about legal and social evolution. He wished to direct comparative law as a juristic enterprise away from these seemingly arcane sociological inquiries about the genesis of law.

Nevertheless, the project of comparative legal history was one to which many of Durkheim's closest collaborators – including Lambert's brilliant young colleague in the Lyon law faculty, the Romanist Paul Huvelin[29] – devoted themselves, combining the study of legal texts with ethnographic, literary and historical materials.[30] Durkheimian sociologists made much use of jurists' comparative studies. Potentially, at least, links at this time between comparatists and sociologists were intimate, even if comparatists might often regard sociologists' inquiries as impractical, ill-informed and too speculative, and sociologists might see comparatists' work as unsystematic, atheoretical and intellectually narrow. Certainly, for the Durkheimians, it was immaterial whether researchers called themselves jurists or sociologists if their work was sociological in orientation.

The early links between comparative law and sociological inquiry at this most ambitious level find faint echoes in the rich texture and broad sweep of some later comparatists' writings. But presenting comparative legal analysis

---

supra, note 25, even treats comparative legal history as synonymous with legal sociology. See Emile Durkheim, *Textes*, vol. III (Paris: Editions de Minuit, 1975), p. 266 [1904]. Lambert, correspondingly, cites Durkheim's *L'Année sociologique* as a primary locus of comparative legal scholarship of this kind. See *supra*, note 20.

[27] Lambert, *supra*, note 20, p. 127.

[28] *Id.*, *supra*, note 25, pp. 886–91. But he also carefully noted sociology's great promise for legal studies. See *id.*, p. 891. See also Christophe Jamin, 'Le vieux rêve de Saleilles et Lambert revisité: à propos du centenaire du Congrès international de droit comparé de Paris', Rev. int. dr. comp., 2000, p. 733.

[29] See Paul Huvelin, 'Magie et droit individuel', (1907) 10 Année sociologique 1; *id.*, *Etudes d'histoire du droit commercial romain* (Paris: Sirey, 1929). Lambert often cites Huvelin's writings on early Roman law approvingly in his *La fonction du droit civil comparé*, *supra*, note 25 (for example, see pp. 644 and 646). The Lyon law faculty also included another key member of Durkheim's sociological group, Emmanuel Lévy, whose work Lambert admired and actively promoted. See Edouard Lambert, 'Préface', in Emmanuel Lévy, *La vision socialiste du droit* (Paris: Giard, 1926), pp. v–xvi.

[30] See Cotterrell, *supra*, note 26, pp. 82–99 and 119–47.

in a contextual matrix embracing entire cultures is a task suited only to those few who can command with assurance the vast range of historical and sociological reference required.[31] Today, the great classics of sociology – the writings of Max Weber, Durkheim and a few of his followers, for example – are still read for this range and for the insight and panache with which they embrace it. But comprehensive comparison of laws, societies or cultures to create panoramic systems of social or legal knowledge has largely ceased to be an objective in either sociology or comparative law. A much more modest stress on comparative law as 'method', distancing itself from broad substantive aims and focusing on multifaceted technical utility, corresponds to some extent with Abrams's 'socio-technics conception' in sociology. Yet, objectives of comparative law are still often proclaimed in terms related to Abrams's sociological conception of enlightenment through education. Comparative law and sociology have largely put to one side the broadest ambitions that might have allied them as parts of a project of interpreting history and social variation in the elaborate, asymmetrical patterns of its evolution. But it would be regrettable if these ambitions were discarded entirely.

There has been only one attempt in Anglo-American literature in relatively recent times to re-open a sustained argument for a general union of comparative law and legal sociology. Jerome Hall's *Comparative Law and Social Theory*, published in 1963, tries to recover the old project of an integrated social science in which comparative law would play a major part. But Hall insists that comparative law is an entirely different enterprise from what he sees as the scientific theory-building of much modern sociology, its methods of observation and data collection modelled partly on those of the natural sciences. Comparative law, like all interpretive legal study, must, in Hall's view, understand and give full account of the values, ideals and ideas of law. A social science modelled on natural science cannot do this. Again, as 'a composite of social knowledge of law',[32] comparative law must study not just positive legal rules but also official action and styles of analysis of legal problems, as well as social practices that relate to law and give it meaning in citizens' experience. As a lawyer, Hall clearly wants to insist that all such matters must be understood interpretively from a Hartian internal aspect and in terms of values, as well as through observation of law as a

---

[31] *Cf.* Curran, *supra*, note 6, pp. 52–4, noting a narrowing of vision over time in US comparative law.
[32] Hall, *supra*, note 7, p. 33.

social phenomenon. For this reason, comparative law could be part only of a *humanistic* legal sociology that stresses interpretive, evaluative aspects of law. It 'could never be reduced to a sociology comprised only of descriptive causal generalizations. For comparative law holds fast to the distinctiveness, autonomy and value of legal ideas.'[33]

In hindsight, the responses Hall's book attracted are as interesting as the work itself. Some reviews were friendly, if bland, but several were very hostile. Hall was criticized for failing to recognize the range of comparatists' aims, or the scope and variety of their work, and for focusing only on 'one possible objective of comparative law scholarship, its potential contribution to social theory'.[34] He was asking the impossible, that comparatists should understand the evolution of the social sciences as well as all developments in their own field.[35] One critic agreed that comparative legal studies should help toward understanding societies but insisted that most comparatists were already engaged in this task.[36] From the sociologists' side, a leading scholar wrote: 'Whatever the opposite of breaking new ground is, Jerome Hall has done it in this book.'[37] He had failed to see the range of work being done in legal sociology. More good research and a comprehensive theoretical framework were needed but the book gave 'reasons for doubting the possibility of either' and the reasons were unconvincing.[38] Some reviews found the book deeply perplexing, with key arguments very hard to understand.[39] Richard Wasserstrom identified what he saw as a basic confusion. For Hall, the natural-science model was inappropriate in studying legal systems because account had to be taken of human purposes, ideals and reasons. But, Wasserstrom noted, it is entirely possible to make general, non-normative scientific statements about, for example, people's ideals.[40] These matters, treated as recordable attitudes or preferences, are not outside the scope of a scientific legal sociology.

---

[33] *Id.*, p. 67.
[34] See Arthur T. von Mehren, 'Book Review', (1965–6) 16 U. Toronto L.J. 187, p. 188. See also John N. Hazard, 'Book Review' (1963–4) 39 Indiana L.J. 411; Rudolf B. Schlesinger, 'Book Review', (1964–5) 50 Cornell L.Q. 570.
[35] See W. J. Wagner, 'Book Review', (1964) 64 Columbia L.R. 985.
[36] Hazard, *supra*, note 34.
[37] Richard D. Schwartz, 'Book Review', (1965) 30 Am. Sociological R. 290, p. 290.
[38] *Id.*, p. 291.
[39] For example, see Wagner, *supra*, note 35; Richard Wasserstrom, 'Book Review', (1964) 17 J. Leg. Educ. 105.
[40] Wasserstrom, *supra*, note 39, p. 109.

Such reactions show that sociology and comparative law had travelled far apart by the 1960s. Their agendas were complex and it was easy to criticize Hall for simplifying or distorting them. In contrast to earlier proclamations, from both comparatists and sociologists, of the closeness or interdependence of the two fields, it seemed misguided to propose any general connection between them. Links could only be for specific purposes and projects. But Hall was right to criticize the limitations of sociology's dominant orientations (functionalism, positivism and scientism) at the time he wrote. Wasserstrom's critique missed the point in claiming that social science could treat values and motivations as data. Hall's book demands exactly the reverse: that social science must appreciate the 'internal', interpretive aspects of law, not just reduce them to measurable data.

Hall calls for a non-positivist project of social science in which comparative law could have a recognized, secure and valuable place. But he wrote before the so-called 'interpretive turn' in legal theory and social research, and so lacked the means to clarify his project sufficiently. There is, indeed, much to be said for the aim of integrating some projects of comparative law and sociology. Given developments in both legal theory and social science, this is far more feasible than at the time Hall wrote. It presumes that there need ultimately be no radical opposition between comparatists' and legal sociologists' perspectives despite the great diversity of objectives of research in their fields; that lawyers' comparative perspectives on legal experience can be informed by broader sociological perspectives; and that sociological perspectives on law must ultimately embrace, interpret, preserve, interact with and contextualize the diverse, varied perspectives of lawyers as legal participants and legal observers. The result should not be a resurrection of sociological jurisprudence (legal practice coloured by social-scientific rhetoric) but a heightened awareness of relationships between the innumerable forms of practical participation in, and observation of, law.

These claims become clearer in their implications if the terms 'sociology' and 'legal sociology', as used in this context, are themselves clarified. One reason why Hall's project of integrative social science embracing comparative law attracted fierce criticism was surely its implication that comparatists must master some other (social science) discipline beyond legal studies or else see their work as subservient to it. In an earlier era, a main reason why jurists were suspicious of the kind of sociology Durkheim proposed and of the enthusiasm with which he and his colleagues advocated cooperation between jurists and sociologists was that sociology as a discipline appeared shamelessly imperialistic.[41] 'My aim', Durkheim wrote, 'has been precisely to introduce [...] [the sociological] idea into those disciplines [such as legal studies] from which it was absent and thereby to make them branches of sociology'.[42]

Such an idea can be made acceptable to comparatists and to other sociologically minded legal scholars only if 'sociology', for the purposes of legal inquiry, is understood not as a discipline but solely as a process of, and aspiration toward, systematic, theoretically oriented and empirically grounded understanding of social life. This process and aspiration is not the monopoly of any particular academic discipline. Sociological perspectives on law use theory, methods, data and research traditions from the social sciences (and other disciplines). Legal sociology is thus an interdisciplinary project, like comparative law itself, focused on empirical and theoretical study of what we choose to identify as the legal aspects of social life.[43] The focus is firmly on 'law' – that is, law not just as lawyers know it in their distinct jurisdictions but law as an aspect or field of social experience more generally. To conceptualize provisionally this aspect or field is a task for social analysis.[44]

Legal sociology seeks perspectives that, unlike those of comparative law, directly apply social theory (theoretical analysis of conditions of social change and stability and of the nature of social relationships in general) and contribute to it. In this sense, legal sociology is more explicitly and systematically focused on exploring the nature of 'the social', as the broader setting of legal doctrine and institutions, than is comparative law.[45] In fact, that exploration may be very important in answering such comparatists' questions as: how far is unification or harmonization of law desirable or feasible and in relation to what kinds of regulation and what kinds of regulated communities? As I shall suggest below, the question of what the social should be taken to be is a complex one for contemporary law. Legal sociology has a major role in conceptualizing the various aspects or regions

---

[41] See Cotterrell, *supra*, note 26, p. 37.   [42] Durkheim, *Rules*, *supra*, note 5, p. 260.
[43] See Roger Cotterrell, 'Why Must Legal Ideas Be Interpreted Sociologically?', (1998) 25 J. L. & Society 171.
[44] Among the problems in fulfilling this task is that of taking account of socially important regulatory systems that reflect cultural traditions fundamentally alien to western legal thought and experience. For example, see Werner F. Menski, *Comparative Law in a Global Context: The Legal Systems of Asia and Africa* (London: Platinium, 2000).
[45] See Roger Cotterrell, 'Law and Community: A New Relationship?', (1998) 51 Current Leg. Problems 367.

of the social. Its task is to show their general significance as environments of legal regulation in relation to which law finds its meaning. Legal sociology provides theories and interpretations of the nature of law within these environments, embedded in, and inseparable from, them. In that way, it can help to clarify epistemological and ontological puzzles that still haunt comparative law as a field of study: questions about what to compare and about the validity of comparisons made. Correspondingly, comparative law's recording and interpretation of legal practices, institutions and ideas are essential to legal sociology. They provide a variety of juristic perspectives on law that must be incorporated into those developed by legal sociology.

In my view, these general ideas should determine comparative law's current relations with legal sociology. Legal sociology's most important potential contribution to comparative law is to clarify the nature of the social, the contextual settings of law and legal institutions in relation to which comparison can usefully take place. How, then, can it do this in relation to current, prominent orientations of comparative law? The remainder of this paper considers three such orientations (Alan Watson's legal transplants thesis, the application of autopoiesis theory to comparative law and the recent use by some comparatists of the concept of 'legal culture') as a basis for examining what a sociological perspective can offer comparatists today.

III

In the present context, the most striking aspect of Alan Watson's influential work is its determined attempt to avoid any dependence of comparative law on sociology. Watson recognizes that the formulation of 'legal problems' (for example, 'rent restriction' or 'alimony on divorce') as a basis for comparison cannot be done in the absence of a study of the social context in which the problems arise and which ultimately defines their nature. Thus, 'the weight of the investigation will always be primarily on the comparability of the problem, only secondarily on the comparability of the law; and any discipline founded on such a starting point will be sociology rather than law'.[46] Watson's solution is to reject comparison entirely and focus instead

---

[46] Watson, *supra*, note 10, p. 5. The problem is discussed in some detail but inconclusively in Zoltán Péteri, 'Some Aspects of the Sociological Approach in Comparative Law', in *id.* (ed.), *Hungarian Law – Comparative Law: Essays for the Eighth International Congress of Comparative Law* (Budapest: Akadémiai Kiadó, 1970), pp. 90–3.

on the processes of reasoning by analogy and borrowing of legal ideas from other systems, which he sees as the keys to explaining legal development. Comparative law, for Watson, is thus 'the study of the relationship of one legal system and its rules with another'.[47] It looks not to sociology but to legal history and jurisprudence as sister disciplines, since its focus is on the nature of law and its processes of development.[48]

Elsewhere, I have analysed Watson's claims about the nature of legal sociology, the recent systematization of these claims by William Ewald and aspects of the general logic of Watson's legal transplants thesis.[49] My purpose here is only to summarize some sociological implications of the approach to comparative law represented by Watson's work.

Watson sees legal change as an essentially 'internal' process,[50] in the sense that sociological influences on legal development are considered generally unimportant. To this extent, comparative law appears to stand as a fully independent discipline, free of any reliance on such sociologically dependent concepts as function, evolution, legal or social problems or interests. The evidence offered to support Watson's position is in his historical studies of legal change, which claim to show, for example: (i) that the transplanting of legal rules between systems is 'socially easy'[51] even when there are great material and cultural disparities between the donor and recipient societies; (ii) that no area of private law is extremely resistant to change through foreign influence[52] (contrary to familiar sociologically oriented claims that culturally rooted law is harder to change than merely instrumental law);[53] (iii) that recipient legal systems need no knowledge of the context of origin and growth of laws received by transplantation from another system;[54] and (iv) that social need does not bring about legal change or explain the survival of laws.[55]

Taking these claims at face value, they raise two fundamental issues which, despite Watson's best efforts, draw legal sociology back into the

---

[47] Watson, *supra*, note 10, p. 6.   [48] *Id.*, p. 7.
[49] See Roger Cotterrell, 'Is There a Logic of Legal Transplants?', in David Nelken and Johannes Feest (eds.), *Adapting Legal Cultures* (Oxford: Hart, 2001), pp. 71–92.
[50] He writes, for example, of an 'internal legal logic' or of 'the internal logic of the legal tradition' governing legal development: Alan Watson, *The Evolution of Law* (Oxford: Blackwell, 1985), pp. 21–2.
[51] *Id.*, *supra*, note 10, p. 95.   [52] *Id.*, p. 98.
[53] For example, see Ernst Levy, 'The Reception of Highly Developed Legal Systems by Peoples of Different Cultures', (1950) 25 Washington L.R. 233.
[54] See Alan Watson, 'Legal Transplants and Law Reform', (1976) 92 L.Q.R. 79, pp. 80–1.
[55] See *id.*, *supra*, note 50, p. 119: 'Law is largely autonomous and not shaped by societal needs.'

comparatist's range of vision, or should do. First, assuming that legal transplants are, as Watson claims, fundamentally important to legal development, what is transplanted and what is the test of success in transplantation? Second, what is the nature of the internal processes of legal development that determine whether legal transplants or adaptations take place?

Addressing the second of these first, Watson claims that it is lawyers with their professional needs, interests, prerogatives and judgements of prestige who mainly control the processes of legal development. Thus, sociological perspectives are excluded only by assuming that legal sociology has nothing important to say about lawyers and legal practice. In fact, however, the sociology of legal professions and of legal practice is one of the central, most highly developed fields of empirical inquiry in legal sociology.[56] Very important studies of the role of lawyers' professional practices in shaping legal change have now been undertaken.[57] If 'external' social influences (i.e., influences other than from lawyers themselves) on legal change are (very controversially) excluded from serious consideration in Watson's thesis,[58] 'internal' influences are no less demanding of sociological inquiry. Indeed, on Watson's own arguments, it would seem impossible to understand why and when legal development occurs without such sociological inquiries about the practices, interests, strategies and politics of legal elites who, according to him, play an overwhelmingly important, usually crucial, role in this development.[59]

Furthermore, Watson's attempt to distinguish internal from external forces of legal development appears incoherent if the internal is identified

---

[56] For samples from a vast literature, see Richard L. Abel and Philip S. C. Lewis (eds.), *Lawyers in Society* (Berkeley: University of California Press, 1988–9), 3 vols.

[57] See, especially, Yves Dezalay and Bryant G. Garth, *Dealing in Virtue: International Commercial Arbitration and the Construction of a Transnational Legal Order* (Chicago: University of Chicago Press, 1996).

[58] For an early critique of Watson's approach by a legal sociologist, see Robert B. Seidman, 'Book Review', (1975) 55 Boston U. L.R. 682, p. 683: 'Because he has already abjured any study of societal factors as "sociology" and not "law", when he is forced to take these factors into account he does so without any careful analysis or testing of hypotheses.' See also Richard L. Abel, 'Law as Lag: Inertia as a Social Theory of Law', (1982) 80 Michigan L.R. 785.

[59] Watson often cites admiration for a foreign legal system as an important independent factor in the decision to adopt legal doctrine from it. For example, see Watson, *supra*, note 50, pp. 109 and 118. 'Admirableness', like 'prestige', remains, however, an entirely opaque concept for explanatory purposes unless the elements that produce it are identified and the relation of these elements explained. Lawyers' ideas about the relative prestige of foreign sources of law are juristic shorthand for reference to a vast sociological portfolio of economic and other interests, ultimate value commitments, affective ties and common or divergent historical experiences which, in various combinations, influence choices of models for law reform.

with the practices or interests of legal elites. These surely relate to the interests of client groups (for example, economic or political) that lawyers serve, and lawyers' concerns need to be understood, at least partly, in terms of their position in society. So, their professional interests cannot be separated from conditions in the wider society that provide the settings for their practices. Equally, we need not think only in terms of relationships of 'interests' to challenge the internal-external distinction. We can refer, for example, to legal 'understanding', 'interpretation' or 'experience'. Legal sociology, from its earliest development, has had much to say on these matters. Here, it is important to insist that none of them is the 'internal' prerogative of legal elites (however defined). Nor are they uniform or invariant for these elites. The ways in which law is understood, interpreted and experienced in different regions of the social are complex, varied, ever-changing matters that can be examined only by combining juristic analysis and sociological inquiry.

A way of avoiding the collapse of any internal-external distinction that keeps sociology out of explanations of legal development may be through the use of systems theory. Autopoiesis theory, whose implications for comparative law have been explored by Gunther Teubner,[60] proposes that law in certain modern conditions can be treated as a distinct, self-renewing system of communication. Teubner criticizes Watson for attaching far too much importance to lawyers' professional practices as such. Teubner sees these practices not as, in themselves, the motor of law's development but rather as the necessary consequence of law's modern character as a distinctive discourse focused specifically on producing decisions that define what is legal or illegal. Because this legal/illegal coding – and not, for example, judgements about morality, efficiency, scientific or historical truth – is law's essential focus as an independent discourse, it cannot be governed by social developments of the kind sociology studies. It may react to these developments but it will always do so in its own normative terms. What Watson sees as the autonomous law-making of legal elites, adherents of autopoiesis theory see as the working out of law's independent destiny as a highly specialized, functionally distinctive communication system.[61]

---

[60] See Gunther Teubner, 'Legal Irritants: Good Faith in British Law or How Unifying Law Ends Up in New Divergences', (1998) 61 Modern L.R. 11.
[61] See generally *id.*, *Law as an Autopoietic System* (Oxford: Blackwell, 1993); Jiri Priban and David Nelken (eds.), *Law's New Boundaries: The Consequences of Legal Autopoiesis* (Aldershot: Dartmouth, 2001).

Law as a communication system in society is linked to other systems (such as the economy) but not through patterns of direct influence. What autopoiesis theory terms 'structural coupling' refers to a much more indirect and contingent set of relations between these systems. And in different societies, the 'coupling' takes different forms. This has extremely important consequences for comparative law's interests in the transplantation of law. Legal rules governing good faith in the law of contracts, for example, might be taken from one legal system and imported into another or imposed generally through European legal harmonization. But whereas Watson's thesis suggests this can be an 'easy' process, Teubner claims that the meaning of legal ideas may well change dramatically in the process of transfer. This is because, apart from any differences in styles and traditions of legal interpretation and conceptualization in different legal systems, the coupling of the system to the economy and other social systems may vary in different national contexts and vary in its 'tightness' or 'looseness' for different areas of law. Autopoiesis theory assumes that movement is occurring toward a global legal discourse but it also recognizes, at least in Teubner's interpretation, major incompatibilities between legal systems arising from their specific social settings.[62] Because this makes the result of transfers of legal ideas between systems theoretically indeterminate, Teubner sees not so much legal transplants as legal 'irritants' occurring, causing unpredictable changes in recipient legal systems.

Implicitly, Teubner's thesis entirely rejects Watson's effort to exclude sociology from the logic of legal transplants and so from a central concern of comparative law. For Teubner, law's coupling with other systems in society puts important limits on the ambitions of some comparatists for unification or harmonization of law. To understand what is possible in the transfer of legal ideas between legal systems, social-scientific knowledge of the legal context is undoubtedly necessary. But, from another point of view, autopoiesis theory gives very little guidance as to how empirical legal sociology can help comparatists. Law's resistance to 'external' social influence is not, as with Watson's thesis, seen as the effect of lawyers' behaviour that could be studied sociologically. It is the consequence of law's self-sufficient, self-producing and self-reproducing discursive character, which autopoiesis theory claims to identify.

[62] See Gunther Teubner, ' "Global Bukowina": Legal Pluralism in the World Society', in *id.* (ed.), *Global Law Without a State* (Aldershot: Dartmouth, 1997), pp. 3–28; Michael King, 'Comparing Legal Cultures in the Quest for Law's Identity', in Nelken, *supra*, note 2, pp. 119–34.

Autopoiesis theory has been applied not just to law but to the study of social systems of communication generally (including, for example, economic systems and administrative systems). Niklas Luhmann, who has pioneered these applications, treats the theory as a basis for all general sociological analysis of the nature of social systems and their mutual relations.[63] But its theoretical claims about the nature and consequences of law's autonomy are very powerful postulates, presented in advance of (and even, perhaps, in place of) the kind of detailed empirical study of social influences on, and through, legal change that comparatists and most legal sociologists are likely to favour. The postulates of autopoiesis theory do not so much guide empirical research as explain conclusively how to interpret anything that this research may discover. Comparatists and (most) legal sociologists might well want to ask why the particular discursive character of law that autopoiesis theory insists on must be taken as the starting-point for analysis; why, for example, is it to be *assumed* that any direct influence of legal ideas between legal systems is likely to be impossible and why is modern law *necessarily* to be seen as merely 'coupled' to (rather than linked in mutual influence with) the economy or other aspects of social life? In other words, comparatists and legal sociologists might be well advised to join forces to ask for more attention to open-minded empirical inquiry and for theory that imports less initial scepticism about the richness and profundity of law's social embeddedness.

IV

In a legal transplant, what is transplanted and what is the test of successful transplantation? This is the other question that was suggested earlier as left open by Watson's transplants thesis. If all that is involved is a transfer of certain rules of positive law, a transplant need be no more than the formal enacting of those rules by the recipient legal system. And if the enactment in itself is what is recognized as transplantation, without any concern for who actually uses the rules, who knows about them or whether they influence social or economic life in any way, mere enactment constitutes success. In so far as Watson's thesis is concerned with lawyers' borrowing of foreign rules and enacting them or adopting them formally in legal practice, his

---

[63] See Niklas Luhmann, *Social Systems*, transl. by John Bednarz and Dirk Baecker (Stanford: Stanford University Press, 1995).

claims about the ease with which successful transplants can occur reduce almost to tautology. If a transplant is no more than the putting of a foreign rule on the statute-book or its adoption in the practice of courts, success in legal transplantation is entirely in the hands of those legal elites that control courts or legislatures. It has nothing to do with what may or may not happen in society beyond the world of professional legal or legislative practice.[64] By definition, sociology (treated by Watson as the study of everything social except lawyers' own practices) is rendered irrelevant: transplants cannot be other than 'socially easy'.

Sometimes, however, Watson has used the term 'legal culture' to refer to conditions governing successful transplantation.[65] These conditions are the outlook, practices, knowledge, values and traditions of the legal elite of the recipient legal system.[66] Legal culture, in this sense, is seen by Watson as a major determinant of law's 'internal' processes of development. But to refer to 'culture' in this way is to appeal to an idea that has, for a long time, been an important focus of social science (especially anthropology). It refers to a compendium of matters of social experience, understanding and practice that clearly invite social scientific analysis and clarification. Again, the problem of the internal–external dichotomy presents itself. If these matters of outlook, values, etc., are important among Watson's legal elites, why are they not important among other social groups that might be crucial in determining whether transplanted law is invoked, applied or enforced?

Here, interesting contrasts with developments in legal sociology can be noted. The concept of 'legal culture' has been much used in sociology of law, especially through the influence of Lawrence Friedman's work,[67] to refer to attitudes toward, and ideas, beliefs and expectations about, law. Most often, the focus has been on these ideas as held by non-lawyers. Watson's use of the term corresponds to what Friedman calls 'internal' (lawyers') legal culture. But Friedman's main concern is with 'external' (i.e., non-lawyers') legal culture. He rejects comparatists' typical categorizations of legal styles or legal systems precisely because these take insufficient account

---

[64] However, Watson assumes, without supplying evidence, that transplanted law will normally strongly control 'lesser officials' and affected citizens. See Alan Watson, *Legal Origins and Legal Change* (London: Hambledon Press, 1991), p. 87.

[65] For example, see *id.*, pp. 100–2.

[66] Sometimes, Watson refers to 'the lawyers' culture'. See *id.*, *supra*, note 50, pp. 117–18.

[67] For example, see Lawrence M. Friedman, 'Is There a Modern Legal Culture?', (1994) 7 Ratio Juris 117.

of differences or similarities in 'external' legal culture, which he sees as crucial determinants of law's social meaning and significance.[68] But, in fact, comparatists might be strongly justified in criticizing the legal sociologists' focus on culture for its conceptual vagueness and potentially unlimited scope of inquiry. Thus, in Friedman's conception, everyone is likely to inhabit an indeterminate number of legal cultures (for example, there may be attitudes to, or beliefs about, law held differentially by rich or poor, men or women, different ethnic or occupational groups or nations or groups of nations). The study of legal culture, in this sense, embraces potentially all kinds of social differentiation without indicating means of defining or relating them or judging their independent significance. A tie to law is given only by *some* attitudinal focus on the official legal system or on something else (for example, disputing, complaining or official behaviour) that might be seen as in some way related to it. The concept of 'culture' in this usage focuses on everything and nothing. It is hopelessly vague and comparatists would do well to avoid it.[69]

Contemporary usage of the term 'legal culture' by some comparatists, though, is clearly quite different from Friedman's or from the use of the term by other legal sociologists to refer not to attitudinal matters but to measurable behavioural patterns related to law (for example, as indicated by litigation rates).[70] Interestingly, Pierre Legrand's approach seems to contextualize the traditional comparative-law concern for contrasting legal styles of different 'families' of law into a much broader focus on legal cultures as distinctive *mentalités* ('modes of understanding reality')[71] informing all aspects of the particular civilization in which law is embedded in a specific time and place. Because Legrand's main concern as a comparatist in using the concept of 'legal culture' in this way is to appreciate and highlight difference between the styles and outlooks of jurists,[72] rather than to make causal claims as with Friedman's legal sociology, his use of the idea of 'culture' seems much less vulnerable to criticism of its vagueness and indeterminate scope. I see it as a provisional interpretive concept of the kind Jerome Hall might have approved for comparative law as humanistic legal sociology,

---

[68] See Friedman, *supra*, note 2, p. 36.
[69] See Roger Cotterrell, 'The Concept of Legal Culture', in Nelken, *supra*, note 2, pp. 13–31. For a careful assessment of the sociological potential of the concept in a variety of contexts, see David Nelken, 'Disclosing/Invoking Legal Culture: An Introduction', (1995) 4 Soc. & Leg. Stud. 435.
[70] See Erhard Blankenberg, 'Civil Litigation Rates as Indicators for Legal Cultures', in Nelken, *supra*, note 2, pp. 41–68.
[71] Legrand, *supra*, note 18, p. 11.   [72] *Id.*, pp. 1–13.

rather than as an explanatory concept of a scientific, theory-building sociology seeking generalizations about social and legal development. The concept of 'legal culture' in this usage can evoke a sense of rich and complex difference that is important in appreciating, in a general, preliminary way, variation between modes of legal understanding or legal styles of analysis and interpretation, even if the elements of difference remain aggregated, diffuse or indistinct and, ultimately, of unspecified individual significance.

From a sociological point of view, the difficulties with any concept of 'legal culture' of this kind are likely to arise only when it is treated as a sufficient basis of predictions about social (including legal) development. Legal culture, in Legrand's depiction, is focused on the accumulated professional traditions, styles of thought and habits of practice of lawyers but (far more subtly than in Watson's use of the concept) it extends beyond these to stress their roots and resonances in much wider aspects of cultural experience. As an aggregate of variables, with its elements not rigorously differentiated, legal culture, in this sense, can run into the same difficulties as the legal sociologists' concept does when it is used in social explanation. It may cover too much and focus clearly on too little to allow it to be used convincingly in explaining social phenomena.

Just as autopoiesis theory encourages us to see law as immune from direct external influence because of its impenetrability as a normatively self-sufficient discourse, so a focus on legal culture as an all-embracing *mentalité* can suggest similar immunities.[73] In both cases, the suggestion of immunity is not necessarily empirically warranted but is the result of presenting a vast diversity of contingently related phenomena as if it were a complex, rather solid *unity*. In autopoiesis theory, law's very diverse forms of knowledge, reasoning and practice are presented as a single, unique discourse. Similarly, in some conceptions of legal culture, the aggregate of extremely diverse elements of experience that might, taken together, be labelled as 'culture' is treated as though it were an integrated unity capable of resisting other cultures, conceived as opposing unities.

No doubt 'each person's cultural context is unique to some extent'[74] and perfect communication across cultural contexts may be impossible (as the illustration of language translation so well shows).[75] From a social scientific standpoint, one of the valuable effects of the recent emphasis among

---

[73] *Cf.* Pierre Legrand, 'European Legal Systems Are Not Converging', (1996) 45 Int. & Comp. L.Q. 52; *id.*, 'The Impossibility of "Legal Transplants"', (1997) 4 Maastricht J. Eur. & Comp. L. 111.
[74] Curran, *supra*, note 6, p. 49.   [75] *Id.*, pp. 54–9; Legrand, *supra*, note 18, pp. 3–4.

comparatists on legal culture is the degree of harmonization on matters of method that it may promote, for certain purposes, between comparative law and social science. An awareness of 'irreducible incomparables',[76] and of deep cultural differences the components of which remain undifferentiated in any conclusive way, points to a 'need to accept that others have different truths' from ourselves.[77] But this does not mean that communication or comparison is impossible. It means rather that communication and comparison demand what anthropologists call 'thick description'[78] – rich, multilayered and detailed accounts of social experience to convey the complexity of cultural difference, to identify points of empathy and thereby to provide some keys of entry into the understanding and appreciation of different cultures. Vivian Curran refers to this method for comparative law as 'immersion comparison'. It involves studying not just legal rules but what attaches to them: values, beliefs, traditions and collective memories, understandings, aspirations and emotions. 'It contemplates a slow pushing against cultural barriers toward an ideal of mutual comprehension, a striving to reach comprehension, and a recognition that some distances will remain.'[79]

If social science has messages of value for comparative law today, I think they can be summed up in the following way. Comparison is more difficult in some contexts and for some purposes than has often been thought in the past, and what is to be compared must be conceptualized in much more complex and subtle ways than previously. The social milieux of regulation need to be understood systematically, empirically and interpretively in their detail and complexity.

Can legal sociology help this understanding? Earlier in this paper, reference was made to a need to conceptualize and clarify the different aspects or regions of the social in relation to law. Most legal study is still focused

---

[76] Curran, *supra*, note 6, p. 91.
[77] *Id.*, p. 91. Ethnocentricism (one kind of failure to accept this) is at least as serious a danger for legal sociologists as for comparatists. For example, 'law and development', a heavily funded major social-science initiative in comparative legal research in the 1960s and 1970s, failed in part because it 'was largely a parochial expression of the American legal style': John H. Merryman, 'Comparative Law and Social Change: On the Origins, Style, Decline and Revival of the Law and Development Movement', (1977) 25 Am. J. Comp. L. 457, p. 479. For further comment on the ethnocentricism issue, see William P. Alford, 'On the Limits of "Grand Theory" in Comparative Law', (1986) 61 Washington L.R. 945.
[78] See Clifford Geertz, *The Interpretation of Cultures* (New York: Basic Books, 1973), pp. 5–10; *id.*, *Local Knowledge* (London: Fontana, 1993), pp. 55–70.
[79] Curran, *supra*, note 6, p. 91.

strongly on the law of nation states but law increasingly seeks to fly free of nation-state jurisdiction in a host of ways. The political society of the nation state is much less obviously than in the recent past the social of law – its environment of significance and authority.[80] Legal sociology has long been concerned to study forms of regulation that have jurisdictions different from those of state law. It has a large literature on legal pluralism – the diversity of legal forms, jurisdictions or regimes that may coexist (or struggle for regulatory supremacy or legitimacy) within or beyond state borders.[81] It has sometimes tried to show (often with polemical intent) how law is created and sustained in patterns of social relations that have very little to do with the state's regulatory activity.[82] And it has tried to understand the varieties of legal experience as forms of subjective social experience.[83]

In contemporary contexts, these socio-legal orientations become concerns with different types of community – ways of being linked socially with other individuals – that law can express in regulating social relationships, groups and organizations.[84] One type of community is instrumental, expressed especially in business relations (extending, with increasing frequency, beyond state boundaries, as in trade and financial systems). Another kind is the link of common beliefs or ultimate values (expressed, for example, in movements supporting international human rights). Many social relations remain strongly territorial in focus, linked to, and defined by, specific localities that, again, may or may not be coterminous with nation-state jurisdictional boundaries. Others are focused on family or friendship groups. The social is thus highly complex and varied as a matter of description or identification.[85]

---

[80] For example, see Patrick Glenn's contribution to this book.
[81] For example, see Sally E. Merry, 'Legal Pluralism', (1988) 22 L. & Society R. 869.
[82] See Eugen Ehrlich, *Fundamental Principles of the Sociology of Law*, transl. by Walter L. Moll (New York: Arno Press, repr. 1975)[1913].
[83] See Georges Gurvitch, *L'expérience juridique et la philosophie pluraliste du droit* (Paris: Pedone, 1935).
[84] See Roger Cotterrell, 'A Legal Concept of Community', (1997) 12 Can. J. L. & Society 75. Gurvitch uses the term 'sociality' to convey this idea of abstract types of community that can be expressed in diverse ways in actual social relations. See Georges Gurvitch, *The Sociology of Law* (London: Routledge & Kegan Paul, 1947), p. 49. But his particular typology of the 'forms of sociality' is, in my view, too intricate and often too obscure in its empirical reference to be generally useful for socio-legal analysis.
[85] For example, see Boaventura de Sousa Santos, *Toward a New Legal Common Sense: Law, Globalization, and Emancipation*, 2d ed. (London: Butterworths, 2002).

All of this is important for comparative law's efforts to survey and compare the variety of systems of regulation that, in some way, express these manifestations of the social or are struggling to emerge so as to do so. And a concern with types of community as expressed in actual patterns of social relationships must involve the effort to appreciate how people *subjectively experience* community and its legal expressions. This is what makes 'thick description' and 'immersion comparison' valuable and old ideas of, for example, 'function', 'evolution' and social problems inadequate for some tasks of comparative study. Despite these complexities, however, comparison of law (as of other aspects of social life) remains possible and necessary, whether to pursue 'socio-technics', 'education' (to borrow Abrams's terms) or other aims. It is not to be jettisoned from the heart of the legal comparatist's enterprise because it often implies difficult links with, and dependences on, social-scientific ideas.

Nor do these links demand or suggest any subordination of one academic discipline to another in a hierarchy of explanation. Legal sociology and comparative law are, for many (but not all) important purposes, interdependent co-workers in the empirical study of law. One aspect of this is that law ought not to be conceptualized (for example, as an autopoietic system or self-contained cultural sphere) in ways that make it harder to see the intricacy and intimacy of influence, interaction and interpenetration between different elements of social life and legal experience. Legal sociologists, no less than comparatists, need to take on board these principles and frame their researches in the light of them. If this is done, it may not be over-optimistic to suggest that a part, at least, of the great aspirations of the past for the unselfconscious integration of comparative law and legal sociology around ambitious projects of comparative study will eventually be realized.

7

Comparatists and languages

BERNHARD GROßFELD

Introduction

The shock experience

Comparative law is without a doubt the most promising part of modern jurisprudence.[1] Josef Kohler (1849–1919) saw comparative law as jurisprudence's 'bloom' and 'blossom'.[2] This great lawyer-artist,[3] an exuberant Catholic inspired by metaphor, made the statement at the 1900 Paris Congress.[4] Kohler came from a French-law background and loved the cultural study of law, regarding it as a way to reconstruct legal scholarship.[5]

Comparative law looks deceptively simple to some.[6] But the reality of comparative analysis for those who actually *do* it is very different. Comparative law provides the *ultimate* shock experience for any nationally trained

---

I am grateful to Helen Brimacombe for her assistance in preparing this paper for publication. All translations are mine.

[1] See Claus Luttermann, 'Dialog der Kulturen', in *Festschrift Bernhard Großfeld* (Heidelberg: Verlag Recht und Wirtschaft, 1999), p. 771 [hereinafter *Festschrift Großfeld*]; Bernhard Großfeld, 'Comparative Law as a Comprehensive Approach', (2000) 1 Richmond J. Global L. & Bus. 1; Basil S. Markesinis, *Foreign Law and Comparative Methodology: A Subject and a Thesis* (Oxford: Hart, 1997); Abbo Junker, 'Rechtsvergleichung als Grundlagenfach', JZ, 1994, p. 921; Kai Schadbach, 'The Benefits of Comparative Law', (1998) 16 Boston U. Int. L.J. 331; Caroline Bradley, 'Transatlantic Misunderstandings: Corporate Law and Society', (1999) 53 Miami L.R. 269.

[2] On Kohler, see Michaela Grzesch, 'Josef Kohler', Zeitschrift für vergleichende Rechtswissenschaft, 1999, p. 2; Bernhard Großfeld and Ingo Theusinger, 'Josef Kohler', RabelsZ, 2000, p. 696.

[3] See Ernst Rabel, 'Josef Kohler', in *Gesammelte Aufsätze*, ed. by Hans G. Leser, vol. I (Tübingen: J. C. B. Mohr, 1965), pp. 340–50 [1919]; Bernhard Großfeld and Ingo Theusinger, 'L'oeuvre de Josef Kohler', Droit et cultures, 2001, p. 167.

[4] See Josef Kohler, 'Über die Methode der Rechtsvergleichung', Zeitschrift für das Privat- und Öffentliche Recht der Gegenwart, 1901, p. 273.

[5] But see, for a critical view, Paul W. Kahn, *The Cultural Study of Law* (Chicago: University of Chicago Press, 1999).

[6] See Hannes Rösler, 'Rechtsvergleichung als Erkenntnisinstrument in Wissenschaft, Praxis und Ausbildung', Juristische Schulung, 1999, p. 1186.

and conditioned lawyer. It throws him into confusion by taking away all language-based feelings of security about understanding the world. The result is a loss of control.[7]

Comparing

My subject-matter is a classic example of this shock experience as the difficulty begins with the two words 'comparatists' and 'languages'. Language has occupied the central place for comparatists.[8] My title seems to assume that there is a kind of vital connection between the two terms. This might be so but what do these words mean? Starting with the first term, 'comparatists', there is a long string of questions to be asked about our status and activities as comparatists. Are we actually comparatists? Do we really compare? What can we compare? If law is a 'living field' or a 'living-room' for exchanges and communications within a culture, is it meaningful to compare 'living fields' or 'living rooms', for instance, your living room and my living room? How can we compare? Does the term 'compare' carry with it the same abstract flair as that which we first experience when studying the geometry of triangles? Does the use of this term imply a kind of geometrical approach (*mos geometricus*) toward human relations even though humans are neither triangles nor quadrangles nor 'angles' at all?

What about languages?

Let us retain this sceptical approach and start to consider the other word in my title, 'languages', which is also connected with so many conventional concepts.[9] What does one mean by this term, 'languages'?[10] A few years ago, I learned that the Chinese identify the expression 'Chinese language' only with their written 'language' because it is this semiotic system – largely independent of voice – that is felt to make someone 'Chinese' and to result in thinking in a 'Chinese' manner. You are accepted as a 'real' Chinese only if you can read and write the identifying written signs.

---

[7] See Bernhard Großfeld, *Rechtsvergleichung* (Wiesbaden: Westdeutscher Verlag, 2001), p. 66.
[8] This is also the case for conflicts lawyers. See Robert Freitag, 'Sprachenzwang, Sprachrisiko und Formanforderungen im IPR', IPRax, 1999, p. 142.
[9] See George A. Miller, *The Science of Words* (New York: Scientific American Library, 1996).
[10] See Jean B. Elshtain, 'How Should We Talk?', (1999) 50 Case Western Reserve L.R. 731.

What is the correspondence within our western laws? What is our language in law? Is it oral or written language? Do we follow the beat of words (the magic flute) or the silent letter of the law (the Holy Scripture)? Do we work with the oral language of the present or with a frozen written language of the past? Can we mix them up under the term 'language'? What about body language[11] or 'pattern language', such as court architecture, procedural rituals and pictures?[12]

Given the doubts thrown up by the topic, I propose to treat these matters in reverse order, beginning with language and inquiring into the status of language in our laws. We have to clarify that status first before we can turn to technical differences in the structure of languages.

Language[13]

The word 'language' is used here in its plain meaning, though doubts can be raised even at this point. Legal language is different from other language since it normally serves particular ends. As Hermann Kantorowicz observed, 'behind opinions stand intention'. In law, language is often used 'not to find the truth but to serve interests'.[14] Even leaving aside this particular aspect of legal language, plain language alone already poses serious questions.[15]

The status of language

Law is part of a wider web of communications, references, experiences and hopes within a culture, the participants in which instinctively feel their place at any given moment.[16] When inquiring into the status of language as

---

[11] See Bernard Hibbits, 'Making Motions: The Embodiment of Law in Gesture', (1995) 6 J. Contemp. Leg. Issues 51; *id.*, 'Coming to Our Senses: Communication and Legal Expression in Performance Cultures', (1992) 41 Emory L.J. 873.

[12] See Christopher Alexander, Shera Ishikawa and Murray Silverstein, *A Pattern Language: Towns – Buildings – Constructions* (Oxford: Oxford University Press, 1999).

[13] See generally Miller, *supra*, note 9.

[14] Hermann Kantorowicz, *Der Kampf um die Rechtswissenschaft* (Heidelberg: Winter, 1906), p. 38. See Vivian G. Curran, 'Rethinking Hermann Kantorowicz: Free Law, American Legal Realism and the Legacy of Anti-Formalism', in Annelise Riles (ed.), *Rethinking the Masters of Comparative Law* (Oxford: Hart, 2001), pp. 66–91.

[15] As for 'language statutes', see the French *loi* no. 94–665 of 4 August 1994, D.1994.L.416. See generally Wolfram Gärtner and Mirek Hempel, 'Das Gesetz über die polnische Sprache im Lichte des europäischen Rechts', [Austrian] Zeitschrift für Rechtsvergleichung, 2000, p. 9.

[16] See Judit Frigyesi, 'Sacred and Secular – What Can Music Teach About Jewish Thought', (1999) 20 Cardozo L.R. 1673, p. 1680. For a more general discussion, see Roger Cotterrell, 'The Concept of

a way of conveying order (and not only as social music), we have to take into account history. Our western concepts of 'language' and 'law' are conditioned by religion. John 1,1 states that 'in the beginning was the word' (and not the letter, as we might add, given that, at the time of writing, we are in 2000, the 'Gutenberg year'). Equally, there is a powerful myth attached to language that is immediately turned into rules. From early childhood on we are taught, for instance, that we must tell the truth and 'nothing but the truth' when we speak or be silent (though that is not a general rule under German law, nor is it a cultural universal).

Not all cultures regard oral language as sufficiently precise to serve as an instrument of order. For example, while the German word '*bestimmt*' (= precise) is derived from '*Stimme*' (= voice), it has no equivalent in Chinese. Consider that other cultures see 'the beginning' in silence (*Lao-tse*) rather than in words. Consider also that the connection of language with truth is not universal. In Papua-New Guinea, for example, to tell the truth is required only between members of the same group, not toward others.[17] Are we obliged, encouraged or even allowed to tell the truth to our enemy? Cannot the criminal defendant in some cultures lie as much as he likes?

From this, we can see that languages are not neutral. They operate powerfully out of often unconscious backgrounds and they reduce a complex reality to make it manageable in our own contexts and in the directions which *we* prefer. This raises doubts about whether a language can fit into another background – not necessarily because of differences in the nature of human beings but because of differences in the way human beings choose and rely on words. What makes us reduce reality in different ways? For instance, what makes us believe in the 'reality' of legal persons? What brings us to a level of abstraction that makes us accept a 'person' that can neither come into 'real' being nor pass away (corporate immortality)? Why do some cultures speak 'scientifically' whereas others use plainer language?[18] Is the explanation to be found in different geography, in different signs?

All of this is not to be understood in terms of absolute contrasts. Word, letter and picture overlap and no culture monopolizes the one in particular

---

Legal Culture', in David Nelken (ed.), *Comparing Legal Cultures* (Aldershot: Dartmouth, 1997), pp. 13–31.

[17] See Michaela Grzesch, 'Die Neuendettelsauer Mission in Papua-Neuguinea vor dem Ersten Weltkrieg', in Bernhard Großfeld (ed.), *Rechtsvergleicher – verkannt, vergessen, verdrängt* (Münster: LIT Verlag, 2000), p. 12.

[18] See Lorraine Daston, 'Can Scientific Objectivity Have a History?', Alexander von Humboldt Mitteilungen, 2000, p. 75.

over the others. But there are differences in degrees and such shades count in comparative law. The comparatist has to deal in shades.

A topiary garden[19]

Turning to language, to speech language in particular, it is not necessary to repeat various references about the parallel between language and law as organic developments, a subject so characteristic of the von Savigny/Grimm/Maitland approach in the nineteenth century.[20] It is a subject that does not need any further discussion.[21] Along with Gottfried Wilhelm Leibniz (1646–1716), we should see language as a mirror of the mind that reflects into the mind and on from there – at least in the western world – into concepts of order. I leave out the Whorfian hypothesis (which I accept), as I cannot add anything new to it:[22] language, and signs in general, shape the world into a topiary garden. We impose both on reality.

The oft-repeated adage that lawyers have only one instrument, language, also deserves short shrift.[23] Every court-house, every ritual, every judicial wig, every trial by jury stands against this proposition, not to speak of the immense vastness of silent legal formants ('cryptotypes'), of *'droit muet'*, which Rodolfo Sacco has analysed so masterfully.[24]

Semiotic competition

Preamble

For our purposes, it is more important to realize that words, letters and pictures compete with each other for status. Emphasizing words and letters

---

[19] See Bernhard Großfeld, 'Literature, Language, and the Law', (1987) 20 De Jure 212; Yadira Calvo, 'Language and the Law', (1998–9) 7 J. Gender Soc. Policy & L. 381.

[20] See Richard Posner, 'Savigny, Holmes, and the Law and Economics of Possession', (2000) 86 Virginia L.R. 535; Marie-Jeanne Campana, 'Vers un langage juridique commun en Europe?', in Rodolfo Sacco and Luca Castellani (eds.), *Les multiples langues du droit européen uniforme* (Turin: L'Harmattan, 1999), pp. 7–34.

[21] See Eric Pederson *et al.*, 'Semantic Typology and Spatial Conceptualization', (1998) 74 Language 557; Michael C. Corballis, 'The Gestual Origins of Language', (1999) 87 American Scientist 139.

[22] See Pederson *et al.*, *supra*, note 21, p. 557.

[23] See George P. Fletcher, 'Fair and Reasonable: A Linguistic Glimpse Into the American Legal Mind', in Sacco and Castellani, *supra*, note 20, pp. 57–70.

[24] See Rodolfo Sacco, 'Legal Formants', (1991) 39 Am. J. Comp. L. 1 & 343; *id.*, 'Droit muet', Rev. trim. dr. civ., 1995, p. 783. For an English rendition, see *id.*, 'Mute Law', (1995) 43 Am.J. Comp. L. 454.

discourages idolatry; strong pictures make us distrust 'dead' letters and 'empty' words.[25] St John expresses this when he first distinguishes the word from the letter (at least, in my interpretation) and then sets them both against the picture ('and the word became flesh [...] and we have seen his glory' – John 1,14 – or 'Jesus did his signs before his disciples' eyes' – John 1,30).[26] This is a decisive difference between the Jewish ('inlibration'), Islamic ('inlinguation') and European–Christian ('incarnation') views.[27] Equally, these semiotic views are mirrored in the 'letter of the law' inscribed by God himself on two tablets, their core being an ethical content;[28] in the beauty of the super-human language (the 'music of the law'),[29] given to the illiterate Mohammed;[30] in the 'pictorial law' of the Middle Ages as expressed in the '*Sachsenspiegel*' (the 'Saxon Mirror' of the 1230s);[31] or in any of the English and Continental cathedrals.

It is not necessary to go so far back. One hears and sees these differences at home even today. Catholics and Protestants can easily be set apart by different feelings toward words, letters and pictures. Luther's 'the word they should let stand' and his '*sola scriptura*' mark a stark contrast to the Catholic '*hoc est enim corpus meum*' or 'see the lamb of God'.[32] Comparative semiotics is central to comparative law. If we neglect comparative semiotics, we miss the point altogether not realizing that within other cultures we can find, in terms of their social position, real equivalents to language. In these cultures, rituals and symbols may 'speak' more and engender more far-reaching influences (for example, Mao swimming in the Yangtze River, the heart of China, at Wuhan, where the 1911 revolution began, and thus starting a 'cultural revolution'). Semiotic systems represent fully differentiated

---

[25] See Erik Jorink, *Wetenshap en werelbeld in die Goulden Euw* (Hilversum: Verloren, 1999).
[26] See also John 1, 6: 'what we have seen with our eyes', 'what we have touched with our hands'.
[27] For example, see Bernard Weiss, 'Exotericism and Objectivity in Islamic Jurisprudence', in Nicholas Heer (ed.), *Islamic Law and Jurisprudence* (Seattle: University of Washington Press, 1990), p. 56.
[28] See Erich Zenger, *Am Fuß des Sinai*, 2d ed. (Tübingen: J. C. B. Mohr, 1998), p. 134.
[29] See Desmond Manderson and David Caudill, 'Modes of Law: Music and Legal Theory', (1999) 20 Cardozo L.R. 1325; Wayne Alpen, 'Music Theory as a Mode of Law: The Case of Heinrich Schenker, Esq.', (1999) 20 Cardozo L.R. 1459; Carl Weisbrod, 'Fusion Folk: A Comment on Law and Music', (1999) 20 Cardozo L.R. 1439; Frigyesi, *supra*, note 16.
[30] See David Kermanin, *Gott ist schön: Das ästhetische Erleben des Koran* (Munich: C. H. Beck, 1999).
[31] See Klaus Luig, 'Staat und Recht in den Emblemen von Andrea Alciato (1492–1550)', in *Festschrift Großfeld*, *supra*, note 1, pp. 727–44.
[32] *Cf*. Händel's (1685–1759) aria 'Meine Seele hört im Sehen' (= 'my soul hears when seeing'). Händel was a former law student. The text is from Brockes, a lawyer–poet (1680–1747).

ranges of conceptual vocabularies that match the slow accumulation of new ideas, of fine distinctions and subtle techniques. Cultures are well aware that signs are '[p]owers/ [w]hich of themselves our minds impress'.[33] Therefore, they tend to condition their members with the leading semiotic system from early childhood onwards (consider William Wordsworth's formulation: 'The Child is Father of the Man').[34] The entrenched subliminal status of signs gives or takes status to, or from, ideas, lending particular dignity to leading ideologies.

Orality v. writing

Staying with language alone, the differing positions toward orality versus writing, the 'linguistic turn', are one of the first riddles to be answered by comparatists. Again, one does not have to look too far for examples.[35] Consider the difference in distance between orality and writing in Germany and England. Germans speak as they write, or write as they speak, that is, letter by letter. The English speak and write differently – phonetically. Now, consider the different styles of court opinions in England, France and Germany.[36] In England, the higher courts traditionally give their opinions orally in a highly personal way. Even today, opinions in the House of Lords are called 'speeches'.[37] In France, judges produce short and abstract written versions, '*more geometrico*'. In Germany, they elaborate long written 'dissertations' in the particular grammatical style of the Latin-language tradition and, thus, quite often in bad German.[38] In England, we find a largely silent constitution, in Germany and in the United States written texts.

The US trial by jury shows another marked difference between orality and writing.[39] The judge instructs the jury orally; the jury normally

---

[33] William Wordsworth, 'Expostulation and Reply', in *Selected Poetry of William Wordsworth*, ed. by Mark Van Doren (New York: Modern Library, 2001), p. 79 [1798] (hereinafter *Selected Poetry*).
[34] *Id.*, ' "My Heart Leaps Up When I Behold" ', in *Selected Poetry*, *supra*, note 33, p. 445 [1807]. See also *id.*, 'The Solitary Reaper', in *Selected Poetry*, *supra*, note 33, p. 469: 'The music in my heart I bore/Long after it was heard no more' [1807].
[35] See Tony Weir, *Wise Men's Counters* (Münster: Westfälische Wilhelms-Universität Münster, 1998), p. 14.
[36] See Hein Kötz, 'Über den Stil höchstrichterlicher Entscheidunge', RabelsZ, 1973, p. 245; Basil S. Markesinis, 'A Matter of Style', (1994) 110 L.Q.R. 607.
[37] See Weir, *supra*, note 35, p. 17.
[38] See Olivier Beaudand and Erik Volkmar Heyen (eds.), *Eine deutsch-französische Rechtswissenschaft?* (Baden-Baden: Nomos, 1999). *Cf*. Bernhard Großfeld, 'Book Review', JZ, 2000, p. 249.
[39] See generally 'The Common Law Jury', (1999) 62 L. & Contemporary Problems, No. 2.

does not read statutes, law books or law-review articles and no bar examination is required for jury members. The courtroom is filled with voice, with body and symbolic language – all only reasonably intelligible to, and assessable by, long-serving members of the culture. The power of the written word is diminished. Writing does not catch the picture; the abstract bridge of an abstract semiotic system is of little use to jurors. It is even controversial whether the jury applies the law or finds the law from oral discussion. The jury does not give reasons and, therefore, no written judgements; this leads to other methods of judicial review. The jury not only stands for the difference between professional and layman but it stands even more for another view of orality and writing. It diminishes the power of written texts. That is why letter-oriented and letter-narrowed European lawyers never cease to be sceptical about the United States's jury system.

Language as garment

Semiotic systems are quite stable. These systems are structures of social organization in space and time. They *are* rituals that give emotional stability and carry the appearance of higher authority and, therefore, of legitimacy 'as it is written'. Only consider the persistence of 'imperial measures' in England versus the metric system on the Continent, of left-side or right-side driving.

Semiotic systems are the texture of times and places, leaving their footprints on the sand of time (discoverable by Oliver Wendell Holmes's 'discerning eye'). However, they never paint objectively. Such systems are subjective and objective phenomena, and subjective phenomena are no more false illusions than objective phenomena are true absolutes. They are both real.[40] They constantly interact with each other in the same way that certain colours, when juxtaposed to one another, cause different visual effects or in the way that billiard balls often roll in unpredictable directions after clicking against each other or touching the cushion. No word is an island.[41] A word is not just a verbal icon but part of a dynamic 'flow',[42] which needs more than the mistakes of a piecemeal approach because such an approach leads to arbitrary hermeneutic choices. We cannot treat the

---

[40] See Daston, *supra*, note 18, p. 37.
[41] See Robert Spoo, '"No Word Is An Island": Textualism and Aesthetics in Akhil Reed Amar's The Bill of Rights', (1999) 33 U. Richmond L.R. 537.
[42] See William K. Wimsatt, *The Verbal Icon: Studies in the Meaning of Poetry* (New York: Noonday Press, 1958).

word as an exclusive 'vehicle of choice for the text-oriented' comparatist.[43] Language does not offer the safe basis which it is often taken to do: 'Woord is but wynd; leff woord and tak the dede' (John Lydgate, 1370?–1450?).

Instead, we have to turn to pictures.[44] Just as our way of thinking is metaphorical, metaphor is the mother of all law[45] – and metaphors 'make' sense.[46] Pictures are the garment of the law. Pictures are the true story behind the stories and they have a right to be seen and heard.[47] Without taking this into account, and by leaving law in the abstract world of word and letters, we are creating a 'fetishism' of law.[48] Legal language tends to beautify the world and offers itself as the basis of happiness. The losers are rarely heard. That is why 'literature and law' is so important:[49] it presents the dark side of law to us when it defines the '*palais de justice*' as '*l'égout de la société*' (the 'sewer of society')[50] or talks about law as an 'order of sufferings'.[51]

Writing

The authority of writing

We talk about language in general but in reality we deal almost exclusively with written language, even to the extent that sometimes we forget how to use voice. Written language, or textism, is the order of the day. We are

---

[43] Spoo, *supra*, note 41, p. 544. *Cf*. Jack Hiller and Bernhard Großfeld, 'Comparative Legal Semiotics and the Divided Brain: Are We Producing Half-Brained Lawyers?', (2002) 50 Am. J. Comp. L. 175.

[44] See Bernard Hibbits, 'Making Sense of Metaphors: Visuality, Aurality and the Reconfiguration of American Legal Discourse', (1995) 16 Cardozo L.R. 229.

[45] Vivian G. Curran, 'Metaphor Is the Mother of All Law', in Roberta Kevelson (ed.), *Law and the Conflict of Ideologies* (New York: Peter Lang, 1996), p. 65; Bernhard Großfeld, *Bildhaftes Rechtsdenken* (Opladen: Westdeutscher Verlag, 1998).

[46] See Hibbits, *supra*, note 44.

[47] See Othmar Keel, *Das Recht der Bilder gesehen zu werden* (Freiburg: Universitätsverlag, 1992).

[48] See Antony Carty, 'The Psychoanalytical and Phenomenological Perspectives of Hans Kelsen and Carl Schmitt', (1995) 16 Cardozo L.R. 1235.

[49] See Uwe Diederichsen, 'Dans le piège juridique – Juristisches aus den Erzählungen Maupassants', NJW, 1999, p. 1904 [hereinafter 'Maupassant']; *id.*, 'Martial: Epigramme', in Wilfried Barner (ed.), *Querlektueren – Weltliteratur zwischen den Disziplinen* (Göttingen: Wallstein, 1999), p. 48; George A. Martinez, 'Philosophical Considerations and the Use of Narrative in Law', (1999) 30 Rutgers L.J. 683.

[50] Diederichsen, 'Maupassant', *supra*, note 49, p. 1908, n. 64.

[51] Bernhard Großfeld, *Recht als Leidensordnung* (Opladen: Westdeutscher Verlag, 1998), p. 1.

'*hommes de la lettre*'. Even at conferences, we present 'papers'. Orality has lost ground, which has been taken over by letters.[52] Though Wordsworth taught us that 'of tones and numbers all things are controlled',[53] alphabet-trained lawyers, and law professors in particular ('*lecturer* in law', '*Vorlesung*'), have lost the feeling for the 'Power of Sound'.[54] In the western world, alphanumerical patterns, acting like algorithms, have become predominant ('according to Scripture', 'as it is written').[55] Small wonder, as writing is the stronger semiotic system, collapsing space and time. Word, picture and ritual vanish, letters endure.[56] This is what enables them to create cultural identity and to appear 'holy'. Thus, 'holy' books do not just reflect life; they 'make' life (consider the 'trees of life').

The authoritative strength of signs and their trustworthiness, however, vary with different cultures. If, for instance, the name of God (10–5–6–5) shall only be written alphabetically in (holy) Hebrew letters, those letters assume a dominant position as they are inseparably associated with the name of God (and with numbers). As members of a 'book religion' (letters identify belief), we are constantly trained to find the final truth in the 'Scripture'. The letter introduces an abstract view in substitution for the evidence which we get from our senses. We receive a letter-view, not a reality-view. A 'higher' truth, not found in worldly things, can be discovered only in the written text. A statement is true because it is written: this is performative writing.[57] To read, to learn, to believe and to remember replace day-to-day experience.[58] Consequently, libraries act as the foundations of society. Today's legal scholar is the natural consequence; he or she is a product of writing and he or she thinks along with alphabet. Library experience takes the place of life experience. A classic cognitive lock-in!

---

[52] See Kathryn M. Stanchi, 'Resistance is Futile: How Legal Writing Pedagogy Contributes to the Law's Marginalization of Outsider Voices', (1998) 103 Dickinson L.R. 7.
[53] Wordsworth, 'On the Power of Sound', in *Selected Poetry, supra*, note 33, p. 36.
[54] *Id.*, p. 35.
[55] See David Berlinski, *The Advent of the Algorithm: The Idea That Rules the World* (New York: Harcourt, 2000).
[56] See Brian Stock, *The Implications of Literacy* (Princeton: Princeton University Press, 1983); Bernhard Großfeld, 'Rechtsvergleichende Zeichenkunde: Gottes Name/Gotteszahl', Zeitschrift für vergleichende Rechtswissenschaft, 2001, p. 90.
[57] See Jan Assmann, 'Inscriptional Violence and the Art of Cursing: A Study of Performative Writing', (1992) 9 Stanford Literature R. 43.
[58] See *id.*, *Fünf Stufen auf dem Weg zum Kanon: Tradition und Schriftkultur im frühen Judentum und in seiner Umwelt* (Munich: LIT Verlag, 1999), p. 1.

Writing's autonomous power

The power of writing is made the stronger as letters exert a hidden influence, which is neither fully controlled by the writer nor fully understood by the reader. Signs interact autonomously with themselves and the outside world. They paint a more abstract, or pictorial, view of the world and of how the world should both be and be seen to be. Hebrew and Chinese writings are superb examples of this proposition.[59] They work differently on different readers. Native speakers interpret the written text more deeply, filling it with more associations while, in contrast, the foreign speaker struggles to understand even the main theme.[60]

The weakness of writing

The strength of writing is coupled with a weakness.[61] Writing is a poorer form of expression as it is always more abstract. This leaves a gap in understanding as compared with orality. It is not just the word that gives meaning to spoken language but the tone ('the tone makes the music'), the strength, the modulation and the speed. It is the music behind the words, the passion behind the music, the person behind the passion (think of eye contact) and the openness to immediate responses (such as exchanges of *views*). Add to this the power of gestures, which promote understanding and consensus. They make the law intimate and give a sense that the law is literally 'made'.[62] All this is lost in the act of inscribing. Written texts are life from tinned preserves; they never taste like the real fruit. Also, the question remains: do we only take back from the sky what we first wrote into it? Is writing a closed shop, a self-referential system? In any event, writing makes translations more difficult. The more abstract the expression, the more ways there are to fill it with different pictures.

Ratio *and writing*

Writing is thus easily equated with a higher '*ratio*'.[63] The medieval monasteries supported this trend. The building made the inhabitants (Goethe,

---

[59] See Hiller and Großfeld, *supra*, note 43.
[60] See Y. Horiba, 'Reader Control in Reading: Effects of Language Competence, Text Type, and Task', (2000) 29 Discourse Processes 223.
[61] See Bernhard Großfeld, 'Language, Writing, and the Law', (1997) 5 Eur. R. 383.
[62] See Hibbits, *supra*, note 11.   [63] See Hiller and Großfeld, *supra*, note 43.

1749–1832).[64] The Benedictine monks, in particular, were surrounded by architectural geometry, a *ratio* made visible by numbers (mathematical harmony) and by writing (copying the Bible). Orality was sidelined as talking was restricted (the obligation of taciturnity).[65] Small wonder that Roman law became '*ratio scripta*' – a '*ratio*' in writing, but also a '*ratio*' from writing. It was not the '*ratio*' of the illiterate majority but of a small minority (about 1 per cent of the population),[66] which was conditioned in a very particular, alphabetical way. Writing even took control of language. Modern German was largely created by Martin Luther's translation of the Bible (language as literacy).[67] Luther's '*sola scriptura*' made German a '*Schriftsprache*' (scripture-language). Remember, Germans speak as they write!

Luther's religious concept of '*sola scriptura*' has thus become even more important (*sic veniat verbum*) for lawyers and law professors alike. Both are more alphabet- than language-oriented. Lawyers learn their job as students almost entirely in libraries for an extended period of time (law as bibliolatry)[68] and are made to overlook Lydgate's decisive 'dede'. They become 'slaves' of the writing system, enlocked in a 'mirrored room' of signs. They are constantly trained to take the fictive world of signs for the real world of facts, as shown in their tendency to 'reify' notions. There are, for example, the words '*juristische Person*' (legal person) that put a fiction on an equal footing with 'natural persons'. I recall a relatively prominent German legal tele-don telling us that files are the backbone of the state! This is particularly 'helpful' for those who adopt a superficially easy approach toward comparative law. Not being aware of the impact of writing, they do not realize the influence that it has on content.[69] This makes comparative law 'easy' and 'scientific' but unreliable.

---

[64] Johann Wolfgang von Goethe, *Wilhelm Meisters Wanderjahre*, bk I, ch. 2 [1829]. The German text reads: '*das Gebäude hat eigentlich die Bewohner gemacht.*'

[65] See Dom Johannes von der Laan, *Der architektonische Raum* (Braunschweig: Vieweg, 1992); Richard Padovan, *Dom Hans van der Laan: Modern Primitive* (Braunschweig: Vieweg, 1994). See also Ingeborg Flage, 'Stonehenge in Vaals', *Frankfurter Allgemeine Zeitung*, 21 August 1999, p. 44.

[66] See Gottfried G. Krodel, 'The Opposition to Roman Law and the Reformation', (1993–4) 10 J. L. & Relig. 221; *id.*, 'Luther and the Opposition to Roman Law in Germany', (1991) 58 Lutherjahrbuch 13.

[67] See Hans Rothe, 'Was ist "altrussische" Literatur?' (Wiesbaden: Westdeutscher Verlag, 2000), p. 9.

[68] See Frederick C. DeCoste, 'Retrieving Positivism: Law As Bibliolatry', (1990) 13 Dalhousie L.J. 55.

[69] See John Goody, *The Logic of Writing and the Organization of Society* (Cambridge: Cambridge University Press, 1986).

Writing styles and hermeneutics

Different writing styles require and create different hermeneutics.[70] Hermeneutics is sign-specific; it is sign-environment- (or geography-) dependent.[71] This is clearly visible when comparing our alphabet with Chinese characters.[72] The difference is even seen when comparing the Hebrew and the Latin (originally Greek) alphabet. The Hebrew alphabet contains only consonants and no vowels and, therefore, affords a greater leeway for interpretation. Accordingly, the aim is not to find the one unique meaning of a written text. The prize goes to the interpreter who finds evermore possible meanings and flexible answers to a concrete situation. The Arabic alphabet (also without vowels) has a similar impact. Things are different under the Latin alphabet. Vowels are ubiquitous and a change of meaning by exchanging vowels is not possible. It is clear that this more rigid structure of writing results in the search for one and only one meaning of the text. It is also much more difficult to adapt the written message of the past to the requirements of today. Thus, owing to these sign-induced different assumptions, legal texts here and legal texts there are not the same and have other effects. The 'letter of the law' indicates smoothness or rigidity and leads to different results according to the 'order of the letters'. Translating different writings precisely is almost impossible.

Add to this the differences in hermeneutics of which there is a general consciousness.[73] These differences reach new proportions when it comes to writing. Are expressions used on a more abstract level to be taken at their face value or do they need to be 'de-rhetoricized'? Do we see the true story behind the stories? May we take it into account? We all know the difference between the Continental and the English approach to interpretation.[74] On the Continent, the statute reigns supreme and is taken as the starting-point for loose explications and wide concepts of analogy. In England, it is the

---

[70] See Arndt Teichmann, 'Die "Europäisierung des Zivilrechts" und ihre Auswirkungen auf die Hermeneutik', in *Festgabe Zivilrechtslehrer 1934–35*, ed. by Walther Hadding (Berlin: Walter de Gruyter, 1999), pp. 629–48.
[71] See Bernhard Großfeld, 'Geography and Law', (1984) 82 Michigan L.R. 1510.
[72] See Jack A. Hiller, 'Law, Language, Creativity and the Divided Brain: Are We Producing Half-Brained Lawyers?', in *Festschrift Großfeld, supra*, note 1, pp. 365–81.
[73] See Günter Abel, *Sprache, Zeichen, Interpretation* (Frankfurt: Suhrkamp, 1999).
[74] For example, see Harm-Jan De Kluiver, 'Harmonisation of Law, Substantive Review and Abuse of Rights in the EC – Some Observations from the Perspective of EC Company Law', in Reiner Schulze (ed.), *Auslegung europäischen Privatrechts und angeglichenen Rechts* (Baden-Baden: Nomos, 1999), pp. 47–61.

other way round, as is expressed in the golden rule, 'adhere to the text as closely as possible'.[75] The aim of the legislative draftsman is not to make the statute easily understood, 'but that it be incapable of being misunderstood by a person who was determined to misunderstand it'.[76] The language of the statute should not be applied to a similar situation: 'The question is not what Parliament was aiming at, but what it has hit.'[77] We find other approaches toward the use of legislative materials quite in vogue in Germany, anathema in European law and rare in England. Here again, the same text (by way of translation) inevitably has different meanings.

The flow of time

Hermeneutics is of central importance in the interpretation of written texts. Is this because it is only when using the other culture's hermeneutics that we have a chance to find a text's contemporary meaning? Are we able to span time the way hermeneutics does? This is most important for written legal texts that appear to be stable in time, even though changelessness is not an appropriate character of law.[78] Law is a product of time (past and present) and is a constant conversation between traditional and current views.[79] We have to catch these dynamics of the flow of time if we want to gain understanding. Otherwise, we lose the texture of other time, miss the utter strangeness of the past. We neglect the 'sovereignty of succeeding generations'.[80] We also lose the fact that any law, in order to survive, 'must be accepted by each succeeding generation that it purports to govern'.[81] Or, to express the same thought in the words of Oliver Wendell Holmes, 'the present has a right to govern itself so far as it can'.[82] The dead hand of the law-giver and the 'almost as dead hands of the reconstructors' run into the problems of today and always end up creating a *new* meaning.[83] Comparative law, then, involves listening to the conversation that the law's

---

[75] See Roderick Munday, 'The Common Lawyer's Philosophy of Legislation', (1983) 14 Rechtstheorie 191.
[76] Weir, *supra*, note 35, p. 21.   [77] *Ibid.*
[78] See John C. Blue, 'The Government of the Living – The Legacy of the Dead', (1999) 33 U. Richmond L.R. 325, p. 329.
[79] *Cf*. Elspeth Attwooll, *The Tapestry of the Law* (Dordrecht: Kluwer, 1997).
[80] Blue, *supra*, note 78, p. 335.   [81] *Id*., p. 326.
[82] Oliver Wendell Holmes, 'Learning and Science', in *Collected Legal Papers* (New York: Peter Smith, 1952), p. 139 [1895] (hereinafter *Collected Legal Papers*).
[83] See Blue, *supra*, note 78, p. 326.

present trustees are conducting with the letters of the past. The comparatist listens to law as social music, as the 'magic flute'. Such blurry anachronism leads to blurry comparative law.

The example of illiteracy

The unbelievable, and mostly secret, strength of semiotic systems tends to paint a world which we take for 'granted'. Our cultural view is mainly bestowed by the 'myth of the alphabet', so highly, though often innocently, praised by lawyers as the 'sorcerer's apprentice' (consider Goethe's poem, '*Der Zauberlehrling*'). Lawyers are trained and made to take the fictive system for reality. The better you are in fictions, the higher you are rated as a lawyer. Elegant language is the lawyer's trademark despite real life's unfortunate lack of elegance. How, then, does language catch reality? What makes us so sure about language? Written language is a self-fulfilling prophecy. You are the best in a world which you yourself have construed from letters.

This is relevant to my experiences when representing illiterates before German courts.[84] It is almost impossible to convince German courts that illiteracy haunts 4 million adults in Germany and that it is a condition that should be respected in law.[85] Illiterates are often not stupid. They just do not fit into the particular semiotic system which we call 'alphabet' and which we use as the yardstick for intelligence. Illiterates are lost in the world of written words. They are spellbound by a spell which they cannot spell. They are semiotic and, *therefore*, intellectual *and* normative outcasts.

A lower German court, not guided by any precedent, refused to grant partial incapacity for a long-term standard cellular phone contract in the following words:

> After hearing the defendant, doubts as to his capacity no longer exist: he could follow the oral arguments, he spoke clearly [...]. His full legal capacity is not put in doubt by the fact that he has great difficulties with reading and writing. Whatever he wants to express when arguing that he is an illiterate with little literacy left – that does not matter. The civil code grants legal capacity also to persons that can neither read nor write if they can distinguish 'good and

[84] See Bernhard Großfeld, 'Analphabetismus im Zivilrecht', JZ, 1999, p. 430. See also *id.* and Oliver Brand, *Das Recht in Goethes Iphigenie auf Tauris*, JZ, 1999, p. 809.
[85] See Shirin Sojitrawalla, 'Der Mythos vom Alphabet', *Frankfurter Allgemeine Zeitung*, 17 July 1999, p. 10.

bad' – and this, the defendant can. Whoever is clearly and distinctively able to present facts and to present them orally to the court is not like a child.[86]

The judge missed the point. He argued from orality, from living words. However, the issue was not about intelligence and the lack of language. The issue was about *writing*. The issue was about dead letters and the ability to cope with them. Could the defendant distinguish 'good and bad' in a particular semiotic system unknown to him? As he could not break the 'code', the defendant saw the world through the 'glasses' of letters.

Beyond language and writing

Logical v. organic development

In Germany, we take for granted that answers from texts should be derived through logical conclusions.[87] The word 'syllogism' reigns supreme (in the sense of finding the true meaning of 'sentences' 'scientifically' through logical operations, as *per* William of Ockham, 1280–1349). This is the rule for legal texts, whereas the process is different, for instance, with national anthems. Why should this be the case? Is the structure of language really sufficiently firm to serve as a basis for geometrical-logical deductions? Is language not Delphic? What is the connecting factor between 'logic' and 'justice'? For English listeners, the questions do not seem to be as taboo as for Germans because in England, logic does not seem to be the standard which makes legal texts authoritative.

England may be maintaining a singular position. In most other parts of the western world, lawyers are trained to believe in magical deductions from magical signs.[88] 'Reason' is the leader in the field of linguistic Abracadabra or alphabetical Kabala. This catchword arrests thought. 'Reason' is repeated over and over again as if its mere repetition can make reason appear. Like 'fairness', 'reasonableness' is an untranslatable concept: it 'functions as a place holder for a range of values'.[89] Typically, they work in favour of those who use them: 'Be reasonable, do it my way.' Such pseudo-objective, but strongly biased words, should have no place in comparative dialogues.

---

[86] Amtsgericht Duisburg, file no. 53/45 C. 434/99, 13 January 2000 (Judge Dueck).
[87] *Cf*. Matthew Finkin, 'Quatsch', (1999) 83 Minnesota L.R. 1681.
[88] See Pierre Schlag, 'Anti-intellectualism', (1995) 16 Cardozo L.R. 1111, p. 1119.
[89] Fletcher, *supra*, note 23, p. 67.

God's numbers

The reliance on logic and reason has deep religious roots, starting again with the Bible. As Hebrew reading and writing is a constant training in arithmetic and algebra, God's name (the 'Tetragram') also appears as numbers first (10–5–6–5 = 26). Small wonder that, from these numerical and mathematical signs, numerical concepts are transferred to the 'one', God Himself. A God who created everything according to measure, number and weight, and who counts every hair on our head, is an eternal mathematician.[90] Small wonder also that we regard mathematical and geometrical concepts as *the* appropriate instruments to understand and order the world as a cosmos and, therefore, as constituting *the* core of legal concepts.[91]

Philosophical underpinnings

This idea received strong support from Pythagoras and Plato ('*Timaeus*') as propagated by Boethius (480–524): 'You [God] enchained the elements under the law of number.'[92] Mathematics received its particular strength after the influx of the 'new' Arabic numbers that arrived in Europe with a Spanish manuscript from 976. These numbers gained a firm hold following Gerbert d'Aurillac's studies in Vich, Northern Spain, in the years 970–6 (Aurillac was a Benedictine monk under Pope Sylvester II, 945/50–1003).[93] Later, Islamic thinkers like Avicenna (b. Buchara 980 – d. Hamada 1037) and Averroes (b. Cordoba 1126 – d. Marrakech 1198) became the figureheads. They forced Aristotle's philosophy (for Thomas Aquinas, '*the* philosopher') into the European mind ('*Latin Averroism*') and encouraged the medieval concepts of '*mos mathematicorum*' and '*deus geometra*',[94] based on the idea that God had created the world starting from numbers, rhythm and harmony.[95] Nicholas of Cusa (Cusanus, 1401–64), in particular, equated the very essence of God with geometry. In his famous book, '*De docta ignorantia*' (1440), Cusa started with the infinite triangle (three equal and rectangular angles with infinite sides) as a symbol for God and, from there, drew conclusions

---

[90] See Großfeld, *supra*, note 56.
[91] See *id.*, 'Comparative Legal Semiotics: Numbers in Law', [2001] South African L.J. 396.
[92] Pierre Riche, *Gerbert d'Aurillac: le pape de l'an mil* (Paris: Fayard, 1987), p. 47.
[93] *Id.*, *passim*. See also Jack Goody, *The East in the West* (Cambridge: Cambridge University Press, 1996).
[94] See Bernhard Großfeld, *Zeichen und Zahlen im Recht*, 2d ed. (Tübingen: J. C. B. Mohr, 1995).
[95] See Riche, *supra*, note 92, p. 46.

about the eternal existence of God.[96] In Cusa's eyes, mathematics and geometry are the leaders in any research based on making comparisons[97] and comparative relations.[98] And we could assert that they continue to be so.

Legal mathematics

It was enticing to introduce these ideas into law. Mathematics suggests a reference to a supernatural order and from there – by way of verbal connections – to an inner-world, 'just' justice. Abstract notions allow all kinds of interrelations to be made by the verbal imagination. Again, the authority of particular signs (here, numbers and geometrical figures) was used to enhance the rhetoric of law and the status of scribes ('clerks', from 'clerical'). Accordingly, through the '*mos geometricus*' in the 'century of Enlightenment' (that is, the eighteenth century), it became characteristic for German legal '*Dogmatik*' to 'construe' the law. This approach reached its height under the influence of Savigny's (1779–1861) formal logical deductions from principles. His epigones, Puchta (1798–1846) and Windscheid (1817–92), became the leaders in the field, notwithstanding Jhering's (1818–92) opposition. Windscheid (who was so influential in the elaboration of the 1896 German civil code) explained his 'jurisprudence' or 'epistemology' as follows:

> It is most important to distil the elements of each notion in order to show their intellectual structure. We can continue this operation to a smaller or lesser extent, as the elements found can themselves be compounds of even more simple elements and so on. The new legal science has the strong tendency to dissolve the notions as far as possible. And this is its merit. As a matter of fact, the full understanding of law requires that we fully exhaust the content of the notions that are used in legal rules. The same is true for their rigorous application. The decision results from a computation ('*Rechnung*'), in which the legal notions are the factors. The result of this computation is the better the safer the value of the factors stands.[99]

---

[96] Nicholas of Cusa, *De docta ignorantia*, XII.
[97] *Id.*, I: '*Comparativa igitur est omnis inquisitio medio proportionis utens*' (= All research is done through comparing by using proportions).
[98] *Id.*, I: '*Omnis igitur inquisitio in comparativa proportione facile vel difficile existit*' (= All research is done by setting comparative relations, be it more or less difficult).
[99] Bernhard Windscheid, *Lehrbuch des Pandektenrechts*, 7th ed., vol. I (Frankfurt: Rütten & Loening, 1891), p. 59.

Textism and mathematics walk hand in hand. In large parts of German legal education, they reign supreme – even today.

The limits of logic

Certainly, we do esteem these intellectual endeavours. We should appreciate the disciplined analysis, one of the fruits of which is the German *Bürgerliches Gesetzbuch*. Here again, the issue is one of shades. However, we do not believe any longer (at least not to the same extent) in 'human' mathematics.[100] Quantum physics,[101] Kurt Gödel's (1906–78) 'limits of logic'[102] and Georg Cantor's (1845–1918) 'infinite sets'[103] were steps toward this reorientation. We are more sceptical about 'legal mathematics'; we distrust a single-minded focus upon reason, logic and analysis in legal education and in the practice of law.[104] But Gods that once were linger. Still, we have learned to appreciate the importance of non-analytical mental processes. This reflects a growing awareness that the creative lawyer must also draw upon the mental processes of the artist.[105] The esteem for the only analytical, half-brained (left-sided) lawyer has passed its peak;[106] the right side of the lawyer's brain, controlling art, intuition and imagination, is no longer his or her forgotten side.[107]

We 'do know [...] that law resists scientization because of its fluid and incomplete character'.[108] We can even go beyond that:

> The scientist's claim to rationality is just part of his ideology, but he is no more reasonable or rational than the witch-hunter or the witch. In insisting on his rationality all he does is dogmatically to impose his method as that appropriate for everyone in pursuit of knowledge. In doing so he ignores the

---

[100] See J. B. Ruhl, 'Complexity Theory As a Paradigm for the Dynamical Law-and-Society System: A Wake-up Call for Legal Reductionism and the Modern Administrative State', (1996) 45 Duke L.J. 849; Jan Stewart, *Does God Play Dice?*, 2d ed. (New York: Penguin, 1997).

[101] See Ulrich Hoyer, 'Quantentheorie und Kausalität', Horin-Vergleichende Studien zur japanischen Kultur, 1999, p. 211; *id.*, 'Klassische Naturphilosophie und moderne Physik', Existentia-Meletai Sofias, 1993–4, p. 7.

[102] See John W. Dawson, 'Kurt Gödel und die Grenzen der Logik', Spektrum der Wissenschaft, September 1999, p. 73.

[103] See Amir D. Aczel, *The Mystery of the Aleph* (New York: Pocket Books, 2000).

[104] See Hiller and Großfeld, *supra*, note 43.

[105] See Graham B. Strong, 'The Lawyer's Left Hand: Nonanalytical Thought in the Practice of Law', (1998) 69 U. Colorado L.R. 759.

[106] See Hiller, *supra*, note 72, p. 365.   [107] See Strong, *supra*, note 105, p. 762.

[108] Vivian G. Curran, 'Cultural Immersion, Difference and Categories in US Comparative Law', (1998) 46 Am. J. Comp. L. 43, p. 63.

wisdom available to those who pursue other methods or work from other background beliefs.[109]

The perils of an uncritical reliance on mathematics are conveyed by a satirical epitaph published in France after the death of John Law (1671–1729), which reads: 'Here lies the celebrated Scotsman, that peerless mathematician who, by the rules of algebra, sent France to the poorhouse.'[110]

Language and religion ('Dieu et mon droit')

There is a kind of myth around and behind signs given their overwhelming importance for the efficiency and for the survival of any society. Again and again, we run into religion: Holy Language, Holy Writing, Holy Picture. Alf Ross thus refers to the interaction of language and religion in his famous article, 'Tu-Tu':

> In this way, it must be admitted, our terminology and our ideas bear a considerable structural resemblance to primitive magic thought concerning the invocation of supernatural powers which in turn are converted into factual effects.[111]

Religion's silent influences go further. Religion controls large parts of the central semiotic systems. Religion is a regiment of signs and rituals. What cannot be seen has to be represented by signs and repeated actions ('liturgies') that become symbols (*cf*. Hebr. 11, 1: 'Faith is the [...] evidence of things not seen'). That is why religion is so deeply, in the truest sense even so 'vitally', concerned with semiotics (remember the notion of cognitive lock-ins raised above). Religion often establishes and reinforces semiotic authority (again, the ideas of Holy Language, Holy Scripture, Holy Picture are pertinent) and their relative position toward each other in social standing, their acceptance and rebuttal (language v. letter v. picture). Religion also directs hermeneutics. Should the interpretation be strict, loose or more

---

[109] Karen Green and John Bigelow, 'Does Science Persecute Women? The Case of the 16th–17th Century Witch-Hunts', (1998) 73 Philosophy 195.

[110] Cynthia Grossen, 'John Law's Currency System Was Worth Its Weight in Gold', *The Wall Street Journal Europe*, 20 July 2000, p. A6.

[111] Alf Ross, 'Tu-Tu', (1957) 70 Harvard L.R. 812, p. 818. *Cf*. Layman E. Allen, 'Some Examples of Using Legal Relations Language in the Legal Domain: Applied Deontic Logic', (1998) 73 Notre Dame L.R. 535.

open to factual circumstances? Is the text supreme, secluded within itself, or is the text open to traditional adjustments, to oral corrections (just consider the oral *Torah*)?

Writing and religion received support from the printing press. Together, they formed a strong triple alliance. The English Bible, for example, made scripture dominate every department of thought. The Bible asserted the supremacy of the English language in a society which, from the eleventh to the fourteenth century, had been governed by French-speaking Normans (*cf*. law-French).[112] Its translation into English coincided with the new invention of printing.[113]

Religious pictures stand behind many rules, which we regard as mundane (this is law as 'latent theology'). The German Imperial Court called the 'fundamental rights' (*Grundrechte*) of the Weimar Constitution, 'the Holy Grail of the German people' ('*Heiligtum des deutschen Volkes*').[114] Take the US Constitution, this 'high temple of constitutional order'. It is treated like a 'sanctified structure', that is, it is interpreted like the Holy Bible ('a sort of constitutional Chartres Cathedral').[115] The binding power of the word as a constituent of contracts follows from religious concepts of the 'Word'. The line between gambling and betting on the one side (unenforceable) and valid contracts on the other side (enforceable), though always difficult to find (*cf*. 'allotment', 'lot' and 'lottery') is drawn by religion. As in Goethe's 'Faust', gambling appears to be the devil's work.[116] Our belief in numbers and mathematics is based on the biblical report that the creation itself is already counted ('first day', 'second day', etc.).[117] As we have seen, the '*mos geometricus*' of the century of enlightment is derived from the medieval '*mos mathematicorum*' and from the '*deus geometra*', who created everything according to measure, number and weight.

Our concept of money also follows from religious cults where tokens were used to replace the real sacrifice (cattle = *pecus*) with a symbol showing

---

[112] See Karsten Kerber, *Sprachwandel im englischen Recht: Vom Law French zum Englischen* (Münster: LIT Verlag, 1997).
[113] See Christopher Hill, *The English Bible and the Seventeenth-Century Revolution* (London: Penguin, 1993), p. 7.
[114] *Entscheidungen des Reichsgerichts in Zivilsachen*, vol. CII (Berlin: Walter de Gruyter, 1921), p. 165.
[115] Blue, *supra*, note 78, p. 329.
[116] See Bernhard Großfeld and Oliver Rothe, 'Spiel und Wette in Literatur und Recht', Zeitschrift für Vergleichende Rechtswissenschaft, 1999, p. 209.
[117] See Großfeld, *supra*, note 94.

the animal (*pecunia* = from *pecus*; *cf*. 'pecuniary').[118] Modern financial markets started with temple taxes (*cf*. Gen. 1, 20; 1 Kings 7, 51; Mt 17, 24) and temple economics (*cf*. Mt 21, 12; Mk 11, 15; Lk 19, 45; John 2, 14; Acts 19, 23). To swear by 'the gold of the temple' became proverbial.[119] The effects of interests and compound interests[120] as pillars of the global financial system were central issues of the Jewish and Christian religious teachings and their antagonisms.[121] Modern accounting technique (originally, the secret knowledge of those who practised the craft) was first publicized by a Franciscan monk, Pacioli, in Venice in 1494.[122] The Franciscans stood behind the first European communal bank, the Monte di Pasci de Siena (1472). Modern capitalism owes much to Calvin's religious doctrines[123] and made subjects like the 'Bible and Exchange' into common topics.[124] A modern version on a cruder level is the Ayn Rand cult, with the dollar as its symbol.[125] Even modern choice-of-law thinking has been compared to theology. Where 'interest analysis' has attained the status of a credo with some, others characterize it as a 'quaking quagmire'.[126]

Procedure

So far, we have concentrated on substantive law and have nearly missed out an equally important part: procedure. Just as it is with jokes, though, so it is with law. What matters is *who* tells the joke *how*. The outcome of cases is much affected by lawyers' and judges' emotional and intellectual legal 'instincts'.[127] Very important, though seldom discussed, are the lawyers' 'flat fees', 'contingency fees' and 'billable hours'. As for judges, civil service structures and their professional ethos are as vital as political affiliations

---

[118] See Bernhard Laum, *Heiliges Geld: Eine historische Untersuchung über den sakralen Ursprung des Geldes* (Tübingen: J. C. B. Mohr, 1924).
[119] Mt 23, 16.
[120] See John H. Biggs, 'The Miracle of Compound Interest: Why Small Differences Make Big Differences', *The Participant*, February 1998, p. 2.
[121] See Johannes Heil (ed.), *Zinsverbot und Geldverleih in jüdischer und christlicher Tradition* (Munich: Fink, 1997).
[122] See Luca Pacioli, *Summa de arithmetica, geometrica, proportioni et proportionalita* (1494).
[123] See Max Weber, *Die protestantische Ethik und der Geist des Kapitalismus* (Tübingen: J. C. B. Mohr, 1934) [1904].
[124] See Gerhard Simson, 'Bibel und Börse: Die religiösen Wurzeln des Kapitalismus', Archiv für Kulturgeschichte, 1984, p. 87.
[125] See Jeff Welker, *The Ayn Rand Cult* (Chicago: Open Court, 1999).
[126] Friedrich K. Juenger, 'A Third Conflicts Restatement?', (2000) 75 Indiana L.J. 404, p. 406.
[127] Hebr. 7, 12: 'When there is a change of priesthood, there is necessarily a change of law as well.'

and dependence on campaign contributions for re-election.[128] These factors carry more weight than 'any niceties of substantive law such as those that preoccupy textbook writers'.[129]

Rules of procedure have a similarly strong impact. Access to court, distribution of costs (legal aid, the rule according to which the loser pays all costs), the way facts are found, how the truth is established (pre-trial discovery, cross-examinations, *Miranda*) are the vital core of any legal order. 'Parties are more likely to regard their treatment at the hands of the law as unjust because of what they perceive to be defects of procedure than because of what they perceive to be defects of substantive law.'[130] Up until now, although the discussion on comparative procedure has been harsh at times, it has not always proved enlightening.[131]

In this respect, Continental Europe, England and the United States are worlds apart. Admittedly, everywhere in the west, lawyers – if they are really good – are 'fact-oriented': *'Da mihi facta, dabo tibi ius'* ('give me the facts, I will give you the law'). Facts are sacred. This is not an English or US peculiarity. But differences are to be found in the handling and discovery of facts. How are facts found (cross-examinations)? When do they matter (*Miranda*)? What is it about hearsay and the confrontation doctrine?[132] What are the rules against self-incrimination or illegally obtained evidence? Does it matter what actually happened or are we concerned only with what is accurately depicted at the trial?

On the Continent, we see a continuing exchange of written texts, punctuated whenever necessary by proof-taking hearings, but with no dramatic climax. In England, the drama is more evident. The trial is the great happening. Thus, the historical common-law jury trial continues to colour English procedure, though jury trial in civil cases is now extremely rare (despite the court having a discretion to permit jury trials to a greater extent). The jury is 'a phantom limb which, though no longer present, profoundly affects the behaviour of the body of which it used to be part'.[133] (A path dependence, reminding us of the refrain, 'Gods that once were...'.) Does the continuing

---

[128] See Mathias Reimann, 'Droit positif et culture juridique: l'américanisation du droit européen par réception', Arch. phil. dr., 2001, p. 71.
[129] Jeremy Lever, 'Why Procedure is More Important Than Substantive Law', (1999) 48 Int. & Comp. L.Q. 285, p. 285.
[130] *Ibid.*
[131] For a pacifying attempt, see John C. Reitz, 'Why We Probably Cannot Adopt the German Advantage in Civil Procedure', (1990) 75 Iowa L.R. 987.
[132] See *Lilly* v. *Virginia*, (1999) 119 S.Ct. 1887.   [133] Lever, *supra*, note 129, p. 296.

tradition reflect a national predilection for drama?[134] The US jury and the US pre-trial discovery, mass torts and class actions need no further elaboration.

These rules of procedure are very strong tacit formants, mostly overlooked. But the consequences for comparatists are clear enough:

> Lawyers from different traditions start from different assumptions about the way in which the law ought to work, and they carry these assumptions through into the way in which they make it work. The greatest problem for the comparatist is to articulate what lawyers of different traditions do not think to explain because they take it for granted. He must especially avoid making value judgments about the respective merits of different systems before establishing the facts and how they work.[135]

The truth of the law lies in its execution. How much suffering are we willing to accept for how long? Comparative law should start here!

Path dependence

This survey shows that law reaches far beyond oral and written language and that it is the product of vital, environmental factors that just grow and which we cannot disentangle.[136] Following Rudolf von Jhering,[137] Oliver Wendell Holmes (1841–1935) used the picture, 'the path of the law'.[138] But how little do we know even about the paths of our own culture, how little do we know about the silent changes brought about by new technical and commercial developments?[139] We do not even know why a path was taken; we just see that there is a path and that we are path dependent.[140] It is impossible to

---

[134] *Id.*, p. 297.
[135] David Edwards, 'Fact-Finding: A British Perspective', in D.L. Carey-Miller and Paul R. Beaumont (eds.), *The Option of Litigation in Europe* (London: U.K.N.C.C.L., 1993), p. 44.
[136] *Cf.* H. Patrick Glenn, *Legal Traditions of the World* (Oxford: Oxford University Press, 2000), *passim.*
[137] *Cf.* Rudolf von Jhering, 'Theorie der juristischen Technik', in Werner Krawietz (ed.), *Theorie und Technik der Begriffsjurisprudenz* (Darmstadt: Wissenschaftliche Buchgesellschaft, 1976), p. 11 [1858].
[138] Oliver Wendell Holmes, 'The Path of the Law', in *Collected Legal Papers*, *supra*, note 82, pp. 167–202 [1897].
[139] See John A. Makdisi, 'The Islamic Origins of the Common Law', (1999) 77 North Carolina L.R. 1635.
[140] See Douglass C. North, *Structure and Change in Economic History* (New York: Norton, 1981); *id., Institutions, Institutional Change and Economic Performance* (Cambridge, Mass.: Cambridge University Press, 1990); *id.*, 'Institutions and Credible Commitment', (1993) 149 J. Institutional & Theoretical Econ. 11.

discern the texture given by informal constraints and encouragements and to evaluate exactly the strength of an individual thread.

This is no reason to give up. We can recognize major conditioning factors, we can evaluate their presence or absence and we can discuss their relative status – though we cannot adequately perceive their interactions and functions under circumstances which we never fully understand. Law is just there and its existence does not need an explanation. The past is more than facts; it is normative.

We may, however, find an answer to the questions why people obey the law and what creates a legal obligation to follow rules.[141] We know that compliance is rooted in the belief in law's legitimacy much more than in the assessment of the likelihood that one will be called to order. Signs and pictures are essential factors in lending law the appearance of legitimacy. Their authority conveys a kind of magical authority to the law. The correct 'spelling' is an important part of the law's magical *spell*.[142]

Comparatists

Having started back-to-front, we now return to the beginning of the topic, that is, to 'comparatists'. What can comparatists do when confronted with the bundle of which language is just one cord? Here again, we need to consider some foundational issues.

Comparison

So far, the discussion has given us new insights into the concept of 'comparison'. As stated, the concept originally came up in the context of mathematics and geometry (Cusanus) and was then extended into law as a kind of '*mos geometricus*'.[143] But we know that human beings are neither numbers nor geometrical patterns; they are not idealized abstract figures and they have more than three dimensions. If this is so, then, comparison gets a different meaning, one detached from mathematics.

We should also take into account that law has to do with 'order'. But what is 'order'? Is it an objective situation or a subjective feeling? Does it have

---

[141] See Tom R. Tyler, *Why People Obey the Law* (New Haven: Yale University Press, 1990).
[142] See Bernhard Großfeld, *Zauber des Rechts* (Tübingen: J. C. B. Mohr, 1999).
[143] For the Roman-law background, see Reinhard Zimmermann, 'In der Schule von Ludwig Mitteis: Ernst Rabels rechtshistorische Ursprünge', RabelsZ, 2001, p. 1.

ethical overtones or undertones? Is 'order' just an environment in which we function easily, depending on individual abilities and inclinations? Is it an '*ordo rationis*', as Thomas Aquinas (1225–74) felt, or is it a '*sentiment du coeur*', as Pascal (1623–62) imagined? We can 'order' vertically/horizontally, historically/systematically or just numerically/alphabetically. We can simply add differences in emphasis and rhythm. Order follows from function and function follows from order. The question remains, though: if we cannot define order objectively, how can we compare it? How can we compare inner feelings? What creates inner feelings: geographical environment, semiotic systems, technical developments? Is it a matter of intuition? What, then, creates our intuitions? Social music? Ponder the Australian aborigines' *dream paths* and *song lines*[144] – are they, and we, dreaming order? ('We are such stuff/As dreams are made on, and our little life/Is rounded with a sleep'.)[145] Indeed, this could be a cultural universal: order as an 'American dream', an 'English dream', a 'German dream', a 'global dream', a dream full-stop.

Functional v. organic approaches

The question of comparison becomes even more critical when we ask for functions. What is the function of a particular rule within the wider context? Given the innumerable interactions between reality, signs and thoughts and given all kinds of unpredictable entanglements along the path, this is difficult to answer. Superficial attempts abound, often decorated with allusions to economic analysis, '*homo economicus*' and transaction costs.[146] None of them are very convincing.[147] Undeniably, law is not only the product of some inexplicable growth as a spontaneous social order but it is also the result of purposive projects, of functions.[148] Yet, how do we find those purposes from the outside? Will we find purposes from texts? The difficulties

---

[144] See Bruce Chatwin, *The Songlines* (London: Jonathan Cape, 1987), *passim*.
[145] Shakespeare, *The Tempest*, IV, 156–8.
[146] See William Ewald, 'Posner's Economic Approach to Comparative Law', (1998) 33 Texas Int. L.J. 381. But see Richard A. Posner, 'Savigny, Holmes, and the Law of Economics of Possession', (2000) 86 Virginia L.R. 535; Anthony Ogus, 'Competition Between National Legal Systems: A Contribution of Economic Analysis to Comparative Law', (1999) 48 Int. & Comp. L.Q. 405.
[147] See Catherine A. Rogers, 'Gulliver's Troubled Travels, or the Conundrum of Comparative Law', (1998) 67 George Washington L.R. 149.
[148] See Piergiuseppe Monateri, 'Cunning Passages: Comparison and Ideology in the Law and Language Story', in Sacco and Castellani, *supra*, note 20, pp. 123–41.

increase when we turn to a legal culture farther away from our own. What are the standards of distance? Do cultures share the same functions and may we be misled into taking our functional views for theirs? Religious laws, in particular, do not allow for asking about functions, as this question takes away from the authority of the law. The law is within God[149] – and God cannot be functionalized. What counts is to *do* the law, to keep it 'in your mouth and in your heart', not to categorize it according to human understanding and temporary needs. Asking for functions may diminish the law's status.

But is this *comparative* law? As we have seen, comparison is a difficult task. We need a '*tertium comparationis*', which we pretend to find through a functional approach. How is this function served here, how is it served there? The function is not only hard to identify, as we have seen, but how do we know if the goal has been served according to the understanding of members of the other culture? The presently pervading textism in our field does not tell us much about this crucial issue as cultures tend to keep their weaknesses taboo toward foreigners. The textual approach gives a false impression of precision and security.

This rejection of the textual approach is not irrational. The basic idea behind the alternative approach is that law largely grows from roots beyond our control that are partially universal.[150] This approach ascribes the development of law to the dynamics of day-to-day experiences, which find their way into the semiotic system through osmotic dynamics, for example, by introducing new oral vowels (in an alphabet without vowels), by encouraging new readings (if *this* is the ethic of hermeneutics), by meeting new challenges (such as the homeland v. diasporas), by the rise of circumventing practices that become standard over time (*cf.* the German '*Sicherungsübereignung*') and by new technical developments (the internet). This is an organic as opposed to a functional/rational approach, or perhaps a *mixture of both*.

The home view

The situation is puzzling. Codes and treatises are, at best, unreliable guides mainly from the past.[151] Indeed, the history of mundane texts is the history

---

[149] See Weiss, *supra*, note 27, p. 53
[150] See Bernhard Großfeld, 'The Invisible Hand: Patterns of Order in Comparative Law', [1997] South African L.J. 648.
[151] See Edwards, *supra*, note 135, p. 44.

of decline. How do they become living experience, how do they affect real life today? Unfortunately, we, national lawyers, often arrive too late on our field of honour.[152] German law students, in particular, are pressed into provincial text-structures by a dull crafts-school training that lasts far too long. How can we escape from this prison of textism, of legal mathematics and geometrical concepts, which students are made to believe is the 'wide-open country' to which they aspire? These students are demotivated into playing wisely and into growing as '*homines ludentes*'. Prisoners so conditioned do not see the prison any more; they do not see the green fields outside. Prison work is the basis for a career in the prison,[153] and the inmates are trained to become epigones since this is the fastest and most comfortable route toward local recognition. Consider that America was not named after Columbus!

There is a strong temptation to apply these inmate views to the outside world, to construe the world according to the geometry and time-concept of the prisoner's emotional and intellectual home-base. The inmate disciples actually create and 'construe' the world, which they pretend to discover, a self-referential approach called the 'science of law' (*Rechtswissenschaft*) or a 'world in a nutshell'.

Transplants

People trained in this prison-like manner eagerly 'jump' on 'transplants' and on 'legal families' when they are finally let loose on the world.[154] Finally, something 'reasonable' that looks reliable and up to standards! They flatter themselves about German or French law being found 'just everywhere' (from South America to China and Japan) and on the common law being admired in exotic places.[155] By the same mental disposition and in the same breath, they regret the influx of 'scientifically inferior and obscure' legal imports. But can 'transplants' help? Not to the extent that they pretend to do.

---

[152] See Pierre Legrand, 'How to Compare Now', (1996) 16 Leg. Stud. 223, p. 241.
[153] See Hans-Christof Kraus, *Theodor Anton Heinrich Schmalz* (Frankfurt: Vittorio Klostermann, 1999). For a review, see Gerd Roellecke, JZ, 2000, p. 198.
[154] See William Ewald, 'Comparative Jurisprudence (II): The Concept of Legal Transplants', (1995) 43 Am. J. Comp. L. 489; Paul E. Geller, 'Policy Consideration: Legal Transplants in International Copyright – Some Problems of Method', (1994) 13 U.C.L.A. Pacific Basin L.J. 199.
[155] *Cf*. Helmut Janssen, *Die Übertragung von Rechtsvorstellungen auf fremde Kulturen am Beispiel des englischen Kolonialrechts* (Tübingen: J. C. B. Mohr, 2000).

Certainly, transplants do exist as legal cultures grow from the absorption of foreign ideas and through borrowing from foreign experiences.[156] Indeed, there is little that is really German in German law. Currently, German corporation law imitates many US innovations.[157] 'Legal transplants' appear to be easily accessible to those looking for new ideas (which are always rare).[158] However, we have to be cautious. Transplants are of little help when they create a false sense of familiarity, of *déjà vu*; they might turn out to be '*faux-amis*'. 'Transplants' are first transplants of signs (including the latent 'content' of signs). As such, they may be 'law out of context'.[159] Separated from their cultural roots, the written signs stay on but they become even more abstract. This makes them more the object of studies in theory of law than the object of veneration and, hence, the carrier of creative influences. Such transplants are often predominantly law for lawyers and for legal philosophers. This may change over time, as happened with Roman law in Germany under the impact of '*usus modernus pandectarum*' from the sixteenth to the nineteenth century. In this case, though, the persistent signs silently gain their new content from the new environment and this makes them less reliable as 'transplants'. It is inevitable, though often unperceived, that the transplanted signs receive another meaning to the extent that the original and receiving environments differ. The magic flutes of cultures play distinctive melodies: 'Things as they are/Are changed upon the blue guitar.'[160] The interaction of static signs and dynamic life leads to unpredictable results. Therefore, transplants are not bulwarks to rest on but invitations to be aware of the versatility of semiotic contents.

The need for immersion

Following our local training, we always start comparative legal work with reading – taking for granted that written law has a fairly similar authority everywhere in the civilized world. This view is a priori mistaken but it leads

---

[156] See Alan Watson, *Legal Transplants*, 2d ed. (Athens, Georgia: University of Georgia Press, 1993); *id.*, 'Legal Transplants and European Private Law', (2000) Electronic J. Comp. L. [http://law.kub.nl/ejcl/44/art44–2.html#N8] (hereinafter 'European Private Law').
[157] See Bernhard Großfeld, *The Strength and Weakness of Comparative Law*, transl. by Tony Weir (Oxford: Oxford University Press, 1990), p. 15.
[158] Watson, 'European Private Law', *supra*, note 156, p. 3.
[159] See *id.*, *Law Out of Context* (Athens, Georgia: University of Georgia Press, 2000).
[160] Wallace Stevens, 'The Man With the Blue Guitar', in *The Collected Poems of Wallace Stevens* (New York: Vintage,1990), p. 165 [1937].

to further undesirable results. We see the foreign world first as letters. But what should be given importance is neither the beauty nor the consistency or logic of semiotic systems. What counts are the effects of those semiotic systems. What do we know about them? Very little and often we do not even care. We must perform some kind of cultural excavation to find the meanings of foreign texts even though we can be sure that we will never be quite sure.[161] This requires a deep cultural immersion into the target culture's identity,[162] into 'the collective programming of the mind which distinguishes the members of one human group from another'.[163] We have to recognize, however, that human cultures are largely impenetrable to each other. Cultures tend to keep their taboos to themselves. 'Distance' is an indispensable companion in order not to be lost in 'immersion'.[164]

The parallax in law

A few facts, at least, are certain. Law is more than language and literature; it is subject and object in a much larger and much more intricate web of experiences and hopes. Legal cultures never work quite the way they appear, or want to appear, in any semiotic system. There is always a semiotic overreach and underreach, a semiotic rhetoric. Law never represents the fullness of life. There is always a shadow, a parallax; in this respect, '[t]he time is out of joint'.[165] Therefore, whoever wants to take exactly the words or the letter of the law becomes an 'order-eccentric', an 'ex-centrist' in the full meaning of the word. The German poet Heinrich von Kleist (1777–1811) makes this point superbly in his famous novel, *Michael Kohlhaas*.

The limits of understanding

The internal working of legal cultures and their interaction with the 'ocean of silence' is barely penetrable from the outside. To what extent does a culture

---

[161] See Spoo, *supra*, note 41, p. 553.
[162] See Curran, *supra*, note 108. See also Bernhard Großfeld, *Kernfragen der Rechtsvergleichung* (Tübingen: J. C. B. Mohr, 1996). For a review, see Vivian G. Curran, 'Book Review', (1999) 47 Am. J. Comp. L. 535.
[163] Geert Hofstede, *Culture's Consequences* (Newbury Park, California: Sage, 1980), p. 19. See also *id.*, *Cultures and Organizations* (New York: McGraw-Hill, 1991).
[164] See Nora V. Demleitner, 'Combating Legal Ethnocentrism: Comparative Law Sets Boundaries', (1999) 31 Arizona. L.J. 737.
[165] Shakespeare, *Hamlet*, I, v, 189.

emphasize communal duties more than individual rights?[166] What are the negotiating styles?[167] What about evasions and circumventions? Marriage annulments may be substituted for divorces; sale and resale practices or general damages may replace forbidden forms of interests and compound interests.[168] Where is the line between pressure and extortion? What illegal acts are regarded as legitimate? How are barristers selected to become Queen's Counsels and what is the function of the 'silk system'?[169]

Normally we know little about 'old-boy networks'. 'Guanxi-relations' are largely impenetrable, the 'cash flow of law and justice' in some cultures might be beyond our expectations. 'Untouchables' leave us stunned. Even if we meet 'democratic systems', there are further considerations – what percentage of the population actually votes and what percentage regards statutes as an expression of *their* worldviews? We also have limited knowledge about why and how some cultures emphasize hierarchy over equality (or vice versa), why some encourage and others discourage litigation.[170] Sometimes, we do not even ask, not being aware that conceivably there are differences.

The 'rebirth' of capital punishment in the United States, the revitalization of 'Southern Trees' (*cf.* Lewis Allen's poem, 'Strange Fruit'),[171] was such an unexpected event. The loss of voting rights for convicted felons in many US states is another example. Even *Buck* v. *Bell*, featuring Holmes's 'three generations of imbeciles', is full of surprises.[172] Path dependence is difficult to recognize for (geometrically minded) lawyers who see the world as a flat plain to be inscribed anew everyday. As to the loss of voting rights, who would have expected the explanation that losing the right to vote is a traditional part of a felon's sentence, based on European laws that pre-date the nation's founding? We are managers of an 'encyclopaedia of ignorance'[173] – or,

---

[166] See Won-Ho Lee, 'Kurzer Abriss über koreanische Recht in Vergangenheit und Gegenwart' in *Festschrift Großfeld, supra*, note 1, pp. 687–700.

[167] See Jeswald W. Salacuse, 'Ten Ways That Culture Affects Negotiating Style: Some Survey Results', (1998) Negotiation J. 221.

[168] See Oliver Brand, *Englisches Zinsrecht* (Tübingen: J. C. B. Mohr, 2002).

[169] See Frances Gibb, 'Watchdog to Check: How QCs Earn Their Fees', *The Times*, 24 July 2000, p. 9.

[170] See Patti Waldmeier, 'Legal Eagles Rule the Roost', *Financial Times*, 11–12 December 1999, p. 12.

[171] There is a discussion of this poem in Judge Reinhard's dissent in *Campbell* v. *Wood*, (1994) 18 F.3d 662, p. 692 (9th Cir.).

[172] (1927) 274 US 200. See Rodney A. Smolla, 'The Trial of Oliver Wendell Holmes', (1994) 36 William & Mary L.R. 173.

[173] Ronald Duncan and Miranda Weston-Smith (eds.), *Encyclopedia of Ignorance* (London: Pergamon Press, 1977).

more encouragingly, an 'encyclopaedia of the unexpected'. Our fate is to be taken by surprise:

> Nota: man is the intelligence of his soil,
> The sovereign ghost. As such, the Socrates
> Of snails, musician of pears, principium
> And lex. Sed quaeritur: is this the same wig
> Of things, this nincompated pedagogue,
> Preceptor to the sea? Crispin at sea
> Created, in his day, a touch of doubt.[174]

The possibilities for comparison

Avoiding perfectionism

There are lots of other questions along the way. Even leaving out the central question of 'what we mean by "law" as the object of all our endeavours?', we could ask how we can translate[175] – and how we can compare? These issues can be left to Pierre Legrand[176] and to Tony Weir,[177] although not without quoting a sentence from Weir: 'The difference between the oral and the written of course is the difference between interpreting a speaker and translating a writer.'[178] In any case, we have to be aware that translation might acquire a new dimension through the use of computers. All of a sudden, language is exposed to a particular algorithm that does not fully represent the human mind.[179] Such an impressive technical device might tend to cover up secret changes in linguistic shades. Just consider the translation of the words 'rule of law' (English – and American?), '*Rechtsstaat*' (German) and '*prééminence du droit*' (French).[180] However, although translation remains imperfect, it *is* possible – at least in a face-to-face situation.[181] 'Perfect' is a

---

[174] Stevens, 'The Comedian as the Letter C', *supra*, note 160, p. 27.
[175] See Susan Šarčević, *New Approach to Legal Translation* (The Hague: Kluwer, 1997). For aspects of 'missionaries' linguistics', see Brigitte Schlieben-Lange, 'Missionslinguistik in Lateinamerika', Zeitschrift für Literaturwissenschaft und Linguistik, 1999, p. 34; Christine Dümmler, 'Die Übersetzungsproblematik in Missionarssprachwerken aus der kolumbianischen Kolonialzeit', Zeitschrift für Literaturwissenschaft und Linguistik, 1999, p. 100.
[176] See Pierre Legrand, *Le droit comparé* (Paris: Presses Universitaires de France, 1999); *id.*, *Fragments on Law-as-Culture* (Deventer: W. E. J. Tjeenk Willink, 1999); *id.*, *supra*, note 152.
[177] Weir, *supra*, note 35, p. 24.   [178] Ibid.
[179] *Cf.* William Safire, 'Numbers War Between the Continents', *International Herald Tribune*, 6 March 2000, p. 4.
[180] For assistance, see Fletcher, *supra*, note 23, pp. 57–70.
[181] See Lutterman, *supra*, note 1, p. 77.

mathematical ('perfect circle') and logical ('perfect proof') concept. It has no outside reality independently from that. We should not become 'perfectionists'. It is now appropriate, therefore, rather to turn to our opportunities – in fields that are often overlooked.

The basis for communication

How, then, do we keep communicating? Clearly, we do not have to give up the comparative endeavour. At least, we adjust to expecting the unexpected; we learn to distrust our localized methods that were conceived for another field of engagement. We have to immerse ourselves into the cultural context in which the legal system operates.[182] By the same token, we learn about factors that shape concepts of order, that shape the '*sentiment du coeur*', and in time we may be able to guess about trends and tendencies. Comparative law is indeed primarily a *way* of finding out not just about others, but about ourselves. It opens up the world. Thus, comparative law creates the basis for a cross-cultural (though imperfect) communication.[183] This stays in line with a great tradition that interprets the 'rule of law' as 'an invitation to a discussion and a debate'.[184] This is more than just 'cherish[ing] differences';[185] it is an attempt to find and to cross bridges.[186] Comparison is an afterthought that has to be handled cautiously in order not to enslave foreign experiences, foreign hopes and foreign worldviews into our notions of how the world should be. Then, the other law is not our slave but our partner. The results will always be imperfect as precise comparison in human relations is impossible:

> Enough of science and of art
> Close up these barren leaves;
> Come forth, and bring with you a heart
> That watches and receives.[187]

Shared experiences

Admittedly, '[t]he effort to justify comparative law by its practical uses sometimes verges on the ridiculous'.[188] Nonetheless, there are possibilities

---

[182] See Curran, *supra*, note 108, p. 51. [183] *Id.*, p. 50. [184] Fletcher, *supra*, note 23, p. 57.
[185] Legrand, *supra*, note 152, p. 240. [186] See Markesinis, *supra*, note 1, p. 194.
[187] This is an extract from a Catholic prayer-book. [188] Sacco, *supra*, note 24, p. 2.

for comparison provided we do not aim too high and stay down to earth.[189] We should start from a point of reference where we share experiences.

Markets

A prime example is the experience with homogeneous goods in common-market environments. This discussion leaves out other day-to-day experiences that are not primarily market-oriented. Certainly, there is a market for love and for marriages but, for our purposes, the concept of 'human dignity' restricts that of market. Value judgements limit or extend the meaning of every notion.

The reference to markets for goods and services as a common ground for the exchange of legal views is a fact familiar from history. The European market starting in the eleventh century with European commercial roads and pilgrimages (*cf.* the 'great pilgrimage of the Middle Ages', the pilgrimage to Santiago de Compostella)[190] led to the reception of the amalgamated canon law and Roman law as the '*jus communis*'. Similarly, the European Common Market preceded European law. Global markets give rise to '*lex mercatoria*' and to global rules of accounting. Markets convey experiences and worldviews, enforce comparisons in many fields and in many languages and are a formidable means of communication (beyond voice and writing).[191] That is why common markets make common semiotic systems, such as weight, measures, money – and law. The market also ensures that the standard meanings of signs remain undisturbed, as trust in signs is indispensable for low transaction costs and for credible commitments to keep customers and clients.[192]

The discussion turns, therefore, to the chances of comparative law with regard to global financial markets. Skipping the extensive debates on the international '*lex mercatoria*',[193] I propose to focus on rules of accounting.[194]

---

[189] *Cf.* Thomas Weigend, 'Book Review', JZ, 2000, p. 41.
[190] One need only think of St James's Palace in London or St James's Street in King's Lynn.
[191] See Werner Krawietz, 'Legal Communication in Modern Law and Legal Systems', in Lucent J. Wintgens (ed.), *The Law in Philosophical Perspective* (Dordrecht: Kluwer, 1999), pp. 69–120.
[192] See Claude Ferry, 'Market Anthropology and International Legal Order', in *Liber Amicorum Richard M. Buxbaum* (London: Kluwer, 2000), pp. 149–55 [hereinafter *Liber Amicorum Buxbaum*].
[193] See Stefan Grundmann, 'General Principles of Private Law and Ius Commune Modernum as Applicable Law?', in *Liber Amicorum Buxbaum, supra*, note 192, pp. 213–34.
[194] See Bernhard Großfeld, 'Global Accounting: Where Internet Meets Geography', (2000) 48 Am. J. Comp. L. 261 [hereinafter 'Global Accounting']; *id.*, 'Loss of Distance: Global Corporate Governance and Global Corporate Actors', (2000) 34 Int. Lawyer 963.

The internet[195]

The concept of 'comparative law' has received a new impetus through the internet, which makes time and distance shrink. It brings cultures together at the tap of a finger, multiplies contacts and creates new markets, which then create new rules. This does not mean, however, that local or personal differences and, therefore, comparative law do not count any more. Global trade depends on local trustworthiness and this turns around local conventions and means of enforcement. That is why the term 'glocalization of markets', as derived from 'globalization' and 'localization', is preferable.

Capital markets[196]

'Glocalization' finds its strongest expression in capital markets for which national borders do not exist any more. Here, the financial landscape has undergone a significant transformation as a result of the internet. We see the rise of a virtual economy in cyberspace. The internet is more than a passive community of people accessing information. As with every other semiotic system, it constitutes an active community of users 'who create content',[197] that is, *new* content. The activities of investors become increasingly global and cross-border transactions[198] and cyber-corporations multiply.[199] Yet, different legal cultures remain. Rules of accounting are among the prime movers of flows of capital around the globe. These actors leave their micro-economic clothes behind and grow into macro-economic actors of unprecedented proportions. They are the cornerstone of international finance and the guarantors of macro-justice in capital markets.

---

[195] See William Twining, 'Globalization and Comparative Law', (1999) 6 Maastricht J. Eur. & Comp. L. 217; Mireille Delmas-Marty, 'La mondialisation du droit: chances et risques', D.1999.Chr.43.

[196] See Dagmar Cöster-Waltjen, 'Accounting, Auditing and Global Capital Markets', in *Liber Amicorum Buxbaum*, supra, note 192, pp. 101–12; Gerard Hertig, 'Der Einfluss neuer Informationstechniken auf das Gesellschaftsrecht und die corporate governance-Debatte', in *Liber Amicorum Buxbaum*, supra, note 192, pp. 265–82.

[197] Bernard Hibbits, 'Changing Our Minds: Legal History Meets the World Wide Web', (1999) 17 L. & Hist. R. 385, p. 385.

[198] See Bernhard Großfeld, 'Cross-Border Mergers: Accounting and Valuation', Zeitschrift für Vergleichende Rechtswissenschaft, 2001, p. 1.

[199] See *id.*, 'CyberCorporation Law: Comparative Legal Semiotics/Comparative Legal Logistics', (2001) 35 Int. Lawyer 1405; *id.* and Josef Höltzenbein, 'CyberLex als Unternehmensrecht', Neue Zeitschrift für Gesellschaftsrecht, 2000, p. 779.

Global accounting[200]

Competing systems of accounting

Global accounting also turns out to be a wonderland with the most practical challenges for comparatists. This is owing to the fact that the information derived from accounting is more useful and more reliable if it can be easily compared with similar information from abroad. It would be a large step in this direction if all enterprises used the same quality of international accounting standards. Unfortunately, this is not the case. Basically, two systems compete with each other: the Europe-inspired International Accounting Standards (IAS) and the United States–American Generally Accepted Accounting Principles (GAAP). At first glance, it looks reassuring that both sets are in English. This suggests that there might finally be a common language basis for comparative law.[201] However, one must ask important questions. Is this language English or American? Where do these languages differ? One must be aware of idiosyncrasies. It is hard to think of any legal terms in these two languages that have the same content. Even when working with International Standards, we cannot leave the problems of language behind.[202] In addition, accounting is a kind of international meta-language, whereas 'law'[203] refers constantly to a local environment, be it in contract, property or company law.

The numbers' war[204]

The present reality in accounting can be described as a 'numbers war' between Europe and the United States.[205] We live in a Babel of accounting

---

[200] See Großfeld, 'Global Accounting', *supra*, note 194; *id.*, 'Common Roots of the European Law of Accounting', (1989) 23 Int. Lawyer 865.
[201] *Cf*. David J. Gerber, 'System Dynamics: Toward a Language of Comparative Law?', (1998) 46 Am. J. Comp. L. 719.
[202] See Campana, *supra*, note 20, p. 7; Olivier Moréteau, 'L'anglais pourrait-il devenir la langue juridique commune en Europe?', in Sacco and Castellani, *supra*, note 20, pp. 143–62; Jacques Vanderlinden, 'Le futur des langues du droit ou le dilemme du dernier orateur', in Sacco and Castellani, *supra*, note 20, pp. 193–221; Hans Hattenhauer, 'Zur Zukunft des Deutschen als Sprache der Rechtswissenschaft', JZ, 2000, p. 545.
[203] See Bernhard Großfeld, 'Normschaffung und Normvermittlung im Internationalen Unternehmensrecht', in *Festschrift für Marcus Lutter* (Cologne: Otto Schmidt, 2000), pp. 47–60.
[204] See *id.*, 'Lawyers and Accountants: A Semiotic Competition', (2001) 36 Wake Forest L.R. 167.
[205] The expression is taken from Safire, *supra*, note 179, p. 4.

languages, which often hides different policy objectives. This increases the costs of accessing multiple capital markets and creates inefficiencies in cross-border capital flows. Also, current discrepancies in accounting practices may be a reason for foreign corporations not to list their securities on US exchanges. Efforts toward the convergence of accounting standards in a global environment are, however, the order of the day. The work is primarily being done through the International Organization of Securities Commissions (IOSCO), which presently numbers 135 members. The aim is to develop a globally accepted, high-quality financial reporting framework. Thus, all of a sudden, a subject that had been largely neglected by comparatists has entered the limelight: comparative accounting.[206] By the same token, accounting has entered macro-economic proportions, also missed by most lawyers, who relegated accounting to bookkeeping and the counting of 'peanuts'. In reality, accounting is the most potent semiotic system in the movement of economic powers, wealth and poverty around the world.

The combination of the internet and accounting has dramatically increased this impact. Accounting activates powers in statistically relevant proportions; it triggers interests and compound interests. This makes it *the* primary actor in world economics. Add to this the need to value assets and firms all around the world, be it for cross-border mergers or financial 'rankings'. A whole new world of language is appearing on the comparatist's horizon.[207]

Global discussion

It is here that comparative law reaches new dimensions. Rules of accounting constantly interact with corporation law and the language in one field interacts with the language in the other field. The same names do not mean the same for both sides in the information process. There is just no 'common' sense (in the original meaning of the term) which would allow for such an equivalence. The clarity of the numbers used covers up strong and irregular undercurrents. Comparative law then becomes a prime instrument of intercultural conversation, of a meeting of minds in a technical and complicated field.

---

[206] See Bernhard Großfeld, 'Comparative Accounting', (1993) 28 Texas Int. L.J. 235.
[207] See *id.*, 'Global Valuation: Geography and Semiotics', (2002) 55 Southern Methodist U. L.R. 197; *id.*, 'Internationale Unternehmensbewertung', Betriebs-Berater, 2001, p. 1836.

The involvement of the internet

Concept Release

The US Financial Accounting Standard Board has presented a comprehensive comparative study of both sets of standards as a basis for an intensive discussion.[208] At this point, the debate reached internet dimensions. The US Securities and Exchange Commission (SEC) has started an exchange of comments on the internet through its 'Concept Release' concerning the recognition of IAS in the United States.[209]

The SEC's move has turned up the heat on a long-simmering debate. Currently, foreign corporations are allowed to list in the United States only under the US accounting rules (GAAP). Up until now, the SEC suspected that under IAS the numerical analysis was less rigorous. Prominent examples are costs for research and development: under GAAP, corporations have to write off these costs immediately, while under IAS they can be written off over time, giving management greater latitude to level out future earnings. A common set of rules would make it much easier for the market to allocate capital efficiently, to compare one set of results to another on a comparable basis. If 'profit' means one thing in one country and something quite different in another, how can actions be decided upon? The SEC's invitation has now moved harmonization efforts onto the front burner. All electronically mailed comments are to be published on the SEC's website. This is an international forum of an as yet unknown size. The publication could turn out to be 'an auspicious instrument of international and comparative analysis'.[210] The internet unlocks market information that allows us to share experiences. Thus, it promotes assimilation through new technology.

Issues

The Release reiterates US reservations against IAS.[211] It takes the position that the traditional 'textism' in comparative law cannot help. Instead,

---

[208] See *The IASC-US Comparison Project: A Report on the Similarities and Differences Between IASC Standards and US GAAP*, 2d ed. by Carrie Bloomer (Norwalk, Connecticut: Financial Accounting Standards Board, 1999). For an introduction, see Donna L. Street and Sidney G. Gray, 'How Wide is the Gap Between IASC and US GAAP?', (1999) 8 Int. Account. Audit. & Taxation 133.

[209] See www.sec.gov/sitemap.shtml.

[210] Amed Olsora, 'Toward an Auspicious Reconciliation of International and Comparative Analysis', (1998) 48 Am. J. Comp. L. 669, p. 669.

[211] *Cf.* James D. Cox, 'Regulatory Duopoly in US Securities Markets', (1999) 99 Columbia L. R. 1200.

the Release looks for effectiveness from proper application and rigorous interpretation. The emphasis is on investors' and analysts' experiences. The SEC asks for answers to three concepts sub-divided into twenty-six questions.

The three main issues are as follows. Are the IAS sufficiently comprehensive, are they of sufficiently high quality and can they be interpreted and applied rigorously and uniformly? The twenty-six detailed questions are concerned, among others things, with the true and fair view as an overriding principle, the option to revalue assets to fair value, the useful life of goodwill and other intangibles, the transition provisions for employee-benefit obligations, the hedges of anticipated transactions and commitments, and the concept of merger of equals.

The outcome of the current assessment work will have far-reaching implications. Depending on the feedback it receives, the SEC could eventually abolish its current requirement that foreign corporations adapt or redo their books according to US GAAP before being listed on US exchanges. The results may be dramatic. If the IAS were to be recognized, then the present balance between the two sets of standards in Germany would probably shift toward them.

Difficulties

Whether the 'standards' or 'principles' will be treated as 'law' need not bother us as long as they are perceived as binding under any standard of fairness. Comparative semiotics is not outflanked. Written language is expressed with a series of symbols that we call 'letters'. Do people agree on what the symbols stand for or do we continue 'gesticulating wildly in a Tower of Babel'?[212] How are the standards to be interpreted – in the English or the US way? What is the US standard – before a judge or before a jury? Given the constant interaction with company law, these questions remain crucial. How do the 'standards' work with different concepts of 'legal personality' and with different feelings about time (a core problem of accounting)?[213] Cross-cultural differences in attitudes and beliefs invariably exist, in accounting as everywhere else. These differences define ethical

---

[212] Safire, *supra*, note 179, p. 4.
[213] See Rosalyn Higgins, 'Time and the Law: International Perspectives on an Old Problem', (1997) 46 Int. & Comp. L.Q. 501.

or methodical behaviour and decide to what extent a formal code shapes decisions.[214]

Our approaches do not change with the internet.[215] Legal orders continue to rely on community consensus surrounding the rules that law and custom embody. The real world will not be fully separated from the virtual.[216] The point of reference for meanings and hermeneutics will continue to be reality before signs. Even logically formulated accounting structures will be differently interpreted 'when the symbols and words representing descriptions or measurements are not empirically related to real world phenomena'.[217] Socio-cultural characteristics will change only slowly.[218] Local legal expertise remains crucial.[219] Mental internationalization and globalization have limits.

The meeting of minds

If we want to stay loyal to our tasks as comparatists, we must never forget that we are dealing with human beings, with human views that are not 'exotic' in their own environment. As long as 'Adam' refers to 'earth', as long as 'culture' is derived from the Latin word '*colere, cultus*', which means 'to work the ground', and as long as 'man is the intelligence of his soil',[220] we need interpreters over space and time. We need comparatists as communicators and bridge builders.[221] To do the job properly, we have to make audible and visible the silent and invisible powers of signs. Content follows signs.

---

[214] See Jeffrey R. Colhen, Laurie W. Pant and David J. Sharp, 'A Methodological Note on Cross-Cultural Accounting Ethic Research', (1996) 31 Int. J. Account. 55.

[215] See David R. Johnson and David Post, 'Law and Borders – The Rise of Law in Cyberspace', (1996) 48 Stanford L.R. 1367; Lawrence Lessig, 'The Zones of Cyberspace', (1996) 48 Stanford L.R. 1403; Edward Soja, 'Afterword', (1996) 48 Stanford L.R. 1421.

[216] See Christopher M. Kelly, 'The Cyberspace Separatism Fallacy', (1999) 34 Texas Int. L.J. 413, p. 415. *Cf*. Curtis E. A. Karnow, *Future Codes: Essays in Advanced Computer Technology and Law* (Boston: Artech House, 1997).

[217] Mohamed E. Hussein, 'A Comparative Study of Cultural Influences on Financial Reporting in the US and the Netherlands', (1996) 31 Int. J. Account. 95, p. 95.

[218] See Tymothy S. Doupni and Stephen B. Salter, 'External Environment, Culture, and Accounting Practice: A Preliminary Test of a General Model of International Accounting Developments', (1995) 30 Int. J. Account. 189; Jeanne H. Yamamura *et al.*, 'A Comparison of Japanese and US Auditor Decision-Making Behaviour', (1996) 31 J. Int. Account. 347.

[219] See Siegfried Böttcher, *Kulturelle Unterschiede: Grenzen der Globalisierung* (Berlin: Duncker & Humblot, 1999).

[220] Stevens, 'The Comedian as the Letter C', *supra*, note 160, p. 27.

[221] See Esin Örücü, 'Critical Comparative Law: Considering Paradoxes for Legal Systems in Transition', (1999) 59 Nederlandse Vereniging voor Rechtsvergelijking 1.

Comparative ordering then reaches far beyond concepts of 'international management' or 'transnational business'.[222] What matters is the meeting of minds across pictorial and semiotic borders.[223] What is needed are 'routers' for a new 'world wide web' beyond national systems.[224] That remains our opportunity and our duty in the future. We can never fully translate space and time but we can go further than we have dared to do so far.

---

[222] For an excellent guide, see Eberhard Dülfer, *International Management in Diverse Cultural Areas* (Munich: R. Oldenbourg, 1999).

[223] See Gardiol van Niekerk, 'Indigenous Law and Narrative: Rethinking Methodology', (1999) 32 Comp. & Int. L.J. South Africa 208.

[224] See Mathias Reimann, 'Beyond National Systems: A Comparative Law for the International Age', (2001) 75 Tulane L.R. 1103.

Comparative legal studies and its theories

8

The question of understanding

MITCHEL DE S.-O.-L'E. LASSER

Comparatists love to wail about the state of their discipline. To read contemporary comparative legal literature is, therefore, to witness a pitiful series of testimonials about the alienation of the comparatist. The discipline of comparative law, it seems, is marginalized in any number of ways.[1] Thus, '[w]e comparative lawyers often complain that our colleagues see our work as peripheral.'[2] Comparative law 'has enjoyed so little prestige in the inner circles of the academy'.[3] This 'marginal status' of the discipline results in, and is reflected by, the lack of 'full-time comparative law scholar[s] on the faculty' of a distressingly large number of prestigious US law schools.[4] Even within the US law-school curriculum, the discipline is but 'a subject on the margin'.[5]

In order to remedy this apparent marginalization, comparatists have argued repeatedly for the adoption and deployment of some form of 'theory'.[6] According to Ugo Mattei and Mathias Reimann, comparative law exhibits 'a lack of methodological reflection and theoretical foundation'.[7] In the

---

[1] See Günter Frankenberg, 'Critical Comparisons: Re-thinking Comparative Law', (1985) 26 Harvard Int. L.J. 411, pp. 418–21.
[2] James Gordley, 'Comparative Law in the United States Today: Distinctiveness, Quality, and Tradition', (1998) 46 Am. J. Comp. L. 607, p. 615. Merryman, in his delightful interview with Legrand, states: 'There was probably some skepticism about the importance of this kind of work among some of my colleagues': Pierre Legrand, 'John Henry Merryman and Comparative Legal Studies: A Dialogue', (1999) 47 Am. J. Comp. L. 3, pp. 21–2.
[3] George P. Fletcher, 'Comparative Law as a Subversive Discipline', (1998) 46 Am. J. Comp. L. 683, p. 683.
[4] Ugo Mattei, 'An Opportunity Not To Be Missed: The Future of Comparative Law in the United States', (1998) 46 Am. J. Comp. L. 709, p. 709.
[5] Mathias Reimann, 'The End of Comparative Law as an Autonomous Subject', (1996) 11 Tulane Eur. & Civ. L. Forum 49, p. 52.
[6] For example, see Frankenberg, *supra*, note 1, pp. 416–18.
[7] Ugo Mattei and Mathias Reimann, 'Introduction' [to the Symposium 'New Directions in Comparative Law'], (1998) 46 Am. J. Comp. L. 597, p. 597.

dialogue between Pierre Legrand and John Merryman, the former decries 'the poverty of legal theory in the comparative field',[8] while the latter simply notes: 'I do not know of anyone who has done substantial theoretical work addressed to what comparative law really is about.'[9] This theoretical imperative has been promoted in many forms. If comparatists could only develop and deploy the proper methodology – whether functionalist,[10] economic,[11] philosophical,[12] cultural[13] or otherwise – comparative law would, it seems, find its rightful place as a discipline.

This paper presents how I have sought to deal with the nagging problems of comparative-law methodology. Its purpose is to offer a straightforward, even naive, presentation of my comparative methodology, and then to confront it with the most powerful sceptical objections that I can muster. The idea is to challenge and push the methodology as much as possible by what I consider to be the arguments most debilitating for the possibility of comparative understanding. Hopefully, this confrontation will raise some of the intractable problems of comparative-law methodology, shed light on some of the challenges facing comparative understanding and suggest some ways to meet these challenges in an earnest and productive manner.

The analysis is structured as follows. The first section presents an intentionally rosy picture of the comparative methodology that I have been working on and have been utilizing over the last few years. This methodology is composed, in so far as I can tell, of three basic elements. The first is a vague but strong belief that the comparatist can gain a certain insight into the conceptual universe of foreign legal systems. The second is a methodological orientation, namely, that the best method to gain insight into how foreign jurists speak or even think is to deploy a rigorous literary analysis of the discourses employed in, and by, those jurists' legal systems. Finally, the third element is the anti-positivist injunction that the deployment of this literary analysis – 'close reading' – should not be limited to legally binding, official and public work-product generated by formal state agencies.

---

[8] Legrand, *supra*, note 2, p. 36. [9] *Ibid*.
[10] See Konrad Zweigert and Hein Kötz, *An Introduction to Comparative Law*, 3d ed. transl. by Tony Weir (Oxford: Oxford University Press, 1998).
[11] See Ugo Mattei, *Comparative Law and Economics* (Ann Arbor: University of Michigan Press, 1997).
[12] See William Ewald, 'The Jurisprudential Approach to Comparative Law: A Field Guide to "Rats"', (1998) 46 Am. J. Comp. L. 701.
[13] See Bernhard Großfeld, *The Strength and Weakness of Comparative Law*, transl. by Tony Weir (Oxford: Oxford University Press, 1990); Fletcher, *supra*, note 3.

The second section confronts this rosy methodological picture with intentionally threatening, sceptical objections. These objections, which are extremely compelling, tend to deny the possibility of comparative (and perhaps any) understanding, thereby undermining not only the methodology presented in the first section, but also, perhaps, any and all comparative projects.

The third section offers a hopeful reconstruction of my methodology, chided, informed and transformed by the sceptical objections raised in the second section. It acknowledges the sceptical critiques and tries to offer a methodology that responds to, and even works with, them. It urges comparatists to adopt a situation-specific approach that fosters detailed, generous, challenging and responsible engagement with the subjects and objects of their comparative analyses.

The rosy methodology[14]

Sympathetic understanding

My comparative methodology rests first and foremost on an optimistic hypothesis, namely, that the comparatist can, in fact, approach and eventually gain entry into the conceptual universe of a legal system other than her own. This optimistic hypothesis is based on nothing more sophisticated than empirical observation. I have, for example, met a small but hardly insignificant number of European and even non-European law professors (not all of whom, by the way, are comparatists) who have become more or less perfectly conversant in the substantive law, jurisprudence and discourse of the US legal system. Exposure to, and study of, a foreign legal system, therefore, *can* lead to a certain fluency in the conceptual universe of that system, just as linguistic and conceptual fluency can be improved with prolonged exposure to, and study of, a foreign language.

Detailed linguistic analysis offers the key to this comparative conceptual fluency. The linguistic and conceptual universe of a foreign legal system is, in fact, more or less accessible to any reasonably talented comparatist willing to put in the requisite time and effort. By working closely with the

---

[14] I would like to beg the (temporary) indulgence of my colleagues: the following description of the tellingly-named 'rosy methodology' offers an intentionally naive and problematic representation of my comparative approach, one that is particularly susceptible to the critiques raised in the second section.

discourses deployed in such a legal system, the comparatist can develop a very good sense of the recurring linguistic and conceptual references that structure and compose its discourses. Some of these references are merely technical and thus quite easy to master. It does not take very much to figure out, for example, the basic structure of the foreign system's criminal procedure. References to particular stages of that procedure or to particular institutional players within the criminal procedure apparatus, therefore, quickly become relatively unproblematic and even intelligible.

Needless to say, however, knowledge of this kind of basic procedure represents barely the tip of the iceberg. Criminal procedure, to stick with the same example, plays out against an extremely dense and complex background of shared and conflicting assumptions. Developing a sense of this background knowledge requires significant (and even endless) study. Thus, for example, criminal procedure operates in a complex socio-political context that informs, and is itself informed by, that procedure. This context ranges from race, class and gender relations, to past and current political debates, to services provided by the welfare state, to historical developments of assorted kinds, to 'high' and 'low' cultural forms, etc. The more the comparatist becomes conversant with such background knowledge, the greater her linguistic and conceptual fluency. In short, the comparatist must become acquainted with the foreign legal *culture*.[15]

Becoming culturally fluent obviously represents a major undertaking. Furthermore, it may well be the case that perfect fluency is more or less impossible to attain, even with respect to foreign legal systems that are not 'radically different' from the comparatist's own.[16] But there can be no question, at least in the context of non-radically different legal cultures, that the comparatist can attain sufficient fluency to get a very good sense of the conceptual parameters within which, and through which, a foreign jurist tends to conceptualize, articulate, debate and resolve legal problems.

Such comparative fluency can manifest itself in several different but interrelated ways. The first is that the student of foreign legal systems can come to recognize certain modes of argument as originating from, or characteristic of, particular legal systems. The identification and recognition

---

[15] See Pierre Legrand, *Fragments on Law-as-Culture* (Deventer: W. E. J. Tjeenk Willink, 1999).

[16] See John Barton et al., *Law in Radically Different Cultures* (St Paul: West, 1983); Walter Otto Weyrauch and Maureen Anne Bell, 'Autonomous Lawmaking: The Case of the "Gypsies"', (1993) 103 Yale L.J. 323.

of such discursive and conceptual characteristics can obviously be more or less sophisticated. At a basic level, for example, students of my one-semester comparative-law course can and do, in fact, learn to identify, with a rather high degree of accuracy, the origin of assorted legal arguments. They can, for example, distinguish between translated French, Italian, German and Japanese documents and can even do so in the context of civil, criminal, administrative and constitutional tribunals. In short, comparatists can learn to identify and recognize the discursive, argumentative and conceptual traits that characterize different legal systems.

This comparative sensibility and the fluency it enables can also be taken to more sophisticated levels. Students of comparative law can learn to appreciate and then to mimic or reproduce legal arguments typical of particular legal systems. They can successfully learn to argue 'in the style of' a French civil judge or of an Italian 'common-core' academic or of any number of other players in any number of legal systems. The quality of such performances obviously varies depending on the expertise and talent of the comparatist. To what extent has the comparatist grasped that a given expression or term tends to be used in some contexts as opposed to others? Thus, for example, has he noted that the first person singular pronoun '*je*' is never used in the collegial French civil judicial decision, but that it is commonly used by French civil judges when arguing to their brethren in their '*rapports*' and yet that it is almost always replaced by the first person plural '*nous*' in French academic arguments? Can he explain, in the manner of a mainstream French civilian academic, what is so misguided about the Holmesian notion that the law is 'what the judge does in fact'? The quality of the comparative imitation, therefore, depends on a combination of empirical study and artistic sensibility. It hinges on whether the requisite research has been performed and whether the analyst has been sensitive to the specificity of the foreign system's discursive universe.

Needless to say, it is more than likely that such comparative imitation will be flawed in some way that is recognizable to a jurist born and raised, so to speak, in the imitated legal system. But this simply does not mean that the comparatist has failed to gain significant access to the conceptual universe in which that foreign jurist functions. Thus, for example, the comparatist may very well be able to sense the shortcomings of some other comparative representation of that foreign legal system and may well be able to express these failings in terms quite similar to those that a local jurist might use.[17] The comparatist can, therefore, gain sufficient discursive fluency in the foreign system to be sensitive to many, or even to most, of its material, argumentative and conceptual conventions and expectations.

Furthermore, and perhaps as a result, the comparatist can translate, however approximately, the discourse and concepts of a foreign system into those of her 'home' system. This translation is bound to be stilted and awkward, as is any translation. The foreign legal discourse possesses at every turn a different set of referents. Each word is steeped in the history of how it has been used in the past. Each concept functions in the context of all the other concepts to which it relates. Every institution or institutional player is embedded in an endless series of associations and references.

The comparatist must seek to impart some of the 'thickness' and detail of this linguistic and conceptual web; and, of course, her translation must necessarily be incomplete and inexact. After all, the only way to re-present the original faithfully would be to present the original. The comparatist must, therefore, engage in the interminable and eventually impossible task of explaining at almost every turn how each term, concept, institution, procedure, character and the like relates to every other. How could she ever produce enough in the way of footnoted (or 'hypertext') explanations to flesh out completely the background – or even the foreground – of what she is translating? But then again, how can a non-New Yorker ever truly grasp the field of referents in a Woody Allen movie? How can someone unfamiliar with upper-bourgeois French society of a certain generation ever truly grasp the signification of Proust? Although extensive use of footnotes can help to explain some of the historical, cultural, literary, linguistic and other references, these footnotes will be somewhat pedantic and will, therefore, detract from the original in other ways. That said, Allen and Proust can be translated, however imperfectly; and these translations can get across quite a bit – though obviously not all – of the original. There is no particular reason to believe that comparatists could not do as well in the legal context as translators do in the literary.[18]

---

[17] For the best and most detailed comparative analysis of a particular concept, see Neil MacCormick and Robert S. Summers, *Interpreting Precedents: A Comparative Study* (Dartmouth: Ashgate, 1997). In this remarkable collection of essays, the authors produce analyses that sensitize the reader to the subtle – and yet utterly foundational – differences between assorted legal systems' conception of prior judicial decisions.

[18] For an interesting description of law as a process of translation, see Lawrence Lessig, 'Fidelity in Translation', (1993) 71 Texas L.R. 1165.

Literary analysis

The form of analysis that I have been suggesting consists of a rigorous literary analysis – or 'close reading' – of the language and discourse of the foreign legal system. The basic idea is to approach the documents or arguments produced by a legal system as if they were serious literary works and thus to treat them with a similar degree of careful, detailed and almost exhaustive attention. The underlying assumption is that these legal texts are meaningful in some way that transcends their already important substantive attributes. In other words, this literary methodology assumes that legislative statutes, academic articles, judicial decisions and other legal texts are significant not only because of the substantive results that they enact, suggest or order, but also because of the way in which those texts are composed. The methodology claims that each of these documents reflects, constructs and presents its own worldview, one that expresses particular conceptions about all of the issues, arguments, institutions, characters and the like to which the documents implicitly or explicitly refer – or do *not* refer – and about the relationships between them. In short, the methodology affirms that legal texts display an implicit conceptual universe that can fruitfully, if imperfectly, be made explicit by meticulous literary analysis.

Close reading suggests that by performing such an analysis, the comparatist can begin to recognize the ways in which the assorted issues, arguments, concepts, institutions and characters tend to interrelate in the different legal texts. She can start to get a sense of the discursive and conceptual patterns that characterize particular kinds of arguments or documents. This awareness allows the comparatist to analyse and recognize the field of referents typically at play in a given type of document. She can appreciate how academics describe and conceptualize the role of, say, legislators, judges or other institutional players, and how each of these players describes and conceptualizes each of the others. Even the most basic questions can send the comparatist down suggestive paths. What are understood to be the sources of law and how have such understandings changed over time? What are the accepted relationships between legal interpretation and law-making? Is adaptive or modernizing interpretation, for example, categorized as law-making? Do different sets of actors in the legal system present different notions about the proper role of the assorted players in that system? What are the schisms within the various groups of actors within the system? How are such schisms presented and in what types of documents? How does each of these types of documents present itself? Is its authorial voice tentative, assertive, personal, magisterial, institutional, sympathetic, paternalistic, emotional, individual and/or formulaic? What does each document have to say about its purpose? How does it portray its own production? How does it represent its relationship to other elements of the legal, political or social systems?

Such questions, and the careful structural and rhetorical analyses that they can provoke, lead the comparatist toward a far greater awareness of the conceptual and discursive parameters of a foreign (or even domestic) legal system. The comparatist can begin to anticipate argumentative patterns and conceptual relationships. She senses almost at once that when a French jurist argues about how something is 'shocking', he is about to ask the court to overturn an 'inequitable' legal rule.[19] She knows that when he mentions a 'controversy within *doctrine*', he is using academic disagreements to highlight an interpretive problem that the court should now resolve by adopting a new and authoritative position.[20] She recognizes immediately that when a French civil court deploys the awkward construction 'but whereas', it is not suggesting countervailing policy interests or alternative interpretive possibilities, but rather is formally refuting an argument advanced by one of the parties.[21] She comes to appreciate that when a French jurist suggests that the courts should adapt or modernize their interpretation of a given code provision, that neither the jurist nor the judges consider this suggestion to violate the injunctions against judicial law-making.[22]

At the same time, such close reading also helps to sensitize the comparatist to the conflicts and tensions within the conceptual universe reflected in, and constructed by, the legal system's discourse. French jurists, for example, constantly deploy the distinctions between 'evolutive' or 'equitable' interpretation, on the one hand, and law-making, on the other. But these distinctions do not prove to be unproblematic. Close reading reveals that these tenuous distinctions are, in fact, maintained by means of a complex conceptual substratum. It is this fundamental conceptual context that supports and permits the maintenance of these otherwise problematic distinctions.

In the French civil context, this conceptual substratum consists, *inter alia*, of the utterly foundational explanation of the 'sources of the law', according

---

[19] See Mitchel de S.-O.-l'E. Lasser, 'Judicial (Self-)Portraits: Judicial Discourse in the French Legal System', (1995) 104 Yale L.J. 1325, p. 1385.
[20] *Id.*, pp. 1374–6.   [21] *Id.*, p. 1341.   [22] *Id.*, pp. 1382–4.

to which only legislation and perhaps custom qualify as veritable 'sources of the law'. This formal definition of what truly constitutes 'law' turns out to be immensely liberating. It allows significant judicial norm-creation and development precisely because it refuses to recognize that these constitute true sources of law. Although a more pragmatic understanding might include such judicial norm-creation and development in its definition of 'law', it might thereby disable the liberatingly 'flexible' French code-based approach. Close reading can thus put the comparatist in a position to identify this characteristic French theoretical conundrum and prepare him to appreciate the ways in which French theory and practice have sought to resolve or, at least, defuse it.

In short, close reading puts the comparatist in the position of *taking seriously* the linguistic and conceptual claims made by the analysed legal system. This meticulous approach induces the comparatist to push the logic of the studied discourse to its maximum. This forces her to visualize the relationships between the assorted institutions, protagonists and concepts at play in that discourse and thus to confront how that discourse constructs and rationalizes them. These relationships, which often turn out to be quite nuanced and complex, then offer a crack through which the comparatist can examine the ways in which other conceptual constructs mediate between and/or support these and other relationships. Close reading advances in this way one step at a time, deepening and broadening the comparatist's familiarity with the legal system's discursive and conceptual universe or worldview. By developing a sufficient familiarity with this discursive and conceptual web, the comparatist can, in time, approach a certain fluency in that legal system's *culture*.[23]

Such close reading, therefore, represents an attempt to come to terms with the discursive and conceptual universe of a legal system *in the terms and according to the logic of that system*. It seeks, therefore, to develop what is in some sense an 'internal' perspective on that system. It must be recognized, however, that close reading also depends on – and perhaps well constitutes – a methodology that is in some sense 'external' to that system. It is a means of approaching and apprehending facets of that system's discursive and conceptual parameters and relationships. It is a methodology that places

---

[23] There is obviously no end to the concepts, referents and images that can and should be considered by the comparatist. As Legrand correctly notes, for example, artistic imagery such as Jacques-Louis David's portrayal of Napoleon writing the civil code may be utterly central to French legal culture: see Legrand, *supra*, note 15, p. 5.

language at the very centre of the analysis and then performs that analysis by structuralist and rhetorical means.

Close reading, at least as I have deployed it, is intimately linked, therefore, with a particular approach to reading texts, one that falls under the general rubric of 'literary criticism'. It represents a certain 'lit. theory' posture toward legal texts.[24] This posture is *not* scientific. It merely represents a suggestive and, in my experience, fruitful means of inducing the comparatist to take a sustained and detailed look at how legal texts are put together and thus to gain a certain insight into what those texts signify about the legal system that produced them.

This posture is not, however, unbiased. It represents a methodology that is brought to the analytic table not from 'within' the observed legal system, but from the 'outside'. In other words, it is deployed by the comparatist; and however much the methodology stresses the language 'internal' to the legal system, it nonetheless represents an 'external' perspective on that 'internal' discourse. That said, the methodology does offer a major analytic advantage: it significantly reduces the extent to which comparative analysis consists of analysing one legal system in the loaded terms and parochial concepts particular to another.[25] As I have explained elsewhere,

> [t]he deployment of literary theory as the conceptual framework for comparative analysis therefore offers some semblance of intellectual neutrality. This neutrality, however, is not unbiased. Rather, the use of literary theory shifts the analytic biases from the biases of a particular legal tradition to those of another discipline. In so far as the biases of literary theory tend toward a careful examination of language and textual interpretation, and insofar as textual interpretation represents a prime judicial and jurisprudential concern, the adoption of such biases appears to offer a reasonable match between the method and the object of analysis.[26]

The deployment of a literary methodology, therefore, pushes the analysis in the desired direction: close reading of the legal system's linguistic and conceptual relations.

---

[24] See Mitchel de S.-O.-l'E. Lasser, ' "Lit. Theory" Put to the Test: A Comparative Literary Analysis of American Judicial Tests and French Judicial Discourse', (1998) 111 Harvard L.R. 689.

[25] The deployment of parochial concepts in the comparative context represents perhaps the most common failing of US comparative analyses of civilian legal systems. See Mitchel de S.-O.-l'E. Lasser, 'Do Judges Deploy Policy?', (2001) 22 Cardozo L.R. 863 [portraying Roscoe Pound, John Dawson, John Merryman and Duncan Kennedy as falling into this trap].

[26] Lasser, *supra*, note 24, pp. 693–4.

The goal of this comparative literary analysis is to grasp and represent the constitutive linguistic and conceptual relationships that characterize the analysed legal system. My methodology, therefore, focuses on how a legal text arranges and relates particular terms and concepts and on how these arrangements and relations come to offer a portrait of the legal text and of the legal system that produced it. By parsing out and analysing the complex relationships between different modes of legal discourse, different modes of interpretation and different modes of relating interpretive decisions to 'governing law', this literary methodology seeks to dive into the depths of a legal system's linguistic and conceptual universe and thus to gain a certain insight into how the legal system understands itself to function. The resulting analysis and explanation should offer a detailed portrayal of the complex relations between the legal system's multiple players and their multiple roles, as depicted in their discourses and as constructed in, and by, their conceptual universe.

Anti-positivist materials

As my comparative literary methodology seeks to analyse legal texts in order to grasp their depictions of the legal universe that produced them, a practical question emerges: what legal texts should be analysed? The comparatist's attention should probably fall first on the official documents produced by the formally-recognized legal institutions of the state. It is, therefore, essential for the comparatist to devote serious attention to the traditional focal points of legal research: constitutional documents, legislation, judicial and administrative decisions and the like. These documents represent the most explicit means by which western legal systems tend to manifest themselves and thus offer the primary means of access to comparative study.

The linguistic and conceptual constructs offered by such official state legal documents are terribly important and deeply meaningful. They constitute the 'official portrait' of a legal system, that is, they form a state-sanctioned representation of how the legal system functions, of the role played by the legal system's assorted cast of characters, of the relationship between assorted legal institutions and between the players who compose them, of the purposes, principles and values that motivate the structure and operation of the system as a whole and of each of its component parts, of the procedures and intellectual processes that govern the functioning of the system, etc. In short, the official portrait produced by such official state documents offers to the comparatist a rich set of materials, conceptions and images about how the legal system functions – or, at least, how it portrays itself as functioning.

By analysing such official state materials, therefore, the comparatist gains access to the rules that construct and govern the public identity or character of the legal system. These rules, and the public practices by which they manifest themselves, constitute the official ethos of that system. These rules, practices and resulting ethos are actually quite accessible to the comparatist, and this for a very simple reason: the whole point of the official portrait is that it is published through documents – such as, *inter alia*, legislation, constitutions, judicial decisions and administrative rules and decisions – and is, therefore, accessible to the general public. This public and official identity or self-portrait frames how the legal system is constructed and also shapes how people and institutions within and without that system conceive of it and function relatively to it. In short, this official portrait informs everything that happens in and around the legal system.

That said, the documents that constitute this official portrait do not represent the be-all and end-all of that legal system. On a practical level, it has become quite clear that the published and official documents of the state legal system tend to give the observer a very incomplete picture of how that legal system actually operates on a day-to-day level. That is the whole point of the now ritual distinction between 'law in the books' and 'law in action'.

This *caveat* functions on the linguistic and conceptual level as well. This observation has, however, rarely been made – let alone been seriously considered – in the comparative context. Just because the published and official documents of the state legal system tend to deploy particular linguistic and/or conceptual constructs does not mean that these constructs adequately represent how actors in the legal system speak, write, argue or reason on a daily basis.[27]

The question, at least for the comparatist, is whether the linguistic and conceptual framework presented by a legal system's official discourse adequately represents how jurists in that system actually speak, write, argue and reason on a routine basis. The answer to this question varies from one

---

[27] See John Bell, 'Comparing Precedent', (1997) 82 Cornell L.R. 1243, pp. 1270–1. A legal system riddled with corruption might offer the prototype of such a disjunction: on the surface, the system appears to be governed by certain legal concepts when, in fact, it is ruled primarily by notions and practices of monetary (or other) exchange invisible in official legal documents.

legal system to the next. The French civil judicial system, for example, offers a particularly clear instance of a legal system in which the official legal discourse does not, in fact, give the comparatist access to that system's routine forms of reasoning and argument. It turns out that there exist within the French legal system several discourses – some more hidden than others – that demonstrate that French jurists (including judges) do not typically reason, argue about or even conceptualize legal issues in the way that the official and public state documents would lead one to believe.

In the end, the underlying issue is whether the jurists of a legal system would see themselves and their linguistic/conceptual processes as being adequately represented by their legal system's official discourse. Thus, for example, when asked whether the discourse of French judicial decisions accurately represents how they think about and decide cases, French judges tend to answer 'not really', 'not entirely' or 'only in easy cases'. This poses an important problem for the comparatist seeking to gain access to the linguistic and conceptual universe of a foreign legal system. If the official products of that system do not entirely reflect how the actors inside the system actually argue and reason about, and eventually resolve, legal problems, then it can only be misleading to base one's comparative analyses entirely on such official documents.

The solution to this problem, needless to say, is for the comparatist to refuse to deploy a positivist conception of legal materials. She must expand the range of materials for study. She must at the very least seek to gain access to other important discourses within the studied legal system, such as academic writings and practitioners' arguments, and incorporate these discourses into her analysis. Such materials can give the comparatist a broader and more detailed sense of the discourses that are routinely deployed within the studied legal system and can, therefore, radically alter the comparatist's analysis. By analysing the arguments produced by counsel, for example, the comparatist can rapidly learn the legal system's argumentative conventions. These debates offer an excellent window on what kinds of arguments are considered acceptable within the system, what seem to be the sources of legal authority, what are the accepted roles of each of the private and institutional players within the legal system, etc. Simply put, these arguments are produced by professionals of the system. It is the business of these professionals to be effective within that system and their work-product, therefore, offers uniquely valuable models of how those within the system understand the system to function.

Academic writings offer yet another useful set of materials. They may well reflect a somewhat different perspective on the operation of the studied legal system than the ones offered by either the official documents or the practitioners' arguments. This alternative perspective can be immensely useful in its own right, as it represents how the theoreticians, apologists, critics and educators of the system analyse, explain and seek to influence that system. It offers implicit understandings of how the system does and should function, understandings that are transmitted as knowledge or goals to the next generation of attorneys as well as to assorted elites within the legal system. As a result, the comparatist can glean from these writings how a particularly influential set of thinkers conceives of, and seeks to resolve, assorted legal issues, ranging from substantive questions about contract law to far more fundamental institutional or structural questions about how assorted institutional actors within the legal system should respond in the face of changing social realities.

The comparatist should also be receptive to the existence of other documents that might offer a glimpse of how assorted institutional actors actually understand their legal system to function. It is, of course, impossible to know in advance what such documents or practices might be and what they might contain and reveal. What is important, however, is that the comparatist be on the look-out for documents or practices that represent important forms of communication between the institutional actors who are primarily responsible for operating the legal system. Such 'internal' legal documents may not be intended for publication, may not be thought of as legally authoritative and, therefore, may not qualify as 'official' state legal documents. But they may nonetheless offer invaluable insights into how assorted institutional actors actually speak to each other, how they seek to influence or convince each other and thus how they seek to operate effectively in the context of some underlying conception of how that legal system and its agents function and interact.

The archetype of such a document may be the judicial bench memorandum, in which one judicial officer deploys a series of arguments in an attempt to convince colleagues to conceptualize and resolve a legal dispute in one way or another. Such a document grants to the comparatist a perspective that official state legal documents, such as published judicial decisions, simply cannot yield. It offers the perspective of judicial officers communicating among themselves and for themselves, rather than of judicial officers producing public arguments of justification intended, *inter alia*, for public consumption. It therefore offers the comparatist relatively direct access to the worldviews, concepts and forms of reasoning that are thought to be compelling to those who operate within the analysed legal system. For this reason, I have argued that such documents offer important 'unofficial' and 'internal' understandings of how the legal system functions. Without some means of plugging directly into the thoughts of others, such documents probably represent the most direct means of gaining access to how foreign judges conceptualize specific legal issues, general legal concerns and the legal system as a whole.

At the same time, gaining access to such routine and representative internal discourses offers more than just a window on how those within the system reason and communicate. This reasoning/communication represents, in and of itself, a significant constitutive element of the legal system. Thus, bench memoranda not only display how judges reason and argue; they also construct and reflect a series of practices within the legal system. The judicial discourse, in short, is a practice; and this practice is a significant facet of the legal system. By widening the field of documents to be studied, the comparatist thus gains access not only to more routine and representative legal discourses, but also to the routine discursive, interpretive, creative and other practices that these discourses represent.

Finally, by gaining access to these documents and their discourses, the comparatist also gets a sense of the relationship between a legal system's many discourses. Each of these discourses not only emerges from, and forms a different facet of, that legal system, but it is also meaningfully related to each of the others. Furthermore, prolonged and detailed study reveals the *conceptual structure* that balances and sustains these somewhat similar but also somewhat contradictory discourses. This structure mediates the tensions between the discourses' somewhat different images of how the legal system can, does and should function. It resolves, as best it can – and often in extremely significant and revealing ways – the apparent conceptual difficulties within the system.

To return to the French example, it is most important to identify the linguistic and conceptual framework that allows the French jurist to reconcile, (i) the official injunction that the French civil judge not create law with (ii) the undeniable fact – recognized by all who work in the legal system – that the French civil judge plays an extremely important and creative normative role in that system. I dare say that it is only when the comparatist has gained sufficient familiarity with the multiple discourses within the French system so as to recognize the existence and resolution of such discursive and conceptual tensions that she has begun to do serious comparative work.

In simplistic summary, then, my comparative methodology rests on three interrelated claims. The comparatist can, in fact, gain a certain insight into the conceptual universe of foreign legal systems. To do so, she should conduct a rigorous literary analysis of the discourses deployed in those legal systems. Finally, such 'close reading' must be practised not only on the official and public work-product generated by formal state agencies, but also on the many other discourses that are produced in and around those legal systems. Comparatists who adopt such an approach can gain sufficient conceptual fluency to engage in fruitful conversations with jurists of the studied legal system, to present and explain that system to others and eventually to appreciate and critique it in a knowledgeable and meaningful way.

The sceptical objection

Problems of understanding

The problems of understanding the 'other' (however defined) have been written about at great length in any number of humanities and social-science fields ranging across, to list but a few, hermeneutics, anthropology, cultural studies, women's studies/feminism and philosophy. This varied literature addresses these problems so relentlessly as to raise the very serious and rather vexing possibility that it may be quite impossible to understand anyone or anything!

Rather than simply accept this sweeping conclusion, let us limit the scope of the issues and the terms of the debate to a level more familiar to legal academics. Even at this level, it is by now commonplace to recognize the tremendous difficulties, and perhaps the impossibility, of arriving at understanding from outside a given community or tradition. Much of the basic thrust of communitarian analysis and theory, for example, consists precisely of such a claim. Similarly, Robert Cover's continuing legacy rests on his dramatic portrayal of 'paideic' communities of understanding and of the 'jurispathic' tendencies of any interpretive intervention originating from outside (and, in some instances, even from within) such a community.[28]

---

[28] Robert M. Cover, '*Nomos* and Narrative', (1983–4) 97 Harvard L.R. 4, p. 12.

Even Stanley Fish's notion of 'embeddedness' would seem to imply the impossibility of cross-cultural understanding, that is, understanding from outside a given interpretive community.[29] This is to say nothing of the far more challenging analyses proposed by the theorists of 'radical difference' in the context of race and gender that explicitly stress the impossibility of understanding even *within* the boundaries of national, local or other communities.

Finally, one need not even venture beyond the existing comparative legal literature in order to find repeated warnings about the impossibility of understanding the other. A short passage from the conversation between Legrand and Merryman illustrates the full extent to which the problematic of external understanding has become an almost automatic assumption within the ranks of legal comparatists:

> PL: [...] In your experience, can the comparatist ever be objective or does he not come to the act of comparison as an 'encumbered self' so that whatever exists 'out there' can only be 'known' through the filter of the comparatist's own cognitive processes and will accordingly find itself being inevitably distorted along the way? In other words, 'cultural familiarity and respectable theory' would help but would never be enough to avoid the projection by the comparatist of his own background?
> JHM: Of course. Does anyone really suppose otherwise?[30]

Even Bernhard Großfeld, by no means as controversial as Pierre Legrand, writes: 'Our knowledge is limited, for complete understanding of a foreign legal institution is almost impossible to attain. Our vision is culturally blinkered, our expertise often built on sand.'[31]

Furthermore, even if we were to refuse to adopt the impossibility of external understanding as an a priori principle of serious comparative analysis, understanding would hardly be at our fingertips. Contemporary comparative scholarship increasingly stresses the daunting *practical* problems involved in seeking to understand a foreign legal system.

These practical problems of external understanding begin with the object of analysis. A legal system, or some part thereof, is not some monolithic object, but a stunningly complex and polivocal entity. It is obviously composed of an enormous number of constitutive and interrelated elements, be they termed 'institutions', 'actors', 'sources of the law' or, according to

---

[29] Stanley Fish, *Doing What Comes Naturally* (Durham: Duke University Press, 1989), p. 141.
[30] Legrand, *supra*, note 2, p. 54.   [31] Großfeld, *supra*, note 13, p. 38.

Rodolfo Sacco, 'legal formants'.[32] Furthermore, as Sacco has convincingly argued, these formants may not be particularly consistent, and may even be in competition, with one another.[33] Thus, a legal system's academic *doctrine*, for example, may well be at odds with – and be actively seeking to supplant – its legislation or *jurisprudence*.

To make matters more difficult, every constitutive element or 'legal formant' of a given legal system reveals itself to be deeply complex and polivocal in its own right. Legal academics, to take an obvious example, hardly constitute a homogeneous block of thinkers/writers. When or where does the academy ever speak as one?[34] The same holds true historically. To stick with the French example, Marie-Claire Belleau has effectively debunked the oversimplified history of French doctrinal thought which tends to present the '*école de l'exégèse*' as the only important player in pre-Second World War French legal academics: 'There is in fact a vibrant critical tradition in French legal scholarship [,] the school of [...] the '*juristes inquiets*' [...] that existed in French legal academia at the end of the nineteenth century.'[35] The assorted legal formants must, therefore, be historicized, as the relationships both within and between them change diachronically.[36] Finally, as the above example of French academic *doctrine* demonstrates, these formants cannot simply be taken for granted as a given, as an object. Rather, they should be analysed as complex and shifting practices, as Evelyne Serverin has shown in the context of French *jurisprudence*[37] and as Philippe Jestaz and Christophe Jamin have described in the context of French academic *doctrine*.[38]

In short, the recognition of the multiplicity of legal formants and of the complexity within each of them results in an enormous problematization of the notion of 'understanding' a foreign legal system, thereby placing the comparatist in a serious quandary. Given the multiplicity of players in a foreign system, why should she focus her analysis, to take obvious examples,

---

[32] Rodolfo Sacco, 'Legal Formants: A Dynamic Approach to Comparative Law', (1991) 39 Am. J. Comp. L. 1 & 343.
[33] *Id.*
[34] See John H. Merryman, *The Civil Law Tradition*, 2d ed. (Stanford: Stanford University Press, 1985), p. 28.
[35] Marie-Claire Belleau, 'The "*juristes inquiets*": Legal Classicim and Criticism in Early Twentieth-Century France', [1997] Utah L.R. 379, pp. 379–80.
[36] See Roscoe Pound, *Jurisprudence*, vol. II (St Paul: West, 1959), pp. 9–12.
[37] Evelyne Serverin, *De la jurisprudence en droit privé* (Lyon: Presses Universitaires de Lyon, 1985).
[38] Philippe Jestaz and Christophe Jamin, 'L'entité doctrinale française', D.1997.Chron.167.

on judges, as opposed to legislators, attorneys or clients? Even within any of these categories of players, such as clients, why should she focus on individual clients of means as opposed to welfare mothers, corporate clients, oppressed minorities, the poor and/or people whose identities straddle and combine several of these and many other categories? Are there any satisfactory a priori answers to such questions?

This quandary leads to a most basic problem. If the point of comparative law is 'understanding', that is, if the point is to seek not so much 'law in books' or even 'law in action', but, to use William Ewald's elegant phrase, 'law in minds',[39] whose 'mind' should we have in mind? This is to say nothing about how a comparatist would ever know whether he had 'understood' the foreign object of his analysis. Who would be in a position to compose and administer the test and on the basis of what standard?

The foregoing analysis and leading questions suggest yet another twist. It is worth pausing to consider whether the complexities outlined in the context of external understanding do not also apply in the context of 'internal' understanding. Thus, even if, for the sake of argument, we could agree that someone actually qualifies as 'inside' a given legal system, it is less than clear whether such a person could be said to 'understand' that system. Once again, whose understanding would that person possess and of what facet of the system? Thus, for example, can it really be said that Rodolfo Sacco, to pick an eminent example, 'understands' the Italian legal system, so that if only we could have access to Italian law 'in his mind' we would understand Italian law? Is his view representative of some general Italian understanding? Does it correspond to the perspective of Italian legislators, of whatever party, never mind to that of Sicilian shepherds petitioning their local administrative authorities? I would venture to guess that his view hardly represents that of the great majority of Italian academics.[40]

Finally, comparatists have long been aware of the peculiar analytic disadvantage of being 'inside' a given legal system. The problem is one of Sartrean blindness, of unawareness of what one carries and takes for granted on a

---

[39] See William Ewald, 'Comparative Jurisprudence (I): What Was it Like to Try a Rat?', (1995) 143 U. Penn. L.R. 1889, p. 2111.

[40] When John Merryman addresses the question of 'Italians dealing with their own legal system', he states: 'Different Italians will deal differently with the same topic. There is no immaculate perception nor is there such a thing as immaculate representation': Legrand, *supra*, note 2, p. 54. I have picked Sacco as my protagonist because I believe that the problematic implications of complexity for comparative understanding are, in fact, implicit in his notion of competitive 'legal formants'. The legal formants, in other words, do not see eye to eye.

daily basis. Mirjan Damaška, for example, argues explicitly for a comparative methodology that adopts the outsider's perspective.[41] Though coming from an entirely different perspective, Legrand speaks in terms of 'critical distance' and even goes so far as to suggest the analytic advantages of 'exile'.[42] From the wildly different perspective of contemporary 'common-core' methodology, Mauro Bussani and Ugo Mattei state: 'we assume that for the purpose of comparative scholarship the internal lawyer is not necessarily the best reporter of his or her own system [...]. The point is [...] that nationals may be less well equipped in detecting hidden data and the rhetorical attitude, because they may be misled by automatic assumptions.'[43] Thus, even if one brackets the problem of the diversity of insider perspectives, it nonetheless remains debatable whether the 'insider's' understanding of her legal system should be privileged over the outsider's.

The problem of understanding in the comparative legal context emerges, therefore, not only as a question of complexity, but also as one of potentially irreducible complexity, that is, of diversity. A massively complex model that might effectively encapsulate and represent a large number of the diverse 'internal' perspectives and understandings of a legal system – whether produced by an 'inside' or 'outside' observer – would unquestionably be of great benefit for a number of descriptive purposes. The greatest benefit of such an exercise might, in fact, be nothing other than the recognition – by the comparatist and her audience – of the daunting complexity of her object of analysis.

But such a model, however complex it might be, can hardly be said to have overcome the problem of 'understanding'. As a practical matter, the model will have had to 'encapsulate', that is, tame, flatten and objectify the multiple worldviews/perspectives/understandings, thereby radically changing them all. It will not have mattered whether the analysis had adopted an 'insider's' or 'outsider's' perspective: each of the understandings is external to the others. The model, in other words, however complex it may be, will apparently not have generated a single 'understanding' along the way, never mind a general understanding of the legal system under analysis.

---

[41] Mirjan Damaška, *The Faces of Justice and State Authority* (New Haven: Yale University Press, 1986).

[42] Legrand, *supra*, note 2, p. 20.

[43] Mauro Bussani and Ugo Mattei, 'The Common Core Approach to European Private Law', (1997–8) 3 Columbia J. Eur. L. 339, pp. 352–3.

Problems in constructing the object of analysis

The above problems of internal and external understanding place the comparatist in a series of terrible binds with respect to his relation to the object of his analysis. The first is that of perspective. As we have just seen, the comparatist can never really be said to be truly 'inside' a foreign – and perhaps even a domestic – object of legal analysis: the object is itself too complex and diverse to be said to have *an* 'inside'.

At the same time, the comparatist can never really be said to be truly 'outside' the foreign or domestic object of analysis. The comparatist engages in a practice that partakes of, has some dialogical relation with, and produces effects on, that object. One need not even get into the intractable problems of subject/object theory to arrive at such a conclusion. Thus, to provide a straightforward comparative law example, Mattei writes fascinatingly on the effect that Rudolf Schlesinger's work had not only in the United States (Schlesinger's adopted 'home' system), but most especially in Europe.[44] The object of comparative description and analysis, in other words, is not left untouched or unaffected by the process of having been treated as an object of analysis.[45] This is to say nothing of the more explicitly problematic process of 'orientalizing' the other.[46] The very interconnectedness of the observer and the observed, therefore, calls into question the possibility of an 'outside' perspective.

This problem of perspective spills into that of methodology and theory. The comparatist must come to terms with the fact that the object of analysis does not simply 'exist' and 'speak for itself'.[47] The comparatist must recognize that she selects what to describe, decides what to focus on and edits the description and analysis accordingly. The adoption of a methodological approach and thus of a theoretical framework, therefore, constructs the object even as it describes it. The functionalist approach, as Günter Frankenberg points out, does not stumble upon its object, but builds it according to its methodological presuppositions.[48] As William Alford suggests, comparatists often produce analyses that say as much or more

---

[44] See Ugo Mattei, 'Why The Wind Changed: Intellectual Leadership in Western Law', (1994) 42 Am. J. Comp. L. 195, p. 211.
[45] Levinas offers particularly interesting thoughts on the transformative aspects of speech acts. See Emmanuel Levinas, *Nine Talmudic Readings*, transl. by Annette Aronowicz (Bloomington: Indiana University Press, 1990).
[46] See Edward W. Said, *Orientalism* (New York: Pantheon, 1978).
[47] See Frankenberg, *supra*, note 1, pp. 434–40.   [48] *Ibid.*

about the theoretical construct deployed as they say about the legal culture examined.[49]

To push this line of analysis further still, a given theoretical/methodological approach can even be said to construct the 'inside'/'outside' dichotomy itself, thereby constructing the very perspectives that it then takes for granted. One need only consider James Gordley's impassioned pleas for a 'transnational legal science'[50] in order to recognize the constructed quality of the 'inside' and the 'outside', the 'domestic' and the 'foreign'. The same even holds true as regards the discipline of comparative law itself. It is less than clear why Japanese legal studies, to take Frank Upham's example,[51] should effectively be placed outside the ambit of the US discipline of comparative law or why the much decried, and yet routine, analytic exclusion of 'Third World' legal systems should continue to persist within the discipline.

The difference/similarity dichotomy poses similar dilemmas. The comparatist must decide when to construct her analysis with a focus on similarity (the tack typically urged by Basil Markesinis, Gordley and Mattei) and when with a focus on difference (the tack typically urged by Legrand).[52] In the face of such a choice, wiser heads may appear to prevail. Thus Merryman replies to Legrand: 'As to your suggested choice between difference and similarity, why must one choose?'[53] The difficult issue, however, is not really whether the comparatist must or must not choose between one and the other alternative. Rather, it is whether the distinction itself is analytically tenable. 'Difference' and 'similarity' do not simply pre-exist the comparatist's descriptive and analytic gaze. The comparatist must construct the analysis, that is, she must at the very least choose the objects of analysis, decide what to focus on and where to lay her stress, and thus she must make – and make something of – the differences and similarities that she only then observes.

---

[49] See William Alford, 'On the Limits of "Grand Theory" in Comparative Law', (1986) 61 Washington L.R. 945.
[50] James Gordley, 'Comparative Legal Research: Its Function in the Development of Harmonized Law', (1995) 43 Am. J. Comp. L. 555, p. 567.
[51] See Frank Upham, 'The Place of Japanese Legal Studies in American Comparative Law', [1997] Utah L.R. 639.
[52] See Basil S. Markesinis, 'Why a Code is Not the Best Way to Advance the Cause of European Legal Unity', (1997) 5 Eur. R. Priv. L. 519, p. 520; Gordley, *supra*, note 50; Mattei, *supra*, note 43; Legrand, *supra*, note 15. In this professional and even filial context, it is quite amusing to find Legrand citing Schlesinger in support of his difference project. See Pierre Legrand, 'Structuring European Community Law: How Tacit Knowledge Matters', (1998) 21 Hastings Int. & Comp. L.R. 871, p. 872, citing Rudolf Schlesinger, 'The Past and Future of Comparative Law', (1995) 43 Am. J. Comp. L. 477, p. 480.
[53] Legrand, *supra*, note 2, p. 42.

This is not to say that objects of analysis are not different and/or alike. Rather, it is to stress that the comparatist partakes of the process whereby 'difference' and 'similarity' are defined, then found and found to be meaningful. What is in question is the construction and deployment of the 'difference v. similarity' construct itself. The relation between the objects, like a metaphor or a metonymy, is in some important sense authored by the comparatist.

Despite the imperative to grapple with such fundamental dichotomies as the insider/outsider or similarity/difference distinctions, the basic and intractable problem, however, is that doing so in no way 'solves' any of the problems of comparative analysis. Working on, as well as with, such dichotomies involves and promotes an awareness of the comparatist's position not as an independent observer, but as an active participant in the construction of the object of analysis. It highlights her role in constructing her position relative to the object and to its analysis as well as her role in composing the methodology deployed and the referents supplied.

But this awareness of one's position does not solve any of the dilemmas of comparative practice. Subjectivity is not just an independent variable. Self-awareness does not put the comparatist in the position of 'discounting', 'accounting for' or 'correcting' her position. The same holds true for her awareness of the dichotomies and of her choice of why to stress one or the other of their poles. The same even holds true for awareness of the 'constructed' quality of the fundamental dichotomies. After all, is not the notion of 'construction' itself a construct, the result of a fabricated dichotomy the other side of which would be 'essence' or 'nature'? The comparatist cannot get out of these positions or dichotomies; she cannot walk away from her own situatedness.[54]

Given that the comparatist cannot escape her subjectivity or her situatedness, she must recognize that her work represents an *intervention* and must, therefore, account for her motives. She must, for example, address the reasons for her choice of object as well as of methodology. She must consider the often very personal (and often very random) reasons for analysing, for example, the Italian legal system.[55] Furthermore, she must account for the motives for her choice of project. That project may range from the

---

[54] See Fish, *supra*, note 29.
[55] Merryman provides such an account in his interview with Legrand. See Legrand, *supra*, note 2, pp. 14–15 [offering, among other reasons, the explanation that 'Italy seemed to be an attractive place']. See also Frankenberg, *supra*, note 1, p. 416 [noting the marginal status of such explanations].

technical, such as John Langbein's, Lloyd Weinreb's or Paul Frase's goal of improving some facet of the 'domestic' legal system,[56] to the transformative, such as Ugo Mattei's goal of overtly constructing a common and economically efficient European civil law,[57] to the political/cultural, such as Pierre Legrand's goal of preserving diversity and pluralism in the face of ever-increasing legal and cultural globalization.[58] Whatever the project, these motives and choices shape and orient the comparatist's work. The comparatist's enterprise, labour and production constitute an intervention in the chosen sphere of operation (and likely in others as well) and the comparatist is, therefore, responsible for engaging in the chosen work in the chosen manner.

The problem, unfortunately, is that there is no assurance that a given comparative methodology, constructed and applied in variable contexts, will or will not yield productive, enlightening, culturally sensitive or otherwise desirable results. Even what seem to be particularly sensitive comparative approaches can, depending on the circumstances, be deployed in quite troubling ways. Günter Frankenberg's comparative methodology, for example, explicitly refuses to make objectivist, materialist or scientific claims. To the contrary, it explicitly critiques and rejects such claims in an attempt to open itself up and be receptive, in so far as possible, to difference.[59] Armed with his sensitive and enlightened self-awareness, Frankenberg then travels to Albania as a consultant for the drafting of its new Administrative Procedure Act.[60] In this capacity, he functions in a manner that he himself terms 'comparative legal practice and the tragically hegemonic self'[61] – and that Fran Olsen describes as politically oblivious.[62] As Frankenberg himself suggests, it is less than clear that his sensitive methodology actually led – at

---

[56] For example, see John Langbein, 'The German Advantage in Civil Procedure', (1985) 52 U. Chicago L.R. 823; Lloyd Weinreb, *Denial of Justice* (New York: Free Press, 1977), pp. 119–37 [arguing for the establishment of an investigating magistracy in the United States, an argument derived from the French model]; Richard Frase, 'Comparative Criminal Justice as a Guide to American Law Reform: How Do the French Do It, How Can We Find Out, and Why Should We Care?', (1990) 78 California L.R. 539.
[57] See Ugo Mattei, 'The Issue of European Civil Codification and Legal Scholarship: Biases, Strategies and Developments', (1998) 21 Hastings Int. & Comp. L.R. 883.
[58] See Legrand, *supra*, note 2; *id.*, *supra*, note 15; *id.*, 'Codification and the Politics of Exclusion: A Challenge for Comparativists', (1998) 31 U. C. Davis L. R. 799.
[59] See Frankenberg, *supra*, note 1.
[60] See *id.*, 'Stranger than Paradise: Identity and Politics in Comparative Law', [1997] Utah L.R. 259.
[61] *Id.*, p. 270.
[62] See Fran Olson, 'The Drama of Comparative Law', [1997] Utah L.R. 275, pp. 277–80.

least on that occasion – to a particularly sensitive or effective comparative practice.

There are, of course, no easy methodological answers. Comparative methodologies, constructed and deployed by different people in different times and places not only yield very different results, but also represent fundamentally different kinds of interventions. Frankenberg's approach represents something altogether different in Frankfurt than it does in Tirana. Similarly, I can still remember attending a conference in Paris in which a young academic adopted a staunchly US style of legal realism. Citing US examples, he argued that French judges ought to adopt the practice of prospective overruling. The young academic was then immediately taken to task by a particularly venerable-looking colleague, who proceeded to explain to him in particularly pointed terms the A-B-Cs of the republican structure of French government. At once amused and frightened by the reactionary response of the elder scholar, I turned to my neighbour. I asked her whether she would introduce me to the progressive Young Turk, the French voice of US legal realism. She looked at me with disbelief. 'Don't you get it?', she said. 'He's the legal academic voice of Le Pen's *Front National!*'

Comparatists, in short, should be deeply sceptical of the idea that there could be a comparative methodology or theoretical approach that could be safely applied in historically variable circumstances. The comparative possibilities are endless, but so are the contexts in which comparative work can be done. The idea of an a priori comparative Theory that might yield transculturally valid results flies in the face of all the misunderstandings that comparatists observe, produce, decry and consume on a daily basis.

The rosy methodology reconsidered

'External' problems

It is important to recognize that the general critiques outlined above raise serious issues for the rosy methodology. This section, therefore, transposes and applies these general critiques to the comparative methodology suggested in the first section and then responds, in so far as possible, to their troubling implications.

First and foremost, these sceptical critiques suggest that the comparatist may never be able to overcome the fact that he is observing a foreign legal system from the outside. His external position, for example, implies that the comparatist can analyse and reproduce only those facets of the legal system that he can perceive from the outside with his already culturally blinkered perspective. The implications of these critiques are quite threatening to the rosy methodology and to its attempt to gain access to the conceptual framework of foreign legal systems by studying and reproducing their varied discursive characteristics. The sceptical critiques raise serious doubts about whether such linguistic analysis and mimicry can get the comparatist anywhere. Is there any reason to believe that such mimicry might actually produce understanding? Does the comparatist get 'inside' the foreign legal system by studying and copying its linguistic surface? Can he ever get beyond his own external apprehension of what this linguistic surface might mean? Can he ever learn and experience the resonance and significance of such a language? Is there even anything 'below' the linguistic 'surface'? Or is it the case that if the comparatist can really 'speak the speak', he then has somehow grasped the system in whose language he is speaking?

I must confess that I find these questions to be among both the most important and the most impossible for comparatists to answer. I cannot say what there is or may be 'under' the linguistic surface of a legal system. I assume that difference exists, real difference that may not and perhaps cannot be bridged. I think it very likely that however well I learn to speak Russian, however well I come to know its 'high' and 'low' culture and however well I can 'pass' for a Russian on the streets of St Petersburg, my heart will not beat quite the same way as some Russians' upon hearing a few lines of Pushkin! I assume, furthermore, that I will probably never truly understand why those Russian hearts beat quite the way they do.

However, I do feel confident that comparatists can, in fact, come to master – more or less well – the linguistic and conceptual habits that characterize a particular group of people. I believe that most law students can come to recognize and reproduce the vocabulary, grammar, logic, reasoning, justifications and references of foreign attorneys or, at least, of attorneys from other western liberal democracies. I believe, in short, that the comparatist can, in fact, gain considerable access to the *ideolects* of foreign legal actors:[63]

---

[63] See M. M. Bakhtin, *The Dialogic Imagination*, ed. by Michael Holquist and transl. by *id.* and Caryl Emerson (Austin: University of Texas Press, 1981), pp. 333–41; Fredric Jameson, 'Post-Modernism and Consumer Society', in Hal Foster (ed.), *The Anti-Aesthetic: Essays on Postmodern Culture* (Port Townsend, Washington: Bay Press, 1983), p. 114.

the comparatist can develop a certain familiarity with the discourses deployed by others, discourses that reflect and produce particular social, ideological and material practices.

This process of linguistic or discursive mastery is not terribly different from that produced by the US legal pedagogical process known as the 'Socratic method'. Although the claim has always been that this method teaches the US law student to 'think like a lawyer', the most one could truly say is that it teaches the student to 'speak or argue like a lawyer'. The student goes through a process of *acculturation* that leads slowly but surely toward the reproduction of a particular set of legal discourses – ranging from formal syllogisms to distinctive forms of policy debate and the like – that mark the student's entry into the professional culture.

Of course, the discursive mastery produced – especially in the comparative context – is likely to be imperfect. The comparatist can see only through her own eyes and this filters what she perceives and how she interprets what she perceives. Her perspective then manifests itself in her work, thereby shaping, at least to some extent, her comparative analyses. That said, a talented and diligent comparatist can come to gain significant appreciation for such foreign legal ideolects. The key is that the comparatist relentlessly confront the discourses produced in, and by, the foreign legal system. Every comparative description or explanation must be founded upon, and checked by, the careful linguistic analysis of specific discourses. At every turn, the comparatist must juxtapose and confront her comparative analyses to further examples of the studied system's varied discourses. If the comparatist constantly engages the foreign system's discourses in this way, then whatever explanations she might produce are likely to be insightful and even rather reliable. Such detailed discursive study both grants a certain access to, and hems in the comparatist's analysis of, the foreign ideolect. The comparatist's conclusions about one facet of the foreign system are always confronted with another facet, for which the comparatist's conclusions must now account and so on and so forth. Little by little, step by step, the comparatist thus develops a growing sense of the myriad elements and interrelationships that constitute the complex linguistic and conceptual universe of the foreign legal system.

Once such a detailed study has been performed, a final and essential test must be passed: are the comparatist's descriptions and discursive reproductions more or less recognizable to those who operate within the studied system? In other words, would the judges, academics, attorneys or others within the studied system – or some significant cross-section thereof – be willing to recognize, or sign off on, the comparative description of their legal system? This is the basic litmus test, the price of entry for serious comparative work. Similarly, can the comparatist's reproduction of the foreign discourses 'pass' fairly well? If it cannot, or if the foreign attorneys are unable or unwilling to recognize the description, then the comparatist has simply not captured the ideolect sufficiently well.

It is important to note, however, that this comparative description and/or emulation of the 'internal' ideolects need hardly represent the totality of the comparatist's work. Once the comparatist has satisfied this fundamental requirement, she is entirely free to analyse and/or critique the foreign system in whatever way she finds most interesting or productive. She can produce mainstream or radical analyses and critiques that may, or may not, be assimilable to analyses or critiques produced within the studied system. That is up to her. She has an ethical and professional duty of *fidelity* to the object of analysis, a duty that is discharged by constantly doing her best to master its material, linguistic and conceptual characteristics and that is confirmed by a general willingness by actors within the studied system to accept her basic description. This duty fulfilled, the comparatist is free to produce law-and-economics, feminist, Marxist, communitarian, post-Freudian, New Historicist, libertarian, literary or any other analyses; she does not require acceptance of her analyses or conclusions by those within the studied system.

It is, of course, impossible to draw a clean line between the descriptive and the analytic. Any description presupposes an analytic framework that identifies and prioritizes what should be described and that determines why and how it should be described. Any description, therefore, represents a certain translation or re-presentation of the object into the terms and concepts deployed by the comparatist's analytic framework. One might, therefore, question what parts of the comparatist's descriptions, explanations, analyses and/or critiques must pass muster with those within the studied system. Where is the line between the description, which must somehow be acceptable, and the analysis, which need not be?

The line may often be less than clear, but the basic requirement of an acceptable description nonetheless holds. Let me take my own work on French civil judicial discourse as an example. It has been my basic proposition that there is much more to French judicial discourse, reasoning and practice than

French civil judicial decisions would lead one to believe. At the very least, I must be able to get most French judges, attorneys and/or academics – or, more realistically, significant groups of French judges, attorneys or academics – to agree that important discourses exist in the French judicial system other than the terse and syllogistic discourse of the French judicial decision. They must be willing to recognize certain factual information that I have reported, such as the existence and role of certain institutional players. Furthermore, I should be able to get them to agree with my description of the basic characteristics of these players' discourses. They should be willing to vouch, for example, for my description of the importance of equity and legal adaptation concerns to French judicial decision-making. In short, the basic (though very important) descriptive elements of the comparatist's work – whether they describe material details, discursive traits or conceptual devices – must be recognizable to those within the described system. This represents the necessary check on the comparatist's data and on his translation.

However, I see no reason to require French judicial or academic approval of how I then organize, analyse and work with this information. Thus, for example, I have often used a simple heuristic device in order to get across the idea that there is more to French judicial discourse than French judicial decisions would lead one to believe. In particular, I have argued that the French judicial system possesses both an 'official' and an 'unofficial' portrait of the judicial role and that the great flaw in past US comparative work has been to focus primarily on the official portrait.

In order to make this point clearly, I have lumped together a number of different discourses under the rubric of the 'unofficial' including, for example, all academic writing as well as the arguments produced by the *avocat général* and by French judges acting as *rapporteurs*. Needless to say, this heuristic device of dividing French judicial discourses into two groups poses certain problems. First, it is obviously simplistic. Second, it is less than clear why certain discourses should be placed under one or the other banner. Is it really so clear, for example, that academic arguments should fall into the 'unofficial' category? French academics, after all, are all state employees who have gone through rather rigid state training and certification. Furthermore, these academics have traditionally played an extremely important and quite well-recognized role in the development of French law. It would, in short, take little effort to argue that French academic discourse should fall into the 'official' category or even that the official/unofficial distinction is inherently flawed.

It is not my purpose here to defend or attack portions of the methodology that I deployed in my first article.[64] Rather, my aim is simply to argue that such debates over how I chose to analyse French judicial discourse, however fascinating, important and potentially fruitful they may be, presuppose an initial descriptive common ground.[65] The points of agreement include at the very least that French academic discourse (i) differs enormously from the discourse of French civil judicial decisions, as is demonstrated by its recurrent and explicit use of equity, legal adaptation and institutional competence arguments; and, therefore, that (ii) it reflects and constructs a very different understanding of the judicial role than that implicit in the judicial decisions. Having gotten French jurists to sign off on these fundamental descriptions, I am free to produce whatever analysis and critique I find most probative for whatever audience in whatever context I am working. At this point, discussions about what to *make* of the described system (and agreement and disagreement over such questions) cannot help but be interesting and enlightening: each of the analyses is likely to reveal and stress a different facet of the French civil judicial system.

Complexity problems

The possibility, and even the necessity, of stressing different facets of the studied foreign system raises another serious issue for the rosy methodology. This methodology is explicitly open to complexity, but only to a point. It is still focused overwhelmingly on what might now be termed the 'quasi-official' facets of that foreign system. In particular, it limits itself to studying the discursive and conceptual characteristics of the more or less official players of the foreign system. This orientation emerges quite clearly in the French context, where my deployment of the methodology has confined analysis to the discourses of judges, legislators, *avocats généraux*, academics and the like.

This critique is unfortunately quite correct. Two arguments should nonetheless be offered in response. First, the methodology, for all of its focus on the ideolects of quasi-official legal actors, is nonetheless decidedly more varied, diverse, complex, detailed and relational than the methodologies

---

[64] I am, in fact, increasingly dissatisfied with the categorizations that I offered in my early work and, therefore, intend to present shortly a more nuanced reading of the French civil judicial system.
[65] I would actually be tempted to visualize heuristic categories (and most anything else) as both descriptive and analytic.

deployed by most traditional US comparative scholarship. In the French context, for example, such traditional work has tended to focus at most on legislation and official judicial decisions, with perhaps some passing references to largely outdated academic writing. As strange as it may seem, the last major US comparatist to take French academic writing relatively seriously may well have been Roscoe Pound![66] In this respect, the rosy methodology's refusal to be utterly dismissive of French academics actually represents, in and of itself, a significant departure.[67]

Furthermore, the methodology's detailed study of what might be termed 'high-professional discourse' – which includes the discourses of not only academics, but also of institutional players such as *avocats généraux* and *juges rapporteurs* – constitutes a fairly significant advance over traditional US comparative scholarship. It provides, for the first time, a window into the varied ideolects of those professional players who significantly influence the daily operation of the French civil legal system.

What is more, because the methodology takes such discourses seriously, it recognizes and tries to deal with the subtle and not-so-subtle differences that distinguish these discourses from each other. As a result, the methodology recognizes, exposes and tries to explain and come to terms with the significant *heteroglossia* that exists even within the relatively narrow confines of such quasi-official discourses.[68] The resulting descriptions and analyses are, therefore, significantly enriched: a greater number of discourses are brought to the table and the relationships between these discourses emerge as a particularly important object of analysis.

The second response addresses the complexity critique in a more direct fashion. This response begins by acknowledging that I find it quite tempting – at least in theory – to include ever-greater amounts of discursive or conceptual material in my comparative analyses. I can only assume that the greater the number of discursive and conceptual sources, the richer the resulting analysis. I would, therefore, be in favour – at least in theory – of adopting a certain 'cultural-studies' approach to comparative legal work.

---

[66] In fact, Pound's knowledge of, and interest in, foreign academic writing is nothing short of remarkable. The sheer breadth and detail of his footnote references are intimidating. For example, see Roscoe Pound, *Jurisprudence*, vol. I (St Paul: West, 1959), p. 178, n. 122 and p. 523, n. 147.

[67] Belleau has been taking a parallel path in the historical context. She has been resurrecting and taking seriously a series of early twentieth-century French academics. See Belleau, *supra*, note 35.

[68] See Bakhtin, *supra*, note 63, p. 428.

Such an approach, however, raises a deeply practical problem. What sources should the comparatist actually seek to study? Perhaps she should approach assorted 'high' and 'low' cultural forms, such as architecture, the visual arts, public-opinion polls, novels, newspaper accounts, oral histories, films and/or television. The problem with adopting such an approach, however, is that I can think of no reliable way to determine what these assorted materials actually represent, never mind to figure out the relationship between these materials and the legal system.

I strongly suspect, for example, that a detailed study of assorted forms of legal iconography cannot help but be fascinating and suggestive. I am unreservedly in favour of the study of such representations *as representations*. The difficulty consists of trying to infer that such representations are in some way *representative* or constitutive of the legal system. Although I am fairly comfortable in asserting that the discursive practices of assorted French legal professionals are fairly representative of these professionals' ideolects, I am not at all sure whether Jacques-Louis David's painting of Napoleon drafting the French civil code – studied on its own – is similarly representative of these professionals' ideolects, or of David's, or of Napoleon's or of anyone else's.[69] I have no doubt that the painting may well influence the French legal professional's ideolect, but unfortunately I have no reliable way to examine or demonstrate this relation. However, having studied in detail the ideolects of assorted players in the French legal apparatus, it can be immensely productive to refer to the David painting as *illustrative* of some facet of those ideolects.[70]

My unease at the prospect of moving beyond my relatively broad (and yet limited) set of materials, therefore, rests on very pragmatic methodological concerns. Rather than seek to (re-)construct some sort of 'public', 'general' or other ideolect, I prefer to limit my analysis to materials that are clearly generated by, or within, the studied legal system's professional culture. *This most certainly does not mean that I believe that the legal system is in any way separate from the general culture.* I assume that public perceptions and general cultural assumptions significantly affect – and even help – to constitute the structure, operation and ideology of a legal system. I recognize that a legal system includes not only the formal structures of, for example,

---

[69] *Cf*. Legrand, *supra*, note 15, p. 5.

[70] In a recent article, for example, I try to use French culinary debates as a means of illustrating French jurisprudential debates. See Mitchel de S.-O.-l'E. Lasser, 'La Macdonald-isation du discours judiciaire français', Arch. phil. dr., 2001, p. 137.

the three branches of government, but also the ways in which most of the population never appears to have direct contact with (or believes that it has no direct contact with), for example, the judicial system. I concede, therefore, that to focus on the discursive practices of the professional legal culture is to focus on a relatively narrow slice of what constitutes the legal system. But I prefer to remain relatively limited in analytic scope (although, again, broader in scope than traditional US comparatists) rather than get embroiled in the analysis of a whole series of cultural forms whose significance or representative-ness I cannot assume or demonstrate.

Finally, it is worth raising a final version of the (lack of) complexity critique. This version of the critique might object to the rosy methodology's apparent refusal to countenance the possibility of *radical* difference *within* the quasi-official discursive materials. In other words, the rosy methodology tends to assume that certain important concepts, theories and practices *mediate* between what appear at first blush to be irreconcilable discourses or ideolects within the quasi-official realm. This assumption, however, rules out the possibility of radically different ideolects within a given legal system.

Once again, this critique is, in fact, quite justified. The rosy methodology actively seeks to locate and analyse not only the patently official state legal discourses (such as legislation or judicial decisions), but also the numerous quasi-official discourses that reflect and constitute the complex, daily, on-the-ground, professional legal ideolects. It is, therefore, only reasonable to expect that there will be significant disjunctions not only between the official and quasi-official discourses/ideolects, but also between the assorted quasi-official discourses/ideolects. The question is what to make of these disjunctions.

It is, in fact, one of the fundamental working assumptions of my methodology that the multiple discourses within a legal system are not likely to be considered irreconcilable by those who deploy them. The first explanation for this assumption is systemic. Given that these discourses all function within a single legal system, and given that each is deployed in the context of the others in order to produce some effect within that system, it seems only reasonable to assume that there exists a certain inter-operability of the discourses. In other words, it seems unlikely that the players operating in a legal system would deploy discourses that they and others would consider utterly irreconcilable with, or irrelevant or even incomprehensible to, the other important discourses in the system. It is only reasonable to suppose, for example, that a government attorney who deploys a particular form of discourse when arguing to an appellate court expects that discourse to be effective in one way or another. She expects (or at least hopes!) that her discourse – and the ideolect that it represents – relates in some way to the official discourse of past judicial decisions and that it will have some effect on that judicial discourse in the present instance. This attorney, in other words, has some integrating theory about how her own discourse and ideolect fits in with, and can even influence, other discourses in the legal field.

This working assumption of discursive and conceptual inter-operability holds precisely because my analyses focus on quasi-official discourses, that is, on discourses deployed by professionals within the legal system. None of these professionals can afford to be radically different than, or radically separate from, or radically incomprehensible to, the other professionals in the field. Each of these professionals – be they, for example, judges, legislators, attorneys or academics – seeks, at least to some extent, to be heard, understood and followed by her professional addressees.

Furthermore, I think it unlikely that the quasi-official players in a legal system would maintain a truly radical disjunction between the official and their unofficial discourses and understandings. It is difficult to prove the validity of this supposition, but I nonetheless believe that few legal actors operate as two-faced, bad-faith manipulators. Rather, most such actors possess broad and overarching theories, worldviews and role definitions that facilitate a certain mediation and co-existence with the official discourses and concepts. In the United States, for example, there is little in the way of radical disjunction between the ideolects of attorneys or academics and that of the official judicial discourse. Even the most explicitly tactical players, such as criminal defence attorneys, tax attorneys or those academics who most explicitly urge tactical behaviour, almost always do so in the context of overarching legitimating claims, such as the role of the attorney as check on the power of the state or the interpretive tradition of the common law.[71] According to such explanations, the role played or urged by these tacticians may be somewhat at cross-purposes with the official discourse, *but only somewhat*: in the end, it is consistently argued, the fundamental purposes of the legal system will be served and advanced. In this respect, these ideolects are, in fact, part and parcel of mainstream legal ideology, according to which, in the end, the common law and the adversary system will out. It is very

---

[71] See Alan Dershowitz, *The Best Defense* (New York: Random House, 1983); Duncan Kennedy, 'Freedom and Constraint in Adjudication: A Critical Phenomenology', (1986) 36 J. Leg. Ed. 518.

rare indeed for legal actors to argue that there is no bridging between the official and their unofficial discourses/understandings and, therefore, that their approach represents a veritable opting out of the legal system. Even proponents of race-based jury nullification argue within the traditional and legitimating construct of the common-law tradition and, therefore, explicitly tie themselves to the official ideolects.[72]

In the end, it is precisely this interplay between the official and quasi-official discourses that is so revealing about a legal system and about the ways in which it operates, both intellectually and practically. This interplay establishes and reflects a series of conceptual and 'on-the-ground' relations between the official and quasi-official discourses, as well as between the assorted quasi-official discourses, that constitute the basic intellectual structure or conceptual framework of the legal system. My comparative methodology is, therefore, geared toward gaining access to these *interrelated* and *mediating* modes of speaking, explaining, justifying and conceptualizing.

'Internal problems'

Perhaps the second section's weakest objection to the rosy methodology is that the methodology represents an 'external' attempt to gain access to 'internal' understandings of a foreign legal system when it is less than clear that those actors who are 'inside' a legal system actually understand how their legal system works.

Although this description of the rosy methodology is on point – it does, in fact, seek to allow a jurist from one legal system to gain access to how the jurists from a foreign legal system conceptualize their legal universe – the critique rests on the deeply problematic suggestion that these foreign jurists might well not understand how their own legal system actually works. This suggestion rests, in turn, on a couple of highly debatable assumptions: first, that there actually exists some objectively correct understanding of how that system works – one that, therefore, focuses not on how people *think*, but on how institutions, state apparatuses and other legal actors actually *function* – and, second, that such an objective account would be best produced from 'outside' the observed system. This critique itself falls prey to all of the criticisms that are traditionally levelled, for example,

---

[72] For example, see Paul Butler, 'Racially Based Jury Nullification: Black Power in the Criminal Justice System', (1995) 105 Yale L.J. 677.

at materialist, 'infrastructure'-oriented analyses. Thus, even if we were to bracket the impossible question of whether we could actually produce an objective description of the material world (a dubious proposition at best), something terribly important would nonetheless be missing from the 'objective' description, namely, the modes of thinking that permeate the legal system under observation.

My methodology operates on altogether different assumptions. It assumes that how those people who function within a legal system believe that legal system to work, how they talk about 'legal' and/or 'non-legal' issues, indeed how they conceive of such things as the 'legal' and the 'non-legal', constitutes a significant facet of what that legal system *is*. This assumption is important not only because modes of thinking and speaking are likely to produce – by means of complex and perhaps unpredictable mechanisms – tangible effects or material manifestations, but also because legal systems comprise not only material apparatuses, but also modes of thought and discourse that are taught and transmitted in complex ways, ranging from formal legal education to the criminal justice system's iconography to official judicial discourse, etc. Thus, even if such modes of thought and discourse do not clearly *determine* the material elements and practices of the legal system then, at the very least, they possess a complex dialogical relationship with them. To ignore such modes of thought and discourse – to ignore the ideolects – on the ground that they are not objective aspects of the legal system is, therefore, to miss the point.

In the end, it is worth noting that to the extent that jurists of a given legal system appear to be blind to certain characteristics of that system or to apparent disjunctions, tensions or contradictions between assorted facets of that system, such apparent 'blindness' may well constitute an important feature of that legal system, of its ways of conceptualizing and describing its relevant reality. At the very least, this supposed blindness is indicative of another way of organizing and understanding the legal universe and thus represents a potentially fruitful focal point for comparative analysis.

The problem of methodology: constructing the object of analysis

The answers given above do not address a final series of interrelated objections raised in the second section. These important objections call attention to the analytic effects produced by constructing and deploying any methodology to describe and analyse any object, including a foreign legal system.

The gist of these sceptical objections is that the construction and deployment of a given methodology produces a constitutive effect on the object of analysis: any methodology contains its own worldview and presuppositions, which it embeds in its own distinctions and definitions and which it then projects onto the object of analysis. As a result, the methodology selects aspects of what it observes and constructs the object according to its own image. According to such critiques, all of the distinctions repeatedly deployed by comparatists, such as, for example, similarity v. difference or internal v. external perspectives, actually play an important constitutive role in the construction of the object of analysis. The problem is not limited to whether, in any given context, the comparatist should describe something as, for example, 'similar to' or 'different than' something else (or both) or whether he should, as a general matter, adopt a methodology that stresses similarity or difference (or both). The primary problem is that the construction of the similarity/difference methodology – and the resulting projection of its two categories – constitute and shape the object of analysis.

To take my own work as an example, it is undeniable that the method that I have deployed in the French and US legal context has significantly affected what I have studied and how I have analysed and described it. The result has been conclusions utterly dependent on, and perhaps even presaged by, the initial choice of methodology. Thus, for example, the division of modes of reading into two broad categories (the 'grammatical' and the 'hermeneutic') has obviously had an enormous constitutive effect on how my analysis has defined and described the observed French and US judicial discourses, which has led to rather foreseeable consequences. In particular, as a result of the construction and deployment of these two broad categories, all forms of interpretation premised on a notion that texts can be read or applied without having recourse to extra-textual considerations were lumped under one rubric, 'grammatical reading'. All other forms of interpretation – that is, those premised on the need to resort to extra-textual means – were then lumped together under the other rubric, 'hermeneutic interpretation'. Needless to say, this fundamental division, for all of its taxonomic usefulness, nonetheless remains quite crude. Under this methodology, for instance, economic-policy analysis and equity discourse both get categorized as 'hermeneutic' forms of interpretation.

The problem with the methodology is that it constructs French and US judicial discourse in a largely foreseeable way. Given the breadth of the categories, is it really surprising that, in the end, French and US judges turn out to deploy variations on the same basic combination of grammatical and hermeneutic interpretation? By dividing the discursive and interpretive possibilities into only two broad categories and by including non-positivistic sources (such as high-professional discourse) within the ambit of the 'judicial', the methodology arrived at what could reasonably – if rather harshly – be considered to be a trumped-up conclusion: Franco-US similarity.

Of course, any methodology falls into the same trap. It would have taken little to produce a contrary conclusion. The traditional US comparative approach has repeatedly consisted of doing just that. By limiting its materials to published judicial decisions, this approach has, in fact, constructed its objects in such a way as to lead to an apparently obvious conclusion: Franco-US difference. Who could help but notice that French and US judicial decisions look very different, use different types of discourses and suggest different forms of judicial interpretation and reasoning? But this conclusion of apparent difference was more or less posited by the decision of how to construct the object of analysis, that is, of what to include in the analysis, of what to put on each side of the comparative scale.

In short, any methodology affects the construction, description and interpretation of the object of analysis. The comparatist must choose a methodology; and her choice necessarily and significantly affects her comparative analysis. How, then, should the comparatist decide upon the selection of a particular methodological approach?

I believe that such a methodological choice can be considered and justified only in a particular comparative context. My own methodological decisions, for example, have been forged in the context of traditional US comparative analyses of the French civil judicial system. These traditional US analyses, as I have repeatedly explained, consistently stressed Franco-US *difference* by deploying deeply parochial, post-realist methodologies. By limiting observation to published French judicial decisions, and by adopting parochial US realist perspectives about the proper sources of the law and about the evils of formalism, these analyses could not help but produce deeply dismissive – and often overtly negative – characterizations of the French civil judicial system.

In this context, my goal was to produce and deploy a methodology that would productively *re-engage* the French materials. The purpose of my methodology was, therefore, to generate a description of French judicial discourse, thinking and practice that would force a serious reconceptualization of the French judicial system. My approach was to contradict the canonical comparative accounts by producing a description that would stress the fundamental *similarities* between French and US judicial discourse and practice. The result was a methodology that promoted the close reading of long quotations culled from a broad set of judicial, professional and academic sources. Framed in this manner, the French civil judicial system could no longer be summarily dismissed as an object lesson on the evils of formalism. It emerged instead as a reasonable, coherent and perhaps even challenging alternative to US legal thought. The methodology, in other words, produced a far richer – and, to my mind, more responsible and representative – portrayal of the conceptual underpinnings and daily practices of the French civil legal system.

My approach to comparative practice, therefore, acknowledges and accepts the critique that any choice of methodology significantly affects the construction, description and interpretation of the object of analysis. My response has simply been to *treat comparative law as a relational practice*. The idea is to forge relationships with prior comparative analyses, with the objects of analysis, with other disciplines (in my case, literary theory and criticism) and with the audience that foster a sense of *responsibility* toward the materials with which one works.

The method consists of stressing those explanations that actively combat facile and dismissive analytic attitudes, explanations that promote instead detailed, generous and challenging engagement with the objects of analysis. Of course, there is no rule about how to produce such an engagement. I assume that in different contexts, different means could and should be used. I believe, for example, that in the context of my recent work stressing Franco-US similarity, the next step toward further engagement will consist precisely of stressing the important discursive and conceptual *differences* that continue to distinguish French from US judicial practice. This next step will likely consist, therefore, of breaking down the broad categories of 'grammatical' and 'hermeneutic' reading in order to offer more nuanced – and thereby more differentiating – descriptions of French and US discourse. By constantly readjusting my methodology in this fashion, I hope that I will come ever closer to appreciating and producing ever-richer comparative representations, hopefully resulting in ever-greater and more challenging engagement with the objects of analysis, the academic disciplines in play and the audiences at work.

I can, therefore, offer no rule about how to arrive at such responsible engagement. The best I can do is to suggest the importance of what Anglo-American jurists might term a certain 'situation sense'[73] or of what Continental academics might regard as a certain Aristotelian '*tekhnè*',[74] that is, a deep contextually embedded judgement about how best to provoke, for different audiences in different disciplines at different times, instances of cross-cultural conceptual insight. It should be stressed, however, that a rigid initial requirement nonetheless continues to apply. The basic description produced by the comparatist must pass muster with at least some significant portion of the players of the studied foreign legal system, be they judges, legislators, academics, attorneys, clients or others, or more likely some significant sub-group within or across any of these general categories. This is the basic price of admission for serious comparative work, or at least for comparative work that takes ideolects into account.

Conclusion

Perhaps the best way to conclude this ponderous explanation of my comparative method is to offer a light-hearted example. At a comparative-law conference held in Chicago some time ago, four Italian colleagues invited me to join them for dinner. After a mediocre meal at a restaurant clearly geared toward tourists, one of my Italian friends ordered an espresso. Holding his thumb and index finger slightly apart, he requested that the espresso be '*corto* ... eh ... short'. For a brief moment, the waiter's confusion was apparent. A short cup of espresso? The waiter quickly regained his composure. 'Well, *our* espresso machine only makes *big* cups of espresso', he explained disdainfully, 'but I can pour half of it out, *if you want*'.

It is my contention that our waiter adopted a cross-cultural approach that, not unlike many US comparative analyses, was inclined to produce an interpretation of the foreign as obtuse. His reading was dismissive – and perhaps even intentionally so – despite the fact that so many other readings were readily available. Perhaps because of his background

---

[73] Karl Llewellyn, 'Remarks on the Theory of Appellate Decision and the Rules or Canons about How Statutes Are to Be Construed', (1950) 3 Vanderbilt L.R. 395, p. 401; *id.*, *The Common Law Tradition* (Boston: Little, Brown, 1960), pp. 60–1.
[74] For example, see Jean-François Lyotard and Jean-Loup Thébaud, *Just Gaming*, transl. by Wlad Godzich (Minneapolis: University of Minnesota Press, 1985), p. 28.

and temperament, perhaps because of his working conditions and perhaps because he had simply never been introduced to the joys of comparative law, the waiter was looking to make his life easy, rather than seeking to engage – to whatever extent possible – the difficult, the complex and the different.[75] He possessed no sense of responsibility to his audience/clients, never mind to his own work. He was prepared to understand the Italian request, but only on his own terms. The only true rule of his game was that his own perspective not be challenged.

The comparative posture or attitude must be radically different than that displayed in the Chicago restaurant. Why would someone from the land of espresso (even the word is Italian, as are the brand names emblazoned on almost every espresso machine in the United States!)[76] make such an apparently nonsensical request? A generous reading of the request would have to acknowledge that the Italian obviously had a very clear idea of how he wished his coffee to be made and/or served and to recognize that it was unlikely that this idea, formulated in his request, was just plain idiotic. At the very least, it seems to me that a comparatist seeking to decipher the request would have an obligation to become fairly well acquainted with Italian coffee discourse and its basic accompanying practices.

In this particular instance, the generous – and thus conscientious – comparatist would engage in sufficient discursive and field research to figure out that in Italian coffee discourse, 'short' does not mean 'small' so much as 'strong'.[77] The Italian was requesting a 'short pull', that is, he wanted only the first part of the stream of espresso to be pushed through the coffee grinds. He did not want this, the strongest and most fragrant part of the stream of espresso – known as the '*ristretto*' – to be diluted by the continuing stream of evermore tasteless coffee that would pass through the same grinds. He wanted the stream of espresso to be cut short, so to speak. Such is the discourse of Italian espresso-making, a discourse that obviously reflects and produces certain practices and that can, therefore, be quite revealing for the committed comparatist. At the very least, the comparatist must be able to generate the kind of basic linguistic and practical explanation offered

---

[75] Disclaimer: as someone who has actually waited on tables, I am, in fact, extremely sympathetic to waiters everywhere, unless, of course, they take it upon themselves to be rude to foreigners.

[76] The machines are typically made by such companies as Gaggia, La Pavoni, DeLonghi, Rancilio and Saeco. Even Starbucks, that quintessentially US company, gives its espresso machines Italian names, such as the 'Barista'.

[77] It is, however, sometimes the case that '*corto*' is used to order a single – as opposed to a double ('*doppio*' or '*lungo*') – shot of espresso.

directly above. She must, in short, be able to grasp and to explain the gist of what was said.

This basic level of explanation represents, of course, but the tip of the comparative iceberg. The comparatist can go into infinitely greater depth in an attempt to offer evermore incisive analysis. Further research should reveal even more of the underlying espresso culture. It should expose certain typical attitudes and recurring practices. It should introduce a whole cast of espresso characters and institutions, from the '*barista*' (the espresso barman), to the bar itself, to the customers, to the importers, to the producers, to the labourers... In short, serious study should generate increasingly rich description.

What the comparatist wants to make, so to speak, of the information she gathers is another story altogether. There is, of course, no end to the ways in which she might analyse the Italian espresso culture. She might focus, for example, on revealing Italian/US difference by analysing the significance of drinking an espresso while standing at a bar versus drinking a cup of coffee while seated at a diner. She might delve into the deeper import of taking a 'short' espresso as opposed to having a 'bottomless' cup of coffee. She might offer compelling accounts of how coffee practices reflect and produce colonial and post-colonial exploitation, as well as race, gender and class divisions.[78] She might buttress her conclusions with revealing data about Italian and US coffee production, distribution and consumption.[79] She might trace the intellectual history of coffeehouse culture.[80] She might study representations of coffee in assorted 'high' and 'low' cultural forms, ranging from novels to movies to advertising posters. Or she might, as my own suggestions tend to demonstrate, focus on the discourses of coffee deployed by assorted groups of *baristas*, waiters, coffee drinkers, roasters and suppliers, wholesale buyers, importers, busboys, food critics and the like.

In short, the comparative possibilities are endless; and, frankly, they all strike me as intriguing and revealing. But whatever approach the comparatist chooses to take, she had better satisfy the initial requirement, namely, that her basic description pass muster with some significant portion of the

---

[78] For example, see Stewart Lee Allen, *The Devil's Cup: Coffee, the Driving Force in History* (New York: Soho Press, 1999).

[79] For example, see Gregory Dicum and Nina Luttinger, *The Coffee Book: Anatomy of an Industry from Crop to the Last Drop* (New York: New Press, 1999).

[80] For example, see Ralph Hattox, *Coffee and Coffeehouses: The Origins of a Social Beverage in the Medieval Near East* (Seattle: University of Washington Press, 1985); Ulla Heise, *Coffee and Coffee Houses*, transl. by Paul Roper (West Chester, Pennsylvania: Schiffer, 1987).

players of the studied coffee-system, be they consumers, producers, servers, critics or others, or more likely some significant sub-group within or across any of these general categories.

Beyond this, it is up to the comparatist to deploy her 'situation sense' or '*tekhnè*' in order to produce an analysis that she believes best reveals and expresses some facet of the studied coffee-system to the particular audience that she is addressing. It may well be that enlightening comparisons can be drawn, for example, between the '*corto*'/'*lungo*' distinction and the 'black'/'regular' distinction.[81] Such a determination obviously depends on any number of factors, ranging from the history of coffee studies to the composition of her audience to the relationship between the coffee-systems under analysis, etc. In the face of dismissive Italian accounts of watered-down US coffee, perhaps an introduction to local US espresso shops is in order. In the face of US franchising of commodified espresso drinks, maybe a short encounter with a Neapolitan *barista* (or even a compelling description thereof) will give reason to pause. And, perhaps, in the face of both, a short course on the purchasing and home-roasting of select lots of green coffee beans might destabilize one's pat understandings of coffee cultures, leading to a new and productive engagement with those cultures and even with coffee itself.[82]

I assume that I will never truly 'understand' what it means for some Italians to order a '*corto*' (also known as a '*basso*'). I will underanalyse and/or overanalyse Italian espresso discourses and practices; I will learn some references and make some connections, but not others; and I will flatten, assimilate and orientalize to various extents. In short, it will never be the same for me to make such an order, or to hear it being made, as it would be for certain people acculturated in some way into the various Italian espresso cultures. But I can certainly study those cultures, learn about and analyse them to some significant extent, convey some of what I have learned by offering imperfect but resonant translations and even present generous, engaging and eventually challenging analyses and critiques of what I have described. In the end, I believe that this represents a comparatively good start.

---

[81] As always, the comparatist must be open to complexity and variation, even in such banal circumstances. As I learned in my high-school 'behind-the-counter' days, there is little agreement on whether a 'regular' coffee includes sugar as well as milk!

[82] For example, see Kenneth Davids, *Home Coffee Roasting: Romance and Revival* (New York: St Martin's, 1996).

9

The same and the different

PIERRE LEGRAND

Pour Casimir et Imogene, qui font toute la différence.
Auch für die, die andere Wege öffnet.

> It is rather like alluding to the obvious connection between the two ceremonies of the sword: when it taps a man's shoulder, and when it cuts off his head. It is not at all similar for the man.
>
> (G. K. Chesterton)[1]

One is at the mercy of others. One's view of oneself, for example, is shaped by the others' gaze. And, beyond specularity, one fears being encumbered by something alien to oneself. In order to accommodate the vagaries of dependency and to contain the threat that others may represent, it becomes necessary to ascertain whether others are friends or foes, which is tantamount to asking whether they are like or unlike one. Difference, then, can be invoked to the disadvantage of those to whom it is applied as when it serves to place an individual's or a community's distinctiveness in jeopardy through oppression, disavowal, exclusion or obliteration. Overt sexual or ethnic discrimination provide evident applications of this discursive strategy. But the logic of betrayal and rejection through differentiation

---

Apart from the few instances where I have chosen to use only an English translation on account of its currency (for example, see *infra*, note 15), I refer to original versions, whether on their own (for materials in French) or in addition to authoritative English translations whenever available (for texts in other languages). Unattributed English translations are mine. I am immensely grateful to Geoffrey Samuel, Nicholas Kasirer, Horatia Muir Watt, Roderick Munday, Georgina Firth, Mitchel Lasser, Peter Goodrich and Michel Rosenfeld, all of whom provided invaluable and emboldening friendship while I was researching and writing this paper. As it seems fair to assume that parts at least of my argument will be met with suspicion (or alarm!), the usual disclaimer appears especially apt.

[1] G. K. Chesterton, *Orthodoxy*, in *The Collected Works of G. K. Chesterton*, ed. by David Dooley, vol. I (San Francisco: Ignatius Press, 1986), p. 335 [1908].

can adopt more insidious forms. Consider the character of the mother in Nathalie Sarraute's *L'usage de la parole*. In differentiating, through a brutal naming of roles, between the various members of the family who had been huddling together on the sofa ('She shook them, she forced them to awake, to detach themselves from one another. You see, here we are: I can help you do the census. Here, in front of you: the father. This is the daughter. Here is the son'), the mother destroys the indistinction of the family bond. As she shatters the intimate embrace of family relations, her words inflict a cruel separation to those around her, who simultaneously find themselves at a distance from her because she has abruptly removed herself from the rest of the family (in the words of the narrator, 'why is it that she, the mother... she was not where she should have found herself, where one ordinarily finds her, between her husband, her daughter and her son. She was as far away from them as a stranger. Had she fled? Abandoned her dignity, her role as mother? 'Your father' 'Your sister'... words like herself, like everything around... icy and hard...').[2]

Ultimately, all linguistic, social and cultural activity is grounded in differential thinking, if only because of the originary and irreducible distance between word and object, between self and other. But difference is polymorphous and need not be apprehended as divisive and impoverishing. It can also be experienced as an affirmation, as an assertion of being. The act of differentiation regularly provides one with a vital capacity for action by enabling one to resist the erosion of boundaries between subjects, by allowing one to elude misrecognition or banishment, by permitting one to avoid violent confusions. Not only is difference, therefore, linked to the very matter of intelligibility (how could understanding – envisaged here as always-interpretation – come from indistinction?), but it is also connected to the possibility of social organization and to the survival of the individual, for it can be construed as aborting all possible totalization. It is this redemptive, empowering feature of differential thought – difference's responsive

---

[2] Nathalie Sarraute, *L'usage de la parole*, in *Oeuvres complètes*, ed. by Jean-Yves Tadié et al. (Paris: Gallimard, 1996), pp. 941 and 943–4 ['*Elle les a secoués, elle les a obligés à se réveiller, à se détacher les uns des autres (...). (...) Vous voyez, nous voici, je peux vous aider à faire le recensement. Voici devant vous: le père. Voici la fille. Ici c'est le fils*'; '*Mais alors, comment se fait-il qu'elle, la mère... elle n'était pas là où elle devait se trouver, où on la trouve d'ordinaire, entre son mari, sa fille et son fils. Elle était aussi loin d'eux qu'une étrangère (...). (...) Aurait-elle fui? Abandonné sa tenue, son rôle de mère? (...) "Ton père" "Ta soeur"... des mots comme elle-même, comme tout autour... glacés et durs...*'] (1980) [hereinafter *Oeuvres complètes*]. I follow Ann Jefferson, *Nathalie Sarraute, Fiction and Theory* (Cambridge: Cambridge University Press, 2000), pp. 56–9.

and responsible *yes* – which this exercise in negative dialectics is committed to celebrating.³

* * *

Negative dialectics, in the expression made famous by Theodor Adorno, refers to a critical mode of reflection which at crucial moments – those moments in the production of knowledge that call upon one to take positions which determine how one gets from one step to the next, from one statement to the next, from one sentence to the next – negates what a discipline affirms. I regard this paper as a variation on the theme of negative dialectics in the sense that it is largely an argument meant to negate clearly and emphatically the positivistic enterprise that (establishment-minded) comparative legal studies wants to be. Negativity, far from suggesting a 'mood' – one need not be a negative person in order to engage in negative dialectics – is a de-position or a dis-position, a distrust in positing and in positivity and in positivists and in the positivistic *Zeitgeist*, which must be *ex-posed* as the most important factor suppressing the contextual dimension of meaningful experience within comparative analysis. In this sense, negativity epitomizes the transformative role of theory as counter-discourse. It is, literally, an *undisciplined* gesture. It effectuates a politics of resistance. It is transgressive (not strictly in a cathartic sense, although it would be unwise to obfuscate the constructive value that the purgative dimension may hold, but in an ecstatic mode, in other words, in the way it is 'critically promot[ing] progressive social transformation').⁴

* * *

Some further liminary observations are apposite, for instance, as regards the notion of 'tradition', which takes us beyond national boundaries and the problematic idea of 'system' and, even more importantly, shows at a meta-stable level how the connection of my present perception with past experience is part of a continuing life-history *along* with it (rather than

---

³ For a key and, *vis-à-vis* mainstream philosophical thought, disruptive treatment of difference as productive force, see Gilles Deleuze, *Différence et répétition* (Paris: Presses Universitaires de France, 1968). I refer to mainstream philosophical thought at *infra*, text accompanying notes 49–57. More generally, see Gilles Deleuze and Félix Guattari, *L'anti-Oedipe* (Paris: Editions de Minuit, 1972), where the authors contrast the Platonic or Christian conception of desire as lack, distress and suffering with the affirmative conception of a desire that is productive and creative.

⁴ Patricia J. Huntington, *Ecstatic Subjects, Utopia, and Recognition* (Albany: SUNY Press, 1998), pp. 10–11 and *passim*. See Johannes Fabian, *Anthropology with an Attitude* (Stanford: Stanford University Press, 2001), pp. 7, 100 and 93. See generally Theodor W. Adorno, *Negative Dialectics*, transl. by E. B. Ashton (London: Routledge, 1973). *Adde*: Susan Buck-Morss, *The Origin of Negative Dialectics* (New York: Free Press, 1977).

being causally affected by it and, therefore, separated from it) and *against* the present, enclosed as it is in its own self-certainty. Tradition, then, is also emancipation from the present. In other words, what comes to one from the past can be a means of drawing one out of oneself, of constituting oneself as historical being – which, as far as law's subjects are concerned, entails the opportunity of escaping from a strategy of world-making predicated on the exclusion of the uncontainable.[5]

Now, I do not claim that legal traditions are sociologically equivalent, but that they are epistemologically comparable despite their uniqueness (in the sense that they constitute 'originary' discourse-producing units, in the way that they represent 'originary' sources of meaning or intention).[6] Legal traditions are, of course, only virtually homogeneous and there is no doubt that they contain internal dissensions. Indeed, one can take as fundamental the facts of fragmentation, incoherence, transgression and conflict within interpretive communities: 'There is no single culture that constitutes an autarchic, self-established, and self-sufficient unity. Every culture cultivates itself with regard to other cultures and is cultivated by other cultures. There is no culture that has not emerged from the configuration of others [...] and has not been co-determined and transformed by these others at every moment of its history. Culture is a *plurale tantum*: it exists only in the plural.'[7] Thus, I accept that the qualifiers 'civil law' and 'common law' do not refer in an exclusive way to one or the other of the western legal traditions. My point is rather that one will find traces of a legal or rhetorical or anthropological or sociological or political economy said to be 'civil law' more easily in jurisdictions having received Roman law and that one will find traces of a legal or rhetorical or anthropological or sociological or

---

[5] To reduce 'tradition' to a massive typological narrative or a vast programme of structural integration, to stress perpetuation over dissemination, as is commonly done, is, therefore, to miss the hermeneutic point. In an important essay, Bruns observes how 'tradition is not the persistence of the same'. Rather, 'it is the disruption of the same by that which cannot be repressed or subsumed into a familiar category'. He adds: 'The encounter with tradition [...] is always subversive of totalization or containment': Gerald L. Bruns, *Hermeneutics Ancient and Modern* (New Haven: Yale University Press, 1992), pp. 201–2.
[6] For a reflection on the interaction between 'law' and 'tradition', see Martin Krygier, 'Law as Tradition', (1986) 5 L. & Phil. 237.
[7] Werner Hamacher, 'One 2 Many Multiculturalisms', in Hent deVries and Samuel Weber (eds.), *Violence, Identity, and Self-Determination* (Stanford: Stanford University Press, 1997), pp. 295–6. See also Bhikhu Parekh, *Rethinking Multiculturalism* (Cambridge, Mass.: Harvard University Press, 2000), pp. 76–9. For a graphic attempt at capturing cultural interaction, see Peter N. Stearns, *Cultures in Motion* (New Haven: Yale University Press, 2001).

political economy said to be 'common law' more easily in jurisdictions not having received Roman law. I ground this argument on my conviction that law is performance (whether voluntary or involuntary) – not a 'being', but a 'doing' – such that what makes civil law 'civil law' and what makes common law 'common law' takes place in a constituting process in which civil law and common law call upon each other as other in order to be able to fashion themselves and be what they are in difference from one another. I further base my claim on my own life experience, which has taken me repeatedly and for extended periods of time to civil-law and to common-law jurisdictions, whether as student, advocate, researcher or teacher. It is also my own life-in-the-law, that of someone without a mother-law, that of someone who was never locked inside the familiarity of one law, that of someone who is free to imagine oneself as either civil-law or common-law lawyer, that of someone who has constantly straddled western legal traditions, which has led me to write explicitly, as I have done on more than one occasion, against essentialism. 'Civil-law' and 'common-law' do not exist a priori as kinds of essences, but only a posteriori in multiple incarnations – none of which is pure. I believe in inescapable hybridity (which, incidentally, is why the notion of 'mixed legal systems' still advocated by many comparatists strikes me as somewhat unsophisticated). I have, therefore, never propounded a theory of 'civil law' or 'common law'. In fact, I cannot relate to the idea of a specifically 'civil-law' or 'common-law' identity. (I do relate, however, to Ezra Pound's line: 'One says "I am" this, that, or the other, and with the words scarcely uttered one ceases to be that thing.'[8]) What I have advanced, and what I continue to advance, is a theory of dissidence or sub-alternity or marginality, that is, a theory of *positioning* which, specifically, adopts the view of common law as antirrhetic and argues that, historically, there can be no other position for the common law than *there* – a historical argument which has nothing to do with the question of the 'intactness' of any given politico-cultural *Lebenswelt*.[9] Against that background, I assert that, understood as epistemological areas, the civil law and the common law, as they partake in a general and non-neutral agnostics which divides

---

[8] Ezra Pound, *Gaudier-Brzeska: A Memoir* (New York: New Directions, 1960), p. 85 [1916].
[9] In this respect, I derive compelling inspiration from Goodrich's erudite publications. See Peter Goodrich, '*Ars Bablativa*: Ramism, Rhetoric, and the Genealogy of English Jurisprudence', in Gregory Leyh (ed.), *Legal Hermeneutics* (Berkeley: University of California Press, 1992), pp. 43–82; *id.*, 'Poor Illiterate Reason: History, Nationalism and Common Law', (1992) 1 Soc. & Leg. Stud. 7; *id.*, *Oedipus Lex* (Berkeley: University of California Press, 1995), pp. 41–67 and *passim* [hereinafter *Oedipus Lex*].

the field of what is called, unconvincingly, 'western law' along the lines of nomothetism and idiographism (in a manner which may involve the staking of claims and the effort to appropriate), are irrevocably irreconcilable, even though we live them simultaneously and manage to reconcile them in an obscure and private economy.[10] (*Quaere*: how, ultimately, could the self exist if the other were reconcilable with it?)

* * *

In a very important sense, the recent history of comparative legal studies must be read as a persistent, albeit not always adroit, attempt to identify sameness across laws and to demote difference to a *modus deficiens* of sameness.[11] As John Merryman observes, '[d]ifferences between legal systems have been regarded [...] as evils or inconveniences to be overcome.'[12] Not surprisingly, '[w]hen differences are discovered, gentility seems to require that [they] be dissolved.'[13] Indeed, as he engages with his (impossible) object of study, 'the comparati[st] *presumes* similarities between different jurisdictions in the very act of searching for them' and assumes differentiating features to be largely indifferent.[14] The desire for sameness breeds

---

[10] I adopt and adapt Jacques Derrida, *L'écriture et la différence* (Paris: Le Seuil, 1967), p. 427.
[11] It would be mistaken to assume that comparatists-at-law always favoured sameness as their privileged epistemological register. For example, Montesquieu expressed his guiding principle in the following terms: 'not to consider as similar those instances that are really different and not to overlook the differences in those that appear similar': *De l'esprit des lois*, in *Oeuvres complètes*, ed. by Roger Caillois, vol. II (Paris: Gallimard, 1951), p. 229 ['*ne pas regarder comme semblables des cas réellement différents; et ne pas manquer les différences de ceux qui paroissent semblables*'] (1748). A genealogy of comparative legal studies also attests to signal and influential contributions to the thematization of difference in sixteenth-century France. This discourse has since been suppressed. But see Jean-Louis Thireau, 'Le comparatisme et la naissance du droit français', Revue d'histoire des facultés de droit et de la science juridique, 1990, Nos. 10/11, p. 153, who offers useful materials toward the recuperation of comparative legal studies's alternative enunciatory site. One is reminded of Benjamin's observation: 'The perception of similarities thus seems to be bound to a moment in time': Walter Benjamin, 'Doctrine of the Similar', in *Selected Writings*, ed. by Michael W. Jennings, Howard Eiland and Gary Smith and transl. by Michael W. Jennings, vol. II: *1927–1934* (Cambridge, Mass.: Harvard University Press, 1999), p. 696 [1933]. For the original text, see *id.*, 'Lehre vom Ähnlichen', in *Gesammelte Schriften*, ed. by Rolf Tiedemann and Hermann Schweppenhäuser, vol. II, t. 1 (Frankfurt: Suhrkamp, 1977), pp. 204–5 ['*Die Wahrnehmung von Ähnlichkeiten also scheint an ein Zeitmoment gebunden*'].
[12] John H. Merryman, 'On the Convergence (and Divergence) of the Civil Law and the Common Law', in Mauro Cappelletti (ed.), *New Perspectives for a Common Law of Europe* (Leyden: Sijthoff, 1978), p. 195.
[13] Richard Hyland, 'Comparative Law', in Dennis Patterson (ed.), *A Companion to Philosophy of Law and Legal Theory* (Oxford: Blackwell, 1996), p. 196.
[14] Joseph Vining, *The Authoritative and the Authoritarian* (Chicago: University of Chicago Press, 1986), p. 65 [my emphasis].

the expectation of sameness which, in turn, begets the finding of sameness. Even a posteriori re-presentations contradicting sameness appear not to prevent comparatists from 'catch[ing] sight [...] of the grand similarities and so to deepen [their] belief in the existence of a unitary sense of justice'.[15] Illustrations of the reigning proleptical orthodoxy abound.

In his general report to the 1900 Paris Congress, Edouard Lambert claimed that 'the comparatist, in order to fulfil his task, must select [as the object of his comparison] the most similar laws.'[16] For a French jurist, therefore, the study of English law ought to occur only 'accessorily'; it must occupy no more than 'a discreet place'.[17] However, 'a comparison can be very usefully drawn between the Latin group and the Germanic group' – that is, among legal 'systems' partaking in the Romanist legal tradition.[18] For Ernst Rabel, '[comparative research] ascertains throughout the world the facts common to all, the common life problems, the common functions of the legal institutions.'[19] Konrad Zweigert and Hein Kötz indeed postulate a '*praesumptio similitudinis*' to the effect that 'legal systems give the same or very similar solutions, even as to detail, to the same problems of life', so that a finding of difference should lead comparatists to start their investigation afresh. In these authors' words, 'the comparatist can rest content if his researches through all the relevant material lead to the conclusion that the systems he has compared reach the same or similar practical results, but if he finds that there are great differences or indeed diametrically opposite results, he should be warned and go back to check again whether the terms in which he posed his original question were [...] purely functional, and whether he has spread the net of his researches quite wide enough.'[20] For Alan Watson, the circulation and reception of legal rules point to substantial sameness across laws. One of the numerous illustrations developed by this author over the years concerns the rules on transfer of ownership and risk in sale: 'Before the *Code civil* the Roman rules were generally accepted in France [...]. This was also the law accepted

---

[15] Konrad Zweigert and Hein Kötz, *An Introduction to Comparative Law*, 3d ed. transl. by Tony Weir (Oxford: Oxford University Press, 1998), p. 3.
[16] Congrès international de droit comparé, *Procès-verbaux des séances et documents*, vol. I (Paris: L.G.D.J., 1905), p. 49 ['*le comparatiste juriste, pour remplir sa tâche, doit choisir (comme objet de sa comparaison) les législations les plus semblables*'].
[17] *Ibid.* ['*à titre accessoire*'; '*une place plus effacée*'].
[18] *Id.*, p. 48 ['*la comparaison pourra être établie très utilement entre le groupe latin et le groupe germanique*'].
[19] Ernst Rabel, 'Comparative Conflicts Law', (1949) 24 Indiana L.J. 353, p. 355.
[20] Zweigert and Kötz, *supra*, note 15, pp. 39–40.

by the first modern European code, the Prussian *Allgemeines Landrecht für die Preußischen Staaten* of 1794.'[21] According to Ugo Mattei, there exists, and there can be discovered, a 'common core of efficient principles hidden in the different technicalities of [...] legal systems'.[22] Thus, 'common core research is a very promising tool for unearthing deeper analogies hidden by formal differences.'[23] Rudolf Schlesinger's own 'common-core' project, which concerned contract formation, was directed toward the formulation of an area of agreement 'in terms of precise and narrow rules'.[24] Various contemporary applications demonstrate the enduring attraction of Schlesinger's *esprit de simplification* and offer fully or partly mimetic variations on his coarse model.[25] For his part, Basil Markesinis argues that 'we must try to overcome obstacles of terminology and classification in order to show that foreign law is not very different from ours but only appears to be so.'[26] Elsewhere, Markesinis observes 'how similar our laws on tort are or, more accurately, how similar they can be made to look with the help of some skilful (and well-meaning) *manipulation*.'[27] This kind of dissembling, this brand of speculative auto-semanticization whereby sameness is equated with thought about sameness, effectively aiming to dispossess the other-in-the-law of his strangeness, readily prompts one to ask whether comparatists who make an ideological investment in sameness believe in their myths, whether they are being tenaciously *delusional* or stubbornly *disingenuous*.[28] Do comparatists, as they disclose a comprehensive attitude

---

[21] Alan Watson, *Legal Transplants*, 2d ed. (Athens, Georgia: University of Georgia Press, 1993), p. 83.

[22] Ugo Mattei, *Comparative Law and Economics* (Ann Arbor: University of Michigan Press, 1997), p. 144.

[23] Mauro Bussani and Ugo Mattei, 'The Common Core Approach to European Private Law', (1997–8) 3 Columbia J. Eur. L. 339, p. 340.

[24] Rudolf B. Schlesinger, 'Introduction', in *id*. (ed.), *Formation of Contracts: A Study of the Common Core of Legal Systems*, vol. I (Dobbs Ferry: Oceana, 1968), p. 9.

[25] For example, see Hein Kötz and Axel Flessner, *European Contract Law*, vol. I (by Kötz): *Formation, Validity, and Content of Contracts; Contract and Third Parties*, transl. by Tony Weir (Oxford: Oxford University Press, 1997); Christian von Bar, *The Common European Law of Torts* (Oxford: Oxford University Press, 1998 and 2000), 2 vols.; Walter van Gerven, Jeremy Lever and Pierre Larouche, *Tort Law* (Oxford: Hart, 2000).

[26] Basil S. Markesinis, 'The Destructive and Constructive Role of the Comparative Lawyer', RabelsZ, 1993, p. 443.

[27] *Id*., 'Why a Code is Not the Best Way to Advance the Cause of European Legal Unity', (1997) 5 Eur. R. Priv. L. 519, p. 520 [my emphasis].

[28] Note that such ideological investment can appear particularly crude as is the case when the measure of good law becomes the maximization of cost-effectiveness. While hiding behind a veneer of disinterestedness purporting to move the debate beyond culture, the quest for low transaction costs does, in fact, rotate the axis of our public conversation on account of the glorification of

preceding the facts which are supposed to call it forth, act out of *wishful thinking* or in *bad faith*?[29] Perhaps more accurately, do they indulge in *double belief* through two contrary reactions, simultaneously recognizing and rejecting 'reality', that is, acknowledging the 'reality' of difference through the persistence of perception and yet disavowing or repressing it in order to make themselves believe something else?[30] Does the main goal of ideology not become the consistency of ideology itself? Another (related) question arises: are comparatists at all aware of the cognitive impairment which their attitude inevitably entails?

In sum, the picture painted by Tullio Ascarelli remains compelling: comparative legal studies is either concerned with unification of laws within substantive or geographical limits or is more philosophically inclined and aspires to a uniform law that would be universal.[31] Under both approaches, the point is not to explain legal diversity, but to explain it away, to contain it in the name of an authoritative ideal of knowledge and truth somehow deemed to be *above* diversity, to be intrinsically diversity-free. Such ideas are, in fact, expressly articulated in Unidroit's *Principles of International Commercial Contracts*, an ostensibly comparative endeavour: 'The objective of the Unidroit Principles is to establish a balanced set of rules designed for use throughout the world irrespective of the legal traditions and the

numbers it effectively propounds. As it instrumentalizes values, economic analysis speaks to our conception of ourselves as moral beings. In the process, it significantly impoverishes us. Consider Deborah A. Stone, *Policy Paradox and Political Reason* (New York: HarperCollins, 1988), pp. 136–7: 'Numbers provide the comforting illusion that incommensurables can be weighted against each other, because arithmetic always "works." Given some numbers to start with, arithmetic yields answers. Numbers force a common denominator where there is none'/'[N]umbers are symbols of precision, accuracy, and objectivity. They suggest mechanical selection, dictated by the nature of the objects, even though all counting involves judgment and discretion. [...] Numerals hide all the difficult choices that go into a count. And certain kinds of numbers – big ones, ones with decimal points, ones that are not multiples of ten — not only conceal the underlying choices but seemingly advertise the prowess of the measurer. To offer one of these numbers is by itself a gesture of authority.' For a comprehensive argument along these lines, see Janice G. Stein, *The Cult of Efficiency* (Toronto: Anansi, 2001).

[29] I borrow the formulae from Duncan Kennedy, *A Critique of Adjudication* (Cambridge, Mass.: Harvard University Press, 1997), pp. 191–4.

[30] For discussion, see Sigmund Freud, 'Splitting of the Ego in the Process of Defence', in *The Standard Edition of the Complete Psychological Works of Sigmund Freud*, transl. by James Strachey *et al.*, vol. XXIII (London: Hogarth Press, 1964), pp. 275–8 [1938]; *id.*, 'Fetishism', vol. XXI (1961), pp. 152–7 [1927]. For the German texts, see *id.*, 'Die Ichspaltung im Abwehrvorgang', in *Gesammelte Werke*, ed. by Anna Freud *et al.*, vol. XVII: *Schriften aus dem Nachlass* (Frankfurt: S. Fischer, 1941), pp. 57–62; *id.*, 'Fetischismus', vol. XIV: *Werke aus den Jahren 1925–1931* (1948), pp. 309–17.

[31] Tullio Ascarelli, 'Etude comparative et interprétation du droit', in *Problemi giuridici*, vol. I (Milan: Giuffrè, 1959), p. 321.

economic and political conditions of the countries in which they are to be applied.'[32] The frantic urge to eliminate difference as a valid analytical focus for comparative legal studies – without any apparent concern for what is being lost along the way – has even prompted James Gordley to write that 'there is no such thing as a French law or German law or American law that is an independent object of study apart from the law of other countries.'[33] The outreach of the dominant and enveloping epistemological discourse that has operated an institutionalization of sameness and ensured the disqualification of difference – that has wanted to bring matters to a kind of degree zero of comparatism – is not in doubt.[34] Through the development of a monistic framework, comparatists have made it their collective and coercive purpose to proscribe what they regard as disorder and to invalidate what they apprehend as dissonance. Difference, then, is in tension with the comparative project of wanting to get things right, to keep things straight. It is in tension with the self-control that purports to characterize comparative legal studies's totalizing, *hygienic* style. In fact, the forgetting of difference within comparative legal studies is so profound that even this forgetting is forgotten (which, I suppose, is a courteous way of saying that comparative legal studies denies difference and denies this denial). The meaningful is the concordant; indeed, the only legitimate discourse is the concordant (such that there emerges a reassuring concordance in the comparatists' lives themselves). In Jean Bollack's words, 'one believes or one wants the text to mean what one wants or believes. This search for non-difference is the strongest censorship.'[35] From the control desks in Hamburg,

---

[32] Governing Council of Unidroit, 'Introduction', in Unidroit, *Principles of International Commercial Contracts* (Rome: International Institute for the Unification of Private Law, 1994), p. viii [hereinafter *Unidroit Principles*]. A related expression of the universalizing agenda is developed in Mireille Delmas-Marty, *Trois défis pour un droit mondial* (Paris: Le Seuil, 1998).

[33] James Gordley, 'Comparative Legal Research: Its Function in the Development of Harmonized Law', (1995) 43 Am. J. Comp. L. 555, p. 566.

[34] In terms of the conditions of 'imposability' within the discipline of comparative legal studies – that is, 'the conditions under which arguments, categories, and values impose and maintain a certain authority' – this unstated dogma points to prevailing institutional and structural constraints and shows the way in which, through politically conditioned criteria of acceptability, normalizing power is exercised, for example, as regards the funding of research projects, the creation of journals or the organization of conferences. I am, therefore, simply unable to agree with Schlesinger, who remarks, without adducing evidence, that '[t]raditionally, [comparatists] have tended to dwell more heavily on differences than on similarities': Schlesinger, *supra*, note 24, p. 3, n. 1. The other quotations are from Samuel Weber, *Institution and Interpretation*, 2d ed. (Stanford: Stanford University Press, 2001), p. 19.

[35] Jean Bollack, *Sens contre sens* (Genouilleux: La passe du vent, 2000), pp. 179–80 ['*On croit ou l'on veut que le texte signifie ce que l'on veut ou croit. C'est la censure la plus forte que cette recherche de la non-différence*'].

Trento, Osnabrück, Maastricht, Rome, Utrecht and Copenhagen, the self-appointed spokesmen of reason, unbeclouded by any personal proclivities, able to take the long and detached view, wage an unceasing campaign to smother difference and bridle chaos, to evict and supplant the disruptive and deregulating impact of (bigoted) local impulses, to cleanse the law of all contingent and transitory traits best regarded as belonging to an obsolete era and as surviving into the present under false pretences, aptly apprehended as resilient distortions (from what?), properly envisaged, ultimately, as something of a scandal, as a morbid state of affairs yearning to be rectified. In their eschatological compulsion to design the absolute set of *regulae ad directionem civitatis*, they need to take the law in hand, to lay claim to it, to make it answerable to their programmes.

* * *

By purporting to wrest comparatists away from narcotizing theology, by trying to drive the received assumptions and the heuristic fictions they generate into productive crisis, I aim to move comparative legal studies beyond resolute technical confidence, synaesthetic or monumental vision and *mathesis universalis*. I argue for a protocol of action foregrounding an interpellative and interlocutionary ethics upon which all other structures organizing the relation between self and other – and between self-in-the-law and other-in-the-law – must rest. The politics of understanding I defend calls for the voice of the other and, specifically, for the voice of the other-in-the-law to be allowed to be heard above the chatter seeking to silence it. It requires comparatists to become addressees of validity-claims made and accepted by the other on the basis of ontological-symbolic premises guiding his statements and actions and taken by him as being either true or correct. The hermeneutic exigencies of a non-totalizing thought, a thought which accepts the other as interlocutor, which finds its closest grammatical analogue in the vocative, which allows the other (and the other-in-the-law) to signify according to himself and to his own *obviousness*, which accepts that the other is not just a modality of the self, which is, ultimately and empathically, *for* the other,[36] wants to be read as an announcement and as a summation, as a demand and as a complaint and, in any event, as the principle of a comparison whereby the comparatist is prepared to engage in self-distanciation from his own assumptions and orientations (which, then, no longer partake in truth), is interested in a variety of responses to 'reality'

---

[36] For a thoughtful reflection on being 'for the other', see Zygmunt Bauman, *Postmodern Ethics* (Oxford: Blackwell, 1993), p. 90.

and is keen to grasp the unique significance of these responses for given communities, such that his understanding of the world is stronger and that he lives more knowledgeably. Unlike mainstream comparative thought, which enunciates itself in the form of progressive exclusions setting aside precisely the cases where there would be ambiguity in order to replace them with the orderly rule of abstract and formal reason, the non-totalizing thought I advocate – 'the anxious thought, the thought in pursuit of its object, the thought in search of dialectical occasions to step out of itself, to break from its own frames'[37] – accepts that 'the little orders and "systems" we carve out in the world are brittle, until-further-notice, and as arbitrary and in the end contingent as their alternatives', that 'the "messiness" will stay whatever we do or know.'[38] (After all, in the end, 'only death is unambiguous, and escape from ambivalence is the temptation of Thanatos.'[39]) Non-totalizing thought takes the view that, rather than assault its *Sache*, it must grant experience in all its looseness and complexity in all its formlessness an open field. As it purports to re-enchant the law-world-as-cultural-form (to allude to a familiar Weberian theme), non-totalizing thought within comparative legal studies immediately invites a consideration of the subject-matter of 'representation'. Is comparison not premised on a belief that, in the context of a transaction between self and other mediated by a third term that is the meeting-point in language, another law is capable of being re-presented?

***

In the process of comparison, something is made accessible. But 'it' becomes accessible only on account of the very act of comparison, under *its* conditions or presuppositions. Although that to which comparison refers exists without comparison, once it is captured by comparison it is affected by comparison and its *Vorstellung* must turn on the act of comparison being itself understood in terms of its determining moments, both historical and structural. In this respect, I claim that one must accept that the critical distance between one and that which is being suspended at the end of one's gaze (let us say, foreign law) accounts for the condition of possibility of all perception itself. Any idea that the comparatist ought to gain access to the legal perspective 'from within' or to the legal community's 'inner perspective' – Hartian or otherwise – and that he ought do so through a strategy of

---

[37] Gaston Bachelard, *Le nouvel esprit scientifique*, 4th ed. (Paris: Presses Universitaires de France, 1991), p. 181 ['*la pensée anxieuse, (...) la pensée en quête d'objet, (...) la pensée qui cherche des occasions dialectiques de sortir d'elle-même, de rompre ses propres cadres*'] (1934).
[38] Bauman, *supra*, note 36, pp. 33 and 32, respectively.   [39] *Id.*, p. 109.

'immersion' is, therefore, to be rejected. Because the disclosure of the other's conceptions and of the symbolic-ontological basis underlying those conceptions may allow the observer to uncover structures that run counter to the observed's self-understanding, critical distance is key: 'A dissenter's exact imagination can see more than a thousand eyes peering through the same pink spectacles, confusing what they see with universal truth, and regressing.'[40] Critical distance remains, in any event, unavoidable since one cannot 'be' the other. Despite the painful (and necessary) exertions of the observer, the gap between that which is being said and that about which that which is being said is being said simply cannot vanish. This *décalage* means that differentiation must be central to any comparative study.

The point is to stress that the assumed link between 're-presentation' and 'resemblance' is mistaken. In fact, denotation lies at the heart of any re-presentative strategy and it stands independently from any notion of 'resemblance'. Consider a painting, any painting, say, Balthus's *La leçon de guitare*. In what way can the piano featured in the painting be said to 'be' a piano? To assert that 'the piano-in-the-painting' resembles a piano would imply that a piano resembles 'the piano-in-the-painting', which, in the case of this particular painting, simply cannot be the case since '[the keys] are zebra-striped – alternating black and white, of equal size and scale, directly next to one another – a far cry from real piano keys, in which the black sharps and flats are smaller and sit atop the larger white ones.'[41] The re-presentative relationship, however, does not require such symmetrical connections; it works otherwise. The fact that 'the piano-in-the-painting' re-presents a piano need not imply that a piano re-presents 'the piano-in-the-painting'. That re-presentation stands independently from resemblance is also apparent when Casimir and Imogene, aged eight and six, use the salter, the pepper pot and the sugar bowl to 'play the metro' at the restaurant. Surely, the salter does not resemble a metro door. Yet, it is made to re-present it.[42] Take another example to emphasize further the distinction between

---

[40] Adorno, *supra*, note 4, p. 46. For the original text, see *id.*, *Negative Dialektik* (Frankfurt: Suhrkamp, 1966), p. 56 ['*Exakte Phantasie eines Dissentierenden kann mehr sehen als tausend Augen, denen die rosarote Einheitsbrille aufgestülpt ward, die dann, was sie erblicken, mit der Allgemeinheit des Wahren verwechseln und regredieren*'].

[41] Nicholas Fox Weber, *Balthus* (New York: Knopf, 1999), pp. 224–5.

[42] Like Jean Piaget, Benjamin took a keen interest in child cognition. Unlike Piaget, however, he insisted on the historical specificity of the development of formal rational operations and drew a link between mimetic capacity, similarity and childhood. For example, see Walter Benjamin, 'One-Way Street', in *Selected Writings*, ed. by Marcus Bullock and Michael W. Jennings and

're-presentation' and 'resemblance'. Assume two cats sitting side by side. Would it occur to anyone to say of cat #1 that it 're-presents' cat #2? But one might comment, of course, that cat #1 resembles cat #2.[43]

At this stage, I suggest a brief visit to Borges's enchanted world. In his *Historia universal de la infamia*, one of the stories tells about an empire where the art of cartography had been developed to such perfection that the map of a single province occupied a whole town and the map of the empire covered a whole province. In time, these enormous maps no longer gave satisfaction and the college of cartographers established a map of the empire which was the size of the empire and coincided with it point for point. Subsequent generations reflected that this inflated map was useless and abandoned it.[44] Not unlike the cartographers' ultimate map of the empire, a comparative practice that purported to mirror the laws being compared and sought to avoid any schematization whatsoever would be devoid of value. The interest of comparative research lies precisely in the fact that it embodies hermeneutic interventions upon laws or schematizations of laws (irrespective of how much transformative ambition the comparatist may, or may not, actually harbour). Comparative work about law offers a tactical attempt to impute intellectual coherence to law as it is perceived. Accordingly, comparative legal studies fashions its account as an instance of transacted simplification or ascribed complexification.

To an important extent, of course, any comparative re-presentation is governed by what is 'there', that is, by that which is being re-presented by the comparatist. But more is involved, for to re-present implies emotional

---

transl. by Edmund Jephcott, vol. I: *1913–1926* (Cambridge, Mass.: Harvard University Press, 1996), p. 465: '[The child's] dresser drawers must become arsenal and zoo, crime museum and crypt. "To tidy up" would be to demolish an edifice full of prickly chestnuts that are spiky clubs, tinfoil that is hoarded silver, bricks that are coffins, cacti that are totem poles, and copper pennies that are shields' [1928]. For the German text, see *id.*, *Einbahnstraße*, in *Gesammelte Schriften*, ed. by Rolf Tiedemann, Hermann Schweppenhäuser and Tillman Rexroth, vol. IV, t. 1 (Frankfurt: Suhrkamp, 1972), p. 115 ['*Seine Schubladen müssen Zeughaus und Zoo, Kriminalmuseum und Krypta werden. "Aufräumen" hieße einen Bau vernichten voll stachliger Kastanien, die Morgensterne, Stanniolpapiere, die ein Silberhort, Bauklötze, die Särge, Kakteen, die Totembäume und Kupferpfennige, die Schilde sind*']. See generally Susan Buck-Morss, *Walter Benjamin and the Arcades Project* (Cambridge, Mass.: MIT Press, 1989), pp. 262–75.

[43] See Jean-Pierre Cometti, *Art, représentation, expression* (Paris: Presses Universitaires de France, 2002), pp. 25–43.

[44] Jorge Luis Borges, 'Histoire universelle de l'infamie', in *Oeuvres complètes*, ed. and transl. by Jean-Pierre Bernès, vol. I (Paris: Gallimard, 1993), p. 1509 [1935]. Reference to the French version of this text is justified by the fact that Borges himself ascribed authoritative status to it over the Spanish original: *id.*, p. 1508.

and intellectual commitments that lead the re-presentation to look this way rather than that: the very fact of cognitive selection displays the contingent character of the product of that selection. The choice of materials by the re-presenter is an act of power, if only because these materials always take the place of other materials that are omitted as part of the re-presentation. The act of selection, therefore, insensibly moves the selector from the descriptive to the prescriptive mode. Thus, the comparatist is *never* merely describing in comparative terms two or three laws which are 'there'. Rather, he is *prescribing* two or three laws through his comparative framework, that is, he is bringing a range of manifestations of the legal into accord with specific intellectual goals by enclosing them within a calculative regime. Because it is never strictly constative (or iconic), description is ascription. And any description that is not strictly 'descriptive' must differ from that which is being 'described'.[45] Because the *Lebenswelt* is antepredicative, the word can only mark a separation from it, which means that the defeat of the *logos* is certain. The unavoidable variations between an original (say, 'the foreign law') and a diagrammatic replica of it, no matter how purportedly totalizing (say, 'comparative analysis'), entail the inevitably limited character of the act of re-presentation. I argue that even 'straightforward' repetition implies the new, such that *any* repetition can be said to *engender* the new, that is, to produce difference.[46] In fact, etymology teaches that a re-presentation is something which is presented *anew*. How, indeed, could the second performance replicate in all respects that of the opening night? How could it not differ? How could re-staging not engender difference? Accordingly, I find it helpful to refer to 're-presentation' rather than 'representation' – to disturb the smooth linguistic surface – in order to mark the distance or the detachment characterizing the (non-)*reprise* and thus move away from the idea of 'representation' as falling under the authority of the principle of identity. (*Quaere*: what intellectual/emotional disposition is required for someone to 'see' that the act of 'reproduction' cannot overcome singularity, that re-presentation is tied in a necessary and non-suppressible fashion to *ex post*

---

[45] *Cf*. Deleuze, *supra*, note 3, p. 74: 'every time there is representation, there is always an unrepresented singularity' ['*chaque fois qu'il y a (...) représentation (...), il y a toujours une singularité non représentée*'].

[46] See Jacques Derrida, *Marges de la philosophie* (Paris: Editions de Minuit, 1972), pp. 374–81, who links the idea of 'repetition' with that of 'differentiation' through his notion of 'iterability' – a neologism which, etymologically, wishes to connote at once 'reiteration' and 'alterity'; Jean-François Lyotard, *La phénoménologie*, 11th ed. (Paris: Presses Universitaires de France, 1992), p. 43. See also Maurice Merleau-Ponty, *Phénoménologie de la perception* (Paris: Gallimard, 1945), pp. 388–9.

facto perception even as the re-presenting statement purports faithfully to account for what was presented? In the end, all depends on openness onto the sphere of what is not one's own or on the consciousness of an interpreter, which is constituted by a dialectical combination of non-presence and presence — a kind of primordial intuition allowing one to know that one does not know or does not know enough.)

This argument can be made in modified terms from a related perspective. Sameness, of course, governs the central strategy of mediation deployed by the comparatist as he aims to show that another law which may initially appear irrational is at least sensible and perhaps necessary. In other words, difference is recast *ab initio* as being well within the limits of understanding, of the comparatist's understanding and, in the final analysis, of sameness (for example, a French comparatist writes that the exponential growth of the tort of negligence in English law — in a context where other torts did not develop along such spectacular lines — recalls the expansive judicial interpretation of art. 1384 of the French civil code). However, at the very moment that sameness is constructed, it finds itself disproved on account of the fundamental difference between observer and observed. Each time sameness emerges, it is simultaneously annihilated by the very fact that it is the product of the discursive power of the observer, who has re-formulated the observed's experience on the basis of something the observed does not know in the way that the observer claims to be able to know (for example, the remark concerning the English law of negligence is a product of the French comparatist's imagination working on the basis of French data not readily accessible or suggestive to an English lawyer and showing how the other is simply disclosed through the self's habitual and antepredicative patterns of thought; indeed, the development of art. 1384 of the French civil code constitutes a move *away* from fault-based liability). It follows that it is impossible for the comparatist-as-observer ever to demonstrate sameness non-ethnocentrically because any understanding on his part assumes integration into his already-understood world, a world he cannot actually reflect himself out of. In other words, it is his privileged vantage point which informs the very formation of sameness (for example, the French comparatist subsumes the indigenous English experience under the correlation between the English law of negligence and art. 1384 of the French civil code).[47] Because the comparatist is being-situated, because he

---

[47] For the parallel between English and French law mentioned in the text, see René David and Xavier Blanc-Jouvan, *Le droit anglais*, 9th ed. (Paris: Presses Universitaires de France, 2001), p. 117.

always comes to the matter armed with his materially embedded, culturally situated understanding – which can, therefore, be apprehended as a 'pre-understanding' as regards what it is that he is studying[48] – explication of (other) meaning is, thus, articulation of difference. Indeed, the more reflective and self-critical the process of understanding another legal culture becomes, the more differential the comparatist's account proves to be.

* * *

It is precisely the irreducibility of difference within the act of re-presentation, seen to be marking the *limits* of re-presentation, that has historically made difference subservient to sameness. Paul Feyerabend offers a somewhat caustic panorama: 'Almost all [philosophers] praised oneness (or, to use a better word, monotony) and denounced abundance. Xenophanes rejected the gods of tradition and introduced a single faceless god-monster. Heraclitus heaped scorn on *polymathi'e*, the rich and complex information that had been assembled by commonsense, artisans and his own philosophical predecessors, and insisted that "what is Wise is One." Parmenides argued against change and qualitative difference and postulated a stable and indivisible block of Being as the foundation of all existence. Empedocles replaced traditional information about the nature of diseases by a short, useless but universal definition. Thucydides criticized Herodotus's stylistic pluralism and insisted on a uniform causal account. Plato opposed the political pluralism of democracy, rejected the view of tragedians such as Sophocles that (ethical) conflicts might be unresolvable by "rational" means, criticized astronomers who tried to explore the heavens in an empirical way and suggested tying all subjects to a single theoretical basis.'[49] Crucial to the process of subjugation of pluralism to unity,

---

[48] The notion of 'pre-understanding' (*'Vorverständnis'*) is famously developed in Hans-Georg Gadamer, *Truth and Method*, 2d ed. transl. by Joel Weinsheimer and Donald G. Marshall (London: Sheed & Ward, 1993), pp. 265–307 [1960]. It is indebted to Heidegger's idea of 'fore-conception' (*'Vorgriff'*). See Martin Heidegger, *Being and Time*, transl. by John Macquarrie and Edward Robinson (Oxford: Blackwell, 1962), p. 191: 'the interpretation has already decided for a definite way of conceiving [the entity we are interpreting], either with finality or with reservations; it is grounded in something we grasp in advance – in a *fore-conception*' [emphasis original] (1927) [hereinafter *Being and Time*]. (I refer to the standard English edition.) For the German text, see *id.*, *Sein und Zeit*, 18th ed. (Tübingen: Max Niemeyer, 2001), p. 150 ['*Wie immer – die Auslegung hat sich je schon endgültig oder vorbehaltlich für eine bestimmte Begrifflichkeit entschieden; sie gründet in einem* Vorgriff'] (emphasis original) [hereinafter *Sein und Zeit*]. Note that there are still those who claim that 'our situatedness is as immaterial to our theoretical enterprises as it is inevitable': Larry Alexander, 'Theory's a What Comes Natcherly', (2000) 37 San Diego L.R. 777, p. 778. I owe this reference to Joanne Conaghan.

[49] Paul Feyerabend, *Farewell to Reason* (London: Verso, 1987), p. 116. For another argument to the effect that the history of philosophy in the west is the history of a philosophy of the same

however, is Plato's negative judgement on mimesis as ontologically derivative and debased.[50] Because only Courage is Courageous – because only the Idea is not anything else than what it is, because only the Idea is ultimately real – those who are courageous can attest only to an earthly manifestation of the quality of Courage. Accordingly, their courage is not identical to Courage; it is a mere copy or imitation of the Idea, a secondary term; it is different from Courage. Given that 'Platonism represents a preference for a stable and hierarchical world where neither persons nor things appear as other than they are',[51] difference is inherently a failure, something negative, a malediction. Ultimately, for Plato, difference is a form of nothingness, since to differ from something is *not to be* like it.[52]

A monistic model thus runs through the ethical tradition from the pre-Socratics to Plato but also from Kant to John Rawls. For all these philosophers, difference is understood as inferiority, a sign of pathology, a disease that only clear and ordered thinking can, should and will overcome.[53] Michel Foucault notes how 'one experiences a singular repugnance to think in terms of difference, to describe discrepancies and dispersions',[54] while Theodor Adorno observes that differences, whether 'actual or imagined', are regarded as 'stigmas indicating that *not enough has yet been done*'.[55] A related observation is Jean-François Lyotard's: 'If there are opponents, it is because humankind has not succeeded in realizing itself.'[56] Referring specifically to cultural diversity, Claude Lévi-Strauss writes that people

---

whose hidden purpose has always been to find a means to attenuate the shock of alterity, see Emmanuel Levinas, *En découvrant l'existence avec Husserl et Heidegger*, 3d ed. (Paris: Vrin, 2001), pp. 261–82 [1949].

[50] For a general discussion of Plato's hostility to reproductive art, see Iris Murdoch, *The Fire and the Sun: Why Plato Banished the Artists* (London: Chatto & Windus, 1977). See also Pierre-Maxime Schuhl, *Platon et l'art de son temps* (Paris: Félix Alcan, 1933). For a well-known illustration of Plato's refusal to accommodate difference, see his *Timaeus*, 35.

[51] Paul Patton, *Deleuze and the Political* (London: Routledge, 2000), p. 33.

[52] See generally Deleuze, *supra*, note 3, pp. 82–9, 165–8, 340–1 and 349–50.

[53] Indeed, for all their critical edge, even Heidegger's ontological analysis of 'Being' and Gadamer's reconciliative hermeneutics ultimately fail to escape this pattern. But see, for a very influential interpretation of Nietzsche as a philosopher of difference, Gilles Deleuze, *Nietzsche et la philosophie*, 3d ed. (Paris: Presses Universitaires de France, 1999) [1962].

[54] Michel Foucault, *L'archéologie du savoir* (Paris: Gallimard, 1969), p. 21 ['on éprouv(e) une répugnance singulière à penser la différence, à décrire des écarts et des dispersions'].

[55] Theodor Adorno, *Minima Moralia*, transl. by E. F. N. Jephcott (London: Verso, 1978), p. 103 [my emphasis]. For the original text, see *id*., *Minima Moralia* (Berlin: Suhrkamp, 1951), p. 184 ['Sie betrachtet die tatsächlichen oder eingebildeten Differenzen als Schandmale, die bezeugen, daß man es noch nicht weit genug gebracht hat'].

[56] Jean-François Lyotard, *Le différend* (Paris: Editions de Minuit, 1983), p. 215 ['s'il y a des adversaires, c'est que l'humanité n'est pas parvenue à sa réalisation'].

have traditionally approached this phenomenon as 'a kind of monstrosity or scandal'.[57] In the words of Michel Serres, 'multiplicity [in the sense of diversity or difference] fosters anxiety and unity reassures.'[58] Turning briefly from philosophy to poetry – an alternative hermeneutic strategy – we see that Rilke captures the general idea in *The First Elegy*: 'We are not very securely at home in the interpreted world.'[59] Nowadays, in fact, the discontent surrounding the notion of 'difference' can be stoked whenever its promotion is seen as subverting the proclaimed Enlightenment commitments to human emancipation and liberty or apprehended as suggesting a regression to a pre-Enlightenment cast of mind, which denied parity for all before the law, favoured exclusion based on status and extolled the mystifying authority of the forces of superstition and tyranny. Remember how, for Zweigert and Kötz, a finding of difference across laws denotes *inadequate research*.[60]

* * *

Difference, of course, suggests a dimension unknown to the self, something like *das Unheimliche*. Difference belongs to thought's unthought realm. Perhaps it even partakes in what thought cannot think. Difference lies beyond the self. It is vexatious, at times maddening. It threatens the death of the self even.[61] And does difference not prohibit any relationship whatsoever?

---

[57] Claude Lévi-Strauss, *Race et histoire* (Paris: Albin Michel, 2001), p. 43 ['*une sorte de monstruosité ou de scandale*'] (1952).
[58] Michel Serres, *Eloge de la philosophie en langue française* (Paris: Fayard, 1995), p. 270 ['*Le multiple propage l'angoisse et l'unité rassure*']. See also Dominique Schnapper, *La relation à l'autre* (Paris: Gallimard, 1998), p. 132: 'the existence of dissonance being a source of uneasiness, it leads the individual to an activity aiming to reduce it' ['*l'existence d'une dissonance étant source de malaise entraîne de la part de l'individu une activité qui vise à la réduire*'].
[59] Rainer Maria Rilke, 'The First Elegy', in *The Essential Rilke*, transl. by Galway Kinnell and Hannah Liebmann (New York: Ecco Press, 2000), p. 77 [1923]. For the German text, see *id.*, p. 76: '*wir nicht sehr verläßlich zu Haus sind in der gedeuteten Welt.*' I have modified the translation slightly.
[60] Zweigert and Kötz, *supra*, at text accompanying note 20. It should be observed, however, that even Enlightenment figures such as Diderot and Lessing forgo any unifying epistemology and, rather than desire pure insight into universal truth (the kind of claim which led Hegel to equate the work of abstraction with the work of death), promote the recognition of multiplicity and polyphony. For Hegel's argument, see G. W. F. Hegel, *Phenomenology of Spirit*, transl. by A. V. Miller (Oxford: Oxford University Press, 1977), nos. 538–95, pp. 328–63 [1807]. For an illuminating commentary on the connections Hegel draws between Enlightenment and death, see James Schmidt, 'Cabbage Heads and Gulps of Water', (1998) 26 Political Theory 4, pp. 19–24. For an essay illustrating the link between 'Enlightenment' and 'difference', see Dena Goodman, 'Difference: An Enlightenment Concept', in Keith Michael Baker and Peter Hanns Reill (eds.), *What's Left of Enlightenment?* (Stanford: Stanford University Press, 2001), pp. 129–47.
[61] This language is not strictly metaphorical as is evidenced by a French contribution to a leading American law review appearing shortly after the First World War: 'divergences in laws cause

In order to be neutralized, it must be erased. By silencing difference, often violently, the longing for universality, the quest for commonality based on some vague conception of the ontic sameness of people (perhaps nurtured by Christian cosmologies for which mankind is ultimately one and the same), allows the comparatist to circumvent the trauma that would otherwise present itself through the painful 'reality' of alternative and contrapuntal worlds: universality dispenses with differentiation. In profound contradiction with the fact that it is this differential 'reality' itself which invited comparative research into being in the first place and to which comparative legal studies, therefore, owes its very *raison d'être*, 'the phantasm of the One charges the whole of politics with its furious, archaic, and terrifying energy.'[62] The humanist ideal of *mastery* inherited from the Enlightenment favours, as an anti-psychosis strategy, the reduction of difference to sameness and legalizes the forgetting of difference in the name of sameness: the self consumes and nullifies alterity, which then shows itself to be merely instrumental to the satisfaction of desire (a pursuit not unrelated to apprehensions of truth and righteousness). Spinoza notes the self's essential tendency to persist or to persevere in its being,[63] while Maurice Blanchot offers a related insight in contemporary – if somewhat less apodictic – terms: 'It is tempting to attract the unknown to oneself, to desire to bind it through a sovereign decision; it is tempting, when one has power over that which is in the distance, to remain inside the house, to call

other divergences that generate unconsciously, bit by bit, these misunderstandings and conflicts among nations which end with blood and desolation': Pierre Lepaulle, 'The Function of Comparative Law', (1921–2) 35 Harvard L.R. 838, p. 857. No doubt the same preoccupation animated the German comparatist Ernst Rabel as he prefaced the 1949 issue of his *Zeitschrift für ausländisches und internationales Privatrecht*, the first to appear since the end of the Second World War: 'After such fearful turmoil our age requires more than ever that the west consolidate its law-making powers. We must work with renewed courage toward the reconciliation of needless differences, the facilitation of international trade and the improvement of private-law systems': 'Zum Geleit', Zeitschrift für ausländisches und internationales Privatrecht, 1949–50, p. 1 ['*Mehr denn jemals, nach einem noch schrecklicheren Wirrsal, braucht unsere Zeit die Zusammenfassung der rechtsbildenden Kräfte des Abendlands. Beherzter als früher muß an der Ausgleichung grundloser Gegensätze, an der Erleichterung des internationalen Rechtsverkehrs, an der Verbesserung der Privatrechtssysteme gearbeitet werden*']. The point of the effacement of legal diversity becomes the taming of international tensions or, to put it more bluntly, the attenuation of the risk of war. The desire for the assimilation of other laws is thus linked to the fact that nationalist forms, which are associated with a territory, terrify. See Pierre Legendre, *Jouir du pouvoir: traité de la bureaucratie patriote* (Paris: Editions de Minuit, 1976), pp. 57 and 246.

[62] Roger Dadoun, *La psychanalyse politique* (Paris: Presses Universitaires de France, 1995), p. 31 ['*le fantasme de l'Un charge tout le politique de sa furieuse, archaïque et terrorisante énergie*'].
[63] *Ethica*, III, 6 [1677].

it there and to continue, in this way, to enjoy the quiet and familiarity of the house.'[64]

* * *

Such attitudes are very apparent as civilians in mainland Europe try to come to terms with the common-law world through the civil-law's time-honoured institutionalized forms of rationality and familiar conceptual grids – a reminder of these Odyssean journeys in which the peregrinations and adventures are but so many accidents on the way back home.[65] A German civilian, blithely experiencing the other as an imperfect approximation of himself, thus asks bluntly why can the common law not be civilian! Why, for instance, can the (deviant) English law not be like the law in Germany, where there prevails a 'refined and liberal approach to statutory interpretation [which] constitutes a considerable advance in legal culture'? It is time for English law to learn the 'lesson [which] has been learnt in Germany [and] which explains the great success of the German Civil Code'. And there is hope because the common law is, after all, not unlike the *Grundgesetz*...[66] Here is a reading betraying a strategy of hierarchization of

---

[64] Maurice Blanchot, *Celui qui ne m'accompagnait pas* (Paris: Gallimard, 1953), p. 152 ['*Il est tentant d'attirer à soi l'inconnu, de désirer le lier par une décision souveraine; il est tentant, quand on a le pouvoir sur le lointain, de rester à l'intérieur de la maison, de l'y appeler et de continuer, en cette approche, à jouir du calme et de la familiarité de la maison*'].

[65] While civilians assert that the common law does not, ultimately, differ from the civil law (for example, see Reinhard Zimmermann, 'Der europäische Charakter des englischen Rechts', Zeitschrift für Europäisches Privatrecht, 1993, p. 4), one fails to encounter arguments by civilians to the effect that the civil law does not, in the end, differ from the common law. In point of fact, similarity by projection (projective identification), which consists in attributing features to another that one confers to oneself, is much more current than similarity by introjection (introjective identification) whereby the individual attributes to himself features that he attributes to another. The point is that individuals like to think that they differ from others more than others differ from them and that others resemble them more than they resemble others. Concretely, this means that the individual accepts better the idea that others belong to his category while he would rebel at the thought that he belongs to the others'. See Geneviève Vinsonneau, 'Appartenances culturelles, inégalités sociales et procédés cognitifs en jeu dans les comparaisons inter-personnelles', Bulletin de Psychologie, 1994, No. 419, p. 422. For a general reflection on 'epistemic self-privileging' or 'epistemic asymmetry' (that is, the conviction that the self is enlightened and that the other is benighted), see Barbara Herrnstein Smith, *Belief and Resistance* (Cambridge, Mass.: Harvard University Press, 1997), p. xvi.

[66] Reinhard Zimmermann, '*Statuta sunt stricte interpretanda*? Statutes and the Common Law: A Continental Perspective', [1997] Cambridge L.J. 315, pp. 321, 326 and 328, respectively. As a German academic asserts such anti-particularism, he is also giving effect to the nineteenth-century view that '[o]nly by transcending what distinguished Swabia from Prussia, or Bavaria from Schleswig-Holstein, could Germany become, in law as in ideology, one.' This quotation is from W. T. Murphy, *The Oldest Social Science?* (Oxford: Oxford University Press, 1997), p. 44, n. 22. For a further illustration of strong German ethnocentrism, see Reinhard Zimmermann,

governmentalities, evidencing a determination to disavow difference and disclosing a will to power which, in failing to specify the confines of its own locus of enunciation, proceeds to individualize otherness as the discovery of its own assumptions. The other is methodologically 'admitted' as another in so far, and in so far only, as he proves compatible with the comparatist's ontological premises.

* * *

Even leaving to one side the critique by eighteenth-century thinkers such as Hamann, Vico and Herder, who decried Enlightenment attempts to override feelings of distinctiveness based on national identity, language, history and culture, there is an important sense, harking back to Hegelian historicism and anti-transcendentalism, in which the Enlightenment project can be said, through its exhilarating quest for power over nature and the world, to have fostered the abandonment of the search for meaning, the commodification of knowledge, the bureaucratization of the *Lebenswelt*, the marginalization of human experience and the disqualification of ethics.[67] Indeed, the sameness across jurisdictions which most comparative research automatically postulates and then seeks to elucidate is *necessarily* based on a repression of pertinent differences located in the contextual matrices within which instantiations of posited law are inevitably ensconced. In other words,

---

'Savigny's Legacy: Legal History, Comparative Law, and the Emergence of a European Legal Science', (1996) 112 L.Q.R. 576, where the author goes so far as to suggest as an inspirational model for European academics a law professor whose (German) nationalistic historicism was always inimical to comparative legal studies, as underlined in Ernst Landsberg, *Geschichte der Deutschen Rechtswissenschaft*, vol. III, t. 2 (Munich: R. Oldenbourg, 1910), pp. 207–17, and whose abiding commitment lay with the institution of a Romanist *Rechtsstaat* in Germany, as shown in James Q. Whitman, *The Legacy of Roman Law in the German Romantic Era* (Princeton: Princeton University Press, 1990). For general evidence supporting the view that German academics tend to address European matters as if *German* history was repeating itself, see John Laughland, *The Tainted Source* (London: Little, Brown, 1997), pp. 22–3, 26, 31–3, 110–11, 116–17, 120 and 137. However, there is little in common between a situation where political power required to suppress pluralism in order to assert its authority and another where the dynamics of market integration assumes pluralism (indeed, the fundamental tenets underlying the Treaty of Rome are that there should be an opening of economic borders within the European Community; that the Member States should recognize each other's law and that 'market citizens' should have the opportunity to select the legal regulation that best suits them).

[67] See Theodor W. Adorno and Max Horkheimer, *Dialectic of Enlightenment*, transl. by John Cumming (London: Verso, 1997), pp. 3–42 [1944]. For the original text, see *id.*, *Dialektik der Aufklärung* (Frankfurt: S. Fischer, 1969), pp. 9–49. See also Alasdair MacIntyre, *After Virtue*, 2d ed. (London: Duckworth, 1985), pp. 51–61; Stephen Toulmin, *Cosmopolis* (Chicago: University of Chicago Press, 1990), p. 201 and *passim*. For a helpful consideration of the work of Hamann, Vico and Herder, see Isaiah Berlin, *Three Critics of the Enlightenment*, ed. by Henry Hardy (Princeton: Princeton University Press, 2000).

the specification of sameness can only be achieved if the historico-sociocultural dimensions are artificially excluded from the analytical framework as is done, for instance, by the proponents of 'common-core' research, who confine their work to what they regard as being acceptably legal.[68] I agree with George Fletcher's observation: 'common-core' research, as it purports to exhume the treasures of the law, all these sadly buried commonalities, is 'a way of thinking designed to suppress difference. It purchases a sense of universality in law but only at the price of the ideas and arguments that make the law a worthy creation of the human intellect.'[69] This is to say that the creation and maintenance of homogeneity across a range of posited laws must be apprehended as a demonstrably artificial enterprise: 'homogeneity [...] is always revealed as fictitious and based on acts of exclusion', which are an inseparable concomitant of every uniformization process.[70] As a matter of fact, the deliberate character which this suppression of information may adopt has been openly acknowledged.[71] Only something like *interpretive closure* – what one might call 'cost-effective reasoning' – can reduce to sameness what is, and should, for the sake of the integrity of the comparative enterprise, remain different. (Needless to add, anything

---

[68] For a critique of Schlesinger's endeavours, see William Ewald, 'Comparative Jurisprudence (I): What Was it Like to Try a Rat?', (1995) 143 U. Pennsylvania L.R. 1889, pp. 1978–82 and 2081, who notes how this project arose from 'a rather crude philosophical picture that seems to appeal to legal scholars when they attempt to serve what they imagine to be the practical needs of corporate attorneys' (p. 2081). A variation on the theme of 'common-core' research is offered by the *International Encyclopedia of Comparative Law* (Tübingen: J. C. B. Mohr, 1971–). For a critical introduction to this venture, see Ewald, *supra*, pp. 1978–84.

[69] George P. Fletcher, 'Comparative Law as a Subversive Discipline', (1998) 46 Am. J. Comp. L. 683, p. 694. See also Ian Ward, 'The Limits of Comparativism: Lessons from UK–EC', (1995) 2 Maastricht J. Eur. & Comp. L. 23, p. 31: 'It is undeniable [...] that in the European scenario, comparative law, at both micro and macro levels, is being used as a means of effecting sameness and suppressing difference.'

[70] Chantal Mouffe, 'Democracy, Power, and the "Political" ', in Seyla Benhabib (ed.), *Democracy and Difference* (Princeton: Princeton University Press, 1996), p. 246. See also Bachelard, *supra*, note 37, p. 114: 'The communion of minds is achieved through negation' ['*La communion des esprits se réalise dans la négation*'].

[71] See Markesinis, *supra*, at text accompanying note 27. An application of the duplicitous strategy advocated by Markesinis is seemingly offered in van Gerven *et al.*, *supra*, note 25, p. 44, where it is asserted that 'English law has *followed* Roman law longer than the Continental legal systems by retaining specific heads of tortious liability, each of which was originally covered by a different "writ" ' [my emphasis]. But the historical fact of nominate torts in English law has nothing to do with 'following' Roman law as is shown, for instance, in D. J. Ibbetson, *A Historical Introduction to the Law of Obligations* (Oxford: Oxford University Press, 1999). Here is the kind of irresponsible simplification that is engendered by a frenetic and hasty search for commonalities-which-clearly-must-be-there-since-we-want-them-there.

along the lines of 'homogenized law' remains entangled in the philosophy of the subject for it is the comparatist, situated in his concrete context and armed with his own interpretive schemes, who determines the meaning of utterances and provides the 'reconstruction' of rules.)

The fact that difference inheres to any identitarian endeavour and that its silencing must, therefore, assume deliberate effacement can be asserted from a more distinctly philosophical perspective. The fundamental argument is that *in effect* identity requires difference in order to assume its being. Identity, because it is a relation, demands, as the condition of its very existence, the existence of a non-identity that exists outside of it. Only the existence of non-identity allows identity to exist as identity, which is to say that identity owes its existence to non-identity, that it takes its being from non-identity or difference. It follows that difference can then be understood not only as somehow 'consubstantial' with identity, but as enjoying a measure of primordiality over identity because it is what allows identity to be itself. Thus, the concept 'cat' (an identity) requires 'cats' in order to exist: cats must come first so as to provoke the mind into conceptualization. The limitations inherent in the 'concept' are illustrated by Vincent Descombes drawing on Kant's example of the 100 *thalers*. In sum, Kant's point is that there is nothing more in the real *thalers* than in the possible *thalers*. The 100 *thalers* I am complaining of not having are the same as the 100 *thalers* that I wish I had in my pocket. These *thalers*, if they ever come to my pocket, will be exactly those whose presence I wanted. The passage from the possible to the real does not, therefore, modify the concept. Be that as it may, there is an important difference between having and not having the 100 *thalers*, between a presence and an absence. What Kant's argument shows us is that the concept is indifferent to this difference and that what ultimately matters – existence or non-existence – requires a site of enunciation that is located beyond the concept.[72] Another example allows a return to the fact of sequential theatrical performances. The first night cannot be the first night if there is not after it the second night. Thus, the second night is not just what comes after the first night, but it is what allows the first night to be the first night. The first night cannot be the first night 'on its own', so to speak, but requires primordial help from the second night. It is through the second night that the first night is first. The second night, therefore, enjoys

---

[72] See Vincent Descombes, *Le même et l'autre* (Paris: Editions de Minuit, 1979), pp. 32–3. The '*thaler*' is a large silver coin current in the German states from the sixteenth century. In English, the word was modified to 'dollar' before 1600.

a kind of priority over the first night in the sense that it exists right from the start as the prerequisite to the firstness of the first night.[73]

Emmanuel Levinas observes that the other always exceeds the idea of the other in me, that the other can never be cognitively or emotionally mastered, that the other is ultimately independent from my initiative and power, that the other interrupts the self on a primordial level, that the other suppresses the self as a subject of experience (what the other experiences lies beyond the self), that the other is, in this sense, transcendent, that it assumes *priority* over the self.[74] The precedence of alterity arising from this structural asymmetry provides the ethical norm and imperative for comparative legal studies as well as the criterion of practical decision for comparatists, whom it summons to emancipation or deterritorialization,[75] responsibility or response. A challenge to the subject's omniscience, it acts as a governing postulate for comparative analysis, helping it to move away from logocentric postulates where '[w]hat counts for the purpose of comparison is the fact of a solution and not the ideas, concepts, or legal arguments that support the solution'.[76] The habitual position is, of course, that '[i]f on a given set of facts the victim of an accident in a friend's apartment can recover damages from the landlord, the fact of recovery overwhelms, in significance, the rationale for the decision. As compared with the hard fact of wealth transferring from one party to the other, the ideas and arguments explaining the flow are of little significance.'[77] It is such reductionism which the comparatist must avoid as he appreciates that raw solutions cannot exhaust the extension of the concept 'law'.[78] Specifically, the redaction of an account

---

[73] See *id.*, p. 170. *Cf.* Jacques Derrida, *La voix et le phénomène*, 2d ed. (Paris: Presses Universitaires de France, 1998), p. 95: 'the same is only the same by being sensitive to the other' ['*le même n'est le même qu'en s'affectant de l'autre*']. For Benjamin, the perception of similarities is derivative behaviour: Walter Benjamin, 'On the Mimetic Faculty', in *Selected Writings*, ed. by Michael W. Jennings, Howard Eiland and Gary Smith and transl. by Edmund Jephcott, vol. II: *1927–1934* (Cambridge, Mass.: Harvard University Press, 1999), p. 720 [1933]. For the original text, see *id.*, 'Über das mimetische Vermögen', in *Gesammelte Schriften*, ed. by Rolf Tiedemann and Hermann Schweppenhäuser, vol. II, t. 1 (Frankfurt: Suhrkamp, 1977), p. 210.

[74] See Emmanuel Levinas, *Totalité et infini* (Paris: Le Livre de Poche, [n.d.]), pp. 39–45 [1971].

[75] *Cf.* Jürgen Habermas, *Knowledge and Human Interests* (Boston: Beacon Press, 1987), pp. 302–17, who develops the notion of 'emancipatory interest'. The German formulation is '*emanzipatorische Erkenntnisinteresse*': *id.*, *Technik und Wissenschaft als 'Ideologie'* (Frankfurt: Suhrkamp, 1971), p. 155. For the idea of 'deterritorialization', see Gilles Deleuze and Félix Guattari, *Mille plateaux* (Paris: Editions de Minuit, 1980), pp. 381–433 ['*déterritorialisation*'].

[76] George P. Fletcher, 'The Universal and the Particular in Legal Discourse', [1987] Brigham Young U. L.R. 335, p. 335.

[77] *Ibid*.

[78] For a sensitive exploration of the conceptual extension of 'law' by a discerning comparatist, see Nicholas Kasirer, 'Honour Bound', (2001) 47 McGill L. J. 237. But *cf.* Ugo Mattei, 'Three

which will not prove unduly distortive of the law being considered must attend to recurrently emergent, relatively stable, institutionally reinforced social practices and discursive modalities (a certain lexicon, a certain range of intellectual or rhetorical themes, a certain set of logical or conceptual moves, a certain emotional register) acquired by the members of a community through social interaction and experienced by them as generalized tendencies and educated expectations congruent with their conception of justice.[79] And this task is greatly facilitated as the anticipation of sameness geared to an examination conducted on the surface level of the posited law recedes into the background to make way for receptivity to the radical epistemological diversity that undergirds the posited law's answers across legal communities and legal traditions.

Cartesianism introduces the *cogito* as an absolute with everything else (including the other) being made relative to it. The being of the other is made equivalent to the being as it is known by the *cogito* (which is another way of saying that the being of the other is made subservient to the self, who controls it). I argue that the challenge for comparative legal studies is thus to position itself as an heir to the Counter-Enlightenment – to borrow Isaiah Berlin's expression[80] – and to exhibit elective affinities with idealism, relativism, historicism and the politics of authenticity, identity and recognition.[81] In other words, I argue that comparative legal studies, in order to overcome the epistemological barrier to knowledge which its logocentric practices have conspired to erect, must operate a Bachelardian *epistemological break*.[82]

* * *

This claim warrants some elaboration as regards the relationship of the thesis I defend with Counter-Enlightenment critique, at least in so far as

---

Patterns of Law: Taxonomy and Change in the World's Legal Systems', (1997) 45 Am. J. Comp. L. 5, p. 13, n. 37: 'I do not wish to enter into the largely sterile and boring discussion of what can be considered law.'

[79] I closely follow Smith, *supra*, note 65, p. 92.
[80] Isaiah Berlin, 'The Counter-Enlightenment', in *Against the Current*, ed. by Henry Hardy (London: Hogarth Press, 1979), pp. 1–24.
[81] In this respect, Bachelard's critique of the reductionism inherent to Cartesian thought remains invaluable: *supra*, note 37, pp. 139–83. For a helpful commentary, see Mary Tiles, *Bachelard: Science and Objectivity* (Cambridge: Cambridge University Press, 1984), pp. 28–65.
[82] Bachelard writes that 'one knows *against* prior knowledge': Gaston Bachelard, *La formation de l'esprit scientifique*, 14th ed. (Paris: Vrin, 1989), p. 14 ['*on connaît* contre *une connaissance antérieure*'] (emphasis original) [1938]. I note that in his contribution to this book, Upendra Baxi, for reasons not wholly unrelated to mine, also calls on comparatists-at-law to perform an epistemological rupture.

the connection with Johann Gottfried Herder's arguments is concerned. I think that an important point must be emphasized at the outset. The fact that twentieth-century racist writers (such as various Nazi ideologues) have appealed to Herder's ideas and invested them with xenophobic and anti-Semitic content cannot be taken to establish that Herder's views were inherently racist. Indeed, when one turns to Herder's programmatic texts and, in particular, to his *Auch eine Philosophie der Geschichte zur Bildung der Menschheit*,[83] one very much finds a variation on the theme of cultural essentialism rather than a theory of evolutionary racialism. In his thorough intellectual history of the relationship between Herder and Kant – Herder was Kant's favourite pupil in Königsberg between 1762 and 1764 and the two eventually formed a close intellectual friendship marked by mutual admiration before diverging when the mature Herder began to express views which his former master could not accept – John Zammito observes that '[Herder's] thoughts on the physical anthropology of race are, for modern eyes, vastly less painful than Kant's.'[84] He adds that, contrary to Kant, 'Herder was skeptical of the fixture of distinct racial groups, precisely for the fear that this would lead to hypostasis of distinctions in their capacities.'[85] While Herder may have been guilty of expressing '*cultural* contempt', say, toward the Chinese, he never engaged in 'Kant's *biological* disqualification of non-Western peoples'.[86] In his *Ideen zur Philosophie der Geschichte der Menschheit*,[87] Herder, in fact, explicitly denies the word 'race'

---

[83] Johann Gottfried Herder, *Auch eine Philosophie der Geschichte zur Bildung der Menschheit*, in *Werke in zehn Bänden*, vol. I: *Schriften zu Philosophie, Literatur, Kunst und Altertum 1774–1787*, ed. by Jürgen Brummack and Martin Bollacher (Frankfurt: Deutscher Klassiker Verlag, 1994), pp. 9–107 [1774]. For an abridged English translation, see *id.*, *Yet Another Philosophy of History*, in *J. G. Herder on Social and Political Culture*, ed. and transl. by F. M. Barnard (Cambridge: Cambridge University Press, 1969), pp. 179–223 [hereinafter *Herder on Culture*].

[84] John H. Zammito, *Kant, Herder, and the Birth of Anthropology* (Chicago: University of Chicago Press, 2002), p. 345.

[85] *Ibid.*

[86] *Ibid.* [emphasis original]. For a further exploration of the significant differences between Kant and Herder with respect to the notion of 'race', see Robert Bernasconi, 'Who Invented the Concept of Race? Kant's Role in the Enlightenment Construction of Race', in *id.* (ed.), *Race* (Oxford: Blackwell, 2001), pp. 11–36. For an examination of Kant's absolutization of racial difference, see Mark Larrimore, 'Sublime Waste: Kant on the Destiny of the "Races"', Canadian J. Phil., 1999, Suppl. Vol. 25, pp. 99–125.

[87] Johann Gottfried Herder, *Ideen zur Philosophie der Geschichte der Menschheit*, in *Werke in zehn Bänden*, vol. VI, ed. by Martin Bollacher (Frankfurt: Deutscher Klassiker Verlag, 1989) [1784–91]. For a contemporary (albeit abridged) English translation, see *id.*, *Reflections on the Philosophy of the History of Mankind*, ed. by Frank E. Manuel (Chicago: University of Chicago Press, 1968).

and rejects the existence of 'races'.[88] Accordingly, H. B. Nisbet, one of the leading students of Herder's thought, remarks that 'although Herder was prepared to classify races aesthetically, he believed that they cannot be classified anthropologically, since he realised (quite correctly, according to most present-day theorists) that racial differences in man are only superficial. Thus, those who, during the Nazi era, used Herder's aesthetic classification to suggest that he considered certain races as anthropologically superior to others, were quite mistaken.'[89] Indeed, Herder's concern for the plight of oppressed black communities – which he expressed, in particular, through his poetry – has been documented in detail.[90] Even less sanguine critics conclude that Herder cannot, ultimately, be held accountable for the subsequent perversion of his thought: 'The truth of the matter was that Herder's ideas were too heady a mixture for a people who were inexperienced in politics and who, as [the poet Heinrich] Heine pointed out, lived in dreams rather than realities.'[91]

Of course, this is not to say that every feature of Herder's new hermeneutic historicism deserves support. Specifically, to the extent that Herder apprehended national communities as constituting organic wholes, I would dissent – although it is not at all clear that Herder's claim in this respect was ever as emphatic as is often assumed.[92] Nor would I accept the idea that communities are driven by an inner spiritual force; indeed, I cannot find any merit to the hylozoist view of a unifying psychological essence, such as *Volksgeist* (which makes me suspicious also of anything along the lines of

---

[88] See Larrimore, *supra*, note 86, p. 106. See also Bernasconi, *supra*, note 86, pp. 28–9.
[89] H. B. Nisbet, *Herder and the Philosophy and History of Science* (Cambridge: Modern Humanities Research Association, 1970), p. 230. See also Gerald Broce, 'Herder and Ethnography', (1986) 22 J. Hist. Behavioral Sciences 150, p. 164.
[90] See Ingeborg Solbrig, 'Herder and the "Harlem Renaissance" of Black Culture in America: The Case of the "Neger-Idyllen"', in Kurt Mueller-Vollmer (ed.), *Herder Today* (Berlin: Walter de Gruyter, 1990), pp. 402–14. The author underlines the positive impact of Herder's thought on contemporary African-American studies.
[91] Gordon A. Craig, 'Herder: The Legacy', in Kurt Mueller-Vollmer (ed.), *Herder Today* (Berlin: Walter de Gruyter, 1990), p. 25. For more on Heine's views of German culture, see Nigel Reeves, *Heinrich Heine: Poetry and Politics* (Oxford: Oxford University Press, 1974).
[92] See Vicki A. Spencer, 'Difference and Unity: Herder's Concept of *Volk* and Its Relevance for Contemporary Multicultural Societies', in Regine Otto (ed.), *Nationen und Kulturen* (Würzburg: Königshausen & Neumann, 1996), pp. 296–9, where the author observes that, for Herder, 'a community's culture [...] is a heterogeneous rather than a homogeneous entity' (p. 296) and notes that Herder 'does not mistakenly think a community's culture is a uniform body with all its parts changing in unison' (p. 297). Rather, 'a community's culture [is] the outcome of a complicated interaction of various environmental forces, individual powers, specific activities and different attitudes' (*ibid.*).

Wilhelm von Humboldt's notion of '*Nationalcharakter*', as outlined in his *Plan einer vergleichenden Anthropologie*).[93] I cannot subscribe to the idea of some external or metaphysical forces deterministically acting upon individuals: culture is but the expression of individuals thinking about their world and acting to change it (on the understanding that their past functions as a condition of possibility, which limits what it constitutes). Nor would I agree, therefore, that the individual is insignificant in the context of historical processes of diffusion and accretion or sedimentation of cultural traits.[94] But the work of writers like Herder and Humboldt can hardly be reduced to *Volksgeist* and *Volksgeister*, to *Nationalcharakter* and *Nationalcharakteren*.

Crucially, these authors contest the Kantian enterprise of a transcendental grounding of reason: universality of human reason across space and time yields to an empirical apprehension of space and time grounded in lived experience (*Erfahrung*). Herder and Humboldt claim that morality is acquired through formal and informal enculturation. The interpreter must, therefore, rather than engage in the construction of elaborate rationalizing systems, attend to the specificity of historical processes with a view to making each factual configuration intelligible in terms of its particular context. In a letter dated 31 October 1767, Herder indeed writes as follows: 'Nothing makes me sicker than the arch-error of the Germans, to build systems.'[95] Rather than formal logic, Herder wishes to stress human sensibility. His goal is to grasp the character of human knowledge. Herder regards the human mind as constitutive of the world of experience, of the reality that is the focus of cognition,[96] which leads him to emphasize the perspectival nature

---

[93] Wilhelm von Humboldt, *Plan einer vergleichenden Anthropologie*, in *Werke*, ed. by Albert Leitzmann, vol. I: *1785–1795* (Berlin: B. Behr's Verlag, 1903), pp. 377–410 [1795].

[94] *Cf*. Zygmunt Bauman and Keith Tester, *Conversations with Zygmunt Bauman* (Cambridge: Polity, 2001), p. 32: 'Culture is a *permanent revolution* of sorts. To say "culture" is to make another attempt to account for the fact that the human world (the world moulded by the humans and the world which moulds the humans) is perpetually, unavoidably and unremediably *noch nicht geworden* (not-yet-accomplished)' [emphasis original]. The words are Bauman's, referring to Ernst Bloch. They connect to the wider phenomenon of 'detraditionalization'. See generally Paul Heelas, Scott Lash and Paul Morris (eds.), *Detraditionalization* (Oxford: Blackwell, 1996).

[95] Johann Gottfried Herder, *Briefe: Gesamtausgabe 1763–1803*, vol. I: *April 1763–April 1771*, ed. by Wilhelm Dobbek and Günter Arnold (Weimar: Hermann Böhlaus Nachfolger, 1977), p. 92 ['*Vor nichts aber graut mir mehr, als vor dem Erbfehler der Deutschen, Systeme zu zimmern*'].

[96] The primacy which Herder grants *poiesis* in the constitution of reality makes him a forerunner of Heidegger and Wittgenstein. For these and other epistemological connections, see Michael Morton, 'Changing the Subject: Herder and the Reorientation of Philosophy', in Kurt Mueller-Vollmer (ed.), *Herder Today* (Berlin: Walter de Gruyter, 1990), pp. 158–72.

of human understanding and generally to highlight the situatedness of cultural forms. According to Ernest Menze, 'Herder's historical relativism was his most important achievement.'[97]

Given that Herder is often portrayed as a rabid nationalist, it may be worth insisting that his intellectual outlook was, in fact, most cosmopolitan. For instance, he expressly acknowledged his intellectual debt to Francis Bacon's empiricism. In a 1764 poem, 'Erhebung und Verlangen', Herder thus recounted his intellectual journey in these terms: 'and listened to Kant/And drifted sidewards after Bacon.'[98] Indeed, 'it was chiefly to Bacon, with his *commercium mentis et rei*, that [Herder] looked as his *theoretical* guide.'[99] Moreover, Herder drew inspiration from David Hume, in particular from his *The History of Great Britain*.[100] Hume's pragmatism exercised a deep influence over Herder, who repeatedly praised him as the greatest historian of the day.[101] Specifically, Herder saluted Hume's scrupulous sense of historicity and welcomed the fact that, rather than fall for arid and oppressive judgements about superficial commonalities, Hume held that 'every class, every way of life has its own mores.'[102] One could easily supply other

---

[97] Ernest A. Menze, 'Königsberg and Riga: The Genesis and Significance of Herder's Historical Thought', in Kurt Mueller-Vollmer (ed.), *Herder Today* (Berlin: Walter de Gruyter, 1990), p. 98. See also Dagmar Barnouw, 'Political Correctness in the 1780s: Kant, Herder, Forster and the Knowledge of Diversity', *Herder Jahrbuch 1994*, ed. by Wilfried Malsch (Stuttgart: J. B. Metzler, 1994), p. 57.

[98] Johann Gottfried Herder, 'Erhebung und Verlangen', in *Werke in zehn Bänden*, vol. III: *Volkslieder, Übertragungen, Dichtungen*, ed. by Ulrich Gaier (Frankfurt: Deutscher Klassiker Verlag, 1990), p. 778 ['*und hörte Kant! (...)/ Und irrte seitwärts Baco nach!*'] (1774).

[99] H. B. Nisbet, 'Herder and Francis Bacon', (1967) 62 Modern Language R. 267, p. 271 [emphasis original].

[100] David Hume's *The History of Great Britain* appeared in six volumes between 1754 and 1762. It has become known as *The History of England From the Invasion of Julius Caesar to the Revolution in 1688*. For a current facsimile edition of the 1778 version, the last to have been revised by Hume himself, see David Hume, *The History of England* (Indianapolis: Liberty Fund, 1985), 6 vols.

[101] For example, see Johann Gottfried Herder, 'On the Transformation of the Taste of Nations in the Course of the Ages', in *Selected Early Works 1764–1767*, ed. by Ernest A. Menze and Karl Menges and transl. by Ernest A. Menze and Michael Palma (University Park: Pennsylvania State University Press, 1992), p. 66 [1766].

[102] *Id.*, *Journal meiner Reise im Jahr 1769*, in *Werke in zehn Bänden*, vol. IX, t. 2, ed. by Rainer Wisbert (Frankfurt: Deutscher Klassiker Verlag, 1997), p. 27 ['*Jeder Stand, jede Lebensart hat ihre eignen Sitten*'] (1810) [hereinafter *Journal meiner Reise*]. For an abridged English translation, see *id.*, *Journal of my Voyage in the Year 1769*, in *Herder on Culture*, *supra*, note 83, p. 76 [hereinafter *Journal of my Voyage*]. See also Amy R. McCready, 'Herder's Theory of Cultural Diversity and Its Postmodern Relative', in Regine Otto (ed.), *Nationen und Kulturen* (Würzburg: Königshausen & Neumann, 1996), p. 191: 'instead of the antagonism that has characterized cultural relations throughout history, adulation marks Herder's descriptions of other times and places. Herder is

illustrations of Herder's cosmopolitanism, such as his noted essay on Shakespeare, where he aimed to 'explain him, feel him *as he is*, use him, and – *if possible* – make him alive [...] in Germany'.[103] Indeed, this passage is revealing of Herder's general openness of mind. Thus, he expressed his abiding cultural ambition in these terms: 'to our Leibnizes [to add] the Shaftesburys and Lockes, to our Spaldings the Sternes, Fosters, and Richardsons, to our Moses [Mendelssohn], the Browns and Montesquieus.'[104] A significant component of Herder's nationalism, therefore, involved the '[assimilation] into a nascent German culture [of] the best of French and British thought'.[105]

To Herder, concern for particularism was perfectly compatible with a cosmopolitan outlook – he himself referred at length to the idea of '*Humanität*' – this common bond of humanity being expressed in the diversity rather than in the sameness of human forms.[106] The point is worth reiterating : 'There was nothing political about Herder's views about belonging. He had little interest in politics and its manifestations and forms. He hated

fascinated with human diversity, and this fascination is reflected in both his method of inquiry and the subjects of his research.'

[103] Johann Gottfried Herder, 'Shakespeare', in *Eighteenth Century German Criticism*, ed. by Timothy J. Chamberlain (New York: Continuum, 1992), p. 143 [my emphasis] (1773). The translation from the German is by Joyce P. Crick and H. B. Nisbet. The German text, which initially appeared as part of the *Sturm und Drang* manifesto, reads as follows: '*zu erklären, zu fühlen wie er ist, zu nüßen, und – wo möglich! – uns Deutschen herzustellen.*' For an edition of the manifesto, see *Von Deutscher Art und Kunst* (Stuttgart: G. J. Göschen'sche Verlagshandlung, 1892). The relevant passage is on p. 53. See generally Zammito, *supra*, note 84, pp. 342–4. See also Robert S. Mayo, *Herder and the Beginnings of Comparative Literature* (Chapel Hill: University of North Carolina Press, 1969).

[104] Herder, *Journal meiner Reise*, *supra*, note 102, p. 33. This passage is omitted in *Journal of my Voyage*, *supra*, note 102. I have used the translation in Zammito, *supra*, note 84, pp. 314–15.

[105] Zammito, *supra*, note 84, p. 315.

[106] According to Herder, even such a notion as '*Humanität*', though, retains its concrete character. This point is well captured in Benjamin Bennett, *Beyond Theory: Eighteenth-Century German Literature and the Poetics of Irony* (Ithaca: Cornell University Press, 1993), p. 259, where the author observes that, for Herder, 'our being is indistinguishable from our being-human, and that our being-human, in turn, our "Humanität", our existence, experience, and history, is exactly coextensive with the invention, operation, and development of language'. See generally Johann Gottfried Herder, *Briefe zu Beförderung der Humanität*, in *Werke in zehn Bänden*, vol. VII, ed. by Hans-Dietrich Irmscher (Frankfurt: Deutscher Klassiker Verlag, 1991), pp. 147–53 [being letters 27 and 28] (1794) [hereinafter *Humanität*]. For an English translation of the relevant letters, see *On World History: Johann Gottfried Herder – An Anthology*, ed. by Hans Adler and Ernest A. Menze and transl. by Ernest A. Menze and Michael Palma (Armonk, New York: M. E. Sharpe, 1997), pp. 105–9. See also Samson B. Knoll, 'Herder's Concept of *Humanität*', in Wulf Koepke (ed.), *Johann Gottfried Herder: Innovator Through the Ages* (Bonn: Bouvier, 1992), pp. 9–19; A. Gillies, *Herder* (Oxford: Blackwell, 1945), pp. 97–113. For a thorough exploration in German, see 'Herders Verständnis von "Humanität"', being part of the commentary ('Kommentar') in *Humanität*, *supra*, pp. 817–37.

centralization, coercion, regulation, imperialism, all of which he associated with the State, a favorite target of his invectives. *His nationalism was not political but cultural.*'[107] In sum, Herder, 'the complete anthropologist',[108] was among the most sensitive, culturally aware and creative respondents to the challenge posed by European expansion and its corollary, the contact with strange cultures. 'Herder stresse[d] the necessity for any adequate understanding of the diverse cultures of human history to grasp the distinctive assumptions and prejudices implicit in the cultural consciousness of any given national community.'[109] Along the same lines, in his *Über die Aufgabe des Geschichtschreibers*, Wilhelm von Humboldt argued that the ultimate goal of the interpreter must be 'understanding' ('*Verstehen*'),[110] which calls for a fundamental appreciation of the 'abilities, feelings, dispositions and desires' ('*Fähigkeiten, Empfindungen, Neigungen und Leidenschaften*') of individuals as agents of history.[111] In my view, the contemporary relevance of the historicist critique of Enlightenment rationalism and of its claim to transhistorical and supracultural rationality very much lies in its strong defence of a pluralistic and non-hierarchical approach to a brand of cultural studies acknowledging the contingency and finitude of individuals and, therefore, underlying the relevance of gnoseological studies (understood in the broadest sense and including, for example, empirical psychology).[112]

*   *   *

Comparatists-at-law must, therefore, reverse the intellectual movement which subordinates difference to identity and emulate Wittgenstein, who said: 'my interest is in shewing that things which look the same are really different.'[113] To quote Günter Frankenberg, '[a]nalogies and the

---

[107] Craig, *supra*, note 91, p. 24 [my emphasis].
[108] Zammito, *supra*, note 84, p. 344. See also *id*., p. 475, n. 33.
[109] Brian J. Whitton, 'Herder's Critique of the Enlightenment: Cultural Community Versus Cosmopolitan Rationalism', (1988) 27 Hist. & Theory 146, p. 154.
[110] Wilhelm von Humboldt, *Über die Aufgabe des Geschichtschreibers*, in *Werke*, ed. by Albert Leitzmann, vol. IV: *1820–1822*, (Berlin: B. Behr's Verlag, 1905), pp. 38 and 41 [1821].
[111] *Id*., p. 49. Herder also insisted on the importance of sentiments. See McCready, *supra*, note 102, pp. 191–2.
[112] For a summary of Herder's contribution to philosophical thought, see the 'nine theses' submitted by Robert S. Leventhal, *The Disciplines of Interpretation* (Berlin: Walter de Gruyter, 1994), pp. 230–4. In the light of Leventhal's excursus, I am minded to address the question which James Whitman puts in his contribution to this book by voicing a somewhat emphatic '*oui*'. *Cf.* Charles Taylor, 'The Importance of Herder', in *Philosophical Arguments* (Cambridge, Mass.: Harvard University Press, 1995), pp. 79–99.
[113] M. O'C. Drury, 'Conversations with Wittgenstein', in Rush Rees (ed.), *Ludwig Wittgenstein: Personal Recollections* (Oxford: Blackwell, 1981), p. 171 [1948].

presumption of similarity have to be abandoned for a rigorous experience of distance and difference.'[114] I claim that comparison must involve a *principium individuationis*, 'the primary and fundamental investigation of difference'.[115] Likewise, Else Øyen remarks that the time has come for comparative research 'to shift its emphasis from seeking uniformity among variety to studying the preservation of enclaves of uniqueness among growing homogeneity and uniformity'.[116] Comparative legal studies must 'recognize and lay out a space of the other within the law. It is a question of identifying the conditions of difference, the places, occasions, energies, and institutional focuses within which difference, as difference, can appear or the other speak.'[117] Ascribing meaning to a legal culture or tradition means 'finding what is significant in [its] difference from others'.[118] This strategy, in turn, assumes a susceptibility to alterity on the part of the comparatist even prior to the inception of the comparative investigation. In this sense, a respect for alterity is not so much the result of a quest for difference as it is its pre-requisite.

***

By contrast, the insistence on a unitary conceptual matrix can lead to remarkable claims. James Gordley, who tells us that 'there is no such thing as a French law or German law or American law that is an independent object of study apart from the law of other countries', makes two other assertions along these lines.[119] First, he writes that '[o]nly in a qualified sense can we even say that the German, the American, and the Frenchman are writing about the law of their own countries. They are addressing a problem that arises in each of their own countries but neither the problem nor its solution

---

[114] Günter Frankenberg, 'Critical Comparisons: Re-thinking Comparative Law', (1985) 26 Harvard Int. L.J. 411, p. 453. See also Vivian G. Curran, 'Cultural Immersion, Difference and Categories in US Comparative Law', (1998) 46 Am. J. Comp. L. 301; *id.*, 'Romantic Common Law, Enlightened Civil Law: Legal Uniformity and the Homogenization of the European Union', (2001) 7 Columbia J. Eur. L. 63. But see, for example, Bernhard Großfeld, *Kernfragen der Rechtsvergleichung* (Tübingen: J. C. B. Mohr, 1996), p. 283.

[115] Michel Foucault, *Les mots et les choses* (Paris: Gallimard, 1966), p. 68 [*'la recherche première et fondamentale de la différence'*]. In this respect (as in many others), comparative legal studies does not differ from anthropology. See Carol J. Greenhouse, 'Just in Time: Temporality and the Cultural Legitimation of Law', (1989) 98 Yale L.J. 1631, p. 1631: 'anthropology is the study of the significance of cultural difference.'

[116] Else Øyen, 'The Imperfection of Comparisons', in *id.* (ed.), *Comparative Methodology* (London: Sage, 1990), p. 1.

[117] Goodrich, *Oedipus Lex*, *supra*, note 9, p. 241.

[118] Charles Taylor, *The Malaise of Modernity* (Concord, Ontario: Anansi, 1991), pp. 35–6.

[119] Gordley, *supra*, at text accompanying note 33.

are any more German than American or French.'[120] Second, he observes that '[w]hen we describe [judicial] decisions as applications of German or French or American law, we mean little more than that the court making the decision had jurisdiction, because the case arose in these countries. There [is] nothing distinctively German, French or American about the decisions themselves.'[121] What assumptions underwrite these statements? I propose to consider this far-reaching version of the monistic argument by way of a 'problem' with which I am familiar on account of prior research, the question of whether – and, if so, to what extent – a seller must volunteer information to his prospective buyer before the agreement is concluded. On the assumption that the 'problem' manifests itself in both legal 'systems' to the extent at least that each legal 'system' regards the issue as suitably 'problematic', I wish to focus specifically on two jurisdictions, England and France.

In England, the common law continues to favour a rigorous application of the *caveat emptor* doctrine.[122] Indeed, the House of Lords takes the view that a principle of 'good faith' is 'unworkable in practice' since it is 'inherently repugnant to the adversarial position of the parties'.[123] In France, however, a statute of 18 January 1992 enacts that 'the seller must, before the contract is entered into, put the consumer in a position to know all the essential features of the thing being sold'.[124] Beginning in 1945 with Michel de Juglart, a number of French writers have pleaded for the recognition of such a legal obligation.[125] Is it a coincidence that the call from Juglart and

---

[120] *Id.*, p. 561.
[121] *Id.*, p. 563. For an amplification of this view, see James Gordley, 'Is Comparative Law a Distinct Discipline?', (1998) 46 Am. J. Comp. L. 607.
[122] For example, see *Bell v. Lever Bros, Ltd*, [1932] A.C. 161 (H.L.), p. 224 (Lord Atkin); *Smith v. Hughes*, (1871) L.R. 6 Q.B. 597, p. 607 (Cockburn C.J.); *Banque Financière de la Cité SA v. Westgate Insurance Co.*, [1989] 2 All E.R. 952 (C.A.), pp. 988–1004 (Slade L.J.).
[123] *Walford v. Miles*, [1992] 2 A.C. 128, p. 138 (Lord Ackner). A striking illustration of the English resistance to the idea of 'good faith' is offered by the judgement in *Director General of Fair Trading v. First National Bank plc*, [2001] 3 W.L.R. 1297 (H.L.).
[124] *Loi* No. 92–60 of 18 January 1992 Reinforcing the Protection of Consumers ('*renforçant la protection des consommateurs*'), art. 2, D.1992.L.129 ['*Tout professionnel vendeur de biens (...) doit, avant la conclusion du contrat, mettre le consommateur en mesure de connaître les caractéristiques essentielles du bien*']. This text was followed by a further *Loi* No. 96–588 of 1 July 1996 on Loyalty and Parity Within Commercial Relationships ['*sur la loyauté et l'équilibre des relations commerciales*'], D.1996.L.295. For a commentary, including observations on the title of the statute, see Christophe Jamin, Rev. trim. dr. civ., 1996, p. 1009.
[125] See Michel de Juglart, 'L'obligation de renseignements dans les contrats', Rev. trim. dr. civ., 1945, p. 1. The best-known argument is in Jacques Ghestin, *Traité de droit civil: la formation du contrat*, 3d ed. (Paris: L.G.D.J., 1993), nos 593–673, pp. 576–653. See generally Muriel Fabre-Magnan, *De l'obligation d'information dans les contrats* (Paris: L.G.D.J., 1992).

those who heard him came when it did, that is to say, at a time when the Vichy regime had been advocating fierce anti-individualism and advancing its programme of regeneration of the national soul through the promotion of team spirit, service to the community and social solidarity?[126] Thus, Juglart's claim – which explicitly invites his readership to envisage the matter of pre-contractual information as 'one of the manifestations of this spirit of solidarity that characterizes our times'[127] – can be connected with the adoption of an ordinance dated 4 October 1945 laying the cornerstone of a new system of social security and of a statute dated 22 May 1946 operating the generalization of social security.[128]

For Gordley's monistic argument to stand, it must be the case that, both in England and in France, the social and legal role and responsibilities of seller and buyer are constructed in the same way by the community; that the social and legal dynamics of the relationship between seller and buyer are constructed in the same way by the community; that the significance and value of information as a commodity and the perception of information as an object of legal duties and responsibilities are constructed in the same way by the community; that the values of self-reliance and social solidarity intervene in the same way in both jurisdictions; that the fear (and realistic likelihood) that a complaint will be made by the buyer to the seller after the sale is experienced in the same way by sellers in both jurisdictions; that the fear that the seller will suffer a social stigma or will find himself the object of legal proceedings as a result of a complaint being made by the buyer after the sale is experienced in the same way by sellers in both jurisdictions (so that

---

[126] *Quid* of the fact that Juglart's paper, published as it was in the immediate wake of the Second World War, may also have been indebted to the unprecedented levels of popularity and support which the French Communist Party and the then USSR enjoyed among the French population on account of the contribution of Communists at home and abroad in the defeat of Nazism. This wave of sympathy for orthodox communism nationally and internationally had a particular impact on French intellectuals who, in the aftermath of the war, were now forced to assess their behaviour and attitudes before and, importantly, during the conflict. Many were determined to be on the side of History, of progress, and to assist in the emancipation of the oppressed. For some, these values took the form of an active agenda for the socialization of law. See generally Jacques Donzelot, *L'invention du social* (Paris: Le Seuil, 1994); François Ewald, *L'Etat providence* (Paris: Grasset, 1986). For a current application of these ideas with specific reference to French contract law, see Christophe Jamin, 'Plaidoyer pour le solidarisme contractuel', in *Etudes offertes à Jacques Ghestin* (Paris: L.G.D.J., 2001), pp. 441–72.

[127] Juglart, *supra*, note 125, no. 1, p. 1 ['*l'une des manifestations de cet esprit de solidarité qui caractérise notre époque*'].

[128] *Ordonnance* No. 45–2250 of 4 October 1945 Concerning the Organization of Social Security ['*portant organisation de la sécurité sociale*'], D.1945.L.253; *Loi* No. 46–1146 of 22 May 1946 Concerning the Generalization of Social Security ['*portant généralisation de la sécurité sociale*'], D.1946.L.237.

the same deterrent effect is at work in this respect); that the stigma, if any, encountered by the buyer-as-complainer is experienced in the same way by buyers in both jurisdictions (so that the same deterrent effect is at work in this respect); that the eventual costs associated with a complaint from the point of view of the buyer are internalized in the same way by buyers in both jurisdictions (so that the same deterrent effect is at work in this respect); that the information regarding available legal rights or remedies in the possession of buyers is the same for buyers in both jurisdictions (so that the same incentive effect is at work in this respect); that access to justice is the same for buyers in both countries (so that the same incentive effect is at work in this respect); that the likelihood of a monetary award being made against the seller in the courts is the same in both jurisdictions and that that information is available to sellers and buyers in the same way in both jurisdictions (so that the same incentive effect is at work in this respect); and that the monetary award has the same impact on the seller's pocket in both jurisdictions (so as to have the same deterrent impact on sellers). These are only *some* of the seemingly countless considerations that a comparatist must take for granted in order to reach the conclusion that 'the problem' of pre-contractual information I have raised is the same in both jurisdictions. In advance of empirical study, I argue that the sameness that is postulated is simply unrealistic.

Now, the issue becomes even more complex if I envisage a situation where an English and a French court would each render a decision involving the matter of 'pre-contractual information'. Let us assume that the facts and the law are precisely the same in both jurisdictions. Clearly, one must still bear in mind that the English judge is English and that the French judge is French. Because of the factors I have just outlined, the way in which the English and French judges will approach the merits of a case involving the matter of pre-contractual information as between seller and buyer will vary. *Inevitably*, the judge comes to 'the problem' – and to the reading of the relevant texts – as a socialized human being, that is, as an individual educated in a specific cultural and legal environment, understood here as a structuring social space, who would have to say, whether in London or Paris, to quote from Philip Larkin: 'Here no elsewhere underwrites my existence.'[129] (Indeed, 'the specific legal practices of a culture are simply dialects of a

---

[129] Philip Larkin, 'The Importance of Elsewhere', in *Collected Poems* (London: Faber & Faber, 1990), p. 104 [1955]. For a very influential argument regarding the way in which 'socialization' impacts upon reading, see Stanley Fish, *Is There a Text in This Class?* (Cambridge, Mass.: Harvard University Press, 1980), pp. 331–2.

parent social speech' and one should not expect a legal culture – which, whatever else it also is, is a cultural practice or product like any other – to 'depart drastically from the common stock of understanding in the surrounding culture'.[130]) But there is more. Different evidentiary rules and doctrines (themselves reflecting different social and political values developed over the long term) will make for a different construction of the facts in the eye of each law. In other words, even if the facts are the 'same' or, more accurately, even if lawyers in both jurisdictions construct the facts deemed relevant in precisely the 'same' way (something which I am prepared to assume for present purposes), it remains that the facts will not be the 'same' in the eye of each law. Likewise, different judicial drafting techniques will thematize certain dimensions of 'the problem' and ignore others. When French decisions, for instance, appeal to the comforting idea of interpretive stability that a grammatical discourse connotes so as to suggest that, although they are clearly not 'the law', they are simply a vehicle allowing for the stable production of the legislative texts' necessary legal solutions, they are doing much more than simply gesturing toward formalism. They are thereby advocating a particular vision of adjudication and of the values served by adjudication. The felt need to obfuscate, or at least to demote, the role of hermeneutic readings of the law in order not to invest the generative structure of the decision with the insecurity associated with purposive hermeneutics is, in itself, of considerable significance to an understanding of judicial governance and, more broadly, of a legal *mentalité*.[131]

The monistic argument, therefore, can hold only if its proponent is prepared to pretend that the problems which the law addresses and the solutions which the law provides to these problems are somehow unconnected to the cultural environment from which the problems and solutions arise. In other words, this kind of claim requires the comparatist to regard social problems and their legal treatment as occurring in a cultural vacuum, that is, to *bracket* historical, societal, political and psychological data. Only if one is willing to ignore the cultural dimension of the law can one say that the problem of 'pre-contractual information' and its treatment by the law can be considered irrespective of geography, of *place*. What remains unclear is

---

[130] Robert W. Gordon, 'Critical Legal Histories', (1984) 36 Stanford L.R. 57, p. 90. Of course, this is emphatically not to say that every manifestation of law within a culture is nothing but an example of that entire culture being acted out.

[131] See Mitchel Lasser, ' "Lit. Theory" Put to the Test: A Comparative Literary Analysis of American Judicial Tests and French Judicial Discourse', (1998) 111 Harvard L.R. 689.

whether the comparatist propounding this monistic approach accepts that law necessarily partakes in the culture from which it emanates but prefers to close his eyes to this fact, leaving the matter to sociologists or other such figures regarded by mainstream lawyers as marginal at best, or whether he takes the view that, unlike art or literature, law is somehow completely disconnected from the society by which it is fabricated (so that law would be permanently dysfunctional). In either case, the proposed approach perpetuates the kind of dreary positivism which relegates comparative legal studies to a technical exercise whose output is deeply flawed and which, on this account, remains largely irrelevant to the matter of understanding alterity in the law.[132] Consider, by way of illustration, Alan Watson's example regarding transfer of ownership and risk in sale and claiming to establish substantive sameness across laws.[133] Now, the fact is that the Roman 'rules' Watson refers to were written in Latin and purported to regulate the dealings of citizens in sixth-century Constantinople. The French rules mentioned by Watson were written in French and intended to govern citizens in pre-revolutionary France. And the Prussian rules addressed by Watson were written in German and were concerned with legal relationships in what remained feudal Prussia. I argue that cultural constructions of 'reality' and of law and of rules in the three settings inevitably harbour certain distinctive characteristics which, therefore, inevitably affect the interpretation of a rule, that is, which inevitably determine the ruleness of the rule according to the distinctive cultural logics of the native laws. These rules, thus, are not the same rules; any sameness stops at the bare form of words itself. Even then, this conclusion would not account for the fact that the inscribed words appear in three different languages with each language suggesting a specific relationship between the words and their content (for example, '[n]o language divides time or space exactly as does any other [...]; no language has identical taboos with any other [...]; no language dreams precisely like any other').[134] Watson, therefore, is only able to argue in favour of sameness by

---

[132] But see Bernhard Großfeld, *The Strength and Weakness of Comparative Law*, transl. by Tony Weir (Oxford: Oxford University Press, 1990), pp. 79–80, where the author shows, to borrow one illustration from his vast reservoir, how 'the problem' of damage caused by the escape of water from one's land differs as it arises in Texas rather than England.

[133] Watson, *supra*, at text accompanying note 21.

[134] George Steiner, *What is Comparative Literature?* (Oxford: Oxford University Press, 1995), p. 10. There is a famous passage of Benjamin's where he reminds us that 'the word *Brot* [...] mean[s] something other to a German than what the word *pain* means to a Frenchman': Walter Benjamin, 'The Task of the Translator', in *Selected Writings*, ed. by Marcus Bullock and Michael

uncoupling the rules from the real experience of law-in-the-world, which he appears to regard as simply not being worthy of esteem. His exclusive concern is with the integration of the rules under examination into a new, shared and immediate conceptual world – an ideological endeavour which operates in a supposedly open, yet, in fact, most conservative manner. It can be seen how perspicacious Gabriel Tarde was when he faulted the tendency 'to exaggerate the number and the extent of the similarities which strike the mind at first sight when comparing bodies of law'.[135]

* * *

I argue that, although it may be inconvenient for lawyers so to acknowledge given the limits of their technical expertise and the fact that they have manacled their lives to rules, law is a cultural fabric, such that the law comparatists address is inevitably indigenous and, therefore, different in the way something which is unique is necessarily different. Because '[t]here is only one thing in this world which cannot be compared, and that is "one thing"',[136] comparison *requires* at least two elements. Now, the comparison of two elements must assume difference between them. The point is Leibniz's: 'By virtue of imperceptible variations, two individual things cannot be perfectly

---

W. Jennings and transl. by Harry Zohn, vol. I: *1913–1926* (Cambridge, Mass.: Harvard University Press, 1996), p. 257 [1923] (hereinafter 'The Task of the Translator'). For the original text, see *id.*, 'Die Aufgabe des Übersetzers', in *Gesammelte Schriften*, ed. by Rolf Tiedemann, Hermann Schweppenhäuser and Tillman Rexroth, vol. IV, t. 1 (Frankfurt: Suhrkamp, 1972), p. 14 ['*In "Brot" und "pain" ist das Gemeinte zwar dasselbe, die Art, es zu meinen, dagegen nicht. In der Art des Meinens nämlich liegt es, daß beide Worte dem Deutschen und Franzosen je etwas Verschiedenes bedeuten, daß sie für beide nicht vertauschbar sind, ja sich letzten Endes auszuschließen streben; am Gemeinten aber, daß sie, absolut genommen, das Selbe und Identische bedeuten*'] (hereinafter 'Die Aufgabe des Übersetzers'). There are many such examples in circulation, some of which are collected in Willis Barnstone, *The Poetics of Translation* (New Haven: Yale University Press, 1993).

[135] Gabriel Tarde, *Les transformations du droit* (Paris: Berg, 1994), p. 34 ['*exagérer le nombre et la portée des similitudes qui frappent l'esprit, à première vue, quand on compare des corps de droit*'] (1893). For a further illustration showing how the urge to derive similarities across different legal traditions can lead to extraordinary claims, see Tony Weir, 'Die Sprachen des europäischen Rechts', Zeitschrift für Europäisches Privatrecht, 1995, pp. 372–3, who rebuts the argument that the English Statute of Frauds is indebted to the 1566 *Ordonnance de Moulins*. For this assertion, see Ernst Rabel, 'The Statute of Frauds and Comparative Legal History', (1947) 63 L.Q.R. 174.

[136] Ferdinand J. M. Feldbrugge, 'Sociological Research Methods and Comparative Law', in Mario Rotondi (ed.), *Inchieste di diritto comparato*, vol. II: *Buts et méthodes du droit comparé* (Padova: Cedam, 1973), p. 213. *Cf.* Mauro Cappelletti, Monica Seccombe and Joseph H. H. Weiler, 'Integration Through Law: Europe and the American Federal Experience – A General Introduction', in *id.* (eds.), *Integration Through Law*, vol. I: *Methods, Tools and Institutions*, t. 1: *A Political, Legal and Economic Overview* (Berlin: Walter de Gruyter, 1986), p. 9: 'Comparative analysis becomes meaningless in conditions of identity.'

similar.'[137] *To accord difference priority is the only way for comparative legal studies to take cognizance of what is the case.* In acknowledgement of the fact that comparative analysis of law is a serious political act – does it not ascertain the other for me and inscribe him to the point where what I write constitutes, in part at least, the other's legal identity (which can always be made to look good or bad) and reconstitutes, in part at least, my own identity? – comparatists must resist the powerful temptation toward the construction of abstract and superficial commonalities and assent to the ineliminability of difference, which it becomes their responsibility to characterize, articulate and justify.[138] Thus, they must embrace thick or deep thought: 'The force that shatters the appearance of identity is the force of thinking.'[139] Indeed, the common denominators that mark the outcome of legal research are common only in the light of a particular research project and its limits as deliberately set. Any finalized unity is, in this sense, strictly mental. In effect, each data holds an infinite complexity, the exploration of which never ceases to relegate the frontiers of homogeneity to the benefit of heterogeneity. To mention Tarde again, 'wherever a scholar digs underneath apparent indistinction, he discovers a wealth of unexpected distinctions': before the telescope, the stars were considered to be homogeneous and before the microscope, the molecules were considered to be homogeneous.[140] Likewise, any sameness identified by comparatists signifies but a transitional state of knowledge, the relevant and fundamental differences being more or less deliberately confined to obscurity.

---

[137] Leibniz, *Nouveaux essais sur l'entendement*, in *Die philosophischen Schriften von Gottfried Wilhelm Leibniz*, ed. by C. J. Gerhardt, vol. V (Hildesheim: Georg Olms, 1960), p. 49 ['*En vertu des variations insensibles, deux choses individuelles ne sauraient être parfaitement semblables*'] (1882). See also Martin Heidegger, *Identity and Difference*, transl. by Joan Stambaugh (Chicago: University of Chicago Press, 2002), pp. 23–4: 'For something to be the same, one is always enough' [hereinafter *Identity*]. For the original text, see *id.*, *Identität und Differenz* (Stuttgart: Günther Neske, 1957), p. 10 ['*Damit etwas das Selbe sein kann, genügt jeweils eines*'] (hereinafter *Identität*). *Cf.* Adorno, *supra*, note 4, p. 184: 'Without otherness, cognition would deteriorate into tautology; what is known would be knowledge itself.' For the original text, see *id.*, *supra*, note 40, p. 185 ['*Ohne sie verkäme Erkenntnis zur Tautologie; das Erkannte wäre sie selbst*'].
[138] The point about anything being liable to laudable or damning redescription is underlined in Richard Rorty, *Contingency, Irony, and Solidarity* (Cambridge: Cambridge University Press, 1989), p. 73.
[139] Adorno, *supra*, note 4, p. 149. For the original text, see *id.*, *supra*, note 40, p. 152 ['*Die Kraft, die den Schein von Identität sprengt, ist die des Denkens selber*'].
[140] Gabriel Tarde, *Monadologie et sociologie*, in *Oeuvres*, ed. by Eric Alliez, vol. I (Paris: Institut Synthélabo, 1999), p. 72 ['*Partout où, sous l'indistinct apparent, un savant creuse, il découvre des trésors de distinctions inattendues*'] (1893). The two examples are Tarde's.

The prioritization of difference satisfies the need for self-transcendence. If comparison aims primarily to show what legal communities all share, then no one needs to revise one's opinions in order to take into account perspectives and experiences beyond oneself. It is only through the assumption that communicative interaction means encountering difference of meaning that I, as observer, am aware of the fact that my position is perspectival – and that I can then act upon this fact. Indeed, it should now be clear that one can pursue a programme of harmonization of law that will secure the allegiance of the various constituencies only by retreating from the imperialist drive to oneness and by doing justice to the profound diversity of legal experience across jurisdictions.[141] Is the key to the sustainability of the ecosystem not biodiversity?[142] In my opinion, the favour which habitual comparative endeavours – including 'common-core' research – continues to enjoy is a good measure of the distance comparative legal studies must still travel before it emancipates itself from monological discourse and, at long last, acquires the intellectual credibility which it has thus far properly been denied on account of its recurrent failure to propound thick or deep understanding.[143]

---

[141] See James Tully, *Strange Multiplicity: Constitutionalism in an Age of Diversity* (Cambridge: Cambridge University Press, 1995) p. 197. *Cf*. René Girard, *La violence et le sacré* (Paris: Grasset, 1972), p. 89: 'where difference is lacking, violence threatens' ['*Là où la différence fait défaut, c'est la violence qui menace*'].

[142] For a useful introduction to the argument from biodiversity, see David Takacs, *The Idea of Biodiversity* (Baltimore: Johns Hopkins University Press, 1996). For stimulating connections between biological and cultural diversity, see Luisa Maffi (ed.), *On Biocultural Diversity* (Washington, DC: Smithsonian Institution, 2001).

[143] For noteworthy – and, of course, non-exhaustive – illustrations of what can be done to make comparative legal studies intellectually respectable, see Bernard Rudden, 'Torticles', (1991–2) 6/7 Tulane Civ. L. Forum 105; Geoffrey Samuel, *The Foundations of Legal Reasoning* (Antwerp: Maklu, 1994); Ewald, *supra*, note 68; Janet E. Ainsworth, 'Categories and Culture: On the "Rectification of Names" in Comparative Law', (1996) 82 Cornell L.R. 19; Gunther Teubner, 'Legal Irritants: Good Faith in British Law or How Unifying Law Ends Up in New Divergences', (1998) 61 Modern L.R. 11; Lasser, *supra*, note 131; Nicholas Kasirer, '*Lex*-icographie *mercatoria*', (1999) 47 Am. J. Comp. L. 653 [hereinafter '*Lex*-icographie']; John C. Reitz, 'Political Economy and Abstract Review in Germany, France and the United States', in Sally J. Kenney, William M. Reisinger and *id*. (eds.), *Constitutional Dialogues in Comparative Perspective* (London: Macmillan, 1999), pp. 62–88; James Q. Whitman, 'Enforcing Civility and Respect: Three Societies', (2000) 109 Yale L.J. 1279; Teemu Ruskola, 'Conceptualizing Corporations and Kinship: Comparative Law and Development Theory in a Chinese Perspective', (2000) 52 Stanford L.R. 1599; Nicholas Kasirer, '*Agapè*', Rev. int. dr. comp., 2001, p. 575 [hereinafter '*Agapè*']; Geoffrey Samuel, *Epistemology and Method in Law* (Dartmouth: Ashgate, 2003) [hereinafter *Epistemology*]. This strictly exemplificational list is deliberately limited to twelve publications covering the period from the early 1990s to the early 2000s. It is arranged in roughly chronological order.

Lucia Zedner's remark is apposite: 'If the comparative project is to produce anything of value we need to develop an acute sensitivity to the peculiarities of the local.'[144]

* * *

Except, of course, to the extent that the self cannot be the other, these observations should not be read to indicate that I regard alterity as being *absolutely absolute* (if only because absolute otherness would imply absolute identity). To suggest the complete impenetrability of alterity would make the very idea of comparison unintelligible and incoherent. The basic point can be formulated thus: 'the other is absolutely the other by being an ego, that is to say, in a certain way, the same as me.'[145] Nor does incommensurability across legal traditions detract from comparability. For example, although, unlike the Fahrenheit and centigrade scales, the German and Spanish languages are incommensurable – because they cannot be assessed by reference to a shared standard of evaluation on account of the non-homology between linguistic grids which, in turn, reflects the differences between the two cultures and their environments as those two cultures have experienced them – they can be compared, say, with respect to the position of the verb within the typical sentence.[146] In other words, and with the exception of situations when understanding someone or something can only mean understanding that person's or that thing's incomprehensibility,[147] even the presence of

---

[144] Lucia Zedner, 'In Pursuit of the Vernacular: Comparing Law and Order Discourse in Britain and Germany', (1995) 4 Soc. & Leg. Stud. 517, p. 519.

[145] Derrida, *supra*, note 10, p. 187 [*'l'autre n'est absolument autre qu'en étant un ego, c'est-à-dire d'une certaine façon le même que moi'*]. In this sense, there *is* a relation between self and other, *pace* Levinas, *supra*, note 74 and *infra*, note 219, *passim*. See also Paul Ricoeur, *Soi-même comme un autre* (Paris: Le Seuil, 1990), p. 387, who notes that ' "he thinks", "she thinks" means: "he/she says in his/her heart : I think" ' [' *"il pense", "elle pense" signifie: "il/elle dit dans son coeur: je pense"* ']. *Cf.* Samuel, *Epistemology*, *supra*, note 143, p. 15, who observes that whether in the civil-law or the common-law world law is about relations between individuals, on the one hand, and between individuals and things, on the other.

[146] The same goes for other examples of incommensurability, such as those offered in Nelson Goodman, *Ways of Worldmaking* (Indianapolis: Hackett, 1978), p. 13. Incidentally, to the contrast that Goodman draws between twelve-tone and eight-tone musical scales one could add the one between jazz and classical music.

[147] *Cf*. Theodor W. Adorno, 'Trying to Understand *Endgame*', in *Notes to Literature*, ed. by Rolf Tiedemann and transl. by Shierry Weber Nicholsen, vol. I (New York: Columbia University Press, 1991), p. 243: 'Understanding [the play] can mean only understanding its unintelligibility, concretely reconstructing the meaning of the fact that it has no meaning' [1961]. For the German text, see *id.*, 'Versuch, das Endspiel zu verstehen', in *Gesammelte Schriften*, vol. XI: *Noten zur Literatur*, ed. by Rolf Tiedemann (Frankfurt: Suhrkamp, 1974), p. 283 ['*Es verstehen kann nichts anderes heißen, als seine Unverständlichkeit verstehen, konkret den Sinnzusammenhang dessen*

radically divergent evaluative standards does not prevent the possibility of understanding another's meaning – at least in the 'weak' sense of achieving an appearance of consensus for, in fact, the possibility of accordance is limited given that 'one understands *differently, when one understands at all*'.[148] Nor does the possibility of understanding another's meaning prevent a finding of incommensurability, *pace* Donald Davidson. Applying Davidson's reasoning to comparative legal studies, if a comparatist were able to render anything within another legal culture sufficiently meaningful so as to make it intelligible, he would have to conclude that the other law is commensurable with his own. In sum, Davidson tells us that cognitive bridges, no matter how fragile, foreclose a finding of incommensurability. But does it follow from the existence of cognitive bridges (imagined or otherwise) that two legal cultures cannot rest on irreconcilable ontological premises? In fact, although Davidson argues that even the merest cognitive connection prevents incommensurability, it seems that cognitive connections represent a necessary *semantic* pre-requisite to the appreciation of *epistemological* incommensurability, a kind of constitutive dialogical threshold. Envisage two laws, one where judicial review is based on reasonableness and the other where it rests on proportionality. There exists between these two laws a semantic commonality or dialogical interface around which members of both legal communities can agree: for both laws, the issue concerns the legitimacy of judicial review. And this semantic commonality or dialogical interface remains, even though each law has its own understanding of what 'judicial review' (and legitimacy) can mean. Now, it is precisely this commonality

---

nachkonstruieren, daß es keinen hat']. Adorno's observation concerned Samuel Beckett's *Fin de partie*.

[148] Gadamer, *supra*, note 48, p. 297. For the German text, see *id.*, *Wahrheit und Methode*, 6th ed. (Tübingen: J. C. B. Mohr, 1990), p. 302 ['*daß man* anders *versteht,* wenn man überhaupt versteht'] (emphasis original). This *caveat* is also captured by Humboldt: 'Nobody means by a word precisely and exactly what his neighbour does, and the difference, be it ever so small, vibrates, like a ripple in water, throughout the entire language. Thus all understanding is always at the same time a not-understanding, all concurrence in thought and feeling at the same time a divergence': Wilhelm von Humboldt, *On Language: On the Diversity of Human Language Construction and Its Influence on the Mental Development of the Human Species*, ed. by Michael Losonsky and transl. by Peter Heath (Cambridge: Cambridge University Press, 1988), p. 63 [1836]. For the original text, see *id.*, *Über die Verschiedenheit des menschlichen Sprachbaues*, ed. by Donatella Di Cesare (Paderborn: Ferdinand Schöningh, 1998), pp. 190–1 ['*Keiner denkt bei dem Wort gerade und genau das, was der andre, und die noch so kleine Verschiedenheit zittert, wie ein Kreis im Wasser, durch die ganze Sprache fort. Alles Verstehen ist daher immer zugleich ein Nicht-Verstehen, alle Übereinstimmung in Gedanken und Gefühlen zugleich ein Auseinandergehen*'].

or interface around the notion of 'judicial review' which allows the comparatist to apprehend the incommensurability of the two approaches, to realize how these two epistemological orientations, these two conceptions, can only signify alterity *vis-à-vis* each other despite a common semantic referent. What rod could the comparatist use to measure one perspective based on the judge-as-participant-in-the-community (the 'reasonableness' approach) and the other founded on the judge-as-agent-of-government (the 'proportionality' model)? Incommensurability is not untranslatability; it can never, therefore, be reduced to a question that would be exclusively or chiefly semantic.[149] Ultimately, incommensurability is best apprehended as an important hermeneutic device allowing the comparatist to protect the identity of any particular cognitive framework and to preserve the variety of epistemic perspectives. Incommensurability can thus be considered as an inherent feature of diversity.

Still as regards the matter of alterity not being *absolutely absolute*, I accept that no comparison can be initiated without a comparatist taking the view that there is an apparent sameness between the objects of comparison, that they seem alike in at least one respect. Inevitably, operating his culturally pre-oriented understanding-enabling background, the comparatist must build a perceptual or cognitive bridge allowing for the apprehension of something as something that can be compared with something else – a claim which finds its resonance in the Heideggerian 'as-structure' of perception.[150] Let us refer to this estimation as the 'condition of possibility' of comparison, the ineliminable sensibility that demarcates the epistemological space within which it becomes possible to study other laws. But this point must

---

[149] For Donald Davidson's position, see his *Inquiries into Truth and Interpretation* (Oxford: Oxford University Press, 1984), pp. 183–98. To the extent that Davidson's argument turns on the fact that the idea of difference between conceptual schemes is unintelligible, one may doubt whether the feeling of *Unheimlichkeit* one experiences upon finding oneself confronted with alterity is aptly articulated in terms of an opposition between 'conceptual schemes'. It seems that rhetorical practice, religious sensibility and cultural suggestibility, to take but three random illustrations, can hardly be reduced to 'conceptual schemes'. My general reply to Davidson owes much to Hans-Herbert Kögler, *The Power of Dialogue*, transl. by Paul Hendrickson (Cambridge, Mass.: MIT Press, 1996), pp. 163–6. As regards the illustration based on judicial review, I have derived assistance from Roger Cotterrell, 'Judicial Review and Legal Theory', in Genevra Richardson and Hazel Genn (eds.), *Administrative Law and Government Action* (Oxford: Oxford University Press, 1994), pp. 13–34.

[150] See Gerald L. Bruns, *Tragic Thoughts at the End of Philosophy* (Evanston: Northwestern University Press, 1999), p. 28. For a related formulation of this point, see Andrew Benjamin, *Philosophy's Literature* (Manchester: Clinamen Press, 2001), p. 2: 'it is the presence of the object as a repetition that allows for interpretation.'

not be understood to mean that comparatists can then legitimately effectuate an approximation of alterity to sameness, that they can then engage in a silencing or obliteration of alterity, that they can then repress alterity by dismissing it as insignificant or reduce alterity by narcissistically assimilating it to sameness. I argue that comparative legal studies must assume the duty to acknowledge, appreciate and respect alterity. Without such recognizance, no ethics is possible. In other words, the *raison d'être* of the comparative project lies in the refusal of national pride, in the rejection of cultural taboos, in the awareness and valorization of difference and in the empathic articulation of the voices of alterity to the point where the self is actually prepared to accept being *othered* by otherness.[151] This agenda, I may add, does not assume the existence of holistic and fixed systems of meaning. It leaves room for human agency and creative practice; it also allows for the contested dimensions of social life. In particular, it is sensitive to the cohabitation within given communities of differentiated meanings ascribed by those in different social positions. Let me reiterate, for example, that the identity of the civil-law or common-law traditions does not exist in the sense of *semper idem* or *semper unum*. In fact, as the Spanish language teaches us, identity need not be understood as a fixed condition or state [*'ser'*] but can be apprehended as fluid, that is, as suggesting movement [*'estar'*].

* * *

If only because a comparatist cannot separate his inherence in his law from his inherence in his act of comparison, there is, of course, a sense in which I construct and maintain difference even as I purport merely to explain it (can the 'real' ever be encountered by a disembodied observer and can the 'real' ever be encountered except through idealization and fantasy – which is *not* to say that the fact that knowledge is subjectively articulated or designed denies it status as knowledge).[152] A law, like a thing, is what it is and it is not

---

[151] I borrow the neologism from Rodolphe Gasché, *Of Minimal Things* (Stanford: Stanford University Press, 1999), p. 324. For a well-known argument to the effect that an encounter with another culture ought to prompt one to reflect critically on one's own cultural situation, see Peter Winch, 'Understanding a Primitive Society', (1964) 1 Am. Philosophical Q. 307. Of course, there is a crucial sense in which the self always-already features an irreducible otherness, an other scene, *ein anderer Schauplatz* – to borrow Freud's designation of the unconscious. Comparison, like psychoanalysis, is a transferential process in which one redefines oneself in the course of renegotiating one's relation with the other and, specifically, with the other-in-the-law.

[152] Gadamer is right to say that '[w]e always find ourselves within a situation, and [that] throwing light on it is a task that is never entirely finished': *supra*, note 48, p. 301. For the German text, see *id.*, *supra*, note 148, p. 307 ['*Man steht in ihr, findet sich immer schon in einer Situation*

one of its ontological characteristics not to be another law: difference has no self of its own. The fact that differences are fundamentally accidental and inessential means that a law is never different as such, but that it is differentiated by the comparatist's hermeneutic thought as he decides when the movement of difference starts and stops – which, therefore, means that the comparatist intervenes performatively in that he does more than simply report on existing data (difference is not in the nature of visual data) but also generates original information (which is why the comparatist's object of study is never an *object*). Difference, then, has no inert existence that could be severed from the various descriptions and qualifications that mediate understanding and compromise the ideal character of the act of referentiality. This is to say that the comparatist inheres in the difference that he experiences. This is also to say that, because it rests on an infinite bringing forth of itself, difference is inexhaustible in that it never ceases to become manifest in new facets as the relationship of power between the comparatist and his 'object' of study fashions the kind of knowledge created by the comparatist about his 'object' of study: that which is compared is not a given but an *assignment* and difference is not a given but an *accomplishment*. Yet, it would be too much to say that the civil-law and common-law traditions, for instance, have no independent existence beyond the individual realizations that accrue from historical awareness.[153] The historical fact of two main legal traditions in the western world (one that received Roman law and the other that did not) delineates an economy of signification that cannot be reduced to a phantasmatic projection (contrary to what the universalist bias of mainstream comparative legal studies would have us believe). Thus,

---

vor, deren Erhellung die nie ganz zu vollendende Aufgabe ist']. At the minimum, I can say that I was born and lived for twenty years or so within a francophone minority, which continues to owe its existence to the fact that it has relentlessly, at least since the early 1960s, asserted its cultural difference from neighbouring anglophone communities. This autobiographical note, of course, alludes to the fact that what I may wish to refer to as my 'subjectivity' incorporates institutionalized sets of assumptions that have constituted me into the comparatist I have become and which, to a significant extent, predetermine any intellectual move I may make despite the lack of any explicit fidelity on my part to my native culture.

[153] For a related argument in the context of literary criticism, see Edward W. Said, 'Orientalism Reconsidered', (1985) 1 Cultural Critique 89, p. 92: 'Each age, for instance, re-interprets Shakespeare, not because Shakespeare changes, but because despite the existence of numerous and reliable editions of Shakespeare, there is no such fixed and non-trivial object as Shakespeare independent of his editors, the actors who played his roles, the translators who put him in other languages, the hundreds of millions of readers who have read him or watched performances of his plays since the late sixteenth century. On the other hand, *it is too much to say that Shakespeare has no independent existence at all*' [my emphasis].

difference cannot be reduced to my psychological state or to the vagaries of my thought.[154] In the words of Bernard Williams, '[k]nowledge is of what is there *anyway*'.[155]

To defend the priority of difference is not to suggest, moreover, that what philosophers might call the 'problem' of difference can ever be resolved. In the way in which I am never done with my responsibilities for the other, in the way in which my exacting answerability to the other is incessant, difference is ultimately intractable. Consider how the 'object' of study which is different is irreducibly independent from the comparatist who thinks or expresses this difference and from its empirical manifestation in the comparatist's speech. The gap, which lies between an always-already-constituted law and a constituting consciousness, continually defers 'object' and thought from coming into coincidence.[156] (The *décalage* is amplified by the fact that any comparison is mediated by the felt need to tell an effective story, one that is at once coherent and persuasive. What is written, therefore, involves both the exclusion of what would undermine the credibility of the narrative and the inclusion of discursive forms that stamp the story with scholarly authority.[157]) This experience of difference – or, perhaps, this

---

[154] To quote Levinas, '[i]t is not difference which makes alterity: alterity makes difference': Emmanuel Levinas, *Is It Righteous To Be?*, ed. by Jill Robbins (Stanford: Stanford University Press, 2001), p. 106 [1988].

[155] Bernard Williams, *Descartes: The Project of Pure Enquiry* (London: Harvester, 1968), p. 64 [emphasis original].

[156] This is the gist of Derrida's famous pun on *'différence'* and *'différance'*: *supra*, note 10, *passim*. See also *id.*, *supra*, note 46, pp. 1–29. *Cf*. Werner Hamacher, *Premises*, transl. by Peter Fenves (Stanford: Stanford University Press, 1996), pp. 15–16: 'Only in the not-yet and never-once of understanding can something be understood.'

[157] What is recounted partakes in a reflection on an experience which once was and, because it has perished, cannot be again. Writing, since it necessarily intervenes at a time that is subsequent to experience, remains as a memory of that which cannot be restored *as such*. Thus, Flaubert in his Egyptian diary: 'Between the I of tonight and the I of that other night, there is the difference between the corpse and the surgeon performing the autopsy': Gustave Flaubert, *Voyage en Egypte*, ed. by Pierre-Marc de Biasi (Paris: Grasset, 1991), p. 125 [*'Entre le moi de ce soir et le moi de ce soir-là, il y a la différence du cadavre au chirurgien qui l'autopsie'*] (1851). The magnitude of the illusion is liable to increase with time. In March 1836, Stendhal told of his crossing of the Grand-Saint-Bernard pass with the Italian army thirty-six years earlier: 'I very well remember the descent. But I do not want to hide to myself that five or six years later I saw an engraving of it, which I thought was a very good likeness, and my recollection is *only* of the engraving': Stendhal, *Vie de Henry Brulard*, in *Oeuvres intimes*, ed. by Victor Del Litto, vol. II (Paris: Gallimard, 1982), p. 941 [*'je me figure fort bien la descente. Mais je ne veux pas dissimuler que cinq ou six ans après j'en vis une gravure que je trouvai fort ressemblante, et mon souvenir n'est plus que la gravure'*] (1890) [emphasis original].

épreuve of difference – reminds us that the position of being responsible (the mastery of the 'I') is more a dignity than a happiness.[158]

* * *

Some of the most obvious implications resulting from the prioritization of difference may now be addressed. At the outset, the focus on difference identifies a practice, a manner, a style of thinking which purports to engage behaviour, to inculcate the propensity to act in a certain fashion and to obtain a modification of consciousness in the way the comparatist sees the world, himself and his relationships with others. It is the expression of a being-in-the-world. It must, therefore, affect what comparatists look for and thus what they get to know – their knowledge-claims – and how they (and others) act on the basis of what becomes known. What is at stake is the shape and contents of the comparative psyche and, ultimately, the idea and ideal of knowledge – let us remember that what we call the 'other' is, in fact, what we *know* of the 'other'. Bearing in mind that every law is able to be considered with respect to its particularity, the aim must be for comparatists to abjure the search for imputed sameness – always superficial, inevitably reductionist – and deliberately to devote their enterprise to the elucidation of specificity, that is, to delve as deeply as possible into the creative matrices of particular legal cultures – to embrace, to quote again from Ezra Pound, 'the method of Luminous Detail'[159] – with a view to yielding knowledge that is neither purposefully logocentric nor willingly exclusionary, that neither engages in intentional foreclosure or abjection: 'one must, through

---

[158] In one of his essays on Hölderlin, Heidegger refers to 'the experience of the foreign' ('*die Erfahrung des Fremden*'): Martin Heidegger, *Erläuterungen zu Hölderlins Dichtung*, 2d ed. (Frankfurt: Vittorio Klostermann, 1951), p. 109. The notion of '*Erfahrung*' as understood by Heidegger is of particular interest for comparatists. For example, see *id.*, *On the Way to Language*, transl. by Peter D. Hertz (New York: Harper & Row, 1971), p. 57: 'To undergo an experience with something – be it a thing, a person, or a god – means that this something befalls us, strikes us, comes over us, overwhelms and transforms us.' For the German text, see *id.*, *Unterwegs zur Sprache* (Pfullingen: Günther Neske, 1959), p. 159 ['*Mit etwas, sei es ein Ding, ein Mensch, ein Gott, eine Erfahrung machen heißt, daß es uns widerfährt, daß es uns trifft, über uns kommt, uns umwirft und verwandelt*']. Interestingly, the French translation for the Heideggerian '*Erfahrung*' is '*épreuve*'. For example, see Antoine Berman, *L'épreuve de l'étranger* (Paris: Gallimard, 1984), p. 147. The English translator has saluted this rendition as being 'much richer' than '*expérience*': *id.*, *The Experience of the Foreign*, transl. by S. Heyvaert (Albany: State University of New York Press, 1992), p. vii. The English language is seemingly confined to the bland 'experience', the extravagant 'ordeal' or the equivocal 'challenge'.

[159] Ezra Pound, 'I gather the Limbs of Osiris', in *Selected Prose 1909–1965*, ed. by William Cookson (New York: New Directions, 1973), p. 21 [1911]. Pound adds that these facts, the 'luminous details', 'gover[n] knowledge as the switchboard the electric circuit': *id.*, p. 24.

the analogies, grasp the differential quality.'[160] There is, in fact, a pair of related formulations in French – a *'parti pris'* and *'prendre son parti'* – which connote at least three meanings that jointly capture the three main facets of my argument. First, one can have a *'parti pris'* in the sense of showing purposefulness. For example, a French sentence could run thus: *'Chez lui, le parti pris de faire du bien se remarquait vite'* ('In him, the determination to do good could easily be noticed'). A variation on this sentence would read: *'Il avait pris le parti de faire du bien'* ('He had determined to do good'). Second, a *'parti pris'* refers to a prejudice, whether positive or negative, as in the sentence, *'il y a trop de parti pris dans ses jugements'* ('there is too much prejudice in his opinions'). Third, *'prendre son parti'* can mean 'to resign oneself'. After one has lost an important vote, it can be said that *'il en a pris son parti'*, that 'he has resigned himself to it'. Purposefulness, prejudice and resignation are three cardinal features of the brand of comparative legal studies I advocate. I claim that comparatists must resign themselves to the fact that law is a cultural phenomenon and that, therefore, differences across legal cultures can only ever be overcome imperfectly. Disclaiming any objectivity (and, therefore, bringing to bear their own prejudices as situated observers), they must purposefully privilege the identification of differences across the laws they compare lest they fail to address singularity with scrupulous authenticity. They must make themselves into *difference engineers*.[161]

There is more. Within the European context, the French or German jurist should ensure that English law forms part of the terms of comparison in that if one compares strictly within one's own legal tradition, one may form the (unwarranted) view that certain epistemological assumptions are necessary or natural while they are simply characteristic of laws in a particular historico-socio-cultural configuration. If the benefits derived from the act of comparison are to be optimalized, the observer needs to be confronted with the breadth of possibilities, something which is best achieved at the level of 'most-different-units design', that is, as it involves a comparison across the civil-law and common-law traditions.[162] Indeed, contrary

---

[160] Francis Ponge, 'My Creative Method', in *Oeuvres complètes*, ed. by Bernard Beugnot, vol. I (Paris: Gallimard, 1999), p. 536 ['*Il faut, à travers les analogies, saisir la qualité différentielle*'] (1961). The title appears in English.

[161] I borrow the label from the sub-title in Keith A. Pearson (ed.), *Deleuze and Philosophy* (London: Routledge, 1997).

[162] *Cf.* Richard H. S. Tur, 'The Dialectic of General Jurisprudence and Comparative Law', [1977] Juridical R. 238, p. 246.

to the view held by those who wish to trivialize comparative studies featuring civil-law and common-law jurisdictions,[163] the fact remains that very much of significance has yet to be written on the civil law and common law as idiosyncratic narratives or discursive strategies.[164] (I also have in mind various features of the discourse of the undisclosed or the unthought, such as the conditions of subjective attachment to the institution; the *mise en scène* of symbols and images, connecting to the questions of constraint and emancipation; the silences;[165] the interdictions and their problematizations.) There is a clear sense in which the ethical encounter, which I argue must govern the act of comparison, has simply not (yet) materialized in the context of civil-law/common-law interactions – a claim which need not deny the indisputable need for comparatists also to move their field-work beyond Europe and North America.

Regard for the prescriptive guidance afforded by comparison-as-difference further helps the comparatist to determine, for example, whether a treatment of German law in the casebook format properly allows the English lawyer to whom it is destined the opportunity of a thick or deep understanding of German law *as German law*.[166] It permits the comparatist

---

[163] For example, see Mattei, *supra*, note 78, p. 23, who regards 'the traditional distinction between common law and civil law [as] a subdivision within a highly homogeneous family of legal systems: the western legal tradition'.

[164] Among the various differences which such epistemological investigations might elucidate in order to understand how they are made, the following motifs, which I introduce somewhat schematically (and, therefore, disputably), appear worthy of especial attention. Civil law is language that is (or wants to be) fixed, settled while the words of the common law circulate in the air as so many stories, sayings and memories. Also, while civil law is assertive of what is the case, common law is responsive to whatever it hears. Civil law is apodictic or propositional form, a system of concepts, while common law is self-reflexive, material, figurative and nomadic language. Civil law is rule-governed and self-contained while common law is spontaneous, open-ended, unrestrained by the law of non-contradiction. Civil law aspires only to what is necessary and universal while common law is singular, contingent and refractory to categories. Civil law is disengaged and monadic, always careful to determine what counts as itself, while common law is porous, exposed, always captivated by whatever is otherwise. Note that these labels are meant mutually to clarify rather than to exclude one another. I closely follow Bruns, *supra*, note 150, p. 2.

[165] The cultural value of silence is evoked by Michel Foucault, *Dits et écrits*, ed. by Daniel Defert and François Ewald, vol. IV: *1980–1988* (Paris: Gallimard, 1994), pp. 525–6 [1983]. See also José Ortega y Gasset, *Man and People*, transl. by Willard R. Trask (New York: Norton, 1957), p. 244. For the original text, see *id.*, *El hombre y la gente*, in *Obras completas* (Madrid: Alianza Editorial, 1994), p. 250 [1957].

[166] For a re-presentation of German law as a collection of cases, see Basil S. Markesinis, *The German Law of Torts: A Comparative Treatise*, 4th ed. by *id.* and Hannes Unberath (Oxford: Hart, 2002). Contrast H. C. Gutteridge, *Comparative Law*, 2d ed. (Cambridge: Cambridge University Press, 1949), p. 91: 'an English comparative lawyer must resist the temptation to approach the study of

to appreciate that the claim that 'one must [...] "anglicize" German law in order to make it more palatable to an English readership' means, in effect, that the English audience is (somewhat patronizingly) denied the experience of the *Germanness* of German law.[167] Indeed, the English readership is made to learn something which is emphatically *not* German law such as 'German tort law'.[168] This approach trivializes the specificity of another legal community's experience by confining it to the observer's own cognitive categories. It involves a manifest expulsion of the values of humility and deference from the relational framework between observer and observed showing the observer to be more interested in the vindication of his own *author-ity* than in the pursuit of ethical communicative action.[169] It is as if the proponents of this analytical framework had been reading US mathematician Warren Weaver: 'When I look at an article in Russian, I say: "This is really written in English, but it has been coded in some strange symbols. I will now proceed to decode".'[170] (Note that the way in which comparatists-at-law must allow the other to realize his vision of his world is not unlike the manner in which the translator must inscribe alterity at the heart of identity by accepting that the original presence of the guest language ought not to be effaced. If a translation aimed to look so 'natural' within the host

a problem in continental law by way of judicial decisions.' For a critique of the use of casebooks as pedagogical instruments for the study of the civil-law tradition, see Ewald, *supra*, note 68, pp. 1968–75. The basic antimony is captured by Samuel who notes that in the common law 'legal reasoning is a matter, not of applying pre-established legal rules as such [as in the civil law], but of pushing outwards from the facts': *Epistemology, supra*, note 143, p. 104.

[167] Gerhard Dannemann and Basil Markesinis, 'The Legacy of History on German Contract Law', in Ross Cranston (ed.), *Making Commercial Law: Essays in Honour of Roy Goode* (Oxford: Oxford University Press, 1997), p. 29. For a critique of Dannemann and Markesinis, see Roderick Munday, 'Book Review', [1998] Cambridge L.J. 222, pp. 222–3.

[168] Markesinis, *supra*, note 166.

[169] For a reply which strains credulity, see Basil Markesinis, 'Studying Judicial Decisions in the Common Law and the Civil Law: A Good Way of Discovering Some of the Most Interesting Similarities and Differences That Exist Between These Legal Families', in Mark Van Hoecke and François Ost (eds.), *The Harmonisation of European Private Law* (Oxford: Hart, 2000), p. 133. But see, for sophisticated reflections on the necessity of attending to alterity's specificity within the communicative and subsequent re-presentational process, Laurence Thomas, 'Moral Deference', (1992) 24 Philosophical Forum 233; Iris Marion Young, 'Asymmetrical Reciprocity: On Moral Respect, Wonder, and Enlarged Thought', (1997) 3 Constellations 340, p. 362, n. 11. For a noteworthy attempt to combat the degradation of communication and elucidate a language of comparison suitably respectful of the rich texture of indigenous experiences of law which would avoid any assertion of 'ownership' over them by the comparatist, see Ainsworth, *supra*, note 143.

[170] Warren Weaver, 'Translation', in William N. Locke and A. Donald Booth (eds.), *Machine Translation of Languages* (Cambridge, Mass.: MIT Press, 1955), p. 18.

language as no longer to appear like a translation, it would, ultimately, be refusing to grant hospitality to alterity. Rather, the translator adapts the host language in order to accommodate alterity and thus avoids denying the entitlement of alterity to exist as alterity – the point of translation being to allow a readership to partake in diversity which cannot, therefore, be obliterated lest the idea of translation itself be betrayed.[171] Indeed, Jacques Derrida perspicuously observes that 'for the notion of translation, one will have to substitute a notion of *transformation*: the regulated transformation of a language by another, of a text by another'. He adds: 'We will never have been involved and never have been involved in fact in the "transportation" of pure signifieds which the signifying instrument – or the "vehicle" – would leave intact and untouched, from one language to another.'[172] Translation does not aspire to a fulfilment of the original. As Walter Benjamin puts it, '[i]t is evident that no translation, however good it may be, can have any significance as regards the original.'[173] In other words, the idea is to apprehend translation not as purporting to achieve unity and truth in language – that is, neither as mere interpretation of the original text nor as mere departure or licence from the original – but rather as that which repudiates the reflexivity of representation – that which disrupts, decentres and displaces representation – through the multiplication and the constant renewal and the ultimate inexhaustibility of meanings and truths. Instead of falling within the logic of sameness, translation acts as an operator of difference; it has difference-creating power.[174])

---

[171] For a compelling argument along these lines, see Antoine Berman, *La traduction et la lettre ou l'auberge du lointain* (Paris: Le Seuil, 1999). Further reflection is offered in Alasdair MacIntyre, *Whose Justice? Which Rationality?* (Notre Dame: University of Notre Dame Press, 1988), pp. 370–88. A fascinating application of the 'linguistics of particularity' is found in A. L. Becker, *Beyond Translation* (Ann Arbor: University of Michigan Press, 1995), p. 71 and *passim*.

[172] Jacques Derrida, *Positions* (Paris: Editions de Minuit, 1972), p. 31 ['*à la notion de traduction, il faudra substituer une notion de* transformation: *transformation réglée d'une langue par une autre, d'un texte par un autre. Nous n'aurons et n'avons en fait jamais eu affaire à quelque "transport" de signifiés purs que l'instrument – ou le "véhicule" – signifiant laisserait vierge et inentamé, d'une langue à l'autre*'] (emphasis original). This statement was made in the context of an interview with Julia Kristeva. For an illuminating analysis of the way in which Derrida's own work was transformed upon being received in the United States, see Peter Goodrich, 'Europe in America: Grammatology, Legal Studies, and the Politics of Transmission', (2001) 101 Columbia L.R. 2033.

[173] Benjamin, 'The Task of the Translator', *supra*, note 134, p. 254. The German text reads: '*Daß eine Übersetzung niemals, so gut sie auch sei, etwas für das Original zu bedeuten vermag, leuchtet ein*': *id.*, 'Die Aufgabe des Übersetzers', *supra*, note 134, p. 10.

[174] See Stephen D. Ross, 'Translation as Transgression', in Dennis J. Schmidt (ed.), *Hermeneutics and Poetic Motion* (Binghamton: SUNY, 1990), pp. 25–42. I owe this citation to Simone

To appreciate the irrefragability of difference further allows comparatists to break the 'charmed circle' of functional inquiry,[175] that is, to move away from Zweigert and Kötz's proclamation that '[t]he basic methodological principle of all comparative [analysis of] law is that of functionality.'[176] Quite apart from the fact that there exist other 'schemes of intelligibility' and that it appears very strange to confine comparative legal studies to one methodological approach which would act as a kind of abecederian narrative,[177] it can only be described as simplistic to regard configurations from different legal cultures as partaking in sameness merely on account of the fact that they perform the 'same', subjectively ascribed, function. I argue that functionalism – a variation on the time-honoured theme of ethnocentric projection – has become unduly attractive as a variance reducer. For instance, it 'has no eye and no sensitivity for what is not formalized and not regulated under a given legal regime'.[178] Crucially, functional analysis lacks a critical vocation because it betrays a fundamentally technical perspective accounting for a view of comparative legal studies as essentially utilitarian.[179] Functionalism offers an application of the idea of formalization, which itself can prevail only if one is prepared to discard the concrete contents of experiences and values and, ultimately, to elide the concrete law (the law that unmarries one, that has one's children taken away from one, that has one lose one's house and so forth). In other words, functionalism is a mechanistic theory which says nothing about understanding. It represents 'a scientific extrapolation and abstract accentuation

---

Glanert. With specific reference to law, this point is compellingly developed in Kasirer, 'Lexicographie', *supra*, note 143; *id.*, 'François Gény's *libre recherche scientifique* as a Guide for Legal Translation', (2001) 61 Louisiana L.R. 331.

[175] Walter Goldschmidt, *Comparative Functionalism* (Berkeley: University of California Press, 1966), p. 14.

[176] Zweigert and Kötz, *supra*, note 15, p. 34.

[177] Anyone who believes that there are no sophisticated alternatives to functional analysis could have attended with great profit a series of lectures which Professor Nicholas Kasirer delivered at the Université Panthéon-Sorbonne in February and March 2002. In the course of his presentations, Professor Kasirer examined and compared the French and English law on altruism not at all in functional terms, but by exploring how law is re-presented in a Norman McLaren film and, conversely, how law represents biblical texts in its ordinary modes of expression. For aspects of this fascinating argument, see Kasirer, 'Agapè', *supra*, note 143. For a non-exhaustive list of five alternatives to functionalism, see Samuel, *supra*, note 143, pp. 301–20 [discussing Jean-Michel Berthelot, *Les vertus de l'incertitude* (Paris: Presses Universitaires de France, 1996), pp. 78–82].

[178] Frankenberg, *supra*, note 114, p. 438.

[179] See Jonathan Hill, 'Comparative Law, Law Reform and Legal Theory', (1989) 9 Oxford J. Leg. Stud. 101, pp. 106–7.

of *one aspect* of a phenomenon simply because it has been thought through *in this form*.[180] Accordingly, 'the functionalist focus on the law's practical consequences neglects much of what might profitably be included as the object of comparative research'.[181] Alan Hunt's conclusion follows: 'the universalism claimed by functionalism is an unsupported assertion which carries the dangerous implication of being likely to result in the misleading imposition of uniformity upon the diversity of social reality.'[182]

The insistence on the values of alterity and authenticity must also lead the comparatist to accept that there is still, in each of the two main legal traditions represented within the European Community, an irreducible element of autochthony constraining the epistemological receptivity to globalization and fostering instead various forms of 'glocalization'.[183] It must further cause the comparatist to welcome the extent to which the syncretization at play at the European level has prompted a revitalization of the national legal heritage, a heightening of legal and cultural self-consciousness. The fact that fragments of local discourse now have their origin elsewhere does not mean that 'transnational culture' has displaced the 'traditionary culture' with

---

[180] Karl Mannheim, *Ideology and Utopia*, transl. by Louis Wirth and Edward Shils (New York: Harcourt Brace Jovanovich, 1936), p. 19 [my emphasis]. See also M. B. Hooker, *Legal Pluralism* (Oxford: Oxford University Press, 1975), p. 42: 'a demonstration in similarity in function [...] does not necessarily imply the same supporting epistemology.'

[181] Hyland, *supra*, note 13, p. 188. For a general critique of functionalism, see *id.*, pp. 188–9. See also Großfeld, *supra*, note 114, p. 10; David J. Gerber, 'System Dynamics: Toward a Language of Comparative Law?', (1998) 46 Am. J. Comp. L. 719, p. 722, who remarks on the 'deracination' process generated by functional analysis.

[182] Alan Hunt, *The Sociological Movement in Law* (London: Macmillan, 1978), p. 53. See also Fletcher, *supra*, note 76, p. 350: 'There are differences among the legal systems of the industrial world which are greater than they appear to the functionalist eye. [...] If everyone is inclined to protect tort plaintiffs, or impose pollution controls, we are inclined to believe that we are all doing the right thing. But this functional resemblance [...] remains superficial unless we know the doctrinal depths from which the instances of convergence emanate.'

[183] Roland Robertson, 'Glocalization: Time-Space and Homogeneity-Heterogeneity', in Mike Featherstone, Scott Lash and *id.* (eds.), *Global Modernities* (London: Sage, 1995), pp. 25–44. For a relevant demonstration, see Teubner, *supra*, note 143, where the author shows, on my reading of his argument, that even as the legal notion of 'good faith' is being 'globalized', cultural embeddedness continues to be strong such that the German model cannot be transferred to Great Britain because it is linked to a specific production regime – what is referred to as 'Rhineland capitalism'. *Cf*. Yves Dezalay and Bryant G. Garth, *Dealing in Virtue: International Commercial Arbitration and the Construction of a Transnational Legal Order* (Chicago: University of Chicago Press, 1996), p. 317, who, writing with specific reference to the field of transnational commercial dispute resolution and addressing the matter of its influence on national laws, observe that 'the impact of internationalization is not automatic or determined in advance.' For an exploration of some of the limits of globalization, see generally James Clifford, *The Predicament of Culture* (Cambridge, Mass.: Harvard University Press, 1988), pp. 1–17. *Cf.* Seyla Benhabib, *The Claims of Culture* (Princeton: Princeton University Press, 2002).

which it mixes and upon which it is superimposed. As a leading naturalist reminds us, '[c]ulture conforms to an important principle of evolutionary biology: most change occurs to maintain the organism in its steady state.'[184] 'Traditionary cultures' remain extraordinarily impervious to disruption so that the civil-law and common-law traditions in Europe can, even today, hardly be reduced to their cosmopolitan facets. By linking the civil-law and common-law traditions, the Treaty of Rome has in fact dramatized their historically rooted cognitive disconnections.[185] Propinquity has made possible a new awareness of epistemological difference – which helps to verify one of Heidegger's fundamental arguments regarding the connection between 'existence' and 'temporality'.[186] As a shared legal framework, far from eradicating the *summa differentia* between the two legal traditions, exacerbates it by sharpening its contours, the focus on alterity demonstrates that it is unjustifiable to advocate the jettisoning of Europe's cultural heterogeneity in the name of an instrumental re-invention of Europeanism dictated by the ethos of capital and technology (and the pathological fear of the ungovernability of ambiguity). I claim that the convergence thesis effectively perpetuates a brand of 'rightwing Hegelianism [which] conceals a stark downgrading of historical contingency and human freedom'.[187] It represents an attack on pluralism, a desire to suppress antinomy, an attempt at the diminution of particularity, a will to erase cultural memory in a context where the two main legal traditions within the European Community

---

[184] Edward O. Wilson, *In Search of Nature* (London: Allen Lane, 1997), p. 107. Social economists refer to the way in which cultures continue to articulate their moral inquiry according to traditional standards of justification as 'path dependence'. For example, see Douglass C. North, *Institutions, Institutional Change and Economic Performance* (Cambridge: Cambridge University Press, 1990), pp. 92–100. See also Mark Granovetter, 'Economic Action and Social Structure: The Problem of Embeddedness', (1985) 91 Am. J. Socio. 481. See generally Cass R. Sunstein (ed.), *Behavioral Law and Economics* (Cambridge: Cambridge University Press, 2000).

[185] Arguably, this situation offers an instance of a wider cultural phenomenon. The intensity of contact among cultural groups often has the paradoxical consequence that it stimulates cultural diversity by confirming group members in their own identity. See Geert Hofstede, *Cultures and Organizations* (London: McGraw-Hill, 1991), p. 238. *Cf.* Feyerabend, *supra*, note 49, p. 274: 'It is true that nations and groups within a society frequently establish some kind of contact, but it is not true that in doing this they create, or assume, a "common metadiscourse" or a common cultural bond.' For a reflection on the production of locality in a globalizing world, see Arjun Appadurai, *Modernity at Large* (Minneapolis: University of Minnesota Press, 1996), pp. 188–99.

[186] Heidegger's words are that 'the meaning of Dasein [human existence] is temporality': *Being and Time, supra*, note 48, p. 380. For the German text, see *id., Sein und Zeit, supra*, note 48, p. 331 ['*der Sinn des Daseins ist die Zeitlichkeit*']. See also Merleau-Ponty, *supra*, note 46, p. 475.

[187] Roberto Mangabeira Unger, *What Should Legal Analysis Become?* (London: Verso, 1996), p. 9. See also *id.*, pp. 72–3 and 76–7.

can best be regarded as epistemic peers, serving equally well by catering to their respective communities' specific historical needs. Indeed, 'the *duty* to answer the call of European memory dictates respect for difference, the idiomatic, the minority, the singular and commands to tolerate and respect everything that does not place itself under the authority of reason.'[188] And 'this responsibility toward memory is a responsibility toward the concept of responsibility itself which regulates the justice and the justness of our behaviour, of our theoretical, practical, ethico-political decisions.'[189] The convergence thesis thus appears as an entirely ahistorical, even antihistorical, argument.

The priority of alterity, in sum, makes it acceptable that complete *Ordnung* should lie beyond one's grasp.[190] It indicates that 'whatever conclusions [the comparative study of law] comes to must relate to the management of difference not to the abolition of it.'[191] Moreover, it illustrates how the comparatist must discard one specific approach to the management of difference aptly described as 'better-law' comparison. To argue, as does the principal text in the field,[192] that comparative legal studies must aim to find the 'better solution' reflects confusion and complacency. Consider the following passage from that book: 'the [English, French, and German] systems attach different legal consequences to the issuance of an offer. [...] The critic is forced to conclude that on this point the German system is best.'[193] Is the suggestion, to quote again from the *Unidroit Principles*, that the German law of 'offer' is to be preferred '*irrespective* of the legal traditions

---

[188] Jacques Derrida, *L'autre cap* (Paris: Editions de Minuit, 1991), pp. 75–7 ['*le devoir de répondre à l'appel de la mémoire européenne* (...) *dicte de respecter la différence, l'idiome, la minorité, la singularité* (... *et*) *commande de tolérer et de respecter tout ce qui ne se place pas sous l'autorité de la raison*'] (emphasis original).

[189] Id., *Force de loi* (Paris: Galilée, 1994), p. 45 ['*Cette responsabilité devant la mémoire est une responsabilité devant le concept même de responsabilité qui règle la justice et la justesse de nos comportements, de nos décisions théoriques, pratiques, éthico-politiques*'].

[190] As I make this point, it is only fair to note that the question of how far one can take the notion of 'difference' does not detain me here. My view is that there exists a fundamental and irreducible epistemological difference across legal traditions which is massively more significant for comparative legal studies than any similarity at the level of posited law across legal 'systems'. For its part, Sacco's theory of 'legal formants' addresses the matter of differences concerning the formulation of posited law *within* legal 'systems' themselves. See Rodolfo Sacco, 'Legal Formants: A Dynamic Approach to Comparative Law', (1991) 39 Am. J. Comp. L. 1 & 343. For some of the questions which inevitably arise if one pursues the matter further and asks oneself, for instance, whether there is a French 'accent' in music or whether Americans drive with an 'American' touch, see Douglas R. Hofstadter, *Le Ton beau de Marot* (London: Bloomsbury, 1997), pp. 40–1 and 284.

[191] Clifford Geertz, *Local Knowledge* (New York: Basic Books, 1983), pp. 215–16.

[192] Zweigert and Kötz, *supra*, note 15, p. 15.   [193] *Id.*, p. 362.

and the economic and political conditions of the countries in which [it is] to be applied'?[194] But how can a law be 'good' or 'better' *in and of itself*? Is it not the case that a law can only be more or less successfully responsive to particular circumstances or be more or less influential in a given environment? And how can the comparatist ever make it his business to operate a 'ranking' of different laws or experiences of law, promoting some and demoting others? Rather, comparative legal studies must favour an ecumenical appreciation of what are but equal evidential claims made by diverse laws on the world. Moreover, the advocacy of 'better-law' comparative legal studies reveals at least two fundamental contradictions in its leading proponents' own theoretical framework. First, how can it be simultaneously asserted that 'legal systems give the same or very similar solutions, even as to detail, to the same problems of life' *and* that comparatists need to identify the 'better' law, a process which must assume the repeated presence of difference across laws?[195] Second, how can it be stated that comparatists must 'insist on purely objective requirements' as they compare the various laws *and* choose the 'better' law?[196]

* * *

To stress difference's *vis affirmativa*, that is, to insist on the value of difference as non-negativity or complementarity (in the sense in which different languages concur in the quest for an understanding of what we call 'reality') is to encourage oppositional discourse in the face of a strategic and totalitarian rationality which, while claiming to pursue the ideal of impartiality by reducing differences in the *Lebenswelt* to calculative and instrumental unity, effectively privileges a situated perspective (the observer's own), which it allows to project as universal. The comparatist must accept, rather than attempt to evade, the necessarily contingent – and, ultimately, determinative – character of cognitive points of departure across legal traditions. To do otherwise, that is, to relegate the cognitive asymmetries between the civil-law and common-law worlds to ignorable differences, to the realm of epiphenomena, is superficial and shows confusion between the legitimate desire to overcome barriers of communication across legal traditions and

---

[194] *Unidroit Principles, supra*, at text accompanying note 32 [my emphasis].
[195] Zweigert and Kötz, *supra*, note 15, p. 39.
[196] *Id.*, p. 44. I argue that comparatists need to dispense with the idea of 'objectivity'. In recognition of the fact that extrication by the comparatist from his circumstances is impossible, comparative legal studies must privilege a reflexive epistemology and foster 'reflection' as a valid category of discovery.

the presumptuous fabrication of 'black-letter' sameness severed from all its constitutive contexts. Insensitivity to questions of cultural heterogeneity fails to do justice to the situated, local properties of knowledge, which are no less powerful because they may remain inchoate and uninstitutionalized. In the way it refuses to address plurijurality at the deep, cultural level, the rhetoric of legal convergence advocated by comparatists simply forfeits intercultural and epistemological validity. The immediate goal, therefore, must be to move toward a variation on what feminists refer to as 'standpoint epistemology' – a standpoint implying a keen awareness of the material and social circumstances under which knowledge emerges and, thus, being understood as 'a hard-won product of consciousness-raising and social-political engagement' as regards the fabrication of knowledge-claims, which insists not only on context, but also on contextualization or complexification of context, that is, on the particularization of the social and institutional practices within which knowledge is formed or produced.[197] Not unlike women, comparatists must attempt to struggle out of their characteristic – and characteristically, in their case, rule-oriented – social position and condition.

* * *

Note that in the quest for thick or deep understanding, the comparatist must maintain alterity in its specificity while at all times avoiding the tendency to essentialize it. I repeat that I am emphatically not in search of uniquely original essences, either to restore them or to set them in a place of unimpeachable honour. It is not that a civilian, for instance, can never

---

[197] The quotation is from Lorraine Code, 'Epistemology', in Alison M. Jaggar and Iris Marion Young (eds.), *A Companion to Feminist Philosophy* (Oxford: Blackwell, 1998), p. 180. For a useful primer, see Alessandra Tanesini, *An Introduction to Feminist Epistemologies* (Oxford: Blackwell, 1999), pp. 138–59. A leading advocate of standpoint epistemology is Sandra Harding, *Whose Science? Whose Knowledge?* (Ithaca: Cornell University Press, 1991), pp. 119–37 and 165–81. An insightful application to law is offered by Joanne Conaghan, 'Reassessing the Feminist Theoretical Project in Law', (2000) 27 J. L. & Society 351. For a critical overview, see Diemut Bubeck, 'Feminism in Political Philosophy: Women's Difference', in Miranda Fricker and Jennifer Hornsby (eds.), *The Cambridge Companion to Feminism in Philosophy* (Cambridge: Cambridge University Press, 2000), pp. 186–91. These various texts show, however, that the assumptions underlying standpoint epistemology cannot be imported wholesale by comparative legal studies. Yet, one can argue that the other-in-the-law must be endowed with something like an epistemic privilege, such that his theorization of 'reality' is granted most significant – albeit non-exclusive – status. The reason why the epistemic privileging cannot be exclusive is, of course, because any group can be deceived about itself and that not even the experiences of suffering or resistance, therefore, guarantee lucid knowledge of self. I am grateful to Joanne Conaghan for calling my attention to standpoint epistemology.

understand the English legal experience – or that a man can never understand womanhood.[198] Rather, the point is that a civilian can never understand the English legal experience *like an English lawyer* because he cannot interpret it from within the culture itself. Understanding there can be, but a *different* understanding it will *have to* be since the civilian cannot *inhabit* English legal culture: English law is something that the civilian observes while it is something that the English lawyer lives through. Note that this *décalage* between understanding and what is the case (for the English lawyer) is indeed crucial if the alterity of the other is to be preserved and if the other's self-understanding (and *Selbstvorverständnis*) is to be critiqued.[199]

Not only does comparative-legal-studies-as-difference not entail essentialism, but it does not even posit a number of stable categories, discrete and monolithic heritages organically tied to specific homelands and considered best kept separate. In this respect, Clifford Geertz draws a helpful distinction between 'difference' and 'dichotomy': '[a difference] is a comparison and it relates; [a dichotomy] is a severance and it isolates.'[200] Hence, Philip Larkin's verse: 'Insisting so on difference, made me welcome:/ Once that was recognised, we were in touch.'[201] I want to stress that the prioritization of difference does not deny their cosmopolitanism to the legal communities being studied. In other words, a focus on difference does not connote nationalism, imperialism, colonialism or isolationism, that is, something like 'cultural fundamentalism'; on the contrary, it very much allows for a transnational public sphere. Nor does comparative-legal-studies-as-differential-analysis-of-juriscultures – or differential comparison of juriscultures – challenge the complex, conflicted and mobile nature of identity. Nor, a fortiori, does it connote ethnicity or race. The fact that the concept of 'difference' can be abused by those who exaggerate the patterning of human action and fall for stereotypical or overdetermined knowledge, the fact that 'difference' may be mobilized in support of sexism and racism, the fact that even such an

---

[198] For an influential apprehension of the epistemological relevance of gender, see Carol Gilligan, *In a Different Voice*, 2d ed. (Cambridge, Mass.: Harvard University Press, 1993). See generally Mary Field Belenky *et al.*, *Women's Ways of Knowing*, 2d ed. (New York: Basic Books, 1997).

[199] Levinas argues that, strictly speaking, a relationship with the other must be a relation without a relation. This is because although an encounter takes place, it does not establish understanding. See Levinas, *supra*, note 74, pp. 79 and 329.

[200] Clifford Geertz, *After the Fact* (Cambridge, Mass.: Harvard University Press, 1995), p. 28. For difference-as-relation, see also Luce Irigaray, *J'aime à toi* (Paris: Grasset, 1992), p. 133.

[201] Larkin, *supra*, note 129, p. 104.

extreme event as the Holocaust – undoubtedly the pre-eminent example of discriminatory practice in recent history – can be regarded as a form of 'differencing', hardly justifies jettisoning 'difference' as an investigative precept. Who would consider no longer resorting to the word 'democracy' because the USSR abused it for much of the twentieth century?

* * *

Today's comparatists in law faculties everywhere, perhaps especially in Europe, are expected to subscribe to a script of underlying unity and transcendent universalism where particularism is assumed to be secondary and fated to play but a peripheral role in the future of human affairs. It is easy to sympathize with the desire for a more orderly, circumscribed world. The obsession to find and impose order possibly answers a most basic human drive. But it is quite another thing to underwrite the search for a monistic unifying pattern not unlike the Platonic or Hegelian belief in a final rational harmony, that is, to endorse reason acting as the corrosive solvent of custom and allegiance. And this is why the programmatic engagement that I advocate for comparative legal studies requires post-Cartesian, post-idealist, post-foundationalist moves that will resist the attempts of conservative academics to reduce alterity to sameness by way of sterile facilitations reminiscent of the *Begriff*-stricken world of nineteenth-century scholarship.

Comparison must not have a unifying, but a multiplying effect.[202] It must stand athwart the self-deluding investment in the excision of the incommensurable. It must avoid complicity in the disregard for different ways of doing things and the ensuing exclusion of alterity, in the refusal to recognize other worlds as other worlds. It must aim at organizing the diversity of discourses around different (cultural) forms and counter the intellectual tendency toward assimilation as already identified by Vico who observed

---

[202] For example, see Jerome Hall, *Comparative Law and Social Theory* (Baton Rouge: Louisiana State University Press, 1963), pp. 48–9, who contends that comparative analysis of law is concerned with 'the delineation of differences against a background of similarities'; Rodolfo Sacco, *Introduzione al diritto comparato*, 5th ed. (Turin: UTET, 1992), p. 11, who observes that 'comparison consists in measuring the differences which exist across a multiplicity of legal models' ['*la comparazione consiste nel misurare le differenze che esistono tra una molteplicità di modelli giuridici*']; Richard L. Abel, 'Comparative Law and Social Theory', (1978) 26 Am. J. Comp. L. 219, p. 220, who argues that '[c]omparison, whether spatial or temporal, allows us to measure differences in the values of our variables – an essential step in formulating and testing hypotheses.' See generally Carol Harlow, 'Voices of Difference in a Plural Community', (2002) 50 Am. J. Comp. L. 339.*Cf*. Gilles Deleuze and Claire Parnet, *Dialogues*, 2d ed. (Paris: Flammarion, 1996), p. 179: 'Philosophy is the theory of multiplicities' ['*La philosophie est la théorie des multiplicités*']. The words are Deleuze's.

that '[t]he human mind naturally tends to take delight in what is uniform.'[203] (That the proponents of uniformization of law aim at the crushing of the indissoluble in the grey crucible of oneness is, of course, crisply expressed in the *Unidroit Principles*.[204]) The comparatist must emphatically rebut any attempt at the extravagant axiomatization of sameness. I argue that comparatists need to recall how the diversity of legal traditions and the diversity of forms of life-in-the-law these traditions embody remain the expression of the human capacity for choice and self-creation, that is, how the differences at issue are not just superficial or technical distinctions but play a constituting role in shaping cultural identity. The (perhaps unelucidated) attachment to a familiar legal tradition must be appreciated as a legitimate and often vital aspect of social existence which, as it helps to define selfhood, deserves to be respected.[205] Not to be prepared to accommodate this fact, not to give legal communities and individuals within these communities their historical due, is necessarily to assimilate human beings within one legal tradition to a different way of speaking and acting and to another notion of *what makes sense*; it is to expect men and women to undergo a religious conversion – something which may not even be *possible*; it is to engage in an act of *totalization* that *neutralizes* the other. Comparison must, therefore, grasp legal cultures *diacritically* (which, once again, need *not* entail an essentialist or fundamentalist understanding of identity). Charles Taylor offers useful guidance: 'the adequate language in which we can understand another society is not our language of understanding, or theirs, but rather what one could call a language of perspicuous contrast.'[206] Ultimately, because difference conditions identity, comparatists must indeed argue that only in *deferring* to the non-identical can the claim to justice be redeemed – a commitment which finds a pithy expression in the exigent work of the Spanish poet Antonio Machado: 'All the efforts of human reason tend to the elimination of [the other]. The other does not exist: such is rational

---

[203] Giambattista Vico, *New Science*, transl. and ed. by David Marsh (London: Penguin, 2001), bk I, sec. 2, no. 47, p. 92 [1744]. I have modified the translation slightly. For the original text, see *id.*, *Principi di scienza nuova*, in *Opere*, ed. by Fausto Nicolini (Milan: Riccardo Ricciardi, 1953), p. 452 ['*La mente umana è naturalmente portata a dilettarsi dell'uniforme*'].
[204] *Supra*, at text accompanying note 32.
[205] As Gadamer observes, tradition is not 'something other, something alien'. Rather, '[i]t is always part of us': *supra*, note 48, p. 282. As regards the second quotation, the German text reads: '*es ist immer schon ein Eigenes*': *id.*, *supra*, note 148, p. 286.
[206] Charles Taylor, *Philosophy and the Human Sciences: Philosophical Papers 2* (Cambridge: Cambridge University Press, 1985), p. 125.

faith, the incurable belief of human reason. Identity = reality, as if, in the end, everything must absolutely and necessarily be one and the same. But the other refuses to disappear: it subsists, it persists; it is the hard bone on which reason breaks its teeth. [There is] what might be called the incurable otherness from which oneness must always suffer.'[207]

* * *

I disagree with fellow comparatists who dismiss the argument for differential comparison as something like a diversionary move into obsolescence.[208] I also disagree with those who condemn it as a brand of methodological 'extremism' – a time-honoured, 'low-cost', marginalization and silencing strategy.[209] I trust I have shown that my claim to change the way in which comparative legal studies is performed is neither spurious nor excessive and I am prepared to let my paper speak for itself on both counts. After all, the condition of the comparatist is primordially being-toward-another-law, such that the notion of 'relation' must lie at the heart of any comparative endeavour. Now, we know that '[relation] secures the difference of things, their singularity.'[210] In my view, therefore, the most important objection to my plea for a new comparative ethics can only lie elsewhere. In arguing for the prioritization of difference, am I not reproducing the totalitarian thinking from which I am trying to escape? Am I not relapsing into transcendental thinking? My answer is that the way toward the singularity of the law, which is a thinking of diversity or cosmopolitanism, which is a thinking of justice, cannot be equated to a totalitarian strategy, except in the most formal (and, therefore, meaningless) sense of the term. Far from partaking in a totalitarian strategy, in fact, differential thinking is characterized by its thorough immanence to actualized, real and, therefore, discontinuous experience, such that if difference is denied, it is life and existence themselves that are denied. Therefore, differential thinking attests to 'a gnawing sense of unfulfilledness, [an] endemic dissatisfaction with itself'. It is 'haunted by

---

[207] Antonio Machado, 'Juan de Mairena – Sentencias, donaires, apuntes y recuerdos de un profesor apócrifo', in *Poesía y prosa*, ed. by Oreste Macrì, t. IV: *Prosas completas (1936–39)* (Madrid: Espasa-Calpe, 1989), II, p. 1917 ['De lo uno a lo otro (...). Todo el trabajo de la fe racional humana tiende a la eliminación del segundo término. Lo otro no existe: tal es la fe racional, la incurable creencia de la razón humana. Identidad = realidad, como si, a fin de cuentas, todo hubiera de ser, absoluta y necesariamente, uno y lo mismo. Pero lo otro *no se deja eliminar: subsiste, persiste*; es el hueso duro de roer en que la razón se deja los dientes. (...) como si dijéramos en la incurable otredad *que padece lo* uno'] (emphasis original).

[208] For example, see Lawrence Rosen's contribution to this book.

[209] For example, see David Kennedy's contribution to this book.

[210] Gasché, *supra*, note 151, p. 10.

the suspicion' that it is never differential *enough* – an anxiety hardly compatible with the reification that must accompany any totalizing frame.[211]

* * *

Perhaps aspects of the argument can usefully be (ampliatively) summarized at this stage. I accept that there is an important sense in which the binary distinction between sameness and difference, like all binary distinctions, must itself be rejected: to describe the other as different from the self implies a knowledge of the other by the self which, ultimately, must deny the other's position as other. Against the background of this aporia, some philosophers have sought to elaborate a non-dialectical theory of difference by developing a concept that never could have been, and never could be, included within the habitual hierarchy and that would, therefore, take us beyond it – I have in mind, for example, Derrida's idea of '*différance*'.[212] I need not follow this route, if only because my concern is not so much to abandon the idea of 'sameness' as to reject the exclusive way in which it has been constituted by comparatists. I react to the fact that, largely since the 1900s, a powerful disciplinarian regime within the field of comparative legal studies, through a repeated assertion of enabling discursive power addressing law exclusively in terms of 'itself', despite the evidence of much broader relationships, and through an insistent denial of the overwhelming weight of a past time, has established this mobile positioning into a fixity by proving eager to strap its interpretations to the Procrustean bed of sameness. This approach has followed the modernist tradition, within which difference is conceived as chaotic on Kantian and neo-Kantian grounds and is apprehended as a flaw or as a fault line, at best as an anxiogenic form of indeterminacy. But, '[w]hat we differentiate will appear divergent, dissonant, negative for just as long as the structure of our consciousness obliges it to strive for unity: as long as its demand for totality will be its measure for whatever is not identical with it.'[213] I argue that the constant repetition of the all-encompassing principle of sameness as a re-presentation of desire within the law is not innocent, that it conceals as much as it reveals, that it is analytically comparable to trauma. I argue that the seemingly inexorable logic of sameness – ultimately moving from *ipse* to *idem* (that is, from 'similarity', which is, after all, a form

---

[211] I adopt and adapt Bauman, *supra*, note 36, p. 80.   [212] *Supra*, note 156.
[213] Adorno, *supra*, note 4, pp. 5–6. For the original text, see *id.*, *supra*, note 40, p. 17 ['Das Differenzierte erscheint so lange divergent, dissonant, negativ, wie das Bewußtsein der eigenen Formation nach auf Einheit drängen muß: solange es, was nicht mit ihm identisch ist, an seinem Totalitätsanspruch mißt'].

of difference, to 'sameness') – hides an active subjectivity which, at the very least, takes the form of a love of order, of an affection for normativity (must not one assume responsibility for the tendency of one's political truth?). Yet, like all desire, the desire for oneness-in-the-law must ultimately fail because it focuses on an impossible object which can exist only as a condensed or abstract version of itself, that is, as something which it is not in fact. The point is, therefore, to avoid the cultural fusionism which 'permits [...] the other of the "own" culture or the other of "culture" *tout court*, to be perceived no longer in its alterity but only as a variant of one's own culture [and further] permits treating one's own culture as a homogeneous, given fact, ignoring its internal tensions, contradictions, and struggles, and giving oneself over to the fantasy that it is a logical continuum without history and does not always *also* contain the demand to transform that history'.[214] The point is to displace the precedence of (purported) sameness-in-the-law in order to show that behind the mask of universality lies a differentiation which has been repressed and which, although unsettling to the dominant and dogmatic discourse, can be recovered in its expressive and excessive dimensions. The point is to reject a topology and propose a topography. The point is to analyse the specific as the specific. The point is to foster hyperawareness. The point is, rather than impose a framework upon something, to derive a framework from something. The point is to impel the comparatist toward an ethical encounter with the other-in-the law.

If only because it is not a standard feature of laws to project their comprehensibility (or their validity) beyond situational barriers, laws (or the seriality of laws) mark a disjunction. As they encounter such a gap, comparatists immediately try to close it, to recuperate it into some form of coherent meaning by resorting to some rhetorical strategy. Ultimately, comparatists cannot bear too much 'reality', that is, they cannot accept that their clarity of vision should find itself threatened on account of instability and fluidity: 'The *prescription* of [their] ideal operates, implicitly or explicitly, by delicate or brutal means, the *proscription* of whatever does not conform to it.'[215] Consider the omission of any mention whatsoever of Gunther Teubner's work in Reinhard Zimmermann and Simon Whittaker's 750-page book on 'good faith' – an extremely audacious gesture.[216] Difference appears as

---

[214] Hamacher, *supra*, note 7, p. 324 [emphasis original].   [215] *Id.*, p. 293 [emphasis original].
[216] I refer to Teubner, *supra*, note 143, being ignored in Reinhard Zimmermann and Simon Whittaker (eds.), *Good Faith in European Contract Law* (Cambridge: Cambridge University Press, 2000).

something contingent, a quality of the merely empirical existent, a disturbance, a pre-eminent disturbance of a universal law. Therefore, comparatists resort to assimilation in order to maintain an imaginary which seems threatened, that is, they employ a strategy of narrativization inviting the reader into identification with a position of coherent and unified vision and into the narcissistic pleasures that go with this. The narrative is made to contain the narrated, the signifier is made to contain the signified. As comparatists produce a narrative space for a specific 'totalization' effect (which yields enjoyment for the comparatist),[217] this narrative space itself produces the comparatists in the sense that it acts as a condition of the comparative work's possibility. Reinhard Zimmermann, Ugo Mattei, Christian von Bar, Basil Markesinis and other *conquérants* – unreconstructed Kelsenians seeking to out-Kelsen Kelsen? – thus fearing a gap in their seamless apprehension of the world (and fearing the questioning of the canonical heritage that institutes them, through patterns of domination and, yes, repression, into the jurists they are and that structures how they re-present the world), proceed in such a way that their imaginary projects onto 'reality' with a view to minimizing the difference between fiction and non-fiction. Difference itself becomes annulled in a homogeneous whole of the differents and is converted into an ultimate sameness. The goal is to tame the gaze of the other – to deny the other's voice epistemic authority – in order to assuage one's own anxious compulsion to be oneself (possibly as a result of the realization that the 'I' cannot see as the other sees, that the 'I' cannot escape the unique point of view from which he sees). How does this surreptitious (and seemingly paradoxical) strategy operate? In Europe, the basic idea is to achieve the self-cancellation of the common law via its opposite, different other. Thus, forgetting that the question is not whether one legal tradition or the other is primordial, but how legal traditions become what they are in their respective difference, Zimmermann refers to the 'European' character of English law – a kind of cannibalistic violence which is the opposite of apositionality.[218]

---

[217] For Levinas, transmutation of otherness into sameness is, in fact, the essence of enjoyment. See Levinas, *supra*, note 74, p. 113.

[218] Zimmermann, *supra*, note 65. This point, of course, assumes the common law's waywardness. But Samuel argues that, contrary to the view which is prone to highlighting the common law's abnormality *vis-à-vis* the civil law, one can regard common-law developments as more 'normal' than what happened in civil-law jurisdictions where medieval jurists made the unlikely decision to adopt as authority an antiquated and foreign text. See Samuel, *Epistemology*, *supra*, note 143, pp. 36 and 310–11 [referring to R. C. Van Caenegem].

According to this very restricted concept, difference is determined by a relation of equalization purporting to cancel terms standing against each other. Here, the interest is in eliminating, through a reciprocal equalizing out of differences, difference itself: inclusion is really disguised exclusion. Rather than emancipate itself from identity, difference eclipses itself and yields to sameness again, to unity, to totality. In other words, difference is made to promote identity; awareness of alterity leads to self-conscious affirmation (rather than to interpellation of self). The seen becomes a scene: there emerges a space of simultaneity, all laws are co-present, the comparatist can move from one to another, from another to one, relating things, judging, knowing.[219] Without needing to argue that every difference is morally salient and without purporting to exoticize difference as absolutely 'other', I reject this syncretism, this sublation of opposites, this spurious synthesis, this annulment of contradictions, this assimilation to a formal principle of equality, this kind of Hegelian *Aufhebung*, and I argue for the need to engage in a process of interior edification, a *Bildungsprozeß*, leading to the realization that the interval that marks the (non-hierarchical) proximity between beings-in-the-law need not be apprehended as an empty void or an opaque space, but that it can be 'occupied' with wonder, attraction, admiration, desire – or, let us say, with something like *recognition*, that is, with the institution of a 'nonobjectifying and nonpossessive relation to the mysterious self-disclosure of others'.[220] To paraphrase Benjamin, comparative legal studies demands a *now of recognition*,[221] which involves a crucial shifting of the balance from repression to recognition.

The singularity of the singular is best appreciated – indeed, can only be appreciated – when failure of desingularization is encountered. (Think of translation which, being particularly attuned to the duplicity of the signifier,

---

[219] See Emmanuel Levinas, *Autrement qu'être ou au-delà de l'essence* (Paris: Le Livre de Poche, [n.d.]), p. 247 [1978].
[220] Huntington, *supra*, note 4, p. 17. For an argument derived from 'admiration' based on Descartes, see Luce Irigaray, *Ethique de la différence sexuelle* (Paris: Editions de Minuit, 1984), pp. 75–84. In any event, it is clear that positive encouragement of alterity requires more than mere tolerance since to tolerate the other's view means to apprehend it as coming toward one's own truth.
[221] See Walter Benjamin, *The Arcades Project*, ed. by Rolf Tiedemann and transl. by Howard Eiland and Kevin McLaughlin (Cambridge, Mass.: Harvard University Press, 1999), pp. 463 and 473 [Convolutes N 3,1 and N 9,7] (1927–40) [hereinafter *Arcades Project*]. For the German edition, see *id.*, *Gesammelte Schriften*, ed. by Rolf Tiedemann, vol. V: *Das Passagen-Werk*, t. 1 (Frankfurt: Suhrkamp, 1982), pp. 578 and 591–2 ['*im Jetzt der Erkennbarkeit*'] (hereinafter *Passagen-Werk*). The expression also appears in correspondence. For example, see a letter from Benjamin to Gretel Adorno in *id.*, t. 2, p. 1148 ['*Jetzt's der Erkennbarkeit*'] (9 October 1935).

shows, perhaps more strikingly than other linguistic processes, that no word exhausts that which is being described and that nothing which is being described goes into a word without leaving a remainder.) Any encounter worth the name, therefore, must assume encountering the other in all the other's singularity and recognizing this singularity (which, of course, requires wrenching it from a minimal horizon of non-singular intelligibility in the first place, if only because appearance of identity is inherent in thought itself). The idea, therefore, is for cognition to bow to concretion, the goal is to move judgement from received certainties to disturbing experiences, that is, from a cognitive to a re-cognitive ground which, because it implies an acknowledgement (in the sense of giving one the recognition that is solicited and deserved or in the related sense of giving a speaker a voice), is also an ethical, political and hermeneutic ground. But, '[i]n order for the recognition of the other to be possible, there must first be respect for the other.'[222] In the words of Seyla Benhabib, '[n]either the concreteness nor the otherness of the "concrete other" can be known in the absence of the *voice* of the other' – who remains entitled to refuse derivation from self.[223] This is why comparatists-at-law must purposively resort to quotations which, because they constitute 'the ultimate accomplishment of the mimetic or representational process',[224] validate and accredit the discourse of the other, that is, produce enhanced reliability by allowing the other to be *as such* and thereby foster a measure of equipollence between their and the other's experiences. (*Quaere*: does the comparison *par excellence* not consist of a montage of one quotation next to another?)[225] Nothing in this strategy denies, of course, that the carving of a quotation remains a function of the observer's choice, a fact which raises the matter of the fidelity to the observed's thought and, indeed, that of the integrity of the process as a whole. For instance, does the observed, through the quotation, assume ethical responsibility, or rather co-responsibility, for the re-presentation?

[222] Hamacher, *supra*, note 7, p. 323.
[223] Seyla Benhabib, *Situating the Self* (Cambridge: Polity Press, 1992), p. 168 [emphasis original].
[224] Louis Marin, 'Mimésis et description, ou de la curiosité à la méthode de l'âge de Montaigne à celui de Descartes', in *De la représentation*, ed. by Daniel Arasse *et al.* (Paris: Gallimard, 1994), p. 84 ['*l'accomplissement ultime du processus mimétique ou représentationnel*']. See generally Antoine Compagnon, *La seconde main ou le travail de la citation* (Paris: Le Seuil, 1979), p. 12, who justifiably comments that 'the quotation represents capital stakes, a strategic and even political site in any practice of language' ['*la citation représente un enjeu capital, un lieu stratégique et même politique dans toute pratique du langage*'].
[225] Benjamin's so-called '*Passagen-Werk*' offers a well-known illustration of such construction. For the English version, see *Arcades Project*, *supra*, note 221.

To desist from subjecting heteronomy to the logic of subsumption, to yield to that which is being described, to its value, to its dignity and to its distinction – to allow something to be seen for what it is ('*etwas* als *etwas sehen lassen*', to borrow from Heideggerian ontology),[226] to allow a law to affirm itself in its difference, to permit a law to reveal itself or to come into being as meaningful by wresting it from the dominant interpretations which obscure its self-revelation – is to do justice to it because it is to engage in a process along the lines of *restitutio in integrum* (while accepting, of course, that the self can never fully overcome the epistemic partiality arising from the fact that human relations are inherently asymmetrical and irreversible).[227]

Needless to say, the 'recognition' that must be sought is emphatically not to be understood as an appropriational relation of knowledge in the sense of 'self-recognition and self-idealization, of self-affection [...] with respect to another who is regarded as pertaining to one's own self, as belonging to oneself alone, as reducible to oneself'.[228] In other words, given that 'individuals desire less to know the world than to recognize themselves in it, substituting for the indefinite frontiers of a fleeting universe the totalitarian security of closed worlds', 'the wish to know must protect itself against the need to recognize everything, which subverts it.'[229] Although recognition allows the other to give meaning to my existence in addition to the meaning I myself give it, although the self can become explicit to itself only through the mediation of an other, although self-consciousness requires a constitutive relation to otherness to confirm and transform its own self-understanding and drive it beyond abstract solipsism of the 'I am I' type,[230] the other is not to be reduced to a simple vehicle for the recovery of the

---

[226] Heidegger, *Sein und Zeit*, *supra*, note 48, p. 33 [emphasis original]. For the English rendition, see *Being and Time*, *supra*, note 48, p. 56: 'letting [something] be seen *as* something'.

[227] See Fabian, *supra*, note 4, pp. 162, 158 [referring to W. J. T. Mitchell] and 171–6; Young, *supra*, note 169. See generally Charles Taylor, *Multiculturalism and the 'Politics of Recognition'* (Princeton: Princeton University Press, 1992); Robert R. Williams, *Hegel's Ethics of Recognition* (Berkeley: University of California Press, 1998).

[228] Hamacher, *supra*, note 7, p. 290.

[229] Marc Augé, *Le sens des autres* (Paris: Fayard, 1994), pp. 131 and 143 ['*les hommes souhaitent moins connaître le monde que s'y reconnaître, substituant aux frontières indéfinies d'un univers en fuite la sécurité totalitaire des mondes clos*'; '*le désir de connaître doit se prévenir contre le besoin de tout reconnaître qui le subvertit*'].

[230] A typically Sartrean illustration showing how the self can be 'othered' would be 'shame': I am ashamed of myself as I appear to the other, such that I am what the other sees. The other within the same prompts a re-identification and, thus, forms part of identity. *Cf*. Levinas, *supra*, note 219, p. 176, who characterizes subjectivity as 'the other in the same' ('*l'autre dans le même*').

self, a mere occasion for self-consciousness, a variation on the theme of my 'I-ness', an opportunity for the self-interested furtherance of self-reflective or monological identity, a maieutics: Egyptians do not owe their existence to egyptologists.

There is one more observation to be reiterated in this regard. The recognition that I advocate in order to move comparative legal studies beyond egology is not to be taken as implying the validation or certification of the other's self-disclosure: critical evaluation remains inherent to the act of comparison.

* * *

In *The Nice and the Good*, Iris Murdoch has an elderly gentleman, Uncle Theo, sitting with his twin niece and nephew while they play on the seashore. The beach is a source of acute discomfort to Uncle Theo. While the children's noise and exuberance bother him, what really makes Uncle Theo most anxious is the multiplicity of things. As if twinness was not enough of an ontological disturbance, there are on the beach all those pebbles. Because each pebble is clamouring in its particularity, the totality of them is threatening the intelligibility and the manageability of the world. Uncle Theo is a man who can only negotiate the possibility of plurality if the many can be reduced to a few or, best of all, to one. While the twins display a childlike delight in variety, Uncle Theo exhibits a plethoraphobic distaste for multiplicity and randomness. His preoccupation with perceptual and conceptual tidiness shows Uncle Theo as the primordial comparatist-at-law, that is, as someone who is dismayed and disturbed by difference.[231] Uncle Theo is the comparatist-at-law comparatists-at-law must learn to unbecome by adumbrating a Heideggerian attunement to the self-disclosure of law focusing not so much on the law-as-disclosed (which would mire us into yet more positivistic immiseration) as on the disclosive process itself.[232]

Clearly, what is involved in the prioritization of difference does not simply relate to the overcoming by the comparatist of obstacles that could be described as 'external' to him (such as institutional frameworks and other structures legitimating uniformity-as-performativity), but also entails overcoming the self as an agent of censorship (after all, the desire not to know about otherness-in-the-law is not simple ignorance; rather, it

---

[231] See Iris Murdoch, *The Nice and the Good* (London: Vintage, 2000), pp. 152–3 [1968]. I closely follow Elizabeth V. Spelman, *Inessential Woman* (London: The Women's Press, 1988), pp. 1–2.

[232] *Cf.* Thomas Sheehan, 'On Movement and the Destruction of Ontology', (1981) 64 The Monist 534, p. 536.

assumes a prescience of what it is that one does not want to know – which suggests that the comparatist's unknown is far from being the simple opposite of his known). In Freudian terms, *Entstellung* (distortion) must yield to *Darstellung* (re-presentation): the deformation that seeks to dissimulate its deformative character by creating a re-presentational façade, the tendentious consciousness abandoning itself to wish-fulfilment – remember Markesinis enjoining comparatists to manipulate data and Zimmermann and Whittaker omitting to refer to Teubner[233] – must yield to the problematization of complexity in terms of ambivalence and conflict, that is, to self-discipline (*Selbstüberwindung*).[234]

Comparatists, then, must learn that there is difference and postponement of meaning. They must favour an ethics of interruption. But, as I have argued, they must learn that there is also nearness – a process which requires much more than textual exposures and demands actual and sustained social interaction (one can know comparison only by living it).[235] This is why the brand of differential analysis or comparison of jurisculures I advocate cannot fairly be attacked as a repudiation of community or as promoting the effacement of any pro-social desire by beings-in-the-law to express themselves coherently in terms of shared meanings or, more crudely, as allowing a lapse into anti-social individualism or existential nominalism and atomism. I acknowledge what Nathalie Sarraute, actually misquoting Katherine Mansfield, calls 'this terrible desire to establish contact'.[236] My argument – which I address to comparatists-at-law – lies elsewhere and aims rather to *intensify* one's engagement in community through a non-repressive and non-dominating form of socialness, to prompt one to move beyond dogmatism and narcissism so as to examine how one's individuality is determined

---

[233] *Supra*, at text accompanying notes 27 and 216, respectively.
[234] See Sigmund Freud, *The Interpretation of Dreams*, in *The Standard Edition of the Complete Psychological Works of Sigmund Freud*, transl. by James Strachey *et al.*, vol. V (London: Hogarth Press, 1953), pp. 524–5 [1900]. For the German text, see *id.*, *Die Traumdeutung*, in *Gesammelte Werke*, ed. by Anna Freud *et al.*, vol. II, t. 3 (Frankfurt: S. Fischer, 1942), p. 529.
[235] This nearness also emerges from the act of writing itself. Thus, beyond the absence it inscribes (*supra*, note 157), the writing also conveys a strong sense of presence: 'One never writes (or describes) something which happened before the work of writing, but that which happens (in all meanings of the word) during this work, in the *present time* of this work': Claude Simon, *Discours de Stockholm* (Paris: Editions de Minuit, 1986), p. 25 [*'l'on n'écrit (ou ne décrit) jamais quelque chose qui s'est passé avant le travail d'écrire, mais bien ce qui se produit (et cela dans tous les sens du terme) au cours de ce travail, au présent de celui-ci'*] (emphasis original).
[236] Nathalie Sarraute, *L'ère du soupçon*, in *Oeuvres complètes*, *supra*, note 2, p. 1568 [1964]. The quotation appears in English.

by assumptions and values and is, in fact, 'embedded within a sociality whose origin in the material and cultural forces of history is incommensurate with powers of the individual to conceptualize or to control'.[237] I am, in other words, arguing for noetic comparative legal studies aiming to make manifest, celebrate, heed and interrogate the *genius loci*. The way forward for comparative legal studies – its *Denkweg* – must not lie with *Ordnung*, but rather with *Ortung*. As '*Ord*' suggests '*Reihe*' and '*Rang*', '*Ort-*' connotes '*Spitze*', that is, by extension, '*Gegend*' and '*Platz*'. What is needed is, indeed, a focus on the law as it is situated, as it is located. What is wanted is an accentuation of the '*Ort-*' of the law. Because particular experience provides the last resort for establishing a weak but respectable veracity and because it is only through the other that it is possible to get behind oneself in a manner not to be achieved simply by way of self-reflection, I am, in the end, through my call for heightened epistemological vigilance, for non-indifference to difference, disclosing a measure of epistemological optimism. I am making a plea for an economy of *indebtedness* which, alone, can help comparatists acquit themselves of the guilt they must otherwise feel on account of the stunningly insistent subjugation of the other to the self that they have been perpetrating, falling for the treacherous seductions of semblance and its constitutive exclusions, effectively removing legal relations from the field of direct experience of particular persons in their mutual involvement, compelling individuals to renounce their autonomy and assigning them to the impersonal forces of the market in legal ideas, replacing a mode of engagement with a perfectly artificial and ideological mode of construction of axiomatic patterns established through strict reference to the formalized and absolutized elements of law. Yes. The only commendable strategy for comparative legal studies today – its urgent and incessant task – is a hermeneutics attending to the constraints of contingency and facticity which features Keats's 'negative capability', a 'quality' he regarded as 'form[ing] a Man of Achievement' and which is present 'when man is capable of being in uncertainties, Mysteries, doubts'.[238] In the words of Heidegger, '[t]his thing that is called difference, we encounter it

---

[237] Cynthia Willett, *Maternal Ethics and Other Slave Moralities* (London: Routledge, 1995), p. 103. Of course, this is not to say that there is not an extent to which the individual's always-particular life-story mediates the background of symbolic and practical fore-structures against which it operates. After all, even shared cultural activities can have an idiosyncratic meaning for individuals.
[238] *The Letters of John Keats*, ed. by Hyder E. Rollins, vol. I (Cambridge, Mass.: Harvard University Press, 1958), p. 193 [being a letter to his brothers, George and Tom Keats, dated 21 or 27 December 1817].

everywhere and always in the matter of thinking, in beings as such – encounter it so unquestioningly that we do not even notice this encounter itself. Nor does anything compel us to notice it. Our thinking is free either to pass over the difference without a thought or to think of it specifically as such. But this freedom does not apply in every case.'[239] My argument is that it does not apply in the case of comparative legal studies.

* * *

The view of comparative legal studies I defend focuses on the decisive historical interests of the comparer and of the compared. Yet, I appreciate that a brief erotic metaphor may make a more lasting impression than all that precedes. Drawing on Zygmunt Bauman, who himself derives inspiration from Emmanuel Levinas,[240] I call for comparison as *caress*, that is, as a gesture that, like the caressing hand, remains open, never tightening into a grip, a gesture which is tentative and exploratory, a gesture which reaches toward the other without any intention of possessing the other and which acts, therefore, as an affirmation of alterity, as opposed, perhaps, to other erotic gestures of pointed invasion, a gesture which nonetheless fosters increased responsibility of the self toward the other since even as I caress the other, as I create an orifice or perhaps just a slit, an opening onto the 'reality' of human (or legal) diversity beyond any purportedly self-contained 'I' (or law), as I exceed the boundaries of self (or self-in-the-law), as I engage in exorbitance, I must answer for the impact of my gesture on the other.

* * *

There are those, no doubt, who wonder why comparative legal studies should be *something that there is a theory of*. And, even though I have purposefully attempted to engage matters 'at ground level',[241] there are those, no doubt, who regard this entire argument about (comparative) intelligibility being a process of differentiation as mere intellectual phantasm. Since a practical justification for this paper might be required, therefore, I shall leave it to an erudite comparatist to make the succinct point for me: in Europe, 'the common law is being squeezed out of significant existence.'[242] Now, is this practical *enough*?

---

[239] Heidegger, *Identity*, *supra*, note 137, p. 63. For the original text, see *id.*, *Identität*, *supra*, note 137, p. 55 ['*Überall und jederzeit finden wir das, was Differenz genannt wird, in der Sache des Denkens, im Seienden als solchem vor, so zweifelsfrei, daß wir diesen Befund gar nicht erst als solchen zur Kenntnis nehmen. Auch zwingt uns nichts, dies zu tun. Unserem Denken steht es frei, die Differenz unbedacht zu lassen oder sie eigens als solche zu bedenken. Aber diese Freiheit gilt nicht für alle Fälle*'].
[240] See Bauman, *supra*, note 36, pp. 92–8.   [241] Bruns, *supra*, note 150, p. 13.
[242] Tony Weir, *A Casebook on Tort*, 9th ed. (London: Sweet & Maxwell, 2000), p. viii.

10

The neo-Romantic turn

JAMES Q. WHITMAN

If I begin by saying that many comparatists have recently taken a 'neo-Romantic turn', it may sound as though I am mounting an attack on the persons responsible. After all, the term 'Romanticism' can have some comical associations and some ugly ones as well. This paper is not by any means meant as an unqualified attack, however. I am more or less in favour of our new Romanticism. Nevertheless, it *is* my goal in this paper to voice some gentle doubts about the new literature.

That said, let me begin by observing that the last couple of years have indeed seen something of a neo-Romantic turn in the philosophy of comparative law. Some of this has involved a revival of the early Romantic philosophers themselves. In particular, the theories of Johann Gottfried Herder, late eighteenth-century philosopher of the *Volksgeist*, have been rediscovered by William Ewald.[1] Some of it has involved later and more difficult representatives of the long Romantic tradition. Thus, a number of different scholars, most prominent among them Pierre Legrand, have revived a mess of ideas from the twentieth-century neo-Romantic tradition of hermeneutics – from the philosophical tradition that conceives interpretation as the enterprise of 'understanding' the 'other', of developing a sympathetic grasp of fundamentally alien cultures and other persons.[2] Alongside Legrand,

---

I gratefully acknowledge the observations of participants in the Conference on an earlier version of this paper as well as the comments of Jack Balkin, Mirjan Damaška, Christian Joerges, Brian Leiter and Annelise Riles.

[1] See especially William Ewald, 'Comparative Jurisprudence (I): What Was it Like to Try a Rat?', (1995) 143 U. Pennsylvania L.R. 1889. I should rush to say that Herder did not himself use the term '*Volksgeist*'. See further *infra*, at text accompanying note 14.

[2] See Pierre Legrand, *Le droit comparé* (Paris: Presses Universitaires de France, 1999); *id.*, *Fragments on Law-as-Culture* (Deventer: W. E. J. Tjeenk Willink, 1999) [hereinafter *Fragments*]; *id.*, 'The Impossibility of "Legal Transplants"', (1997) 4 Maastricht J. Eur. & Comp. L. 111 [hereinafter 'Impossibility']; *id.*, 'European Legal Systems Are Not Converging', (1996) 45 Int. & Comp. L.Q. 52 [hereinafter 'European Legal Systems'].

the names that should be mentioned here include notably those of Vivian Curran and Nora Demleitner;[3] of the anthropologist Annelise Riles;[4] and, from an older generation, that of Josef Esser as well.[5] All of these scholars have been working to breathe new life into the grand tradition of Romanticism, insisting on the importance of the cultural 'difference' in the diverse legal systems of the human world and resisting anything that smacks of a belief in some single 'natural law'.

This has certainly pushed comparative law in a new, and welcome, direction. These scholars have made comparative law a little more like cultural anthropology, have given it more sensitivity to the deep differences in human value-orders. That sort of sensitivity can help to remedy many ills. Our comparative literature is full of articles and books that can seem weirdly innocent of the fact that human societies differ. Most of these articles and books constitute what we really ought to call comparative *doctrine* rather than comparative *law* – more or less useless studies that casually lump together the law of wildly different countries and climes. Ewald and others are surely right to deplore this literature.[6] Some of our comparative law literature employs the 'functionalism' of Konrad Zweigert and Hein Kötz, which declares that the goal of comparative law is to show how different societies use different doctrinal and procedural means to solve the same social problems.[7] Functionalism is an approach with many strengths, but it starts from at least one doubtful assumption: that all societies perceive life as presenting more or less the same social problems. Esser is surely right to attack this assumption.[8] The tone-deafness to difference in our comparative law literature has grown worse, moreover, as a result of the

---

[3] See Vivian Curran, 'Cultural Immersion, Difference and Categories in US Comparative Law', (1998) 46 Am. J. Comp. L. 43; Nora Demleitner, 'Combating Legal Ethnocentrism: Comparative Law Sets Boundaries', (1999) 31 Arizona State L.J. 737.
[4] See Annelise Riles, *The Network Inside Out* (Ann Arbor: University of Michigan Press, 2001).
[5] See especially Josef Esser, *Vorverständnis und Methodenwahl in der Rechtsfindung: Rationalitätsgarantien der richterlichen Entscheidungspraxis* (Frankfurt: Athenäum, 1970) [hereinafter *Vorverständnis*]; id., *Grundsatz und Norm in der richterlichen Fortbildung des Privatrechts: Rechtsvergleichende Beiträge zur Rechtsquellen- und Interpretationslehre*, 2d ed. (Tübingen: J. C. B. Mohr, 1990) [hereinafter *Grundsatz*].
[6] See especially Ewald's discussion, *supra*, note 1, pp. 1961–89; Curran, *supra*, note 3, pp. 60–1.
[7] Konrad Zweigert and Hein Kötz, *An Introduction to Comparative Law*, 3d ed. transl. by Tony Weir (Oxford: Oxford University Press, 1998), pp. 32–47.
[8] Esser, *Vorverständnis*, *supra*, note 5, pp. 19 and 60. Also problematic, in my view, is another implicit claim of the functionalist approach. This is the claim that it matters relatively little what doctrinal and procedural means are used to solve a particular problem. This claim understates the social consequences of the choice of one particular means over another.

situation in Europe. Many European scholars have been eager to develop a common European private law and this has sharply diminished their interest in the problem of understanding cultural differences.[9] Scholars who want to identify some European common ground do not much care to talk about how societies vary. While these scholars may perhaps succeed in producing a common European code, or even some kind of European common law, they risk impoverishing the intellectual life of comparative law in the process. It is understandable that Legrand has raised his voice in protest.[10]

It is indeed in general a very good thing that these critical voices have been sounded. Still, I hope we can all agree that we should not let ourselves get too carried away by our love of 'difference'. After all, if the Romantic tradition is famous for its authentic sensitivity and occasional profundity, it is also famous for generating moments of colossal silliness and of distasteful moral relativism as well. Do we really want to throw in our lot with Herder? Thoughtful scholars have been troubled by the idea of the '*Volksgeist*', and more broadly by Herder's relativism, for generations – and not entirely without reason.[11] Do we really want to wade into the swamp of the philosophy of 'otherness'? Surely we all have a sense of what Hans-Georg Gadamer, the sharpest of hermeneutic philosophers, calls 'the dubiousness of Romantic hermeneutics'[12] – a sense of the danger that our fascination with sheer 'otherness' will deteriorate into a kind of thumb-twiddling reverie. Talking about 'difference' has its grandeur at times; but at other times, it can be a worrisome and intellectually slippery business.

It is with these worries and slipperinesses in mind that I try to present a relatively tame version of the Romantic/hermeneutic approach to comparative law. I do not think any of the scholars working the new vein will necessarily disagree with what I have to say. On the contrary, I hope that they will agree with me that scholars who perceive only 'difference' in the world tend to get a little dizzy, a little unsteady on their scholarly feet. I

---

[9] For example, see the many distinguished contributions to the *Zeitschrift für Europäisches Privatrecht*.
[10] See Legrand, 'European Legal Systems', *supra*, note 2.
[11] For nineteenth-century doubts, see the discussions of the *Völkerpsychologen*, addressed more fully *infra*, at text accompanying note 23; and for modern doubts within the grand Continental Romantic tradition, see Martin Heidegger, 'Die Zeit des Weltbildes', in *Holzwege*, 6th ed. (Frankfurt: Vittorio Klostermann, 1980), pp. 90–1 [1938].
[12] Hans-Georg Gadamer, *Wahrheit und Methode*, 2d ed. (Tübingen: J. C. B. Mohr, 1990), pp. 177–222 ['*die Fragwürdigkeit der romantischen Hermeneutik*'].

also hope that they will agree that dizzy Romanticism is not what we want. Rather, we want some way of speaking intelligently and sensitively about the diversity of the human legal world without losing our bearings. We want to be able to talk about differences without becoming opaque or oracular or simply confused.

In the effort to develop a comparative law that is steady on its feet, I critically discuss two propositions in this paper. Both propositions represent centrally important claims that grow out of the 'difference' orientation in the new literature. The first is Ewald's claim that comparative law should aim at understanding the 'inner' perspective, the view of a given legal system that is consciously held by actors within that system itself.[13] The second is a claim that has been made by Legrand, by Esser and by myself as well: that comparative law should be concerned with the Gadamerian *Vorverständnis*, the unspoken, taken-for-granted body of assumptions and beliefs that inform and motivate the law in different societies.[14] I think both of these claims are correct. But I also think that both can make for inadequate and misleading accounts of what comparative law can and should do. By showing their inadequate and misleading character, I hope to bring us closer to identifying the limits of 'difference' methodology in comparative law.

In the first section of the paper, I survey some of the long history of the Romantic tradition in an effort to cultivate a deeper perspective on our problems. In the second section, I discuss the methodological issues raised by the hunt for the 'inner' perspective and for *Vorverständnis*, using the example of some of my current research on comparative dignitary law.

I

When comparatists today talk about the problem of 'understanding' the 'other' or of law as 'culture', they are drawing on a tradition that can be traced to late eighteenth- and early nineteenth-century Germany. At the cost of repeating commonplaces, I begin by reviewing some of that tradition in the hope of bringing some historical wisdom to our discussion. We will

---

[13] See most recently the statement in William Ewald, 'Legal History and Comparative Law', Zeitschrift für Europäisches Privatrecht, 1999, p. 553.
[14] See Legrand, 'Impossibility', *supra*, note 2, p. 114; Esser, *Vorverständnis*, *supra*, note 5; James Q. Whitman, 'Enforcing Civility and Respect: Three Societies', (2000) 109 Yale L.J. 1387. See also Curran, *supra*, note 3, p. 51.

think more clearly about the methodological problems of comparative law today if we bear in mind some of the insights and failures of the last couple of centuries – if we remember both the sensible Romanticism and the silly Romanticism of the past.

The best-remembered bit of the Romantic tradition is undoubtedly the idea of the '*Volksgeist*'. In the late eighteenth century, a number of German scholars, enamoured of local German culture and hostile to French influence, began to insist on the values of irreducible socio-cultural diversity. Their ideas came to first philosophical fruition in the writings of Herder, who initiated a tradition of talking about the peculiarities of each national 'spirit', of each '*Volksgeist*', as Hegel would dub it.[15] This idea, which owed an obvious debt to Montesquieu and Voltaire, contributed mightily to a widespread desire among the first Romantic scholars to get beyond what seemed the obtuse self-confidence of Enlightenment philosophies of 'natural law'. Of course, '*Volksgeist*' is not a self-explanatory idea and, from the beginning, the notion that there were peculiar national 'spirits' seemed troubling to some of Herder's readers among the jurists, who found it difficult to abandon the idea that law should somehow be regarded, as it were, *sub specie universalitatis*. Thus, even jurists with a palpable sympathy for Herder's point of view, like Gustav Hugo, continued to write texts on 'natural law'.[16] And Herder's most famous and influential follower in the world of German law, the great jurist Friedrich Carl von Savigny, had a hard time producing a theory of the 'Germanness' of German law that seemed ultimately satisfying.[17] Nevertheless, especially under Savigny's influence, many lawyers made intense, and sometimes thrilling, efforts to understand law as having a peculiarly national character. In particular, they did brilliant work in 'historical jurisprudence', that is, in studies of national peculiarities as formed historically.

Indeed, Herderian historical jurisprudence exercised an influence on legal historians and sociologists which can still be felt down to the present day. In particular, a remarkable variety of modern ideas can be traced back to the *Germanisten*, the early nineteenth-century specialists in 'Germanic' law.

---

[15] For the general history, see still Siegfried Brie, *Der Volksgeist bei Hegel und in der historischen Rechtsschule* (Berlin: Walther Rothschild, 1909). For another useful account, see Nathan Rotenstreich, 'Volksgeist', in *Dictionary of the History of Ideas*, ed. by Philip P. Wiener, vol. IV (New York: Scribner's, 1973), pp. 490–6.

[16] See Gustav Hugo, *Lehrbuch des Naturrechts*, 4th ed. (Berlin: August Mylius, 1819).

[17] For my own account, see James Q. Whitman, *The Legacy of Roman Law in the German Romantic Era* (Princeton: Princeton University Press, 1990), pp. 102–50.

These jurists tried to pin down what they often called the 'spirit' of Germanic law, by which they meant basic principles of legal reasoning that distinguished Germanic texts from Roman ones.[18] In particular, they argued that values like 'trust', 'honour' and 'orality' characterized primitive Germanic legal reasoning;[19] whereas Roman legal reasoning was characterized, they thought, by a variety of values that all reflected the kind of assertive individualism described by Rudolf von Jhering in his *Spirit of Roman Law*.[20] This picture of sharp value-differences between the German and Roman legal traditions caught the imagination of many intellectuals of the period leading up to the Revolution of 1848, not least among them Karl Marx.[21] It also proved profoundly influential on the making of later nineteenth-century sociology. Much of the fundamental contrast between *Gemeinschaft* and *Gesellschaft*, as it developed in the later nineteenth century, began its intellectual life as a contrast between the 'spirit' of German law and the 'spirit' of Roman law.[22] This nineteenth-century hunt for the 'spirit' of different legal systems has survived, moreover, in an interesting series edited by Alan Watson,[23] just as it has survived in some form in William Ewald's thinking. Both in the Watson series and in Ewald's writings, we can see that the key idea of the nineteenth-century *Germanisten* – the idea that different legal systems betray the

---

[18] See famously the satirical observations of Rudolf von Jhering, *Scherz und Ernst in der Jurisprudenz*, 3d ed. (Leipzig: Breitkopf & Härtel, 1885), pp. 3–6.

[19] For a classic Germanist text, see Wilhelm Eduard Wilda, *Das Strafrecht der Germanen* (Halle: Schwetschke, 1842). For further discussion and literature, see Whitman, *supra*, note 17, pp. 122–3 and 205–8.

[20] Rudolf von Jhering, *Der Geist des römischen Rechts auf den verschiedenen Stufen seiner Entwicklung*, 10th ed. (Aalen: Scientia, repr. 1958), vol. I, pp. 102–18; vol. II, part 1, pp. 133–55 [1852]. There was an important confusion in the way all these early nineteenth-century scholars argued. They made no distinction between what we would now call 'law' and what we would call 'society'. They simply assumed that the 'spirits' they found in their legal texts were also the 'spirits' of social relations in the societies that produced those texts. This obscured a distinction that lovers of the Herderian tradition might well want to maintain. It may be that 'law' displays values that are only problematically related to the values displayed by 'society'.

[21] See especially Karl Marx, *Debatten über das Holzdiebstahls-Gesetz*, in *Marx-Engels Gesamtausgabe (MEGA)*, vol. I (Berlin: Dietz, 1975), pp. 199–236 [1842].

[22] See Ferdinand Tönnies, *Gemeinschaft und Gesellschaft: Abhandlung des Communismus und des Sozialismus als empirischer Kulturformen* (Leipzig: Fues, 1887).

[23] See Calum Carmichael, *The Spirit of Biblical Law* (Athens, Georgia: University of Georgia Press, 1996); John O. Haley, *The Spirit of Japanese Law* (Athens, Georgia: University of Georgia Press, 1998); Richard H. Helmholz, *The Spirit of Classical Canon Law* (Athens, Georgia: University of Georgia Press, 1996); Geoffrey MacCormack, *The Spirit of Traditional Chinese Law* (Athens, Georgia: University of Georgia Press, 1996); Alan Watson, *The Spirit of Roman Law* (Athens, Georgia: University of Georgia Press, 1995); Bernard Weiss, *The Spirit of Islamic Law* (Athens, Georgia: University of Georgia Press, 1998).

influence of different fundamental normative commitments – has a lasting strength.

Other lines of Herderian thought developed in the nineteenth century too. Particularly noteworthy (though generally forgotten today) was so-called *Völkerpsychologie* or 'national psychology', an aspiring new social science invented by Moritz Lazarus and Heymann Steinthal in the 1860s and continued by Wilhelm Wundt later in the century. The *Völkerpsychologen* aimed to be scientific Herderians, avoiding the vagueness and occasional mysticism that clung to the '*Volksgeist*' idea. Thus, they discarded the notion that there was some collective national 'spirit', focusing instead on the way in which *individual* psychology is moulded by the experience of national traditions and institutions.[24] They did not limit themselves to law, talking also about social manners, art, language and whatever else might contribute to an understanding of what made French individuals *french*, or German individuals *german*. But they did have some striking things indeed to say about national characteristics in law.[25] This interesting approach would continue to find advocates in such twentieth-century scholars as Maurice Halbwachs, Alfred Schütz and Erik Erikson, all of whom asked, in one form or another, the same fascinating sociological question: how is it that individuals learn to behave in recognizably 'national' ways?[26] This aspect of the Herderian tradition is perhaps less alive, in our current comparative law scholarship, than one might like. One can very easily imagine interesting studies indeed that focused on how individual legal actors learn specifically national behaviours. But such studies are, at best, few.

Herderianism represented, in any event, only one early strand in the history of the Romantic/hermeneutic tradition. A second early strand, which is less widely known but which has come to influence a number

---

[24] See the programmatic statement in Moritz Lazarus and Heymann Steinthal, 'Einleitende Gedanken über Völkerpsychologie', Zeitschrift für Völkerpsychologie und Sprachwissenschaft, 1860, p. 1; Wilhelm Wundt, *Völkerpsychologie: Eine Untersuchung der Entwicklungsgesetze von Sprache, Mythus und Sitte*, 3d ed., vol. I (Leipzig: Wilhelm Engelmann, 1911), pp. 7–11.

[25] For interesting examples, see Paul Laband, 'Die rechtliche Stellung der Frauen im altrömischen und germanischen Recht', Zeitschrift für Völkerpsychologie und Sprachwissenschaft, 1865, p. 179 [discussing the economic foundations of differences between the Roman and Germanic legal treatment of women]; Wundt, *supra*, note 24, vol. IX [offering a wealth of observations about the mental structures and symbolism of the law].

[26] Maurice Halbwachs, *La mémoire collective*, 2d ed. (Paris: Albin Michel, 1997), pp. 51–142; Alfred Schütz and Thomas Luckmann, *The Structures of the Life-World*, 2d ed. transl. by Richard Zaner and H. Tristram Engelhardt, vol. I (Evanston: Northwestern University Press, 1973), p. 293; Erik Erikson, *Identity and the Life Cycle* (New York: Norton, 1980), pp. 17–50.

of comparatists, grew out of the so-called 'hermeneutic' theories developed by Lutheran theologians and classical philologists. Early nineteenth-century theologians and classicists shared a common, and very difficult, task: that of understanding mysterious texts written in remote times and places. The Lutheran theologians set the tone in approaching this interpretive task. Following Martin Luther's lead, they argued that readers of scripture, by immersing themselves in the text, could succeed in grasping, through an intuitive leap, the meaning intended by the Holy Spirit. Classical philologists did not talk about the Holy Spirit. But they too thought that long immersion in the primary sources would eventually allow the individual philologist to make an intuitive leap of understanding, grasping the 'spirit' that informed the text before him and indeed the grander 'spirit' of the ancient Greeks. Such, then, was the early nineteenth-century hermeneutic tradition. Deeply Lutheran in character, it was one that spoke generally of understanding profoundly alien 'spirits' through intuitive leaps.[27]

This Lutheran tradition of talking about grasping the 'spirits' of texts and cultures largely died out during the middle decades of the nineteenth century. But, at the end of the nineteenth century, it enjoyed a great revival that has largely continued into the present. This revival began under the banner, on the one hand, of the neo-Kantian philosophers of Marburg and south-west Germany and, on the other hand, under the banner of the first modern hermeneutic philosopher, Wilhelm Dilthey. To have an informed understanding of the hermeneutic tradition, we must know something about these philosophers and about their many and varied disciples as well. For it is the ideas of the neo-Kantians, and especially of Dilthey, that set the principal pattern for thinking about the problem of 'culture' down to our own day not only among anthropologists and sociologists, but also among some of the neo-Romantic comparatists.

The neo-Kantian philosophers were primarily concerned with a topic that seems, indeed, very promising for any philosophy of comparative law: the proper methodologies of various disciplines. In the last decades of the nineteenth century, they began, in particular, to make arguments about

---

[27] For these traditions, see Joachim Wach, *Das Verstehen: Grundzüge einer Geschichte der hermeneutischen Theorie im 19. Jahrhundert* (Tübingen: J. C. B. Mohr, 1926–33), 3 vols.; Gadamer, *supra*, note 12; Benedetto Bravo, *Philologie, histoire, philosophie de l'histoire: étude sur J. G. Droysen, historien de l'Antiquité* (Cracow: Polskiej Akademii Nauk, 1968); Helmut Flashar, Karlfried Gründer and Axel Horstmann (eds.), *Philologie und Hermeneutik im 19. Jahrhundert* (Göttingen: Vandenhoeck & Ruprecht, 1979).

the special character, and peculiar problems, of the *Geisteswissenschaften* – normally translated, not entirely satisfactorily, as 'the human sciences'.[28] In particular, the neo-Kantians set out to distinguish the *Geisteswissenschaften* from the *Naturwissenschaften*, the natural sciences. This is a project that they approached in ways that are easiest to grasp if we recognize their essentially Christian inspiration and, in particular, their concern with broadly Christian ideas of the nature of the free will. The neo-Kantians saw the 'natural' world as a world of mechanical causation and the 'human' world, by contrast, as a world of uncaused free will. Since uncaused free will determined the character of the human world, human affairs could never be fully 'explained'; explanation (*Erklärung*) of appropriately mathematical precision was possible only in the world of mechanics. All that the student of the 'human' world could do was to understand, to *verstehen*; all he could do was to grasp the human world through an effort of imaginative understanding (*Verstehen*), which allowed him to comprehend what processes of the free will had produced it. Moreover, since the free will was uncaused and, therefore, unpredictable, it always produced results that varied unpredictably and infinitely. Every feature of the human world was irreducibly different from every other feature. Features of the human world were, in Leibniz's terminology, 'monadic', irreducibly individual, with an individual dynamic of development. This meant that the human sciences, in the famous neo-Kantian formulation, were not 'nomothetic' but rather 'idiographic': they did not lay down causal laws, but simply described individual characteristics.[29]

This neo-Kantianism obviously lent itself to a resuscitation of early nineteenth-century hermeneutic thought; and it is just such a resuscitation that we find in Dilthey's philosophy of *Verstehen*. Dilthey, drawing especially on the theologian Friedrich Schleiermacher's writings, returned forcefully to the problem of how we can imaginatively recapture vanished and alien societies and texts. In the philosophy of Dilthey, interpretation reassumed its classic Protestant guise, becoming once again the exercise

---

[28] As Gadamer has pointed out, this term was originally coined as a translation for Mill's 'moral sciences': see *supra*, note 12, p. 9. See further Klaus Köhnke, *The Rise of Neo-Kantianism*, transl. by R. J. Hollingdale (Cambridge: Cambridge University Press, 1991), pp. 87–8. The deeper difficulties with the translation 'human sciences' have to do, of course, with the loss of the complex connotations and associations of '*Geist*'.

[29] For an introduction, see Thomas Willey, *Back to Kant: The Revival of Kantianism in German Social and Historical Thought, 1860–1914* (Detroit: Wayne State University Press, 1978). See also the literature cited *infra*, note 31.

of intuitively grasping the totality of the *Geist* of a text or a culture after long immersion in the primary sources. And the accent, for Dilthey, was on 'totality': he thought understanding required the painfully difficult, indeed nearly impossible, business of grasping, as an organic whole, everything that informed the alien culture or the alien text.[30]

With this late nineteenth-century revival of hermeneutic thinking, we are on the road that will lead to much of the new comparative law thinking of our own day. The late nineteenth-century revival had indeed a powerful influence on all of the twentieth-century 'cultural' sciences. But curiously, it had almost no influence (as far as I can see) on the comparative law of its own time. To be sure, the very greatest comparatist of the age, Max Weber, stood under the influence of the neo-Kantian philosophers.[31] But, in this as in most things, Weber has been, scandalously, largely forgotten by comparatists. The other great figures of the comparative law of the day, Albert Hermann Post and Josef Kohler, do not seem to have cared about the problems that exercised other specialists in the 'alien'.[32] In fact, it is hardly before our own day that the great tradition of hermeneutics has begun to make its influence strongly felt among comparatists.

Before coming to our own day, though, let me continue with this brief summary of the development of the grand hermeneutic tradition, laying out a few points that will help us to evaluate the new hermeneutic literature in comparative law. The tradition as it developed in the early part of the twentieth century can be usefully broken down into three strands:[33] the historical, the social scientific and the philosophical. These three strands differed sharply on an important point: the historians remained strongly faithful to the radical Romantic tradition, generally treating different 'cultures'

---

[30] Here, I draw principally on the discussion of Gadamer, *supra*, note 12, pp. 222–46.
[31] For discussions, see Wolfgang Schluchter, *The Rise of Western Rationalism: Max Weber's Developmental History*, transl. by Guenther Roth (Berkeley: University of California Press, 1981), pp. 19–24; Friedrich Tenbruck, 'Die Genesis der Methodologie Max Webers', Kölner Zeitschrift für Soziologie, 1959, p. 11; Gerhard Wagner and Heinz Zipprian, 'Max Weber und die neukantianische Epistemologie', in Hans-Ludwig Ollig (ed.), *Materialien zur Neukantianismusdiskussion* (Darmstadt: Wissenschaftliche Buchgesellschaft, 1987), pp. 184–216.
[32] Kohler's typically sparkling early essay, *Das Recht als Kulturerscheinung: Einleitung in die vergleichende Rechtswissenschaft* (Würzburg: Stahel, 1885), can fairly be described as straightforwardly Herderian in approach. I think it is fair to describe his later work – most famously in *Shakespeare vor dem Forum der Jurisprudenz*, 2d ed. (Leipzig: Walther Rothschild, 1919) – as oriented toward identifying human universals. Human universals were also the interest of Albert Hermann Post, *Grundriss der ethnologischen Jurisprudenz* (Oldenburg: Schulze, 1894), 2 vols.
[33] I oversimply here and I also neglect in particular both psychological hermeneutics, especially Freudian, and literary hermeneutics.

as unconquerably alien to each other. Social scientists and philosophers, by contrast, tended to take a more sober view, regarding 'otherness' as something that could be, and regularly was, overcome.

To begin with the historians. Early twentieth-century historians often remained deeply committed to the strong Romantic belief in the unbridgeable otherness and to the Diltheyan organic 'totality' of alien cultures. A number of early twentieth-century historians, some of them very sophisticated, some very vulgar, embraced a radical version of the Romantic tradition that mixed Herder with Dilthey. Among these were ugly nationalistic German authors such as Houston Stewart Chamberlain, whose ideas of the peculiarities of the German '*Geist*' formed an important item among the intellectual wares of the Nazis. The writings of Chamberlain and his followers did a great deal to discredit the Romantic tradition in historiography.[34] But among the early twentieth-century Romantics were also brilliant cultural historians like Oswald Spengler and Max Weber's unjustly neglected brother, Alfred Weber. Spengler, in particular, constructed an account of human history that assumed that different civilizations, each caught up in an individual cycle of rise and fall, were incomprehensibly alien to each other – so incomprehensibly alien that even mathematics, in the famous Spenglerian claim, did not have the same meaning in one culture that it had in another. Contact between civilizations was, to Spengler, in a fundamental sense impossible; what civilizations tended to experience was not contact, but conflict. Indeed, the stuff of human history was the stuff of conflict between civilizations: between Persians and Greeks, Christendom and Islam, Occident and Orient.[35] Other historians, like Alfred Weber, saw more room for communication between civilizations; but Alfred Weber too thought that the fundamental alienness of 'other' cultures meant that the stuff of human history was inescapably the stuff of conflict – though he thought that substantial borrowings were a constant feature of this conflict-ridden human history.[36]

---

[34] See Houston Stewart Chamberlain, *Die Grundlagen des neunzehnten Jahrhunderts*, 13th ed. (Munich: Bruckmann, 1919). For discussion, see Geoffrey Field, *Evangelist of Race: The Germanic Vision of Houston Stewart Chamberlain* (New York: Columbia University Press, 1981).

[35] See Oswald Spengler, *Der Untergang des Abendlande: Umrisse einer Morphologie der Weltgeschichte* (Munich: C. H. Beck, 1980) [1923]. See also the essays in Alexander Demandt and John Farrenkopf (eds.), *Der Fall Spengler: Eine kritische Bilanz* (Cologne: Böhlau, 1994).

[36] See Alfred Weber, *Ideen zur Staats- und Kultursoziologie* (Karlsruhe: Braun, 1927). Alfred Weber thought that even as fundamentally alien civilizations fell into decline, their discoveries were borrowed by other, rising civilizations – mathematics, for example, having been borrowed from

But if early twentieth-century historians tended to treat the irreducible 'otherness' of cultures as a given, both sociologists and philosophers did not. Indeed, what came to characterize both thoughtful hermeneutic sociology and thoughtful hermeneutic philosophy throughout the twentieth century was the rejection of the strong neo-Romantic, Diltheyan position on 'otherness'. To most of the best thinkers who approached the topic, the goal of the hermeneutic tradition was not to surrender to 'otherness', but to explain how understanding is possible *despite* otherness.

Among sociologists, the most important figure here is, of course, the elder Weber, Max. Max Weber, deeply preoccupied with the ideas of the neo-Kantians, insisted that sociology had to be what he called '*verstehende Soziologie*', a sociology of *Verstehen*, of understanding in the classic hermeneutic sense. But he took a sober position on *Verstehen*. He had little interest in the more mystical beliefs of the Protestant hermeneutic tradition. He did not talk about grasping the ineffably total '*Geist*' of society and he was not troubled by the notion that other cultures were inaccessibly alien. (Indeed, he was cheerfully confident of his ability to understand almost any human society.) Instead of dwelling on these Romantic conundra, Weber sought to apply the technique of imaginative comprehension to the understanding of human *action*. As Weber understood it, the subject of sociology was meaningful action. The meaning of human actions grew out of the fact that they were performed in relation to other human actions. The task of a *verstehende* sociology was to comprehend, imaginatively, the meaning of mutually related human actions. Thus, it was the task of sociology to understand how an investor invested in the market *in the expectation that other investors would respond in particular ways*. Equally, it was the task of sociology to understand how a charismatic prophet behaved *in the expectation that his listeners would respond in particular ways*. Human society was made up of a vast complex of mutually related actions, each of which could be 'understood' through a deeper understanding of its expected responses.[37]

In Weber's account, moreover, human action was always accessible to our understanding for another reason as well: because it always displayed the same general structure. Human action was always purposive (*zweckrational*), obedient to large normative commitments (*wertrational*),

---

the declining Hindus by the rising Muslims, only to be borrowed from the declining Muslims by the rising Europeans.

[37] See Max Weber, *Wirtschaft und Gesellschaft: Grundzüge der verstehenden Soziologie*, 5th ed., vol. I (Tübingen: J. C. B. Mohr, 1976), pp. 1–16 [1922].

concerned with upholding tradition (*traditional*) or emotional and primordial (*affektuell*). The ends, values and traditions that humans pursued and obeyed, and the emotions they experienced, might be endlessly diverse. Nevertheless, because their action always fitted into the same general categories, the general structure of their activities could always be grasped. We can understand *that* another person should be rationally pursuing some end, even if we cannot always understand *why*. We know what purposive behaviour is and we know what tradition-bound behaviour is, even when the purposes and traditions in question seem to us bizarre. Thus, even in the midst of a human world of often profound strangeness, we are always capable of understanding the structure of human action.[38]

Philosophers similarly treated the hermeneutic problem as one that could be *solved*, that is, they treated 'otherness' not as unconquerable, but as philosophically challenging. Particularly important was the tradition of phenomenology, especially as represented by two riveting German philosophers, Max Scheler and Martin Heidegger. Investigating their solutions to the hermeneutic problem would carry us well beyond the bounds of anything that is reasonable here. Nevertheless, it is important to have some sense of what they said. Scheler approached the problem of understanding the 'other' largely through ringing critical variations on Hume's concept of sympathy. Scheler argued that we achieve understanding of other persons through *identification* and, indeed, through identification of a quasi-animal kind.[39] Heidegger's much-discussed approach to the problem of 'the hermeneutic circle' is more than I can examine here; but it is worth observing that Heidegger's solution in many ways resembled Max Weber's: Heidegger too focused on the way we understand *actions* rather than worrying about how we understand *persons*, *texts* or *cultures*. To Heidegger, it seemed clear that we are endowed with a pre-conscious ability to grasp useful actions.[40] At any rate, both Scheler and Heidegger declined to believe that 'otherness' meant unconquerable mutual incomprehensibility.

Even the philosophers who talked most about mutual incomprehensibility – Heidegger's existentialist followers – tried not to treat 'otherness' as a problem defeating all philosophical efforts. On the contrary, particularly in the hands of Sartre and others, existentialist philosophy succeeded in

---

[38] *Id.*, pp. 12–13.
[39] See Max Scheler, *Wesen und Formen der Sympathie*, 6th ed. (Bern: Francke, 1973) [1913].
[40] So, at least, I interpret the famously difficult material in Martin Heidegger, *Sein und Zeit*, 18th ed. (Tübingen: Max Niemeyer, 2001), pp. 142–60 [1927].

making very refined arguments that the encounter with the unknowable 'other' is itself a productive activity.[41] For it is in the effort to grapple with the other – with *das andere Ich*, as German phenomenologists sometimes liked to put it – that we largely are able to define and understand ourselves.

There are many other philosophers who deserve to be mentioned. After all, the fundamental hermeneutic problem of 'understanding' the 'other' dominated twentieth-century Continental philosophy.[42] Inevitably, I leave almost all of them aside. Nevertheless, it is important to say at least a word about one major figure, Hans-Georg Gadamer, author of the much-admired *Wahrheit und Methode*. Gadamer too has always worked from the assumption that the problem of 'otherness' is a problem to be solved. Like Heidegger, Gadamer understands hermeneutic interpretation of the world to be interpretation aimed at furthering freely willed action. Interestingly, this emerges with particular clarity in his long and revealing discussion of juristic hermeneutics. To Gadamer, the goal in 'understanding' is not simply to *know* a thing or a proposition or a form of action, but to *apply* that thing or proposition or form of action. That process of application involves *Vorverständnis*, pre-understanding, which is inarticulate and difficult to communicate. Gadamer however, has never treated this *Vorverständnis* as *impossible* to communicate. On the contrary, by studiously rejecting the Diltheyan claim that all understanding must be 'total' understanding, he has tried to make the hermeneutic problem tractable.[43]

And what of comparative law? Strangely, the highly sophisticated hermeneutic tradition that I have described had, for a long time, almost no influence on comparatists, even though comparatists are surely among the scholars who have their eyes most fastened upon the 'other'. In this as in other respects, twentieth-century comparatists could sometimes remain weirdly innocent of methodological self-reflection. Indeed, in law in general, we must wait until the work of Emilio Betti in the 1950s before serious hermeneutics much penetrates.[44]

Betti nevertheless did introduce modern hermeneutics into Continental legal philosophy and his work, in turn, triggered a major hermeneutic

---

[41] See especially Jean-Paul Sartre, *Being and Nothingness*, transl. by Hazel Barnes (New York: Citadel, [1965]), pp. 361–430 [1943].
[42] Among many, it is important to cite, if not to discuss in detail, Emmanuel Levinas.
[43] See Gadamer, *supra*, note 12, pp. 222–46.
[44] See Emilio Betti, 'Zur Grundlegung einer allgemeinen Auslegungslehre', in *Festschrift für Ernst Rabel*, vol. II (Tübingen: J. C. B. Mohr, 1954), pp. 79–168.

movement in Germany, led by Helmut Coing and Karl Larenz.[45] Gadamer's hermeneutics also penetrated somewhat later into US interpretive theory. This is no place to discuss the details of either movement but one figure has to be mentioned. This is the German Josef Esser, who made an important effort to apply some of Gadamer's lessons to the study of comparative law. In his book *Vorverständnis und Methodenwahl*,[46] Esser tried to apply Gadamer's notion of 'pre-understanding' to the analysis of law, and especially of judicial decision-making, arguing that a wide variety of unarticulated and ill-thought-through assumptions guided judges. The same idea informed his comparative study of legal procedure, *Grundsatz und Norm*.[47] Esser's claims were sharply attacked by the sociologist Hubert Rottleuthner, who found Esser's concept of *Vorverständnis* ill-defined. To Rottleuthner, Esser's *Vorverständnis* added up to an oddly assorted hodgepodge of things that were all 'pre-' in irritatingly different ways.[48] Rottleuthner's attack has probably done something to limit Esser's influence on the Continent. To US readers, most of what Esser writes will probably seem like relatively crude legal realism. Nevertheless, Esser pointed the way to a form of analysis that is of very real value, as I will argue below.

Recently, finally, some younger scholars, particularly in the United States, have picked up on one hermeneutic strand or another. In one form or another, most of these efforts have been founded on the idea that understanding a legal system is closely akin to understanding a 'culture'. Operating principally in the tradition of Dilthey, the new scholars have imagined their task as akin to the task of cultural anthropologists or historians. Thus, they have generally put the accent strongly on the 'otherness' of other legal systems, insisting that the special task of comparative law is to appreciate the depth of difference between legal traditions – just as it is the task of scholars in the cultural sciences to appreciate the depth of differences between cultures.

---

[45] See Helmut Coing, *Die juristischen Auslegungsmethoden und die Lehren der allgemeinen Hermeneutik* (Cologne: Westdeutscher Verlag, 1959); Karl Larenz, *Methodenlehre der Rechtswissenschaft*, 6th ed. (Berlin: Springer, 1991). See also Monika Frommel, *Die Rezeption der Hermeneutik bei Karl Larenz und Josef Esser* (Ebelsbach: Rolf Gremer, 1981).
[46] Esser, *Vorverständnis, supra*, note 5.   [47] *Id.*, *Grundsatz, supra*, note 5.
[48] Hubert Rottleuthner, 'Hermeneutik und Jurisprudenz', in Hans-Joachim Koch (ed.), *Juristische Methodenlehre und analytische Philosophie* (Kronberg: Athenäum, 1976), pp. 7–30, especially pp. 19–23. For another critical evaluation, see Hans-Joachim Koch, 'Zur Rationalität richterlichen Handelns. J. Essers "Vorverständnis und Methodenwahl in der Rechtsfindung" ', Rechtstheorie, 1973, p. 183.

There are, to be sure, real differences in the way representatives of the new literature have treated the problem of the 'otherness' of legal systems. To some, 'otherness' has meant something close to fundamental unknowability. Thus, Nora Demleitner, for example, writing in what we can think of as an existentialist vein, treats foreign law as ultimately unconquerably alien. She does not mean this, though, as a recipe for despair. She thinks, as those writing in the existentialist vein have long thought, that it is in the encounter with the 'other' that we form our own identity and thus concludes that comparative law can further some triumphant refashioning of our selves.[49]

Other authors have made less heavy weather about the unknowability of 'other' cultures. Instead, they have portrayed comparative law as involving the difficult but not impossible business of doing more or less what cultural anthropologists do when they interview local informants – the business of learning to understand a given foreign legal tradition as its participants understand it. Thus, to Vivian Curran, the task of comparative law remains fundamentally the classic hermeneutic one, as developed in the philosophy of Dilthey and pursued by his many disciples in the cultural sciences: it is the task of 'immersing' ourselves in the primacy of immediate experience of the foreign system, in order to develop an (at least partly intuitive) grasp of its spirit.[50] Similarly, to Pierre Legrand, author of unusually sophisticated and influential articles, the work of comparative law involves something Gadamerian/Heideggerian. For Legrand, as for Esser, it involves coming to know the *Vorverständnis*, the taken-for-granted knowledge that lies behind foreign legal practices. Like Gadamer or Heidegger, Legrand does not regard this as an impossible undertaking at all, but only as a strenuous one. Nevertheless, it seems fair to say that Legrand puts the accent on difference – on the need, as he puts it, to 'privilege alterity'.[51] 'Law', according to Legrand's very Diltheyan slogan, '*is* culture', and cultures differ.[52]

William Ewald takes a somewhat different stance, one that he arrives at, presumably, more through reflection on the thought of H. L. A. Hart than through reflection on the thought of Gadamer. To Ewald, doing proper comparative law involves acquiring the 'inner' perspective of the foreign system, understanding its presuppositions as its practitioners do. As Ewald puts it: 'If one's aim is to understand the ideas that lie behind the foreign

---

[49] See Demleitner, *supra*, note 3.   [50] Curran, *supra*, note 3.
[51] Legrand, 'Impossibility', *supra*, note 2, p. 124.   [52] See *id.*, *Fragments*, *supra*, note 2, *passim*.

legal system (and I argue at length this *should* be the aim of comparative law) the sociological data and rule-books alike are unable to furnish what we want, which is a grasp, from the inside, of the conscious reasons and principles and conceptions that are employed by the foreign lawyers.'[53] This search for the 'inner' perspective, as Ewald presents it, certainly requires a rich appreciation of how different the mentalities of foreign lawyers can be. Ewald begins his well-known argument with an account of something very 'other' indeed: the early sixteenth-century prosecution of the rats of Autun and their defence by the wonderful Renaissance jurist Barthélemy de Chasseneux. Ewald challenges his reader to make the effort to understand how such a proceeding could take place and suggests that it is the proper role of comparative law to equip the student to grasp the underlying views of the world that permitted something like the trial of rats – to adopt the 'inner' perspective of Chasseneux and his contemporaries. Turning to modern law, he argues that the same effort to grasp the 'inner' perspective is necessary even when we confront more modern, and less obviously alien, legal traditions. In particular, he tries to show that modern German law is thoroughly imbued with values drawn from the philosophies of Herder and especially of Immanuel Kant. German law cannot be understood by those who do not know this philosophical background.[54]

Nevertheless, if Ewald is concerned with 'difference', just as so many of his contemporaries are, it is important to recognize that his approach is distinctive. To be sure, Ewald too bows in the direction of Dilthey (among others).[55] At the end of the day, though, he stands more in the tradition of Herder than in the grand tradition of hermeneutics. As he puts it, his interest is in '*conscious* reasons and principles' and, correspondingly, he is not so much in the business of hunting for the taken-for-granted, inarticulate *Vorverständnis* of foreign lawyers. In this, Ewald's approach resembles that of the *Germanisten* or of Jhering. Like these nineteenth-century predecessors, Ewald wants to develop a sound account of the basic values that inform the foreign legal system and that are already in essence acknowledged by participants in that system. Moreover, like these nineteenth-century predecessors, he believes the best way to do it is through an understanding of the historical development of those values. The 'inner' perspective that one needs to cultivate, Ewald continues, is inevitably one that is formed *historically*.

---

[53] Ewald, *supra*, note 13, pp. 555–6.   [54] See *id.*, *supra*, note 1, pp. 1990–2045.
[55] *Id.*, *supra*, note 13, p. 556.

Inner perspectives develop over time, which means that comparative law must be largely a species of legal history, concerned with mastering the 'inner' history of the foreign system.

II

This diffusion of neo-Romantic approaches into comparative law, whether in the tradition of Herder or in the tradition of Dilthey, is exciting and overdue. Certainly, I agree that good comparative law has to begin by mastering the 'inner' perspective. Certainly, I agree that we must grasp the *Vorverständnisse* that inform and motivate the activity of foreign lawyers. Certainly, I believe that both approaches can do a lot to improve what is often a literature of wretchedly low quality. Nevertheless, I do not think that either the 'inner' perspective or the pursuit of *Vorverständnis* is enough. My reasons have to do largely with my own current research and I would like to present a brief account of that research in order to make the grounds for my objections clear.

That current research concerns dignitary law. This is a matter on which Americans and Continental Europeans differ dramatically. 'Dignity' and 'personal honour' are regarded as fundamental values in the law of Continental Europe. In the law of the United States, by contrast, the same values play strikingly little role. The contrast shows up again and again, over a striking range of topics, from criminal to civil to constitutional law, in questions both familiar and arcane. Among the familiar examples are many involving one variety of 'dignity', '*human* dignity'. These include some hot-button issues: Europeans, for example, condemn the death penalty as a violation of human dignity in a way that Americans do not quite grasp or, at least, that US majority culture does not grasp. Bioethics is another familiar case. The new French bioethics law, to take the most striking example, sharply limits anything that might even approach commercialization of the body parts and products on the grounds that any concession to the temptation to deny supreme value to the integrity of the human body would undermine the social commitment to human dignity.[56] The dignitary difference extends well beyond these familiar controversies, though. In punishment practice, Americans and Europeans have experienced a profound parting

---

[56] See *loi* no. 94–653 of 29 July 1994, D.1994.L.406 and *loi* no. 94–654 of 29 July 1994, D.1994.L.409. For a description of the law and the justifications offered for it by Judge Noëlle Lenoir, see 'France Weighs Restrictive Biomedical Science Law', *The Boston Globe*, 23 October 1993, p. 6.

of the ways. In the United States, over the last thirty years or so, prison terms have become ever-longer, punishment for drug and other morals offences has become harsher, prison conditions have continued their descent into pure hellishness, criminal liability has been extended to minors as young as six or seven and old-style shame sanctions have been reintroduced. In Europe, over exactly the same thirty years, prison terms have become ever-shorter, morals offences have been broadly decriminalized and prison conditions have been the subject of ongoing reform legislation – all in the name of 'human dignity'.[57] In the law of privacy too, the contrast between Europe and the United States is stark and is growing starker. In the name of dignity, Europeans have aggressively tried to guarantee that individuals control all uses and appearances of their names and their images.[58] Nothing of the kind is true in the United States. In the law of sexual harassment, now slowly spreading into Europe, the same contrast is to be found again: 'dignity' has made little headway as a protectable value in US sexual harassment law; by contrast, it is precisely around 'dignity' that European sexual harassment law revolves. There is more, too. Not least, on the supranational level, there is the jurisprudence of the European Court of Human Rights and the literature surrounding the European Convention on Human Rights. These have become the leading force in the making of high dignitary law in the world today. They are rich in rules and norms that differ dramatically from the rules and norms that prevail in the United States.

Continental Europe and the United States thus differ, and differ in ways that make nonsense of the familiar claim that all modern legal systems are 'converging'. Why is this? Why is it that the Europeans have so much 'dignity' while, at least by European standards, Americans have so little?

This is a problem to which there is an answer very commonly given by European lawyers – an 'inner' answer that seems, at first blush, both plausible and appealing. This answer has to do with *human* dignity, in particular, and it takes the form of asserting that 'dignity' established itself in Europe as part of a reaction against Fascism. The Nazis in particular, it is said, practised systematic violations of human dignity. Once they and other Fascist movements were overcome through the supreme, and in some ways only lucky, efforts of the allies, lawyers recognized the need to establish

---

[57] This is the topic of research I present in my *Harsh Justice: Criminal Punishment and the Widening Divide Between America and Europe* (New York: Oxford University Press, 2003).

[58] For comparison, see most recently Basil S. Markesinis (ed.), *Protecting Privacy* (Oxford: Oxford University Press, 1999).

human rights, and dignitary values, on an unshakeable legal footing. Fifty years of post-Fascist efforts have followed, culminating in the dignitary legal cultures we see today, which sanction Kantian, and broadly Christian, values.[59] This argument has an interesting, but somewhat distressing, implication: that Americans have suffered by their failure to experience Fascism. Never having known Fascism, Americans have never learned to value human dignity.

But is this 'inner' account, frequently repeated by Europeans, true? Anybody who has spent time with lawyers knows that their accounts of the history of their own systems are rarely correct. Moreover, anybody who has spent time in Germany or France knows that the European culture of 'dignity' is much older than 1945 and that 'dignity' is often thought of in ways that do not seem to have much to do with Kant. Is it not possible that Europeans are in some sense wrong about their own system?

In fact, as I try to show in my current research, they *are* wrong.[60] The 'inner' account of the rise of European dignitary law is both seriously incomplete and quite misleading. Moreover, understanding the shortcomings of the 'inner' account can help us to understand why comparative law should not be like some caricature of cultural anthropology – why it is not our business simply to interview local informants.[61]

In point of fact, European dignitary traditions are much older than 1945 and the place of the Fascist period in their development is complex and ambiguous. 'Dignity' as it is protected in Europe today grows largely out of old traditions of the protection of 'personal honour' and especially out of traditions of the protection of aristocratic and high-status personal honour. This is something we can see, to take one important example, in the history and sociology of a dignitary issue that is hotly debated in the United States today, that is, law enforcing interpersonal respect and, in particular, the law of hate speech. Many Americans have advocated some kind of hate-speech regulation, of law protecting minorities against insulting and disrespectful speech. And many of these advocates of hate-speech regulation have looked abroad, pointing admiringly to European, and especially German, models. And there is indeed hate-speech law in Germany – law both against '*Volksverhetzung*', against inciting popular hatred, and against '*Beleidigung*',

---

[59] See the discussion in Whitman, *supra*, note 14, pp. 1283–4.
[60] In what follows, I summarize generally work presented in *id.*, *supra*, note 14.
[61] This is something that careful cultural anthropologists, of course, fully understand. For an example, see Riles, *supra*, note 4, p. 73.

against insult. Really to understand this law, though, we must know a great deal about matters that have nothing to do with hate speech as such. German hate-speech law, as I have tried to show at length, is the outgrowth of a legal culture surrounding the criminal law of 'insult'. The criminal law of insult purports to protect the 'personal honour' of *all* Germans, not just of minorities and it belongs to a lively, and sometimes comical, everyday culture in which insulted Germans are convinced that they have been victims of a criminal offence. The ideas of 'respect' and 'personal honour' that inform the current law and culture of insult are, in turn, deeply rooted in German society and in German social history. In particular, the law of insult, as it exists today, has aristocratic sources. Germans involved in insult litigation display a kind of touchy sense of their own 'honour' that is very much reminiscent of the old aristocratic duellists' world of the eighteenth and nineteenth centuries. And, in fact, the law of insult, as it exists in modern-day Germany, is a kind of living fossil, preserving features that date to a pre-modern era in which German law was concerned with maintaining elaborate norms of social hierarchy and deference. The law of insult, which today applies to all Germans, once upon a time generally applied only to certain high-status ones. Moreover, the substance of the contemporary law of insult grows, strikingly enough, largely out of old *duelling* practices. Legally cognizable 'insults' that we see today generally began as insults offered to duelling aristocrats. These roots of the law of insult in pre-modern social hierarchy go almost entirely unmentioned in the juristic literature that presents the 'inner' German view. But they are of deep importance for understanding what it is that sets this striking German legal culture of insult apart from anything we can find in the United States. In the last analysis, what distinguishes the United States from Germany in this respect is not that the United States has not had Fascism, but that US law does not have a strong tradition of protecting 'personal honour'.

What is more, the role of Fascism in the tale of this aspect of dignitary law turns out to be a surprisingly complex one. The critical extension of a claim to 'personal honour' for *low-status* Germans is something that took place partly *during* the Nazi period. While ideas about the broad social extension of 'honour' circulated during the early twentieth century and while German jurisprudence did begin a slow process of change before Hitler, it was the Nazi seizure of power that really brought fundamental change. It was really the Nazi movement, with its strong insistence that 'honour' should be the basis of national German law, that extended the legally enforceable claim to respect to Germans of all social classes – at least, 'Germans' as the Nazis defined them. Indeed, ironically enough, it was the Nazis who created a large part of the basis of the law of group insult that now protects Jews.

This history is not what our German native informants recount. Yet, it has left a real mark on the German law of hate speech, which in a host of ways is still deeply coloured, and indeed haunted, by very traditional ideas of personal honour just as German society is still haunted by traditional ideas of personal honour. I have presented the details elsewhere. Let me simply say that the German law of hate speech looks, to US eyes, thoroughly inadequate in many ways and its inadequacies have much to do with the fact that it remains, in its substance and its view of the world, a rehash of early-modern duelling law.

Similar stories can be told about many other European dignitary institutions, for example, about the law of prison conditions, in which old high-status forms of imprisonment have been extended to all European inmates; or about privacy law, in which distinctly high-status protections are now being gradually extended throughout the population of northern European countries; or about aspects of the social welfare state such as the effective right of German workers to take Mediterranean vacations. To be sure, not every institution of European dignitary law shows the same pattern. But many indeed do. And this is so because the deep social history of dignity is different in Europe from what it is in the United States. Behind the contemporary European culture of human dignity lies a long history of hierarchical tradition. What is now protected as 'human dignity' was once protected as 'personal honour'; more particularly, what is now protected as the 'dignity' of all persons was once protected as the 'honour' of aristocrats and other members of the social elite alone. Generalizing about this, we can say that the legal cultures of Continental Europe have experienced what I would call '*levelling up*'. In these societies, the cultural memory of an age of social hierarchy is strong and the commitment to modern egalitarianism has been a commitment to the proposition that all persons should stand on the highest rung of the social hierarchy. Egalitarianism in countries like France and Germany is an egalitarianism that proclaims 'we are all aristocrats now'; and, in practice, this has been an egalitarianism of widely generalized norms of dignity. US egalitarianism, by contrast, is an egalitarianism of *levelling down*; it is an egalitarianism that proclaims, in effect, 'there are no more aristocrats', that we all stand together on the lowest rung of the social ladder. One consequence is an egalitarianism of the lowest rung, which has often proven to be an egalitarianism without any commitment to the protection of dignity in the law.

III

Now, in trying to understand all this, I think the danger of taking exclusively the 'inner' point of view is clear. How much of European dignitary law will we understand if we treat comparative law as though it should use the cultural anthropologist's technique of interviewing local informants? Some, but by no means all. Interviewing local informants is a very poor way of fully understanding what is going on in European dignitary law. The participants themselves do not understand where their system came from, nor why it takes the form it takes.

Indeed, there is an inherent bias in everything our 'local informants' tell us about *any* legal system. *Participants in a legal system are unusually poor informants.* This is true for a reason we can see very clearly in the examples that I have given. Legal systems are normative systems and any person involved in a given system is always likely to give an account whose aim is to *justify* its practices (or sometimes to condemn them). Indeed, as Ronald Dworkin has argued, what jurists typically do can be described as striving to construct the most normatively attractive account of their system that they can offer.[62] This is indeed exactly the variety of normative striving that we see European jurists engaging when they re-characterize their dignitary traditions as 'anti-Fascist' traditions. They want to see their dignitary traditions in the most normatively attractive light possible and thinking of them as anti-Fascist does exactly that. Because they aim at this kind of normative reconstruction, it is rare indeed that our informants will be able to take the kind of Nietzschean stance that would allow them to see their practices in the cold light that non-normative description requires. European lawyers feel a real need to talk about the struggle against Fascism in order to justify their activities, in order to capture their own sense of the justness of their cause, in order to range their law on the side of the good in a more or less Manichaean picture of the moral universe.

From a normative point of view, there is absolutely nothing wrong with this. What European lawyers have done under the banner of anti-Fascism

---

[62] For example, see Ronald Dworkin, *Law's Empire* (Cambridge, Mass.: Harvard University Press, 1986), pp. 400–13.

is wonderful and laudable; and in any case, legal systems do not function without justifications of this kind. Moreover, from the descriptive point of view, the European belief in the centrality of the reaction against Fascism – the 'inner' perspective – is of indispensable, if partial, importance. That 'inner' perspective serves a fundamental function in the working of European dignitary law. Legal systems are systems founded on normative beliefs and those beliefs serve as guides to actions. A description of any system that was not also a system of its 'inner' justificatory beliefs could accordingly never be fully adequate. In that measure, William Ewald is entirely right.

Nevertheless, there is more to understanding what European lawyers are up to than grasping their own account of what justifies and motivates their legal reasoning. The cold Nietzschean stance has a lot to offer us, especially if we want to develop the kind of sound understanding of a foreign system that will permit thoughtful comparative analysis. Whether or not they recognize it themselves, the thinking of European lawyers is conditioned and motivated by taken-for-granted assumptions – by matters of *Vorverständnis*, in Gadamer's famous term – which they have not articulated as normative justifications. Terms like '*Vorverständnis*' are ones we should, of course, use sceptically and cautiously. As sensible critics like Rottleuthner have complained, the use of words that begin with the prefix 'pre-' is often an invitation to murky thinking. Nevertheless, as the example of comparative dignitary law suggests, there really are deep cultural differences in our unarticulated assumptions about what kinds of legal rules are justified. Participants in the German and French legal cultures typically take it for granted that persons should be entitled to a certain measure of respect for their 'personal honour'. Over many generations of development, this taken-for-granted assumption has motivated some significant comparative differences between Continental European law, on the one hand, and US law, on the other. German workers are protected against insult at work; US workers are not. Sexual harassment law in both Germany and France aims to guarantee norms of interpersonal respect in a way sexual harassment in US law does not. And on it goes. These are differences that can be understood only if we understand matters that European lawyers themselves do not consciously 'understand'.

Correspondingly, our job as comparatists has to involve more than mastering Ewald's 'inner' perspective. Indeed, all too often, the 'inner' perspective will amount to a species of what we in the United States call 'law-office history': thin, mostly whiggish, stuff that falls far below the level of what any careful historian should accept. Even when the 'inner' perspective is well worked out, moreover, it will be misleading. Dworkin is right: the 'inner' perspective always represents an effort at normative beautification, an effort at improving and reconceiving the principles of the law. And if Dworkin is right, then Ewald is, in the last analysis, wrong. We must begin with the 'inner' perspective, but we would be doing a poor job as descriptive comparatists if we stopped there. Fully describing a foreign system means not only surveying its articulated normative beliefs, but also its unarticulated assumptions. Indeed, uncovering differences in unarticulated assumptions will frequently be the most revealing and gratifying work a comparatist can do.

IV

Thus, I agree with Josef Esser and Pierre Legrand that we should investigate *Vorverständnis*, the unarticulated, taken-for-granted assumptions that underlie the law. At the same time, let me rush to say that I also agree with Rottleuthner that we need to use concepts like '*Vorverständnis*' cautiously. These sorts of concepts are dangerous, as Gadamer himself has been at pains to emphasize; unless we are careful, we can easily find ourselves drawn into a pathless academic murk. It is when we begin to talk about *Vorverständnis*, indeed, that we risk stumbling into the darkness of the more tangled of Romantic jungles. In particular, we must resist a number of excessive Romantic tendencies. (1) While we certainly do want to grasp various *Vorverständnisse*, we must not suppose that the *only* way to understand foreign legal practices is by understanding the *Vorverständnisse* that underlie them. (2) We must not succumb to the vulgar Heideggerian error of thinking of legal actors as somehow unmoveably 'rooted' in the 'cultures' constituted by their *Vorverständnis*. (3) We must not suppose, in particular, that practices are so 'rooted' that they can never be 'transplanted'. To the extent Legrand and others suggest otherwise, they threaten to mislead us. These are points I would like to make by focusing on one example in particular from my current research: the example of the spread of sexual harassment law into Continental Europe.

First, it is not meaningless to speak of 'understanding' legal practices even if we have not fully plumbed all of the *Vorverständnis*, all of the underlying sensibilities, that inform and motivate them. This is true, first of all, because (to echo Weber and Gadamer) what we aim to 'understand' is not total *culture* – an impossibility. What we aim to understand is human *action* – a much less daunting undertaking. It is also true because legal practices represent a particular kind of human action: they represent action that decides the fates of persons and that sort of action is accessible to sympathetic understanding, as I would like to suggest, in peculiar ways.

'Law' is a form of human action. Moreover, in Weber's terms, it is generally 'rational' action. Weber's scheme for the description of rational action has some well-known shortcomings, which I do not want to rehash here. For my purposes, it is enough to deploy Weber's useful terminology. Legal practices are sometimes usefully understood as *zweckrational* – as calculated to achieve a particular result. When US lawyers speak of their law of commercial paper as aiming to guarantee 'security of transactions', they are speaking in *zweckrational* terms. Sometimes, legal practices are usefully understood as *wertrational*, as aiming to maintain fidelity to some normative ideal. When US lawyers argue that affirmative-action programmes unacceptably undermine ideals of equality before the law, they are speaking in *wertrational* terms. *Like other kinds of rational action, legal practices have a structure that makes them always in principle comprehensible.* It is a feature of the human condition that we are able to grasp the structure of forms of action that aim to engineer a particular result or that aim to maintain the integrity of a certain normative ideal – as Heidegger recognized no less than Weber.

This is true even of law that belongs to 'radically different' societies. Thus, we may find Chasseneux's defence of the rats of Autun bizarre; but we recognize that he was engaged in some kind of purposive activity and to that extent we understand the structure of his action. Indeed, Ewald's discussion proceeds from the assumption that Chasseneux's activity must have had *some* goal. The same is true of other similarly bizarre examples like the interpretive 'rule of the black beans' developed in *mimansa* reasoning and described in Robert Lingat's *The Classical Law of India*. That rule and similar interpretive rules apparently aimed at maintaining obedience to the normative authority of Vedic sacrificial ritual.[63] We may find the idea of legal practices that aim to maintain the authority of sacrifical ritual very strange. Nevertheless, once we accept that strange idea – once we accept,

---

[63] Robert Lingat, *The Classical Law of India*, ed. and transl. by J. Duncan M. Derrett (Berkeley: University of California Press, 1973), p. 151.

that is, the proposition that some legal rules might aim to maintain the authority of the Vedas – we *can* comprehend the reasoning of the Hindu *mimansa* jurists. We can follow the way in which they reason, even as we puzzle over the question of *why* they would want to reason in that way.

The same is true of European perceptions of US sexual harassment law. US sexual harassment law aims to protect a *material* interest, not a dignitary interest: it vindicates, in particular, women's rights to career advancement and financial gain. This is so alien to European understandings that, in my experience, Europeans find it difficult even to grasp that US sexual harassment law could have such a purpose – if they do not find it quite as bizarre as trying rats, they nevertheless find it exceedingly strange. Europeans simply take it for granted that any sexual harassment law *must* revolve around women's dignitary interests. To some extent, then, Europeans can be said not to 'understand' US sexual harassment law. Nevertheless, they do grasp what we can call the 'structure' of US sexual harassment law as an example of action. They understand that it is protective in purpose, that it identifies a class and aims to safeguard it against certain kinds of depradation.

What is more, they understand something else, too, something that has to do with the very important fact that law decides the fates of persons. When we witness foreign legal acts, there may be much that we cannot grasp; but typically we can always grasp that somebody's fate is on the line and that fact makes even the most 'foreign' law peculiarly accessible to outside observers. Take the example of female genital mutilation, one of the most fiercely debated topics in our literature on comparative and foreign law and one that Nora Demleitner, in particular, has made a basis for her arguments about the methodology of comparative law.[64] On the one hand, female genital mutilation is profoundly 'foreign'. Most westerners find it difficult to form any sympathetic grasp of the normative beliefs that motivate it; there are, indeed, few practices that seem to us more normatively strange. On the other hand, strange as the practice is, we have absolutely no doubt that we 'understand' what is going on in an act of female genital mutilation. We see a young woman whose fate has been (wrongly) decided. We are so confident of our understanding, indeed, that even if the young woman herself does not object, we are quite prepared to say that *she* has not understood what is 'really' going on.

---

[64] See Demleitner, *supra*, note 3.

Why are we so confident of our ability to understand such acts? It is, I suggest, because they represent decisions about the fate of persons and we always have a *sympathetic identification* with persons whose fates are being decided. Here, I draw on the philosophies of Walter Burkert and Bernard Williams, who emphasize our sympathy with victims of fate,[65] as well as on the philosophy of Scheler, who argues that understanding rests on identification with others.[66] We put ourselves in the shoes of persons whose fates we see being decided and that represents a very important form of understanding. The fate in question may be the fate of Sophocles's Oedipus or it may be the fate of a contemporary supporter of the Falun Gong. Either way, any decision about the fate of a person engages, *for every human observer*, the normative faculties. We all always ask, *was that fate rightly decided*? And because our normative thinking is always triggered by any legal decision, we always have the sense that we can comprehend any legal act, however strange. Legal acts trigger what we may call 'normative sympathetic understanding'. Whatever else may be incomprehensible to us in a given legal act, we always feel ourselves capable of identifying with its 'victim'.

That kind of sympathetic understanding is also present for European observers of US sexual harassment law: they may not quite get the 'why' of the US law, but they do understand that the fate of the 'victim' of an act of harassment is being decided – though to be sure, they (like Americans) may sometimes view the 'victim' as the accused rather than the accuser.

Such normative sympathetic understanding is, of course, not the only kind of understanding we could have or seek. Indeed, it is quite an inadequate form of understanding: people who spend all their time sympathizing with the victims of fates imposed by foreign law make very poor comparatists. Nevertheless, the fact that we always sympathize with the victims of foreign law tells us something important about the nature of legal diversity in the human world. There is a vast and complex range of differences among human legal orders. Certainly, it would be a grave mistake to try to reduce all of those legal orders to any single set of natural-law principles. Nevertheless, while there is not a single natural law in the human world, it

---

[65] See Walter Burkert, 'Greek Tragedy and Sacrificial Ritual', (1966) 7 Greek, Roman & Byzantine Stud. 87; Bernard Williams, *Shame and Necessity* (Berkeley: University of California Press, 1993).

[66] See Scheler, *supra*, note 39.

remains the case that normative legal orders generally address themselves to the same, relatively narrow, range of predicaments. Law is always roughly concerned with decisions about fates: who should die, who should profit, who should be subjected to the authority of whom. While we may find the normative justifications and tacit *Vorverständnis* of a given foreign legal system strange, we are usually able to identify with the predicaments of the parties whose interests are at stake, though we also usually have normative views of our own about how those predicaments should be dealt with. This too is a meaningful form of understanding.

Now, how unmoveably rooted are legal actors in the world created by their *Vorverständnis*? Here again, we must be on our guard. It is easy to slip into the dubious belief that people can never escape their *Vorverständnis*. Scholars working in the Romantic tradition have a long-standing tendency to think of their task as that of 'understanding' the culture of people who remain attached to their native cultural values in the way that the peasants that the early nineteenth-century Romantics loved so much were supposedly attached to their traditional ways. Yet, it is wrong to suppose that foreign lawyers cannot be convinced to see their systems differently. Even peasants can be persuaded to see their world differently from the way their ancestors saw it and so can lawyers.

Indeed, law is in some ways peculiarly susceptible to changed 'understandings'. This is for a reason that highlights once again how deeply different comparative law is from cultural anthropology. In law, when we describe *Vorverständnisse*, we *change* them – and, indeed, we often aim to change them. *Vorverständnis*, in its unstudied, unexamined form, is inarticulate. It is, indeed, in its very nature that it remain *unausgesprochen*, tacit. Yet, what we aim to do when we describe the *Vorverständnis* is to *articulate* it. To articulate legal *Vorverständnis* is, however, to alter its nature, since it is inevitably to subject it to the process of articulate normative critique. What has been *expressed*, in the law, must inevitably be debated and defended.

This may sound like some blathery post-modern claim, but it is something that happens all the time. The best examples involve the changing legal status of women – of which, of course, the rise of sexual harassment law is a prime example. The last thirty or forty years have seen a large-scale articulation of what were once tacit assumptions about the roles and rights of women in western societies everywhere. The very articulation of those assumptions has placed the question of the status of women on the normative agenda, as it were: it has transformed what were once matters of *unausgesprochenes Vorverständnis* into propositions that are openly and energetically debated in the express justificatory reasoning of western legal systems. This does not mean that all western systems are converging on the same normative answers; they surely are not. What it does mean is that the nature and the dynamic of all of these systems has changed to take account of roughly the same normative problem.

To the extent comparatists busy themselves articulating *Vorverständnis*, they thus threaten to change it and to shift the terms of normative debate. Explicating the tacit assumptions of lawyers is indeed something that one can do only with the hope, expectation or fear that one will change them, for lawyers *read* what is written about them and (at least sometimes) they change their minds as a result. This is once again true, to stick with my example, of sexual harassment law in Europe. To the extent that we make it clear that European ideas of sexual harassment law rest on ill-considered assumptions about the dignity of women, we are inevitably opening those assumptions up to normative critique. Such is indeed the aim of Susanne Baer's important book *Würde oder Gleichheit?*, a comparative study of US and German assumptions that is intended as a critical study of any dignity-based sexual harassment law.[67]

This too sets the activity of comparative law sharply apart from the activity of cultural anthropology. Cultural anthropologists never aim to change the *Vorverständnis* of their subjects. They aim to document the 'cultures' they study; and they assume that, if they change those cultures, they have in some fundamental way tainted or destroyed them. The 'cultures' that cultural anthropologists study must remain in some fundamental way unaffected by the act of description, or they will perish. This is why anthropologists engage in 'salvage ethnography'. The same is not true of what comparatists do; it would be correspondingly strange to speak of doing 'salvage comparative law'. This is an important indication that law is *not* culture in the way that some of our new literature – and, perhaps, particularly the writings of Legrand – suggests.

Lastly, we must be careful not to slip into the error of believing that legal practices can be so rooted in their 'cultures' that they can never be transplanted. This is an idea that has exerted a distinct attraction on

---

[67] Susanne Baer, *Würde oder Gleichheit? Zur angemessenen grundrechtlichen Konzeption von Recht gegen Diskriminierung am Beispiel sexueller Belastigung am Arbeitsplatz in der Bundesrepublik Deutschland und den USA* (Baden-Baden: Nomos, 1995).

Ewald and Legrand, both of whom have mounted thoughtful attacks on Watson, the leading defender of the notion that transplants drive legal development.[68] These attacks have some justice to them, which I do not want to dispute here. While Watson's theoretical statements are often quite nuanced, the details of his work often imply that legal rules, and especially rules drawn from the Roman legal tradition, can be more successfully 'transplanted' than one readily believes. Nevertheless, in raising doubts about the 'transplantation' of legal institutions, we run the risk of neglecting what is unquestionably a fundamentally important issue: legal systems *do* permit transcultural discussion and transcultural change. Indeed, they undergo transcultural change all the time.

This is something that we can illustrate once again with the example of the spread of sexual harassment law into northern Europe. Sexual harassment law has been borrowed throughout western Europe from the prestigious US legal order. This is indeed one of the most interesting developments of contemporary comparative law. The 'borrowing', though, is producing a sexual harassment law that is strikingly different from its US model, as we have seen. Predictably, the new European sexual harassment law focuses on *dignitary* interests in a way that its US model does not. To speak of this process of borrowing as a 'transplant' is thus at best misleading because the metaphor 'transplant' suggests that what we see is somehow the same 'plant' in different soil. The plant itself is however being more deeply transformed than the metaphor is capable of conveying.

Nevertheless, *some* kind of a borrowing is surely taking place and we need *some* account of what is going on. Such an account would have to be partly an account of cultural prestige, of what it is that makes Europeans want to adopt aspects of specifically US law. But what I would like to emphasize is that it would have to be largely an account of the *normative character* of US sexual harassment law. US sexual harassment law makes an articulated normative claim: the claim that women are being wrongly treated in some daily encounters. Like all articulated normative claims, it tends to trigger debate and reflection. Indeed, it belongs to the phenomenology of our experience of the world that *we cannot be confronted with an articulated normative position without responding to it. We may accept it or we may*

---

[68] See William Ewald, 'The American Revolution and the Evolution of Law', (1994) 42 Am. J. Comp. L. 1701; Legrand, 'Impossibility', *supra*, note 2.

challenge it, but we always feel we must answer. Europeans, confronted with the articulated normative position represented by US sexual harassment law, have been driven to reflect on the question of whether their own law is normatively adequate. Can we, they are compelled to ask, continue to treat women as we do? Indeed, as Williams has argued at length, moral relativist positions are impossible: whether we like it or not, when we witness an act with 'moral' significance, we take a position on it.[69] Europeans have taken a position on sexual harassment too. They have responded to the US example by making changes in their law, though those changes, of course, obey distinctly European normative beliefs and tacit assumptions. What is happening is thus not that a US institution is being adopted wholesale. What is happening is rather that a US normative claim has propelled European normative debate in new directions.

Behind this lies an important fact about our 'understanding' of foreign law. If law is action that we can in principle always comprehend, it is also action that we can always in principle imitate – and, indeed, may frequently feel *challenged* to imitate. This is true for a reason that is simple enough: law claims, once again, to be *normatively justified*. Law is not only purposive action, it is also action that purports to represent the right thing to do. When law spreads, it typically spreads because it makes that kind of normative claim.

V

In general, my argument in this paper has to do with the simple and obvious fact that legal systems are *normative* systems. 'Law' is not best thought of as a rooted set of cultural facts that can be 'understood' only in cultural context. 'Law' is best thought of as an activity that aims at normative justification of certain human acts and of the exercise of the authority of some humans over others. Different societies unquestionably offer different normative justifications for different acts; moreover, different societies work with different sorts of tacit *Vorverständnis* that bear on the operation of their 'law'. These differences are deep-seated and important – and comparatists should be in the business of studying and articulating them.

---

[69] See Bernard Williams, *Morality: An Introduction to Ethics* (New York: Harper & Row, 1972), pp. 20–5; *id., Ethics and the Limits of Philosophy* (Cambridge, Mass.: Harvard University Press, 1985), pp. 156–73.

Nevertheless, a set of normative justifications and tacit assumptions is not the same thing as a total 'culture'. First of all, normative legal systems are *constructions*, that is, they are efforts at a kind of normative beautification, as Dworkin has contended. This means that the 'inner' perspective is never adequate. Furthermore, it is in the nature of normative justifications that they are subject to *debate*. Indeed, all normative systems are always in flux. As for tacit *Vorverständnis*, it can cease to be tacit and itself become the subject of articulate normative debate. This does not mean that normative systems do not have a momentum, a stickiness, a character of tradition that is hard to shake. They certainly do. Nevertheless, really radical change *is* possible, as the revolution in relations between the sexes in our time suggests more forcefully than almost any other example.

As I see it, all this means that the business of comparatists is fundamentally no different from the business of any other type of legal scholar. All good legal scholars are interested in carefully working out normative justifications for human action and for the exercise of human authority. We should be interested in the same thing. What sets us apart is our knowledge of other possible normative conceptions, of other conceptions of what sorts of action need justification and of other conceptions of what sorts of justifications for action count. What sets us apart is also a certain native scepticism about the possibility of reaching definitive ultimate answers. But we are, or ought to be, engaged in the same general debate about the law as everybody else.

That does not commit us to the proposition that there is some single right answer, some 'natural law'. Normative debate is *debate*; there is no escaping the cacophony of human morality. Nevertheless, there is a great difference between informed debate and ill-informed debate and the best thing we can aim to do is to make some of our colleagues in other branches of the law more aware of how scanty their information remains.

11

The methods and the politics

DAVID KENNEDY

Comparative law as governance

The broad mainstream of comparative law today is careful to distance itself from the work of governance and the choices of political life. Discomfort with politics is common to comparatists who seek knowledge about foreign legal systems more or less for its own sake and those who see themselves as technicians in a project whose political direction has been determined elsewhere. This has not always been true of comparative law and it distinguishes the field from other legal disciplines today. This essay explores the argumentative machinery that generates comparative law's apolitical sensibility and asks whether this practice itself has a politics. I develop some hypotheses about its historical origins and disciplinary specificity and end with some thoughts about its contribution to global governance.[1]

A professional discipline might be thought 'to be political' or 'participate in governance' in a variety of ways. Sometimes, disciplines participate actively in ideological debates within the broader society, taking positions we can associate easily with the left, centre or right. Sometimes, they harness their expertise to the interests of one or another social group, so that we identify their work with the interests of workers or industrialists, men or women. Disciplines may take positions on the broad choices governments make, promoting, say, centralization over decentralization or assimilation

---

I am grateful to all those who very helpfully commented on these arguments as presented at the Sixth General Meeting of the Common Core of European Private Law held in Trento on 13–15 July 2000; at the Northwestern University School of Law Faculty Conference 'Rethinking the Masters of Comparative Law' held in Chicago on 18 March 2000; and at the Conference from which this book emerges. I would like to thank Dan Danielsen, Jorge Esquirol, Janet Halley, Duncan Kennedy and Alejandro Lorite for their help with this essay.

[1] This essay builds on ideas I published initially in David Kennedy, 'New Approaches to Comparative Law and International Governance', [1997] Utah L.R. 545.

over cultural diversity. Professions may urge their members to participate in public life, exercising the levers of governmental authority by applying the profession's special knowledge or viewpoint. Some disciplines encourage professionals to experience their work as the ongoing exercise of power, to see themselves making choices framed, but not compelled, by their professional context and expertise.

Comparative law today distances itself from politics and rulership in each of these senses, eschewing identification with ideological positions and social interests, retreating to the academy from public life and from the application of comparative knowledge. The discipline encourages its practitioners not to take positions on issues facing government and to think of their professional work as the exercise of academic good judgement rather than political choice. Comparative law today is about knowing, not doing.

Perhaps the largest comparative-law undertaking now underway – the effort to uncover and describe a 'common core' in European private law under the loose auspices and funding of the European Union – well illustrates the attitudes of many mainstream comparatists toward engagement with the choices involved in governing. Although the European Union has a clear project of harmonization and unification, those involved in the common-core project present themselves as coming to the effort agnostic about the existence or shape of the common core they are exploring. Their work will be objective, descriptive and scientific. In the words of Mauro Bussani, co-founder of the project:

> We wish to correct this misleading information; we do not wish to force the actual diverse reality of the law into one single map to attain uniformity [...]. This project seeks only to analyse the present complex situation in a reliable way. While we believe that cultural diversity in the law is an asset, we neither wish to take a preservationist approach nor do we wish to push in the direction of uniformity.[2]

Or, later:

---

[2] Mauro Bussani, 'Current Trends in European Comparative Law: The Common Core Approach', (1998) 21 Hastings Int. & Comp. L.R. 785, p. 787. The first two studies from the 'common-core' project have now appeared as Reinhard Zimmermann and Simon Whittaker (eds.), *Good Faith in European Contract Law* (Cambridge: Cambridge University Press, 2000) and James R. Gordley (ed.), *The Enforceability of Promises* (Cambridge: Cambridge University Press, 2001). See also Mauro Bussani and Ugo Mattei (eds.), *Making European Law: Essays on the Common Core Project* (Trento: Università degli Studi di Trento, 2000).

It is true that through the use of the comparative method many common features that remained obscure in traditional legal analysis will be unearthed. This is because the instruments and techniques provide more accurate and correct analysis, not that they force convergence where it does not exist [...]. It is also true that common core research may be a useful instrument for legal harmonization in the sense that it provides reliable data to be used in devising new common solutions that may prove workable in practice. But this has nothing to do with the common core research itself, which is devoted to producing reliable information, whatever its policy use might be.[3]

Of course, many professional and academic disciplines struggle, now as in the past, to protect their reputation for objectivity, scientific neutrality, technical precision and insulation from ideological distortion. Still, the contemporary comparatist stands out, particularly from the perspective of the US legal tradition. Other contemporary legal disciplines seem far more comfortable with rulership and with the idea that they could be said to have a political project. They are more comfortable thinking of their work in ideological terms or associating it with particular social interests. They move more easily toward application of their expertise and think of themselves as exercising power with less hesitation.

In many ways, this comfort is the legacy of a century-long methodological effort to break down the barriers – psychological, institutional, doctrinal – between the work of law and the work of politics. The methodological revolution in legal thought begun by sociological jurisprudence, US legal realism and interests jurisprudence aimed in various ways to connect law with what seemed the realities of social and political life. As this methodological assault slowly became common sense in the years following the Second World War, most legal disciplines replaced the notion of a specific 'legal method' with the more pragmatic idea that 'thinking like a lawyer' means drawing on a range of different disciplines and methods in an intuitive effort to solve problems and exercise good judgement. As anti-formalism became the dominant professional vocabulary, it brought with it both methodological eclecticism and more comfort with the politics

---

[3] Bussani, *supra*, note 2, p. 796. Bussani goes on to differentiate the common-core project from 'any restatement-like enterprise. The latter involves the pursuit of rationality, harmony and reform ideals, whereas the Common Core Project implies the selection of the legal rules and materials best suited for the task. The restatement-like enterprise discards whatever does not fit into its framework. This approach is anathema to an analytical perspective: the very fact that rules and materials exist in a legal system requires that they be taken into consideration in the analysis and become part of the final "map" ': *ibid.*

of policy management. Most legal workers – lawyers, judges, scholars, bureaucrats and activists – now take it for granted that legal work is a practical matter of balancing, negotiating and managing competing political visions, ideals and outcomes.

That said, lawyers and legal scholars vary widely in their comfort level with rulership. Some are quite comfortable with the idea that their expertise expresses an ideological commitment, others are not. Some would be offended if accused of preferring one social interest to another, others not. Most are proud to think of their work as a contribution to governance, although few experience the exercise of professional judgement as the making of political choices. Although some legal disciplines embrace the work of governance (think of torts, local government law or any public regulatory field), in other fields (think of property or contracts) rulership remains an acquired taste, even if comfort with the politics of law has long since become the coin of the realm. The many shadings of the word 'policy' in legal thought mark a range of professional positions between 'it's-all-politics' and 'it's-all-law'. For some, 'policy argument' is a limited and regrettable necessity for judges who must sometimes look to legislative intent or social context to complete their interpretive mission. For others, legal 'policy-making' by administrators, legislators or judges is a sophisticated and specialized professional practice, drawing on cost-benefit analysis, welfare economics, sociology, psychology and more. For most, the ambition is a law which embraces the politics of reason, progress, welfare maximization and institutional pragmatism while rejecting the politics of bias, passion and ideology.

In my own field of public international law, to take an example, the dominant posture is somewhere in the middle. International lawyers are generally proud of their contribution to the resolution of 'disputes' in society, if by this they usually mean the rarefied society of states. The contribution they propose is more often procedural than substantive and they distance their work from disputes about the distributions of wealth or power in society, all but the clearest and most egregious of which seem to happen below the line of national sovereignty and, therefore, outside their normal purview. They understand themselves to have a disciplinary position in broad political debate among right, left and centre positions, but it is a very vague humanist position, cosmopolitan, tolerant, open. They often speak as if they sought engagement with the institutions of government and were confident that the more they were allowed to participate in global governance, the better off the world would be. But they also seem more comfortable advising, criticizing or desiring power than exercising it.

Comparative law today does not share even this ambivalent comfort with rulership. On the contrary, comparatists are sensitive to 'accusations' that their work might have anything one could regard as a politics. To my ears, their sensitivity on this point can seem so extreme that it is hard to think of it as fully ingenuous. This is particularly so when one reflects on the history of comparative law. Early comparatists were significant players in the broad methodological assault on law's seeming parochialism and isolation from political and social life. At the 1900 Paris Congress often thought to have inaugurated the field of comparative law, comparatists shared a professional vision about their contribution to the management of international society and established the comparative profession to pursue it. Looking back, their shared vision seems political in a variety of ways which would be extremely unusual in the field today. Many participated actively as comparatists in public life, indeed, were eager to participate in governmental and academic management. Associating law with the realities of social, economic and political life translated easily into concrete projects associated with ideological positions (generally, but not exclusively, on the left) or with the interest of particular groups (labour, commerce) or nations. They promoted comparative law in the name of quite specific cosmopolitan, internationalist, humanist and socially progressive political visions. They meant comparative law to be applied and harnessed their expertise to broad projects of unification and harmonization of law.

If we jump ahead to the post-1945 period, the aspiration to establish a 'profession' has been fulfilled. Post-war comparatists are part of a stable academic profession. Their work differs from their predecessors' in two crucial respects: the insistent anti-formalism has been replaced by a sensible methodological pluralism and they have become far less comfortable thinking of their work politically in any of these senses. Indeed, methodological pluralism has become the mark of political detachment and both have come to seem necessary for comparative law to remain a professional endeavour.

It is a puzzle to understand how this came about and what the politics of this professional practice and self-image might be. In most other post-war legal fields, methodological pluralism accompanied pragmatic engagement with policy-making – only the methodologically nimble being able to move easily across the boundaries between science and politics.

If we think of post-war legal intellectuals on a continuum from more to less comfort with policy-making, comparative law offers an opportunity to understand the professional practices of the extreme-discomfort end. Why should comparatists have come to associate professionalization with both methodological pluralism and withdrawal from politics? And can we say anything about the politics of this sort of professional project?

The first part of this essay examines the standard professional activity developed by post-war comparatists – writing articles and books which identify and explain similarities and differences among legal regimes. The common-core project is an excellent example of this work. To pursue this activity with methodological eclecticism and political disengagement is no easy task and the rhetorical machinery which generates the effects of methodological eclecticism and political innocence gives us important clues to the politics of the practice.

For a start, placing this activity at the centre of the field narrowed considerably what it means to be a comparatist, pushing to one side foreign-law experts who did not 'compare'. Foreign-law specialists, particularly those who studied the diverse legal systems of Asia and Africa, and, increasingly after 1950, specialists in socialist law, found themselves outside the field. So did those using foreign-law knowledge to build international commercial and governmental regimes. So did foreign-law experts interested in law reform, importing or exporting legal rules to solve economic or social problems in the First World or the Third. The law-and-development movement rose and fell outside comparative law. All the more overt political projects of the pre-war period disappeared from the field – at most, we find vague exhortations to a more cosmopolitan and humanist world. In their introduction to comparative law, published in various editions over the last decades, Konrad Zweigert and Hein Kötz draw the boundaries of the field firmly:

> The neighboring areas of legal science which also deal with foreign law, and from which comparative law must be distinguished, are private international law, public international law, legal history, legal ethnology, and finally sociology of law.[4]

---

[4] Konrad Zweigert and Hein Kötz, *An Introduction to Comparative Law*, 3d ed. transl. by Tony Weir (Oxford: Oxford University Press, 1998), p. 6. Twining replies that 'there would not be much left if one excluded from a bibliography of comparative law parallel studies, students' works on particular foreign legal systems or parts thereof, and some of the most respected examples of twentieth century scholarship that involved sustained study of "foreign" legal phenomena or materials from more than one jurisdiction. A clear distinction between the study of foreign law and comparative law cannot be sustained either in theory or in practice': William Twining,

Significantly, scholars who mobilized foreign-law expertise to participate in the philosophical or methodological debates of the post-war academy were also outside the core comparative activity. Zweigert and Kötz give a sense for this hostility to methodological rumination:

> According to Gustav Radbruch, 'sciences which have to busy themselves with their own methodology are sick sciences' [citation omitted]. Though generally true, this is not a diagnosis which fits modern comparative law. For one thing, comparatists all over the world are perfectly unembarrassed about their methodology, and see themselves as being still at the experimental stage. For another, there has been very little systematic writing about the methods of comparative law. There are thus no signs of the disease in question.[5]

Meanwhile, the training and experience to succeed as a professional comparatist – to attain the intuition and judgement needed to compare without falling prey to the false shortcuts of method – seemed to become evermore burdensome, requiring language study, immersion in numerous legal cultures, years of training, intense interdisciplinary knowledge. William Twining laments the fact that 'serious comparative study is more like a way of life than a method'.[6]

You put all this together and the comparative law discipline, properly so called, became an ever-narrower place after 1950. By 1998, Twining could propose the 'bold hypothesis' that 'few experienced comparatists compare – and for good reasons'.[7] If it were not for resources poured into the field by the common-core effort and related projects, it might be hard to find much well-done comparative-law work – although there would be no shortage of calls for such work, descriptions of its virtues and comment on its regrettable absence. Post-war comparatists seemed determined to

---

'Comparative Law and Legal Theory: The Country and Western Tradition', in Ian Edge (ed.), *Comparative Law in Global Perspective* (Ardsley: Transnational, 2000), p. 47.

[5] Zweigert and Kötz, *supra*, note 4, p. 33.

[6] Twining, *supra*, note 4, p. 57, where he comments in these terms on Max Rheinstein's famous advice for beginners on how to prepare for a career in comparative law (see Max Rheinstein, 'Comparative Law – Its Functions, Methods and Usages', [1968] 22 Arkansas L.R. 415): 'It was quite simple and is easily summarised: first, master your own system of law; second, acquire genuine familiarity with one of the principal systems belonging to another family. This will involve systematic study for at least two years in the relevant country and mastery of at least one foreign language, preferably more. Do not focus merely on the rules of the foreign system; you must also study the mentality and basic concepts and techniques as well as the machinery of justice and the procedural context. "Try to forget that you have ever studied law" and study the local culture on its own terms. If possible, obtain some practical experience of that system in operation. After that one may be ready to start to compare.'

[7] Twining, *supra*, note 4, p. 47.

establish a professional practice more earnest and boring than many of them could actually stand to pursue.

The second part of the essay places today's eclectic and disengaged posture against the background of earlier more overtly political and methodologically assertive comparative work.[8] The no-method method and the no-politics politics of comparative law arose together after 1945 and came to dominate the discipline's mainstream over the next generation as comparative law routinized itself in the North American and European legal academies. It is hard to see how the post-war aspiration to professionalize became associated with disengagement from method and politics or settled on so difficult and sterile a professional activity. This was in many ways an odd development. Exactly as anti-formalism – a fighting faith for pre-war comparatists – became mainstream common sense, post-war comparatists retreated from political assertiveness and reinterpreted the method as an eclectic muddle.

More historical work would be necessary to figure this out, although it had something to do with the move to the United States, something to do with the Cold War. Methodological eclecticism and political agnosticism was the project of a generation in rebellion, establishing a new academic foothold, less in Europe than in the United States, and part of a new common sense in the field about the appropriate role for political and philosophical controversy in law.[9] My own intuition – and it is no more than that – is that comparative law's post-war disengagement is in some way the symptom of

---

[8] The history of disciplinary commitment has often been obscured in histories of the discipline written by its post-war practitioners. For an excellent overview of this forgotten history, see Twining, *supra*, note 4, p. 39, who remarks on the absence in histories written by insiders of any reference to philosophical or methodological engagement: 'To an outsider, there seem to be some striking omissions from the orthodox histories: first, there are passing nods at classic forerunners, especially Montesquieu, Ihering, and Maine, but there is scarcely any reference to developments in legal theory in the twentieth century and especially since the Second World War. Legal theory and legal philosophy are treated as subjects apart, debates about positivism are ignored, recent developments are not cited and the virtual disappearance of historical jurisprudence is left unexplained. The main exception is the alleged "functionalist" approach, which contains rather feeble echoes of the early Roscoe Pound and possibly of the Free Law School.'

[9] In their 1998 edition, long after they were widely regarded as representatives of an establishment which had itself peaked a decade or two before, Zweigert and Kötz, *supra*, note 4, continue to present their functionalism as a youthful attack on a discipline gone stale. See Twining, *supra*, note 4, p. 56, n. 103. Twining sees something similar in efforts by younger scholars in the field, such as Pierre Legrand and William Ewald, to promote methodological engagement while attacking their predecessors for lacking a defensible 'method'. See Twining, *supra*, note 4, p. 54, n. 99.

a kind of academic post-traumatic stress disorder. The men who developed the practice of analysing similarities and differences without method or politics seem to have remembered pre-war comparative work to have been entangled in inconclusive philosophical debates about what law is and could become – indeed, they remembered far more methodological disagreement than actually characterized their field. And they remembered these debates to have been fraught with political meaning and, more specifically, with ideology.

They adopted the professional project of mapping and explaining similarities and differences as an escape from philosophy and the politics of ideology. Their quotidian work, identifying legal phenomena, mapping, comparing, turning repeatedly back from method and from politics, reminded them of their new profession's neutrality and objectivity. The comparatist's routine practice reassured him constantly that no, that was before – now we are practical men who have not fallen for endless speculation, nor become embroiled in ideological battle. My intuition, in short, is that there is something almost compulsive about the post-war comparatist's political and methodological renunciation.

As an argumentative or rhetorical effect, moreover, methodological eclecticism is unstable, the argumentative apparatus which supports it is full of elisions, ambiguities, hidden contradictions, understatements and overstatements which can be, and often are, the object of criticism, often from other comparatists. These criticisms are often successful, in the sense that a comparative effort which seemed – to its author, to others – to have foresworn methodological commitment can be shown to have nevertheless been insufficiently open, to have fallen for false and premature closure in the search for descriptive knowledge. The posture of political disengagement is similarly fragile, open to successful criticism that the author has fallen prematurely for a conclusion which betrays an ideological predisposition. In this sense, the comparatist's eclectic posture is an ongoing performance and it works only when, and for as long as, it remains plausible for a given author, audience or reader. Because no one has discovered a fool-proof way to avoid such criticism, the posture is consistently under threat. To complete a professional analysis of the similarities and differences among legal regimes, the effect of methodological openness and political disengagement must be sustained throughout.

But the escape from politics and method remains a wish. When compulsives repeatedly wash their hands, they do obscure the trauma, the memory and fear of something dirty. But compulsive hand-washing is also traumatic and keeps one's mind preoccupied, if not with dirt, then with cleanliness. Something similar is going on in comparative law. To the extent the routine choices made in comparing law do have a politics or have beaten a path of methodological preference, the agnostic fog sustains, legitimates and obscures it. By holding firm to pluralism and neutrality, by continuing the enumeration of similarities and differences, the profession is able to obscure the ongoing contribution it makes to global governance – but it does not eliminate it. The constant rejection of remembered methodological dispute and political taint nevertheless keeps comparative law preoccupied with the terms of those disputes. And these common-sense assumptions and default practices turn out themselves to have a politics.

The essay ends by speculating more concretely about the politics of contemporary comparative law. Post-war comparative law can often be politically evaluated in the same terms used to understand the politics of pre-war comparatists. Sometimes, they slip off the wagon and one can associate their work with ideological positions or social interests in the broader society. Sometimes, they do promote broad social reform efforts – legal harmonization, diversification, pluralism – which track choices made by government. They do sometimes do applied work or find themselves managing institutions in the academic, governmental or business worlds. But more often, they are careful to avoid doing so. Their methodological choices and professional enthusiasms are extremely difficult to associate with political positions in any of these senses.

As a result, identifying the politics of comparative law after the Second World War requires a different sort of inquiry – into the effects of the discipline's default judgements and background assumptions. It turns out these may well have identifiable effects which we can associate with positions in debates we think of more readily as political. To the extent that these political effects are obscured by the field's apolitical posture, contesting them will mean drawing that posture and the discipline's fluid common sense into question. To my mind, there is no going back on methodological proliferation and there is much to be said for the development of eclectic professional judgement in the weighing and balancing of factors whose significance will always remain open to challenge. Although eclecticism can obscure – even for comparatists – the association of their work with ideological debates and social interests, it does not guarantee political neutrality or disengagement. A routine identification of the politics of comparative intellectual work would permit contestation and encourage a more engaged professional life.

The rhetorical practices of methodological eclecticism

In its pure and simplest form, the basic comparative-law performance is a written account of similarities and differences among legal regimes. The European common-core project, for example, consists of many such accounts. This basic comparative performance sets to one side legal writing which considers foreign legal systems in their own terms. No US or European law professor will understand Chinese law in its own terms as well as the best minds at Beijing University – the comparatist's value-added lies in the account of similarities and differences.[10] We must also set aside writing which seeks to apply knowledge about foreign legal systems – whether in developing transnational litigation strategies and institutions, in conducting international commercial arbitration or in identifying regulatory strategies for international economic or social life. For the comparatist, these applications of comparative knowledge come only at the price of hurrying. In rushing to application, we are likely to forgo the objectivity and generality of training necessary to execute a sophisticated comparatist performance. Better to slow down, prepare, train, learn – until the virtues of patience replace the firm channels of method.

The comparatist builds an account of the similarities and differences among legal regimes in four distinct steps, which I develop here in rough schematic terms. At each stage, the inquiry may be derailed into application or methodological disputation. Only by stilling the will to conclude, by forgoing philosophical conclusions or being drawn into methodological debate, can the performance be completed. It is this forbearance which generates the effect of methodological eclecticism and political neutrality.

[10] According to Bussani, *supra*, note 2, p. 794, n. 22, in the European common-core project, they took it as a starting-point that 'the domestic lawyer is not necessarily the best reporter on his or her own system. She or he may control more information about the system than a foreign lawyer, and it is an understatement to say that committed nationals of all member States are a big asset to our project. Nationals, however, may be less well-equipped to detect the hidden data and the rhetorical attitude of the system because they are misled by automatic assumptions [...]. The participants in our project are comparatists, and as comparatists, are asked to deal with the questionnaires as if they had to describe their own law.'

Identify interesting differences and similarities among legal phenomena in different legal regimes

We begin by finding a legal phenomenon in one legal regime which can be 'compared' with a legal phenomenon in another. The 'legal phenomenon' could be a rule, an institution, a practice, an approach to an economic problem, a custom, a professional ethic, just about anything.[11] Often, comparatists set out with a hunch or loose first impression. Perhaps they visited Mexico and found a whole world of family law which seemed outside the range of variation they were used to in the United States. Maybe they learned Japanese in the army and got interested in Japan – now that I am a law professor, let us see how the Japanese handle a problem I am interested in. Sometimes, it is a matter of broader academic fashion – it is the late 1970s and everyone is trying to figure out why Japan is hot and Europe is cold or it is the 1990s and everyone is talking about US dominance of the high-tech/internet sector: I am a law professor, perhaps there is a legal explanation.

Of course, hunches like this do not just happen – there is usually also a wish. Perhaps that the United States be more or less like Japan or that differences and similarities be understood in a new way by some relevant elite. But these purposes, projects, motives will generally not be visible on the surface of the work. Quite the contrary – the comparative performance presents itself as coming upon the materials it compares disinterestedly, accidentally. For many comparatists, the starting-point is assigned – in the European common-core project, for example, teams have been assigned to canvass a range of jurisdictions to map similarities and differences in contract rules about 'good faith', property rules about 'adverse possession' and so forth, with the goal of eventually covering the whole of private law for the whole of Europe. And doing so without any a priori wish for more or less uniformity.

Once underway, comparatists have preferences about how to define the phenomena to be compared. Some start with formal rules which interest them, others start with aspects of the legal context or social outcomes which seem to stand out. These may be relatively abstract social functions (how do these regimes strengthen kinship or encourage entrepreneurship?) or, as in the common-core project, specific fact-patterns whose legal treatment

---

[11] Indeed, there is a little sub-literature on the question whether there are things which cannot, in their nature, be compared. Although opinions differ, the non-comparability list, even of enthusiasts, is very short. For example, see H. Patrick Glenn, *Legal Traditions of the World* (Oxford: Oxford University Press, 2000), pp. 30–55; *id.*, 'Are Legal Traditions Incommensurable?', (2001) 49 Am. J. Comp. L. 133.

can then be compared. The 'legal regimes' which host the legal phenomena to be compared can also be identified in different ways. Some define the regimes in formal jurisdictional or national terms, others in looser cultural and economic terms. For some, legal regimes are organized in a roughly hierarchical stack – local, national, international – while for others, they are more fluid, interpenetrating and overlapping. Looking at this work, we might say comparative performances could be seen to make choices along a continuum, as in figure 11.1.

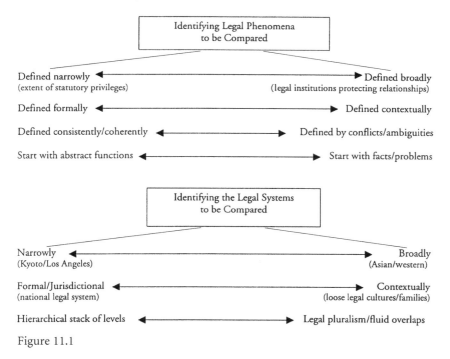

Figure 11.1

Although these preferences sometimes are disputed in methodological terms, more often regimes and legal phenomena are identified in a very fluid and *ad hoc* way.[12] Legal phenomena can be narrow or broad, multiple or

[12] To get a sense for the extreme fluidity of this practice – even when described in methodological terms – see Wenceslas J. Wagner, 'Research in Comparative Law: Some Theoretical Considerations', in Ralph A. Neuman (ed.), *Essays in Jurisprudence in Honor of Roscoe Pound* (Indianapolis: Bobbs-Merrill, 1962), p. 519: 'What should be the subject matter of comparative studies? Legal principles and rules can either be similar or dissimilar both in space and time, and occasionally they have no counterpart in other legal systems. In the tremendous maze of materials from which the comparatist may draw, which should he select for his research? The simple and obvious reply is that the answer to this question should depend on the purpose of the study undertaken.

specific, formal or situationally embedded; regimes can be of any number and situated at almost any degree of difference from one another.[13] At the end of this 'research' phase, we have a loose map. Divorce as a legal institution is *this* in a legal regime we call 'Japanese' and *this* in what we call the 'legal regime' of the United States.

When these preferences *do* become the focus of methodological debate, the comparative work of the article ends. Taking a methodological tack aborts the analysis. The point of the article could then be to demonstrate either the correct way of identifying or the extreme difficulty of identifying phenomena in a methodologically defensible way. The difficulty of identifying what should and should not be in the 'divorce regime' in numerous places might illuminate a general argument about the embedded and contextual nature of law. The ability to identify phenomena which 'function' as adjudication in widely varying cultures might substantiate an argument for the centrality of adjudication to the abstract transhistorical or transcultural thing we call 'law'. This moves the discussion to questions of legal philosophy – we have an essay about what law is rather than an account of similarities and differences among legal regimes.

The best contemporary comparative work simply aggregates these points of view, multiplying ways of thinking about the phenomena to be compared. Indeed, doing so seems the only way to keep going with the comparative project – to avoid becoming entangled in a philosophical debate. It is abstentions such as these which honour the memory of the method 'war-as-tar-baby'. Do not go there – we have had those philosophical debates and they did not end well, no one won a decisive victory, they distracted us from learning anything useful or interesting, they entangled legal scholarship in ideology. It is the echo of this memory which stays the comparatist's hand from methodological rumination and permits the analysis to continue.

And in this vagueness, this abstention from method, there is a default position. By far the most common default remains the national legal system – one compares the legal phenomenon of 'divorce' in, say, Japan and

Zweigert states, in this connection, that "the comparative jurist will mainly refer to such legal systems which are likely to supply him with a special stimulation for the problem to be examined".' The reference to Zweigert is Konrad Zweigert, 'Zur Methode der Rechtsvergleichung', (1960) 13 Studium Generale 193, p. 195.

[13] Legrand synthesizes these choices into two broad traditions, that is, 'the exposition of families of legal systems and the juxtaposition of (mostly private law) rules': Pierre Legrand, 'Comparative Legal Studies and Commitment to Theory', (1995) 58 Modern L.R. 262, p. 263. Twining synthesizes them as 'macro-comparison' and 'micro-comparison': *supra*, note 4, pp. 31–2.

the United States, or 'administrative discretion' in South Korea and Austria, without too much attention to the coherence of the idea that there is a 'Japanese legal system'. These sort of pairings are then aggregated into more complex arrangements – a number of European, American or Asian national systems might be cross-compared. Perhaps the Japanese legal regime is part of a broader 'Asian' legal order or family of law, perhaps not.

We have already here some clues to the work of methodological abstention – or eclecticism – in contemporary comparative law. There is a problem, what to write about, there is a set of choices, arranged in terms which might be, even have been, methodologically disputed. There is a methodological agnosticism. And then there is a default, wrapped in the enigmas of abstention. If the default has a politics, it will be protected here. Likewise the wish which animated the endeavour.

Where there are similarities, deal with the 'transplant' hypothesis

The next step is to determine whether any similarities between the two legal phenomena so identified result from the 'transplant' of a legal idea or institution from one place to another or to both places from the same third source. It is hard to understand why the relationship of 'influence' gets such preliminary and, therefore, prominent, treatment in comparing. Of course, there is no question that legal regimes influence one another. If things which seem similar in two places are similar because one has influenced the other, one need look no further for an 'explanation'. Perhaps the similarities in Japanese and US legal codes about divorce are rooted in the post-1945 US occupation of Japan. Perhaps the North Korean administrative code is really still based on a German implant from the nineteenth century which continues to have echoes in Austrian law. To the extent one has influenced the other, perhaps the places are really not different and no 'comparison' is possible.

That said, comparatists differ a great deal in how seriously they pursue the search for evidence of transplantation or influence. As a result, there are choices to be made at this stage as well. The more formally one defines the phenomena to be compared, the more often similarities which seem to arise from transplant will strike one. The more one thinks of law as an autonomous professional practice, or as a universal problem-solver, and the less one thinks of it as a cultural expression, the more one will be interested in similarities and the more transplantation will seem a good starting-point for analysis. Again, comparative work might be arranged along a continuum, as in figure 11.2.

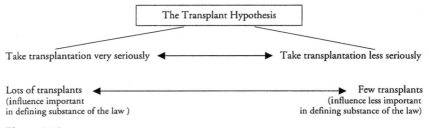

Figure 11.2

There is a further point. In searching for influence, one might focus on differences as well as similarities. Although the transplant idea has been used disproportionately to explain similarities rather than differences, we might imagine that patterns of cultural influence would as readily produce differences as similarities. Failed transplant efforts, indigenous reactions against transplantation, intentional or accidental misreadings of transplanted material, ideas at the source of the transplant about what was needed 'in the periphery' might all generate differences. The more one thought of law in formal terms, the more likely one might think of influence as a matter of similarities. The more one focused on the historical and social context, the more likely one would foreground the hand of influence in resistance, misreading and difference. We could add an axis of choice open to the comparatist at this stage of the work, as in figure 11.3.

Figure 11.3

Most of the choices encountered in this second phase of the comparative performance have been the subject of a quite polarized methodological debate within comparative law, in which each side views the other to be short-circuiting the analysis.[14] Those hostile to transplantation question

[14] The main proponent of the significance of influences and transplantation has been Watson. For example, see Alan Watson, *Legal Transplants*, 2d ed. (Athens, Georgia: University of Georgia Press, 1993) [hereinafter *Legal Transplants*]; *id.*, *Law Out of Context* (Athens, Georgia: University of Georgia Press, 2000); *id.*, 'Legal Transplants and European Private Law', (2000) Electronic J. Comp. L. [http://law.kub.nl/ejcl/44/art44–2.html#N8] (hereinafter 'European Private Law'). Perhaps the clearest denunciation of the transplant hypothesis has come from Legrand, *supra*, note 13; *id.*, 'Against a European Civil Code', (1996) 60 Modern L.R. 44; *id.*, 'The Impossibility of "Legal Transplants"', (1997) 4 Maastricht J. Eur. & Comp. L. 111 [hereinafter 'Impossibility'].

whether it is possible, in the sense of 'intellectually defensible' or 'logically coherent', to identify legal phenomena in one place as having an 'identity' which could be moved. The degree of legal autonomy necessary for there to be a transplant hypothesis to investigate reflects, from this point of view, a failure to continue the search for a cultural/contextual/historical understanding of what has happened. On the other side, transplantation proponents question the coherence of the category of 'culture' as anything other than a default name for social or economic needs and functions which have not yet been explained. For these people, one should continue the analysis until all aspects of a legal order can be understood as either learning or innovation in solving problems or performing functions which are universal, at least within a given type of economy or stage of development.

We have here not the memory, but the living potential for disciplinary death by method. Taking the transplant hypothesis too seriously – either way – sidetracks the basic comparative project, moving us off into legal theory – to what extent is law a universal problem-solver or form of professional specialized knowledge and to what extent is it rooted in, and expressive of, local cultural life?[15] Indeed, participants on both sides of this debate say that they do so out of dissatisfaction with the conventions of comparative-law practice. For the sophisticated comparative analyst embarking upon a project as ambitious as mapping the common core of European private law, it does not pay to become entangled in such debates. Instead, we find agnosticism, restraint and reasonableness about whether to stress similarities or differences. In this work, metabolized into the mainstream comparative activity, the transplant debate simply blurs the edges of legal phenomena and regimes identified in the first phase of the work – perhaps these phenomena are not so similar, perhaps these regimes are not so different. We can think further about the importance of influence later

---

[15] Taking either side of these debates too seriously would undermine the comparative endeavour completely. We see this in Watson's fear that opponents of influence or convergence explanations would support a kind of cultural relativism, which would render legal regimes incommensurable, and in his opponents' fear that taking influence too seriously would eliminate the space for cultural particularity altogether. These fears animate the debate on 'incommensurability' (see *supra*, note 11). Having heard debate on this subject at numerous conferences, I can report that it is standard to accuse one's opponent of hyperbole and to claim the high ground of sensible eclecticism for oneself. If you favour serious investigation of the transplant hypothesis, you do not say that you want to eliminate cultural particularity – you say that your opponents are cultural relativists. And *vice versa*. For the mainstream comparatist, both sides sounds shrill and you can observe the older and wiser scholars in the room go silent, as if waiting for a storm to pass. They have learned not to get entangled in such a controversy in the first place.

in the work, transplant will be one among many explanations of the degree of difference or similarity among legal phenomena in various regimes.

Although this eclecticism protects the enterprise, here too there is a default position – the priority accorded hypotheses about transplant focuses the comparatist's attention first on similarities and on reception, while foregrounding the autonomy of legal phenomena from context. And here too, if this default has a politics, it is methodological restraint which defends it.

Allocate the similarities and differences which remain variously to cultural and technical factors

This is where the real work begins. We have a map of similarities and differences among legal phenomena in different legal regimes. We are heading for an explanation of variation. In this phase, the comparatist identifies the factors, other than transplantation, which might go into the explanation. Generally speaking, there are two broad types of factors, which we might call 'cultural' and 'technical'. The preliminary separation of cultural and technical factors is largely a matter of intuition or common sense.

On the culture side, we have, obviously, different legal cultures: Japan is Japan and the United States is the United States. Legal cultures could be defined as national legal regimes, but they could also be loose descriptions – the Japanese 'way of resolving disputes' or the 'US approach to business' – which float a bit free of their moorings in national legal regimes. Legal cultures might be framed as large cultural families (Asian law, African law, European law, Socialist law and so forth) or more parochially (the New York regulatory system, California law, Inuit practice in a specific community with this much Canadian influence, etc.). As one begins to allocate some of the similarities and differences one has uncovered to 'culture', all these possible ideas about what legal cultures are will be in play. Indeed, the word 'culture' itself may or may not be used – sometimes these factors are more fashionably described as 'social' or 'socio-economic' or simply 'contextual' considerations.

On the technical side, something similar is at work. The idea is to identify a technical dimension of society which might be responsible for legal phenomena in more or less the same way as a legal 'culture'. We start with the common-sense idea that there are, obviously, different economic/social systems in the world, different levels of economic advancement, from primitive hunter/gatherer economies right up through late industrial democracy and advanced industrial capitalism. A legal phenomenon might be part of the 'advanced industrial capitalism' package in the same way it might be part of the 'Japanese legal culture' package. Technical levels might be drawn in very broad historical terms – primitive society, underdeveloped economies and late industrial capitalism (or feudalism and bourgeois capitalism). But the technical factors responsible for legal phenomena might also be associated with broad economic functions – resolving disputes, securing debt, facilitating price signalling, etc. – which might cut across historical stages of economic development. Like legal cultures, moreover, technical factors might also be framed more narrowly – the specific needs of an urban global banking centre or a complex commodities market. As we begin to associate the legal phenomena we have identified with different aspects of the regimes in which we have found them, all these various ways of framing technical explanations will be in play.

So, let us say we have decided that something called a 'divorce regime' can be identified in both Japan and the United States. And let us say we decide that the Japanese and the US legal systems are different enough to make comparison worthwhile – maybe they are Asian and we are western, maybe they are just Japanese and we are American, maybe it is Kyoto and Los Angeles, whatever. And let us say we eliminate the transplant hypothesis in assessing similarities (and maybe even differences) between the Japanese and US divorce regimes. We can imagine that Japan and the United States are both culturally different (perhaps Asian/western) and culturally similar (modern democratic consumer societies, for example). And we can imagine that they are both technically similar (perhaps both late industrial capitalism) and technically different (perhaps industrial systems based on different functional relations between work-family, for example). Now we need to figure out, with more or less precision, which of the aspects of each divorce system should be attributed to culture (Asian/western, say) and which to *tekhnè* (late industrial capitalism, say).

In allocating similarities and differences in legal phenomena to cultural and technical differences and similarities among legal regimes, the comparatist faces a series of choices. How much should be attributed to culture, how much to *tekhnè*? How should the cultural and the technical be defined? Individuals will have preferences. Some comparatists favour broad 'family-like' cultural categories, others more local cultural contexts. Some work more with stages of economic development, others with social/

economic functions. Some think in terms of broad categories, others in more narrowly defined institutional or sectoral terms.

These preferences are analogous to others we have seen. It is easy to imagine that a comparatist sympathetic to a formal identification of legal phenomena, to the transplant hypothesis, to the autonomy of law and legal professionals or to law as a universal phenomenon, might lean toward a broad sense about legal cultures. Comparatists who tend to think of legal cultures as large-scale families of law may well lean toward thinking of the technical in terms of broad historical phases of economic development. We might line these choices up, more or less as follows, in figure 11.4.

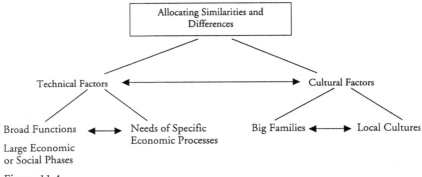

Figure 11.4

These choices certainly could be debated in methodological terms and these debates might well – on analogy to debates about transplantation – be joined in strongly polarized terms. In the best contemporary comparative work, however, this tends not to happen. Instead, the cultural and the technical are understood in very loose terms – a looseness which blunts the emergence of bold methodological claims. This is encouraged by the loose overlap of the terms: is 'modern democratic consumer society' a cultural type or a stage of technical development? What about 'industrial economy with communal work-family structures'? The process of allocation is guided less by method than by the hand of professional good judgement, intuition and experience. One allocates bits here and there as seems to make sense, given one's judgement as a scholar about how things work.

A number of background assumptions are nevertheless at work, such as that technical explanations can be validated by data from other places, while cultural explanations can be validated by data from other legal or social dimensions of the same location. The technical is, in this sense, global, the cultural local. The technical is somehow a more rational, the cultural a more irrational domain. The cultural requires an explanation in the language of history and meaning and leaves room for – indeed, *is* the room for – the mysteries of social connectedness. The cultural seems linked to the domains of either private life or national public patriotism, while the technical seems linked to the intermediate spaces of commerce and the economy and expresses itself in the language of function and performance rather than meaning. Where these background ideas have a politics, where their extension participates in a broader political project, the professional judgements of comparatists to stress one or the other contribute to that politics. And that support would be shrouded in the fog of methodological restraint and eclectic good sense.

Default judgements also emerge in this phase of the work. *Similarities* between legal phenomena in different locations (once the transplant hypothesis has been dealt with) tend to be allocated to economic stages or functional necessities, while *differences* tend to be allocated to cultures. The most conventional comparatist piece might well suggest that differences in the Japanese and US divorce regimes reflect cultural differences and similarities reflect the common economic or functional situation of women and families in modern industrial democracies. This common default arises from the common-sense idea that what modern economies *are*, are similar, rational, regardless of where they are located, and what cultures *are*, are different.

Although this is the default judgement, it is only a default. It can be, and often is, confounded, if not directly contested. It just turns out that in allocating things to the technical and the cultural, it sometimes comes out the other way. So, we often find legal similarities allocated to culture (Japan and the United States turn out to be culturally similar on this point) and differences allocated to the technical (but the functional needs of different industrial models for workers places different demands on the divorce system in the two locations). Two different economic models can turn out, on this point, to be similar, while two very similar cultures can, paradoxically, turn out to be different. In the same way, similarities in legal phenomena can be allocated to differences in technical or cultural positions, just as legal differences can be allocated to technical or cultural similarities.

These choices are loosely analogous to choices we have seen made at earlier stages in the work. When people associate legal similarities to cultural or technical differences or legal differences with cultural or technical similarities, they make law an outlier to the general situation. When they associate legal similarities with cultural/technical similarities and differences with differences, by the same token, they make law expressive of cultural or technical identity. And, naturally enough, we can imagine that comparatists would differ in their tendency to treat law as an outlier, either to economic/functional or cultural identities. We might organize these choices in the following way, as in figure 11.5.

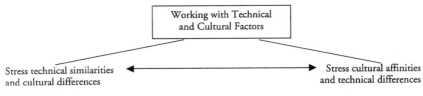

Figure 11.5

The sophisticated comparatist appreciates the range of different ways of articulating cultural identity and achieving economic objectives in a given system and is attentive to the possibility that particular legal phenomena can play a variety of roles, even conflicting ones, in these different domains of social life. One simply does the best one can in developing an understanding of the differences and similarities between these legal phenomena and these legal regimes, taking all of this into account. But if there is a default here, and that default has a politics, it is defended and obscured by this open and pragmatic methodological eclecticism.

Generate a plausible causal account of what you have mapped

The most capable hands have picked their way slowly, meanderingly, to this point, resisting methodological contestation.[16] And some comparative work simply stops here, as if to say, 'here are some similarities and differences among legal phenomena and legal regimes, suggesting cultural and technical differences and similarities of various kinds – I thought you would like to know'. In Twining's words, '[t]he concern is with description

---

[16] In describing the effort to uncover patterns of influence and transplantation, Collins despairs that 'no one ever succeeds in pursuing this method satisfactorily, for the budding comparatist always leaves out one of the dimensions of culture, society, economy, history, politics, and legal logic': Hugh Collins, 'Methods and Aims of Comparative Contract Law', (1991) 11 Oxford J. Leg. Stud. 396, p. 398.

and analysis rather than evaluation and prescription.'[17] For the hardy, however, there is more – some sort of an explanation – the 'analysis' part, which can pull it all together.

What we want here is a story which qualifies our original identification of the 'same phenomena in different regimes' in important ways, but which does not run us into philosophical disputation or political commitment. Staying descriptive is helpful. After study, it might turn out that what is really going on is a bit of transplantation, so the regimes are not really different, some cultural specificity, which makes the legal phenomena more different than we thought, but also some economically or technically driven uniformity. But it can be difficult to develop a stable and plausible account with such a range of diverging factors and interpretive modes.

One common method for doing so is to invent some idiosyncratic intermediate models which combine cultural and technical similarities and differences. Having looked at the legal phenomena of 'good faith' across Europe, we might find that there are two or three different regime types and a couple of outlier countries. We might find, say, a Dutch model and a corporatist model and a full-liability model, with Iceland and Greece as outlier regimes. Stories about these types can contain a range of thoughts – about the effects or purposes of one regime or another, about the intentions of legislators foiled and achieved and so forth. There might be a reference to distributional consequences – perhaps the 'Dutch' way of thinking about 'good faith' reflects a commitment to consumers, as a cultural trait or political achievement. A description of this type preserves the absence of methodological or legal-philosophical controversy. The best description you are likely to get will be custom-tailored to the complexity of these legal phenomena and regime types. It all turns out to be very complex, indeed.

Such an account can be extended in time. Relations among the models might suggest the process of cultural consolidation, or of convergence of technical rationality, or of cultural variation or of technical experimentation. It is hard to avoid an illustration of the sorts of background narratives which can be confounded or confirmed by analysis, as in figure 11.6.

But an eclectic description calls for an eclectic temporal explanation – a combination of historical influences and functional/evolutionary developments. No culture has come to dominate but neither have cultures disappeared, no economic function has figured out the one and only best

---

[17] Twining, *supra*, note 4, p. 34.

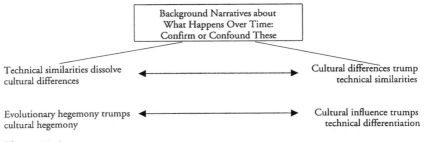

Figure 11.6

practice. Still, some cultures are getting stronger, others weaker, and the field of technical possibility has undoubtedly been usefully narrowed. The more complex the story, the more intricate the history, the harder it is to think of such an account as illustrating a method, much less having a politics. The more eclectic the descriptive account, the more likely we have to conclude that although things have come a long way, there is a long way still to go.

If we look back at the various stages in the development of a comparative performance, the comparatist faced choices at every point. How to identify legal phenomena or regimes, how to identify and weigh the significance of transplantation, how to assess the relative weight of cultural and technical factors in understanding similarities and differences, how to assemble these factors into a satisfactory descriptive account and analysis? All of these choices seem ripe for methodological controversy – they raise eternal questions about the nature of law which have been the stuff of methodological debates in most other legal fields (figure 11.7).

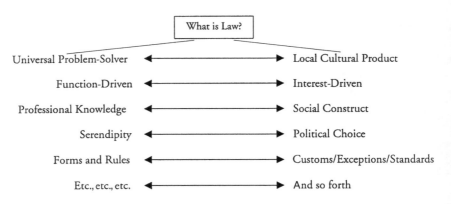

Figure 11.7

Were legal philosophy the queen of the sciences, there would be no cost and some benefit in leaving comparative analysis to pursue such questions. We would expect young scholars seeking to make their mark and elder statesmen seeking to sum up what they have learned to abort the comparative inquiry at the first plausible moment. Legal scholars in other fields have often felt strongly that these philosophical choices had political consequences. So have comparatists of earlier generations. Knowing that law was one way rather than the other would legitimate some political endeavours and delegitimate others. Different law-reform proposals seemed consistent with the left- and right-hand columns.[18] If comparatists had political projects to pursue, it would not be surprising to find them mobilizing their expertise on behalf of one or the other of these methodological alternatives.

This does sometimes happen, of course.[19] But the posture of the common-core project expresses the professional standard – agnostic about these questions, even hostile to their overt exploration. That said, these alternatives have not been discarded in favour of other inquiries and debates. These choices continue to define the factors to be taken into account in respectable professional accounts of similarities and differences. They constitute the background common-sense of the field and the vocabulary of the comparatist's expertise. Nor are comparatists able to complete their work on a perfectly ambivalent knife-edge. Despite the posture of careful doubt and ambiguity, default paths emerge. It is the politics of this vocabulary and these default practices which mature good judgement denies.

The rise of the comparative law professional and the fall from method and politics

The replacement of political and methodological engagement with eclectic professional judgement was the work of post-war comparatists – people like Konrad Zweigert and Hein Kötz, Otto Kahn-Freund, Max Rheinstein, Rudolf Schlesinger, Wolfgang Friedmann and Arthur von Mehren – who

---

[18] See Duncan Kennedy, 'Form and Substance in Private Law Adjudication', (1976) 89 Harvard L.R. 1685; David Kennedy, 'When Renewal Repeats: Thinking Against the Box', (2000) 32 New York J. Int. L. & Politics 335.

[19] For a particularly striking example, see Rodolfo Sacco, 'Diversity and Uniformity in the Law', (2001) 49 Am. J. Comp. L. 171. Sacco's succinct and extremely general reflections on the virtues and likely extent of legal diversity and uniformity, built on a tissue of class-room examples, contrast nicely with the apparently endless and agnostic common-core project described by Bussani, *supra*, at text accompanying notes 2 and 3.

were all eager to establish the field as a respected academic discipline.[20] These men wrote more about method than about politics. They stressed the need to differentiate comparative work from political engagement. Methodologically, they differed on many points – most famously on the relative weight to be accorded cultural and historical developments as opposed to social or economic functions in explaining diverse legal phenomena. But they wrote as if it were imperative to keep methodological disagreements from getting out of hand. Each wrote as if methodological controversy was elsewhere – in other people's work, in earlier work, in the work of younger colleagues. Each pitched his project as a resolution of methodological divergence. Taken collectively, their project was to escape politics and intellectual controversy into methodological eclecticism. If for their predecessors comparative law had been an anti-formalist crusade with clear consequences, for them it was prudent common sense. Such political enthusiasm as remained was chastened and vague, the loose politics of universal humanism. Their passion was directed rather to the professionalization of knowledge and improvement of legal education. The virtues and necessities of systematic comparative knowledge and professional capacity loomed far larger in their aspirations.

Far more work needs to be done on the intellectual history of comparative law to figure out how and why this professional voice emerged. There is something resigned or world-weary in the tone. Deeply learned, these men did not wear their knowledge lightly. They wrote as if they had learned the futility of methodological debate, had lost confidence in their ability to resolve methodological controversy productively. It is hard not to imagine that this had something to do with the large number of German political

---

[20] In reflecting on the common project of the post-war figures, Twining stresses their efforts to defend the professional 'usefulness' of their agnostic inquiries: see *supra*, note 4, pp. 51–3 (focusing on his own teacher, F. H. Lawson). Of course, not all post-war comparatists were methodologically and politically agnostic. McDougal, who proposed an overt political and methodological project for comparative law in the post-war years – clarifying values for use in building a new world-system – never became part of the comparative canon or profession. For example, see Myres S. McDougal, 'The Comparative Study of Law for Policy Purposes: Value Clarification as an Instrument of World Democratic Order', (1952) 1 Am. J. Comp. L. 24. It is not surprising that as this post-war generation fades, younger scholars attack their professional agnosticism in methodological and political terms. Most notable here would probably be Alan Watson, but we might include Pierre Legrand, Upendra Baxi, Mathias Reimann, Günter Frankenberg, Ugo Mattei and many others. For most comparatists in what might be termed the second post-war generation, however, the agnostic and eclectic sensibility established after 1945 continues to define good work in the discipline – I am thinking here of people like Mauro Cappelletti, Mirjan Damaška, Mary Ann Glendon or John Merryman.

refugees in this generation – Wolfgang Friedmann, Otto Kahn-Freund, Clive Schmithoff, F. A. Mann, Max Rheinstein, Friedrich Kessler, Albert Ehrenzweig, Rudolf Schlesinger – it is a long list.[21] The intriguing thing is that these men succeeded in routinizing their intellectual and political trauma, transforming it into a professional training, restaged in the memory of individual comparatists as they put away political or methodological commitments to adopt the mature voice of the detached professional.

The original nature of post-war agnosticism stands out by comparison both to those who founded the discipline between the 1900 Paris Congress and the Second World War and to those precursors interested in foreign law who were not part of the project of disciplinary establishment. Many of the most significant nineteenth- and early twentieth-century legal and social theorists, historians, economists and sociologists wrote about relationships among legal systems – think of Weber, Maine, Durkheim, Marx: the list is almost as long as the canon of western social and political thought during that period.[22] There were also numerous lawyers, practitioners and academics, who developed an interest in things foreign and wrote expansively about relations between legal systems. Of these, perhaps the best known was Dean John Wigmore, of Northwestern University.[23] But however brilliant and insightful, these early authors have not become part of the canonical discipline of comparative law. I was struck at a comparative-law conference when a leading US comparatist insisted that these people simply could not now get tenure at any leading North American law school as comparatists and we should be wary of taking them too seriously.

---

[21] See Twining, *supra*, note 4, pp. 37–9. See also Bernhard Großfeld and Peter Winship, 'The Law Professor Refugee', (1992) 18 Syracuse J. Int. & Comp. L. 3; Kurt Lipstein 'The History of the Contribution to Law by German-Speaking Jewish Refugees in the United Kingdom', in Werner E. Mosse *et al.* (eds.), *Second Chance: Two Centuries of German-Speaking Jews in the United Kingdom* (Tübingen: J. C. B. Mohr, 1991), pp. 221–8.

[22] The texts most remembered in the discipline today are probably Max Rheinstein (ed.), *Max Weber on Law in Economy and Society* (New York: Simon & Schuster, 1967); Henry Sumner Maine, *Ancient Law: Its Connection with the Early History of Society, and Its Relation to Modern Ideas* (London: John Murray, 1861). On Maine, see, for example, Annelise Riles, 'Representing In-Between: Law, Anthropology, and the Rhetoric of Interdisciplinarity', [1994] U. Illinois L.R. 597. On Max Weber, see, for example, Ahmed White, 'Weber and the Uncertainties of Categorical Comparative Law', in Annelise Riles (ed.), *Rethinking the Masters of Comparative Law* (Oxford: Hart, 2001), pp. 40–57.

[23] See Annelise Riles, 'Wigmore's Treasure Box: Comparative Law in the Era of Information', (1999) 40 Harvard Int. L.J. 221; *id.*, 'Encountering Amateurism: John Henry Wigmore and the Uses of American Formalism', in *id.*, *supra*, note 22, pp. 94–126.

There are probably many reasons for this and we should not feel too badly about it – many of these people have secure places in the canons of other fields. Even Wigmore has found a home in the law of evidence. But when 'comparative law' took off as a discipline at the 1900 Paris Congress, these people were not part of it. They shared neither the political projects nor the methodological commitments of the field's founding fathers. In retrospect, it is hard not to be struck by their amateurish and undisciplined way of proceeding. As comparatists, they do seem to lack methodological rigour or discipline. They were not eclectic or pluralist in any contemporary sense – they were simply outside the set of methodological alternatives about which we have since become agnostic. The factors they considered, the range of questions they asked about legal phenomena, seem all over the map. They were not at all careful in their differentiation of technical and cultural explanations, were not even focused particularly on similarities and differences. They often had completely different intellectual agendas and dipped into knowledge about different legal regimes en route to conclusions about other things. They were, in short, simply not working in what would become the professional idiom.

At the same time, their comparisons of different legal systems were part of a wide variety of diverging political projects – efforts to introduce particular legislative changes in one place by reference to laws in place elsewhere, efforts to promote commercial opportunities in far-flung locations by suppression of local laws, efforts to govern and understand colonial possessions, efforts to strengthen the universal appeal of laissez-faire liberalism or legitimate the peculiarities of 'bourgeois law' or 'freedom to contract' by comparative historical accounts of the move from feudalism. From a contemporary perspective, their work is far too politically engaged to be respectable. But this does not place them outside the field – the masters of the comparative canon shared and expressed a political agenda for the discipline they founded. The problem with people like Maine or Marx is that they did not share the discipline's specific political projects. No method, wrong politics.

The great comparatists of the pre-war period – people like Raymond Saleilles, Edouard Lambert, Frederick Pollock, Roscoe Pound, Ernst Rabel, Karl Llewellyn – promoted a more self-conscious discipline of comparative law and shared a loose methodological and political consensus.[24]

---

[24] Pollock's critique of Maine for speculation and unsystematic use of historical evidence illustrates this desire for a discipline: see Frederick Pollock, 'The History of Comparative Jurisprudence', (1903) 5 J. Society Comp. Legis. 74.

In methodological terms, they were all exuberant participants in one or another way in the rise of anti-formal and sociologically attuned legal thought. They focused on the questions which continue to structure comparative analysis – how should one identify the legal phenomenon and regimes to be compared, how significant is influence in accounting for similarities, what is the mix of cultural and technical factors which account for variation, how broadly or narrowly might cultures or economic/social phases of development be identified? Their answers all fell to the right end of the various alternatives sketched in the last section. Their common project was to align law with what they saw as a transformed social and economic world – to make it at once more international, more expressive of cosmopolitan and humanitarian values and more responsive to social and economic needs. None shared Bussani's agnosticism about the desirability of uniform international rules – all were committed internationalists and all favoured more harmonization of law. Method seemed to have social and political consequences – awakening legal science to anti-formalism through comparison would strike a blow for humanist liberal cosmopolitanism. Some went further – comparative anti-formalism offered a mode of progressive or leftish engagement on behalf of the socially disadvantaged or the culturally different. All felt comfortable participating in public life, making choices and advocating positions on issues facing government on the basis of their comparative knowledge.

Of course, these early masters of comparative law also differed in both their methodological and political emphases. Should law be internationalized by universal codification or by exhortations for each legal order to develop an embedded response to what were increasingly universal social and economic problems? What was the place of cultural specificity in the law being developed for the newly international economic system? Was the comparatist's contribution better made from the academy or in public service? How could law best respond to the needs of social development, how best to ameliorate the sharp edges of industrialization? How left-wing is the project of responding to new social needs or economic conditions? What social interests should the legal system be newly attentive to – commercial interests, labour? Still, they shared broadly anti-formal methodological styles and broadly reformist political motives. No one advocated preserving law's detached autonomy or protecting corporate and governmental institutions from demands for social change.

There was not much debate among these early comparatists about either method or politics. They seem to have been in only rather loose contact with one another and to have been far more influenced by philosophical traditions in other jurisdictions – sociological jurisprudence, interests jurisprudence, the Free Law school, legal realism – than by the particular styles of comparative work. Each had a way to use their common vocabulary to promote his own particular project without feeling the need to disassociate from the others. Each took from the anti-formal vocabulary different pieces which, in retrospect, can seem at odds with one another. Each seems to have been far more interested in his political and institutional projects than in refining his comparative method. It bears returning to at least three of these figures – Lambert, Pound and Rabel – to remember how strikingly they differed from their post-war successors. They represent probably the leading comparative voices of the inter-war period in France, the United States and Germany, respectively.

Lambert was not shy about the social import of his project.[25] Comparative law was to be a law-reform project designed to develop more uniform and international rules and to do so with a view to ensuring that the new rules would be better suited to the social needs of a new industrial economic order. Lambert concludes his essay on the sources of comparative law as follows:

> La constitution de cette science internationale du droit privé représente la contribution qui incombe aux juristes dans l'effort collectif pour passer du stade de la concurrence coupe-gorge entre les nationalismes, dont chacun ne veut supporter d'autre loi que la sienne, à un régime de concurrence réglée et de coopération internationale. Mais cette nouvelle forme de la science juridique en est encore à ses premiers balbutiements. [...] Les juristes polonais, roumains, tchécoslovaques et yougoslaves ont d'ailleurs fort bien compris que leur participation au mouvement d'ensemble de la jurisprudence comparative était un des meilleurs moyens de s'outiller pour travailler à une codification unificatrice de leurs lois nationales.[26]

---

[25] My understanding of Lambert's comparative project and its influence relies heavily on two excellent recent studies: Amr A. Shalakany, *The Analytics of the Social in Private Law Theory: A Comparative Study*, Harvard Law School SJD dissertation (April 2000), on file with the author; Marie-Claire Belleau, 'Cross-Atlantic Fertilization: Edouard Lambert and Roscoe Pound on Comparative Law', paper presented at the Northwestern University conference 'Rethinking the Masters of Comparative Law', 18 March 2000, on file with the author.

[26] Edouard Lambert, 'Sources du droit comparé ou supranational: législation uniforme et jurisprudence comparative', in *Recueil d'études sur les sources du droit en l'honneur de François Gény*, vol. III (Paris: Sirey, 1934), p. 502.

The profession of comparative law, institutionalized under Lambert's direction in the law faculty at Lyon,[27] was directed to train a cadre of elite legal professionals capable of understanding law across national contexts, soothing international tensions and finding uniform solutions to modern social problems. To do so, they would need to bring new voices to the table – not just the law of jurists, but the law made by social actors, such as unions, professional associations or chambers of commerce. In reflecting on the significance of the 1900 Paris Congress, Lambert says:

> *Depuis 1900 les perspectives ouvertes à l'action du droit comparé se sont singulièrement élargies. Elles se sont élargies, elles s'élargissent chaque jour un peu plus, sous l'action d'un triple courant d'idées qui se dessine dans l'ensemble de la communauté internationale des peuples industrialisés. C'est d'abord l'éveil de l'esprit international créé par les conséquences économiques de la guerre [...]. Ce sont ensuite les réclamations, de plus en plus énergiques, des opinions publiques des divers pays en faveur de la socialisation du droit, c'est-à-dire d'une interprétation plus souple et plus éclairée de lois et de précédents judiciaires datant souvent d'un autre âge, et de leur adaptation aux conditions économiques de la vie contemporaine. [...] Le mouvement vers la socialisation et le mouvement vers l'internationalisation du droit se prêtent un mutuel appui et l'un et l'autre subissent la poussée d'un troisième mouvement dont la concurrence accélérera de plus en plus leur marche. Ce troisième mouvement, c'est l'entrée en compétition avec le droit des juristes des droits faits, pour leur discipline intérieure et pour le règlement des rapports économiques entre leurs membres, par les groupements de justiciables, tels que les syndicats professionnels ou les chambres syndicales et les associations corporatives des diverses branches du commerce et de l'industrie. [...] Dès sa naissance [le droit de ces groupements de justiciables] prend une humeur internationale parce que les activités, dont il règle et rationalise la concurrence, sont déjà, et deviennent chaque jour davantage, des activités internationales.*[28]

---

[27] For example, see id., *L'institut de droit comparé: son programme, ses méthodes d'enseignement* (Lyon: A. Rey, 1921).

[28] Id., 'Rapport fait à la séance d'inauguration de la session de 1929 à La Haye sur le rôle d'un congrès international de droit comparé en l'an 1931', in *Travaux de l'Académie internationale de droit comparé*, vol. II (1929), fascicule 1, pp. 4–5. Lambert describes the objectives of the congress in these terms: 'La tâche essentielle d'un pareil Congrès sera de préparer et de mettre en mouvement le travail collectif et réfléchi de l'élite des juristes des divers pays par lequel la profession légale internationale – c'est-à-dire le vaste groupement naturel formé par les hommes qui se consacrent à l'étude et l'application du droit – adaptera son activité scientifique d'ensemble aux devoirs et aux sources d'influence sociale que lui crée la naissance de cette communauté économique et politique supra-nationale' (id., p. 8).

In pursuing this project of '*la socialisation et* [...] *l'internationalisation du droit*', Lambert was clear that codification, both nationally and internationally would be useful. Indeed, Lambert's comparative legal study was anything but agnostic on the desirability of more international and uniform law – solutions would not be found in parochial national traditions:

> Le moment n'est-il pas venu pour la science du droit de réagir, par une orientation de ses disciplines dans le sens de l'universalisme, contre les causes de mésintelligence juridique qu'elle a semées entre les nations par la dispersion antérieure de son travail? N'a-t-elle pas maintenant le devoir de rapprocher ses ramifications locales et de leur infuser une humeur internationale?[29]

At the same time, the international legal regime would find its roots in sociological, economic and cultural realities:

> Au-dessous de ses sources formelles et secondaires, – de ce que j'ai pris l'habitude d'appeler ses matrices, – le corps de droit international ou supra-national, qu'étudie le droit comparé, a aussi ses sources matérielles ou primaires fournissant la matière première – le donné, comme dit Gény – des produits façonnés – ou construits – par ses matrices. C'est l'ensemble des forces économiques, sociales ou morales, qui chaque jour resserrent un peu plus la solidarité ou l'interdépendance entre tous les éléments de la communauté internationale. Les plus nombreuses, les plus tenacement agissantes sont d'ordre économique. [...] Parallèlement à ces facteurs économiques, il y a aussi des forces éthiques ou des forces spirituelles – de grandes vagues de l'opinion publique ou de parties agissantes de l'opinion publique mondiale – qui contribuent puissamment à élaborer la matière première d'un droit supra-national.[30]

Lambert promoted codification on the basis of standards rather than rules and emphasized the need for a uniform private law to be achieved through local enforcement, interpretation and implementation. The key to a successful codification, in Lambert's mind, was to engage successfully with customary law and to allow international rules to root in the soil of each legal regime. Only then could unification be part of a broader cultural development toward shared understanding. To succeed, international legislation would need to harmonize the specifics of national social conditions with the need for uniformity:

---

[29] *Id.*, 'L'enseignement du droit comparé: sa coopération au rapprochement entre la jurisprudence française et la jurisprudence anglo-américaine', in *Annales de l'Université de Lyon*, vol. II (1919), fascicule 32, p. 94.
[30] *Id., supra*, note 26, p. 491.

Toute oeuvre de législation internationalement uniforme doit faire face à la tâche essentielle qui s'impose aux législations nationales ou locales: trouver la conciliation opportune entre les deux aspirations opposées de tout ordre juridique, un besoin d'assurer la sécurité des relations juridiques qui ne pourrait être pleinement satisfait que par une uniformité et une immobilité complètes du droit, et un besoin d'adaptation du droit aux exigences changeantes de la vie sociale et économique qui exige l'ouverture de jours et de soupapes de sûreté dans l'ordonnancement juridique. Selon que, dans la matière qu'elle traite, l'un de ces deux intérêts l'emporte plus ou moins fortement sur l'autre dans leur dosage naturel, elle sera amenée à s'orienter vers l'uniformisation cherchée dans la loi uniforme de Genève sur le change [i.e., rules], *ou celle dont se contente l'Organisation Internationale du Travail* [i.e., standards], *ou vers des types intermédiaires d'uniformisation.*[31]

As a participant in the then emerging tradition of sociological jurisprudence, Lambert's methodological commitments were as significant as his political project. For Lambert, both national and international law were full of gaps in which the existing formal legal materials provided no guidance. The work of the jurist was to assist the judge in developing solutions which responded to new social needs and economic conditions. And it was here that the study of comparative law could make its contribution:

---

[31] *Id.*, p. 490. Lambert considers the difficulty, the need and the method for achieving this harmonization in these terms: '*L'impérieuse leçon des faits a vite appris à ceux qui ont eu à la diriger* [i.e., the enterprise of unifying labour law after the Versailles Treaty and the establishment of the International Labour Organization] *[...] qu'il serait chimérique de poursuivre, même sur les terrains les mieux choisis, les plus préparés de ce domaine, une uniformisation matérielle des dispositions des diverses lois d'Etats. Que tout ce qu'il était possible d'obtenir à la longue et par étapes, c'était l'établissement d'une équivalence générale ou moyenne entre ces dispositions, l'acceptation de directives communes, susceptibles d'être adaptées aux conditions particulières de chaque pays, de chaque région et d'être conciliées avec les nécessités propres à chaque branche de l'activité industrielle et commerciale. Un droit international du travail, plus encore que cette branche de législations nationales, ne peut manifestement se développer que sous la forme qui est en contraste le plus net avec un régime de règles uniformes et par conséquent rigides [...]. L'établissement entre nations d'un droit véritablement uniforme [...] aboutirait à immobiliser les parties du droit pour lesquelles [il] s'établirait, à empêcher l'adaptation progressive de leurs principes aux transformations d'un milieu social et économique, qui est en perpétuelle évolution, qui, même à certaines heures – comme l'heure présente – remue avec une intensité inquiétante de puissance de renouvellement. Ou bien, malgré l'existence d'une législation uniforme, les Etats reliés par elle apporteront chacun dans leur version nationale de la législation uniforme les perfectionnements nécessaires à son maintien en harmonie avec le mouvement général de leurs institutions et leurs moeurs économiques, et alors l'uniformité sera vite rompue. Ou, pour maintenir cette uniformité, on s'abstiendra, de part et d'autre, de légiférer sur la partie du droit uniformisée. Mais alors ce sera l'obstacle à tout progrès législatif en cette matière*': *id.*, pp. 487–8.

L'existence, parmi les fonctions judiciaires, de cette délicate mission de découverte du droit, est elle-même la conséquence d'un phénomène sociologique que l'oeuvre de Gény a fait ressortir en une éclatante lumière: la présence inévitable dans tous les corps du droit, – qu'ils soient principalement législatifs, comme ceux des pays de droit civil, ou principalement judiciaires, comme ceux des pays de common law – de lacunes qui, à mesure qu'on arrive à les combler sur certains points, se reforment nécessairement sur d'autres. C'est encore à Gény que revient le mérite d'avoir précisé [...] le rôle qui revient, dans la poursuite des cas non-prévus, à la libre recherche scientifique, et les conditions dans lesquelles elle doit être maniée pour ne point tomber dans l'arbitraire et l'anarchie des doctrines du 'libre droit'. Elle a besoin, à cette fin, de faire appel à tous les instruments qui peuvent lui faciliter la découverte de la solution la plus conforme à ce que Gény appelle la 'nature des choses positives' ou à ce que j'appelle l'infrastructure économique et sociale du droit. Sugiyama ne s'est certes point trompé en signalant [...] le droit comparé comme le principal, et le plus naturellement indiqué de ces instruments.[32]

To contemporary eyes, Lambert's comparative-law writing seems refreshingly direct – there is a clear social objective and a sense of methodological self-confidence. The broad outlines of methodological choices which now seem more fraught with difficulty are here – law as a social fact in particular contexts alongside law as a response to universal social and economic needs or conditions, law as the self-conscious work of a scholarly elite who would look for inspiration in the customary laws of private enterprises, unions and other economic actors, a broad assault on the arid disengagement of existing formal law from social conditions to be achieved by codification, uniform codification to be achieved by local interpretation of broad standards.[33]

In retrospect, many of Lambert's proposals seem contradictory and idiosyncratic. For later scholars, the codes which emerged from anti-formalist enthusiasm in the 1920s would seem as out of touch with social reality as the national legal traditions Lambert sought to overcome through codification. Were we to trace the choices described in the last section through Lambert's work, he would seem to lurch from one spectrum to another. His individual propositions today seem bold and, in a sense, naive, unaware of

---

[32] *Id.*, p. 492.
[33] Lambert's methodological and political self-confidence on this score was shared by many of his contemporaries. For an interesting international law parallel promoting anti-formalism, interdisciplinarity and connection of law with sociological and political realities, all through codification, see Alejandro Alvarez, 'The New International Law', *Transactions of the Grotius Society*, pp. 35–51 (16 April 1929).

the range of possibilities from which they had been plucked and, therefore, not well defended from criticism. A comparatist would no longer write as Lambert did, because he or she would have introjected these potential critics, and we might understand the move from pre- to post-war comparativism as the introjection of these cautions. Anti-formalism is no longer a self-confident assertion, but a set of opposing factors among which only a chastened judgement is possible. But all this was yet to come.

If we take Roscoe Pound, a leading US proponent of comparative law during the inter-war period, we find a similarly self-confident political and methodological project for comparative law. Pound saw comparative law as part of a broader enterprise of sociological jurisprudence.[34] The formal precepts of a given law were not sufficient to understand or work successfully in a legal order. Looking beyond the formal law seemed to blend with looking beyond one's own legal system – looking comparatively would force looking behind formal legal doctrines:

> Matthew Arnold used to say that one who knew only his Bible knew not his Bible. May we not say that one who knows only the laws of his own jurisdiction knows not the laws of his jurisdiction?[35]

Formal legal precepts rested upon a social process or 'technique' which gave them nuance and meaning and to comprehend a legal system, comparatists would need to master its technique:

> Comparison of judicial and juristic technique is the beginning of wisdom in comparative law. It is also a prerequisite of professional use in any one country of the law books of another. One only has to have seen highly trained students from Continental universities trying to use English or American law books, or intelligent American lawyers trying to use Continental or Latin American codes, to perceive how hopeless it is to seek the law of another land from its law books without mastery of the technique of that law.[36]

---

[34] On the relationship between sociological jurisprudence and comparative law, see Roscoe Pound, 'Scope and Purpose of Sociological Jurisprudence (Part I)', (1911) 24 Harvard L.R. 591, pp. 616–18; *id.*, 'Philosophy of Law and Comparative Law', (1951) 100 U. Pennsylvania L.R. 1; *id.*, 'Introduction', (1952) 1 Am. J. Comp. L. 1; *id.*, 'The Place of Comparative Law in the American Law School Curriculum', (1934) 8 Tulane L.R. 163. My understanding of Pound's comparative work relies on the excellent study by Mitchel de S.-O.-l'E. Lasser, 'Comparative Readings of Roscoe Pound's *Jurisprudence*', (2002) 50 Am. J. Comp. L. 719.

[35] Roscoe Pound, 'What May We Expect from Comparative Law?', (1936) 22 Am. Bar Assoc. J. 56, p. 60.

[36] *Ibid.*

Managing a legal order rooted in the social fabric can easily go awry – judges and others may rely too much on the formal rules or might be tempted to substitute their own preferences for the law. For Pound, all this was particularly worrying when, as he experienced the 1930s, the legal system needed not only to be managed, but defended:

> A time of transition, a time of creative lawmaking, a time of legislative and judicial and juristic experimentation, a time of novel theories as to what the law is or of theories that there is no law – that there is only a process none too thoroughly concealed with a camouflage of technical development of the grounds of its operation from the authoritative materials – such a time demands a deeper and wider knowledge of the technique and of the materials of judicial and administrative determination than is called for in an era of stability and quiescence. In the latter minute and accurate information as to the legal precepts recognized and applied by the tribunals of the time and place could make a learned and effective lawyer. In the former these precepts are on trial. They are not thought of as finally established, but as subject to inquiry as to their force and validity. Hence one who merely knows them as they are in comparison to themselves, is likely to be found wanting.[37]

As a result, Pound had a very concrete project in mind for the discipline of comparative law and proposed a particular method of work to achieve it. Comparative law was to be enlisted in the struggle within the legal intelligentsia against those – the 'new realists' or 'radical new realists' – who would see law only in its effects or would root law in the subjective and personal attitudes of particular judges. At the same time, the legal establishment needed to defend itself against those who would seek to disconnect law from social life, either retreating into the 'old systems of natural law' or, like the 'analytic jurists' of the previous century, ignore the urgent need to align law with social needs and ideals. The legal order must be grounded in reality, which, for Pound, meant the reality of what ought to be done:

> Let it be repeated. Faithful portrayal of what courts and law makers and jurists do is not the whole task of a science of law. One of the conspicuous actualities of the legal order is the impossibility of divorcing what they do from what they ought to do or what they feel they ought to do [...]. Critical portrayals of the ideal element in law, valuings of traditional ideals with respect to the

---

[37] Ibid.

actualities of the social and legal order, and the results to which they lead in the social and legal order of today, are as much in touch with reality [...] as psychological theories of the behavior of particular judges in particular cases.[38]

The way to do this was to uncover the 'ideal' elements in a legal system and use them both as a basis for rationalizing and systematizing legal rules and to give nuance and flexibility to the interpretation of formal legal rules. These 'ideals' are a part of the law, but may easily be overlooked or not understood.[39] It is here that the comparatist can be helpful – by comparing the law of a legal system with itself over time and with other legal orders, the ideal element within it can be illuminated:

> But I look forward most, for the purposes of the immediate future, to a study of the ideal element in law, a study of the received ideals of American law, which, if it is to be what it should be, must be carried on comparatively. It must be comparative as to the received ideals of the past, in different stages of legal development, in comparison with those of yesterday and today. It must be comparative as to the ideal element in different bodies of law in comparison with each other [...]. I look forward to a comparative philosophical jurisprudence which shall be able the better to do the needed work upon the ideal element.[40]

By identifying the ideal element in law through comparative study, it will be possible to animate and defend the legal order without relying on the attitudes of particular judges, but also without making the 'mistake [...] to set off the ideal element as something of independent validity above the law – as in the old systems of natural law, and [...] to set it off in order to ignore it, as did the analytical jurists of the last century'.[41]

Comparative study would not only reinforce the authority of the established legal order, but it would also encourage the legal system to become more international as legal elites become more aware of the 'universal character of law'.[42] Through comparative work, jurists will learn that:

---

[38] *Id.*, 'A Call for a Realist Jurisprudence', (1931) 44 Harvard L.R. 697, p. 700.
[39] On the importance of the ideal element of law in Pound's sociological jurisprudence, see *id.*, 'A Comparison of Ideals of Law', (1933) 47 Harvard L.R. 1, pp. 3–4.
[40] *Id., supra*, note 35, p. 60.   [41] *Id., supra*, note 39, p. 4.
[42] See *id., supra*, note 35, p. 60; *id.*, 'Comparative Law in Space and Time', (1955) 4 Am. J. Comp. L. 70, pp. 83–4.

law is general, tending more and more to be universal, while it is laws that are local [...]. The legal order (*ordre juridique, Rechtsordnung*) is general and tends to be universal with the continually increasing economic and cultural unification of the world. Advent of comparative law as a practical subject of study, writing and teaching is but an item in the process of world unification which has gone on increasingly on every side in the history of civilization. War of small town with small town, of clan with clan, tribe with tribe, country with country, empire with empire, and today reaching to continent with continent, shows a process of erasing the minor distinctions that make for local polities and jurisdictions and call for local legal orders and multiplied local laws [...]. And, what is specially significant, the foregoing items of closer jural relations of peoples with peoples today do not have behind them any movement toward an omnicompetent universal super-state. On the contrary, peoples are insistent as ever upon local political independence [...]. Today comparative law becomes, as it were, a book of sketches toward a map of a law of the world, not a chart of a tangle of Main Streets leading nowhere.[43]

Pound's reflections on comparative law are as methodologically self-confident and politically brash as those of Lambert. They share Lambert's broadly anti-formal and social orientation, as well as his internationalist and universalizing objectives. Like Lambert, Pound manages to put together things which no longer combine so easily – universal ideals which are part of the law of particular places or ideals which are facts of a legal culture. He developed elaborate models of stages of legal development, which were both historically specific to particular legal traditions and more general trans-historical phenomena.[44] He privileges neither customary nor legislative materials in accounting for foreign legal orders:

> A developed body of legal precepts is made of two elements, an enacted or imperative and a traditional or habitual element.[45]

Pound's programme is not Lambert's – locating hidden legal ideals is not learning the customary laws of unions and commercial associations. Countering the American realist challenge is not building a more socially

---

[43] *Id.*, 'The Passing of Mainstreetism', in Kurt Nadelmann, Arthur von Mehren and John Hazard (eds.), *Twentieth-Century Comparative and Conflicts Law: Legal Essays in Honor of Hessel E. Yntema* (Leiden: Sijthoff, 1961), pp. 12–14.

[44] For an excellent account of this ambivalence in Pound's comparative writing, see generally Lasser, *supra*, note 34.

[45] Roscoe Pound, *Jurisprudence*, vol. II (St Paul: West, 1959), p. 9, as quoted in Lasser, *supra*, note 34.

progressive legal order in the sphere of French legal influence. Encouraging jurists to navigate by universal ideals is quite a long way from promoting codification of standards which will be interpreted to accord with local social and economic needs. Although Pound and Lambert are not in methodological debate – they both develop their comparative-law ideas as if they spoke for a consensus in the field – the material for a recollection of methodological struggle is there. Once one has learned both, anti-formalism offers choices, not solutions, and we are ready for the emergence of eclecticism.

In Germany, Ernst Rabel was the most significant comparatist of the inter-war period.[46] Rabel began as a historian of Roman law, turning to comparative law only after the First World War. In the years before emigrating to the United States just before the outbreak of war, Rabel sat on numerous arbitral tribunals, served several times as an *ad hoc* judge at the Permanent Court for International Justice, was an active advisor to a wide range of German commercial interests and was the founder and director of the Kaiser-Wilhelm Institute for Foreign and International Private Law in Berlin, where he was also professor. Like Lambert, Rabel saw the institutionalization of comparative legal work as an important project. Looking back on his career after the war, these other more engaged roles slipped from view and it was his work building the institutional and professional resources for sustained comparative work which he remembered as his most lasting contribution – and which he repeatedly urged on his US colleagues.[47]

Like Lambert, Rabel was a lifelong enthusiast of uniform international legal rules for private law and a passionate advocate of codification. He worked extensively preparing for the Hague Conference on the

---

[46] I am indebted to two excellent recent studies of Rabel's comparative legacy. See David J. Gerber, 'Sculpting the Agenda of Comparative Law: Ernst Rabel and the Façade of Language', in Riles, *supra*, note 22, pp. 190–208; Bianca Gardella Tedeschi, 'Anti-formalist Strands in Comparative Legal Thought' (2001), on file with the author. Representative works by Rabel in English are: Ernst Rabel, 'Draft of an International Law of Sales', (1938) 5 U. Chicago L.R. 543 [hereinafter 'Draft']; *id.*, 'On Institutes for Comparative Law', (1947) 47 Columbia L.R. 227 [hereinafter 'On Institutes']; *id.*, 'The Hague Conference on the Unification of Sales Law', (1952) 1 Am. J. Comp. L. 58; *id.*, 'Unpublished Lectures: *Schriften aus dem Nachlass*', RabelsZ, 1986, p. 282 [being a series of speeches and lectures by Rabel in English on a variety of topics in comparative law] (hereinafter '*Schriften*'); *id.*, 'Private Laws of Western Civilization', (1950) 10 Louisiana L.R. 1, 107, 265 & 431 [hereinafter 'Private Laws']. See also *id.*, *The Conflict of Laws: A Comparative Study* (Chicago: Callaghan, 1945), 4 vols. [hereinafter *Conflict*].

[47] See Rabel, 'On Institutes', *supra*, note 46, p. 227. Rabel cited Pound on the significance of comparative law as 'a chief weapon in the armory of the American jurist': *id.*, p. 225.

International Sale of Goods and devoted effort as well to the potential codification of a uniform law of conflicts. He was a strong supporter of the American Law Institute's restatement projects:

> We are pleased to imagine what it would mean, if over great stretches of the earth for the first time a central chapter of the law of obligations would be governed by uniform legislation. What a field for judges like Holmes and authors like Williston, what interchange of solutions, methods, systems! It is not true that unification is practically useless without a common court of appeals. Good decisions have a persuasive power. Common legal science is a greater benefit than is generally imagined. Within each country the international sales law would rival the domestic law by intrinsic strength, as did in Rome the *ius gentium* with the *ius civile*. Looked at in this way, it is well worthwhile to help the international law of sales to come into existence.[48]

Rabel was anything but agnostic about the relative desirability of uniformity and diversity in law. At his most fair-minded, he admitted that divergences would need to be attended to – but similarity was the objective:

> On the international plan, of course, we would not dare to play down the differences. We have to ascertain dissimilarities as well as similarities. Both are equally important and we have to investigate the causes of both. Nevertheless, at the present stage consideration of the common features and the basic ideas are still in the foreground.[49]

Rabel consistently advocated comparative legal study in practical terms – as a guarantee against provincialism, a source of better regulations and rules. During the inter-war period, he also advocated comparative law as an urgent aid in resolving European conflicts by promoting an international spirit for the solution to international problems. But he was also a strong advocate of German national ambitions and saw more professional comparative law as offering competitive advantages to Germany, German business and German lawyers:[50]

> The reconstruction of the fatherland and its strengthening vis-à-vis the outside world require a sharpened perception of the events of the world. The new tasks must also find the jurists armed.[51]

---

[48] *Id.*, 'Draft', *supra*, note 46, p. 565.
[49] *Id.*, '*Schriften*', *supra*, note 46, pp. 319–20.   [50] See Gerber, *supra*, note 46, p. 14.
[51] Ernst Rabel, 'Das Institut für Rechtsvergleichung an der Universität München', Zeitschrift für Rechtspflege in Bayern, 1999, p. 3, as quoted in Gerber, *supra*, note 46, p. 198.

Only through comparative engagement with foreign law could German commercial interests be defended internationally and only through engagement with an international 'spirit' could German national and commercial interests be achieved on the world stage.

In methodological terms, Rabel was influenced by the German 'jurisprudence of interests' and by sociological jurisprudence. His uptake of these ideas reflected the influence of the distinctively German nineteenth-century legal tradition in which he was trained – but this tradition urgently needed reformation to permit German commercial interests to achieve their objectives on the world stage. Specific legal rules were best understood in the context of the 'system' of which they were a part. Understanding a legal system, in turn, required first, historical analysis of the system's development, second, an awareness of the existing legal system as it worked in practice and third, an understanding of a broader 'component that penetrated philosophy, where historical and systematic legal science, together with legal philosophy, examine the deepest issues of the evolution and impact of law'.[52] Although Rabel began as a legal historian, he focused most of his inter-war comparative effort on an attempt to understand the working of foreign legal systems in practice. He never devoted much energy to the 'deepest philosophical issues' and his methodological commitments are never very clearly articulated. He expressed eagerness to pursue comparative law as a 'pure science' by looking beneath the surface of legal language and doctrine to understand the workings of legal rules in practice. And his analysis of legal rules was consistently attentive to the needs and interests of commercial players.

In the United States after the war, Rabel completed a number of short reflective essays and speeches and two major projects. The largest of these was a multi-volume study of comparative conflict of laws rules sponsored by the American Law Institute and intended to serve as the basis for an international effort to unify conflict of laws.[53] Without methodological or historical gloss, these lengthy descriptions focus on the outcomes achieved through various conflicts rules in different systems. His one post-war comparative study was a magisterial overview of the 'Private Laws of Western Civilization' published in a series of articles by the *Louisiana Law Review*.[54] These lectures consider Roman law, the French civil code, the German and

---

[52] *Id.*, p. 2, as quoted in Gerber, *supra*, note 46, p. 197, n. 18.
[53] See Rabel, *Conflict, supra*, note 46.   [54] Rabel, 'Private Laws', *supra*, note 46.

Swiss codes and the common and civil law in historical terms, enumerating various salient differences and similarities. If there is a common theme, it is the identification of the difficulty, encountered differently in each tradition, of escaping the practical constraints of legal formalism to allow for a more practical attention to 'the social purposes more than the technical qualities of the law'.[55]

In comparison to Lambert and Pound, Rabel's focus was far more on the practical outcomes of legal rules as they were encountered by practitioners and commercial actors. He places little emphasis on ideals or normative commitments, although his historical surveys often conclude that a system is committed to a specific idea, such as legalism, precedent, etc. In peering through the language of the law to practice, he was not looking for customary law and, unlike Lambert, was not seeking the views of business people or union leaders about what the law was or should be. He was seeking to canvass the practical outcomes which resulted as different legal systems were in fact applied – and he was confident that these could be harmonized by legislative codification.

Max Rheinstein describes Rabel's methodological preoccupations this way:

> As a comparatist, Rabel had, of necessity, to apply the method which has come to be called in Germany that of the jurisprudence of interests and in this country that of sociological jurisprudence. This method has often been stated to be opposed to that of conceptual jurisprudence. No such opposition existed in Rabel's thought. In his view law was to be treated as a body of rules and concepts arranged harmoniously and systematically. It was his aim to improve the 'system', to refine its concepts, and to prevent their obfuscation [citation omitted]. For him the good lawyer was he who would master the concepts and handle them deftly and cleanly for the achievement of the ends of good policy. A policy would not be good policy, however, if it neglected to consider the experiences of two millennia which had come to be precipitated in the concepts of the Civil Law. Only on rare occasions did Rabel articulate

---

[55] *Id.*, p. 9. Rabel credits Roman law with inventing the idea that 'the judge should evaluate evidence brought before him according to his own conscientious conviction, and not bound by formalized legal rules determining what this or that document is worth, how many witnesses are needed, of what kind, *et cetera*': *id.*, p. 10. See Gerber, *supra*, note 46, p. 10. Rabel traces the historically specific fate of this idea in the other systems, which have very different attitudes toward written law – the rather loose Swiss, the more detailed German code, the French conception of legality, the British opposition of formal rules and equity, the US experience with precedent and so forth.

these methodological convictions of his. Indeed, he avoided participation in the methodological controversy by which German juristic thought was agitated. He simply handled the legal concepts in his own way both in his writing and his teaching.[56]

We can hear in Rheinstein's 1956 eulogy the voice of the post-war eclectic – the image of methodological choice as a 'necessity', the evasion of methodological ambivalence in earlier work, the focus on the practical jurist, deftly aiming to use law for 'good policy'. Putting Lambert, Pound and Rabel together, we can say that by the end of the inter-war period, the broadly anti-formal comparative-law project had been elaborated in a range of quite different directions – emphasizing ideals, social facts, practical effects – and in quite different institutional and ideological projects.

René David illustrates what began to happen next.[57] David is also in the anti-formalist tradition and is committed to transforming law so as to align it with changing social and economic needs.[58] He speaks as one

---

[56] Max Rheinstein, 'In Memory of Ernst Rabel', (1956) 5 Am. J. Comp. L. 185, p. 187.

[57] Basic references for David include René David, *Traité élémentaire de droit civil comparé* (Paris: L.G.D.J., 1950). In relation to this book, David himself later said, in a collection of articles, speeches and essays written over more than thirty years, grouped by topic, and introduced by a general comment on the place of the particular topic in David's work, that it was generally out of date, but that the methodological and theoretical dimension of the work, which was its real focus and purpose '*mérite encore d'être lue*': id., *Le droit comparé: droits d'hier, droits de demain* (Paris: Economica, 1982), p. 39 [hereinafter *Le droit comparé*]. See also id., *Les grands systèmes de droit contemporains*, 11th ed. by Camille Jauffret-Spinosi (Paris: Dalloz, 2002), translated into English, from earlier editions, as id. and John E. C. Brierley, *Major Legal Systems in the World Today*, 3d ed. (London: Stevens, 1985); id., *Les avatars d'un comparatiste* (Paris: Economica, 1982) [hereinafter *Avatars*]. In this, his autobiography, David mainly discusses the methodological/theoretical orientations of his comparative work: see id., pp. 258–68, being c. 18 entitled '*Mon oeuvre*'. On David's comparative work, see Jorge L. Esquirol, 'René David: At the Head of the Legal Family', in Riles, supra, note 22, pp. 212–35.

[58] For example, see David, *Le droit comparé*, supra, note 57, p. 66: '*En vérité, tout le monde le sait, [les juges] jouent dans nos pays comme dans les pays de common law un rôle important de création du droit. On peut, à l'occasion, leur demander et obtenir d'eux une "interprétation" de la loi plus orientée vers une solution de justice que commandée par la volonté du législateur ou par des textes que celui-ci a prescrits*'. And later on, in the same piece: '*Le droit n'a jamais été statique. Toujours il a dû s'adapter à des changements qui se produisaient dans les circonstances, dans les techniques, dans les idées, et qui conduisaient à concevoir d'une manière nouvelle la justice. L'on doit néanmoins reconnaître que cette évolution a pris, dans nos sociétés actuelles, un caractère révolutionnaire parce que le droit, au lieu de se fixer pour tâches essentielles le maintien de l'ordre et la garantie de droits individuels, vise aujourd'hui, à un degré égal et parfois supérieur, à transformer l'ordre social existant et à donner effet à un type nouveau de droits: droits économiques et sociaux, droits collectifs ou diffus*': id., p. 71. Or, in his most classic piece of work: 'When considering a foreign law, we must however bear in mind that the manner in which such law is presented in its formal sources

who stands on the shoulders of giants, praising the great comparatists of the preceding generation.[59] He wears his cosmopolitan commitments on his sleeve.[60] But the tone has shifted – David is also writing against this tradition. The objectives have become mild, universalist, vague. David lists the excellent uses that can be made of comparative law – improving legal theory, understanding legal history, improving national law, contributing to the development of a 'coherent private international law' by ending the 'anarchy' of the currently conflicting legal systems, contributing to an 'understanding of foreign peoples [and] assist[ing] in the creation of a healthy context for the development of international relations'.[61] But when he gets to the 'role of comparatists' in all this, he steps back a bit – the comparatist's 'principal task is to prepare the ground, so to speak, in order that others can, with profit, adapt the comparative method to their specific tasks'.[62]

In methodological terms, David treats his predecessors as having made crucial methodological errors. Against Pound, David argues that

is not necessarily the only factor conditioning social relations in that country': *id.* and Brierley, *supra*, note 57, p. 13. At the same time, David sets aside the view that 'considered comparative law as no more than an aspect of the sociology of law': *ibid.*

[59] The first three pieces in David, *Le droit comparé*, *supra*, note 57, are eulogies for Lambert ['*Edouard Lambert a été un grand comparatiste (...). Il a été de ceux qui, parce qu'ils croyaient à la communauté internationale et parce qu'ils savaient se donner tout entier à un idéal, ont le mieux servi l'intérêt de leur pays; il a été un grand Français*': *id.*, p. 20], Harold Gutteridge ['*un des maîtres inconstestés du droit comparé*': *id.*, p. 21] and Felipe de Solà Cañizares ['*l'oeuvre scientifique de Solà est considérable, et elle aurait suffi à elle seule à le classer comme un grand comparatiste*': *id.*, p. 33]. Elsewhere, he cites Pound as a reference for the sociological dimension of comparative studies in law, referring to '*l'oeuvre de Roscoe Pound, le grand comparatiste américain*': *id.*, *Avatars*, *supra*, note 57, p. 259. He also presents Lambert as an example: '*Mon modèle était plutôt Edouard Lambert, quoique je me méfiasse des tendances un peu chimériques auxquelles l'avait porté sa générosité naturelle*' (*id.*, p. 294).

[60] For example, see *id.*, *Le droit comparé*, *supra*, note 57, p. 63 : '*Je ne conçois pas en effet que l'on puisse "se spécialiser" dans son droit national, et tout ignorer des conceptions différentes du droit, de son rôle, de ses techniques, que l'on peut avoir dans telle ou telle région du monde: aux Etats-Unis qui pour notre bonheur ou notre malheur sont aujourd'hui la puissance dominante dans la politique et l'économie du monde, – dans l'Union soviétique qui met en cause, dans leur fondement même, nos institutions, – dans les pays d'Europe occidentale, avec lesquels nous voudrions nous unir étroitement, – dans les pays du tiers-monde, dont la misère pose un problème angoissant pour la morale universelle et la paix du monde. Se replier sur la seule étude de notre droit national me paraît être aujourd'hui une position – peut-être malheureusement une tendance – anachronique, sans que je fasse à cet égard une différence entre les "grandes puissances" – celles qui se qualifient de telles, disent les Brésiliens, – et les plus petits pays, – ceux qui ont plus de modestie ou une conscience plus nette de leur poids dans le monde contemporain. Tous ceux qui veulent regarder le droit comme une science, tous ceux qui sont conscients de la nécessité d'élaborer un ordre international nouveau fondé sur la justice [...] adhéreront à la conviction qu'un juriste digne de ce nom doit avoir quelque connaissance de ce que sont les principaux systèmes de droit dans le monde contemporain.*'

[61] *Id.* and Brierley, *supra*, note 57, p. 8.   [62] *Ibid.*

law is not universal in its ideals – the Chinese, the Islamic are simply too different to be assimilated in this way to the western legal tradition.[63] Against Lambert, David argues that the comparison of legislation and the aspiration for codification were both too formalist and too positivist – which could lead to a politics of apology for totalitarian departures from culturally embedded freedoms.[64] At the same time, one can go too far toward the culturally particularist end of the spectrum, a position David associates with Lambert's predecessor, François Gény. Such a position could also lead to cultural/racial justifications of totalitarianism which underestimated the positive force of the universal rights of man.[65] Anti-formalism has given rise to a choice.

In building a middle way which could avoid these extremes, David is careful to give appropriate weight to both cultural and functional/technical aspects of law. Though distinct, both culture and function are crucial to an understanding of similarities and differences among legal regimes.[66]

[63] For example, see *id., Le droit comparé, supra*, note 57, pp. 93–4: 'Concernant la définition du droit, on trouve aux Etats-Unis d'Amérique une formule célèbre, selon laquelle le droit n'est pas autre chose que la prédiction raisonnable de ce que les cours de justice pourront décider dans telle ou telle affaire si celle-ci vient à leur être soumise [...]. Transportons-nous [...] en pays d'Islam. Le droit musulman (shâr'ia) consiste dans les préceptes, rattachés à la religion, qui doivent gouverner la conduite des Musulmans dans leurs rapports les uns avec les autres, s'ils ont la préoccupation de leur salut éternel [...]. Le droit tel que le définit Holmes et le droit musulman sont deux choses toutes différentes.' And, further: 'En France, en Angleterre, en Allemagne, aux Etats-Unis d'Amérique on souhaite que la société vienne à être aussi complètement soumise que possible au droit; [...] le droit est symbole de justice, les citoyens sont invités à lutter pour assurer son règne. Dans l'Extrême-Orient au contraire, la philosophie traditionnelle voit dans le droit un pis-aller, une technique bonne tout au plus à discipliner les barbares; l'honnête citoyen ne se soucie pas du droit, il se tient à l'écart des tribunaux et ignore les lois pour vivre selon les règles de la morale, de convenance et d'étiquette, héritées des ancêtres, que lui dicte son sentiment d'appartenance à une certaine communauté. Ici encore il est difficile, on en conviendra, de comparer les deux types de droit: celui qui représente un idéal de justice et celui dont on espère qu'il aura le moins possible lieu d'intervenir': *id.*, p. 94.
[64] See Esquirol, *supra*, note 57, pp. 218–23.
[65] *Id.*, pp. 223–9. As Esquirol points out, there was not only an overt liberal politics in this methodological project but David also had a nationalist agenda, for it was in French legal culture that the two extremes had been avoided and the universal rights of man given cultural form. It is interesting to note that both Lambert and Rabel shared this combination of nationalist pride and humanist cosmopolitanism at some point in their career. On Rabel, see, for example, Gerber, *supra*, note 46. For a glimpse of Lambert's post-war slightly nationalist (and slightly anti-German) undertones, see, for example, Lambert, *supra*, note 29, pp. 6–10.
[66] For example, see David, *Le droit comparé, supra*, note 57, p. 7: 'le droit comparé, c'est essentiellement la lutte contre les idées fausses et les préjugés, engendrés par l'attitude isolationniste qu'ont prise les juristes dans la plupart des pays. Une première idée fausse consiste à penser que le droit est considéré en tous pays de même manière que chez nous: que partout il jouit du même prestige et qu'on y voit partout l'assise fondamentale de la société. Une seconde idée fausse est de croire que le droit est partout conçu comme étant un ensemble de normes, ayant pour les intéressés et pour les

David proposes a series of 'legal families'. These go through various iterations in his work – in *Major Legal Systems in the World Today*, he distinguished 'Romano-Germanic, Common Law, Socialist systems, Muslim-Hindu-Jewish, and Far East'.[67] These broad families, straddling cultural and technical similarities and differences are simply suggestive:

> These discussions, however, if pushed too far, do not make very much sense in the end. The idea of a 'legal family' does not correspond to a biological reality: it is no more than a didactic device. We are attempting no more than to underscore the similarities and differences of the various legal systems – and, in that light, almost any systematic classification would serve the purpose. The matter turns upon the context in which one is placed and the aim in mind. The suitability of any classification will depend upon whether the perspective is world-wide or regional, or whether attention is given to public, private or criminal law. Each approach can undoubtedly be justified from the point of view of the person proposing it and none can, in the end, be recognised as exclusive.[68]

The eclectic voice for post-war comparative law is born. From this point, the canon of great comparatists becomes increasingly modest about its aims, eclectic in its methods and distant from the wisdom of earlier comparatists. But the middle ground to be provided by David's legal families turns out itself to be unstable and subject to attack.

The main alternative to David's legal families idea was the functionalism of Konrad Zweigert and Hein Kötz. Like David, they situate themselves firmly in the anti-formalist tradition:

> juges un caractère impératif. Le droit comparé va dissiper les illusions qui nous font attribuer à nos manières de voir une valeur universelle. Il appelle notre attention sur le fait qu'il existe d'autres recettes que le droit pour aménager les rapports sociaux et que, même chez nous, la société ne saurait être gouvernée exclusivement par le droit. Il nous révèle la souplesse qu'il est possible de donner au droit, lequel ne consiste pas nécessairement en un ensemble de normes impératives, mais peut à l'occasion proposer seulement des modèles ou se borner, sans régler le fond des litiges, à instituer des procédures permettant de rétablir l'ordre et la paix. Le droit comparé enfin fait ressortir le caractère accidentel, lié à des circonstances diverses, de maintes classifications et de maints concepts dont nous pouvons être tentés de croire qu'ils correspondent à des exigences de la logique et qu'ils représentent des vérités absolues lorsque nous considérons notre seul droit national.' For a careful balancing of the functional and cultural (in this case, ideological) dimension of law and comparative law, see *id.*, pp. 141–58 [reproducing his 1963 article entitled 'Le dépassement du droit et les systèmes de droit contemporains', where he addresses the problem of 'overcoming law' from the perspective of the distinction/opposition between bourgeois/socialist legal systems]. See also David and Brierley, *supra*, note 57, pp. 20–1 [discussing the 'criterion for the classification of laws into families' and arguing that cultural and technical criteria must both be given their due].

[67] David and Brierley, *supra*, note 57, pp. 23–31.   [68] David and Brierley, *supra*, note 57, p. 21.

The jurisprudence of interests, the *Freirechtsschule*, the sociology of law, legal realism – all these have played a part by criticizing purely national conceptualism, deprecating scholarship which is territorially limited, and emphasizing that legal science should study the actual problems of life rather than the conceptual constructs which seek to solve them. Law is 'social engineering' and legal science is social science. Comparative lawyers recognize this: it is, indeed, the intellectual and methodological starting-point of their discipline. Comparative law is thus closely in tune with current trends in legal science when it asks what the function of legal institutions in different countries may be, rather than what their doctrinal structure is, and when it orders the solutions of the various systems upon a realistic basis by testing them for their responsiveness to the social needs they seek to fill.[69]

But the critique of legal formalism is no longer avant-garde – it has become more of an ongoing rearguard activity against backsliders:

> Though the hollowness of the traditional attitudes – unreflecting, self-assured, and doctrinaire – has increasingly been demonstrated, they are astonishingly vital. New and more realistic methods, especially those of empirical sociology, have been developed, but it is mere wishful thinking to suppose that they characterize our legal thought. One of these new methods is comparative law and it is preeminently adapted to putting legal science on a sure and realistic basis.[70]

The aim is inward – toward legal science: 'The primary aim of comparative law, as of all science, is knowledge.'[71] To that end, 'the scholar should exert 'sober self-restraint''.[72] The ideal scholar is himself agnostic – Zweigert and Kötz quote Rabel: 'if the picture presented by a scholar is coloured by his background or education, international collaboration will correct it.'[73] If there is a political objective associated with their anti-dogmatism, it is not a particularly progressive one. Rather, a realistic comparative study can help make the law more efficient in its functioning, can lead to 'better' law, more realistic law, more attuned to whatever 'social needs' the law itself might seek to fill.[74] Their project is a technical one – offering knowledge

---

[69] Zweigert and Kötz, *supra*, note 4, p. 45.
[70] *Id.*, p. 33.   [71] *Id.*, p. 15.   [72] *Id.*, p. 41.   [73] *Id.*, p. 47.
[74] *Id.*, pp. 33–4: 'Comparative law not only shows up the emptiness of legal dogmatism and systematics, but because it forces us to abandon national doctrines and come directly to grips with the demands of life for suitable rules, it develops a new and particular system, related to those demands in life and therefore functional and appropriate. Comparative law does not only criticize what it finds, but can claim to show the way to a better mastery of the legal material, to deeper insights into it, and thus in the end, to better law.'

about how common problems are solved elsewhere to the legislator or judge. They are careful to distinguish 'theoretical-descriptive' comparative law from 'applied' comparative law and caution that applied comparative law, which 'suggests how a specific problem can most appropriately be solved under given social and economic circumstances' and 'provide[s] advice on legal policy' can place comparatists under 'considerable pressure'.[75]

For Zweigert and Kötz, there is no particular reason to think the result will be more uniform law or more international law. The most one might shoot for would be to 'reduce the number of divergencies in law, attributable not to the political, moral or social qualities of the different nations, but to historical accident or to temporary or contingent circumstances'.[76] Their concern is far more for the science of law itself, which can now be carried out on an international basis:

> It now becomes unmistakably clear that an international legal science is possible. After a period of national legal developments, producing academically and doctrinally sophisticated structures, each apparently peculiar and incomparable, private law can once again become, as it was in the era of natural law, a proper object of international research, without losing its claim to scientific exactitude and objectivity. To this recognition of the fact that law, and especially private law, may properly be studied outside national boundaries, comparative law has greatly contributed, though other legal disciplines also have long been pointing the way. [...] What we must aim for is a truly international comparative law which could form the basis for a universal legal science. This new legal science could provide the scholar with new methods of thought, new systematic concepts, new methods of posing questions, new material discoveries, and new standards of criticism: his scientific scope would be increased to include the experience of all the legal science in the world, and he would be provided with the means to deal with them. It would facilitate the mutual comprehension of jurists of different nationalities and allay the misunderstandings which come from the prejudices, constraints, and diverse vocabularies of the different systems.[77]

Their aspiration for comparative law is oriented toward enhancing a 'scientific' understanding of law and 'no study deserves the name of science if it limits itself to phenomena arising within its national boundaries.'[78] The echoes of sociological jurisprudence survive in the aspiration that comparative law provide a good heuristic for what have become pragmatic mental habits. Training in comparative law

[75] *Id.*, p. 11.   [76] *Id.*, p. 2.   [77] *Id.*, pp. 45–6.   [78] *Id.*, p. 15.

shows that the rule currently operative is only one of several possible solutions; it provides an effective antidote to uncritical faith in legal doctrine; it teaches us that what is presented as pure natural law proves to be nothing of the sort as soon as one crosses a frontier, and it keeps reminding us that while doctrine and categories are essential in any system, they can sometimes become irrelevant to the functioning and efficacy of the law in action and degenerate into futile professional games.[79]

Zweigert and Kötz place themselves proudly in the history of comparative law, but they are not entirely sanguine about the work of their predecessors.[80] They stress the range of diverse methods and approaches which have been taken to the subject and the numerous sources and influences on the comparative profession. For them, the discipline has come into its own as an institutionalized profession through the establishment of 'special institutes, fully equipped with the personnel and plant needed for sustained work, and finally, the representation of comparatists from all countries in the *Association internationale des sciences juridiques*'[81] – and, most importantly, through methodological consolidation.

For Zweigert and Kötz, the pre-war comparative-law world offered a number of alternative approaches, among which Rabel had emerged as the dominant voice:

> The methods of Rabel and his contemporaries at home and abroad have won through. The problems they identified and the programmes they established constitute the tasks of comparative law today.[82]

The only puzzle here is that Rabel was not in a method war with Lambert or any other comparatist. The specific differences which divided Rabel and Lambert – more or less attention to customary law in codification, say – are not what concern Zweigert and Kötz. They are agnostic about choices of this type. Nevertheless, in some way Rabel has come to stand for a tradition which is more practical in its orientation, more interested in uniform practical needs and less in cultural differences, while Lambert has come to stand for a comparative law more attuned to history, culture,

---

[79] *Id.*, p. 22.
[80] *Id.*, p. 3 [discussing the importance of Lambert's and Saleilles's initiative to launch the 1900 Paris Congress]. Zweigert and Kötz examine the history of the discipline in their short chapter entitled 'The History of Comparative Law': *id.*, pp. 48–62.
[81] *Id.*, p. 62.
[82] *Ibid.* Besides themselves, they counted among Rabel's functionalist successors Rheinstein, Kessler and Kahn-Freund.

context, difference. Rabel and Lambert have come to stand for opposite ends of the various spectrums sketched in the last section.

For Zweigert and Kötz, the pull of practicality and uniformity leads to a comparative legal science which could resist both the tendencies of cultural particularism or rule-scepticism and of traditional formalism, by focusing on 'function':

> The basic methodological principle of all comparative law is that of *functionality*. From this basic principle stem all the other rules which determine the choice of laws to compare, the scope of the undertaking, the creation of a system of comparative law, and so on. Incomparables cannot usefully be compared, and in law the only things which are comparable are those which fulfill the same function. This proposition may seem self-evident, but many of its applications, though familiar to the experienced comparatist, are not obvious to the beginner. The proposition rests on what every comparatist learns, namely that the legal system of every society faces essentially the same problems, and solves these problems with quite different means though very often with similar results. The question to which any comparative study is devoted must be posed in purely functional terms; the problem must be stated without any reference to the concepts of one's own legal system.[83]

In a sense, nothing could be further from David's contemporaneous notion of 'legal families'. 'Legal families' and 'functions' do mark poles of the cultural-technical spectrum for comparative law in the 1950s. And yet, just as David's legal families were proposed as a middle way between cultural particularism and universalism, so the idea of function is designed to float between universals and the particularities of specific contexts and ensure that the comparatist has fully grasped the details of each legal regime's specificity.[84]

---

[83] *Id.*, p. 34. Although Rabel is remembered as the founder of the functionalist approach, and as a forerunner to Zweigert and Kötz, in Rabel's last large comparative study, I was unable to locate the word 'function'. See Rabel, 'Private Laws', *supra*, note 46. *Cf*. Rodolfo Sacco, 'One Hundred Years of Comparative Law', (2001) 75 Tulane L.R. 1159, p. 1167: 'Following Rabel, the comparatist began to pose questions that had to be grappled with in functional terms.'

[84] For example, see Zweigert and Kötz, *supra*, note 4, pp. 35–6: 'The beginner often jumps to the conclusion that a foreign system has "nothing to report" on a particular problem. The principle of functionality applies here. Even experienced comparatists sometimes look for the rule they want only in the particular place in the foreign system where their experience of their own system leads them to expect it: they are unconsciously looking at the problem with the eyes of their own system. If one's comparative researches seem to be leading to the conclusion that the foreign system has "nothing to report" one must rethink the original question and purge it of all the dogmatic accretions of one's one system. [. . .] This, then, is the negative aspect of the principle of

The post-war comparative discipline of David and Zweigert and Kötz had become a respectable participant in the mainstream of post-war antiformalist thought. The social and practically engaged projects and energy of Pound, Lambert or Rabel have disappeared, replaced by far more modest objectives for the professionalization of the discipline itself. It would be easy to associate Lambert, Rabel or Pound with ideological positions and social interests – far less so David or Zweigert and Kötz. In a sense, as the academic establishment of the comparative profession was consolidated, its social aspirations diminished. The new profession would make a contribution more to knowledge than policy.

On the methodological side, the story is more complex. David and Zweigert and Kötz write both more and more explicitly about method. David and Zweigert and Kötz do differ on method and talk about their method, but they each present their own method as a mediation of a methodological controversy which they locate in the past. Zweigert and Kötz associate this earlier division with the names of Lambert and Rabel, David with the names of Pound, Lambert and Gény. They each propose a methodological synthesis. And yet, looking back, their own proposals have become marks for the methodological alternatives of cultural differentiation and technical universalism. Indeed, in retrospect, it is easy to overlook their efforts at synthesis – 'functionalism' has been remembered as a technical assault on the embeddedness of law, rather than as a heuristic to ensure attention to differences.[85] 'Legal families' seems like a crude substitute for careful attention to similarities, differences and influences.[86]

The methodologically eclectic and politically neutral comparative-law sensibility reached its first best expression in the work of Rudolf Schlesinger's

---

functionality, that the comparatist must eradicate the preconceptions of his native legal system; the positive aspect tells us which areas of the foreign legal system to investigate in order to find the analogue to the solution which interests him. The basic principle for the student of foreign legal systems is to avoid all limitations and restraints. This applies particularly to the question of "sources of law"; the comparatist must treat as a source of law whatever moulds or affects the living law in his chosen system, whatever the lawyers would treat as a source of law, and he must accord those sources the same relative weight and value as they do. He must attend, just as they do, to statutory and customary law, to case-law and legal writing, to standard-form contracts and general conditions of business, to trade usages and custom. This is quite essential for the comparative method. But it is not enough. To prepare us for his view of the full requirements of the comparative method, Rabel says: "Our task is as hard as scientific ideals demand [...]."'

[85] There has been much criticism of the functionalism in comparative law for its assumptions of universalism. A good selection is cited by Twining, *supra*, note 4, p. 37.

[86] See Watson, *Legal Transplants*, *supra*, note 14, p. 4.

influential Cornell project of the 1950s, which provides the methodological origins for the ongoing effort to identify the common core of European private law.[87] In many ways, it was Schlesinger who routinized the professional activity of post-war comparatists. His project was enormously ambitious, involving dozens of students over many years. The objective was to compile as accurate and complete a picture as possible of similarities and differences among leading private-law systems. Schlesinger offers none of the broad social or cosmopolitan political justifications of Lambert or Pound. His concerns are directed exclusively toward the development of knowledge and the enrichment of legal education.

This work was to be carried out in the tradition of anti-formalism, but Schlesinger's objective was neither to demonstrate the truth of anti-formalist insights nor to mobilize them in a project of legal reform. His goal was to generate an accurate description and analysis of legal similarities and differences among legal regimes. Anti-formalism provided a taken-for-granted background conception of what law is so as to guide the comparatist in identifying legal phenomena for comparison.

In doing comparative work, Schlesinger exhorted his students, it was important to deal with the 'living law'. To do so, one should use a 'factual' rather than a 'concept-oriented approach'.[88] Schlesinger was interested in

---

[87] See Rudolf B. Schlesinger (ed.), *Formation of Contracts: A Study of the Common Core of Legal Systems* (Dobbs-Ferry: Oceana, 1968), 2 vols. [hereinafter *Formation of Contracts*]. These are the published results of the Cornell project. The introduction particularly deals with the methodology of the project and the 'factual approach': *id.*, 'Introduction', in *id.*, vol. I, pp. 2–58. See also *id.*, 'The Common Core of Legal Systems: An Emerging Subject of Comparative Study', in Nadelmann, von Mehren and Hazard, *supra*, note 43, pp. 65–79 [hereinafter 'The Common Core']; *id.*, *Comparative Law: Cases and Materials* (New York: Foundation Press, 1950). The preface, in particular, deals with 'Objective and Method': *id.*, pp. ix–xvi. This reference is to the first edition, the book currently being in its sixth. See also *id.*, 'The Past and Future of Comparative Law', (1995) 43 Am. J. Comp. L. 477 [hereinafter 'The Past and Future']. See generally Ugo Mattei, 'The Comparative Jurisprudence of Schlesinger and Sacco: A Study in Legal Influence', in Riles, *supra*, note 22, pp. 238–56.

[88] Schlesinger, 'The Common Core', *supra*, note 87, p. 73: 'It is a well known truism in comparative law that different legal systems, even in the countless instances in which they arrive at identical results, usually proceed along divergent conceptual routes. [...] Misunderstandings among lawyers brought up in different legal systems can be effectively minimized if *a segment of life is chosen as the focus and the normal unit of discussion*. In this way, and only in this way, can one be sure that all members of the group always address themselves to the same point, and that they penetrate through the layers of classification and concept with which each legal system covers its actual solutions of social problems. [...] If used by a team of comparatists, the case-oriented factual method forces each participant to face and to answer the question: how does your legal system react to this particular fact situation? What remedy, if any, does your system make available to the plaintiff in this case? If the question is posed in this form, functional

cultural differences and sympathetic to the idea that these differences might well run in families. But he was not pursuing a global taxonomy of legal systems. Rather, he was seeking a micro-description of similarities and differences. He was sympathetic to the functionalist idea and often suggested that an accurate identification of the 'same' legal phenomena in another legal culture required attention to whatever in that culture performed the same 'function'. But his functionalism was instrumental to his descriptive endeavour. The key for Schlesinger was the use of hypothetical fact-patterns or 'problems' against which the reactions of various legal systems can be compared.[89] Investigators from various legal systems were asked how a given fact-pattern would be assessed in their own legal regime so as to facilitate understanding of similarities and differences free from the distraction of pre-existing ideas about legal rules and categories, but also from preferences rooted in particular cultural needs or technical functions.

Distance from practical engagement with government is explicitly promoted by Rodolfo Sacco, the Italian comparatist who provides the link between the Cornell project and the current effort led largely by Sacco's students to mobilize researchers for a description of the common core of European private law.[90] Sacco goes out of his way to deride efforts to justify comparative legal study on the basis of its usefulness:

> Like other sciences, comparative law remains a science as long as it acquires knowledge and regardless of whether or not the knowledge is put to any further use [...]. Comparative law is like other sciences in that its aim must be the acquisition of knowledge. Like other branches of legal science, it seeks knowledge of law.[91]

---

similarities between legal systems will be uncovered upon which a concept-oriented approach would throw no light. It will be found in countless instances that many or all legal systems reach a similar result, although they do so by the use of widely divergent theories and labels' [emphasis original]. Schlesinger adds moreover: 'In a comparative research project, as in other contexts, it is doubtless convenient to use reported cases as ready-made materials for discussion; but it does not follow that one should either limit oneself to reported cases, or use them without constant appraisal of their real importance as living law': *ibid.* On the relevance of history and historical context in comparative work, see also *id.*, 'The Past and Future', *supra*, note 87.

[89] The practical details of the 'factual method' are presented in the general introduction to the Cornell project's results in the area of contract law in *id., Formation of Contracts, supra,* note 87, pp. 30–41. On the relationship between the 'functional' and the 'factual' method, see *id.,* 'The Common Core', *supra*, note 87, p. 74.

[90] For a comparison of Sacco and Schlesinger, see Mattei, *supra*, note 87.

[91] Rodolfo Sacco, 'Legal Formants: A Dynamic Approach to Comparative Law', (1991) 39 Am. J. Comp. L. 1 & 393, p. 4.

Even the objective of increased international understanding and harmony seems to be going too far:

> In general, then, the use to which scientific ideas are put affects neither the definition of science nor the validity of its conclusions. Jurists are generally aware of this truth. They do not think their work is valid because it can be used to achieve this or that practical end. In the case of comparative law, however, a different standard is applied, or at least it was thirty years ago. Those who compare legal systems are always asked about the purpose of such comparisons. The idea seems to be that the study of foreign legal systems is a legitimate enterprise only if it results in proposals for the reform of domestic law. [...] The effort to justify comparative law by its practical uses sometimes verges on the ridiculous. According to some sentimentalists, comparison is supposed to increase understanding among peoples and foster the peaceful coexistence of nations. According to that idea, the statesmen who triggered the two world wars would have stopped at the brink of catastrophe had they only attended courses in comparative law. Napoleon himself would have given up his imperialistic dreams had he spent less time over the code that bears his name and more on the *gemeines Recht* and the *kormchaia pravda*.[92]

Sacco's approach to comparative law is also rooted in his anti-formalist conception of law. Sometimes, as for Schlesinger, anti-formalism seems a background assumption which guides good comparative practice. Comparison of legal systems and rules from the most diverse socio-economic and political traditions is possible only if one pushes behind law's formal appearances, avoiding false similarities and differences.[93] At other times, anti-formalism seems an idea of which jurists constantly need

---

[92] *Id.*, pp. 1–2.
[93] Thus, for example, Sacco exhorts us that the 'operative rules of [...] two systems may be more similar than the vocabularies in which they are expressed': *id.*, p. 13. Or: 'it is wrong to believe that the first step toward comparison is to identify "the legal rule" of the countries to be compared. That is the typical view of an inexperienced jurist. It is a misleading simplification which the student of comparative law has a duty to criticize. Instead of speaking of "the legal rule" of a country, we must speak instead of the rules of constitutions, legislatures, courts, and, indeed, of the scholars who formulate legal doctrine. The reason jurists often fail to do so is that their thought is dominated by a fundamental idea: that in a given country at a given moment the rule contained in the constitution or in legislation, the rule formulated by scholars, the rule declared by courts, and the rule actually enforced by courts, have an identical content and are therefore the same': *id.*, p. 21. Or: 'We should not think, however, that we understand a legal system when we know only how courts have actually resolved cases. Knowledge of a legal system entails knowledge of factors present today which determine how cases will be resolved in the future. We must not only show how courts have acted but consider the influences to which judges are subject': *id.*, p. 23.

to be reminded, for which purpose comparative law provides a good heuristic:

> A comparative method can thus provide a check on the claim of jurists within a legal system that their method rests purely on logic and deduction. [...] The comparative method may thus be a threat to any process of legal reasoning which does not employ comparison. The threat is most direct to those 'scientific' methods of legal reasoning that do not measure themselves against practice, but formulate definitions that are supported solely by their consistency with other definitions. In destroying the conclusions reached by these methods, comparison may provide an alternative method that is more valid.[94]

Law is simply 'society's response to the need of social order', and these responses might be extremely varied. There is certainly a functionalist echo here, but the aim is broader – an engagement with the largest category of social needs across human societies at all stages of economic and social development.

For most post-war comparatists, this anti-formalist idea seemed to suggest at least a weak preference for greater international harmonization. National differences were forms – pushing through them to understand how common problems were solved or how a broader cultural family approached the issue seemed bound to lead not only to greater understanding, but also to the possibility of greater harmonization. Not so for Sacco, whose agnosticism is a more thorough one. Attaining uniformity might be a good idea, 'worthy of encouragement', but there are also advantages to diversity, which might also be useful to progress. There is no compelling proof, moreover, that comparative law has led to uniformity, although comparative study might well illuminate similarities which had hitherto been unknown. The roots of Bussani's insistent agnosticism about the valence of the common-core project lie here.

Sacco is best known for introducing the term 'legal formants' into comparative law's methodological lexicon. In many ways, legal formants play the same role in Sacco's scheme that 'factual problems' do in Schlesinger's Cornell project.[95] They offer a point of reference for the comparatist identifying and analysing similarities and differences in legal

---

[94] *Id.*, p. 24.
[95] On the relationship between Sacco and Schlesinger, see *id.*, pp. 27–30 [where Sacco mentions the Cornell project as an important step in the same direction as the theory of legal formants]. See generally Mattei, *supra*, note 87.

phenomena across different legal regimes which are neither technical nor cultural, providing a middle way between attention to formal rules and social contexts. But where Schlesinger's problems seemed to direct the comparatist to identify the one solution which would emerge in different legal systems, Sacco's notion of 'legal formants' makes it possible to keep the ambivalence and multiplicity of legal rules in each system at play in the comparison. The truly careful comparatist will write an account of similarities and differences among legal phenomena which keeps in mind that legal phenomena are often, even quite often, multiple, contradictory and ambivalent, even within one legal culture:

> Thus even the jurist who seeks a single legal rule, indeed who proceeds from the axiom that there can be one rule in force, recognizes implicitly that living law contains many different elements such as statutory rules, the formulations of scholars, and the decision of judges – elements that he keeps separate in his own thinking. [...] [W]e will call them, borrowing from phonetics, the 'legal formants'. The jurist concerned with the law within a single country examines all of these elements and then eliminates the complications that arise from their multiplicity to arrive at one rule. He does so by a process of interpretation. Yet this process does not guarantee that this is, in his system, only a single rule. Several interpretations will be possible and logic alone will not show that one is correct and another false. Within a given legal system with multiple 'legal formants' there is no guarantee that they will be in harmony rather than in conflict.[96]

The 'legal formant' idea permits investigation of elements within a legal system which are in tension with one another:

> Comparison recognizes that the 'legal formants' within a system are not always uniform and therefore contradiction is possible. The principle of non-contradiction, the fetish of municipal lawyers, loses all value in an historical perspective, and the comparative perspective is historical par excellence.[97]

The 'legal formant' idea is not intended as an intervention in debates about what law or government should be or do, nor does it take sides in methodological debates between, say, functionalism and the tradition of legal families.[98] For Sacco, the aim is simply anti-dogmatic:

---

[96] *Id.*, pp. 22–3.   [97] *Id.*, p. 24.
[98] It would certainly be possible to read Sacco's theory of 'legal formants' as a challenge to functionalism, both as a method of comparison and as an idea about law and society, as Michele Graziadei does elsewhere in this book. The different levels or spheres in which law operates,

The comparative method is thus the opposite of the dogmatic. The comparative method is founded upon the actual observation of the elements at work in a given legal system. The dogmatic method is founded upon analytical reasoning. The comparative method examines the way in which, in various legal systems, jurists work with specific rules and general categories. The dogmatic method offers abstract definitions.[99]

In both Europe and the United States, the comparative-law discipline of Schlesinger or Sacco is methodologically eclectic and careful to remain 'objective', neutral and disengaged from ideological debate and the application of its insights by government. Post-war comparatists speak much less in terms which resonate easily with ideological positions in the broader society and are less easily linked with particular social interests (labour, German commerce, etc.) than their pre-war predecessors. They participate less readily in public life or governmental work. They hesitate more about the application of their knowledge and insist more intently on the virtues of disengaged knowledge than their predecessors.

They do speak a great deal about method. But the methods they propose are extremely nuanced mediations of more extreme methodological alternatives identified with comparative work in the past or with work done by others. Nevertheless, their methodological middle-positions continue to differ, or to seem in retrospect to differ, and to do so in a more structured way than did those before the war. We might say that the post-war authors are insistent eclectics, whose debates occupy an ever-shrinking centre of the anti-formalist spectrum, while their pre-war predecessors were more pluralist in their anti-formalism, ranging more widely among the methodological options.

How can we make sense of this story? The clearest story would be the chastening of overt political commitment by anti-formalism in legal science. The comparative-law profession has been, from the start, insistently anti-formalist about legal materials. For the founders, anti-formalism and sociological realism seemed vital methodological assaults on the mainstream legal science of the time. They were associated with strong projects

---

each quasi-autonomous *vis-à-vis* the other, suggest the importance of differing legal forms even where the results for one or another hypothesized 'function' are identical, and the fact that legal orders are often in contradiction within themselves suggests a critique of universalism, as well as of the idea, hidden but present in functionalism, that societies do things differently to express their 'cultures' in a world of universal functions.

[99] Sacco, *supra*, note 91, pp. 25–6.

of internationalization and law reform, with defences of particular social interests against others and with projects of governance and modernization. After the war, as anti-formalism became mainstream – and as the discipline moved from Europe to the United States – the tone shifted. Anti-formalism now would guarantee comparative law's disciplinary place in the mainstream legal academy and would serve pedagogic purposes in helping 'beginners' overcome parochialism and the common tendency to overestimate the importance of legal forms. Anti-formalism remains the vocabulary for comparative work. Comparatists in each generation are insistent on the need to awaken the legal establishment to anti-formalism. But the anti-establishment and anti-parochial edge of early work has been redirected against those who are naive – students, beginners – who need comparative legal education to become sophisticated participants in establishment life. The project in society has become a knowledge project.

Within this story lies a second – the role of debates within the anti-formalist tradition in bringing about that chastening. For each scholar in the founding generation, anti-formalism had a relatively clear meaning – for Lambert, attention to social and economic needs and desires; for Pound, attention to legal ideals; for Rabel, attention to practical outcomes. These were all offered as departures from textual positivism and as corrections for overinvestment in existing legal forms. We could situate all of them on the right end of the spectrums of the last section; each was proposed and defended as an assault on those who thought about law in terms we now associate with the left-hand columns. And yet, looking back, these were quite different ideas, which were understood to have quite different ideological associations and social consequences. With hindsight, we could say that in some way the spectrum between anti-formalism and traditional jurisprudence repeated itself in the choice between, say, legal ideals and social needs or between social needs and practical results, between codification by legislation and codification by custom and so forth. The rift with the establishment became a rift *within* anti-formalism. Social and political choices were sublimated by methodological choices.

If we were to align our comparatists on the spectrums developed in the last section from relatively more formal and universal to relatively more cultural and differentiated, the results would look something like figure 11.8.

We could say that the 'great debate' between embedded social/cultural needs/ideals and universal functions has continued. But something has

Pound .... is to .... Lambert
                                   as
Rabel .... is to .... Pound
                                   as
Zweigert/Kötz .... is to .... David
                                   as
Schlesinger .... is to .... Sacco

Figure 11.8

changed: the debate has become both muted and muddy. Muted, in the sense that the positions are getting closer together – the debate is evermore a matter of the narcissism of small differences. Schlesinger's 'factual problems' and Sacco's 'legal formants' are more similar than Zweigert and Kötz's 'functions' and David's 'families'. Although 'fact problems' lies further to the universal/technical end of things than 'legal formants', both were proposed as middle positions, efforts to bridge the gap between culturally embedded and universal/technical emphases. And the same could be said of 'families' and 'functions'. As the space of the debate narrows, the extremes disappear into the past, into the naivety of youth, into the positions of unnamed extremists.

The debate has also become muddy in the sense that it is evermore difficult to tell what goes where. Figuring out where to put Pound in the story suggests the difficulty. Compared to Lambert, Pound seemed far less interested in the details of factual difference and far more interested in the discovery of universal ideals. And yet, his ideals were also specific to a culture – by looking abroad, understanding the 'ideal element' in law, one could see the factual presence of an 'ought' in one's own legal culture. Compared to Rabel's attention to practical commercial outcomes, Pound's orientation seems very much to the culturally embedded side of the spectrum.

The fluidity of association among the various positions – among the various choices enumerated in the last section – is what makes it possible to mute the debate over time. The left-to-right alignment of the choices comparatists make within the anti-formalist tradition is a matter only of loose analogy. We might say there is an iron law at work here: the more scholars seek to find a middle way between these methodological alternatives, the muddier the terms will become. But the more what had seemed

Figure 11.9

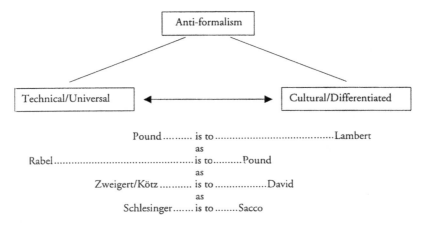

Figure 11.10

diverse preferences within a large tradition will come to seem analogous choices between two unpalatable extremes.

It might be possible to redraw figure 11.8 to take into account something like perceived degrees of separation between the terms. Looked at in 1935, it might appear something like figure 11.9. Looked at in 1955, it might appear something like figure 11.10. And from 2000, it looks like figure 11.11.

This trend highlights a third story – the effects of the slow coming to consciousness of these first two stories. The key difference between the pre- and post-war comparatists is a shift in the tone with which these methodological matters are discussed. The pre-war comparatists cast themselves as outsiders to convention, as engaged social and political actors and as methodological mavericks. The post-war comparatists, by contrast, present themselves more often as insiders, neutral scientists and methodological mediators. This posture reflected in large part, of course, changed circumstances. After the war, largely in the United States, the field of comparative law was aligned with the legal academy's mainstream post-realist common sense. But methodological pronouncements also seem chastened by awareness of

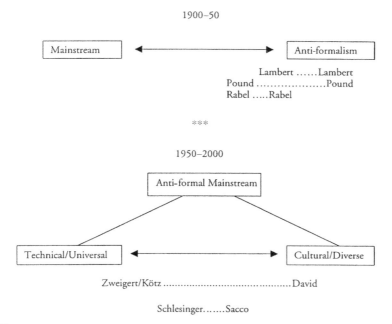

Figure 11.11

the earlier methodological struggle. There certainly was intellectual and political struggle in the 1930s – just not much in comparative law. Standing on the shoulders of giants after 1950 meant seeing their feet of clay – their relative methodological naivety – and reading it as an extreme. Writing yourself into the field after 1950 meant writing yourself against extremism – and against your predecessors. For our predecessors, methodological choices were there to be made – for us, they are there to be balanced, managed, blended, avoided.[100]

The process of disengagement from methodological commitment seems to have been repeated as the field progressed. The 'great' comparatists seem great because they had a strong, if idiosyncratic, methodological formulation. But it is increasingly difficult to find a comparatist who associates with – or even can state clearly – the methodological position of these

---

[100] Duncan Kennedy has written the best study I know of the post-war anti-formalist consciousness of factor balancing. See Duncan Kennedy, 'From the Will Theory to the Principle of Private Autonomy: Lon Fuller's "Consideration and Form"', (2000) 100 Columbia L.R. 94.

early masters. When a great comparatist enters the canon, he is proposing a method which seems like common sense, good professional judgement. At least some people are willing, at least for a moment, to affiliate themselves with this work. Each person who affiliates with a master will want to tweak the method, amending and complexifying it, adding elements from other places, before settling down to wise professional judgement of his own. Indeed, to write as a master, one must write one's predecessors into the margins and occupy the sensible methodological middle. The earlier master is increasingly remembered not for good sense, but for tilting too far and being too preoccupied with methodological matters. Taken together, past masters stand for clear methodological positions, current masters are mature eclectics. In this sense, the moment of methodological division, the clean separation of the poles in the above lists, is always happening and never happened at all.

It is not surprising that scholars of later generations, among them my own contemporaries, are tempted to unsettle the eclectic post-war comparatist by insisting on the significance of methodological clarity. And there have been periodic outbreaks of methodological extremism – the Pierre Legrand–Alan Watson debate might be an illustration.[101] But I do not think these efforts have laid much of a glove on the sensibility of the post-war generation. And indeed, the practical work of the common-core project proceeds with a post-war method of pragmatic eclectic judgement. From the point of view of the field's elder statesmen, these new debates have a definite 'been there, done that' quality.

I have a great deal of sympathy for their reaction – it does seem too late to put the genie of methodological scepticism back in the bottle. An eclectic and unstable effort to pick one's way among all these choices seems unavoidable in thinking about similarities and differences among legal regimes. But this methodological conclusion leaves us with no sense for what has become of the social and political engagements of comparative law. My intuition is that the post-war generation were fleeing more than methodological controversy, that they fled to the method-of-no-method as a sublimation of politics and as a retreat from engagement with governance projects. From my point of view, the problem with the post-war generation was not

---

[101] For example, see Legrand, 'Impossibility', *supra*, note 14; Watson, 'European Private Law', *supra*, note 14.

its methodological eclecticism, but the politics-of-no-politics which this eclecticism facilitated.

It was much easier to understand pre-war comparatists as political actors. They offered polemics for large-scale law-reform projects – to harmonize and codify international rules, to make domestic law more international or social in orientation, to strengthen commercial interests and so forth. They easily associated methodological choices with ideological positions and social interests. To be an anti-formalist about law implied something about one's political commitments and building a more anti-formal legal order seemed hard to distinguish from building a legal system more attuned to 'social' interests, international harmonization, etc. As a more eclectic methodological spirit overtook the field, comparatists seemed to withdraw from politics. Polemics for legal reform were replaced by careful agnosticism about the desirability of, say, legal harmonization. We find instead polemics for the autonomy and neutrality of comparative research. At the same time, methodological commitments became harder to associate cleanly with ideological and social positions.

These may simply have been parallel developments – methodological maturity and political disengagement. But eclecticism also contributed to disengagement. To the extent methodological commitments could still be easily associated with ideological positions or social interests, post-war eclecticism blurred the picture. After the war, moreover, 'anti-formalism' no longer seemed the natural methodological vocabulary of the left alone. With eclecticism came an attenuation of the associations between methodological commitments and ideological positions or social interests. This attenuation compounded the distance post-war eclectics felt from political engagement and seems to have strengthened their determination not to launch polemics for projects of law reform. Or, perhaps more accurately, attenuation sapped something of their confidence as participants in law-reform polemics. For pre-war comparatists, methodological commitments – to various strands of anti-formalism – had provided not only the language, but also the authority, for political engagement. Once anti-formalism ceased to provide stable political guidance, and comparatists ceased to feel stable in their anti-formal commitments, they felt incapacitated from overt political engagement.

To reframe the work of contemporary comparatists in political terms does not mean resurrecting a reliable drive-shaft between method and politics, although if it could be done it might be welcome. The challenge is to render the projects and commitments of methodological eclecticism visible and contestable, disputing the intuitively appealing idea that avoiding methodological dogmatism avoids or neutralizes political effects. My proposal is that doing so may embolden comparatists to pursue political projects even in the absence of clear methodological guidance – harnessing their mature eclectic pragmatism to political objectives which can be embraced or contested. But doing this requires a sharper sense for what it means to say that a professional discipline 'participates in governance' or 'has a politics'.

The politics of contemporary comparative law

The apparent un-politics of today's global regime results in large part from the fact that those who govern are not the people we normally think of as global governors – they are rarely politicians and only very rarely work for foreign ministries or international governmental agencies. Nor are they shadowy 'capitalists' plotting behind closed doors. The international world is largely governed by professional people exercising their expertise: by lawyers and economists, by political scientists and policy professionals, by engineers and business managers.

The most important impediment to appreciating the governing role of experts managing the background norms and institutions of global society is the widespread sense that their work is simply not political or contestable because they *are* experts, managers, pragmatic problem-solvers, technical people. The norms and institutions they manage lie in the background, their professional work involves advising, implementing or interpreting rather than deciding, their decisions seem compelled by their expertise, their expertise rarely takes the form we think of as the terms of political debate. Their vocabularies do not seem like the vocabularies of power – they seem like vocabularies of advice, implementation, technique, know-how.

To contest the politics of expert governance requires that we both identify the decisions these experts make and then associate them with the ideological positions and social interests we usually imagine when we think of contesting something 'politically'. Contesting professional choices requires translation – from the key of knowledge to the key of power, from the vocabulary of expertise to the vocabularies of ideology and interest. A discipline like comparative law participates in global governance when people practising the discipline do things – decide things, place some and not other knowledge in play, argue in one way and not in another – which have consequences that can be associated either with the ideological positions in the broader society through which political debate happens or with social interests which we understand to be in political contestation. This process of translation can be relatively easy or more difficult.

When comparative work is put to use by non-comparatists in their more overtly political projects, it is usually rather easy to associate it with the ideological positions or social interests implicated in those projects. Once comparatists identify two types of legal regime – say regimes of 'status' and of 'contract' – we might well predict that someone else will make it their project to move from one to the other. If such a move can plausibly be thought to benefit 'the left' or 'the right', we can contest the comparatist's contribution in these terms. Should comparative analysis reveal that the global hegemon has a different rule about a problem than whatever prevails locally, someone else – a hegemonic investor, a local politician, a business or labour group – will likely make adoption of the hegemonic approach their own political objective. It may be easy to see this new rule as benefiting one social interest over another and to contest it in those terms.

Associating the *uses* made of comparative work with ideology or interest can often be done even where the work itself is insistently neutral or agnostic. Indeed, claims to neutrality may simply enhance the effectiveness of the work and strengthen its association with politically contestable positions. If the European Union seeks to harmonize European private law and funds an inquiry into the existence of a common core of private law, it may not matter if the project discovers a core or not – if not, the work strengthens the impetus to legislate. Either way, the project's self-conscious agnosticism about the desirability of uniform rules strengthens its authority and its contribution to the Union's political project.

Once we depart from the use or application of comparative law, it becomes more difficult to translate it into politically contestable terms. In the most compelling case, we would identify *effects* of the comparative work and associate those effects with ideology or interest. The whole point of a knowledge project like comparative law is to affect what people know. If knowing *this* rather than *that* will strengthen one ideological position, legitimate or channel elite action to strengthen one social interest, we can contest the comparative work as an act of governance. It is easy to imagine comparative work having an effect on those who consume it, changing their ideas about law and the world in some way which could affect what they do.

Sometimes, these effects arise because experts are pursuing a political agenda, either within the discretionary space offered by their professional vocabulary or by subverting its terms. In these cases, we could say the discipline has been *captured* by ideology or interest. Professionals may proclaim their ideological commitment and interest or they may keep them to themselves. In the easiest case, the expert says 'I do this for labour' and his action does help labour. Somewhat harder is the case where the expert says 'I do this for labour' and the decision misfires or has unexpected effects which hurt labour, or the expert was mistaken or dissembling about his intention. These cases will benefit from sociological attention to the effects, rather than the intention or expressed justification for professional judgement. They encourage us to take professional expressions of interest with a grain of salt. But government by expert makes these easy cases rare indeed. The vocabularies experts use to make and justify decisions are rarely vocabularies of interest or ideology.

Experts generally say something more like 'I do this as an exercise of professional judgement.' In these cases, we can simply ignore what the expert said and focus on the effects of their decisions. If we focus on effects and patterns emerge favourable to one or another interest or ideology, and we do not think the discipline has been 'captured', we will be inclined to think the effects result from the materials and methods of the discipline itself – perhaps from its default practices and background assumptions, perhaps from some bias in the vocabulary of professional judgement. The expert may not have been aware of the effects of his decision, much less of their association with ideology or interest. We might say that the discipline has a *bias* or *blindspot* which affects – even swamps – the discretion of professionals working in it.

We can also try to translate the *professional vocabularies* experts use to make decisions directly into the political vocabularies of ideology and interest. Sometimes, expert vocabularies give us clues to the ideological impact of their work, even where they eschew saying directly 'I do this for labour.' The vocabulary experts use for discussing their background assumptions and default practices – the vocabulary of method – may give us clues to the political biases of everyday professional practices. Sometimes, these methodological commitments offer quite reliable predictors for the political valence and impact of expert decision – think of 'strict interpretation' in debates about US constitutional interpretation. More often, however, it is difficult to associate methodological commitments with ideology or interest without investigating the impact of decisions in concrete cases. And, of course, not everything experts do by default will have given rise to overt methodological discussion. Sometimes, there are background assumptions shared across methodological lines of which professionals may be only partly conscious. Nevertheless, when assumptions and defaults are brought to the attention of the professional as methodological commitments, they sometimes can be associated with ideology or interest in ways which will make them seem political.

This can sometimes be done without reference to outcomes or effects. Imagine an expert saying 'I do this applying the blue method', a method widely associated with the interests of labour but which it is impossible to demonstrate will generate decisions favouring labour in any determinate way. Imagine this particular 'blue-method' decision has consequences which are themselves difficult to associate with labour or that it has no identifiable consequences. There may even be cases 'applying the blue method' which were deeply harmful to labour and this might be such a case. It might nevertheless turn out that saying 'I do this applying the blue method' strengthens the position of labour-friendly rhetoric among elites or allows labour-friendly experts to identify and ally with one another, strengthening their position for *other* projects. Where this happens, we can associate the expression of methodological commitment with an ideology or interest even if the comparative work done using this method has no significant effects favouring that ideological position or interest.

Identifying the political stakes in expert work is most difficult where the expert says, in effect, 'I am not doing anything and I am not applying any method, but I thought you would like to know about this.' This posture makes it more difficult to identify the choices experts make – choices to make *this* known rather than *that* – and removes any clue in the expert's vocabulary to the ideological or interest impact of the decision. It makes it difficult to see the methodological expression as making an independent contribution to the rhetorical power of one or another ideology or interest among elites. Professionals who are proud of their neutral disengagement will often criticize one another's work for ideological or other bias. They work hard to pull one another back from application and use – to cleanse one another's projects of any clue to an association with interest or ideology. Their disengagement from ideology and interest is self-enforcing. This is the posture exemplified by the post-war comparatist, making it particularly difficult to locate a contestable politics or participation in governance.

In this sense, it has become far more difficult to identify the politics of comparative law since the Second World War. Before the war, comparatists associated their own work with ideological positions, social interests and governance choices in ways which seemed plausible and which provided the basis for their participation in large-scale efforts of legal and political reform. Others pursuing related reform projects could recognize these comparatists as allies because they spoke a methodological language which translated easily into political terms. Pre-war comparatists pursued a wide range of projects in the broad methodological vocabulary of anti-formalism which were easy to associate with ideology and interest. They used the anti-formal vocabulary to express rebellion against what they saw as the mainstream of their profession and to express solidarity with broad reform efforts to make law more responsive to political reality, more attuned to social needs and interests, more modern, international and uniform. Sometimes, they expressed more specific political projects and affiliations – assist German commercial interests, defend US legal tradition against realist scepticism, transform the law in the French colonial sphere of influence.

The pre-war anti-formalist tradition had lots of pieces which had not yet been systematized into a series of choices to be made or avoided. And the vocabulary seemed compatible with – seemed even to express – a range of quite different political initiatives. We would need more sociological work to determine whether their ideas about the politics of comparative law were realistic. Did comparative work focusing on the needs of commerce actually benefit German commercial interests? Would comparative attention to legal ideals really strengthen the US democratic order in a time of crisis? Would replacement of legal forms by the voice of customary law provide the basis for more harmonious international life or advance the interests of social forces, labour and so forth? But comparatists were both confident that their anti-formalism would contribute to these political projects and willing to say so. After the war, the situation became far more complex. The anti-formal tradition had become mainstream and many of its internal ambivalences and ambiguities had been systematized as loosely homologous choices. Seen with post-war hindsight, pre-war anti-formalism seemed far more uniform politically – if diverse methodologically – than it had seemed to those who inhabited it. Post-war comparatists, having become eclectic and agnostic, also inhabited a vocabulary which supported a fluid range of political associations – but these associations had become far less easy to identify or contest.

Although post-war legal professionals in many other legal disciplines are more comfortable making 'policy' or contributing to 'governance' than comparatists, they share comparativism's eclecticism about method and historical relationship to the tradition of anti-formalism. The argumentative choices which structure analysis of similarities and differences among legal regimes have much in common with the routine arguments of many allied fields.[102] Although the comparatist's political disengagement is rather extreme, a sensibility which allies methodological pluralism and modesty about governance or detachment from ideological debates is quite common elsewhere. Understanding how to translate the work of post-war comparatists into a politically contestable vocabulary is suggestive for thinking about the politics of other legal fields which share this methodological history and broad sensibility.

My colleague Duncan Kennedy is developing a hypothesis about the history of legal method and doctrine over the last century and a half which might provide a basis for translating professional performances into more overt projects, contestable in ideological or interest terms. He identifies three quite different projects of legal 'globalization' within the lifetime of comparative law – 'classical legal thought' from 1850 to 1900, 'social legal thought' from 1900 to 1950 and 'policy/rights consciousness' from 1950 to 2000. Each period was characterized by an enormous collective effort to develop and spread a specific way of doing law and politics which combined ideas about law, priorities for legal and political work, methodological commitments for lawyers and legal scholars.[103] Moreover, each period saw the primary influence of a national legal system, German to French to US, and focused attention on a set of political priorities and concerns, from laissez-faire individualism through various social-welfare projects to global commerce, development and human rights.

---

[102] My own work on public international law and international economic law turned up a strikingly similar set of argumentative choices with a similar history and sensibility. See David Kennedy, *supra*, note 18; *id.*, 'The International Style in Postwar Law and Policy', [1994] Utah L.R. 7.

[103] See Duncan Kennedy, 'Receiving the Three Globalizations: Classical Legal Thought, Social Legal Thought and Contemporary Rights/Policies Legal Consciousness' (2001), on file with the author. See also *id.*, 'The Rise and Fall of Classical Legal Thought' (1975), on file with the author; *id.*, 'Toward a Historical Understanding of Legal Consciousness: The Case of Classical Legal Thought in America 1850–1940', (1980) 3 Research L. & Society 3.

Comparative legal work has played a range of supporting roles in broad global endeavours of this kind – sorting targets of opportunity, conveying knowledge about the project from the centre to the periphery, legitimating its ideas about law, politics and the world. It is now clear that inter-war comparatists played a significant role in spreading anti-formal and socially orientated ideas about law. A great deal of excellent work has already been done tracing the involvement of comparatists in these projects of the global legal intelligentsia.[104] It is reasonable to imagine that their post-war successors participated in the development and spread of more eclectic, agnostic and pragmatic ideas about law and politics. But these post-war knowledge-projects are more difficult to translate into the languages of political contestation.

To do so, we must focus attention more firmly on default practices or deeply shared background assumptions than upon overt methodological commitments. Direct expression of ideological commitment or interest will be rare. We will need to be alert to the effects of broad ideas about how economies develop, about the relationship between public and private law, about the spatial arrangement of the globe's cultural or economic centre and periphery and more, which we might learn to translate into politically contestable terms. We should attend to the persuasive burden this discipline shoulders for its disciplinary neighbours. Indeed, comparative law often supports projects of international lawyers which are easier to interpret in ideological or interest terms.[105] And we should be alert to the role comparative law might play in the rise and fall of broad ideas – Keynesianism, socialism, neo-liberalism, planning, laissez-faire, etc. In a disaggregated political culture, the ebbs and flows of such ideas can affect decisions in widely dispersed places in ways which we might more easily understand in ideological or interest terms. And sometimes, the comparatist's methodological vocabulary can provide the basis for expressing political sympathies and identifying allies even where these expressions are not turned into decisions whose effects can be associated with ideological positions or interests.

---

[104] See Shalakany, *supra*, note 25; Diego López-Medina, *Comparative Jurisprudence: Reception and Misreading of Transnational Legal Theory in Latin America*, Harvard Law School SJD dissertation (2000), on file with the author; Jorge Esquirol, 'The Fictions of Latin American Law: An Analysis of Comparative Law Scholarship', [1997] Utah L.R. 425; Marie-Claire Belleau, *Les 'juristes inquiets': Critical Currents of Legal Thought in France at the End of the Nineteenth Century*, Harvard Law School SJD dissertation (1995), on file with the author.

[105] See Kennedy, *supra*, note 1.

A quick general example will illustrate the potential – but also the difficulties – of identifying the politically contestable effects of background assumptions and defaults in post-war comparative work. In multijurisdictional big-firm practice, people often compare laws with a motive. Lawyers might compare insurance laws in twenty-five European countries to figure out where to base a new venture offering, say, direct-mail cross-border insurance services. (I once did such a study.) Unlike an academic comparative study of the same regimes, a study generated in law practice will focus on differences in the distributional consequences of various regimes – which ones are good for insurers, reinsurers, consumers, business clients and so forth. By contrast, academic comparatists talk about distributional effects like accidental tourists, as if to suggest 'I do not myself care which way this goes' or 'I certainly have no stake' in the distributional issue. Gone is the insistent tone used to assess whether a legal phenomenon is or is not part of a national culture, is or is not a solution to a general problem in late industrial capitalism, is or is not part of the legal fabric as the result of a transplant from elsewhere and so forth. This is a decision by the comparatist – to downplay distributional consequences in assessing similarities and differences among legal regimes, to investigate and highlight technical similarities or cultural differences. It could be otherwise – indeed, commercial lawyers do the opposite quite routinely.

To translate this decision into politically contestable terms we first need to identify its effects – perhaps its effects on the ideas people who consume comparative study have about law. Here are some hypotheses. Comparative work of this sort might contribute to ignorance about the distributional consequences of legal regimes. And it might turn out that a legal regime whose distributional effects remain unseen will be different and affect interests and ideological positions differently from one whose effects are more visible for contestation. It might be easier to export or import a legal regime which could seem to be managed without references to distributional consequences. The authority of regime managers might be strengthened by the perception that their work did not involve distributional choices. The particular types of law studied by comparatists, often private-law regimes, may come to seem particularly innocent of distribution. This idea might strengthen ideas about appropriate relations between the economy and the state and so forth.

And then we need to associate these effects plausibly with ideological positions or social interests which struggle with one another in our polity.

Much will depend on time and place. More overt attention to the distributional consequences of legal regimes by comparatists might make it easier for left-wing regulators to generate redistributional proposals – but this effect might be swamped by the knowledge now also in the hands of their opponents or by the delegitimation effected by attention to distribution on the status of the field as a whole. And so on. The work of translating knowledge projects into politically contestable terms will need to be done in very specific contextual terms.[106] It is often tempting to forgo inquiry into the context-specific effects of a discipline's default practices or background assumptions and rely instead on the associations people in the field themselves make between their broad methodological commitments and ideological positions or social interests. Although eclectic agnosticism will make this difficult, it may still be possible from time to time. But it can be very misleading.

Inattention to distribution could be either an overt methodological commitment or something which somehow just keeps happening, the result of a blindspot in the dim reaches of professional consciousness, of character, of sensibility or professional training. Either way, once contested, the decision to background distribution would be brought forward to methodological consciousness. Now imagine that a 'distributionist' school emerges. Proponents of the school might defend distributionalism in political terms – perhaps as a progressive strategy to make left-wing legislative experiments more likely or to reset the field's centrist balance by removing an anti-progressive bias. But they could also do so in apolitical terms – as a scientific desire to 'tell the whole story'. And the mainstream, now conscious of its inattention to distribution, might defend it as scientific neutrality. But they might also do so as centrist politics – or even as a bulwark against

---

[106] For example, see Esquirol's investigation of the role played by comparatists in a variety of particular legal elites in Latin America in the second half of the twentieth century, *supra*, note 104. Esquirol contends that Latin American comparatists throughout the post-war period propounded an understanding of Latin American law as essentially 'European' and equated this cultural affinity with a relatively formal, and often quite specific, conception of law. In his analysis, this attitude about the 'nature' of the local legal system came to be shared more widely among legal elites and had a series of identifiable political consequences. As he sees it, this conception strengthened the hands of those within particular elites who, at various times, sought to blunt North American inspired reforms, at first coming from the left and then from the right. At other times, it helped consolidate the hold of a nineteenth-century 'liberal' political elite in its resistance to locally inspired populist legislative and democratic reforms, keeping the same elite from feeling implicated in the public-law transformations wrought during periods of dictatorship and so on.

leftist efforts to make rent-seeking too prevalent in transnational regulatory projects. In reading this exchange, we might well be struck by the apolitical commitment of *both* sides. Or we might find the difference expressed in sharply ideological terms. Either way, we should be sceptical. The association of oneself or one's opponent with an ideological position can represent a professional commitment *and/or* itself be a political strategy.

The associations post-war eclectics make between their routine practices and social interests or ideological positions are particularly likely to be misleading because post-war comparatists use methodological debates to signal political preferences to one another in ways which are cut off from any sense about consequences. It is as if, in taking their vows of disengagement, they also preserved a kind of shadow vocabulary for discussing their personal political preferences with one another. This signalling vocabulary is largely built from fragments of earlier methodological debates and is based on a memory that anti-formalism before the war had been associated with the left. As we have seen, this memory is inaccurate – anti-formalism was associated with a range of political initiatives. Nevertheless, the idea of pre-war left-wing anti-formalism survives as a kind of genetic political tag on the expression of methodological choices on the anti-formal *end* of all the choices *within* the post-war anti-formalist mainstream vocabulary. As post-war comparatists identify and analyse similarities and differences between legal regimes the choices they make seem coded more or less as in figure 11.12.

Right / Mainstream Anti-formalism / Left

relatively formal	relatively antiformal
law as *tekhnè*/function	law as cultural/social practice
lots of transplants	few transplants
autonomous legal profession	legal formants
exoticize the orient	exoticize the neighbor
familiarize the neighbor	familiarize the orient
identify 'best practices'	promote understanding of differences
promote 'our' system	favour cosmopolitan understanding/tolerance
emphasize uniformity comparative law	emphasize diversity
as apology/explanation	comparative law as criticism
functionalist efficiency	normative liberalism/protect weak social constituencies
legal orders tend to coherence/equilibrium	legal orders are in conflict/contradiction
favour outsider's perspective	favour insider's perspective
society's point of view	loser's point of view
autonomous law	embedded law

Figure 11.12

This sort of identification can be significant – if only because saying it is so can sometimes make it so. If comparatists with leftist sympathies use particular methodological arguments to recognize one another and to consolidate their positions within the field, and if the field then does become engaged in a political project, this language can become the vocabulary of their progressive gesture – even without a persuasive link between thinking about law in these terms and, say, redistributing income.

For post-war comparatists, however, these method fragments carry only a very light and tentative political charge. The new eclecticism encourages people with all sorts of different projects to pick among these methodological bits in an *ad hoc* way so that any given piece of comparative-law work will contain a range of method fragments, each of which will help neutralize the political charge of the others. It has also become easy to imagine a leftish argument in the language of universal/technical functionalism or a right-wing argument in the language of cultural identity. Moreover, agnosticism about political commitment and enthusiasm for disengagement have stilled the impulse to investigate the effects of comparative work in ways which could substantiate associations between any of these methodological choices and social interests or ideological positions.

Consequently, internal disciplinary discussions in this shadow vocabulary are far too vague and mushy to provide the basis for much common political engagement – or for reliable assessments on our part of the relations between comparative work and ideological positions or social interests. At the start of a comparative-law conference, I heard the participants getting to know one another by speaking very generally about their discipline in a way which seemed charged with political energy. But just what were these people communicating about their political character? The code has become so uncertain that I became increasingly suspect that they liked talking about their politics in terms which both announced and obscured their commitments. To give you an idea of what I mean, here is what I came up with after a couple of hours – perhaps you can rearrange these quotations more successfully:

Left:

'attention to the losers';
'everyone has a standpoint';
'we can certainly learn from the subaltern – what we learn is critique, engagement';

'we must judge and engage from where we are, comparative law is a political process';
'colonialism is a general phenomenon, but we must engage it in its particularity';
'anthropology';
'functionalism'.

Centre:

'standpoint analysis always underestimates the powers of resistance – losers are savvy';
'We can learn from other legal orders – Canada borrows from Inuit sentencing circles';
'Judgement is unavoidable, but we should focus on sensitivity and not engagement';
'When you analyse a colonial situation, the point is to generalize, of course, but it could also be valuable to know if and to what extent it was specific';
'functionalism'.

Right:

'I'd like to contrast work which focuses on description, on analysis, from that which focuses on judgement';
'the aim should be a description without an agenda';
'you can only really judge where you are from yourself – so not in comparative work';
'the story of progress to modernization remains the central story for comparative law';
'To me, colonialism is interesting as history, but otherwise only if we can generalize from it in some way';
'best practices can only be identified if we understand the efficiencies';
'there is an inner world of differences and an external world of similarities – communication and understanding are about similarities, coherences';
'functionalism'.

I am sure I got code quite off – but I bet they did too. Moreover, it seems unlikely that the consequences of adopting these methodological commitments could be associated with ideological positions with enough plausibility to provide much guidance about the discipline's participation in the work of rulership or governance. Let us take one which is rather clear: 'attention to the loser'. That does signal 'left' (maybe 'left fuzziness') in today's academy, but it does not seem at all clear that comparative-law work which either repeated this phrase a lot or described legal phenomena with extreme sensitivity to the viewpoint of the loser could be said to participate in governance as a leftist – to be a left political act, as it were. That would totally depend on who read it and what they did with it. For all we know, it could end up identifying targets for winners.[107]

Of course, even post-war eclectics also do sometimes discuss the effect they hope their work will have in terms we should be able to associate with political interests or ideological positions. These tend to be private backroom conversations, strategic assessments which range from furtive to bumptious and from cynical to idealistic. At a recent meeting of comparatists involved in the common-core project, many were willing to speak to me between sessions in terms which contrasted sharply with the agnosticism of Bussani's description and with the eclectic restraint of the actual work they were producing. Restricted to background conversation, these political strategies remained vague and untested, their fantastic, almost magic realist tone conflicting sharply with the modest restraint of the comparative work itself.

For some, the project would spread legal anti-formalism and ideas about 'legal formants' to other areas of legal thought – on the view that this would be a more significant (maybe leftist?) political intervention than anything which might come from any increase in either harmonization or differentiation. Others thought people in those other fields, once contaminated by anti-formalist thinking, would experience a Brechtian moment of alienation from the naturalization of their own working assumptions, wake up and join the vanguard. Well, maybe. Or perhaps the project would give academics access to a process of law reform which would otherwise be handled by technocrats in Brussels, in the hopes that this would make it more... progressive or humanist or who knows. Perhaps the agnostic self-presentation will tip the balance back from a pro-unification agenda and

---

[107] At another point, we were discussing 'the state' and whether it was an important way of defining the 'regimes' whose legal phenomena would be compared. Someone asked what we meant by 'the state' and it immediately emerged that for some the key idea, or moment of state creation, was the consolidation of force across a territory in the criminal law, for others the consolidation of boundary control, for others the consolidation of administration, for others the consolidation of the welfare state, for others the consolidation of Keynesian monetary policy. Each of these seemed to signal a political affinity, though I must say I found this code even more obscure. An exercise to try at home: figure out which signals left, which right, which centre.

should be understood, in that sense, to be an anti-federal intervention. Or maybe the idea is to train students working on the common-core project in a mode of scholarship (attentive to all possible conflicting legal formants) which, when used by them in law firms, will have some good political effect, sharpening their critical impulses precisely by modelling how to eschew the critical. All expressed confidence that a known law would be more reasonable and democratic than an obscure and local law – that obscurantism is the totalitarian devil's plaything.

The interesting point is that these assertions and motives remain beneath the surface, hunches, private hopes – despite the fact that they would often make excellent hypotheses for comparative study. Does it turn out that obscurantism lines up with extremism and totalitarianism, clarity about rules with calm and centred democracy? It sounds possible, but we can quickly think of counter-examples, different interpretations of the relationship between democracy and the mystical, reason and fascism. The puzzle is the hesitation to speak about these possible political projects concretely enough to assess their plausibility.

To identify and assess the politics of an agnostic project like the common core, we need better hypotheses about the possible effects of this kind of work. Where these effects seem plausible and can be associated with ideological choices or social interests we might then contest them. We might develop hypotheses about individual comparative-law projects in particular contexts, about the effects of the field's routine default practices or background assumptions on the thinking of elites who consume comparative legal work and about the role of the comparative-law profession itself in the broader intellectual division of labour and the distribution of comparative legal services.

The projects of individuals and groups in the comparative discipline

Sometimes, of course, comparatists do work intended to have effects which are easy to interpret in political terms. One might compare capital punishment regimes to find out how to make one work more effectively, just as one might do so to assess their different effects on minority communities. The projects of pre-war comparatists were easier to identify and more attention to their effects would give us a better sense for their politics. Amr Shalakany's study of the work of Lambert and his Egyptian student Sanhouri seeking simultaneously to modernize, Islamicize and socialize Egyptian law provides a model for understanding the politics of such an effort.[108] But post-war comparatists also sometimes contribute directly to projects whose politics we can assess and might contest.

Many comparatists have helped build the international private-law regime – staffing institutions to restate and reform private-law rules, elaborating a scholarly consensus on the most reasonable or workable rules for international commerce, building institutions to resolve disputes through arbitration, advising legislators in the periphery on how such matters are handled in the most advanced economies or advising at the centre on the applicability of common commercial rules in peripheral settings. Sometimes, it is easy to associate the regime which results with ideological positions and interests, even if it is not overtly biased in one or another direction.[109] The participation of agnostic and eclectic comparatists in the elaboration of the private-law regime strengthens the claim that it reduces the 'risks' associated with national politics and regulatory distortion by eliminating politics altogether from the law governing international commercial transactions. The particular rules which emerge from comparative harmonizations may well be stripped of their exceptions or formalized in ways which will seem to favour some interests over others.

Generally, however, the reform projects of post-war comparatists are altogether less visible than this. In one model effort to identify the politics of such a project, Robert Wai analyses the widespread effort of Canadian judges to transform Canadian private-law and conflict of laws rules to align Canadian law with what they saw, after careful comparative study, to be the needs of 'internationalism' or 'globalization'.[110] It is easy to understand how such a project could emerge and how acknowledging it openly could

---

[108] Shalakany, *supra*, note 25. Abu-Odeh performs a similar political analysis of the strategies of judicial elites in managing the modernization of family law in various Arab societies. See Lama Abu-Odeh, 'Modernizing Muslim Family Law: The Case of Egypt' (2001), on file with the author. See also Kerry Rittich, *Recharacterizing Restructuring: Gender and Distribution in the Legal Structure of Market Reform*, Harvard Law School SJD dissertation (1998), on file with the author [hereinafter *Recharacterizing*]; *id.*, 'Gender and the Concept of Distributive Justice in the World Bank', in Veijo Heiskanen (ed.), *The Legitimacy of International Organizations* (New York: United Nations University Press, 2001), pp. 438–81; *id.*, 'Feminism after the State: The Rise of the Market and the Future of Women's Rights', in Isfahan Merali and Valerie Oosterveld (eds.), *Giving Meaning to Economic, Social and Cultural Rights* (Philadelphia: University of Pennsylvania Press, 2001), pp. 95–108.

[109] For a particularly nuanced appraisal, see Amr Shalakany, 'Arbitration and the Third World: A Plea for Reassessing Bias Under the Specter of Neoliberalism', (2000) 41 Harvard Int. L.J. 419.

[110] See Robert Wai, *Commerce, Cooperation, Cosmopolitanism: Private International Law in an Era of Globalization*, Harvard Law School SJD dissertation (2000), on file with the author.

seem to erode its power or break its magic. Were Canadian judges to have proposed changes in the private-law rules by reference to the interests and ideologies which would be enhanced by their adoption, rather than in the language of deference to 'internationalism' and the findings of comparative study, the rules and the effects might well have been different.

In my experience, eclectic post-war comparatists often find themselves doing work which they have an intuitive or semi-conscious sense will be part of a project one might understand in ideological or interest terms. Imagine that you work for a United Nations agency developing a training programme to provide technical assistance to government staff from developing countries who will soon participate in a round of GATT negotiations. You teach negotiating skills, assertiveness training, procedural rules. You may well have an agenda in providing this training – some combination of strengthening their hand for the negotiation to come and assimilating their countries to the institutional structure of the free-trade regime. Under the new rubric of 'transparency', GATT negotiators promote awareness of the domestic legislation affecting trade in each state party. Your students' governments will need to make their legislation available. But what legislation 'affects' trade and what will the strong players be looking for? You commission and present a comparative study of legislation in other developing nations which participate in GATT. You know that your presentation will send two messages – how to comply with GATT by removing obvious subsidies and barriers to trade and how to hide an industrial policy in a newly transparent world. How these two messages are weighted and taken up by your students may affect the range of regulatory objectives they feel able to pursue. It may be quite easy to anticipate the distributional effects of maintaining different regulatory laws on different social interests. The choices you make in putting the comparative presentation together will influence the message which your students learn and will make them feel empowered to maintain some, but not other, regulatory initiatives.

The effects of shared knowledge practices: what are the legal regimes?

If we revisit the choices post-war comparatists make as they analyse similarities and differences among legal regimes, we will often be able to identify default choices and background assumptions which we can interpret in political terms. The first step was to identify two (or more) legal regimes which are different enough to merit a comparison of legal phenomena found within them. Both *how* this is done and the fact *that* it is done may have contestable effects. Imagine that comparatists' default choices reinforced the idea that differences between African and European law were more salient than differences among legal regimes within Africa or within Europe. There might be an underlying idea here that African law is more primitive or more communal. 'Knowing' this might change how some elites – in Africa, in Europe, elsewhere – evaluate specific legal reforms. Europeans might be convinced to export simplified or stripped-down legal formula which would have different distributional consequences than the more complex regimes they also know. African elites might be strengthened in their resistance – or in their assimilation. People in and outside Africa might invoke the 'African example' when debating communitarian legal schemes and find their proposals accredited or discredited by the association.

The eclectic practice of identifying legal regimes in both cultural and technical terms strengthens the idea that legal regimes both float freely from their context, and communicate with one another, while also somehow remaining connected to political and social history. Identifying legal regimes to compare bears witness to the quasi-autonomy of law. 'Knowing' this may strengthen the hand of those pursuing more concrete governance projects – perhaps nationalist projects to root law more firmly in culture and perhaps cosmopolitan projects to loosen the grip of culture in the name of international understanding and tolerance. Separating legal regimes for comparison strengthens the idea that differences signal local cultural roots, similarities an affiliation with the foreign, the international or the universal. Knowing this channels expression of elite impulses to national self-determination or international cooperation. This comparative witness can affect the choices professionals in neighbouring disciplines make. In building a public international law regime, international lawyers under comparative tutelage may become more committed to doctrines marking jurisdictional limits along the territorial lines between states or treating differently things which happen within a territory, things which pass between two territories and things which happen 'above' or 'outside' the territorial plane altogether.

The default tendency to identify and differentiate legal regimes in loosely *national* terms might make some governance projects seem more or less legitimate.[111] Reassured about the coherence and identity of legal regimes,

---

[111] In his contribution to this book, Patrick Glenn stresses the irony that comparativism has reinforced the idea that legal heritages are national.

a governing elite – national or international – might be more or less willing to 'intervene' from one 'into' another. The map of 'similar' and 'different' might mark natural areas for legitimate and illegitimate intervention. To assess these political effects, we would need to understand better whether an elite metabolized 'difference' as an excuse to stay home or seek conquest, or whether they saw it as natural to ally with those who were the same or different. Annelise Riles provides a suggestive model for this exploration in her study of the quite different ideas nineteenth-century British international lawyers had of 'culture' in Europe, where it promised communication, and in Africa, where it legitimated control.[112]

Imagine that instead of defaulting to national regimes, comparatists separated legal regimes governing different industries across national lines – comparing at will employment or good-faith contracting in the 'pharmaceutical legal regime' with the same phenomena in the 'automotive legal regime'. As elites learned from these new comparatists, we can imagine their sense of possible political initiatives changing in ways it would be hard, but not impossible, to predict. Take a decision by General Motors to require ISO 9000 quality standards in all contracts wherever it does business which sparks a global transformation of quality-control management, first in the automotive industry and then more broadly.[113] Should we celebrate or worry about the extension of US law to Thailand or Automotive law to Textiles? Re-mapping the legal world in industrial terms might make the initiatives of non-state actors – whether shareholders or protestors – seem more or less legitimate. Elites might be more inclined to think of income differences within the 'automotive' regime as they now think of differences within Brazil or the United States and differences between income distributions in 'automotive' and 'textile' regimes like those between countries.

The idea that knowledge professionals contribute to various imperial and neo-colonial projects when they strengthen stereotypes about the east and the west, the north and the south, the modern and the primitive, the familiar and the exotic and so forth has become familiar. Most eclectic comparatists

---

[112] See Annelise Riles, 'Aspiration and Control: International Legal Rhetoric and the Essentialization of Culture', (1993) 106 Harvard L.R. 723.

[113] Stepan Wood is working on an intriguing study of 'voluntary' standards in the environmental area. See Stepan Wood, 'The New Global Environmental Standards', (2000) 93 Proceedings of the American Society of International Law 220; *id.*, *Governing the Green Globe: Environmental Management System Standards and Environmental Regulation*, Harvard Law School SJD dissertation (in progress), on file with the author.

avoid charges of 'orientalism' by avoiding 'normative' interpretations of the differences between legal regimes and by describing similarities and differences in complex ways which avoid simple contrasts between east and west or north and south. But the default practices of this post-orientalist practice – distinguishing regimes in loose cultural 'families' and economic 'stages' of development – may also reinforce elite notions about natural affinities and differences in ways which affect policy-making. It is easy to imagine, for example, that elites will think differently about efforts to link Israeli and Egyptian law if they see these two regimes as 'European/late industrial capitalism' and 'Islamic-traditional/underdevelopment' rather than as two 'post-colonial/developing' legal regimes.[114] Assisted by comparative-law study, European elites understand relations among European Union Member States in terms of 'cohesion' or 'subsidiarity' and relations with central European countries in terms of 'preparing' less well developed nations to 'catch up'. Knowing this affects both the way they shape internal regulatory systems and the way they relate to the international trade system. This interpretive frame makes Greece and Denmark seem more similar than they otherwise might appear, Austria and Slovenia more different.[115]

Dividing legal regimes for comparison in this way can also make it seem evident that *the* question for 'other' societies is whether and how to modernize and westernize. 'Knowing' this may strengthen or weaken the hands of some elites – 'modernizers' perhaps – against others. Imagine a small 'transitional' central European regime when the post-orientalist comparatists come to town with the precise intention of explaining the rich diversity within the European/Modern Capitalist tradition. They come not to dominate, but to empower by pointing out the range of choices available. And they may well – but they also bring the message that there is such a thing as legal modernity. However various its forms, the modernization of legal culture in one of these ways is what it means to transit the transition. When this happens, the agnostic comparatist has participated in governance – delivered a message whose effects we can associate with ideological positions and social interests. The comparatist offers lenses through which the centre can know itself and interpret the periphery, the global can know itself by contrast to the local, and lenses through which the periphery and the local can express their identity and understand the centre. The impact

---

[114] See Yishai Blank, 'Legal Education and the Archeology of Israeli Law', on file with the author.
[115] For an explanation of this effect, see David Kennedy, 'Turning to Market Democracy: A Tale of Two Architectures', (1991) 32 Harv. Int. L.J. 373.

of this work might be felt in the self-confidence and strategy of both the international policy class and culturally remote elites.

The effects of shared knowledge practices: what are the legal phenomena?

As in the identification of legal regimes, both *how* legal phenomena are identified for comparison and the fact *that* they are identified at all in comparative terms may have effects. The phenomena comparatists select for comparison affect what the elite knows. If comparatists spend lots of time on financial regulations and little time studying family law, this may encourage an elite to think of financial regulations in comparative terms and family law in local terms. This may affect the choices these elites make among doctrinal alternatives in each of these fields. Knowing how foreign legal systems manage health care, not how they regulate sports, how they deal with intellectual property, but very little about what they do with real property, lots about comparative private law but very little about public law, may influence the range of regulatory options elites consider or the strength of their attachment to some, but not other, local laws. Preferences of this type are often easy to associate with ideological commitments or the interests of different social groups.

In selecting phenomena suitable for comparison, the comparatist also bears witness to the 'fact' of law's quasi-autonomy. Legal regimes are made up of rules, institutions, practices which are instances of something more general also found in other legal regimes. For eclectic comparatists, it is neither all transplants nor incomparable difference. Legal phenomena in different regimes 'are' similar enough – and different enough – to make comparison worthwhile. In some places, knowing this may strengthen elites proposing technical reform or cultural modernization. Or it may help justify distributions effected by legal rules by placing their origin somewhere outside politics and culture. Or it may make it seem more plausible for judges to fill gaps in legislation without themselves legislating. Knowing that law is quasi-autonomous may make the import of harmonized legal rules seem more palatable by making them seem the product of technical necessity, cultural influence or accidental professional borrowing rather than political contestation.

Like other legal knowledge-makers, comparatists develop and reinforce a typology of legal phenomena. As they distinguish legal phenomena for comparison, they allocate *this* to divorce, *that* to contract, *this* to dispute resolution and so forth. When elites learn the default typologies which emerge, they will have their imagination about regulatory initiatives and reforms channelled in particular ways. Those seeking to improve the status of women may find their imagination limited to the category of law about women – especially if that category has a transcultural force. This sort of effect may occur even where the comparatist compared precisely in order to open up imagination about how a divorce regime might be structured.

The default typologies in comparative work routinely reinforce the idea that public and private law are different – essentially, technically, transculturally – in ways which are not a function of local culture, politics or legal history. Public law is hierarchical, constitutional, procedural, disciplinary, political, distributional and linked very closely with regime identity. Private law is horizontal, consensual, produced by individuals, about problem-solving and economic efficiency, relatively apolitical and only loosely linked with regime identity. These differentiations reinforce the idea that the work of governments and the work of markets are different. Markets make themselves, while governments need to be constructed. Governments originate in mystical historical moments of constitutionalization, markets emerge from numerous pragmatic decisions by individual market actors and so forth.

The default typologies comparatists use to identify legal phenomena for comparison also shape what elites think can appropriately be placed in one or another category. When comparatists work with public law, they represent it to lie closer to cultural and historical developments than private law. And they identify elements within public law for comparison in ways which highlight procedural and technical aspects of a constitutional order. It makes sense to compare a phenomenon like 'constitutional adjudication' or 'judicial review' in different national western legal systems, say, Austrian, Italian and US. The comparison might sensibly focus on the presence and powers of the constitutional court in each system. Differences which emerge might be attributed to national culture and history or we might compare them in philosophical terms – which is more Kantian, more Rawlsian, more in tune with Montesquieu.

These defaults can affect how elites think about constitutional choices. Imagine the authors of a comparative study of constitutional courts describing their work in an eastern European capital in the period of transition and constitutional reform. Our authors are eclectic, agnostic, they come not to influence, but to inform. They have been careful not to express preferences among the regimes, nor to privilege either cultural or technical modes of evaluation in their report. Like their colleagues bringing a comparison of intellectual property regimes, they will bring a message about what it means to be modern and the direction of the transition. But more concretely, they will clarify options for members of an eastern European elite. Perhaps the east European consumers of this comparative performance have long preferred John Rawls to Kant or felt more culturally attuned to Austria than Italy. Perhaps they feel priority should be given the legislature or that the regions should dominate the centre. On all these points, the study will be helpful. But let us say someone represents the farmers' party or wants to know which system will best preserve the power of the ex-*nomenklatura*, be most favourable to women or be most likely to get the country into the European Union fast. He or she will have to infer, reason back from what is manifest in the study and perhaps come to understand that this is not really an appropriate way to think about constitutional reform.[116] The comparatist's default typology for legal phenomena has reinforced the invisibility of some political considerations while foregrounding others for contestation.

The effects of shared knowledge practices: comparing phenomena across regimes

The default choices post-war comparatists make as they identify similarities and differences among legal phenomena for comparison can also have effects we might associate with ideological positions or social interests. By foregrounding the transplantation of similarities and underemphasizing the role of influence in establishing differences, comparatists reinforce the idea that differences should be thought of as aspects of tradition, culture, history. This can make local strategies of resistance and misreading seem more rooted in tradition, culture and history than efforts at assimilation.[117] Comparatists can strengthen the idea that differentiation is naturally a matter of struggle, linked to culture and history, while assimilation is a more benign process, linked to technical alignment with best practice and economic

---

[116] For an excellent study of the process by which the distributional allocations between men and women lost visibility in the legal reforms which accompanied the east/central European transition, see Rittich, *Recharacterizing, supra,* note 108.

[117] For an excellent study of the effects of misreading, see López-Medina, *supra,* note 104. See also Doris Sommer, 'Attitude, Its Rhetoric', in Marjorie Garber, Beatrice Hanssen and Rebecca L. Walkowitz (eds.), *The Turn to Ethics* (New York: Routledge, 2000), pp. 201–20.

development. All these differences can change the balance of authority or legitimacy felt by different elements in a national elite.

The distinction between cultural and technical dimensions of legal regimes which lies at the heart of the post-war comparative endeavour can also have effects. Knowing that legal regimes can be broken down in this way strengthens international legal regimes whose legitimacy is based on the claim that there *is* a relatively technical domain in which they can exercise authority without disturbing local culture. Default ideas about what counts as technical and what as cultural – treating the economy as technical, the family as cultural – can also influence the distribution of governmental regulatory attention. Associating a group or activity (women, the religious, children, the educational) with 'the cultural' changes the legitimacy of political measures which affect it. International regulators propose far more dramatic interventions to deal with balance of payments problems, environmental damage or agricultural development, than they do when they think of themselves regulating the status of women or religion – even when it can clearly be predicted that the more technical intervention will, in fact, have a more intense impact on the lives of women or on the incidence of religious belief in society.

In a more general way, moreover, the default associations of cultural and technical with irrational and rational, mystical and instrumental, local and global, social connection or meaning and economic function, all influence the relative legitimacy of elite projects. Elites might feel quite differently about regulatory initiatives were they to understand global governance as 'cultural' and local initiatives as 'technical'. The association of culture with location makes it seem less legitimate to 'intervene' in far-away places without a good reason. Knowing that a divorce regime is part of such a thing as 'Japanese legal culture' makes it seem less legitimate to argue that 'the French system is just better' and makes arguments about 'women's rights' seem automatically to be about foreign cultural intervention. We might see this as an anti-imperialist bias in comparative work, despite the apparent agnosticism about whether difference or similarity is to be desired.

Being a discipline in the intellectual class

Comparatists differ in the ambitions they have for their profession. Some urge the profession to commit itself methodologically in ways we are urged to interpret in ideological or interest terms. In this book, Upendra Baxi urges us to adopt a stance of empathy with those who have little, who have been marginal or losers in one or another way. But simply being – and being seen to be – a profession may also have political effects, if only as the size and prestige of the profession multiplies the effects of comparative work. Moreover, the effects of comparative work will vary with the distribution of comparative capacity.

Imagine that you work for an international agency aiding countries making the transition from socialism to capitalism. The agency sponsors legal reforms which introduce at least legislative simulacra for the legal institutions of a 'market society'. Let us say you promised your board or parliament that you would produce a market in mortgage-backed securities in a given recipient country and they gave you a lot of money to do so. You spent the money moving the legislation which seemed necessary for a market in mortgage-backed securities through the local political process. Then there is a snag. In the recipient country, it turns out that the name of any person with a security interest in a mortgage, even a secondary one, must be registered, making it impossible for bonds secured by mortgages to change hands fluidly. You came up with a technical solution and sold it to the locals with an interest in getting the necessary legislation off the ground – appoint a representative of the bondholder class and register his name. Your favourite ministry supports this idea, but the ministry of justice has not certified this to be in compliance with the local law and has not yet been willing to register representative members of a class. You are not sure why – perhaps someone in the justice ministry is attached to the principle of registration, perhaps no one seriously thinks there will soon be a market in mortgage-backed bonds, perhaps this technical question has become symbolically part of other political machinations between ministries, between forces in the government favourable and hostile to 'opening' the economy.

You could apply political and economic pressure, try to influence the internal balance of power between the various ministries, hold up payment of the next aid package. And you might commission a study of how this 'problem' is handled in an array of countries which share, let us say, the 'civil-law' culture of the aid recipient but which do have secondary-mortgage bond markets. The existence of a profession which can transform this sort of political problem into a description of technical solutions to a problem common in different cultures – or different technical solutions within the same legal family – may affect the relative strength of participants in the debate, even if the report is never completed. The influence may be more pronounced if access to comparative study is differentially distributed, more available, say, to the 'haves' than the 'have-nots'.

Moreover, like other disciplines, comparative law is a tiny life-world of its own, within which resources, honours and opportunities are distributed in various ways. The consolidation of methodologies, the availability of funding, the projects of individuals in the field – both their own will to power in the profession and their projects in the broader establishment – will affect the distribution of resources among members of the profession. This process is, if in a small world, also a project of governance, a form of politics. We can often associate gains and losses in this small world with broader ideological positions or social interests; and the politics of this small world can affect other elites. Small victories can alter the broader balance of power among forces within the larger elite.

Putting all these hypotheses together, it is striking how little we know about the politics of comparative law and how difficult it is to translate the work of eclectic post-war professionals into politically contestable terms. It is not hard to imagine that knowing one thing rather than another might affect what rulers do, but we are not accustomed to translating knowledge work into political work. Post-war comparative law has successfully insulated itself from the taint of association with the choices of political life. All we have are hypotheses, directions, hints for rendering its eclectic and agnostic surface in the politically contestable terms of ideological commitment and social interest. By following these leads, we might nurture the habit of reading professional judgements as political acts. Imagine each comparative-law project coming with an ideological and interest 'impact statement', articulating the effects that knowing this, rather than something else, might have on the distribution of ideas and things in the world. Become a habit, this heuristic might heighten the comparatist's experience of himself as a ruler. Whether they seemed compelled by expertise or open to eclectic discretion, the quotidian choices professionals make would routinely be understood to have politically contestable consequences and to be part of the fabric of global governance.

And why, might you ask, should we do this? Surely there is also a politics to making known the politics of the profession – to translating our knowledge vocabularies into vocabularies of political contestation. Post-war comparative law is animated by a powerful urge to know. Bussani, speaking of the European common-core project, puts it this way:

It is true that through the use of the comparative method many common features that remained obscure in traditional legal analysis will be unearthed. This is because the instruments and techniques provide more accurate and correct analysis, not that they force convergence where it does not exist. Of course, from better knowledge may follow more integration, and therefore, the common core research may also be considered as pushing indirectly towards more uniformity and less diversity. This objection, however, should not impress us. Change following knowledge is a phenomenon that can be avoided only through obscurantism.[118]

But this urge falls still at the threshold of political life. And the discipline obscures its political effects. I do not know what changes will come as the politics of the profession become known. I have an intuition that the profession does more to sustain than remedy the world's *status quo* injustice, that expression will bring contestation and contestation change. But it is only an intuition. I am wary of a disciplinary power whose politics can barely be glimpsed through the hedges of its agnostic and eclectic professionalism. And I worry about an urge to knowledge which averts its eyes just as it would enter the terrain of contestation. But I am sure I also sometimes share with the post-war comparatist the perfectly human wish to enjoy the Dionysian pleasures of acting precisely when we know not what we do.

[118] Bussani, *supra*, note 2, p. 796.

Comparative legal studies and its futures

12

Comparatists and transferability

DAVID NELKEN

Introduction

Law is on the move. Social engineering through law, for all that it is somewhat out of fashion 'at home' in many industrially developed societies, is increasingly practised abroad. The range of societies currently caught up in what many still describe as 'legal transplants', but which I shall be calling 'legal transfers', is not confined to those in the developing world, though even this covers places as different as China, south-east Asia or Latin America. It also includes almost all of the ex-communist countries and, in many respects, even the countries seeking to harmonize their laws within the European Union. Indeed, the developments associated with the globalization of markets and communication mean that few, if any, places are now immune. If the 'law-and-development' movement is thus in its second (some say third) wave, the question has been raised of how to avoid repeating the 'mistakes' made the first time round.[1] A selective overview of some of the debates concerning the possibility and appropriateness of legal transfers may perhaps make a contribution to this task.

Three sets of interrelated issues will need be considered. How far is it possible to understand other peoples' law? What can be done to ensure that only that law is transferred which 'fits' into its new setting? Finally, in what ways are current wider political, economic and social developments affecting processes of legal transfer? I shall try to explore these questions with special reference to the possibilities of closer collaboration between sociologists of law and comparatists.[2] There are good reasons for trying to encourage such cooperation. Even if the extent of mutual citation is still

---

[1] See Armin Hoeland, 'Evolution du droit en Europe centrale et orientale: assiste-t-on à une renaissance du "*Law and Development*"?', Droit et société, 1993, No. 25, p. 467.
[2] See also Roger Cotterrell's contribution to this book.

regrettably poor, it would often be difficult to draw a useful line between these two bodies of scholarship. Both these academic endeavours are interested in understanding the way legal transfers are affected by interests, mentalities and institutions. Each is struggling to make sense of developments such as Europeanization and globalization which are producing new configurations of the legal, the economic and the political spheres. Sociologists can gain much from comparatists' often first-hand descriptions of efforts at legal transfers and reflections on the obstacles encountered.[3] Some comparatists, for their part, look to the social sciences (with exaggerated expectations) for a 'theory' which could explain and predict the likely result of legal transfers. Faced with strategic or tactical questions in transferring law, comparatists need to consult the existing social science literature so as to learn the lessons of past efforts at social change through law. Comparatists, in turn, have something to teach sociologists about the dangers of ethnocentrism when moving law from one culture to another.

Despite these potential gains, comparatists and sociologists often prefer to ignore or criticize each other's work rather than engage with it.[4] Sociologists typically accuse comparatists of focusing too narrowly on legal doctrine and 'law in the books' and of neglecting the way law operates in practice in its relation to the wider social structure. For their part, comparatists accuse sociologists of neglecting legal doctrine and intellectual history. In contrast to the normative thrust of much comparative work, most sociologists of law tend to have a more explicit commitment to scientific theory-building, testing and experimentation. But the modernist paradigm is under siege and confidence in the possibilities of social engineering may well need to be tempered by the wisdom coming from comparative work more rooted in the humanities. In practice, moreover, some comparatists involved in recommending legal transfers demonstrate an equally blind faith in legal know-how and do-it-yourself social science. And even social scientists often mix the explanatory and normative registers, as I shall seek to show with reference to their efforts to establish the likely or past 'success' of legal transfers.

---

[3] For example, see Thomas W. Waelde and James L. Gunderson, 'Legislative Reform in Transitional Economies: Western Transplants – A Short-Cut to Social Market Economy Status?', (1994) 43 Int. & Comp. L.Q. 347; Gianmaria Ajani, 'By Chance and Prestige: Legal Transplants in Russia and Eastern Europe', (1995) 43 Am. J. Comp. L. 93.

[4] But see David Nelken and Johannes Feest (eds.), *Adapting Legal Cultures* (Oxford: Hart, 2001).

Even if there are important differences between these approaches, it could be argued that it is just these differences which provide the starting-point for collaboration.[5] But any proposed division of labour must also take account of internal differences within each camp. Thus, while some comparatists seek a common core in the laws of different societies,[6] others stress the distinctiveness of legal cultures.[7] Many sociologists seek positivist or functionalist explanations of patterns of legal life,[8] but some insist on the need to interpret their inner meanings.[9] Some – even if perhaps not most – comparatists continue to raise fundamental doubts about the contribution that social scientists can make to the understanding of legal transfers. The assumptions and models of sociology of law may even be seen as more a part of the problem than the solution. On one view, social scientists easily underestimate how profoundly law is embedded in its environing culture. They need to realize that they can never put themselves in a position to grasp other people's law as they themselves understand it – and that this is a *sine qua non* of effective transplantation. On another view, the problem is the opposite. Here, sociologists are described as greatly exaggerating the degree to which law needs to 'fit' the society in which it is currently found. They fail to recognize the very existence of legal transplants as something which undermines any attempt to construct a sociology of law.

It is tempting for sociologists to ignore what may seem extreme and, therefore, unconvincing objections to their work.[10] But this would be a mistake. Certainly, these arguments cannot be accepted in the form in which they are presented. But they do contain partial and complementary insights into the problems involved in seeking to understand the possibilities and limits of legal borrowing. In the following effort to rethink legal transfers, I

---

[5] See David Nelken, 'Puzzling Out Legal Culture: A Comment on Blankenburg', in *id.* (ed.), *Comparing Legal Cultures* (Aldershot: Dartmouth, 1997), pp. 58–88.
[6] For example, see B. S. Markesinis (ed.), *The Gradual Convergence* (Oxford: Oxford University Press, 1994).
[7] For example, see Pierre Legrand, 'European Legal Systems Are Not Converging', (1996) 45 Int. & Comp. L.Q. 52.
[8] For example, see Erhard Blankenburg, 'Civil Litigation Rates as Indicators for Legal Culture', in Nelken, *supra*, note 5, pp. 41–68.
[9] For example, see David Nelken, 'Studying Criminal Justice Comparatively', in Mike Maguire, Rod Morgan and Robert Reiner (eds.), *The Oxford Handbook of Criminology*, 2d ed. (Oxford: Oxford University Press, 1997), pp. 559–76.
[10] For example, see Lawrence Friedman, 'Some Comments on Cotterrell and Legal Transplants', in Nelken and Feest, *supra*, note 4, pp. 93–8.

shall begin by trying to extract the important elements of truth contained in these critiques.[11] I shall seek to demonstrate that even if these criticisms point to the errors of some sociological approaches, they also prove the need for such inquiry. This is because little progress can be made by continuing to argue *whether or not* law should be treated as an inextricable part of the wider society and culture. Instead, we need to look for the best route to capturing the way law both does, and does not, 'fit' society and culture and identify the way this is changing under current conditions. As Gunther Teubner has argued, the study of legal transfers thus offers an ideal opportunity 'to get beyond dichotomies which juxtapose cultural dependency and legal insulation or social context and legal autonomy'.[12]

Does respecting difference rule out a social science of legal transfers?

How well must we understand another society before being in a position to bring about legal transfers? Pierre Legrand, in a succession of learned articles, has warned of the difficulties that face the scholar who wishes to understand the law of other legal cultures, especially if he or she wants to grasp it in the way it is understood by the natives of that culture.[13] Once we understand law in its richest sense,[14] the best that can be achieved is to give people a taste of 'otherness' – what it would be like, for example, to be part of French or German legal culture.

---

[11] In counterposing the writings of Pierre Legrand and Alan Watson as competing critiques of functionalist sociology (see *infra*), I do not intend to suggest any other symmetry in their work. Watson purports to be using historical facts (as well as some comparative work) to show the impossibility of existing sociological theorizing about law. For his part, Legrand is more concerned with the impossibility of transplants whoever advocates them. While Legrand actively argues against legal transplants, it is not clear how far Watson would actually want to encourage them rather than merely insist on their inevitability. Legrand is even more critical of Watson than of sociology, though both might agree about the constitutive role for legal culture of what are not merely technical-legal distinctions.

[12] Gunther Teubner, 'Legal Irritants: Good Faith in British Law or How Unifying Law Ends up in New Divergences', (1998) 61 Modern L.R. 11, p. 17.

[13] For example, see Legrand, *supra*, note 7; *id.*, 'Against a European Civil Code', (1997) 60 Modern L.R. 44; *id.*, 'What "Legal Transplants"?', in Nelken and Feest, *supra*, note 4, pp. 55–69 [hereinafter 'What "Legal Transplants"?'].

[14] For Legrand, 'What "Legal Transplants"?', *supra*, note 13, p. 60, comparative law is more than the study of legal rules and institutions: 'The comparatist must adopt a view of law as a polysemic signifier which connotes *inter alia* cultural, political, sociological, historical, anthropological, linguistic, psychological and economic referents.'

But if the scholar cannot fully understand another culture, still less is this possible for a judge or lawyer. Legrand severely criticizes the work of those of his comparatist colleagues who seek to demonstrate or produce legal convergence, to reveal an underlying 'common core' of principles and so forth. Any attempt to interpret and apply a 'borrowed' law or institution is bound to be different from the interpretation which would be made of it by those participating in a different 'legal *epistémè*'. Hence his radical conclusion that 'legal transplants' are, strictly speaking, impossible. Meaning cannot survive the journey: 'there could only occur a meaningful "legal transplant" when both the propositional statement as such and its invested meaning – which jointly constitute the rule – are transported from one culture to another. Given that the meaning invested into the rule is itself culture-specific, it is difficult to conceive, however, how this transfer could ever happen.'[15] Attempts at harmonization are, therefore, bound to fail and even to cause harm. Legrand thus connects the appropriate strategy to adopt in understanding another culture to the assumption that difference is something we should treasure and protect. For both theoretical and practical reasons, we should 'prioritize' difference.[16]

Much of Legrand's argument is valuable and timely. He is surely correct to warn of the theoretical errors and political dangers of any functionalist approach, which assumes that all societies face the same 'social problems' – to which law can and must provide a solution. Variation in how 'problems' are conceived, and even whether given situations are treated as problems, is the very stuff of cultural analysis. He is also right to remind us how much law is bound up with meaning, identity and the sense of community and tradition. Some social science approaches do tend to underestimate these factors. Moreover, social science cannot claim any certainties in interpreting 'other' cultures. Indeed, there are leading anthropologists, like Clifford Geertz,[17] whose celebration of 'local knowledge' forms part of an attack on the conventional methods of social scientific disciplines, such as the anthropology of law.[18] But these considerations do not stop Geertz, any more than Legrand himself, from attempting to offer accounts of other societies.

---

[15] *Ibid.*   [16] See Pierre Legrand's contribution to this book.
[17] See Clifford Geertz, *Local Knowledge* (New York: Basic Books, 1983).
[18] Post-modern anthropologists such as James Clifford and George Marcus, of course, go even further in questioning the possibility of objective accounts of other cultures. See James Clifford and George Marcus (eds.), *Writing Culture: The Poetics and Politics of Ethnography* (Berkeley: University of California Press, 1986); James Clifford, *The Predicament of Culture* (Cambridge, Mass.: Harvard University Press, 1988).

And the call to privilege difference would make no sense if comparison was actually impossible. Yet, it is far from obvious how far Legrand wishes his arguments to be taken. On the one hand, some might argue that they do not go far enough. What about the belief that particular cultures are *sui generis*, as with the debates over Japanese 'uniqueness' or the insistence that certain religious traditions can only be understood from within? How about those versions of 'perspectivism' according to which certain truths can be grasped only from a specific standpoint such as that provided by membership of categories like women, the working class or intellectuals? On the other hand, does Legrand stop short of relativism and does he want to?[19] Is it plausible to believe that modern cultures are so distinct as to be incommensurable? Why not say the same of differences between sub-cultures? How can we understand the past?

Legrand does seem to place exaggerated stress on the study of difference rather than similarity. Reflection on our own (contrasting) cultural 'starting-point' is always of crucial importance in any comparison and should be taken very seriously when planning legal transfers.[20] But whether or not it is better to concentrate on showing the existence of differences rather than similarities depends on the context and purpose of comparison. Many societies are only too aware of being perceived as different! Academic work which shows surprising and unexpected similarities between these and other societies may be of as much value as that which demonstrates difference and may carry important implications for the possibility of legal transfers. More generally, it is hard to imagine any process of identifying differences which does not require the capacity to distinguish them from similarities. The same applies to the process of deciding which differences count. If difference is 'inexhaustible', how do we decide what differences are important? When is a difference a difference?

Much the same applies to the conclusions Legrand draws for the practice of legal transplants. Taken at its strongest, Legrand's thesis is incontrovertible, but also unhelpful. If by 'legal transplants' we mean the attempt to use laws and legal institutions to reproduce identical meanings and effects in different cultures, then this is indeed impossible. But is there anyone who argues that this is in fact possible? Certainly not Alan Watson, who

---

[19] See Luke Nottage, *Convergence, Divergence, and the Middle Way in Unifying or Harmonising Private Law*, European University Institute Law Department Working Paper 2000/1 (2001).

[20] See David Nelken, 'Telling Difference: Of Crime and Criminal Justice in Italy', in *id.* (ed.), *Contrasting Criminal Justice* (Aldershot: Dartmouth, 2000), pp. 233–64.

popularized the term and who is the direct target of Legrand's criticisms. Who says that what is wanted is an exact transplant? So everything depends on what we mean or wish to mean by 'transplants' and how seriously we take this metaphor.[21] It can hardly be gainsaid that legal transfers are possible, are taking place, have taken place and will take place. What exactly is happening or is likely to happen in such transfers is another story.

In his most recent work, Legrand sets out to clarify — and also perhaps modify — his earlier claims.[22] He admits that it would be a contradiction for us to assert that cultures are totally incommensurable and their communications untranslatable. He concedes that it is possible to go a long way in understanding 'the other' — indeed, that our possibility to dialogue with others presupposes likeness. He even suggests that to assert difference is not to argue for a dichotomy but for a relationship. When it comes actually to carrying out comparative research, he acknowledges that we need to identify some similarities in an institution or practice before we can even talk of differences. Furthermore, he admits that assertions of given 'difference' are culturally contested and that the observer constructs differences in the course of trying to identify them (given that re-presentation is as much prescriptive as descriptive). But none of these concessions are allowed to do much to modify his overall stance. Legrand still insists on what he calls 'radical epistemological diversity'[23] and the impossibility of ever comprehending others as they understand themselves. Whatever similarities we may presuppose or find, '[our] responsibility [is] to characterize, articulate and justify [the ineliminability of difference].'[24]

A puzzling feature of Legrand's argument is his assumption that the goal of the comparatist must always be to try to see foreign law as 'the native' does. It is no small matter to decide which native should serve as the measure of our successful understanding of another culture. But, more than this, depending on our purposes, we may be seeking more or less understanding than that which the native possesses. Not only may the outsider sometimes see more than the native does,[25] but the natives themselves may be more interested than Legrand admits in what they can learn from the

---

[21] See *id.*, 'Beyond the Metaphor of Legal Transplants? Consequences of Autopoietic Theory for the Study of Cross-Cultural Legal Adaptation', in Jiri Priban and *id.* (eds.), *Law's New Boundaries: The Consequences of Autopoiesis* (Aldershot: Dartmouth, 2001), pp. 265–302.

[22] For example, see Pierre Legrand's contribution to this book. [23] *Ibid.* [24] *Ibid.*

[25] Legrand talks of natives having a '(perhaps unelucidated) attachment to a familiar legal tradition': *ibid.* But this makes it clear that we cannot assume that all natives know their own tradition or use this knowledge as the criterion by which a tradition is defined.

relatively external perspective of the foreign lawyer or social scientist (and this seems especially true where policy-driven legal transfers are being considered). Legrand's argument should probably, therefore, not to be taken as a recommendation concerning comparative methodology *tout court*. In the context of legal transplants, the issue is less the 'scientific' validity of our interpretation of law than the need to understand (and predict) how the 'native' lawyer or judge or scholar will act upon 'reception' of a foreign law. Legrand's demonstration of our inability to put ourselves in the place of the native is then to be understood as a warning to the outsider to respect the integrity and independence of the tradition which it is the task of insiders to unfold.[26]

But if the reason to stress difference is as much political as it is intellectual, this raises a new set of questions. Is it always politically sound to privilege difference? Is this what natives always want to do? Legrand denies that his position has anything to do with nationalism or cultural fundamentalism. His is rather a defensive move intended to counterbalance those comparatists who, he claims, see particularity as epiphemenonal and treat difference as an evil to be overcome at all costs. But many contemporary legal transfers are bound up with deliberate transitions from apartheid, Fascism or communism. If we were to concentrate here mainly on how best to preserve existing differences, we would surely be missing the point.

Though couched in general terms, it might be said, however, that Legrand intends his arguments to be limited to contexts similar to the current attempts at greater harmonization of law within the European Union (stigmatized by him as 'an instrumental re-invention of Europeanism dictated by the ethos of capital and technology').[27] But the reflections of a comparatist about the importance of preserving cultural differences are unlikely in themselves to provide enough of a guide for resolving complex issues of socio-legal policy-making. Surely all depends on the purpose, reach and likely effects of a given legal transfer? The link between the descriptive and the prescriptive parts of Legrand's argument is, in any case, somewhat forced. He objects in principle to legal transfers whose explicit aim is to try to make societies more alike rather than encouraging them to develop the distinctiveness of their own traditions. The fear is of what would be lost if 'success' in such enterprises actually resulted in the smoothing out of

---

[26] Legrand speaks of traditions as 'epistemic peers, serving equally well by catering to their respective communities' specific historical needs': *ibid*.

[27] *Ibid*.

differences. But, at the same time, Legrand also believes that underlying differences in legal *epistémès* mean that such efforts are, in any case, bound to fail – even ending up, as he says, by accentuating differences.[28] But, if this is so, why the fear about the loss of distinctiveness? Why oppose efforts toward European Union harmonization in the name of protecting diversity if we can be confident that transferred law will actually lead to more divergence?

Legrand's arguments are at their most persuasive if we take them to show only that existing differences do sometimes need to be defended. But we need to be sure that we know exactly what we are trying to protect. Legrand writes mainly about the need to preserve the distinctive legal traditions of common law and civil law. What is the relationship, however, between the intellectual concept of 'legal *epistémè*' which he employs and the socio-political entity represented by the integrity of a legal culture or a legal tradition – and how far are these ethnocentric concepts which themselves belong to a specific legal-cultural context? Do such categories coincide with, or transcend, nation states, pointing us toward rejecting or toward respecting national differences? What of regional and local differences within nation states? It is difficult to be consistently in favour of difference because this would lead to insisting on the existence of evermore micro-differences even within the same tradition. But where does the right to difference stop?

We also need to ask how a tradition maintains its distinctiveness. The meaning and boundaries of traditions are not unchangeable. What defines the boundaries of a tradition and what falls outside it? And who has the power to formulate this definition? The constitutive role of those engaged in arguing about and constructing tradition seems all-important here, a point Legrand accepts. Indeed, if the achievement of tradition is to make 'the past live in the present', no hard and fast line between invented and reworked tradition is possible.[29] Some apparently long-standing 'traditions' are relatively recent 'inventions',[30] others pertain to 'imagined communities'.[31] Moreover, all traditions are in some sense hybrids, even if many bearers of tradition do their best to deny this. Traditions do not evolve only in

---

[28] Legrand, *supra*, note 7, p. 69: 'a common European law, far from eradicating the *summa differentia* between the two legal traditions, would exacerbate it by sharpening its contours.'
[29] See Martin Krygier, 'Law as Tradition', (1986) 5 L. & Phil. 237.
[30] See generally Eric Hobsbawm and Terence Ranger (eds.), *The Invention of Tradition* (Cambridge: Cambridge University Press, 1983).
[31] See Benedict Anderson, *Imagined Communities* (London: Verso, 1983).

accordance with some underlying or evolutionary logic but are frequently transformed as a result of voluntary or forced engagement with other cultures whereby something new emerges. Hence the appropriateness and assimilability of proposed legal transfers is itself an essential element of such internal disagreement over the boundaries of tradition.[32]

A hermeneutic approach such as that recommended by Legrand could help us identify some of the factors (even if not all of them) which are appreciated by the social actors concerned, which serve to make their tradition coherent. But the external observer should not necessarily endorse any given vision, least of all the idea that difference – and the rejection of foreign models – is in itself a value. By taking a stand in favour of some differences rather than others, there is a risk that the observer could end up imposing hegemonic claims of similarity and coherence made by some interpreters of the tradition at the expense of others. Opposing larger-scale changes, the observer may unwillingly offer comfort and assistance to those attacking lower-level or other internal differences within their tradition – and the groups or minorities bearing such ideas and practices. In this way, Legrand's ideal comparatist would become just as much a participant in claims about the need or possibility of seeking to take ideas from elsewhere as those purporting to promote transfer or harmonization. But – according to his own argument – they would be participants without the capacity to understand fully the tradition they would be seeking to defend.

Is there any point in asking whether legal transfers will fit the societies in which they are adopted?

The upshot of the argument so far is that, despite the strictures of Legrand, there will sometimes be situations in which natives and others will want to consider when and how to transfer law. But evidence of the continuing importance of the issues raised by Legrand can be seen in the way those engaged in such exercises themselves often ask how they can best ensure that the transferred law will 'fit' well into its new environment. But it is exactly this sort of inquiry which other writers insist is, in many respects, both unnecessary and useless. In particular, the view regularly proposed and re-proposed by Alan Watson is that legal transplants just happen and

---

[32] For an illustration, see Antoine Garapon's description of the tensions within present-day French legal culture: 'French Legal Culture and the Shock of "Globalization"', (1995) 4 Soc. & Leg. Stud. 493.

that they happen all the time, quite irrespective of whether they have any broad socio-economic or other 'fit' with the society for which they are suggested or in which they are adopted.[33] Social scientists stand accused not, as with Legrand, of advocating impossible legal transplants, but of failing to recognize the significance for their understanding of law of the very ease and inevitability with which legal transfers take place.

Watson's argument (which was also directed against some styles of work in comparative law as much as to sociology of law) is that a large proportion of law in any society is a direct result of 'legal transplants' and thus owes its form and content to its origins in other times and places. Rules of private law, in particular, are often out of step for long periods with the needs and aspirations of society or any particular group or class within it. This includes bodies of law having a great impact on practical life, such as contract law or land law. Other major branches of law, such as conflict of laws, also develop with no input at all from society. Watson denies that such law is shaped by the purposes of politics, arguing that '[o]ver most of the field of law, and especially of private law, in most political and economic circumstances, political rulers need have no interest in determining what the rules of law are or should be (provided always, of course, that revenues roll in and that the public peace is kept)'.[34] 'It follows', says Watson, 'that usually legal rules are not peculiarly devised for the particular society in which they now operate and also that this is not a matter for great concern'.[35]

Other comparatists, such as William Ewald,[36] follow Watson's lead in arguing that the frequency of legal transplants demonstrates the fallacy of attempting to produce a sociology of law. These comparatists describe the sociological view they reject as the 'mirror theor[y] of law' and attribute this idea somewhat indifferently to all sociologists of law.[37] While an interest in the problem of how law relates to society is certainly a defining characteristic of their work, evidence that all sociologists rely on such a crude theory

---

[33] For example, see Alan Watson, *Legal Transplants*, 2d ed. (Athens, Georgia: University of Georgia Press, 1993) [hereinafter *Legal Transplants*]; id., *Social and Legal Change* (Edinburgh: Scottish Academic Press, 1977); id., *Law Out of Context* (Athens, Georgia: University of Georgia Press, 2000) [hereinafter *Law Out of Context*].

[34] Id., *Roman Law and Comparative Law* (Athens, Georgia: University of Georgia Press, 1991), p. 97.

[35] Id., *Legal Transplants*, *supra*, note 33, p. 96.

[36] See William Ewald, 'Comparative Jurisprudence (II): The Logic of Legal Transplants', (1995) 43 Am. J. Comp. L. 489.

[37] Id., p. 492.

(or metaphor) is certainly exaggerated. It would be enough to consider the historical sociology of Max Weber. It is true that, at the outset of his career, Emile Durkheim did argue that law could be treated as an 'index' or mirror of society.[38] But his concern was less with what shaped law than with how law could be used to map long-term changes in types of social solidarity.[39] Moreover, Durkheim saw law as playing a key role in reproducing and not merely reflecting society. Yet, the key point here is that Durkheim's claims have been criticized by virtually all later sociologists.[40] In fact, he himself soon modified his arguments, for example, by finding an independent role for the political as well as by rethinking the relationship between ideas and social practices.[41]

The larger charge that sociologists of law always reduce law to an epiphenomenon of society is also misleading. Thus, Ewald cites Lawrence Friedman as an illustration of the way contemporary sociologists treat law as overly dependent on society.[42] But Friedman's thesis, that 'law is reshaped by change, that nothing is historical accident, nothing is autonomous, everything is moulded by economics and society',[43] is no more and no less than the claim that, taking the longer view, law changes over time in response to social developments. Can this be doubted?[44] It is enough, as Friedman suggests, to compare the similarities in the form and substance of law in all modern industrial societies with their own previous pre-industrial legal regimes.[45] In addition, throughout his writings, Friedman has sought to stress how law is an instrument and the result of group conflict, both of which are aspects of law incompatible with the 'mirror' metaphor. Comparatists often fail to

---

[38] See Emile Durkheim, *The Division of Labour in Society*, transl. by W. D. Halls (London: Macmillan, 1984) [1892].

[39] See Roger Cotterrell, *Emile Durkheim: Law in a Moral Domain* (Edinburgh: Edinburgh University Press, 1999), pp. 70–4.

[40] In the words of Cotterrell, 'the index thesis, as [Durkheim] explains it, seems to show the worst aspects of the positivist orientation of his sociology': *id.*, p. 33.

[41] See Emile Durkheim, 'Two Laws of Penal Evolution', in Mike Gane (ed.), *The Radical Sociology of Durkheim and Mauss* (London: Routledge, 1992), pp. 21–49 [1901]. The translation is by T. Anthony Jones and Andrew T. Scull.

[42] Ewald, *supra*, note 36, p. 492, referring to Lawrence M. Friedman, *History of American Law*, 2d ed. (New York: Simon & Schuster, 1985).

[43] Friedman, *supra*, note 42, p. 595.

[44] Strictly speaking, though, Friedman's claim is overargued. Why should law be exempted from the effects of 'historical accident'?

[45] See Lawrence M. Friedman, 'Comments on Applebaum and Nottage', in Johannes Feest and Volkmar Gessner (eds.), *Proceedings of the Second Oñati Workshop on Changing Legal Cultures* (Oñati: International Institute for the Sociology of Law, 1998), pp. 139–49.

distinguish the functionalist claim, that law matches the 'needs' of something we call 'society', from the pluralist or conflict-theory argument, that law serves as part of the strategies of certain groups in society and that the 'law in the books' and, even more, the 'law in action' reflect the changing balance of forces in society. Friedman is a follower of the second of these theories. And such an approach in no way commits him or anyone else to the idea that law must always arise from within the society concerned, rather than be borrowed from abroad or even imposed from the outside.

Watson makes much of the fact that which legal rule is transferred depends on the accident of which foreign university lawyers attended, chance encounters between scholars or chains of mistaken interpretations of ancient texts. But his own theory (or refusal of theory), which claims that law serves no one's interests because it so often has foreign roots and is just the special province of lawyers, is highly implausible. To show Watson's claim to be accurate, more needs to be done than illustrate the survival of socially irrelevant legal distinctions and doctrines or provide examples of the contingent, the unforeseen, and the apparent 'inertia' of law. What would be required would be exactly that careful sociological investigation of the relationship between different branches of law and their social significance which Watson wants to reject a priori.

Paradoxically, whatever his actual claims about the ease of legal transplants, Watson's chosen metaphor strongly suggests that transplanting laws is, and should be, an arduous affair.[46] Certainly, medical transplants are highly planned and not something one undergoes lightly! And botanical transplants too are often carefully programmed. In practice, even Watson sometimes admits that what happens *after law has been transferred* depends on exactly those matters of social context which law-and-society scholars take to be central. He admits the possibility of barbarization or failure and the fact that law can be influential even when totally misunderstood. And he points out that the impact of legal transplants in a new setting will typically be very different from that in their society of origin: 'The insertion of an alien rule into another complex system may cause it to operate in a fresh way.'[47] He observes further that '[t]he whole context of the rule or concept has to be studied to understand the extent of the transformation.'[48] These are arguments which bring his approach very close to those espoused by sociologists.

---

[46] See generally Nelken, *supra*, note 21.
[47] Watson, *Legal Transplants, supra*, note 33, p. 116.   [48] *Ibid.*

The real importance of Watson's claims do not lie in their capacity to undermine a mirror theory of law, which has few, if any, adherents. Rather, the evidence of incongruity between legal rules and social life which he offers can be used to challenge and enrich our understanding of the various and varying forms taken by the relationship between law and society. And it is exactly that problem – the shared concern for how law connects to or 'fits' society – which represents the mainstream paradigm of sociology of law.[49] Such a paradigm allows for – indeed, presupposes – considerable disagreement over what is meant by 'law', what is meant by 'society' and what is meant by 'fit'.[50] For example, very different conclusions will be reached if law is seen as governmental order, as an aspect of social control, as the institutionalization of community norms, as cultural *epistémè* (as Legrand would favour) or as an aspect of the ideology of lawyers as a professional group or sacred clique (as Watson would prefer). Few of these starting-points have much to do with the idea of law as a mirror of society. If law as 'governmental social control' begins where community ends, it clearly cannot mirror social norms.

Empirical investigation of law's relation to society covers a wide range of what fits with what, how it fits, when it fits and which is the best way to study such fit. Theory and research may focus on macro-social change, such as the transition from 'status to contract' (and back again?) or on Durkheim's (flawed) arguments about the change from mechanical to organic solidarity or on Niklas Luhmann's examination of the relationships between the legal and other sub-systems, which maintain the high level of complexity achieved in the transition from modern to late-modern society. The macro-fit between modern law and modern society can be sought in the idea of 'equivalence' generated within the capitalist mode of production (as identified by Pashukanis)[51] or in the needs and problems created by advanced technology and the accompanying culture of expressive individualism.[52]

---

[49] See Robert Kidder, *Connecting Law and Society* (Englewood Cliffs, New Jersey: Prentice-Hall, 1983).

[50] As a policy inquiry, the question of 'fit' also connects with the famous 'gap' problem in social studies of law, which focuses on the question whether laws achieve the goals they are supposed to be fulfilling. See David Nelken, 'The "Gap Problem" in the Sociology of Law: A Theoretical Review', (1981) 1 Windsor Yearbook of Access to Justice 35. The relevance of this question for debates over legal transfers hardly needs to be spelled out.

[51] See Evgeny B. Pashukanis, *Law and Marxism: A General Theory*, transl. by Barbara Einhorn (London: Ink Links, 1978) [1924].

[52] See Lawrence M. Friedman, *The Republic of Choice* (Cambridge, Mass.: Harvard University Press, 1990).

Alternatively, attention may be given to more micro-social connections between law, social norms and social action, as in the attempt to discover how the norms of contract law actually influence business relationships, or to the degree of interdependence between legal norms and other sources of order.[53]

All of these inquiries, and others, can provide valuable insights into the potential problems involved in transferring law from one socio-economic and cultural context to another. At the same time, however, sociologists of law have long been aware that law does not always fit society. As the discussion of Legrand and Watson suggests, the relationship may, on the one hand, be so close that the question of fit does not even arise. On the other hand, it may be out of phase with social change, whether it is behind or ahead of other developments, or, more subtly, it may allow social change by not itself changing.[54] Law can 'belong' not only to other places, but also to the past, to a previous social and economic order, to tradition and to history, as much as to the present. Or it can aim at the future, acting as an index of *desired* social, political and economic change, of what society would like to become (or *should* like to become).

Over the last few years especially, attention has increasingly been directed at theorizing exactly these aspects of law.[55] Such attempts to rethink the 'law-and-society' relationship have, in some respects, gone in directions parallel to the opposing comparative critiques we have been discussing. Arguments for an identification between law and social life have been strengthened by research into 'law as ideology', 'law in everyday life' or, as some writers would have it, law as 'constitutive' of society.[56] Work emanating from the 'law-as-literature' movement, or the study of 'law as communication' more generally,[57] also supports Legrand's warning about the importance of seeing law as a way in which society transmits and reinterprets its myths,

---

[53] See Robert C. Ellickson, *Order Without Law: How Neighbours Settle Disputes* (Cambridge, Mass.: Harvard University Press, 1991).

[54] See Karl Renner, *The Private Institutions of Private Law and their Social Functions*, ed. by Otto Kahn-Freund and transl. by Agnes Schwarzschild (London: Routledge & Kegan Paul, 1949).

[55] For example, see David Nelken, 'Beyond the Study of "Law and Society"?', [1986] Am. Bar Found. Research J. 323; *id.*, 'Changing Paradigms in the Sociology of Law', in Gunther Teubner (ed.), *Autopoietic Law: A New Approach to Law and Society* (Berlin: Walter de Gruyter, 1987), pp. 191–217.

[56] For example, see Alan Hunt, *Explorations in Law and Society: Towards a Constitutive Theory of Law* (London: Routledge, 1993).

[57] See generally David Nelken (ed.), *Law as Communication* (Aldershot: Dartmouth, 1996).

rather than treating it merely as an instrument used for the purpose of achieving regulatory goals.

But social theorists have also stressed the need to overcome the idea that there is any necessary link between a given social context and a given form of law. Some stress law's capacity to transcend and transform social contexts.[58] Others debate the nature and implications of law's autonomy from other social discourses and the way this relates to the autonomy of art, religion or science.[59] Autopoietic theorists, for their part, put forward a sophisticated account of the way that legal operations are linked to other legal operations rather than directly to other sub-systems of modern society.[60] In short, law not only has a social context, but it also makes its context.[61] A future task for sociology of law (and not only for sociology of law) is to reconcile these competing understandings of law. At stake, among other things, is the prospect of getting a better grip on what is involved in deliberate efforts at legal transfer.

Can we make a success of legal transfers?

Watson may be right that legal transfers often just happen but he tends to belittle the importance of cases where transfers occur either by direct imposition or as part of larger socio-legal changes. The conclusions he draws from his historical examples are also of little help if we are called upon to take a part in promoting or assessing such transfers. To be told that the details of such legal transfers are of interest only to lawyers and scholars while business people just want the greatest posssible harmonization so as to get on with their affairs seems altogether too slim and skewed a basis for policy-making. We will need to think more systematically if we wish to explain why some laws remain a dead letter while others are transformed out of recognition. This will require us to pay attention to the way the

---

[58] For example, see Roberto Mangabeira Unger, *False Necessity: Anti-Necessitarian Social Theory in the Service of Radical Democracy* (Cambridge: Cambridge University Press, 1987).

[59] For example, see Roger Cotterrell, 'Why Must Legal Ideas Be Interpreted Sociologically?', (1998) 25 J. L. & Society 171; David Nelken, 'Blinding Insights? The Limits of a Reflexive Sociology of Law', (1998) 25 J. L. & Society 407.

[60] See Gunther Teubner, *Autopoietic Law* (Oxford: Blackwell, 1993).

[61] For a reflection on getting the law 'out of context', see David Nelken, 'Getting the Law "Out of Context"', (1996) 19 Socio-Legal Newsletter 12. Watson's volume by the same title (*Law Out of Context*, *supra*, note 33) is disappointing because it does not mark any real progress toward this goal.

relationship or 'fit' between law and society varies culturally and thus overcome ethnocentric ideas about how law must fit society.

One way of taking such matters further is to examine debates over 'success' and 'failure' in writing about transnational legal transfers. For it is in this 'mixed discourse', which combines aspects of technocractic and normative evaluation, that sociology of law and comparative law are most likely to cross paths. Talking about a successful transfer always invokes evaluations, even when the term is used by social scientists. At the extreme, it could sometimes be more appropriate to describe 'resistance' to legal transfer as success. But even those most opposed to a social-engineering approach to law find it difficult to avoid recourse to descriptive claims about what is likely or not likely to happen when they argue in favour or against given projects of legal transfer. But the conceptual and empirical difficulties that face any inquiry into the potential success of legal transfers do not end here.[62] We shall need to distinguish three sets of problems. What do we mean by 'success'? What are the conditions which make legal transfers more or less successful? Finally, and most importantly for present purposes, how far are problems in assessing success bound up with cultural variability in the way people think, or should think, about the fit between law and society? I shall discuss these matters in turn.

There is no consensus about how to define success, nor about the way it should be measured. Should we view the type of legal pluralism that characterizes areas such as south-east Asia, which has played host to a series of legal transfers,[63] as an example of success or failure? Apparent success at one level can conceal underlying failure at another. The introduction of modern law in Japan is technically a success. But, according to some insiders, it has left a feeling of inauthenticity linked to the idea that if modernity had to be imported, Japan is not really Modern.[64] We can even ask if success is always good. The introduction of new legal rules can either stabilize or unsettle existing normative practices, just as it can consolidate or

---

[62] See David Nelken, 'The Meaning of Success in Transnational Legal Transfers', (2001) 20 Windsor Yearbook of Access to Justice 349 [hereinafter 'The Meaning of Success']; *id.*, 'Towards a Sociology of Legal Adaptation', in *id.* and Feest, *supra*, note 4, pp. 7–54.

[63] See Andrew Harding, 'Comparative Law and Legal Transplantation in South East Asia: Making Sense of the "Nomic Din"', in Nelken and Feest, *supra*, note 4, pp. 199–222.

[64] See Takao Tanase, 'The Empty Space of the Modern in Japanese Law Discourse', in Nelken and Feest, *supra*, note 4, pp. 187–98. This interpretation of Japanese experience, albeit controversial, lends some support to Legrand's argument about the impossibility of legal transplants ('What "Legal Transplants"?', *supra*, note 13).

undermine competing expertises.[65] Legal innovations – whether at home or abroad – may sometimes be considered 'too successful' if they 'colonize' or displace other established normative or technical patterns of regulating social relationships without the use of law, leading to 'juridification'.

Other conceptual problems have to do with who has (and who should have) the power to define success. Put differently, whose goals count? Those of the country 'exporting' its law or those of the country receiving it? What about the differences among competing economic interests, among members of governmental and non-governmental organizations (NGOs), parliamentarians, judges, lawyers and other professionals as well as all the other groups likely to be most affected by the law? Should success be judged in terms of an outside observer's assessment of results and effects or in terms of the views of the insiders promoting or being affected by the transfer? How do the criteria used by outsiders and insiders relate to each other? Are we interested more in the experience of politicians, policymakers, judges, scholars, lawyers, business people, ordinary working people or immigrants and those on the margins of society?[66] What if members of the receiving society want different or even contradictory things? Is success a matter of actually achieving the right fit between law and society or rather the capacity to have one's claims about this accepted?

A second set of issues concerns the conditions for success. The sociology of law textbooks tell us that the likelihood of successful social change through law in *national* contexts depends on what is being transferred, by which source, the way the transfer is introduced, the number of social groups involved, as well as a potentially unlimited number of wider background factors and previous historical experiences.[67] Many of these considerations, such as the authoritativeness of the source of law or the mediating role of institutions, will also be applicable to transfers between countries.[68] But some postulated conditions only beg the question. What does it mean, for example, to say that '[l]aw must appear compatible with cultural assumptions'?[69] Other claims in this literature border on the ethnocentric: the alleged special

---

[65] See John Flood, 'The Vultures Fly East: The Creation and Globalisation of the Distressed Debt Market', in Nelken and Feest, *supra*, note 4, pp. 257–78.

[66] See Eve Darian-Smith, 'Structural Inequalities in the Global System', (2000) 34 L. & Society R. 809.

[67] For example, see Roger Cotterrell, *The Sociology of Law*, 2d ed. (London: Butterworths, 1992), pp. 44–65.

[68] See *id.*, 'Is There a Logic of Legal Transplants?', in Nelken and Feest, *supra*, note 4, pp. 70–92.

[69] *Id.*, *supra*, note 67, p. 59 [discussing the views of William M. Evan].

difficulties of regulating family life or the need to present projects of legal change in ways that do not make them seem utopian are problems which are perceived very differently in different legal cultures.[70] As importantly, proposing legal transfers to other societies raises distinctive questions. In a national law-reform setting, law will often do no more than accompany or register long-standing processes of social change. In transnational legal transfers, however, it is *typical* for law to be asked to jump-start the wider process of social change and leap-frog over long-standing social and cultural obstacles.

How far are the 'conditions' of success beyond our control? It can be helpful to distinguish between what we might call the 'objective' and 'subjective' aspects of this question. As an example of objective condition, we might consider the debate over whether legal change in newly developing or in ex-communist countries has to proceed following the same stages as taken in the west. Is the existence of a certain type of legal profession a pre-condition for certain types of social change? Societies going through a post-communist transition also face the problem whether the extension of competition and the 'free market' should precede, accompany or follow the construction of effective multi-party democracy. Some studies of democratic transitions from Fascist and communist regimes emphasize the need to resolve the problem of creating democratic politics before tackling the construction of free-market capitalism.[71] But the Japanese experience seems to show that successful modernization can equally well be brought about by effective collaboration between a relatively authoritarian government bureaucracy and private industry.[72]

Yet the success of legal transfers depends not only on past or present objective circumstances but also on how far social actors decide to treat these as if they were unchangeable and beyond their control. Martin Krygier argues that we should distinguish between 'pessimistic' and 'optimistic' approaches to legal transplants.[73] Such attitudes regarding the feasibility of changing established institutions or the possibility of overcoming cultural obstacles to change are often manifested with reference to the question of

---

[70] *Id.*, p. 60.
[71] For example, see Juan J. Linz and Alfred Stepan, *Problems of Democratic Transition and Consolidation* (Baltimore: Johns Hopkins University Press, 1996).
[72] See Tanase, *supra*, note 64.
[73] Martin Krygier, 'Is There Constitutionalism After Communism? Institutional Optimism, Cultural Pessimism, and the Rule of Law', (1996–7) 26 Int. J. Sociology L. 17.

how far back in history it is necessary to go in seeking an explanation for the present problems to which a transplanted remedy is being proposed.

What, finally, of the connection between arguments about success and ideas of 'fit'? Many issues concerning legal transfers are discussed as if they are only a matter of appropriate pre-conditions, of getting the 'timing' right. But they also go to the heart of the theoretical question of the 'fit' between law and society. Is it a mistake to deregulate prices before implementing competition law? (Can things be done the other way round?) At what stage should a society opt for more market and when for more regulation? Do markets produce rules or rules markets? Must stable institutions precede rules? Should we characterize the nexus between law and the market in capitalist societies as a system of unstable predictability or predictable instability? All these matters rely on implicit ideas about how law does, and how it should, relate to other aspects of society and culture. Sometimes, these are made explicit. In considering whether the 'developmental state' must follow the model of law-and-capitalism in the first capitalist societies, Tom Ginsburg asks: 'How does a system based on personalistic social relations and close ties between business and government move toward a more open and transparent system governed by generally applicable rules? What configuration of political interests are required to initiate and sustain such a transformation?'[74]

Many insightful scholars return from trips abroad where they have been asked to give advice about potential transfers convinced more than ever of the way legal reforms depend on culturally specific presuppositions about the appropriate fit between law and society. Thus, Edward Rubin tells us that his experience in China confirmed him in the view that the type of administrative law used in the United States depends on the presence of a litigious culture and the presumption that party involvement by numerous interest groups can be relied upon to comment on, and improve upon, bureaucratic regulations. Hence, it would not be currently appropriate in China. Rubin's conclusions are worth reporting in full: 'by a sort of double reflection, the characterization of American law that China's distance illuminates becomes a way of perceiving what the underlying characterization of a Chinese law would be. That law draws upon the hierarchy, centralization and governmental prestige in the Chinese system. It would

---

[74] Tom Ginsburg, 'Does Law Matter for Economic Development? Evidence from East Asia', (2000) 34 L. & Society R. 829, p. 851.

create governmental supervisory agencies, independent of other agencies, but possessing the full power and prestige of government, to enforce statutorily required procedures. The ultimate lesson is that little can be borrowed, but much can be learned, from foreign law.'[75] On which, one might comment that often, for better or worse, borrowing is also a way of learning.

However, it would be a fundamental mistake to confine discussions of legal transfers to questions of how new rules, ideas or institutions 'fit' *what already exists*. Legal transfers are frequently – perhaps predominantly – geared to fitting an imagined *future*. Most legal transfers are imposed, invited or otherwise adopted because the society, or at least some groups or elites within that society, seek to use law for the purposes of *change*. The goal is not to fit law to what exists but to reshape what exists through the introduction of something *different*. Hence ex-communist countries try to become more like selected examples of the more successful market societies or South Africa models its new constitution on the best that western regimes have to offer rather than on constitutional arrangements found in its nearer neighbours in Africa. Thus, rather than aiming to reproduce past or present conditions or ideals, law aims to overcome these. The hope is that law may be a means of resolving current problems by transforming society into something more like the source of the borrowed law. In this way, a legal transfer is part of the effort to become more democratic, more economically successful, more secular (or more religious). In what is almost a species of sympathetic magic, borrowed law is deemed capable of bringing about the same conditions allowing for a flourishing economy or a healthy civil society that are found in the social context from which the borrowed law has been taken.[76] In some cases, such as in the modernization of Japan or in Italy, after the recent collapse of the ruling political parties,[77] the search, more modestly, may be for institutions which will make societies more 'normal'. But even this quest for achieved normality can easily be self-defeating.

---

[75] Edward Rubin, 'Administrative Law and the Complexity of Culture', in Anne Seidman, Robert Seidman and Janice Payne (eds.), *Legislative Drafting for Market Reform: Some Lessons from China* (London: Macmillan, 2000), p. 108.

[76] See Julie Mertus, 'The Liberal State vs. the National Soul: Mapping Civil Society Transplants', (1999) 8 Soc. & Leg. Stud. 121.

[77] See David Nelken, 'A Legal Revolution? The Judges and Tangentopoly', in Stephen Gundle and Simon Parker (eds.), *The New Italian Republic: From the Fall of the Berlin Wall to Berlusconi* (London: Routledge, 1995), pp. 191–206.

The search for dissimilar legal models is perhaps most likely where the legal transfer is imposed by third parties as part of a colonial project and/or insisted upon as a condition of trade, aid, alliance or diplomatic recognition. But it also characterizes the efforts of international organizations, such as the International Monetary Fund (IMF), when they seek to reshape societies according to a supposedly universal pattern of political and financial integrity. And it may be requested or agreed upon mainly as a way of marking a willingness to accept the 'rules of the game' of the wider global economy. This explains the adhesion to the intellectual property or anti-trust provisions of the World Trade Organization by countries which have few ways of enforcing such rules or little need to do so.

All of this complicates any attempt to use the criterion of 'fit' as a way of measuring success in introducing new law. Is the appropriate fit that which corresponds to the understanding or working of the law or institution in its society of origin? Or is it that which results when it is successfully 'reworked' for the society in which it now has to operate? Without prior research, we should also not assume that we actually know how law worked even in its original context. The study of legal transfers presents us with a challenge to document the considerable socio-cultural variation in the extent to which law actually conditions social action, both in the society of origin and in that of arrival. But we also need to consider differences in whether *it is thought to need to do so*. This has important implications for assessing typical claims that transplanted law must 'fit' the society to which it is introduced if it is to be 'effective' – and it also helps us predict when and where such claims are likely to be made.

Future empirical research is likely to illustrate the point that what is actually being exported in the present round of legal transfers, along with any given legal institution or procedure, is a culturally specific ideology. The legal philosophy which underpins current law-and-development activity is broadly describable as that of 'pragmatic legal instrumentalism'. It promotes *the very idea that law is something which does or should 'work'*, together with the claim that this is something that can or should be assessed in ways which are separable from wider political debates. Time will tell, for example, how far NAFTA will succeed in altering a legal culture such as Mexico's where, we are told, 'law institutes without regulating'.[78] But it will often be difficult to draw a clear line between economic and political change, on

---

[78] Sergio López-Ayylon, 'Notes on Mexican Legal Culture', (1995) 4 Soc. & Leg. Stud. 477, p. 479.

the one hand, and cultural change on the other. In either case, in Pierre Legrand's terms, legal transfers may be more a means of changing local narratives, rather than continuing them.

Legal transfers in changing contexts: an agenda for research

Every instance of legal transfer has its own history and needs to be examined in its own right. The idea that 'theory' can provide us with a means of predicting what will, or must, happen to legal transfers will usually prove misplaced or at least elusive; 'thick' description may be the best that we can achieve.[79] But the social scientist should also try to say something about the larger context in which these transfers take place. In particular, in order to make progress in rethinking legal transfers, we shall have both to clarify what is special about current developments and also ask whether existing models of legal transfer offer appropriate and comprehensive frameworks for understanding them.

In seeking to classify the kinds of legal transfers which are currently taking place, we may want to distinguish *different* processes of legal transfer happening at the same time. Take, for example, the following types of transfer (which do not begin to exhaust all the possible ways of distinguishing different mechanisms and processes of legal change):

1. Cases where one country borrows or submits to new laws introduced from another society (though there are likely to be very important differences between cases where this takes place as part of colonial imposition or as a result of other forms of influence).
2. Processes involving the spread of standards, regulations or 'soft law', for instance, through attempts at harmonization of private law within the European Union; conventions on biodiversity, genetic engineering or the internet; labour regulations by the International Labour Organization or international taxation agreements.
3. Cases where 'third cultures', such as arbitration fora in Paris or Zurich, reflect and further processes of globalization of law.

But we may also be interested in examining what *unites* present initiatives. For example, we may choose to explore the way transnational activities of legal transfer are linked to national, international and transnational

---

[79] Clifford Geertz, *The Interpretation of Cultures* (London: Fontana, 1973), p. 7.

actors – and how NGOs, such as the IMF or large charitable foundations, intersect or reconstitute these boundaries. We will need to bear in mind not only such central legal activities as those connected to legislation and standard-setting, adjudication, regulation, mediation and dispute settlement, but also mutual exchange and networking as with international meetings of judges, lawyers, academics, police or customs officers, as well as efforts to create new legal, economic, political, social and educational institutions.

It is tempting to summarize present developments as all, in one way or another, illustrating the globalization of law. But it is important not to make one-sided assumptions about what is meant by 'globalization' or the way it affects law.[80] Globalization is a process which has multiple and often contradictory aspects (social, cultural, economic, political, technical, etc.). There are major changes taking place in world trade and communication. But their effects are neither uniform nor easily predictable. The label is often used to cover developments which could be understood in other terms; and it would be wrong to attribute to globalization what are simply parallel but indigenous processes. Most importantly, globalization does not mean that the world is necessarily becoming more homogeneous or harmonized. Much of the economic and financial integration which characterizes globalized markets of production and consumption also presupposes, and produces, divergence and difference or inclusion and exclusion.[81] Sometimes, globalization actually strengthens the local.[82] If globalization often marginalizes the local, it is in part through its ability to define others as 'merely' local. For some observers, globalization should even be seen as no more than a temporary vogue for neo-liberal policy choices dressed up in the language of economic inevitability.[83]

Law can act as the bearer of globalization but it can also form part of the resistance to it. To say that legal innovations are usually part and parcel of

---

[80] See Wolf Heydebrand, 'From Globalization of Law to Law under Globalization', in Nelken and Feest, *supra*, note 4, pp. 117–37; *id.*, 'Globalization and the Rule of Law at the End of the Twentieth Century', in Alberto Febbrajo, David Nelken and Vittorio Olgiati (eds.), *Social Processes and Patterns of Legal Control: European Yearbook of Sociology of Law 2000* (Milan: Giuffrè, 2001), pp. 25–127 [hereinafter 'Globalization and the Rule of Law'].

[81] For example, see David Nelken, 'The Globalization of Crime and Criminal Justice: Prospects and Problems', in Michael Freeman (ed.), *Law and Opinion at the End of the Twentieth Century* (Oxford: Oxford University Press, 1997), pp. 251–79.

[82] See Francis Snyder, 'Governing Economic Globalization: Global Legal Pluralism and European Law', (1999) Eur. L.J. 334, p. 336.

[83] For example, see Allan Scott, 'Globalization: Social Process or Political Rhetoric?', in *id.* (ed.), *The Limits of Globalization: Cases and Arguments* (London: Routledge, 1997), pp. 1–24.

longer-term social changes does not mean that law can be reduced to an inevitable concomitant or expression of such larger trends of convergence or globalization.[84] A weak feature of such a 'convergence thesis' is that it fails to explain how far, when and why law, or some components of law or any particular model of law, becomes a necessary part of doing things as compared to other forms of securing market certainty, political legitimacy or whatever.

If we are to take a stand for or against the globalization of law (for example, in the name of protecting diversity), we need to take care not to get any one aspect of these developments out of focus. For example, in his stringent criticisms of efforts geared to harmonization of law within the European Union, Pierre Legrand suggests that the law-making and law-enforcing activities of Europe's central agencies risk imposing the style and substance of civil-law at the expense of common-law legal culture.[85] By contrast, Maria Rosaria Ferrarese sees the globalization of law as essentially a process by which Anglo-American legal culture is systematically overpowering its civil-law competition by facilitating and promoting 'marketization'. Ferrarese points to the way corporations are becoming the new crucial legal actors as law comes to be linked to the needs of business rather than to national jurisdictions. She illustrates her argument with examples of many telling changes, ranging from the redefinition of the 'public' and the 'private' to the increasing use of oral proceedings.[86] No doubt there is evidence of both trends but it is important to recognize that matters are not one-sided.

Globalization of private and public law involves legislative, judicial or other efforts to extend cross-frontier trade and communication including e-commerce, the melding of 'private' and 'public' in international trade litigation and the creation or regulation of 'third spaces'. Although this is claimed to be in the general interest of free trade, we would be wrong to assume that all trading nations or all types of businesses gain equally. As an example of the globalization of criminal law, we can take the creation of international war tribunals or measures to permit the pursuit of crimes across national boundaries. Many initiatives aim to curb what are said to be common social problems, such as organized crime, money laundering, corruption, paedophilia, unauthorized immigration, environmental pollution, unregulated scientific experimentation, breach of copyright, counterfeiting or computer hacking. Sometimes, these measures also involve proposed

---

[84] See Lawrence M. Friedman, 'Is There a Modern Legal Culture?', (1994) 7 Ratio Juris 117.
[85] See Pierre Legrand, 'Against a European Civil Code', (1997) 60 Modern L.R. 44.
[86] See Maria Rosaria Ferrarese, *Le istituzioni della globalizzazione* (Bologna: Il Mulino, 2000).

solutions, as with the extension of transnational ethics in pharmaceutical research or common rules on asylum for refugees. But, again, whether, and how far, such problems are really the same in all the societies concerned and who benefits most from the struggle against them remains moot. Another important example of the globalization of law is found in the effort to spread human rights, as seen, for example, in international campaigns against wife-beating or female circumcision. Here, the success of globalization can be measured in the ability to deny that gains for victim groups are being bought at the expense of loss of cultural diversity.

Our theories of legal transfer are also likely to be affected by these social changes. Some writers make perhaps overstrong claims arguing that the interdependencies created by globalization require us to re-examine the whole comparative project. Wolf Heydebrand, for example, talks of the 'tension between the more or less static and interpretative comparative project and the dynamic longitudinal project imposed by the resumption of globalization'.[87] For her part, Maureen Cain suggests that where there are common causes and concerns, old-style comparison no longer has a point and risks ending up as either 'occidentalism' or 'orientalism'.[88] The assumptions which lie behind officially sponsored moves to legal transfer also change over time and place. Tom Ginsburg tells us that the new law-and-development movement is characterized by a focus on the techniques appropriate for transferring legal and political institutions, as if these can be abstracted from culture and from wider social change: 'today's development policy assumes that a country must adapt the proper institutions to facilitate growth and that institutions can be transferred across borders.'[89]

The theoretical models we use must make allowance for the variety of ways in which legal transfers can take place. Lawrence Friedman suggests that we should distinguish between processes of borrowing, diffusion or imposition.[90] Writers who draw on autopoietic theory likewise propose distinguishing between *ad hoc* contacts, systemic linkages and

---

[87] Heydebrand, 'Globalization and the Rule of Law', *supra*, note 80, p. 110.
[88] Maureen Cain, 'Orientalism, Occidentalism and the Sociology of Crime', (2000) 40 Brit. J. Criminology 239.
[89] Ginsburg, *supra*, note 74, p. 833. See also Wojciech Sadurski, 'On the Relevance of Institutions and the Centrality of Constitutions in Post-communist Transitions', in Jan Zielonka (ed.), *Democratic Consolidation in Eastern Europe*, vol. I: *Institutional Engineering* (Oxford: Oxford University Press, 2001), pp. 455–74.
[90] See Lawrence M. Friedman, 'Borders: On the Emerging Sociology of Transnational Law', (1996) 32 Stanford J. Int. L. 65.

co-evolution.[91] This also suggests the need to think more carefully about the relationship between such different processes and the commonly used metaphor of 'legal transplants'. Despite its continuing popularity, this metaphor seems ill-equipped to bring out such differences. Even with reference to straightforward attempts to introduce new legal institutions, the metaphor can easily prove misleading. In biological or botanical adaptation, success may indeed be a matter of 'survive or perish'. But, in the case of adapting legal systems, a far wider range of outcomes is possible – and, indeed, likely – and it will often not be clear whether survival refers to the legal system (or a given institution within it) or to the larger society itself.

It would be a mistake to see the problem here as simply requiring us to avoid resorting to metaphors. The use of 'living' or 'dead' metaphors is an intrinsic and unavoidable element of all our analogies and explanations. Rather, we need to become more aware of the implications of different metaphors. For example, what is illuminated and what is obscured by the alternative metaphor of 'palace wars', which Yves Dezalay and Bryant Garth suggest as the key to understanding the way legal ideas are now fought over by social elites at home and abroad?[92] Even the anodyne term 'legal transfers', which I chose for its very inoffensiveness, conjures up a sense of geographic mobility of law that could be misleading with respect to some processes by which law comes to be imitated abroad.

In line with my general argument, it is important to appreciate how different metaphors mobilize and favour different ideas about how law fits society. 'Mechanical' metaphors of legal transfer, for example, are those which use the language of borrowing, export, diffusion, circulation or imposition. They tend to accompany talking about law in the language of 'impact' and 'penetration' and reflect a vision of law as a working institution, as an instrument and as a technique of social engineering. Organic metaphors, however, speak about 'grafts', 'viruses' and 'contamination' and, of course, 'transplants' (whether medical or botanical). Legal transfers, when they succeed, thus 'set root' or 'blossom' and are described as 'fertile'. The use of these metaphors is likely to belong to a functionalist model of law as an interdependent part of a larger whole. Thus, to talk of 'legal adaptation' is to

---

[91] See John Paterson and Gunther Teubner, 'Changing Maps: Empirical Legal Autopoiesis', (1998) 7 Soc. & Leg. Stud. 451. See also Gunther Teubner, 'Global Bukowina: Legal Pluralism in the World Society', in *id.* (ed.), *Global Law Without a State* (Aldershot: Dartmouth, 1997), pp. 3–38.

[92] Yves Dezalay and Bryant Garth, 'The Import and Export of Law and Legal Institutions: International Strategies in National Palace Wars', in Nelken and Feest, *supra*, note 4, pp. 241–56.

use a metaphor derived from the language of functionalist survival. Finally, discursive metaphors apprehend law as communication, as narrative and as myth. Transferring law, on this approach, is to be understood mainly as a matter of translating and reformulating explicit and implicit meanings.

Law can be treated as an instrumentality, as part of a functioning whole or as communication. Depending on the purposes of our research into legal transfers, we may wish to privilege the exploration of one or more of these aspects of law. In replacing the metaphor of 'legal transplants', we should be careful to ensure that we are able to address all these aspects as and when relevant. Gunther Teubner's proposal to substitute the metaphor of 'legal irritants' does touch on all these three aspects of law. His work is also important because of the way it shows how theorizing about the possibility of legal transfers must be, and can be, linked to the understanding of new legal and social developments. In elaborating his critical account of judicial efforts to bring about legal harmonization in Europe, Teubner draws on Luhmann's social-systems theory and, in particular, on his idea of legal autopoiesis so as to show the way in which the binding arrangements between law and society have changed in conditions of late modernity.[93]

However, Teubner's arguments are not free of ambiguities.[94] His proposed new metaphor is unlikely to solve all our problems in understanding legal transfers. Thus, Teubner argues that legal transfers tend to lead to the 'creation of new cleavages in the interdependence of operationally closed social discourses'.[95] Because this unpredictability suggests the need for caution in undertaking legal transfers, Teubner's ideas have been quickly embraced for political-normative reasons rather than for theoretical-explanatory purposes. But some scholars who cite his work have no real interest in, or sympathy for, the theory which provides the framework for his argument. They fail to note that an insistence on the need for hermeneutic and interpretive exploration of legal culture and legal meaning would be quite incompatible with Teubner's attempts to apply Luhmann's observer-based systems theory. Nor is the idea of distinct legal *epistémès* consistent with Luhmann's 'scientific' attempt to postulate a universalistic definition of law. Finally, Teubner himself is by no means as pessimistic about the possibility of legal transfers as he is sometimes made to seem.[96]

---

[93] See Teubner, *supra*, note 12.   [94] See Nelken, 'The Meaning of Success', *supra*, note 62.
[95] Teubner, *supra*, note 12, pp. 31–2.
[96] His actual argument is that 'legal irritants' force the specific *epistémè* of domestic law to a reconstitution in the network of its distinctions and also provoke the social discourse to which law is closely tied to a reconstruction of its own. See Teubner, *supra*, note 12.

From the perspective of the sociology of law, a defect of much comparative work, both in theory and in practice, is the failure to engage in sufficient empirical research into what else is happening in the societies promoting or receiving legal transfers. There would seem to be little point in seeking to protect legal distinctiveness if other things in the society or culture concerned were already changing so as to achieve harmonization even without resort to law. Take, once again, the debates over harmonization within the European Union. There is currently considerable legal discussion over the appropriateness or otherwise of introducing harmonized European criminal proceedings as a means of tackling the considerable problem of frauds against the European Union budget.[97] But no one engaged in this controversy seems in the least worried about the well-established common auditing methods used by agencies such as the European Court of Auditors! To take a different example, many of the governmental and international agencies which promote legal change in developing countries focus on formal as opposed to informal institutions. These are easier to identify, analyse and engineer in ways that can produce the measurable results by which such bureaucracies justify their existence. Yet, there are likely to be informal institutions, less amenable to change by external interventions, which already carry out many of the tasks of the formal institutions whose performance the agencies are seeking to improve.[98]

Much the same applies to what may *not* be happening in receiving societies as compared to those doing the exporting of legal institutions or ideals. In considering current (renewed) efforts to export the 'rule of law', both to former communist countries or to emerging economies, careful attention needs to be given to the differential pace of technological revolutions and other social developments. William Scheuerman has put forward a schematic but provocative analysis of the effects of technical change on business life under late-modern forms of capitalism, arguing that the political and legal infrastructure of globalization bears little resemblance to the liberal model of the rule of law.[99] The rule of law was particularly useful to business people when it met their aspirations to make time and space manageable so as to reduce uncertainty based on distance and duration of commercial exchange. Now, however, the compression of time and space

---

[97] For example, see House of Lords Select Committee on the European Community, 'Prosecuting Fraud on the Communities Finances – The Corpus Juris', 62d session, 9th Report (1998–9).
[98] See Ginsburg, *supra*, note 74, p. 850.
[99] William E. Scheuerman, 'Globalization and the Fate of Law', in David Dyzenhaus (ed.), *Recrafting the Rule of Law: The Limits of Legal Order* (Oxford: Hart, 1999), pp. 243–66.

which characterizes globalization means that there is less of an elective affinity between capitalism and the rule of law. The risks the rule of law helped reduce are now, Scheuerman argues, better dealt with by the time-space compression made possible by modern technology: communication via computer is much quicker than creating and enforcing legal agreements. Against this background of social change, law increasingly loses its autonomy and becomes porous and open-ended. Flexibility is now all-important and business people have less need of standard and consistent norms. They thrive instead on the opportunities provided by difference between legal regimes. Arbitration is treated as the best option in cases of dispute.

No less importantly, the rule of law used to be valued because it protected business transactions from arbitrary interference by the state. But now, argues Scheuerman, at least as far as multinational business is concerned, companies often have the same rights as states themselves (as with NAFTA). The fact that poorer states need the investment which these businesses bring them means that the balance of power is no longer to their advantage. There follows a competition to reduce legal safeguards and there is, by now, considerable evidence that economic globalization flourishes where lower standards in protecting labour, health and the environment are exploited by powerful companies.[100] It would be misleading to ignore these or other similar factors when assessing the likely outcomes of introducing the type of separation between the state and the market identified with the classical (but now somewhat dated) idea of the 'rule of law'.

---

[100] See Fiona Haines, 'Towards Understanding Globalization and Corporate Harm: A Preliminary Criminological Analysis', paper presented at the Law and Society Association annual conference, Chicago, 2 June 1999, on file with the author.

13

Comparatists and extraordinary places

ESIN ÖRÜCÜ

Introduction

What can contemporary comparative legal studies say in a world radically different from the one covered by such studies up until now? Can the comparatists of today enter this new and different world with their existing strategies and accommodate differences by building on, or modifying, these strategies and so extend the scope of comparative analysis beyond the jurisdictions ordinarily dealt with? In my view, the future entails change, both in the perception and practice of comparative legal studies and in its interaction with other disciplines investigating the phenomena of legal and social cultures.

Traditionally, most comparatists have come from the western legal traditions. They have been mainly interested in the comparison of common law and civil law and in the expansion of these two legal traditions, considering the 'totally other' only in this context. The emphasis has either been on similarities between similars, or even between differents, and differences between differents – but rarely between similars. Each of these strategies has its own agenda. Sometimes, the purpose is to indicate that the world is divided between two traditions, sometimes to show that there is a global *rapprochement* or, at least, a *rapprochement* between common law and civil law and, more recently, between socialist law and civil law. Sometimes, the goal is to point out that 'never the twain shall meet' and, sometimes, to show that 'we are all changing and changing in the same direction, so what do the differences matter anyway?' The inescapable fact, however, is that in most 'totally other' legal systems – those left behind by western comparatists – massive law-reform is taking place and that these legal systems are now themselves looking at the west, though sometimes with extensive encouragement from it. At present, a number of such legal systems are experiencing fundamental upheaval. Some are reshaping themselves with the help of outside models chosen from competing systems. This is so in social, economic and legal terms. These are systems in transition. Some, operating within certain regions or groupings, are fundamentally affected by reciprocal influence. Some are swayed by globalization, a term much used in our day. How should western comparatists approach this new world?

Hiding behind proclamations such as 'comparative law as we know it cannot cope with renewal', 'law is culture and lawyers cannot understand any other culture than their own', 'legal history is the only path to be followed by comparatists', 'the only true explanation of legal change is through economic analysis of law', 'comparative law must be legal theory, therefore we must be "comparative jurisprudents" so as to understand other laws' or 'transplants are impossible' will not solve the actual problems facing comparatists. We cannot ignore the reality of transmigration, nor can we ignore the reality of 'difference'. Whatever their stance, western comparatists must be prepared to go out to 'extraordinary places'. Indeed, 'comparison in extraordinary places' is vital in our 'extraordinary times'.

What is an 'extraordinary place'?

An 'extraordinary place' can be one of several things.

First, it can be a place not ordinarily covered by conventional comparative law. In this sense, 'ordinary' would mean civil-law and common-law jurisdictions, usually limited to France, Germany, Italy (and recently Spain), on the one hand, and England and the United States, on the other. Any legal system outside these would be regarded as a system in an 'extraordinary place'. This place can also be one, of course, where the legal system or the law is based on, or heavily determined by, religion or belief.

Secondly, an 'extraordinary place' can be a place in which out-of-the-ordinary things are happening. Examples are Hong Kong, where in terms of its relationship with China there is talk of 'one country, two systems'; Hungary, where there was a civilian tradition without a civil code followed by a socialist era with freedom of sorts for the civilian tradition to live on and where there is now a new era of transformation and preparation for European Union membership; or Turkey, where the dominant elite had a vision which entailed changing not only the legal culture, but also the socioculture by employing foreign legal models leading to the erasure of the indigenous and ending up in a 'limping marriage' with the European Union.

Thirdly, an 'extraordinary place' can be a place where there has been transmigration of laws between legal systems characterized by both a legal and socio-cultural diversity creating either legal pluralism, a mixed jurisdiction, a hybrid system or unexpected results under pressure from a dominant elite.

Sometimes, there are overlaps between the three phenomena and a place can be 'extraordinary' in all these senses. It is, in fact, from such places that examples will be drawn in this study. These illustrations defy the theory of 'legal families', traditional paradigms being inadequate to account for them. An important point must be made at this early stage, however, which is that legal systems in 'extraordinary places' are not necessarily the so-called 'exotic' legal systems. When juxtaposing legal and socio-cultural systems from 'ordinary' and 'extraordinary' places, the 'extraordinary' may well prove similar to the 'ordinary'. This similarity may be socio-cultural and legal-cultural or legal-cultural only. If there is socio-cultural similarity but legal-cultural diversity between the two systems under review, comparatists then tend to seek refuge in historical explanations or hide behind the term 'historical accident'. In such instances of similarity, the task of the comparatist, however, is to analyse the reasons for the similarity bearing in mind that there are no identicals in law since even after very successful *transpositions*,[1] an evolutionary dynamism emerges and systems go their own way. Incoming concepts or institutions, now living in a different environment, begin to change; an internal 'contamination' occurs. But what can the comparatist do when the 'extraordinary' is totally different from the 'ordinary', beyond trying to explain the reasons for the difference or divergence? This difference can be both socio-cultural and legal-cultural or socio-cultural only or legal-cultural only. When the divergence is socio-cultural and yet there is legal-cultural similarity, the term 'historical accident' is again resorted to in order to explain this anomaly. Of course, transmigration from the system of an 'ordinary place' into that of an 'extraordinary place' may give rise to incompatibility or mismatch as the deeper values and purposes of the two may be seemingly irreconcilable.[2] Indeed, if reciprocity and mutuality were to be achieved between legal and cultural systems, then they would all become 'contaminants' and 'irritants' of each other. In this case, comparatists would find themselves being the bridge-builders

---

[1] This term is analysed below.
[2] See David S. Berry, 'Interpreting Rights and Culture: Extending Law's Empire', (1998) 4 Res Publica 3, p. 14.

between traditional cultures and western-style expressions of norms and standards.

The future of comparative legal studies is tied both theoretically and practically to an appreciation of diversity. In fact, I argue that the more 'extraordinary' the place, the more important comparative legal studies becomes. Comparative legal studies must get involved in a search for, and an explanation of, divergences, especially between the seemingly similar.[3] This task should be undertaken constructively with the aim of enhancing our understanding of law and legal and social cultures. Also, because reciprocal influence and transposition will dominate the twenty-first century, comparatists must consider 'extraordinary places' and how mismatches are resolved. The 'convergence thesis' can be challenged without going down the path followed by Pierre Legrand that legal transplants are impossible.[4] Borrowing and imitation are of central importance in understanding the course of legal change since original innovation in law is very small.[5] Nevertheless, the current 'transplant' theory is in need of some conceptual refinement. For example, though Gunther Teubner does not support Alan Watson,[6] he claims that the conceptual refinement needed would 'allow us to analyse institutional transfer in terms different from the simple alternative of context versus autonomy', as the contemporary ties of law to society change.[7] Concluding that transplantation is hazardous, John Allison points to the need for considering 'both the present and proposed contexts of a transplant'.[8] In this respect, I have developed the concepts of 'transposition' and 'tuning'.[9]

Though ill-considered transplants are dangerous, the use of transplants has been, and is, inevitable, especially in 'extraordinary places'. A colourful vocabulary highlighting nuances in individual instances of transmigrations of legal institutions and ideas, such as 'grafting', 'implantation', 're-potting' and 'cross-fertilization', has supplemented the terminology used in

---

[3] For example, see Vivian G. Curran, 'Dealing in Difference: Comparative Law's Potential for Broadening Legal Perspective', (1998) 46 Am. J. Comp. L. 657; Nora V. Demleitner, 'Challenge, Opportunity and Risk: An Era of Change in Comparative Law', (1998) 46 Am. J. Comp. L. 647.

[4] Pierre Legrand, 'The Impossibility of "Legal Transplants"', (1997) 4 Maastricht J. Eur. & Comp. L. 111.

[5] See Rodolfo Sacco, 'Legal Formants: A Dynamic Approach to Comparative Law', (1991) 39 Am. J. Comp. L. 1 & 343, p. 395.

[6] Alan Watson, *Legal Transplants*, 2d ed. (Athens, Georgia: University of Georgia Press, 1993).

[7] Gunther Teubner, 'Legal Irritants: Good Faith in British Law or How Unifying Law Ends Up in New Divergencies', (1998) 61 Modern L.R. 17.

[8] John W. F. Allison, *A Continental Distinction in the Common Law* (Oxford: Oxford University Press, 1996), p. 16. See also *id.*, p. 236.

[9] Esin Örücü, 'Law as Transposition', (2002) 51 Int. & Comp. L.Q. 205.

classical statements of this mobility, such as 'imposition', 'transplant' and 'reception'.[10] New bases for analysis are being developed, such as 'collective colonization', 'multiculturalism', 'legal pluralism', 'contaminants', 'legal irritants', 'layered law', 'hyphenated law' and 'competing legal systems'. It is recognized that influences exist not only between legal systems, but also between socio-cultures and legal systems and that legal culture and legal systems must be contemporary bases for analysis. 'Contamination', 'irritation', 'inoculation' and 'infiltration' thus are all appropriate terms for describing the encounters taking place today and 'reception', 'imposed reception' and 'concerted parallel development' can be used to account for the relevant processes. Although the term 'legal transplant'[11] is the usual one being applied interchangeably to all of these phenomena, I regard the word 'transposition' to be more apt.

The importance of legal transposition in 'extraordinary places'

In instances of massive change based on competing models, the term 'transposition', as used in music, is indeed more appropriate. Here, the 'pitch' is changing. In musical transposition, each note takes the same relative place in the scale of the new key as in the old, the transposition being made to suit the particular instrument or the voice-range of the singer. In the context of legal transposition, each legal institution or rule is introduced and used in the system of the recipient, as it was in the system of the model, the transposition occurring to suit the particular socio-legal culture and needs of the recipient. Since no given model is systematically used by any recipient, there will occur a number of transpositions. Contemporary developments can be seen as instances of such transposition, both in 'ordinary' and 'extraordinary' places, 'tuning' becoming the key to success.

---

[10] For the latter series, see Watson, *supra*, note 6, p. 30, n. 53, where he also mentions 'imposed reception', 'solicited imposition', 'crypto-reception' and 'inoculation'. For a more complete list within the former series, including 'cross-pollination', 'engulfment', 'emulation', 'infiltration', 'infusion', 'digestion', 'salad-bowl' and 'melting-pot', see Esin Örücü, 'A Theoretical Framework for Transfrontier Mobility of Law', in R. Jagtenberg, *id*. and A. de Roo (eds.), *Transfrontier Mobility of Law* (The Hague: Kluwer, 1995), pp. 5–8.

[11] Monateri claims that the term 'legal transplant' as used by Watson for 'scholarly purposes' is today being taken over by 'purposive practical lawyers' involved in the project of 'exporting their own legal systems': Piergiuseppe Monateri, 'The "Weak" Law: Contaminations and Legal Cultures', in *Italian National Reports to the XVth International Congress of Comparative Law, Bristol, 1998* (Milan: Giuffrè, 1998), p. 83.

When elements from different internal logics come together,[12] the usual outcome is a mixed or mixing system. At one extreme is the situation where transposition has not worked and the official legal system has 'curdled', as is the case in Burkina Faso, a most 'extraordinary place'.[13] The other extreme is where the transmigration works very smoothly, either because of extensive similarities in structure, substance and culture and because of fine-'tuning' or a strong push from a ruling elite or the legal profession, that is, from the legal actors. Between these extremes lies a spectrum with a range of 'extraordinary places'.[14] The end-product depends on conditions such as the size of the transmigration, the characteristics of the legal movement, the success or otherwise of transpositions and 'tuning', the element of force or choice inherent in the move and the social culture of the new environment.[15] The first type of 'extraordinary place' would be one in which elements attesting to socio-cultural similarity but legal-cultural difference come together, forming a mixed jurisdiction of the 'simple' kind, the so-called 'mixing bowl', the ingredients being in the process of blending but in need of further processing if a 'purée' is desired. An example is Scotland. Next come the 'complex' mixed systems, 'extraordinary places' where the elements are both socio-culturally and legal-culturally different. This type can be called the 'Italian salad bowl', where, although the salad dressing covers the salad, it is easy to detect the individual ingredients clearly through the side of the glass bowl. Algeria would be a good example of this. Then, there is the 'English salad plate', the ingredients sitting separately and far apart on a flat plate with a blob of mayonnaise at the side into which the different pieces of the salad can be dipped before consumption. Examples could be the Sudan and Zimbabwe. This is more or less the other end of the spectrum, the examples becoming more 'extraordinary' along the path, ending in 'curdling', that is, with a dysfunctional official legal system, as already mentioned.[16] But how do we account for Turkey, an 'extraordinary place' to be considered below, which could have been an example alongside Algeria but which is, in fact, a civilian 'purée'?

---

[12] See Esin Örücü, 'An Exercise on the Internal Logic of Legal Systems', (1987) 7 Leg. Stud. 310.
[13] See generally Sally Falk Moore, *Law as Process: An Anthropological Approach* (London: Routledge & Kegan Paul: 1978); *id.*, *Social Facts and Fabrications: 'Customary' Law on Kilimanjaro, 1880–1980* (Cambridge: Cambridge University Press, 1986).
[14] See Örücü, *supra*, note 10, pp.10–12. See also *id.*, *supra*, note 9.
[15] See *id.*, *supra*, note 10, p. 9.
[16] It has been suggested to me that other categories could be developed to correspond to the 'Japanese sushi', seen as window-dressing, or a Jewish clear chicken soup with Kneidlach balls, which may float or sink depending on how they are made but never disintegrate.

I have approached these products of transmigration of law elsewhere under four headings:[17] 'the paths of migration', that is, colonization, resettlement, occupation, expansion and interrelationships; 'the method and specific techniques of migration', such as imposition, reception, imposed reception, co-ordinated parallel development, infiltration, imitation and variations and combinations of these; 'consequences' of such migration, that is, systems in transition and mixing, mixed jurisdictions, interrelated systems, evolving systems, continuous state, layered law, hyphenated legal systems, harmonization, unification and standardization; and finally, 'the conceptual and future implications of migration', such as redefinition of law, legal concepts, legal rules and legal system, clashes between culture and law (legal cultures in diversity, legal cultures in affinity), top-down and bottom-up explanation of law-making, law reform, legal systems in transition and a new approach to legal traditions or families.

Whereas the main emphasis in the past has been on historical transplants,[18] today reciprocal influence must be examined in other ways since the emphasis of transmigration of law, its consequences and the means used to achieve it have changed. The most prominent 'reciprocal influence' in Europe today is taking place within the European Union but transpositions from the western legal traditions to the eastern and central European legal systems are of equal, if not greater, importance.[19] Other cross-fertilizations are occurring elsewhere, such as that between China and Hong Kong. Thus, we witness the birth of a 'new *genre* of *mixité*',[20] more 'extraordinary places', the blurring of the demarcation lines between the generally

---

[17] See Örücü, *supra*, note 10, pp. 10–2.
[18] Competing visions of modernity are on offer for systems in 'extraordinary places'. These range from emulating the west in the construction of a modern, market-oriented society to altogether different visions. However, not all advocates of modernization see it as appropriate to rely on foreign models. For example, Kulcsar doubts the value of comparisons between societies as diverse as Ethiopia and Hungary and notes that he sees 'the most important characteristic of modernity in whether a society is capable of continuous social change by utilising its own, internal conditions': Kalman Kulcsar, *Modernisation and Law* (Budapest: Akadémiai Kiadó, 1992), p. 18.
[19] In Europe today, the primary task for comparative legal studies is in 'new *jus commune*' studies aimed at facilitating integration and making a case for the success of legal transpositions as the basis for convergence. In its relations with the extra-European scene, Europe seeks the support of comparative legal studies in exporting legal ideas and institutions to places both 'ordinary' and 'extraordinary' and aiding law reform by providing a convincing display of competing models from a pool representing western European legal systems. A further point is the competition of the United States with European systems to sell her law, specifically in central and eastern European states, in preference to any European model.
[20] See Esin Örücü, 'Mixed and Mixing Systems: A Conceptual Search', in *id*., Elspeth Attwooll and Sean Coyle (eds.), *Studies in Legal Systems: Mixed and Mixing* (London: Kluwer, 1996), p. 351.

accepted classifications of legal families and the emergence of new clashes between legal cultures themselves or legal cultures and socio-cultures. The means are apparently voluntary reception rather than colonization and imposition as in the past, though imposed receptions are more prominent in some instances.[21]

Against that background, a number of issues are being raised by scholars. The question of whether the current needs of the post-socialist economies are met by 'new legal models' is thus highlighted by Gianmaria Ajani. He stresses the fact that for importation to be successful, there must be adaptation to the conditions of the recipient countries. For example, looking at the borrowings that have taken place in the three Baltic states, he observes that in those jurisdictions a civil code is regarded as a 'symbolic document'.[22] Latvia has re-enacted a pre-socialist code. However, Lithuania has followed the Hungarian and Polish examples and, while preserving the general outline of her old code, has gradually renewed the earlier original text. Estonia, for its part, has elected to adopt a new text, largely borrowed from Germanic models.[23] Ajani shows the extensive role of comparative legal studies in the Baltic states by undertaking a 'comparative analysis of competing models'.[24] He then deals with the 1995 Russian code, 'based on the deep-lying traditions of Russia's codified civil law, which has a history of almost two centuries', an initiative which has been legitimized in the following words:

> [T]he draft of Part I [...] has absorbed, like a sponge, many new statutes of foreign legislation and progressive civil law thought. Great assistance in the recognition of the essence of these new statutes and ideas has been rendered by Dutch, Italian, American and German jurists, who have co-operated to great effect with Russian jurists engaged in the preparation of the draft civil code of Russia. [...] The ideas of our foreign colleagues that were deemed acceptable were embodied in specific articles by the Russian lawyers with the observance of all the traditions of codified Russian civil law.[25]

---

[21] In the case of central and eastern European legal systems, the term 'collective colonization by the European Union' can be used.

[22] Gianmaria Ajani, 'The Role of Comparative Law in the Adoption of New Codifications', in *Italian National Reports to the XVth International Congress of Comparative Law, Bristol, 1998* (Milan: Giuffrè, 1998), p. 70.

[23] For the influence of the Louisiana civil code, see Paul Varul and Heiki Pisuke, 'Louisiana's Contribution to the Estonian Civil Code', (1999) 73 Tulane L.R. 1027.

[24] Ajani, *supra*, note 22, p. 70.   [25] *Id.*, p. 72.

As new legal models are sought, even though they may be transitional texts and incorporate existing conditions, the old models are abandoned with 'optimistic normativism'.[26] However, 'a transplanted legal system that is not compatible with the (legal) culture in the receiving country only creates a virtual reality' and importing a western legal model does not necessarily lead to economic success.[27] In order for the transposition to work, it must be accompanied by the 'training of a new generation of judges and advocates, a reordering of the procedures and practices of the courts, the establishment of an impartial, civilian and strong police force, and a concerted effort to subject the decisions of the administration to the scrutiny of independent judges'.[28] These requirements must be seen as part of the vital 'tuning' process.

Sampling some 'extraordinary places'

On the new edge of 'Europe'

Western comparatists have failed to bring about a true understanding of the legal cultures of eastern Europe, Asia and Africa, the comparisons made tending to remain formalistic. They have taken an unreflexive, positivistic standpoint, reductionist in its operation and involving a process of uncritical description. Sociological realities have been instrumentalized by an a priori functionalist type of analysis.[29] Though a living legal culture reflects the evolution of society as effected by social interaction, reductionism loses sight of cultural diversity, distinctiveness and complexity. A new, reflexive, non-traditional approach must be adopted as a major law-reform movement is taking place in central and eastern Europe. Such an approach is particularly important in the comparison of all 'differents' and is required for comparison in all 'extraordinary places'.

---

[26] *Id.*, p. 68. See also *id.*, 'La circulation des modèles juridiques dans le droit post-socialiste', Rev. int. dr. comp., 1994, p. 1087.
[27] Jan M. Smits, 'Systems Mixing and in Transition: Import and Export of Legal Models – The Dutch Experience', in Ewoud H. Hondius (ed.), *Netherlands Reports to the Fifteenth International Congress of Comparative Law* (Antwerpen: Intersentia, 1998), p. 55. See, however, the Turkish example as developed below.
[28] Roger Scruton, 'The Reform of Law in Eastern Europe', (1991) 1 Tilburg Foreign L.R. 7, p. 8.
[29] See Bogumila Pulchalska-Tych and Michael Salter, 'Comparing Legal Cultures of East Europe: The Need for a Dialectical Analysis', (1996) 16 Leg. Stud. 157. See also Esin Örücü, *Critical Comparative Law: Considering Paradoxes for Legal Systems in Transition* (Deventer: Kluwer, 1999), pp. 118–26.

Though the central and eastern European systems are often addressed together, it is important to note a fundamental difference between the two, both as to past legal culture and socio-culture. The central European systems have fewer problems as they face western models in that they already featured considerable civilian characteristics before they were subject to massive impositions and imposed receptions from the socialist socio-cultural and legal-cultural tradition. As such, the socialist tradition was partly a derivative of the civilian tradition. The legal systems in this group can be thought of as returning to the western legal tradition. However, the western legal tradition is itself no longer solely civilian in character since within it, new encounters are taking place either directly between socialist law and common law[30] or between civil law and common law in the context of European Community law.

The eastern European group, however, is more problematic. This group includes two sub-groups, each facing different difficulties. Members of the first sub-group have had no substantial previous legal contact with the civil-law or common-law systems, which are now offered to them as competing models for law reform. As Akmal Saidov points out, in Uzbekistan, for example, the principal formal elements of Romano-Germanic law were introduced when the Russians occupied central Asia and then again during the era of Soviet law.[31] He states that it is only now that not just the form, but the content of the law actually conforms to Continental law.[32]

In this sub-group, Albania can be mentioned as an example of an 'extraordinary place'. After spending 400 years under Ottoman rule with the majority of its population being Muslim, Albania was isolated from the west. It became independent in 1912 and subsequently turned Fascist and Communist. The country's civil code of 1994 is influenced by some of the elements and structure of the old Albanian code of 1928, which was mainly based on the French model and on the 1865 Italian civil code. As regards commercial law, the Albanian code of 1992 was influenced by the French, German and Italian models. Here, the need to harmonize with European Union law may further complicate matters. The pervasive Italian influence is remarkable also through the impact of the 1989 Italian code of criminal procedure with its strong commitment to the Anglo-American accusatory

---

[30] As a result, 'trust' has entered the Russian civil code.
[31] See Akmal Saidov, 'Le droit comparé et le droit ouzbek', Rev. int. dr. comp., 1996, p. 481.
[32] Id., p. 484. We know that prior to the socialist era, Russian law was not totally civilian either.

system, which has become a 'tempting model for some post-socialist lawmakers'.[33]

A process of transposition must take place to resolve the new clashes between traditional/socialist, socialist/civilian, socialist/common law and common law/civilian combinations in this first sub-group. Systems in the second sub-group, however, are similar in many ways to the central European legal systems, which had already been in contact with the civilian tradition. This is the occasion to recall John Merryman's retrospective observations to the effect that '[s]ocialist legal principles appear [...] to have been at most a sort of temporary superstructure erected on a legal base that was largely Western in character', that 'the Western legal body appears to have rejected the socialist transplant' and that '[t]he attempt to build a socialist legal order now looks more like a temporary deviation than a new direction.'[34] This view must be seen as simplistic; it will no doubt be tested as the new borrowings and transpositions start to work. Merryman's remarks are also reductionist in so far as they cast the shadow of the 'ordinary' over the 'extraordinary' and, therefore, blur the outline. The new 'irritants' may easily stimulate the old answers. Thus, it can hardly be assumed that all countries in central and eastern Europe will shape the legal foundations for their economic systems on the European Community model.

Turkey

A fundamental mismatch between model and recipient may result in a 'mixed jurisdiction', a 'mixed legal system' or 'legal pluralism',[35] with the diverse elements coexisting in the resultant 'extraordinary' legal system. Any intermingling depends on a number of things. It may be that there is no socio-cultural diversity, but only a legal-cultural one so that in time the diverse elements will blend. It may be that one of the elements becomes the dominant one owing to political factors or, again, that, from the very beginning, one of the elements is systematically erased by authoritarian power. Turkey offers an example of such an 'extraordinary place'.

Regarded as Asian, Caucasian, Middle Eastern and European all at once and made up of many races, the Turkish population has been exposed to

---

[33] Ajani, *supra*, note 22, pp. 74–80, especially p. 74, n. 17.
[34] John H. Merryman, 'The French Deviation', (1996) 44 Am. J. Comp. L. 109, p. 109.
[35] See Örücü, *supra*, note 20, pp. 344–5.

a process of social engineering from the time of the Ottoman Empire and more extensively under the Republic. This continuous process, started in 1839 and at its strongest between 1924 and 1929, culminated in a civilian legal tradition, a modern legal framework, secularization and a blending of the incoming elements with the existing ones into a purée, erasing the indigenous where deemed necessary.[36] The present legal framework in Turkey is the product of law imported from Switzerland, Italy, France, Germany and, recently, the United States and the European Union, that is, from societies and laws socio-culturally and legally-culturally very different from her own. Turkish law has been constructed through a succession of imposed receptions, voluntary receptions, imitations and adjustments, the elements of chance, choice, historical accident and the prestige of the competing legal models all playing important roles.[37] Both the legal and the social culture are 'hyphenated'. The courts still refer to the 'source laws' as they interpret and adapt, that is, as they carry out the process of transposition and 'tuning' of the law according to local circumstances and needs.

Early reform efforts in Turkey rested solely on legal import from 'ordinary' jurisdictions as the country went through a major process of total modernization, westernization, secularization, democratization and constitutionalization while it reshaped its private, administrative, constitutional, criminal, civil, commercial and maritime law and procedure. This wholesale reform of the legal system was accompanied and complemented by the adoption of a series of social laws aimed at changing the people's ways. The overriding force and desire of the elite to eliminate custom combined with the establishment of a legal system based on legislation to make history irrelevant to law. As we assess the diverse elements of the legal 'compound', let us do so against the vision that binds the Turkish Republic together.

A good starting-point is to recall that the law in force at any given time is the outcome of a complex competitive relationship between various sources of influence. Since the Turkish legislature is intent on keeping control over both the legal and the social fabric, the courts by and large address the

---

[36] For an analysis of the Turkish experience, see generally Esin Örücü, 'The Impact of European Law on the Ottoman Empire and Turkey', in Wolfgang J. Mommsen and Jan A. de Moor (eds.), *European Expansion and Law* (Oxford: Berg, 1992), pp. 39–58; *id.*, 'Turkey: Change Under Pressure', in *id.*, Attwooll and Coyle, *supra*, note 20, pp. 89–111; *id.*, *supra*, note 29, pp. 80–118; *id.*, *supra*, note 10, pp. 13–14.

[37] It must be noted here that choosing a number of different models gave the reception 'cultural legitimacy' as the legal system was not seen to be beholden to any one dominant model, though it clearly owed an overall debt to 'western culture'.

wording and the spirit of the formal system. Yet, they cater to diverse interests that present themselves through the cases reaching them. But do the various systems at work in Turkey successfully interlock? An illustration will show that the important role of the civil, administrative and constitutional high courts, serving as 'melting-pots' in the processes of transposition, adjustment and 'tuning', cannot be overemphasized. Thus, the *Yargitay*, the High Court of Appeal, is extremely cautious in the application of section 134 of the civil code as amended in 1988, introducing divorce by mutual consent. The court believes that divorces apparently based upon mutual consent may, in fact, not be so based. Women, who are socially the weaker partners in Turkish marriages, may be forced by their husbands to accept divorce. According to the court, the conditions of section 134 must, therefore, be strictly met: the marriage must have lasted for at least a year; the judge must himself hear both parties separately and be convinced that each is expressing his/her will freely; and the court must endorse the arrangements made by the parties as regards the financial consequences of the divorce and the care of the children. As a result, the High Court does not recognize a divorce decree obtained abroad if the foreign judge has not ensured that these various conditions are met. Here, we see the court holding on to the legal framework and, at the same time, acting as the protector of women and children by taking into consideration the realities of Turkish society. Thus, the 'layered law' is transformed into a 'hyphenated law' through the efforts of judges, the 'legal navigators', with a view to smoothing out differences and welding the various layers together. The behaviour of each layer, as it interacts with the one that precedes or follows it, is the law.[38]

From its inception, the Turkish legal system has mixed with, and at the same time has tried to transform, indigenous legal, social, political, ideological, religious and economic systems. Thus, Turkish law is not internally homogeneous and its roots lie wide, whether at home or abroad. Nor is the interlocking of her systems complete. Whether this will ever be so remains open to question.

In time, the top-down model became linked to the Turkish reality, which is that of an economically, culturally and socially divergent people. With the hyphenated nature of her systems and peoples, Turkey lives in a 'limping marriage' with the 'ordinary' and with the 'cluster of the ordinary' that is

---

[38] See Elisabetta Grande, 'Preface', in *id.* (ed.), *Transplants Innovation and Legal Tradition in the Horn of Africa* (Trento: L'Harmattan, 1995), p. 14.

represented by the European Union. In other words, the formal legal system performs a balancing act: Turkey can mirror the 'ordinary' at certain levels without ever losing the character of being 'other'. The predominant layer within the Turkish legal system is, clearly, the 'modern' one, which reflects the 'hyphenated' nature of the law and the systems. However, the interaction between the modern layer and the underlying traditional and religious layers is of the utmost importance. The received legal institutions have not been profoundly transformed upon transfer and the hidden pluralism is enveloped within the monolithic legal system. This system reflects various legal cultures tied to each other, blending their socio-cultures with the local socio-culture, living in a world where each is the environment of the other. A most remarkable case can serve as an example of the interlocking of the social, religious and formal legal cultures.

This is a decision of the *Yargitay* reached in 1979. The case concerned the sexual involvement of an under-age village boy with a neighbour's cow. The owner of the cow, rather than suing for bestiality under the criminal code, claimed damages from the father of the boy. He argued that his cow could not be sold or its meat and milk consumed, since, according to religious sources which he cited, it had become untouchable. The case was dismissed by the lower court for lack of legal grounds as Islamic law is not a recognized source of Turkish law. The owner appealed. The *Yargitay* overturned the decision of the lower court, saying that, although religious rules could not form the basis of any claim, if the complainant could prove by means of expert evidence that there were local religious or moral beliefs or customs to the effect that the meat and the milk of such an animal could not be consumed, then the animal would be considered to have lost its market value, in which case, through application of the 'noxal' rule of Roman law, the cow should be given to the father of the boy and the claimant should be given the market value of the cow by the father.[39] The formula is a fine

---

[39] 79/1644; 79/14383; 21.12.1979. In a more recent case where the lower court decided that the claimant had no legal claim as there was no 'medical objection' to the utilization of the meat and the milk of an animal, the *Yargitay* overturned the decision declaring that when there is no codal provision applicable to a given matter, then, according to section 1 of the civil code, tradition and custom are to be resorted to. According to the court, 'since facts are not in dispute in this case, tradition and custom have to be investigated in line with the claim, and if custom, tradition, religious and moral beliefs and conceptions are in line with the claim, then the existence of damages cannot be questioned. The claimant should be asked whether he wishes to surrender the animal to the defendant in return for the market price, and if not, then reasonable compensation must be decided upon. This is a case of economic loss': 98/2632; 98/3249; 24.3.1998; 24 *YKD*, 1998, p. 834 [my translation].

example of how the *Yargitay* avoids openly facing religious issues and resolves disputes within the formal legal system. The case shows how the 'layers' of systems may interlock.

If 'unity in diversity' is to be the norm, then 'hyphenated' systems have a special place. Here, we have many peoples with diverse backgrounds and, therefore, diverse socio-cultures, but one legal system and seemingly one official socio-culture. In such an 'extraordinary place', the layers can easily become unlocked and isolated, and progressively more self-referential, unless finely 'tuned'. This kind of an 'extraordinary place' is truly 'extraordinary' in all the senses referred to above.

Hong Kong

Hong Kong, another 'extraordinary place', a system in transition *par excellence*, a dependency of the United Kingdom from 1843 until 1997, and now an administrative region of China, is today experiencing another 'extraordinary' phenomenon: 'one country, two systems'. A legal system regarded as part of the common-law tradition, though a mixture of sorts with the traditional and cultural values of a Chinese population, now lives within the parent system of China, which itself has a civilian legal framework but a socialist ideology and institutions reflecting both that ideology and Chinese socio-culture.

Common law was the overlay of the Hong Kong legal system as the imposed element. Today, it is one of the underlays while the other underlay, the Hong Kong Chinese local custom, is rapidly gaining strength in this new environment. The overlay is now the legal system of mainland China. Whether Hong Kong remains a common-law enclave is doubtful in spite of the notion of 'one country, two systems' being seemingly officially guaranteed. What is certain, however, is that it will always continue as an 'extraordinary place' with a 'Hong Kong-style' common law, a 'locally seasoned common law' developing its 'localism' further than it did under the dominance of the British legal system and precedents.[40]

Common law, of course, is the overlay in many other mixed legal systems, usually those living within a common-law environment and nurturing their civil-law tradition. In Hong Kong, however, the situation is reversed and

---

[40] See Chenguang Wang and Guobin Zhu, 'A Tale of Two Legal Systems: The Interaction of Common Law and Civil Law in Hong Kong', Rev. int. dr. comp., 1999, p. 917. The authors also compare with, and highlight the differences from, Louisiana and Quebec: see *id.*, pp. 920–1.

more complicated in that the new parent system, China, is not 'ordinary' either. The common-law system can hardly be regarded as being well established and ingrained in the local community and serving as the foundation of a society where a large percentage of the population does not even speak the original language of the common law.[41] Because the Chinese legal system is not in a position to replace it, the reciprocal influence is bound to be strong. Transposition and 'tuning' will have to be delicate if traditions, cultures and laws are to be integrated. 'Unity in diversity' must be the slogan for success and a layered law may well prove to be the outcome in this most 'extraordinary place'.[42]

Shared elements

Although 'practical utility is the basis for much of a reception of law',[43] in 'extraordinary places' the element of 'chance' has often been even more important – and chance is something that can hardly be predicted.[44] In today's transpositions, however, the element of 'chance' has been largely superseded by that of 'prestige' and the respective 'power profiles' of competing legal systems as well as 'economic efficiency'. The crucial part played by elites and 'intellectuals' is another element to be stressed. Piergiuseppe Monateri thus talks of competing elites in search of legitimation.[45] The text legitimating the 1995 Russian civil code is pertinent in this context.[46] In addition, the Turkish case already discussed provides an example of the far-reaching role that an elite can play in the reshaping of a people.[47]

The element of 'choice', however, often seems to be lacking and is more problematic. For example, at the time of the breakdown of the socialist

---

[41] See Derry Wong, 'Language Discrimination and the Hong Kong Jury', (1995) 1 J. Chinese & Comp. L. 153. See also D. W. Ling, 'Confucianism and English Common Law: A Chinese Lawyer's Observations', (1995) 1 J. Chinese & Comp. L. 72.

[42] I have written elsewhere that 'common law is now surrounded by Chinese law, a variation on the civilian tradition, in structures if not in content, and will be sandwiched between the traditional first bottom layer and a Chinese/civilian third top layer': Örücü, *supra*, note 29, p. 36. Wang and Zhu predict that 'separation with unity' will be the future of Hong Kong: *supra*, note 40, pp. 922–3.

[43] Alan Watson, 'Aspects of Reception of Law', (1996) 44 Am. J. Comp. L. 335, p. 335.

[44] For example, 'a particular book may be present in a particular library at a particular time; or it may not': *id.*, p. 339.

[45] See Gianmaria Ajani, 'By Chance and Prestige: Legal Transplants in Russia and Eastern Europe', (1995) 43 Am. J. Comp. L. 93. See also Ugo Mattei, 'Why the Wind Changed: Intellectual Leadership in Western Law', (1994) 42 Am. J. Comp. L. 195.

[46] *Supra*, at text accompanying note 25.   [47] *Supra*, at text accompanying note 39.

systems more than a decade ago, a clear choice was made to move outside the existing legal tradition. Thereafter, 'choice' was replaced by 'necessity'. The new desire and vision preclude real choice now. That is why the term 'imposed reception' is more appropriate in depicting what is taking place. Nonetheless, there is an element of limited choice as to which sub-models to follow or imitate. Here, the influence of foreign models is a diffuse one, since there is foreign suggestion but national choice. Imports have only persuasive authority and no single legal model has been imported wholesale. Economic factors play a predominant part, although western fundamentalism as to democracy, the rule of law and human rights gives an added impetus to the western export. In Turkey, the choice is that of the elite. In Hong Kong, there has never been choice.

Ugo Mattei points to 'prestige' as the paramount element in the search for 'economic efficiency',[48] which encourages choice from a pool of models emanating from competing legal systems and may ultimately necessitate convergence. Gianmaria Ajani, discussing the role of 'prestige' and 'political opportunity', specifically comments on commercial law and says that most commercial legislation in central and eastern Europe shows the influence of German law, the choice being 'driven by the prestige of the model'.[49] Although Rodolfo Sacco also accepts that one of the fundamental causes of imitation is 'prestige' – 'usually, reception takes place because of the desire to appropriate the work of others [which] arises because this work has a quality one can only describe as "prestige"'[50] – he states that comparative law has no definition of 'prestige'. Monateri, however, is scathing about the whole idea. He observes that all depends on a prestigious *presentation* of the model 'sometimes with reference to "efficiency" as a magic key-word in the rhetoric of borrowing elites'.[51] It must be remembered, of course, that the most 'efficient' model may not be the most 'prestigious' one.

The incoming tide consists of legal culture, legal structure and legal substance. Structure and substance can be transposed with less difficulty than legal culture, itself part of socio-culture. Both the transpositions themselves and the distortions which may appear during the fitting to the existing traditions will certainly have a serious effect on how the structure and substance

---

[48] Ugo Mattei, 'Efficiency in Legal Transplants: An Essay in Comparative Law and Economics', (1994) 14 Int. R. L. & Econ. 3, pp. 6–8. Economic efficiency may be understood in the sense of 'practical utility'.
[49] Ajani, *supra*, note 22, p. 80.   [50] Sacco, *supra*, note 5, pp. 398–400.
[51] Monateri, *supra*, note 11, p. 95.

operate. What the transposed 'irritants' produce by way of 'antibodies' and the general health of the 'extraordinary' systems in transition can be assessed only in the future. The difficulties do not lie in the transposition of techniques and forms but in the values and contents which in turn 'contaminate' the forms in practice. However, the use of the concept 'import and export of legal rules' suggests their 'commodification'.[52] This may be especially so in relation to former socialist countries and to Turkey, where legal rules are regarded as 'commodities' not tied to legal history or to legal culture. All our 'extraordinary places' suffer from problems of mismatch of culture, structure and substance in their own ways.

When we survey the present experience of systems in transition and in 'extraordinary places' as to form and content, we observe that the experience as to form indicates that the technique employed, predominantly codification, is national in most cases and not imported, since most of the legal systems had already codified their laws. This is obvious for members of the socialist tradition. Their codes were, however, mostly based on foreign models, that is, on the classical Continental models. Later, codification became a landmark of the socialist tradition also. Nevertheless, in most cases, the new codifications signify a break with the immediate past and there is, therefore, urgency in the production of these codes. Additional problems are expected in Hong Kong because of the marriage between common-law and civil-law/socialist-law techniques,[53] but no further difficulties will arise in Turkey in this respect.

The experience as to content in central and eastern Europe shows that law is eclectic, though predominantly civilian, most provisions being meant to facilitate a free-market economy. There is also some US input as to content if not as to form. For example, in Russia Continental and Anglo-American experts work together to help in the preparation and in the installation of a model fashioned to fit the needs of the Russian socio-culture. Legal advice is provided, not just in the abstract, but also in a practical way during the drafting process.[54] The new models are not only the classic ones, but feature those of the European Union, uniform laws, international conventions, the Anglo-American experience and newly modernized frameworks, such as those of the Netherlands and Quebec. The outcome of the Hong Kong experience in this respect remains to be seen.

---

[52] *Id.*, pp. 84–5.
[53] For these worries, see Wang and Zhu, *supra*, note 40, pp. 933–44; Ling, *supra*, note 41, pp. 85–90.
[54] See Smits, *supra*, note 27, p. 64.

Models and mismatch in 'extraordinary places'

Many systems in 'extraordinary places' look toward systems that are socio-culturally or in a legal-cultural way very different from their own. Differences in legal cultures can be as to sources of law, methods of legal reasoning or legal institutions. The more fundamental differences underlying these are those related to socio-cultures and values. There is never a perfect match between model and recipient. Though Watson claims that legal rules can be equally at home in many places and that 'whatever their historical origins may have been, rules of private law can survive without any close connection to any particular people, any particular period of time or any particular place',[55] one must doubt whether this is correct. Such models cannot work unless they are delicately transposed and 'tuned'.

Ian Ward asks: 'Are we identifying difference, and cherishing it, or are we trying to suppress it, by effective sameness?'[56] He suggests that the 'sameness and difference debate' dominates most of 'theoretical comparativism'. It is true that the last thing needed is 'distinctiveness for its own sake'[57] and that comparative legal studies is used today mainly as an instrument of integration. However, this must not be allowed to challenge the virtues of 'distinction' or 'diversity', which are the significant features within 'extraordinary places'. Have divergences been overstated in the past and are similarities being overstated today?[58] Can it be said that showing the similarity between some selected single rules even in their detail, whether as to substance or function, is enough to negate the 'difference approach' and confirm the 'convergence approach'?[59] Or should the function of comparative legal studies,

---

[55] Alan Watson, 'Legal Transplants and Law Reform', (1976) 92 L.Q.R. 79, p. 81. For an analysis of Watson's work, see William Ewald, 'Comparative Jurisprudence (II): The Logic of Legal Transplants', (1995) 43 Am. J. Comp. L. 489.

[56] Ian Ward, 'The Limits of Comparativism: Lessons from UK–EC Integration', (1995) 2 Maastricht J. Eur. & Comp. L. 23, p. 31.

[57] Eric M. Clive, 'Scottish Family Law', in John P. Grant (ed.), *Independence and Devolution: The Legal Implications for Scotland* (Edinburgh: Green, 1976), p. 173.

[58] See Luigi Moccia, 'Historical Overview on the Origins and Attitudes of Comparative Law', in Bruno De Witte and Caroline Forder (eds.), *The Common Law of Europe and the Future of Legal Education* (Deventer: Kluwer, 1992), p. 619. See also Rudolf B. Schlesinger, 'The Past and Future of Comparative Law', (1995) 43 Am. J. Comp. L. 477, p. 477, who talks of periods of 'contractive' or 'contrastive' comparison, with the emphasis on differences, alternating with periods of 'integrative' comparison, with the main accent being on similarities. He concludes that the future belongs to 'integrative comparative law'.

[59] See Peter-Christian Müller-Graff, 'Common Private Law in the European Community', in De Witte and Forder, *supra*, note 58, p. 251. See also the editorial by Bruno De Witte, 'The Convergence Debate', (1996) 3 Maastricht J. Eur. & Comp. L. 105.

whatever the findings, be the building of bridges, with the acceptance that legal systems and cultural systems can 'live apart together'?[60] Comparative legal studies in 'extraordinary places' does indeed perform a 'bridging' role and eases the mismatch by helping transpositions to take place. There are serious bridging problems, however, when legal systems from diverse traditions such as the socialist, religious or traditional ones, look toward civilian or common-law systems.[61] This must be of particular concern for legal systems which have never been fully part of a single legal tradition. Consider, for example, the US Uniform Commercial Code in Uzbekistan or the German code of bankruptcy in the Kyrgyz Republic. Such issues are of particular importance for legal and social systems in 'extraordinary places', which have always been at the receiving end of movements from civil-law and common-law jurisdictions, that is, 'ordinary' models.

How is the obstacle of *mentalité* to be bridged? Within Europe, this hurdle has to do with the structure of what is accepted and the technique of how it is accepted, rather than with the principle of the acceptance of a given rule or solution about which there is little room for negotiation, such as putting into effect a European Union directive. So, the real question is not about refusing the medicine,[62] but how to take it. Should it be chewed or swallowed whole, with or without water, in a thimble or a cup?

Models from 'ordinary places' are competing to sell their export to 'extraordinary places'. We know, for example, that the new Dutch civil code has won the competition as a favoured model in the preparation of the Russian civil code and that the systems of the United States, the European Union and the individual Member States of the Union are competing in line with their 'power profile' and with reference to their previous contacts

---

[60] Müller-Graff, *supra*, note 59, p. 254.

[61] Even systems from the same legal tradition have problems when borrowing from each other. The British courts, for example, tend to consider other common-law jurisdictions where socio-cultural and legal-cultural affinity is deemed to exist. But, occasionally, one comes across cases where New Zealand or Australia are found to be too progressive or to rely on other philosophical and social premises. For such cases, see Esin Örücü, 'The United Kingdom as an Importer and Exporter of Legal Models in the Context of Reciprocal Influences and Evolving Legal Systems', in John Bridge (ed.), *UK Law for the Millennium*, 2d ed. (London: U.K.N.C.C.L., 2000), pp. 206–47.

[62] See Konrad Zweigert and Hein Kötz, *An Introduction to Comparative Law*, 3d ed. transl. by Tony Weir (Oxford: Oxford University Press, 1998), p. 17, for Jhering's famous words: 'The reception of foreign legal institutions is not a matter of nationality, but of usefulness and need. No one bothers to fetch a thing from afar when he has one as good or better at home, but only a fool would refuse quinine just because it didn't grow in his back garden.'

with the systems in central and eastern Europe now in transition. Maybe Dutch law appears as particularly well equipped to fulfil its exporting task because in the past the Netherlands was itself an importing country and the new Dutch civil code of 1992 is influenced by German, French and English law and proves to be the outcome of thorough comparative studies.[63] It is claimed that these factors are part of its attraction as an ideal model and as a source of inspiration.[64] As a consequence, Dutch legal advice is playing a more important role than that given by US, German and Italian experts.[65] Dutch experts participate in the drafting of model civil codes, criminal codes and codes of criminal procedure in Russia, Belarus, Kadzakistan, the Kyrgyz Republic, Ukraine, Mongolia, Georgia, Armenia, Moldova, Azerbaijan and Uzbekistan. For example, in Armenia, another 'extraordinary place', Dutch, US and Armenian experts were all involved in the drafting of the new penal code and of the code of criminal procedure in co-operation with the Council of Europe.[66]

Assessment

Legal systems in 'ordinary places' are today competing to become the ones selected for foreign import to 'extraordinary places', even as they themselves try to modernize. In central and eastern Europe, in Asia and Africa, the process of import can create acute problems. For example, how will the Dutch model fare in Russia? Can it be that a jurisdiction that is itself 'extraordinary' would constitute a better model and would be more acceptable to recipients in 'extraordinary places'?

A degree of mismatch is inevitable as there can never be a tailor-made model. The major question remains: how do we address this mismatch? Can it be dealt with through the imagination and creativity of the recipient upon reception, that is, through the 'tuning' process? What is the measure of success? These are questions still seeking satisfactory answers.

The legal systems in 'extraordinary places' can be regarded as 'layered systems', 'hyphenated systems', 'limping marriages' or simply 'mixed systems',

---

[63] See Smits, *supra*, note 27, p. 63.
[64] *Id.*, pp. 47, 51 and 63. It is of interest to note that the various central and eastern European law-reform projects rely on a consultation process involving close co-operation with the Rule of Law Consortium established by two major US commercial consultancy firms.
[65] *Id.*, p. 63.
[66] *Id.*, p. 57. The Dutch Ministry of Justice also funded drafting consultancies to modernize Polish legislation.

depending on the pervasiveness of the seepage and the degree of resolution of internal contradictions between layers of law and culture.[67] Successful transposition and fruitful cross-fertilization do not require similarity, and even the misunderstood has been successfully transposed. However, though differences between national rules do not seem to prevent their importation, legal-cultural and socio-cultural differences often affect their internalization and efficacy.[68] When two different interpretive communities come together, how can they tap into each other and mesh, bringing about successful 'cultural conversation'? Only transposition and 'tuning' at the time of transplant can realize a 'fit'.

Many legal systems, both in 'ordinary' and 'extraordinary' places, are in transition, albeit to differing extents. Most are, and will continue to be, looking into the reshaping of their social as well as of their legal framework. Comparative legal studies will be asked to help and even to provide answers. Increasingly, comparatists will concentrate on the way in which legal institutions are connected, disconnected and transposed and will extend their subject beyond the traditional and 'ordinary' borders, both geographic and substantive, well into the 'extraordinary'.[69] Comparative legal studies must, therefore, be fully involved in all discussions of the redefinition of law, legal concepts, legal rules and legal system; clashes between culture and law; top-down and bottom-up explanation of law-making; law reform; new definitions of modernization or modernity; legal systems in transition and legal pluralism; and deregulation of legal families. Moreover, comparative research must make it possible to surmount the problems created by diversity and affinity.

---

[67] As pointed out by Großfeld, as soon as we leave the European region for Africa or Asia, a whole Pandora's box of problems opens up. See Bernhard Großfeld, *The Strength and Weakness of Comparative Law*, transl. by Tony Weir (Oxford: Oxford University Press, 1990), p. 47. For an insightful contribution to comparative-law scholarship in this regard, see Werner F. Menski, *Comparative Law in a Global Context: The Legal Systems of Asia and Africa* (London: Platinium, 2000), pp. 1–49 and 533–52.

[68] *Cf.* Volkmar Gessner, 'Global Legal Interaction and Legal Cultures', (1994) 7 Ratio Juris 132, who says that the argument for universal harmonization is completely detached from the cultural dimension of law – a major problem for European integration.

[69] Thus, Mattei claims that '[c]omparative law has matured from the *common core* approach to *legal transplants*, from *legal formants* to the idea of legal traditions as a phenomenon of *path dependency*, and on to the notion of the *mute* dimension of the law': Ugo Mattei, 'An Opportunity Not to Be Missed: The Future of Comparative Law in the United States', (1998) 46 Am. J. Comp. L. 709, p. 715 [emphasis original]. See also Anthony Ogus, 'Competition Between National Legal Systems: A Contribution of Economic Analysis to Comparative Law', (1999) 48 Int. & Comp. L.Q. 405, pp. 405–6 and 418.

Systems in transition and in 'extraordinary places', looking at the pool of competing models available in western Europe, America and the Far East with the purpose of redesigning and modernizing their legal, economic and social systems, will be involved in more import as the 'ordinary' models compete to sell their legal products, each one packaging its own model as the most efficient, the one to be preferred to others, with the aim of putting a foot in the door of the economic markets in 'extraordinary places'. The time is one of imposed reception, that is, a voluntary activity of import under circumstances where exporters hold the trump cards. While this activity accelerates, will systems in 'extraordinary places' become the 'ordinary' systems of the future? Will there be increased harmony or discord? Will there be harmony falling short of integration?

Clearly, the future lies in 'diversity' and in 'unity in diversity' rather than in 'unity through uniformity and standardization'. As 'ordinary' places cease to be the main focus of attention, the new *genre* of '*mixité*' in 'extraordinary places' will remain a major concern of comparatists. It is in 'extraordinary places' that the comparatist can best observe, analyse and understand the interaction between legal cultures and socio-cultures and that he can best appreciate the value of 'tuning' in transpositions. Yet, paradoxically, it is in 'extraordinary places' that the comparatist of today is least equipped to work.

Conclusion

14

Beyond compare

LAWRENCE ROSEN

Although a great deal has changed in the years since the 1900 Paris Congress, a significant number of issues have remained constant for students of comparative law. When our predecessors convened at the turn of the last century, they were very much in the throes of a kind of scientism that coloured what they foresaw for their subject of study and, indeed, for the future of law itself. Their evolutionary orientation, their assumption that legal systems would become more universally alike, their continuing belief in the science of law as both a method for unbiased analysis and the discovery of the classifiable nature of all legal systems may seem both naive and self-deceptive from our current stance. But it says much about the difficulties that will have to be faced by future contributors that a good deal of comparative law still remains bound to the programmes and assumptions of that earlier era. By beginning with some of the laments – and some of the grounds for lamentation – my intention is not to be gratuitously insulting. Rather, I think it important to underscore that, as heirs to certain issues and approaches, comparatists have not entirely shaken free from some of their less defensible earlier positions.

There are, for example, the continuing complaints about the state of the art – 'scholars crocheting with rules'[1] – and the articulation of remarkably imprecise and old-fashioned legal taxonomies, ranging from indefensible categories like 'traditional' law, unexamined ones like 'religious' law and simply resigned ones like my own favourite, 'other' conceptions of law.[2]

---

[1] The words are John H. Merryman's. See Pierre Legrand, 'John Henry Merryman and Comparative Legal Studies: A Dialogue', (1999) 47 Am. J. Comp. L. 3, p. 62.

[2] On the former two, see Ugo Mattei, 'Three Patterns of Law: Taxonomy and Change in the World's Legal Systems', (1997) 45 Am. J. Comp. L. 5. The latter category is found in René David, *Les grands systèmes de droit contemporains*, 11th ed. by Camille Jauffret-Spinosi (Paris: Dalloz, 2002), no. 16, p. 16 and no. 21, pp. 20–1. It has also been suggested that a new category, 'African' law, is emerging. There is even a particularly strange reference in these discussions to 'the

There is even the view of those who, continuing to see the differences between the British and the Continentals as a matter of geography, can unabashedly state: 'Convinced, *perhaps from living by the sea*, that life will controvert the best-laid plans, the Englishman is more at home with case-law proceeding cautiously step-by-step than with legislation that purports to lay down rules for the solution of all future cases.'[3] (This latter is particularly distressing since I had thought that if comparative studies had demonstrated anything it was that the perverse attachment by the British to the common law was, in fact, due to a surfeit of marmite at a formative stage of youth, combined with the restricted blood flow to the brain that comes from wearing rubber wellies and fingerless gloves!)

In these, and in so many less risible examples, as often as not, comparative law appears not to have been about comparative law at all, but about something else. Certainly, one can point to its uses over several centuries to further one or another political agenda. At various times, comparative law has (as in the case of Montesquieu's *De l'esprit des lois*) served as a veiled critique of the existing political order, as a vehicle for the extension of colonial powers, or even (as in the case of Wigmore) as a way of demonstrating that academic lawyers were true cosmopolitans whose discipline deserved appropriate respect in university hierarchies. At other moments, comparison has promoted the rules of doing business in forms most favourable to those used to practising by them (from the promulgation of commercial codes in the colonies to the 'New World Order' of George Bush and James

---

Arabian countries', whatever that is supposed to include. See Konrad Zweigert and Hein Kötz, *An Introduction to Comparative Law*, 3d ed. transl. by Tony Weir (Oxford: Oxford University Press, 1998), pp. 65–6. Analogous complaints regarding questionable categories have been made about the field of international law. For example, see David J. Bederman, 'I Hate International Law Scholarship', (2000) 1 Chicago J. Int. L. 75.

[3] Zweigert and Kötz, *supra*, note 2, p. 70 [my emphasis]. The authors must have thought they mollified their tone from the second edition of their book where they said: 'Convinced, perhaps from living by the sea, that life will controvert the best-laid plans, the Englishman is content with case-law as opposed to enactments': *id.*, *An Introduction to Comparative Law*, 2d ed. transl. by Tony Weir (Oxford: Oxford University Press, 1987), p. 71. The quoted passage in the third edition is preceded by these sentences: 'On the Continent lawyers operate with ideas, which often, dangerously enough, take on a life of their own; in England they think in pictures [...]. If we may generalize, the European is given to making plans, to regulating things in advance, and therefore, in terms of law, to drawing up rules and systematizing them. He approaches life with fixed ideas, and operates deductively. The Englishman improvises, never making a decision until he has to: "we'll cross that bridge when we come to it". As Maitland said, he is an empiricist. Only experience counts for him; theorizing has little appeal; and so he is not given to abstract rules of law': *id.*, *supra*, note 2, pp. 69–70.

Baker) or simply as a way of marketing a western product (in this case, the expertise that goes with western legal forms) to developing countries of eastern Europe and the Third World. It may also be that the old debate about whether one should stress differences or similarities when drawing comparisons may take on new political implications: to stress difference may be to validate the empowerment of weak ethnic or social groups, whereas stressing similarity may serve to move us toward pan-national relationships and avoidance of what are taken to be the inevitable evils of ardent nationalism. Comparative law may, of course, also serve as justification for the superiority of one's own approach to matters both organizational and cultural, as proof that one's nation is becoming 'modern', as the perpetuation of the role of law professors or law schools in their respective educational and social structures and as support for claims, sometimes put forth with breathtaking simplification, that since the descent to decadent relativism passes through the misguided ministrations of comparatists, one should avoid comparison altogether and instead redirect attention back to the secure ground of 'natural law'.[4]

Whatever the respective merits of these approaches, it is vital to understand both the value that inheres in some of the negative implications of comparative legal studies and the reasons why what may seem negative actually connects with so much that is positive. Fortunately, in this regard, comparative law is itself often more interesting than some of the things that have been said under that rubric. Someone once introduced the great student of Jewish mysticism, Gershom Scholem, by saying that what he studies is nonsense, but the way he studies it – 'ah, that', said the speaker, 'that is scholarship'! For comparatists, it has sometimes been the opposite: in a sort of reverse alchemy they have managed to turn gold into lead, the subject being far more interesting than some of the things done with it. And yet we have to notice the accomplishments which, I do want to emphasize, are often positive precisely for being negative. It has proven crucial, for example, to show that grand theories are often overblown – and it is comparative law that has often demonstrated exactly why this is so; it is vital to see that it is precisely the range of variation, rather than the purity of type, that is at the heart of the nexus of law and history; it is of inestimable value constantly to demonstrate that it is neither an intrinsic flaw in a field of study nor a

---

[4] The latter argument is exemplified by Heidi Margaret Hurd, 'Relativistic Jurisprudence: Skepticism Founded on Confusion', (1988) 61 Southern California L.R. 1417.

hindrance to the refinement of more informed understanding to appreciate that in legal studies (as in science and the humanities) the search for better criteria of analysis is not inherently antithetical to the involvement of one's own orientations and judgement. Indeed, to see more specifically what I mean by the positive aspects of our negative contributions and what, I would like to suggest, may be some of the directions comparatists might choose to pursue before the next of these centenary occasions, let me begin by taking us right back to the basics and ask quite simply what it is that comparison does for us.

In an oft-quoted passage, Clifford Geertz writes: 'Santayana's famous dictum that one compares only when one is unable to get to the heart of the matter seems to me [...] the precise reverse of the truth; it is through comparison, and of incomparables, that whatever heart we can actually get to is to be reached.'[5] This is so, I think, because what we need to understand are the premises, the implications, the ways of making sense of actions and orientations within a given culture and its law. Now, that can very easily be obscured when we fall into the trap of thinking that the way we have come to view the connections among various aspects of a culture are the ways those connections 'naturally' tend to take shape. Much depends, of course, on the assumptions and position from which one starts the comparison. It is easy to get into a situation like that of the Texan who boasted to one of his new ranch-hands: 'You can drive my car all day long and still be on my land.' 'Yeah', responded the worker, 'I had a car like that myself once'! In the case of law, it is not only that the prospect of making category mistakes may be alleviated by comparison but that – and this is the point I want most to emphasize – otherwise unforeseen connections (and, indeed, unforeseen consequences) may also be missed. I will comment on some of the positively negative aspects of broad theories in a moment but let me elaborate this first point with just a few examples concerning the relation of law and colonialism, the relation of culture to legal reasoning, the role of functionalism, the formation of legal classifications and the elaboration of a unified set of human rights.

As our studies of colonialism have grown more sophisticated, we have begun to see some connections between the law of the colonizer and that of the colonized that had not previously been so apparent. The assumption long held sway, for example, that the law of each colonizing power was itself

---

[5] Clifford Geertz, *Local Knowledge* (New York: Basic Books, 1983), p. 233.

a unity, that it was essentially homogeneous and that when it came into contact with the law of the colonized, its diverse effects were a function of a one-to-one reaction. We had long since recognized the enormous amount of reciprocity that occurs in law, as in other domains, when cultures come in contact, as in the Crusaders absorbing elements of Islamic law or the Romans incorporating aspects of Greek practice. But we can now see – thanks to our studies of legal jurisdiction and local variation – that quite often the law of the colonist was itself quite heterogeneous, that even though there may have been institutional continuity it did not necessarily mean that there was concomitant cultural continuity. The availability to affected peoples of diverse ways of using the multiple jurisdictions and principles of colonial law may actually have contributed to (rather than undermined) interregional order. Indeed, it may even be that, in their early stages, colonial powers were less like states monopolizing legal control than contributors to the *multiplication* of culturally and religiously based local communities.[6] Looked at comparatively, we can not only add to our appreciation that (as, for example, in India) colonial powers sometimes reified religious laws by their own codifications but begin to appreciate that local groups were very creative in exploiting the heterogeneous elements of the colonizers' own law in ways that reinforced local diversity which, in turn, often survived through to independence to become a force to be reckoned with by the new nation.[7] Having come at matters through comparative law, rather than just

---

[6] See Lauren Benton, *Law and Colonial Cultures: Legal Regimes in World History, 1400–1900* (Cambridge: Cambridge University Press, 2002), pp. 31–126. In her conclusion, Benton argues: 'Colonial states did not in an important sense exist *as* states in the early centuries of colonialism. They did not claim or produce a monopoly on legal authority or on the assignment of political and legal identity. Indeed, colonial conditions often intensified the fluidity of the legal order and enhanced the strategic importance of personal law by multiplying claims made by, and on behalf of, cultural and religious communities to their own legal authorities. There was dominance, undeniably, but both colonizing factions and colonized groups were not irrational or deluded when they sought advantage in the fractured qualities of rule': *supra*, p. 259 [emphasis original]. See also *id.*, 'Colonial Law and Cultural Difference: Jurisdictional Politics and the Formation of the Colonial State', (1999) 41 Comp. Stud. Soc. & Hist. 563. For examples of very creative adaptations by local groups to colonial law, see Maria Teresa Sierra, 'Indian Rights and Customary Law in Mexico: A Study of the Nahuas in the Sierra de Puebla', (1995) 29 L. & Society R. 227; Marc Galanter, *Law and Society in Modern India* (Delhi: Oxford University Press, 1989), pp. 33 and 49.

[7] Much the same applies to instances in which local customary practice has been stimulated, rather than repressed, by the lingering implications of colonialism. For example, see Hillel Frisch, 'Modern Absolutist or Neopatriarchal State Building? Customary Law, Extended Families, and the Palestinian Authority', (1997) 29 Int. J. Middle East Stud. 341 ; William L. Rodman, ' "A Law Unto Themselves": Legal Innovation in Ambae, Vanuatu', (1985) 12 Am. Ethnologist 603. See

political history, these forces now play a much more central part in our overall assessment of the course and effects of colonialism generally.

Similarly, we can grasp that in the course of political change – and perhaps especially in the elaboration of democratic forms – groups are forged *through* the political process and not just as a result of it. Here again looking at law brings these features to the fore. Oliver Wendell Holmes's assertion that jurisdiction is power is no mystery to the colonized and their responses were often to forge sets of associations in terms of the ways they had to respond to such jurisdictional possibilities. But whereas some colonial powers reified diversity and homogenized it by applying the same historical assumptions to all groups similarly, studies that focus on comparative law show, better than many other focal points, that the historical impact of exchange or political pluralism actually led to very different local patterns. And when matters are then brought to the present, we can see that if one takes too uniform an approach to the effects of colonialism on local history one may be tempted to apply the same idea of what constitutes appropriate 'rights' to all groups identically, thus erasing the contexts and outcomes that will affect what these 'rights' will mean in any particular circumstance.[8] This is not, as I will indicate in a moment, a mindless plea for comparative law to be in service of utter relativism, any more than it is a brief against broad-scale human rights standards. Rather, I want to underscore that without comparative legal studies we might, like the colonial powers themselves, well stumble into treating the circumstances of each localized encounter as if they were all the same and hence that the 'solutions' to whatever we take to be the problems should also be the same. Since difference is inescapable, comparatists can do much to remind the world of it; otherwise, we may blunder into unforeseen outcomes when local groups are sufficiently perverse as not to have read and followed our instructions for them.

It is also enormously important to appreciate that the way things seem to fit together may look very different when we shift the kaleidoscope a bit to consider their integration within a rather different cultural pattern. Take, for instance, the question of analogic reasoning. From the perspective

---

generally Lawrence Rosen, 'Law and Social Change in the New Nations', (1978) 20 Comp. Stud. Soc. & Hist. 3.

[8] See, in this context, the stimulating remarks by Mahmood Mamdani, 'From Conquest to Consent as the Basis of State Formation: Reflections After a Visit to Rwanda'; Veena Das, 'The "Human" in Human Rights: Universalization Versus Globalization', papers presented at the Princeton University conference 'Universalizing from Particulars: Islamic Views of Human Rights Declarations', 24 May 1996, on file with the author.

of common-law systems, analogic reasoning can arguably be said to work horizontally in the sense that it links judges to one another through a running system of categorizing moves. By contrast, in Islamic legal contexts it could be said (in the absence of significant case reporting and citation) that analogic reasoning works vertically in the sense that it links precepts to social consequences: seemingly similar cases may appear to outsiders to be decided differently, whereas to Muslims similarity lies in the way cultural assumptions are given legal implementation through a distinctive style of analysis rather than through the uniformity of specific results. Of course, we could argue over various interpretations and we could also argue about what we think makes for a 'common-law style of analogic reasoning' but however we come out on those issues, the very fact that we consider the way analogy operates – and particularly how it integrates with other elements of the cultural style of reasoning at large – will no doubt take us a long way toward seeing connections we might otherwise have missed. Thus, as in the case of Islam, law becomes not a study in itself, but an excellent vehicle for seeing what assumptions are being made about human nature and human relationships, what relationships or consequences are being equated and thus why, for Muslims, justice, reinforced by a host of religious and cultural conceptualizations, is seen not as equality but as equivalence.[9]

An emphasis on particularities and connections, even when put negatively, also has a positive effect when it comes to so hoary a question as the classification of legal systems. Here, I really will try to restrain myself from citing a long list of genuinely silly classificatory schemes, except to say that, as in biology, some of them can be enormously amusing. There are those wonderfully old-fashioned biological categories, such as animals that are 'educable' and those that are 'ineducable' or 'fruits ordinary' and 'fruits outlandish'. And those who have served as the head of an academic department may particularly appreciate my own favourite division of creatures into the categories of 'animals unsuspicious' and 'animals infuriate'.[10] But here too comparison alone can lead us to greater understanding of relationship rather than positivistic categories. The key, as in modern evolutionary thought, is variation, not purity of category, and when we think this way we begin, as do contemporary biologists, to expand our range beyond what

---

[9] See Lawrence Rosen, *The Justice of Islam: Comparative Perspectives on Islamic Law and Society* (Oxford: Oxford University Press, 2000), pp. 153–75.

[10] Harriet Ritvo, *The Platypus and the Mermaid and Other Figments of the Classifying Imagination* (Cambridge, Mass.: Harvard University Press, 1997), pp. 36–9, 21 and 189, respectively.

we had previously thought might be included. Thus, it may be said of comparative law, as Stephen Jay Gould has said of other realms of knowledge, that it would be 'a fine example of the methodological principle that sample sizes can often be increased only by recognizing proper analogues in other classes of objects'.[11] Once we begin thinking in this way, the result is not a set of rigidified pigeon-holes but (to push, as one possibility, my own heuristic criteria for classifying legal systems) an appreciation of the ways in which power is distributed and cultural ideas brought within the ambit of the law and hence how legal systems make their various 'solutions' to power and culture connect to other aspects of their overall design.[12] It may even make sense to realize that people may also perpetrate a category mistake in the revision of their own legal systems. Thus (to promote my own goods one last time), it can be argued that Islamic fundamentalists have mistakenly assumed that they can apply Islamic law as an arm of the state when, if I am right, Islamic law is really more of a common-law variant that presses decisions down to local levels and allows changing cultural concepts to have direct incorporation – hence the failure of every Islamic fundamentalist regime to apply strict Islamic law begins to make some sense.

Such circumstantial contributions can also lead us back, but now in a much revitalized way, to some of those classic concerns that have characterized our field of study, universalism and functionalism not being the least among them. At the 1900 Paris Congress, most comparatists were willing to counter what they saw as the undesirable movement away from the unity of the Roman-law tradition through new national codes and the Romanticization of nation-focused individualism by asserting what one called 'the profound unity of human nature of which the law is a necessary manifestation'.[13] But suppose that we were to try to give the best scientific assessment of human nature we have at the present time: how would such a claim be framed and how might it affect our approach to comparative law? Briefly, I would summarize the argument this way. Human beings are the only creatures who create the categories of their own experience. Having attained this capacity for culture before we achieved

---

[11] Stephen Jay Gould, *Eight Little Piggies* (New York: Norton, 1993), p. 171.
[12] For an attempt at such a classificatory scheme, see my 'Islamic Law as Common Law: Power, Culture, and the Reconfiguration of Legal Taxonomies', in Rosen, *supra*, note 9, pp. 38–68.
[13] I quote Giorgio del Vecchio's 'Science of Universal Comparative Law', as reported in Richard Hyland, 'Comparative Law', in Dennis Patterson (ed.), *A Companion to Philosophy of Law and Legal Theory* (Oxford: Blackwell, 1996), p. 186.

our present speciation, we have, for all intents and purposes, replaced instinct with the capacity to create the categories we take as real and to which, in turn, we have had to adapt. Thus, at the heart of our distinctiveness lie two fundamental propositions. First, we are constantly generating categories – distinctions, differences – by which we grasp reality. Second, because we do this through the symbols that shape and convey our distinctions, thought is extrinsic (rather than living in 'the secret grotto of the mind'), available to be worked upon and recovered by all. It is by this ability to generate our own profusion of potentials that we retain the capacity to reconfigure our behaviour so as best to suit our understanding of our own circumstances.[14]

And what might be the implications of such a view? For one thing, it could mean that we are always generating new categories and that while some of these may certainly lead to the amalgamation of prior categories, the very propulsion to create new distinctions almost invariably has the *opposite* effect, that of generating differentiation. Moreover, categories are not pristine, but often rather imprecise – even when the attachment to the differences each imports is stronger than the ability to articulate the distinction. So, we can manage without social structures that are not as precise as some earlier theorists made them out to be – 'passing acquaintance' may do in many instances – because this keeps open the ability to adapt to changing circumstances. When Joseph Raz says that our knowledge often extends beyond our ability to articulate it[15] or when particular cultures simultaneously structure both a 'rage for order' and a 'rage for chaos' (in the sense of randomization), they may be keeping alive, through practice and structure, an ability whose particular uses may never be given unambiguous form.

Law, among other cultural phenomena, may, in part, be connected with this process in several key ways. First, by being a forum through which the categories of collective experience are made to seem real, law both tests and reinforces, through its effects on actual relationships, the ways that experience will itself be grasped. Second, legal systems may share more by their styles of attending to category-formation than by what they actually

---

[14] See E. Galanter and M. Gerstenhaber, 'On Thought: The Extrinsic Theory', (1956) 63 Psychological R. 218; Clifford Geertz, *The Interpretation of Cultures* (New York: Basic Books, 1973), pp. 55–83 and 213–20.

[15] See Joseph Raz, *Engaging Reason: On the Theory of Value and Action* (Oxford: Oxford University Press, 2000), *passim*.

produce at any given moment.[16] If the idea that thought is extrinsic has merit we can also readily escape the sterile question whether we can ever get to know another culture from the inside – the answer being 'of course, we can' and 'of course, we cannot' – because thought, being accessible in its symbolic containers, can be unpacked by all, but we do not have to be able to point to every nuance of personal meaning to be able to say a great deal about the logic of the culture that is conveyed to its own members. Cultures are neither impenetrable nor transparent through their histories: they are neither unapparent to their members nor evident to them or outsiders in all their workings. Indeed, it is crucial to any culture that its various domains be so connected with one another that everyday life can appear both self-evident and natural. Similarity or difference is not the question that can be usefully addressed so much as how the processes of differentiation and interconnection play out with distinctive implications for the people who orient their lives with reference to these very concepts and relationships.

I do not mean to suggest that I have now solved all the hard issues that exist for comparatists. Rather, I simply want to indicate some of the possible advantages that might accompany this view of humankind. Take, for example, the classic issue of universalizing law. I suppose nowadays much of this would be put in terms of the rhetoric of globalization – that economies that are more integrated necessitate legal systems that are more transnational. The result is much the same, though for a very different reason, as that unity seen by our predecessor conferees in 1900. But if this other view has merit, both comparatists and social scientists might, like the devil in the Kipling poem, need to 'limp up and explain it all over again'. No, my friend (we would say), notwithstanding the McDonaldization of the world people will always create differentiating categories and just when you think you have it all moving toward the same thing, you are likely to get bitten in the backside by some local surprise. And the reasons why those of us operating from the western tradition may tend not to see this – and why comparison becomes so crucial – may lie on two fronts. First, there is the common tendency in the west to see things as progressing in some direction. We are no more immune from this view than were our predecessors – whether it be in the insupportable political/economic view that a 'rising tide raises all boats' or

---

[16] This is quite different from the vague notion of 'legal style' commended by Zweigert and Kötz, which, we are told, is discoverable through surprise: 'One indication of the "importance" of a feature in a legal system is if the comparatist from another system finds it very surprising': *supra*, note 2, p. 68. This, of course, simply replaces one unknown with another.

the equally insupportable 'scientific' assumption that the biosphere always tends toward greater complexity.[17] In the process, we miss the second key point, namely, that it is variation, not directionality, that best represents the world of nature and human society and that the extension of one form over others can mask the truth, as applicable in non-biological domains as in that of life forms, that greater expansion in some domains does not mean that everything is moving together in the same direction.[18] To emphasize localization, then, is *not* (as in the 'McDomination' case in France)[19] just an example of provincial chauvinism. For myself, I confess that I have a tendency to think of globalization (to borrow the phrase coined many years ago by Claire Boothe Luce, of all people) as so much 'globaloney'. And I do think that we comparatists, though hardly claiming ours to be a predictive science, may yet be able to detect just such signs of localization when everyone else is marching to the drum of globalism – and with it, to detect concerns that others have failed to note.

Another one of those classic issues that has exercised comparatists is, of course, the role of functionalism. Functionalism in comparative law, as Pierre Legrand has admirably demonstrated,[20] is connected to the eighteenth- and nineteenth-century attempt to show that all forms of law are in some sense similar – even though in my own discipline of anthropology, functionalism mainly played the reverse role in that it tried to show that different social and legal systems 'worked' and 'made sense' in every bit as refined a way as those of 'more developed' societies.[21] Indeed, functionalism

[17] 'Evolution was once equated with progress and increasing complexity; life seemed to march up, up, up, from primordial jellies to the Victorian upper classes. Now it is thought that some species succeed in life by going backward. Viruses were once considered a half step between inanimate matter and cellular life; certain minute microbes (rickettsia and mycoplasmas) were thought to represent a primitive stage between viruses and bacteria. Now these tiny microbes are seen as stripped-down versions of more complex ancestors; they shed all the internal machinery they could and borrowed from hosts': Arno Karlen, *Biography of a Germ* (New York: Pantheon, 2000), p. 81. See also Carol Kaesuk Yoon, 'Biologists Deny Life Gets More Complex', *The New York Times*, 30 March 1993, p. C1.

[18] On the argument from biology in this regard, see Stephen Jay Gould, *Full House: The Spread of Excellence from Plato to Darwin* (New York: Harmony Books, 1996).

[19] José Bové, a French farmer, was convicted of criminal vandalism for attacking a McDonald's restaurant in October 1999, an action that was broadly supported in France by many who thought the restaurant chain represented the US destruction of French values and US domination of the French economy. See Suzanne Daley, 'French Farmer is Sentenced to Jail for Attack on McDonald's', *The New York Times*, 14 September 2000, p. A13.

[20] See Pierre Legrand's contribution to this book.

[21] For example, see Max Gluckman, *The Judicial Process Among the Barotse of Northern Rhodesia* (Manchester: Manchester University Press, 1955); id., *The Ideas in Barotse Jurisprudence*

appears to have come into prominence in various disciplines at somewhat different times and in response to each discipline's own intellectual history. Thus, in the period just after the First World War, functionalism could serve anthropology as a counterweight to Social Darwinism's claims for directionality, which denied the subject of anthropological studies anything but a precursive validity. Ironically, at just the time anthropology sought to avoid the scientific model, comparative law, working from the nineteenth-century view of 'the science of law', sought to justify comparison by using evolutionism as a form of scientific validation for its studies. Around the same time, architecture was attracted to functionalism, under Louis Sullivan's rubric that 'form follows function', as it sought to free itself from the classical elaborations attendant on increasing decoration. Sociology, by contrast, did not come to adopt functionalism until just before and after the Second World War, when it became a vehicle for contending with the perversion of social studies by the Fascists. Functionalism served some sociologists as a means for asserting a non-politicized style of analysis while for others it constituted a justification for involvement in radical sociology based on the premise that certain public policies could be working against the 'functional prerequisites' of a working society.[22] In a sense, functionalism succeeded the same wherever it took hold: it showed connections and led to new theories to explain relationships. But it also failed differently in each place it took hold: in anthropology for not dealing with change, in sociology for failing to point to the dysfunctional and ignoring politics (which came back with a vengeance during the McCarthy era and the 1960s), in architecture for disallowing any decoration that seemed to have no function and in law for reinforcing rule-centrism and formalism.

In some sense, of course, we are all functionalists and that is all to the good inasmuch as it leads us to see connections we might not otherwise have thought obtained. It is less admirable when, just to re-emphasize the case of my own discipline of anthropology, it has led to an inability to generate interesting ideas about social and cultural change since everything – witchcraft accusations, feuds, caste systems and all the other sins out of

---

(New Haven: Yale University Press, 1965), who argued that the Barotse had a system worthy of being called 'jurisprudence'; E. E. Evans-Pritchard, *Nuer Religion* (Oxford: Oxford University Press, 1956), who claimed that the Nuer possessed a well-developed 'theology'.

[22] See Kingsley Davis, 'The Myth of Functional Analysis as a Special Method in Sociology and Anthropology', (1959) 24 Am. Sociological R. 757; D. F. Aberle *et al.*, 'The Functional Prerequisites of a Society', (1950) 60 Ethics 100.

which anthropologists have made a good living – has been seen as functional for the continuing operation of the system as a whole. Moreover, comparatists, like all others, are faced with analytic problems attendant on functionalism that can never be fully resolved. What, for example, is 'the function' any structure is supposed to be addressing? Is the function of a rule of inheritance to move property through a specific line, to establish certain relationships by means of property distribution, to reinforce a worldview that turns on the differential nature of gender or all of the above? Such matters do not answer themselves just because we collect more information, nor is bias automatically neutralized by a more extended search: the grounds for inclusion are not self-executing but are entirely dependent on our implicit or explicit theories about connections and the reasons they exist. Thus, the following assertion by Konrad Zweigert and Hein Kötz is utterly insupportable both as method and as theory:

> The basic methodological principle of all comparative law is that of *functionality* [...]. [T]he comparatist can rest content if his researches through all the relevant material lead to the conclusion that the systems he has compared reach the same or similar practical results, but if he finds that there are great differences or indeed diametrically opposite results, he should be warned and go back to check again whether the terms in which he posed his original question were indeed purely functional, and whether he has spread the net of his researches quite wide enough.[23]

Here again, one encounters the issue of similarity versus difference that continues to exercise comparatists when so many other disciplines have moved away from this concern. It is true that, at first blush, speaking about sameness and difference seems both obvious and unavoidable: if one is going to compare, does not one first have to decide what is alike, and thus worthy of comparison, and what is different? But the issue is really both false and misleading. It is false because there are no natural lines of differentiation that, in some science-like quest, we can discover: to the contrary, the whole point is that where it is best to draw analytic distinctions depends on what it is one is trying to explain. It is context that matters – relationships and connections – and the lines of inclusion or exclusion are not naturally given. Like functionalism, the assumption that there are 'true' bases for categorization has different disciplinary histories. In anthropology, no one would argue the issue of political empowerment of the weak in terms of

---

[23] Zweigert and Kötz, *supra*, note 2, pp. 34 and 40 [emphasis original].

similarity/difference. We 'solved' that issue to our own satisfaction through an emphasis on relativism: cultures can be 'separate but equal' without that leading to such policy implications as support for segregation by race (quite the reverse). Anthropologists moved on to other questions about the context of various elements within cultural and social forms. In law, the similar/different dichotomy has been connected at various times with such propositions as that the law works itself through to its own pure results or that, since efficiency will out, if the law accords with such market-like forces the 'correct' categories of analysis will be self-evident.[24] True believers will never be dissuaded from their acceptance that the categories through which they see the world are naturally given but scholarship demands a higher standard.

Moreover, it is very common, in the sciences as in the arts, that some ways of putting issues simply fall into disuse not because they are demonstrably false, but because we can no longer find new things to say through them. It is in this sense that focusing on the similarity/difference dichotomy is also literally misleading in that it leads us away from other questions that may be more productive of insight. If discerning difference or similarity is no longer in service of any goal that can be justified on intellectual, rather than political, grounds, it must be recognized that it has simply worn out

[24] Fuller, for example, argued that codified law 'does not carry with it the burdens and doubts of its origins, and it cannot therefore – in the famous words of Lord Mansfield – "work itself pure" by the process of comparison, reexamination, and rearticulation that characterizes the common law': Lon L. Fuller, *Anatomy of the Law* (New York: Praeger, 1968), p. 106. Fuller went on to assert the moral superiority of the common law because its logic tends to exclude evil: 'I shall have to rest on the assertion of a belief that may seem naive, namely, coherence and goodness have more affinity than coherence and evil. Accepting this belief, I also believe that when men are compelled to explain and justify their decisions the effect will generally be to pull those decisions toward goodness, by whatever standards of ultimate goodness there are. Accepting these beliefs, I find a considerable incongruity in any conception that envisages a possible future in which the common law would "work itself pure from case to case" toward a more perfect realization of iniquity': *id.*, 'Positivism and Fidelity to Law – A Reply to Professor Hart', (1958) 71 Harvard L.R. 630, p. 636. As to the idea that law is best understood as a self-contained domain, see, for example, Alan Watson and Khaled Abou el Fadl, 'Fox Hunting, Pheasant Shooting, and Comparative Law', (2000) 48 Am. J. Comp. L. 1. Watson and Fadl do not look at actual court proceedings, nor do they even regard as texts large bodies of material that bear directly on their chosen topic. Like those who used to think all history was diplomatic history – before we began to enlarge our idea of what constituted a 'text' – they reproduce the same tautology: because they are not part of the recognizable domain of law, such additional sources have no bearing on law. What they miss, among many other things, is the way in which cultural assumptions inform legal processes, the range of institutions and relationships that form part of peoples' idea of their own legal system and the broader sources of legitimacy that render a legal system both recognizable and acceptable.

its usefulness, at least until we know something we presently do not, and one should move on to more productive conceptualizations.

I will return in a moment to the question of when a field of study needs to give up unresolved issues but would note here that far more accurate, I think, is the point made not by a comparatist, but by Albert Camus when he said: 'Indeed it is not so much identical conclusions that prove minds to be related as the contradictions that are common to them.'[25] His point was right on the mark for us as well: it is not functional goals that bear comparison, but how each society resolves what it sees as contradictions and how the resulting set of concepts and relationships come to appear as a matter of common sense to their adherents. And when one seeks the various ways by which these processes work themselves out over time, the formulation of analytic categories may indeed prove useful. Here, to take my final example, we return to the old question of whether there is a taxonomy of legal systems 'out there'. The nearest analogy, again, is best found in modern approaches in the natural sciences. As Stephen Jay Gould has put it: 'classifications are not passive ordering devices in a world objectively divided into obvious categories. Taxonomies are human decisions imposed upon nature – theories about the causes of nature's order.'[26] Moreover, as Arno Karlen has said: 'Classifications endure only if they explain more than alternatives do, withstand endless reexamination, and accommodate new facts as they appear.'[27] Admittedly, this is one of those domains in which we are all somewhat hypocritical: botanists and lawyers alike have a way of saying that we know that all systems of classification are just constructions of our own making and, in the next breath, of suggesting that whatever system we are attached to is, of course, true! The point, surely, is to get away – as most natural scientists have – from thinking of our subjects of study as organized like a stamp album or a set of pigeon-holes, ask whether we can see connections by trying out various combinations of associations and appreciate what the non-comparatists may ignore, that by widening our categories we see associations others have been missing.

---

[25] I quote Camus, as reported in Charles W. Nuckolls, *Culture: A Problem That Cannot Be Solved* (Madison: University of Wisconsin Press, 1998), p. 270.
[26] Gould, *supra*, note 18, p. 39. See also *id.*, *The Flamingo's Smile* (New York: Norton, 1985), pp. 160–1. For my own uses of these ideas for legal taxonomies, see Rosen, *supra*, note 9, pp. 38–68, especially pp. 45–6 and 63–8.
[27] Karlen, *supra*, note 17, p. 45.

Perhaps some of these features, then, can be drawn together in ways that, without demanding that everyone follow the same path, suggest some common themes for our future orientations. G. K. Chesterton once said: 'the function of imagination is not to make strange things settled, so much as to make settled things strange.'[28] Comparative law, so much a part of the imagination, surely ought to claim a similar role. Of course, the process of shaking up our expectations involves many elements, none of them susceptible to a simple cookbook application. But a feature I commend to you is one that anthropologists often engage in without quite realizing it. It was noted at a recent celebratory conference organized by the small city in Morocco in which we have worked for several decades when Clifford Geertz, in a quite wonderful remark about how all of us who had studied the place had gone about our work, said: 'We had to make ourselves parochial in order to make ourselves cosmopolitan.' Surely, that is a good idea for comparative law too, for by immersing ourselves in others' laws we make our own systems appear just odd enough to grasp features we may otherwise have taken for granted. If, for some, that suggests being a 'subversive discipline' for challenging our own views of ourselves, I cannot fault them (as long as that is not all that comparison is about);[29] if, for others, it is a way of forcing ourselves to see unforeseen connections, that too has obvious merit. Comparative law cannot be expected magically to yield answers to every teleological issue or practical effect; it cannot resolve such questions as whether there are universal values or whether one's own law should focus on process, original intent or majority desires. But it can help us understand the actual content of these claimed bases rather than permit the easy leap to conclusions that, absent such knowledge, never really escape parochialism for all their claim to cosmopolitanism.

Indeed, we have to reconfigure some of our basic orientations if we are to get back to them. We would do well to convert some of our ends to means as, for example, in the use of classificatory systems. We also need to realize that some *topics* of study should not be regarded as appropriate *subjects* of study. Legal transplants may qualify as an example in this regard. Admittedly, I have a rather irreverent response whenever I hear of legal transplants: I tend to think of them as being less akin to botanical or organ transplants and more like hair transplants – they seldom cover the underlying condition completely and always seem, at least to those with some sense of history, a

---

[28] G. K. Chesterton, *The Defendant* (London: Dent, 1922), p. 84 [1901].
[29] George P. Fletcher, 'Comparative Law as a Subversive Discipline', (1998) 46 Am. J. Comp. L. 683, p. 695.

touch contrived. More seriously, while such borrowings no doubt occur and vary in their success, given their dependence on professional application and their cultural entanglement, they do not alone form a useful way of framing issues of process, nor do they help generate theories about interconnection. Like a biological category that lumps together 'all things that go bump in the night', if genuine insights are not produced from the framing categories, it is time to abandon them, reconfigure the issues and move on – even though the topic appears to have some existential value. Certain categories (such as 'peasants' or 'play') that may once have produced comparative insights and may for a time have gained their own disciplinary apparatus (for example, *The Journal of Peasant Studies* or *The Society for the Anthropological Study of Play*) may have generated knowledge that can no longer be usefully contained within their own rubrics. Indeed, if one cannot supply a good answer to the question why is this a useful way of framing the subject – if the topic of study appears to cover so varied an array of instances as to be analytically unproductive – then it is time to forsake it lest its 'natural' appearance continue to lead us into further mistakes of reification.

Instead, we need boldly to seek out the meaning – the connectedness – of key concepts and relationships *for any given situation* if we are to be able to show why, in many situations, that which may seem to be inadequately articulated makes sense in the light of matters that cross-cut the domain of law rather than remain wholly discernible from within law itself. Comparative law could, for example, then be used to re-develop elite theory in sociology, the articulation of cosmologies as understood by anthropology, the moment when trust is established through mediating institutions in economic theory or the attribution of intentionality as considered by philosophy. If one only comes back to law, when issues demand that they be followed into whatever domains they lead, neither legal understanding nor disciplinary theory-building will be advanced.

This does not mean that all comparatists have to become social scientists and it does not mean that we are unable to say anything if we do not generate, for comparative law, a set of distinctive theories. Georges Gurvitch's somewhat elusive notion that 'too little sociology leads you away from law and too much leads you back' is worth considering so long as it is not taken as a prescription for sociological reductionism. I like very much Mitchel Lasser's reference to comparative law as a 'relational practice',[30] though I am a bit more partial (to extend what Huxley said in another context) to

---

[30] See Mitchel Lasser's contribution to this book.

thinking of comparative law as a conversation. It means that we comparatists are, as a matter of fact, hybrids, mongrels: we are the universal donors of legal studies. We cross boundaries precisely because law crosses boundaries. Comparative law (to paraphrase Maitland in reverse) certainly does not have to become (fill in the blank: anthropology, sociology, history) or nothing at all: the appropriateness of one or another set of helpful theories should depend on the issue that one is studying and so long as we keep pushing the boundaries and looking for connections, it may continue to prove true for our intellectual contributions, as for so much else in life, that change comes mostly from the margin. In the process, it is not just having to contend once again with some of our more provincial law-colleagues that can present problems. We may have to resist the blandishments of our own supporters. If you have ever been approached by someone who loved what you were doing but had not got it quite right, you can appreciate what I mean. It is rather like the professor who, after a talk, was greeted by an enthusiast who gushed, 'Oh, Professor, your lecture was wonderful, absolutely superfluous'! 'Well, then', replied the professor, who no doubt thought his own sense of irony equal to the task, 'perhaps I should publish it posthumously.' 'Oh, yes, sir', came the response, 'I think you should get it into print just as soon as you possibly can'!

It is in just such a vein that we can be both optimistic and humble in the face of our chosen field of study. Mongrels that we are, we may never have a home entirely of our own but must drift endlessly across boundaries, eclecticism our natural terrain, resistance to all the reductions of locale and discipline our fated role. But there is a deep satisfaction that comes from this study, from seeing how our fellow human beings try to make sense of the worlds in which they live and give effect to the decisions that must be made in ordering their relations with one another. Their worlds are ours too, their quests ones we can better understand and communicate when we see how they also connect the elements of their world into a meaningful whole. And we replicate that motion too when, at the end of another century, at the beginning of another century, we accept that we may have to renounce comparative law as we have at times known it in order to save it.

INDEX

Abel, Richard, 299
Abrams, Philip, 135–6, 138, 153
Abu-Odeh, Lama, 422
accounting, 175, 189–93
Adorno, Theodor, 242, 252, 258, 279, 281–2, 302
Adorno, Theodor and Max Horkheimer, 261
Ainsworth, Janet, 290
Ajani, Gianmaria, 474, 483
Albania, 476–7
Alexander, Larry
  critique of, 256
Alford, William, 217
Algeria, 472
Allison, John, 470
Althusser, Louis
  logic of indifference and, 48, 53
  repression and, 69
Ambedkar, B. R., 68
Aquinas, 32–5, 39–40, 42–3, 170, 179
Aristotle, 32–5, 42–3, 170
Armenia, 487
Ascarelli, Tullio, 248
Augé, Marc, 307
Austin, John, 67, 70
autopoiesis, 8, 145–7, 150, 452, 462–4

Bachelard, Gaston, 251, 262, 265
Bacon, Francis, 269
Baer, Susanne, 341
Balthus, 252
Baltic states, 474
Bar, Christian von
  critique of, 304

Bauman, Zygmunt, 250–1, 268, 301–2, 311
Baxi, Upendra, 265, 370, 430–1
Becker, A. L., 291
Beckett, Samuel, 281–2
Belleau, Marie-Claire, 214, 227
Benhabib, Seyla, 306
Benjamin, Andrew, 283
Benjamin, Walter, 245, 252–3, 264, 277, 291, 305–6
Bennett, Benjamin, 270
Benton, Lauren, 497
Berlin, Isaiah, 265
Bernasconi, Robert, 266
Betti, Emilio, 325–6
Bhaskar, Roy, 74
Blanchot, Maurice, 259–60
Boethius, 170
Bollack, Jean, 249
Borges, Jorge Luis, 253
Bourdieu, Pierre, 70
Bruns, Gerald, 243, 311
Burkert, Walter, 339
Burkina Faso, 472
Bussani, Mauro, 216, 346–7, 355, 369, 373, 399, 420, 432–3

Cain, Maureen, 462
Cambridge Conference (2000), 3–22, 25, 27–8
Camus, Albert, 507
Cañizares, Felipe de Sola, 388
Cantor, Georg, 172
capital markets, 187–8
Cappelletti, Mauro, 109, 370
central Europe, 472, 474, 476, 482–4
Chamberlain, Houston, 322

511

change, legal, 450–2
　functionalism and, 118–26
　see also transfers, legal
Chesterton, G. K., 13, 240, 508
Clifford, James, 293, 441
Clive, Eric, 485
Code, Lorraine, 297
Cohen, Felix, 107
Coing, Helmut, 326
Collins, Hugh, 366
colonial law, 58–62
　affection and, 60–1
　appropriation of land and, 66
　conquest and, 59
　constitution of subjects and, 68
　constitutional legality and, 69–70
　genetic policing and, 67
　genres of, 52–3
　interpretation of, 59
　legal paternalism and, 60
　legal pluralism and, 59–60
　loyalty and, 60
　making of, 52
　resistance to, 52–3, 61, 72, 74–5
colonial mind-set
　survival of, 49–51
　globalization and, 49, 73
　universality and, 49
colonialism
　armed forces and, 65
　'Caliban syndrome' and, 49
　civil freedom and, 62–5
　detraditionalization and, 64
　England and, 51–2, 55, 59, 60–1, 67
　ethics and, 47
　Euro-American images of, 49
　France and, 52–3, 59
　governmentality and, 57–8
　history and, 47–8
　India and, 50–2, 55–6, 60–1, 497
　Kant and, 47
　legal inheritance of, 47
　mercantilism and, 57–8
　modernity and, 49
　neo-colonialism and, 53
　Portugal and, 53, 59
　post-colonialism and, 50–2, 57, 75

post-modernity and, 49
　Savigny and, 47–8
　transactions and, 46
　violence and making of, 48
common-core research, 280
　Cornell project, as, 107–9, 120, 395–7
　critique of, 261–2
　Trento project, as, 100, 346–7, 350–1, 355–7, 361, 369, 397, 406, 409, 420–1: critique of, 117–8
common law
　colonial legality and, 61, 70
　reasoning and, 498–9
　systemics and, 38
Compagnon, Antoine, 306
comparative legal studies
　coffee culture analogy and, 236–9
　colonialism and, 46–50, 56, 59, 62–3, 75, 86, 494, 496–8
　commercial interests and, 54
　comparatists and attitudes toward, 197–8
　constitutional law and, 53
　construction of object of analysis and, 212–21, 232–6, 253–6, 284–5, 296
　cultural anthropology and, 331, 340–1
　culture and, 110, 148–51: critique of, 114–16, 122, 126, 149
　difference and, see difference
　epistemic communities and, 46–7
　epistemology of, 46–8, 108–18, 131–42, 154–5, 178–87, 193–4, 199–239, 440–6
　eroticism analogy and, 311
　ethics and, 250, 264, 284, 289–90, 301, 303, 306, 309
　ethnocentrism and, 46–75, 151
　European Union and, 294–5, 473
　exclusionary narratives and, 50, 56, 59, 62, 109–11: see also comparative legal studies, privileging sameness, as,
　extraordinary places and, 467–89
　Foucault and, 53
　functionalism and, see functionalism

genres and limitations of, 46–50, 56, 59, 62–3, 75, 131–2, 151–3, 162–5, 167–8, 180–3, 186–7, 313, 345–433, 438–9, 465, 467–8, 475, 493–510
governance and, 345–55, 408–33
heteroglossia, 227
ideolects and, 222–32
informants and, 334–5
instrumentalism and, 54
internet and, 188
jurisprudence and, 154
languages and, 154–94
legal culture and, *see* culture, legal
legal tradition, 77–99
literary analysis and, 203–7
marginal status of, 197–8
mentalité and, 149, 276, 486
method, as, 101
methodology of, 198–239, 345–408
national law and, 76–7, 79–80, 84, 495, 500
politics and, 279, 345–55, 408–33
positivism and, 207–12
privileging sameness, as, 108–9, 245–50, 261–3, 272–8, 313–4
relational practice, as, 235
sociology and, 131–53, 437–9
source materials and, 207–12, 227–31
understanding and, 18, 150–1, 183–5, 199–239, 250–2, 281–3, 297–8, 326–9, 334–43, 440–6
US practice of, 206, 226–7, 404
writing and, 286, 304, 306
conflict of laws *see* private international law
Cotterrell, Roger, 448, 454
Cover, Robert, 212–3
Craig, Gordon, 267
criminal justice
  colonial legality and, 61, 70
culture, legal, 110, 148–51, 154, 183–5, 193, 205, 227–8, 243, 268, 275–6, 288, 341, 344, 361–8, 424, 445, 464, 468–9, 473–4, 483, 485, 488, 496, 500–2

critique of, 114–6, 122, 126, 149, 468
technique and, 362–8, 418, 430
Curran, Vivian, 109, 151, 172, 313, 327
Cusa, Nicholas of, 170–1, 178
custom
  appropriation by colonial elites, 51–2

Dadoun, Roger, 259
Damaška, Mirjan, 216, 370
David, Jacques-Louis, 205, 228
David, René, 387–90, 394–5, 403–5
  critique of, 493
Davidson, Donald
  critique of, 282–3
Dawson, John
  critique of, 206
Deleuze, Gilles, 242, 254, 264, 299
Deleuze, Gilles and Félix Guattari, 242, 264
Demleitner, Nora, 313, 327, 338
Derrida, Jacques, 62–3, 245, 254, 264, 281, 286, 291, 295, 302
Descartes, 305
Descombes, Vincent, 263
Dezalay, Yves, and Bryant Garth, 293, 463
dialectics, negative, 241–2
Diderot, 258
difference
  civil law/common law and, 243–5, 285, 288–9, 294–7
  comparative legal studies and, 44–5, 108–18, 121–5, 150–1, 240–311, 313–4, 330, 339, 344, 467–70, 475, 485–6, 488–9, 498–9, 502–3
  critique of, 218–9, 442, 444, 446, 494, 505–6
  laws and principles distinguished, 31–4, 40–5
  pluralism and, 49
  sameness and, 218–9, 355–69, 424–30
Dilthey, Wilhelm, 319–21, 323, 326, 329
  Verstehen and, 320
Dimock, Wai Chee, 48, 64

Durkheim, Emile, 62, 133, 136–8, 140–1, 371, 448, 450
Dworkin, Ronald, 334–5, 344
  critique of, 53

eastern Europe, 472, 474, 476, 482–4, 494–5
Eco, Umberto, 8
eco-feminism, 52
eco-history, 52
Ehrenzweig, Albert, 371
Empedocles, 256
English law
  disclosure in, 273
  enforcement of contracts in, 40
  good faith in, 273
  judgements in, 160: foreign law and, 486; persuasive authority and, 486; practices of writing, 23–6
  logic and, 169
  negligence in, 255
  statutory interpretation in, 166–7
  trial in, 176–7
epistemic communities
  colonialism and, 63
  comparative legal studies and, 46–7
  power of, 48
epistemology, 46–8, 108–18, 131–42, 154–5, 178–87, 193–4, 199–311, 345–408, 493–510
  ontology, distinguished from, 132–3
  standpoint, 297
Erikson, Erik, 318
Esquirol, Jorge, 389, 416
Esser, Josef, 313, 315, 326–7, 336
European Law
  consumer contracts in, 36
European Union
  model for law reform, as, 484, 486
Evans-Pritchard, E. E., 504
Ewald, William, 215, 262, 290, 312–3, 315, 317–8, 327–8, 341–2, 352, 447–8
  critique of, 335–6
existentialism, 324–55, 327

Feldbrugge, Ferdinand, 278
Ferrarese, Maria Rosaria, 461

Feyerabend, Paul, 256–7, 294
Fish, Stanley, 213, 275
Flaubert, Gustave, 286
Fletcher, George, 37, 262, 264, 293, 508
forest law
  colonial legality and, 61
Foucault, Michel, 47–8, 55, 58, 62–3, 69, 257, 289
Frankenberg, Günter, 217, 271–2, 292, 370
  critique of, 220–1
Frase, Paul, 220
Fraser, Nancy, 66
French law
  bioethics in, 329
  doctrine in, 214
  enforcement of contracts in, 35–6, 39–40
  judgements in, 160, 201
  Lasser, Mitchel, on, 233–5
  pre-contractual information in, 273–4
  privacy in, 43
  rhetorics in, 204–5, 209, 211–3, 224–6
  strict liability in, 34
Freud, Sigmund, 248, 284, 309
Friedman, Lawrence, 148–9, 448–9, 462
  critique of, 149, 448
Friedmann, Wolfgang, 369, 371
Fuller, Lon, 506
functionalism, 100–27, 133, 217, 390–4
  alternatives to, 100–1, 114–18, 125–6
  comparative methodology and, 100–18, 125
  critique of, 108–18, 125–7, 179–80, 292–3, 313, 441, 475, 503–4, 507
  historical antecedents of, 103–8
  legal change and, 118–26
  private international law and, 103–6

Gadamer, H.-G., 256–7, 282, 284, 300, 314, 320, 325–7, 336–7
Gandhi, Mohandas, 55, 74

Garapon, Antoine, 446
Gasché, Rodolphe, 284, 301
Geertz, Clifford, 295, 298, 441, 496, 508
Gény, François, 389, 395
Gerber, David, 293
German law
    Constitution: *Grundgesetz*, 40; Weimar, 174
    enforcement of contracts in, 36–9
    hate speech in, 331–3
    illiteracy and, 168–9
    judgements in, 160
    logic and, 169
    privacy in, 43–4
    strict liability in, 35
Gerven, Walter van
    critique of, 262
Gessner, Volkmar, 488
gift, 41
Ginsburg, Tom, 456, 462
Girard, René, 280
Glendon, Mary Ann, 370
Glenn, H. Patrick, 356, 424
globalization, 49, 51, 54, 98, 188, 293, 437, 460–2, 502–3
    glocalization and, 188, 293
Gluckman, Max, 503–4
Gödel, Kurt, 172
Goethe, J. W., 164–5, 168, 174
Goodrich, Peter, 244, 272, 291
Gordley, James, 218, 272–4
    critique of, 249, 274–7
Gordon, Robert, 275–6
Gould, Stephen Jay, 500, 507
Gramsci, Antonio, 56–7, 69
Graziadei, Michele, 400
Greenhouse, Carol, 272–3
Großfeld, Bernhard, 213, 277, 488
Guha, Ranajit, 61, 66–7
Gurvitch, Georges, 152, 509
Gutteridge, Harold, 10, 133–4, 289–90, 388

Habermas, Jürgen, 264
    critique of, 53
Halbwachs, Maurice, 318
Haldane, Richard, 7

Hall, Jerome, 138–40, 299
Hamacher, Werner, 243, 286, 303, 306–7
Hamann, J. G., 261
Heck, Philipp, 106
Hegel, G. W. F., 258
Heidegger, Martin, 256–7, 268, 279, 287, 294, 307, 310–11, 324, 327, 336, 337
Heine, Heinrich, 267
Heraclitus, 256
Herder, J. G., 261, 265–71, 312–4, 316, 328–9
heritage
    colonialism and, 46
hermeneutics, 166–8, 250, 283, 285, 306, 312, 314, 318–26, 446, 464
Herodotus, 256
Heydebrand, Wolf, 462
historiography
    colonial legality and, 73–5
    feminist narratology and, 52
    narrative hegemony and, 46, 48
    post-colonialism and, 51
    silencing and, 46
    subaltern narratology and, 67–8
Hofstadter, Douglas, 295
Hofstede, Geert, 183
Holmes, Oliver W., 161, 167, 177
Hong Kong, 468, 481–4
Hooker, M. B., 293
human rights
    colonial governance and, 52, 70–2
Humboldt, Wilhelm von, 267–8, 271, 282
    Nationalcharakter and, 267–8
    Verstehen and, 271
Hume, David, 269
Hungary, 468
Hunt, Alan, 293
Huntington, Patricia, 242, 305
Hyland, Richard, 245

international organizations, 423, 458–60
Irigaray, Luce, 305
Islamic law
    reasoning and, 499–500

James, Scott, 67
Jamin, Christophe, 6–7, 214
Jason, Kathrine, 15
Jestaz, Philippe, 214
Jhering, Rudolf von, 177, 317, 328, 486
Juglart, Michel de, 273–4
juridical world outlook (*juristische Weltanschauung*), 54–7
　exclusion and, 54–5
　progress and, 54–5
　repression and, 55–7
　resistance and, 56

Kahn-Freund, Otto, 369, 371, 393
Kant, Immanuel, 47, 257, 263, 266, 328, 429
Kantorowicz, Hermann, 156
Karlen, Arno, 503, 507
Kasirer, Nicholas, 264, 292
Keats, John, 310
Kelsen, Hans, 304
Kennedy, David, 413
　critique of, 301
Kennedy, Duncan, 248, 405, 413
　critique of, 206
Kessler, Friedrich, 371, 393
Kipling, Rudyard, 22, 502
Kleist, Heinrich von, 183
Kötz, Hein, 36
Kohler, Josef, 154, 321
Krygier, Martin, 455
Kulcsar, Kalman, 473
　Ethiopia, on, 473
Kyrgyz Republic, 486

Lambert, Edouard, 6–7, 136–7, 246, 372, 374–9, 382–3, 386–9, 402–5, 421
Landolfi, Tommaso, 15–6
Landsberg, Ernst, 261
Langbein, John, 220
language, 155–69
　mathematics and, 171–3
　oral v. written, 160–9
　reality and, 157–8, 162
　religion and, 173–5
Larenz, Karl, 326
Larkin, Philip, 275, 298

Larrimore, Mark, 266–7
Lasser, Mitchel, 224–6, 228, 233–5, 509
Laughland, John, 261
Law, John, 173
law-and-development, 151, 350, 437
law-making, approaches to, 34–40, 43–4
Lazarus, Moritz, 318
Legrand, Pierre, 122, 149–50, 185, 197–8, 205, 213, 216, 218, 220, 244, 285, 312, 314–15, 327, 336, 352, 358, 360, 370, 440–7, 450–1, 453, 459, 461, 470, 503
　critique of, 341–2, 406, 442–5, 470
Leibniz, G. W., 158, 279, 320
Lepaulle, Pierre, 258–9
Lessing, 258
Leventhal, Robert, 271
Levinas, Emmanuel, 217, 256–7, 264, 286, 298, 304, 307, 311, 325
Lévi-Strauss, Claude, 257–8
limitations
　colonial legality and, 61
Lingat, Robert, 337
Livingstone, David, 64
Llewellyn, Karl, 20, 48, 372
logic
　English law and, 169
　German law and, 169
López-Ayylon, Sergio, 458
　Mexican legal culture, on, 458
López-Medina, Diego, 429
Louisiana, 474
Luce, Claire Boothe, 503
Luhmann, Niklas, 57–8, 147, 450, 464
Luther, Martin, 159, 165, 319
Lydgate, John, 162, 165
Lyotard, Jean-François, 254, 257

McCready, Amy, 269–70
McDougal, Myres, 370
Machado, Antonio, 300–1
Maine, Henry, 62, 371–2
Malinowski, Bronislaw, 64
Mamdani, Mahmood, 51
Mandela, Nelson, 74
Mann, F. A., 371

Mansfield, Katherine, 309
Marcus, George, 441
Marin, Louis, 306
Markesinis, Basil, 10, 290
    critique of, 247, 262, 289–90, 304, 309
Márquez, Gabriel García, 26–7
Marx, Karl, 60, 62, 317, 371
mathematics
    legal, 155, 171–3
    philosophy and, 170
Mattei, Ugo, 118, 197, 216–8, 220, 247, 370, 483, 488
    critique of, 247–8, 264–5, 288–9, 304, 493
Mehren, Arthur von, 369
Merryman, John, 197–8, 213, 215, 218–9, 245, 370, 477, 493
    critique of, 206, 477
Monateri, Piergiuseppe, 471, 482–3
Montesquieu, 118–19, 245, 316, 428, 494
Mouffe, Chantal, 262
Munday, Roderick, 23–6
Murdoch, Iris, 308
Murphy, W. T., 260

Nader, Laura, 53–4
    predatory legality and, 65
Naipaul, V. S., 74
Naples
    language and, 15–6
national law
    codification and, 83
    colonialism and, 86
    content of, 84
    exclusivity of national sources in, 83–4
    foundational element of, 83
    indigenous peoples and, 94
    intermediary, as, 99
    legal system and, 82–3, 91
    persuasive authority and, 76, 91–5
    resistance to, 90–9
    stare decisis and, 83, 93–4
    state and, 78
    tradition, as, 91

natural law, 31–4, 495
    cartography and, 81–2
    Hugo, Gustav, and, 316
Netherlands, The, 484, 486–7
Nietzsche, Friedrich, 61, 257
Nisbet, H. B., 267

Øyen, Else, 272
Olsen, Fran, 220

Paris Congress (1900), 3–5, 131, 136, 154, 246, 349, 371–2, 375, 393, 493, 500, 502
Parmenides, 256
Pascal, 179
Pashukanis, Evgeny, 450
path-dependence, 177–8, 184, 294
Pavlov, [Ivan], 23
Pearson, Keith, 288
phenomenology, 324–5, 342–3
Piaget, Jean, 252
Plato, 170, 256–7
pluralism
    legal, 51, 54
    logic of difference and, 49
Pollock, Frederick, 372
Ponge, Francis, 287–8
Post, Albert, 321
Pound, Ezra, 244, 287
Pound, Roscoe, 206, 227, 372, 374, 379–83, 386–8, 395–6, 402–5
privacy
    European and US law compared, 330
private international law
    alternatives to, 98
    differences in national laws and, 85
    functionalism and, 103–6
    globalization and, 98
procedure, 175–7
progress
    variation of idea within European countries, 67
    western legal institutions as, 49–51, 62, 66
Prosser, William, 38
psycho-history, 52

public international law
  alternatives to, 97
  erosion of, 97–9
  globalization and, 98
  governance and, 348–9, 413, 424
  hegemony of, 86–7, 97–9
  legitimation of state territory by, 84–5
  Roman law and, 85
  state law and, 85
  western character of, 85, 88–9
Pythagoras, 170

Quebec, 484

Rabel, Ernst, 104–6, 246, 259, 278, 372, 374, 383–7, 389, 391, 393–5, 402–5
racism
  epistemic, 53
Radbruch, Gustav, 351
Rawls, John, 257, 429
  critique of, 53
Raz, Joseph, 501
Reimann, Mathias, 197, 370
revenue law
  colonial legality and, 61
review, judicial, 282–3
Rheinstein, Max, 54, 133, 369, 371, 386–7, 393
Ricoeur, Paul, 281
Riles, Annelise, 313, 425
Rilke, Rainer Maria, 258
Rittich, Kerry, 429
Robertson, Roland, 293
Rodney, Walter, 51
Roman law, 165
  European reception of, 77–8, 187, 243
  German law and, 182, 316–7
  public international law and, 85
  systemics in, 38
Romanticism, 158, 312–29, 336, 340
  historians and, 322–3
  philosophers and, 324–5
  sociologists and, 323–4
Rorty, Richard, 279

Rosen, Lawrence
  critique of, 301
Ross, Alf, 173
Rottleuthner, Hubert, 326, 335
Rubin, Edward, 456–7
  Chinese law, on, 456–7
Rudden, Bernard, 7, 113
Russia, 474, 476, 482

Sacco, Rodolfo, 115–17, 120, 158, 215, 299, 369, 394, 397, 399, 403–5, 483
  cryptotypes, 116, 125–6
  legal formants, 116–7, 125–6, 177, 213–4, 295, 399–401, 420
Said, Edward, 285
Saidov, Akmal, 476
  Uzbekistan, on, 476
Saleilles, Raymond, 4–6, 372, 393
Samuel, Geoffrey, 10, 108, 281, 290, 292, 304
Sarraute, Nathalie, 241, 309
Sartre, Jean-Paul, 324
Savigny, Friedrich Carl von, 158, 171, 316
Scheler, Max, 324, 339
Scheuerman, William, 465–6
Schleiermacher, Friedrich, 320
Schlesinger, Rudolf, 217–8, 247, 369, 371, 395–401, 403–5, 485
  critique of, 249, 262
Schmithoff, Clive, 371
Schütz, Alfred, 318
Scotland, 472
semiotics, 156–62, 168, 183, 187, 193
Serres, Michel, 258
Serverin, Evelyne, 214
sexual harassment law
  Continental Europe and US compared, 330, 338–9, 341–3
Shakespeare, 179, 183, 269–70, 285
Shalakany, Amr, 421–2
Simon, Claude, 309
Smith, Barbara Herrnstein, 260, 264–5
Sophocles, 256
Spencer, Vicki, 267
Spengler, Oswald, 322
Spinoza, 259

state
    boundaries of, 80–3: resistance to, 87–90
    carte blanche and, 82, 86, 96
    corruption and, 96
    definition of, 78–9
    erosion of, 87–99
    European decline of, 91–3
    European export, as, 85–6
    Locke and, 86
    Maimonides phenomenon and, 99
    non-European, 95–6
    normative authority of, 80
    obstacles to emergence of, 80
    resistance to, 87–90
    territory of, 79–82
Steiner, George, 277
Steinthal, Heymann, 318
Stendhal, 286
Stevens, Wallace, 182, 185
Stone, Deborah, 248
Stone, Julius, 65
Sudan, 472
Sullivan, Louis, 504

Tanase, Takao, 453
    Japanese law, on, 453
Tarde, Gabriel, 278–9
Taylor, Charles, 300
Teubner, Gunther, 124–5, 145–7, 293, 303, 309, 440, 464, 470
    critique of, 147, 464
Thireau, Jean-Louis, 245
Thomas, Laurence, 290
Thompson, E. P., 50, 57
Thucydides, 256
tradition, 242–3, 445–6
    legal, 77–99, 243
transfers, legal, 118–26, 142–8, 181–2, 341–3, 359–68, 437–89, 508–9
    culinary analogy and, 472
    functionalism and, 118–26
    musical analogy and, 471, 475
translation, 15–17, 201, 290–1, 305–6
    legal, 150, 185
transplants, legal *see* transfers, legal
transposition, 469, 471, 477
    see also transfers, legal

Turkey, 468, 472, 477–84
Twining, William, 350–2, 358, 366–7, 370

Unger, Roberto, 294
Unidroit
    critique of, 248–9, 295–6, 300
United States
    model for law reform, as, 484, 486
Upham, Frank, 218
US law
    capital punishment in, 184, 329
    Constitution, 40, 174
    criminal law in, 329–30
    freedom of expression in, 39–40, 43
    impact of European law on, 77–8
    jury trial in, 160–1
    Lasser, Mitchel, on, 233–5
    privacy in, 38
    procedure in, 176–7
    rhetorics in, 230
    strict liability in, 37
    voting rights in, 184
Uzbekistan, 486

Vico, Giambattista, 261, 299–300
Vining, Joseph, 245
Vinsonneau, Geneviève, 260
Völkerpsychologie, 314, 318
Volksgeist, 47–8, 267–8, 314, 316
Voltaire, 316
Vorverständnis, 255–6, 298, 315, 325–6, 328–9, 336, 340–1, 343–4

Wagner, Wenceslas, 357–8
Wai, Robert
    Canadian law, on, 422–3
Ward, Ian, 262, 485
Watson, Alan, 8, 121–2, 126, 142–5, 147–8, 246–7, 317, 360–1, 370, 440, 442–3, 446–52, 470–1, 482, 485
    critique of, 123–5, 144–5, 277–8, 342, 406, 452, 485
Watson, Alan and Khaled Abou el Fadl,
    critique of, 506
Weaver, Warren, 290
Weber, Alfred, 322–3

Weber, Max, 54, 59, 62, 73, 138, 321–3, 337, 371, 448
  Verstehen and, 323
Weinreb, Lloyd, 220
Weir, Tony, 185, 278, 311
Whitman, James, 261, 271, 315
  dignitary law, on, 329–34
Whorf, Benjamin, 157
Wigmore, John, 371–2, 494
Willett, Cynthia, 310
Williams, Bernard, 286, 339
Wilson, Edward, 294
Winch, Peter, 284
Windscheid, Bernhard, 171–2
Wittgenstein, Ludwig, 20, 27–8, 268, 271
Wood, Stepan, 425
Wordsworth, William, 160, 163

Xenophanes, 256

Young, Iris Marion, 290

Zammito, John, 266
Zedner, Lucia, 280–1
Zimbabwe, 472
Zimmermann, Reinhard
  critique of, 260–1, 304
Zimmermann, Reinhard and Simon Whittaker
  critique of, 303, 309
Zweigert, Konrad, 358
Zweigert, Konrad and Hein Kötz, 3–4, 101–3, 106, 109, 245–6, 258, 350–2, 369, 390–5, 403–5
  critique of, 103, 109–10, 114, 292, 295–6, 493–4, 502, 505

For EU product safety concerns, contact us at Calle de José Abascal, 56–1°, 28003 Madrid, Spain or eugpsr@cambridge.org.

www.ingramcontent.com/pod-product-compliance
Ingram Content Group UK Ltd.
Pitfield, Milton Keynes, MK11 3LW, UK
UKHW010856060825
461487UK00012B/1150